THE BOOK
OF JAPANESE LANGUAGE

Alex Ad

THE BOOK OF JAPANESE LANGUAGE

*Learn Japanese in a logical
and comprehensive way*

by

Alex Adler

Written, Designed & Published by Alex Adler

alex-adler.com

CONTENTS

FOREWORD

The Book of Japanese Language is the result of the desire to compile in a single volume the holistic knowledge necessary to understand the Japanese grammar and vocabulary needed to be able to speak Japanese comfortably.

The problem that Japanese language learners face when dealing with learning the language is the complexity of its grammar, which is completely different in nature from that of European languages.

When faced with learning a new language, it is usually wise to learn it organically, gradually acquiring new phrases and words as you begin to interact with native speakers. The problem with Japanese is that its grammar is so different from English that it would not be easy for the student to organically learn how to speak in a grammatically correct manner.

This is why the English speaker must have a solid foundation in Japanese grammar before he or she wants to speak the language, a foundation that also will facilitate his or her learning progression overall.

In this book, I have tried to compile in a single volume what I consider to be the most relevant principles of Japanese grammar, accompanied with comprehensive explanations and examples.

I have also seen fit to complement this with an exhaustive vocabulary part—for without words, one cannot speak any language—and two extra parts thought to be used for reference: Expressing yourself in Japanese, in which grammatical forms are grouped by their typology so that the student can look for them from an English language point of view; and Grammar Dictionary, a dictionary of grammatical forms listed alphabetically.

Thus, The Book of Japanese Language is intended to be a thorough and complete book for the learner of Japanese at any level, for he can use the book as a learning guide and also as a reference guide.

The Book of Japanese Language

ACKNOWLEDGMENTS

This book would never have been released had it not been for the candid and generous help of all the backers in the crowdfunding campaign done on Kickstarter in September 2019.

My sincere thanks to all backers and contributors.

Special Mention to:

A.J.A. van der Schoot

Aaron Maxwell

Adam Andrzej Jaworski

Andres Yutaka Ohno

Andrew Henri

Andrew Smith

Arthur Teranishi

Ashli Tingle

Ava Mandeville

Bob Covey

Brad Hansen

Brent Atkinson / Graybar Electric

Brian Honnigford

Bryce O Platt

Charles Wilson

Chris Bishop

Christian N

Clay Gardner

Craig Cooper

Craig Sider

Daniel G Weese

David Blake

David Brown

David Hill

David J Poulten

Dean Szonyi

Deborah L Auld

Denis Teo

Dennys Antunish

Dr Michael Walz

Ebrahim AlBishri

Elle Dimopoulos

Eric Edquist

Eric J Wells

Faye Salwin

Franklin E. Powers, Jr.

Georgeanna Curbo

Gonçalo V. Faria

Grace Leigh

Grant P

Gus Ferencz

Henning Colsman-Freyberger

Ian Barclay

Ian Brillembourg

Jade Mouchous

Jamie Chau

Jeff Murphy

Jenny Reed

John M Berry

john sustento

Jonathan Benjamin

Vauhkonen

Joseph Estepa

Joshua Torres

Josiah C. Bailey

Kevin To

Kristopher Volter

Lior Weinstein

Luke Gerhardt

Magnus Løkkås Ulriksen

Maria-Bethlehem Pal-laya

Marian Zsemlye

Marina Turovsky

Mark Miller

Maurice Schlagheck

Michael Itkin

Michael Williams

Michail Drakomathioulakis

Monica Lang

Naomi Colby

Patrick Farrace

Paul Anguiano

Randy Girdhari

RAOULT NOEL

Ro Olufunwa

Robert Moser

Ross Williams

Ryan Wallace

Schuyler Pittman

Sean Pelkey

Seth K Jackson

Shakita Blow

Shawna LaDelpha

Sherman Ying

Sherwin Emmanuel M. Madrid

Stephen Russell

Sterling Lau

Thomas Delalonde

Thomas Keller

Tim Monticchio

Timm Knape

Tony Luong

Tyler Romeo

tyler schmidt

Vesko Gavrilov

Werner Kercher

William Bidlack

William Hartley

William Macrae

William Wurzbach

Xeon Xai

Yangjae Hwang

Yoshiaki Obara

PREFACE

Here we will explain the characteristics of this book in order to be able to use it in an understandable and useful way.

Book Parts

This book is divided into four distinct parts, in addition to a preliminary section. Here we explain the characteristics of each part.

- PRELIMINARIES: In this part we explain the general characteristics of the Japanese language and the necessary background knowledge to be able to study the language.

- VOCABULARY: In this part we present the most common Japanese words divided into parts of speech and then into semantic sets of related meanings.

- GRAMMAR EXPLANATIONS: In this part Japanese grammar is explained in a detailed and progressive manner.

- EXPRESSING YOURSELF IN JAPANESE: This part lists the various Japanese grammatical forms and particles grouped by their typology insofar as they can be looked up from equivalent English expressions.

- GRAMMAR DICTIONARY: This part lists Japanese grammatical forms and particles alphabetically so that they can be looked up from Japanese to English.

Interlinks & Numeration

Throughout the book, references and links appear within the book itself to indicate certain things mentioned in other parts of the book. For ease of reference, each section and subsection within the book is numbered.

The five different parts of the book are referenced by two corresponding initials:

PR: Preliminaries • VO: Vocabulary • GE: Grammar Explanations • EY: Expressing Yourself in Japanese • GD: Grammar Dictionary

Within each part, the main sections are numbered with Roman numerals and subsections within sections with Arabic numerals.

If, for instance, we come across the following link [☞ EY:VI.5.5], we will understand that it is pointing to the part of Expressing Yourself in Japanese (EY), chapter VI, section 5 and subsection 5.

When a link is made within the same part of the book in which it appears, that part of the book is not pointed out. Therefore, if in the Grammar Explanations part, we come across the following link [☞ XII.1.3], we will understand that it is sending us to the chapter 12 within the same part (Grammar Explanations), section 1, subsection 3.

Symbols

Throughout the book, a series of symbols are used in order to gather more information in a smaller space. Starting on the next page, we provide a detailed breakdown of all the symbols that appear in the book.

All abbreviations and symbols used throughout the book are listed here.

ABBREVIATIONS

Different abbreviations used in the explanatory notes in Vocabulary, Expressing Yourself in Japanese and Grammar Dictionary.

Honorifics & Register

hum.	humble	**for.**	formal	**lit.**	literary
hon.	honorific	**fam.**	familiar		
		col.	colloquial	**mas.**	masculine speech
pol.	polite			**fem.**	feminine speech

Parts of Speech & Grammatical Function

n.	noun			NOM	nominative case
num.	number	**pre.**	prefix	ACC	accusative case
	(numeral)	**suf.**	suffix	DAT	dative case
adj.	adjectival	**i.**	inflection	AGENT	agentive case
adv.	adverb			GEN	genitive case
v.	verb	**dep.**	dependent	COM	comitative case
cop.	copula			PRIV	privative case
p.	particle	**c.**	case	TOP	thematic case
con.	conjunction	**m.**	mood		(topic)

Explanations

f.	form	**s.o.**	someone		
u.	used	**s.t.**	something	**reg.**	register
w.	with			**gen.**	gender
m. u.	mostly used	**fig.**	figuratively /		
r. u.	rarely used		figurative	**J.**	Japanese
obs.	obsolete	**pos.**	positive	**O.J.**	Old Japanese
		neg.	negative	**C.J.**	Current Japanese

SYMBOLS

Symbols used for grammatical forms, particles and vocabulary used in all parts of the book except Preliminaries.

Color Codes

non conjugable lexeme
prenominal[1]
conjugable verb

conjugable verbal adjective
colloquial abbreviation
polite form
obsolete form

Honorifics & Register

[*col.*]	colloquial	[*pol.*]	polite	[*mas.*]	masculine
[*lit.*]	literary			[*fəm.*]	feminine
[*for.*]	formal	[**hum.**]	humble		
[*fam.*]	familiar	[**hon.**]	honorific	[*obs.*] obsolete

Explanations & Frequency

(I)	infinitive form of verbs	↝	conjugation
		☞	link to another part of the book
{D}	any form of the copula		
{p}	any particle	=	equal to
		≈	equivalent to
~	place holder for a verb		
...	place holder for a noun or phrase	Ⓣ	very high frequency word (roughly equivalent to JLPT level 5)
♣	notes on grammatical usage		
♣	notes on connotative usage (meaning)	Ⓗ	high frequency word (roughly equivalent to JLPT level 4)
♣	notes on related vocabulary, orthography or pronunciation	Ⓔ	medium frequency word (roughly equivalent to JLPT level 3)
➤	derivation		

Parts of Speech

N	noun	A	adjective	P	prefix
V	verb	B	adverb	S	suffix

---

[1] Word that only appears before nouns.

			$\boxed{S}$	subsidiary verb[3]			
$\boxed{I}$	intransitive verb				Ⓥ	verb inflection	
$\boxed{T}$	transitive verb		Ⓢ	strong verb	Ⓐ	adjectival verb inflection	
			Ⓦ	weak verb			
$\boxed{A}$	auxiliary verb[2]		Ⓘ	irregular verbal	Ⓝ	copular inflection	

Grammatical Forms

Grammatical forms or types of words to which an inflection, particle or grammatical structure is attached.

[]	word to which a grammatical form is attached	**[TA]**	perfective form of a verb (past form)
⟦⟧	word to which a grammatical form is attached as it appears within an explanation	**[V]**	realis or perfective form of a verb
		[TE]	gerundive form of a verb
		[E]	subjunctive form of a verb
⟨⟩	place holder within a gramatical form	**[Ō]**	presumptive form of a verb
		[BA]	provisional form of a verb
[N]	noun, pronoun or numeral	**[I]**	infinitive form of a verb (*masu* stem)
[N(p)]	noun followed by a particle		
[n]	noun form of nominal adjectives (stem of *na* adjectives)	**[A]**	irrealis form of a verb (negative stem)
[C]	classifier	**[na]**	attributive adjectival copula after a nominal adjective
[s]	stem of a verbal adjective	**[na]**	attributive adjectival copula after a noun or nominal adjective
[i]	realis form of a verbal adjective (plain form)	**[no]**	attributive nominal copula after a noun
[U]	realis form of a verb (dictionary form)	**[P]**	phrase or clause

Etymology

C	Chinese (Sino-Japanese) etymological origin	F	French etymological origin
		G	German etymological origin
J	Japanese etymological origin	M	Mandarin Chinese etymological origin
E	English etymological origin		
P	Portuguese etymological origin		
D	Dutch etymological origin	‖	extensive notes on etymology

2 Verb that can be added to the infinitive form of another verb.

3 Verb that can be added to the gerundive form of another verb.

PRELIMINARIES

PRELIMINARIES

This section provides a detailed and extensive introduction to the specific characteristics of the Japanese language, especially as opposed to the English language.

This part of the book presents the necessary notions to comprehend how Japanese grammar works and the terminology required to understand all the explanations in this book properly.

This part is divided into three parts:

I. **Typology & Morphology**: Grammatical and compositional features of the Japanese language.

II. **Phonology**: Sounds and pronunciation of the Japanese language.

III. **Writing**: Japanese writing system.

I. TYPOLOGY & MORPHOLOGY

Studying Japanese is a time-consuming and dedicated task since its structure and vocabulary are very different from those of the English language. Japanese is indeed one of the most, if not the most, distant languages from English, so it is important that the student gets to know the differences between the two languages through an understanding of the characteristics of Japanese.

To make that possible, in this chapter, we will explain in an analytical way the typology and morphology of the Japanese language, that is, the type of language it is—its **typology** [☞ I.1]—in comparison to English or other Indo-European languages, and also how Japanese words are formed and structured: its **morphology** [☞ I.2].

I. TYPOLOGY

In this section, we will look at the key characteristics that define Japanese as opposed to languages such as English by reviewing aspects such as its linguistic classification in terms of syntax and lexicon, its peculiar focus on topic and context, the nature of its verbal conjugations and the use of formality, its taste for repetition and chiming in, and its propensity for leaving some sentences unfinished.

I.1 Generalities & Classification

Japanese is an agglutinative language, meaning that it constructs its words and grammatical forms by adding a series of suffixes or endings to a usually unchanging stem. That also implies that suffixes or particles added to nouns and verbs are extensively used for functions that conjunctions and prepositions would perform in Indo-European languages, which are themselves categorized as inflected languages. Another fundamental characteristic of agglutinative languages and Japanese as a member of this group is that words that modify a different word (modifiers) appear before it. Thus, for example, the adjective always goes before the noun.

The word order in Japanese is also peculiar in regard to its comparison with English, for the Japanese word order is strictly SOV, that is, subject + object + verb. This implies that in Japanese, the verb must invariably go at the end of the sentence in all grammatically well-formulated sentences.

Beyond a structural categorization such as the already mentioned agglutinative languages, Japanese cannot yet be grouped within any language family in terms of linguistic relationship, as there is not enough supporting evidence to help us see a connection between Japanese and other languages[4]. While there are some striking

---

[4] Strictly speaking, Japanese can be grouped within the Japonic language family, but this family is only extant in the islands of Japan and only includes Japanese and the Ryukyuan languages from Okinawa, which are in danger of extinction. The Japanese family itself does not have a proven relationship with other language families.

grammatical, morphological, and even lexical parallels with Korean, and some scholars have pointed out that there may also be a relationship between Japanese and Altaic languages—due to characteristics such as the vocal harmony found in that language family —or even with Austronesian languages—due to their phonological resemblance—the consensus remains, nonetheless, that Japanese is an isolated language.

What we have discussed here so far gives us an idea of the complexity that approaching the Japanese language can entail for any non-Japanese student, since such a student—unless, perhaps, he or she knows the Korean language—will not initially find any familiarity with the target language.

1.2 Theme & Context

Japanese has a distinctive grammatical feature that is absent in European languages: the syntactic focus on the **topic** of conversation, which makes Japanese a topic-prominent language. This means that certain grammatical functions develop according to the central theme of the discourse [☞ GE:II.1.1].

The fact that Japanese is a topic-prominent language also implies that the inflections and other grammatical specificities in many cases do not refer so much to the subject, number or time, but rather to more subjective elements such as the aforementioned topic, the speaker's emotion, or the perceived social status of the persons involved in the conversation (formality). This also means that in Japanese conversations it is often not possible to guess just by the words or grammatical forms given who is the subject of the sentence or at what time an action is performed. This implies that speakers must, in many instances, be aware of a given context to fully comprehend what is being said. Let us use the simple Japanese word *taberu* (食べる) as an example. *Taberu* is the imperfective form (non-past form) of the verb 'to eat', but this word as it is, if there is not a context, has several possible English translations such as 'I/you/he/she/it/we/you/they eat(s)' or 'I/ you/he/she/it/we/you/they will eat'. It is necessary, then, with words or sentences like this, to know the previous context in order to determine the specific meaning of that given word or sentence.

1.3 Conjugation & Formality

That Japanese is a topic-prominent language is mainly determined by the fact that its verb conjugations do not allude in any way to the subject, i.e. who performs the action defined by the verb. Japanese verb conjugations and inflections and the various grammatical suffixes refer only to the aspect—how the action or event takes place in time—or to the modality—the attitude of the speaker with respect to the verb in question. Japanese nouns and adjectives do not even refer to either number or gender so that without a given context, those will remain ambiguous.

Given the need to know the context to understand a Japanese sentence because the conjugations or grammatical forms do not allude to the subject, one might think that, as in English, the subject could be stated, but the fact is that the mention of the subject is profusely avoided in Japanese sentences, so if the listener or reader encounters a particular phrase without knowing the context and does not have any other external clue, he or she will often have to determine it by means of the formality register used.

Japanese has a rich system of formality—or formal language, *keigo*[5] in Japanese— which is another feature that differentiates it from European languages. In these languages, formality is established chiefly through the use of some limited vocabulary. In contrast, in Japanese, formality is established not only through the use of certain vocabulary but also through the use of specifically formal verbal conjugations and grammatical forms. Thus, for a plain, familiar, polite, formal, colloquial, and even literary register, specific verbal conjugations and grammatical endings exist. Then, each conjugation or form will only be used in a context that matches its sociolinguistic register.

Let us illustrate this with the word used as an example in the previous section: *taberu* ('I/you/he/she/we/you/they eat'). Such form is the plain or informal version of the verb, but it also has a formal version, *tabemasu*, which means the same thing but said within a formal context. This applies to all Japanese verbs and conjugations, which do not determine person or number but do determine the degree of formality. In Japanese, however, formality involves not only the register in which one speaks, but also sometimes the hierarchical relationship between the speaker and the listener or between the speaker and the person he or she speaks about, for there are two additional degrees of formality regarding the social and hierarchical positions of the people involved in the discourse: a honorific degree, which is used to show respect to the listener by elevating him or her; and a humble degree, which is used to show respect to the listener by putting oneself below him or her.

As far as formality is concerned, the most relevant things have already been said, but there is one more thing to note in regard to register. Although Japanese verbs or adjectives do not mark gender in the sense that the pronouns or nouns are considered neither masculine nor feminine, there are certain grammatical forms that are related to the speaker's gender, since some of these forms are considered to be of masculine register and others of feminine register, which means that they are used almost exclusively by men or masculine characters in one case and by women or feminine characters in the other.

1.4 Repetition & Backchannels

In Indo-European languages such as English, repeating the same word in succession is usually avoided, but in Japanese this is not a problem. So much so that questions are usually confirmed by repeating the verb in the affirmative form or denied by repeating it in the negative. Then, for example, the question *taberu?* ('are you going to eat?') is usually confirmed with *hai, taberu* ('yes, I'll eat') or denied with *tabenai* ('no, I won't eat'). Word repetition is also commonly used to stress or emphasize a statement, especially when using interjections such as *daijobu daijobu* ('it's okay') or *dōzo dōzo* ('please, go ahead').

Another concept that differentiates Japanese from other languages is the so-called phenomenon of *aizuchi*, which is the repeated use of what in linguistics are called 'backchannels', or confirmatory expressions that are 'chimed in' by the listener in the middle of the speaker's discourse. This practice, which in English can sometimes be considered sarcastic, is deemed polite in Japanese, as it denotes that the listener is actively

---

5 敬語 'respectful language'.

listening. The expressions most commonly used with *aizuchi* are affirmative interjections such as *hai* ('yes') or allusive ones such as *sō* ('that') [☞ GE:VIII.1.1].

1.5 Aposiopesis & Emphasis

Related to the need for an implicit context [☞ I.1.2] and the use of backchannels [☞ I.1.4], there is another phenomenon in Japanese that is not so wide-spread in Indo-European languages either. This is the phenomenon of leaving sentences unfinished, which is called *aposiopesis* (from Greek 'becoming silent') and commonly appears in Japanese due to two factors: 1. That the Japanese verb always comes at the end, 2. That the listener is often expected to insert confirmatory interjections (*aizuchi*). The first factor enables the possibility of not having to say the verb if there is enough context, while the second factor prompts the speaker to do mid-sentence pauses in order to leave a space for the listener to chime in.

The phenomenon described is sometimes reinforced by the emphasis given to certain words through the use of particles [☞ GE:I.5.1] before a pause, which unmistakably implies that the interrupted sentence will be shortly continued.

2. MORPHOLOGY

Morphology is the study of the word-formation process, which is different for each language. For 'word' we understand a meaningful element of speech that can be used with others to form a sentence[6]. The Japanese language, being agglutinative, usually forms its words by combining several morphemes that are left unchanged for the most part. The term **morpheme** refers to the smallest units of meaning within a language. Such a combination of morphemes, however, is subject to different parameters depending on the origin and grammatical functionality of the word in question.

In order to understand Japanese morphology, we will review in this section the origin of Japanese words, their functional structure and, finally, we will dive into the formative or morphological parameters themselves.

2.1 Origin of Words

In lexical terms, Japanese is a language that historically has been and continues to be prone to adopt foreign influences. From the Middle Ages until almost the 19th century, this influence has been almost exclusively Chinese. Classical Chinese had an invaluable impact on the Japanese language, so much so that today about sixty percent of Japanese words are of Chinese origin, whereas only thirty percent are of purely Japanese origin. The remaining ten percent are words of foreign origin other than Chinese, mostly from English, but the

---

[6] In languages written with the Latin alphabet, words are distinguished by being separated with spaces. Japanese is written without spaces [☞ III], but they are introduced, nonetheless, in the transliteration of Japanese into the Latin alphabet.

current trend is for a greater influx of English words that in certain contexts come to replace existing native or Chinese words.

This differentiation in the origin of words in Japanese is not simply an etymological curiosity, since the use and connotation of words, and even some of their grammatical behavior, vary according to their origin. Words of Chinese origin often form doublets with a purely Japanese word—as it occurs in English with some words of Germanic origin and others of Latin origin—or even triplets when a new word of English origin appears. The origin of words is also a determinant factor in Japanese morphology.

Words of purely Japanese origin—or native words—are called *wago*[7], and while they form only about thirty percent of the corpus of words in Japanese, they are the most commonly used, as they predominate in familiar speech, everyday words, and most grammatical forms.

Words of Chinese origin—or Sino-Japanese words—are called *kango*[8] in Japanese and have been used since the Middle Ages to name concepts and objects imported from Chinese civilization as well as all kinds of abstract terms. The adoption of Sino-Japanese words to denote abstract concepts continued until the 19th and early 20th centuries, when many new concepts imported from the West were expressed in Japanese by combining several Chinese characters with their Sinitic pronunciation adapted to Japanese phonetics, a process called *waseigo* (和製語)—'words made in Japan'—which, however, is hardly productive anymore.

New concepts are expressed now with words of foreign origin other than Chinese. The vast majority of these words—called *gairaigo*[9] in Japanese—are actually English words adapted to Japanese phonetics.

We can, therefore, summarize the etymological bulk of Japanese words in three major groups:

- **Native Words** (*wago*): Of purely Japanese origin, they make up about 30 percent of the vocabulary, but their use is the most familiar and commonplace.

- **Sino-Japanese Words** (*kango*): Of Chinese origin, they make up about 60 percent of the vocabulary, but their use is generally more formal.

- **Foreign Words** (*gairaigo*): Imported from foreign languages, mainly English, they are used for naming new concepts in use since the second half of the 20th century.

When there is a purely Japanese word, a Chinese word and an English word for the same concept, their use varies depending on the context. Purely Japanese words tend to be familiar, Chinese words tend to be considered more formal and more cultured, and English words tend to be considered more fashionable, more youthful and more commercial.

---

[7] 和語 'Japanese words'

[8] 漢語 'Chinese words'

[9] 外来語 'Words coming from abroad'

2.2 Functionality of Words

If we look closely at the grammatical functions of Japanese words, we will see that etymologically there are only three types of words with regard to functionality: nouns, verbs and particles. All other types of morphemes with different functionalities [☞ IV.1] such as adjectives, adverbs, suffixes or conjunctions are thus originated or derived from nouns or verbs. In Sino-Japanese words (*kango*), the functional typology is further reduced, since all these words are originally nouns.

Strictly and technically speaking, adjectives as an independent category do not exist, because although two types of adjectives [☞ IV.1] are formally distinguished for more practical analysis, these are actually a form of qualifying verbs called adjectival verbs or a type of noun called adjectival nouns. Similarly, most pronouns and adverbs also behave grammatically in Japanese as nouns or were originally nouns.

2.3 Formation of Words

In a language there are, at a glance, two large groups of words: simple words and compound words. Simple words are equivalent to a semantic **stem** and are themselves lexical morphemes. By lexical morpheme, we mean morphemes that have meaning independently or through grammatical inflections. The lexical morpheme is contrasted with the grammatical morpheme, which are exclusively non-independent morphemes used to change the grammatical behavior of a lexical morpheme.

The bulk of simple words in Japanese are native or foreign nouns. Japanese compound words can be formed by various methods depending on the origin and functionality of the word. In principle, there are three main methods of word formation that can be distinguished: combination, derivation and inflection:

- **Compounding**: Combination of two or more morphemes. In native words, this is usually done by combining two words. Sino-Japanese words, on the other hand, are mostly combinations of two or three non-independent lexical monosyllabic morphemes of Chinese origin.

- **Derivation**: Combination of a word with non-independent grammatical morphemes (suffixes). The result of derivation is a new word with a new meaning.

- **Inflection**: Combination of a non-independent lexical morphemic stem with non-independent grammatical morphemes (i.e. 'lexemes'). All words formed through inflection in Japanese are verbals[10], that is, conjugable words. The result of inflection is a grammatical variant of an original lexeme.

---

[10] Verbs, nominal verbs and adjectival verbs [☞ IV.1]

II. PHONOLOGY

In this section, we will explain the phonology of Japanese, that is, the system of sounds that is used in the language. To understand this system, we can divide phonology into two main sections: **phonetics** and **prosody**. Phonetics explains the set of sounds or 'phonemes' used in Japanese, while prosody explains how these sounds behave together through intonation.

To begin to explain the Japanese pronunciation and phonetic system, we will do it first using the Latin alphabet, since this will allow us to understand how the Japanese sounds work without having to go into the complex Japanese writing system, whose understanding, however, will be more reliable if we already know beforehand how the Japanese pronunciation is.

In this book, we will use a slighted modified[11] version of the transliteration system from Japanese into the Latin alphabet known as 'Hepburn romanization', as it is by far the most widely used.

1. PHONETICS

Japanese phonetics is considerably simple compared to English, having only five vowels (*a*, *i*, *u*, *e*, *o*) and a small number of consonants. Below there is a summarizing table of the set of phonemes used in Japanese. Each of these sounds will be explained in detail in the various corresponding parts within this section: vowels and consonants.

Japanese Phonemes

Vowels			Consonants			
short	long	semi-vowels	root voiceless	derived voiceless	derived voiced	root voiced
a	aa		k		g	n
i	ii	y	s	sh	z; j	m
u	uu	w	t	ch; ts	d; (dj); (dz)	r
e	ee / ē		h	f		
o	oo / ō		p			

---

[11] These modifications are specified in the section dedicated to Writing [☞ III].

1.1 Vowels

The Japanese language has only five vowel qualities—**a, i, u, e, o**—which are very similar to the five vowels of Spanish or Italian. However, these five vowels have two potential contrasting phonemic lengths, meaning that they can be pronounced either short or long. Short vowels are considered simple vowels, and long vowels are considered double vowels. Most of the time vowels are simple, but when they are double, this is indicated by the spelling.

Simple Vowels:

Simple vowels have an invariable sound (phoneme) and are as follows:

a   Open central unrounded vowel /a/[12]: Open means that the tongue is away from the roof of the mouth (with the mouth quite open); central means that the tongue is placed in the middle, neither at the back near the throat nor at the front near the lips; unrounded means that the mouth is wide open instead of circular in shape. It is more or less pronounced like the *a* in 'father'.

i   Close front unrounded vowel /i/: Close means that the tongue is close to the roof of the mouth (with the mouth almost closed); front means that the tongue is close to the opening of the mouth but not touching the teeth. It is more or less pronounced like *ee* in 'meet' but with a shorter length.

u   Close back unrounded vowel /ɯ/: Back means with the tongue slightly retracted; rounded means with the lips in a rounded shape, with the lateral corners of the lips close to each other. It is pronounced roughly like *oo* in 'food' but with a shorter length.

e   Mid front unrounded vowel /e/: Mid means that the tongue is positioned somewhere in the middle of what is done in an open or closed vowel. It is pronounced roughly like the *e* in 'let'.

o   Mid back rounded vowel /o/: It is pronounced approximately like the *o* in 'for' or the first part of the *o* in 'so'.

Double Vowels:

The five single vowels mentioned above can increase in length giving rise to double vowels. Double vowels are pronounced for about twice as long as a single vowel. It should be noted, however, that double vowels can be pronounced either all at once as a long vowel or by separating them into two consecutive single vowels, hence the name *'double* vowels'. Double vowels are as follows:

/aː/   Transcribed as **aa**; equivalent to **a** but articulated twice as long.

/iː/   Transcribed as **ii**; equivalent to **i** but articulated twice as long.

---

[12] The phonetic symbology according to the International Phonetic Alphabet (IPA) is written here between slashes.

/ɯː/ Transcribed as **uu**; equivalent to **u** but articulated twice as long.

/eː/ Transcribed as **ee** or **ē**[13]; equivalent to **e** but articulated twice as long.

/oː/ Transcribed as **oo** or **ō**[14]; equivalent to **o** but articulated twice as long.

Within these double vowels, the most common is **ō**, followed by **ē** and **uu**. **Ō** reflects an old pronunciation *ou* that is no longer extant, while **ē** reflects an old pronunciation *ei* that today is only perceptible in conscientious recitation but not in everyday speech. The double vowel **ii** is frequent in adjectival verb endings ending in *-shii*. The double vowels **aa** or **ee** are infrequent in the pure Japanese language, but appear with some frequency in words imported from English.

When several double vowels follow one another in a sentence—between words—the speaker makes a stop between them in order to differentiate between them.

The length of the vowel sometimes serves to distinguish words from each other as we can see in the following examples:

toru 取る: 'to take' • tooru 通る: 'to pass through'

sato 里: 'village' • satō 砂糖: 'sugar'

Semivowels:

Semivowels are vocalic phonemes that function phonotactically as consonants by acting as a boundary in a syllable, not being able to form a syllable on their own. Semivowels are **y** and **w**.

y   Similar to the approximant palatal sound /j/ represented by the English y in words such as 'you'.

This phoneme only appears at the beginning of a syllable before **a**, **u** or **o** in native or Sino-Japanese words. After a consonant, it also occurs in words of Chinese origin, in combinations of a consonant (C) plus the vowels **a**, **u**, **o**, thus forming the combinations C+**ya/yu/yo**, or with the double vowels **uu** and **ō**, creating the combinations C+**yuu/yō**.

w   Pronounced similarly to the English w but in a compressed manner /ɰᵝ/, i.e., with the lips retracted without forming a fully rounded shape.

The semivowel **w** appears only at the beginning of a syllable and never after a consonant. This phoneme in native or Sino-Japanese words only appears before **a**.

Diphthongs:

---

13 **ee** when in Japanese script it is written with two characters equivalent to /e/, one after the other; **ē** when in Japanese script it is written with the characters equivalent to e + i (ei) [☞ II.1.1].

14 **oo** when in Japanese script it is written with two characters equivalent to /o/, one after the other; **ō** when in Japanese script it is written with the characters equivalent to o + u (ou) [☞ II.1.1].

Diphthongs are the combination of two vowels pronounced at once in a single syllable. In Japanese, phonetic diphthongs themselves only occur after the semivowel y, as in the other cases where two or more vowels are combined, their pronunciation can be done either as a whole or stopping slightly on each vowel depending on the speed of the speech. This is due to the fact that the relevant phonemic units in Japanese are not really syllables, but rather smaller units called *morae*, which will be explained later in the Prosody section [☞ II.2].

Vowel combinations in native Japanese words are **ae**, **ai**, **ao**, **au**, **oi** and **ui**. These vowel combinations are not phonemic diphthongs per se, as each vowel can be pronounced at once or separately in slower or more careful speech. These vowel combinations could be considered phonetic diphthongs only in the case of a single pronunciation. Formally, there is also the diphthong **ei**, but as we mentioned before, it is pronounced in common speech like a long *e* (/eː/), represented in this book as **ē**. The pronunciation as *ei* with the vowels separated is mostly used in the isolated citation of words containing such a combination or while performing a very careful and formal dictation.

In very informal contexts, the phonetic diphthongs **ai**, **oi** and **ui** can undergo a monophthongization process and be articulated as **ee**.

Exceptionally, the combination **iu** also appears in the word *iu* 言う ('to say'), but this combination is pronounced *yuu* (with the semivowel *y*).

Iotized Diphthongs:

The consonant plus semivowel above occurs almost exclusively in words of Chinese origin. These diphthongs are called *iotized*[15] diphthongs, and are made up of the semivowel plus the vowels a, u, or o, thus giving the diphthongs C[16]|**ya**, C|**yu** or C|**yo** and their variants with double vowels C|**yuu** or C|**yō**.

Devoicing:

In Japanese, there is a phenomenon in the pronunciation of the vowels i and u in some environments known as devoicing, which means that their articulation is devoid of laryngeal vibration and their duration is shortened (/i̥, u̥/), sometimes, especially in the case of u, becoming imperceptible. Devoicing is more frequent in contexts where informal language is used than in contexts where formal language is used, and, at the same time, it may be more prominent in some dialects—such as Tokyo's—than in others. In addition, as a general rule, women are less likely to use devoicing than men.

The devoicing of **i** and **u** can appear after **f**, **h**, **k**, **s**, **sh**, and **ts**.

hito 人: 'person' → h'to [hi̥to]

takusan たくさん: 'very' → tak'san [taku̥sãɴ]

The devoicing in the word *desu* ('to be') [☞ VI.1.3] and in the formal ending *-masu* [☞ VI.1.1] is widely used and pronounced even in formal speech.

---

[15] Because they consist of a vowel sound similar to that of the letter i, called iota in Greek.

[16] C stands for 'consonant'.

desu です: 'to be' → des' [des(ɯ̥)]

In very informal contexts, the devoicing of **u** may also appear before an initial **m**.

umai うまい: 'nice' → 'mee [ɯ̥meː]

The vowels **a** and **o** can be devoiced in the first syllable of words when the following syllable has the same vowel.

kokaru こかる: 'to take' → k'karu [kḁkaɾɯ]

kokoro 心: 'heart' → k'koro [ko̥koɾo]

Glotal Stop Insertion:

At the beginning or end of Japanese sentences that start or end with a vowel, there is usually a glottal stop—pronounced with the glottis in the throat—similar to the glottal sound produced in English at the end of words ending in *t*.

1.2 Consonants

There are two main consonant groups in Japanese:

- **Voiceless Consonants**: Pronounced without using the vocal cords, with an absence of vibration.
- **Voiced Consonants**: Pronounced by emitting sound with the vocal cords, emitting vibration (voicing).

There are eight **root consonants** within the two groups mentioned above. Five of them are voiceless (**k, s, t, h, p**) and three voiced (**n, m, r**). The rest of the existing Japanese consonants (**g, sh, z, j, ch, ts, d, f, b**) derive from the four voiceless root consonants.

Root Voiceless Consonants:

The most common consonants in Japanese are the group of root voiceless consonants: **k, s, t, h, p**. Voiceless consonants mean that they are pronounced without using the vocal cords. It is important to point out the characteristics of these vowels because their pronunciation often varies from that of the English phonemes represented by these letters.

k   Velar plosive /k/, pronounced with the back of the tongue making contact with the palate, like the *k* in 'kiss' but less aspirated (expelling less air through the mouth).

s   It is always a voiceless sibilant /s/ like the *s* in the English word 'sit' and not voiceless /z/ like the *s* in the word 'easy'. This consonant never appears before **i**.

31

t   Dental plosive /t/, pronounced with the tip of the tongue touching the teeth, like English *t* but without aspiration, that is, without expelling air through the mouth. This consonant never appears before **i** or **u**.

h   Normally pronounced glottally /h/ as in English, just as the *h* in 'hey' is pronounced. When **h** comes before **i**, however, it is pronounced palatally /ç/, meaning that the tongue is raised almost until it touches the roof of the mouth, similar to the digraph *ch* in the German word 'ich' or the *h* in 'hue'. This consonant never appears before **u**.

p   Bilabial plosive /p/, pronounced by forcefully pressing and releasing the lips together, similar to the *p* in 'spin' or the *p* in 'pack' but without aspiration.

Derived Voiceless Consonants:

There are other voiceless consonants that derive from the root voiceless consonants. They appear as the combination of one of those consonants with some specific vowel (b or **u**). These derived voiceless consonants are **sh**, **ch**, **ts**, **f** and **p**.

sh   Derived from **s**, it only appears before **i**. Alveolo-palatal fricative /ɕ/, pronounced by placing the back of the tongue in contact with the palate letting the air pass over the tongue, producing a sound similar to the English *sh* (/ʃ/) but considerably softer.

ch   Derived from **t**, it only appears before **i**. Alveolo-palatal affricate /tɕ/, pronounced by placing the back of the tongue in contact with the roof of the mouth without letting air pass over the tongue, producing a sound similar to that of the English *ch* (/tʃ/) in 'chimney' but somewhat softer.

ts   Derived from **t**, it appears only before **u**. Alveolar affricate /ts/, pronounced as a combination of *t* and *s*, like the digraph *ts* in the English word 'cats'.

f   Derived from **h**, Japanese **f** is bilabial /ɸ/ instead of labiodental like its English counterpart. This means that it is pronounced only by the movement of air between the lips, without joining the teeth with the lips as in English. This phoneme only appears in native or Sinitic words before the vowel **u**, but in words of foreign origin (*gairaigo*) it can also appear before other vowels.

Derived Voiced Consonants:

There is also a set of voiced consonants that derive from root voiceless consonants: **g**; **z**; **j**; **d**; **b**. As a general rule, these consonants are pronounced like their voiceless counterparts but with the added sound of the vocal cords.

g   Derived from **k**, the sound represented by **g** always corresponds in Japanese to a plosive velar consonant /g/, i.e. equivalent to the *g* in 'get' and never similar to the *g* in 'gene'.

     In the Tokyo dialect, when a *g* appears between two vowels, the *g* sound is usually articulated nasally /ŋ/ as *ng* in the word 'singer'.

z   Derived from **s**, it is a voiced sibilant /z/, pronounced like the z in the word 'zoo'. This phoneme never appears before **i**.

     The combination **zu** at the beginning of a word takes the allophone /dz/, which, unlike /z/, is pronounced by cutting the air inflow, as if /d/ was pronounced before /z/, similar to the digraph *ds* in the word 'kids'. This pronunciation /dzu/ can also appear in places other than the beginning of words in some speakers' refined language.

j   Derived from the phoneme **sh**, it is an affricate alveolo-palatal consonant /dʑ/ and pronounced by placing the back of the tongue in contact with the roof of the mouth without letting air pass over the tongue while vibrating the vocal cords.

     When this phoneme appears in syllables that do not begin a word, it admits the fricative variant /ʑ/, which is pronounced like its equivalent affricate but letting the air pass over the tongue.

d   Derived from **t**, voiced dental plosive /d/, it is pronounced like the d in 'done'. This letter, in native or Sino-Japanese words, never appears before **i** or **u**.

b   Derived from **p**, voiced bilabial plosive /b/, pronounced like the b in 'boat'.

Root Voiced Consonants:

In addition to the voiceless consonants and their derivations, we also have three voiced root consonants: **n**, **m** and **r**, which are pronounced with the help of the vocal cords.

n   The Japanese **n** has different allophones, which means that they are pronounced differently depending on which letters it appears around. The different allophones of *n* are as follows:

     /n/   Sound equivalent to the English *n*. Before **s**, **z**, **t**, **ts**, **d**, **r**, **n** or before a vowel except **i** when *n* starts a syllable.

     /ɲ/   Palatal nasal sound, pronounced with the tongue touching the palate. Thus pronounced before **i** when *n* starts a syllable.

     /ŋ/   Velar nasal sound, equivalent to the English digraph *ng* in the word 'song'. Thus pronounced before **k** or **g** in any circumstance. Before a vowel when *n* is the final letter of a syllable and the vowel starts a new syllable.

     /N/   Uvular nasal sound, pronounced similarly to /ŋ/ (*ng*) but with the back of the tongue almost touching the uvula. Thus, it is pronounced at the end of a vowel—which produces a nasalization of the vowel, at the end of a sentence or at the end of a syllable followed by **y**, **w**, **s**, **sh**, **z**, **h** and **f**.

     /m/   Sound equivalent to the English *m*. Thus pronounced before **m**, **p** or **b**.

m   Bilabial nasal /m/, pronounced like the *m* in 'mine'.

r   The Japanese **r** is an alveolar flap /ɾ/, meaning that it is pronounced with the tongue touching the alveolar ridge (hard palate above the inner part of the teeth) for a very short period of time. It is a sound very similar to the r in the Spanish word 'pero' or the sound indicated by the letters dd in the American English word 'buddy' when it is pronounced conversationally.

This phoneme also admits a lateral variant /l/ when it appears at the beginning of a syllable. The pronunciation of this variant is similar to the English l sound at the beginning of a word.

Double Consonants:

In Japanese, there is also the phenomenon of gemination. Gemination involves a lengthening or doubling of consonants which also, as with double vowels, sometimes serves to differentiate one word from another:

oto 音: 'sound' • otto 夫: 'husband'

ana 穴: 'hole' • anna あんな: 'such'

These double vowels are pronounced for about twice as long as single consonants. This is important to keep in mind as an English speaker because although many consonants are written as doubles in that language, they are mostly pronounced as one. The most similar sound in English occurs between words. It appears, for example, in the distinction between the word combinations 'seat top' and 'sea top', as the pronunciation between the two t's in the combination 'seat top' takes place over a longer period of time than the *t* in the combination 'sea top'.

In native or Sino-Japanese words only voiceless consonants (**k**, **s**, **t**, **p**, **sh**, **ch**, **ts**) can be doubled. The consonants **h** and **f** can also be doubled, but in the form **pp** instead of *hh or *ff[17].

In words of foreign origin (*gairaigo*), there are also double sounding consonants:

handobaggu ハンドバッグ: 'handbag'

beddo ベッド: 'bed'

1.3 **Sound Changes**

In Japanese, a phenomenon occurs wherein certain sound qualities of some phonemes may change under certain circumstances in word formation [☞ I.2.3][18].

Sound changes are also especially relevant in verb conjugations, which are explained in the corresponding section in Grammar Explanations [☞ GE:III].

I will now go on to explain the different types of sound changes produced in Japanese.

Voicing:

---

[17] This is because in Japanese both the sounds *h* and *f* are derived from an original *p* phoneme.

[18] This phenomenon is called *sandhi* in linguistic terms.

Voicing is the most common phenomenon of sound change in Japanese, and it consists of the transformation of initial voiceless consonants into their derived voiced variants. The Japanese term for this phenomenon is *rendaku* 連濁, which means literally 'sequential voicing'.

When a word beginning with a voiceless root consonant acts as the second component of a compound word, sometimes that consonant is transformed into a voiceless derived consonant.

Voicing Patterns

From Root Voiceless:	k → g	s → z	t → d	h → b
From Derived Voiceless:	sh → j	ch → j	ts → z / dz*	f → b

※ Original phoneme /dz/, now it is more commonly pronounced as /z/ in the contemporary language.

One instance in which this phenomenon always occurs is in nouns with a reduplicated element:

hito 人 (*person*) + hito 人 (*person*) → hitobito 人々 (*people*)

In other circumstances, however, this phenomenon is not universal, and there are cases in which, despite the context described before, such transmutation does not occur:

oo 大 (*big*) + saka 坂 (*field*) → oosaka 大阪 (*Osaka city*); *and not* *oozaka

One consideration to keep in mind is that it is regarded as cacophonous (bad sounding) to have two voiced consonants in the same compound:

hitori 一人 (*one person*) + tabi 度 (*travel*) → hitoritabi 一人旅 (*traveling alone*); *and not* *hitoridabi

In Sino-Japanese compounds, composed of two morphemes of Chinese origin, the same phenomenon can occur, although more occasionally:

chuu 中 (*middle*) + koku 国 (*country*) → chuugoku 中国 (*China*)

The phenomenon is even rarer in compounds of two Sino-Japanese words and even more infrequent in words of foreign origin.

Plosivization:

Sometimes, the consonants **h** and **f**, especially in Sino-Japanese compounds, undergo a transmutation into **p** or **pp**:

ki 切 (*cutting*) + fu 付 (*token*) → kippu 切符 (*ticket*)

In this case, the transmutation is universal if the member of the first component ends in **n** or **m**.

bun 文 (*writings*) + hō 法 (*law*) → bunpō 文法 (*grammar*)

Gemination:

Some words containing a single consonant admit a doubling of that consonant for emphasis in informal speech. This process is known as 'gemination'.

amari あまり (*too much*) → ammari あんまり (*way too much*)

bakari ばかり (*only*) → bakkari ばっかり

Only the following consonants can be doubled in native Japanese words: **k**, **sh**, **ch**, **ts**, **p**, **n** and **m**.

The letter **h** can also be reduplicated but by a previous transformation into double **p**:

yahari やはり (*as expected*) → yappari やっぱり

As a side note, it should be added that in the colloquial language the gemination process can exceptionally occur even in voiced consonants:

sugoi すごい (*amazing*) → suggoi すっごい (*really amazing*)

Vowel Transmutation:

In certain Japanese native compounds, the final vowel of some one-syllable or two-syllable native words changes from **e** to **a**.

te 手 (*hand*) + motsu 持つ (*to hold*) → tamotsu 保つ (*to maintain*[19])

Assimilation:

Assimilation in Japanese is a phenomenon that involves the fusion of the syllables **tsu**, **ku**, **chi**, **ki**, and occasionally **fu** and **h** with a following consonant that turns double. Like other sound transmutation phenomena, this phenomenon is not universal, but it is overwhelmingly present in syllable compounds of Chinese origin.

itsu 一 (*one*) + sho 緒 (*twine*) → issho 一緒 (*together*)

gaku 学 (*learning*) + kō 校 (*school*) → gakkō 学校 (*school*)

This consonant contraction or assimilation is also prominent in numeral compounds [☞ VO:III]:

---

[19] The etymology in English is the same, for 'maintain' is composed of 'main' and 'tain', whose Latin original roots 'manus' and 'tenere' signify 'hand' and 'to hold' respectively.

ichi 一 (*one*) + fun 分 (*minute*) → ippun 一分 (*one minute*)

1.4 **Phonotactics**

Phonotactics deals with the possible combinations of sounds (phonemes) within a language. As far as Japanese is concerned, this combination is comparatively limited, resulting in a small number of possible syllables. This is due not only to the fact that the number of vowels and consonants is not too large, but also to the fact that in Japanese all syllables end in a vowel or n. Hence, apart from combinations of n plus a syllable beginning with a consonant, there are no consonant clusters within the language.

Japanese phonotactics, in short, can be summarized in the following combinations for each syllable:

$$(C) \ \mathbf{V} \ (N)$$

$$(C) \ Y + \mathbf{V}^{20} \ (N)$$

$$W + A \ (N)$$

※ **C** stands for a consonant; **V** for a single or double vowel; the letters in *italics and red* represent the phoneme indicated by those letters. Parentheses represent optionality.

2. **PROSODY**

Prosody is the study of the intonation patterns of a language. The intonation of the Japanese language is particularly subject to patterns that affect words differently, although these differences in intonation only in a few cases are determinant in differentiating the meaning of homonyms. Japanese prosody becomes more relevant to sound natural when speaking the language.

As a note for clarification, it is worth mentioning that Japanese intonation is not based on stress like English, since its intonation system relies mainly upon the **pitch accent** [☞ II.2.2]. In order to understand pitch accent, we will have first to explain the distinction between **syllables** and **morae**.

2.1 **Syllables & Morae**

The traditional way of dividing words by phonetic units relevant to intonation is done in most languages through syllables, which are sound units containing at least one vowel and normally also some adjacent consonants. The division of syllables is made in each language taking into account the phonotactics of that language. Japanese syllables usually consist of a vowel, a diphthong (combination of vowels) or a consonant followed by a vowel or diphthong.

---

[20] Except **e** and **i**.

In Japanese, however, the relevant sound units for pronunciation and intonation are not syllables but morae. A **mora** is a smaller unit than the syllable. Morae can be a simple vowel, a consonant and a simple vowel, or a consonant and an iotized vowel. The letter *n* following a vowel acts as a separate mora, and double consonants count as two morae.

What is a mora:

V

C + **V**

C + *Y* + **V**

N after **V**

C before **C**

※ C stands for a consonant; V stands for a simple vowel; letters in italics and red represent the phoneme indicated by those letters.

Examples:	wa	kyō	mata	ryokan	gakkō
Syllables	wa	kyoo	ma-ta	ryo-kan	gak-koo
Morae	wa	kyo-o	ma-ta	ryo-ka-n	ga-k-ko-o
# of Syllables	1	1	2	2	2
# of Morae	1	2	2	3	4

2.2 Pitch Accent

Japanese intonation is governed by pitch accent. The expression 'pitch accent' is used to refer to the accentuation of morae within a word through their pitch, i.e. the degree of highness or lowness of the tone with which the morae are pronounced. This is unlike English, where syllables are accentuated through stress and emphasis.

Within a word, then, there will be some morae with a high tone and some other morae with a low tone. It is important to emphasize that tone does not mean stress; therefore, when a mora has a high tone, it does not mean that it has to be pronounced with more sonority or volume, simply it will be pronounced with a higher pitch.

The tonality of words in Japanese cannot be predicted and varies according to dialects; however, there is, in standard Japanese, a pattern that restricts the tonality of words and following particles to five types[21]:

---

[21] The corresponding traditional nomenclature is as follows: I. *hēbanshiki* 平板式 "flat style"; II. *atamadakagata* 頭高型 "head-high form"; III. *nakadakagata* 中高型 "middle-high form"; IV & V. *odakagata* 尾高型 "tail-high form"

I.   **Flat High Tonality**: The first mora of the word has a low tone and the remaining morae have a high prolonged (flat) tone, including the following particle.

II. **Initial High Tonality**: The first mora of the word has a high tone and the remaining morae have a low tone, including the following particle.

III. **Medial High Tonality**: The first mora of the word has a low tone, the second mora has a high tone and the remaining morae have a low tone, including the following particle.

IV. **Final High Tonality**: The first mora has a low tone, the two following morae have a high tone, and the remaining morae and following particle have a low tone.

V.   **Long Final High Tonality**: The first mora has a low tone, the three following morae have a high tone, and the remaining morae and following particle have a low tone.

We see, then, that the Japanese accentuation of words, rather than consisting of stressed or non-stressed syllables, is formed by a series of morae that maintain a low or high tone. While not strictly necessary for communication or understanding, these tonalities are useful for, when applied within a pattern, making the non-native speaker sound more natural. That is why in this book each Japanese word is marked with its tonality by the use of accent marks in the following manner:

- **Ascending Accent** [ó]: High tone mora that makes the following morae or unaccentuated particle also take a high tone.

- **Descending Accent** [ò]: High tone mora that makes the following morae or unaccentuated particle take a low tone.

- **No Accent** [o]: Mora or particle that follows the tone marked by the previous accent mark, or else: an unaccentuated mora in a low tone.

With this system of tonal representation we can reliably represent homophones with different intonations like the following:

hashì 橋: bridge • hàshi 箸: chopsticks • hashí 端: edge

In the previous example, the following particle would take a low pitch in the first *hashi*, also a low pitch in the second *hashi* and a high pitch in the third *hashi*.

Pitch Accent Chart				
	Flat (I)	Initial (II)	Medial (II)	Final (III)	Long Final (IV)
	o	ò			
1 mora	↗●	↘●			
	na 名	ki 木			

2 morae	o ó ↗ ─ • mizú 水	ò o ↘ __ • àki 秋	o ò ↗ ↘ • hanà 花		
3 morae	o ó o ↗ ── • kaísha 会社	ò o o ↘ __ • tènki 天気	o ò o ↗ ↘ • okàshi お菓子	o ó ò ↗ ─ ↘ • otókò 男	
4 morae	o ó o o ↗ ─── • daígaku 大学	ò o o o ↘ ___ • bùngakü 文学	o ò o o ↗ ↘ __ • yukiguni 雪国	o ó ò o ↗ ─ ↘ __ • saíjìki 歳時記	o ó o ò ↗ ── ↘ • otótò 弟
5 morae	o ó o o o ↗ ──── • chuúgokugo 中国語	ò o o o o ↘ ____ • shàabetto シャアベット	o ò o o o ↗ ↘ ___ • fukyùuritsu 普及率	o ó ò o o ↗ ─ ↘ __ • yamánòbori 山登り	o ó o ò o ↗ ── ↘ _ • kogáta bàsu 小型バス
6 morae	o ó o o o o ↗ ──── • keńbutsunin 見物人	ò o o o o o ↘ _____ • kènmohororo けんもほろろ	o ò o o o o ↗ ↘ ___ • omàwarisan おまわりさん	o ó ò o o o ↗ ─ ↘ __ • kińkònshiki 金婚式	o ó o ò o o ↗ ── ↘ __ • kokúgo jiten 国語辞典

※ The symbol • represents a following particle; the color ■ represents a high pitch and accent; the color ■ represents a low pitch and accent.

Sentence Pitch Accent:

The pitch accent of words is affected in the flow of sentences. While words maintain their pitch accent in slow and cautious speech, in fast everyday speech, the pitch accent adapts to sentences' flow.

The most important thing to keep in mind is that once the intonation is lowered, the lowered intonation is maintained throughout the sentence until a pause is made after a particle or verb.

sushì o tabèru (*I eat sushi*) → sushì o taberu

Question Intonation:

As in English, Japanese interrogations are marked with an intonation change in which the interrogative phrase is held in a high intonation or pitch accent throughout.

III. WRITING

The Japanese writing system is one of the most challenging aspects faced by Japanese language learners. The Japanese writing system is unique in the world in the sense that it does not use a single set of representational graphemes but three, and on top of this, one of these sets is not only phonemic but also logographic, meaning that each graph of that set does represent not only a sound but also a meaning.

The three sets of graphic representation used in Japanese writing are called **hiragana**, **katakana** and **kanji**. Hiragana and katakana are syllabaries and kanji are logograms of Chinese origin (Chinese characters). The syllabaries are composed of different graphemes that represent syllables (vowels or sets of vowels and consonants), while the logograms are graphemes that represent a specific meaning as well as a sound. The hiragana and katakana syllabaries are made up of 46 characters respectively and the set of kanji for official use prescribed by the Japanese Ministry of Education amounts to 2136 characters.

Kanji are used to represent most words of Chinese origin and the root of many native Japanese words of common use. Hiragana is mainly used to write grammatical endings and particles and also to represent some Japonic or Sinitic words that lack kanji associated with them. Finally, katakana is used to represent words of foreign origin (other than Chinese), add emphasis to some words in lieu of exclamation marks or capital letters in the Latin alphabet, or represent onomatopoeic words and for the names of some animals and plants.

Japanese writing seamlessly combines these three sets of symbols in most texts, which can be written both horizontally—from left to right—or vertically—from right to left[22]—and always without spaces between words.

1. SYLLABARIES

Japanese syllabaries—called *kana*[23] in Japanese—are sets composed of characters that can represent a vowel (a, i, u, e, o), a consonant-plus-vowel compound, or the letter n. This is because each character in the syllabary technically represents a mora[24] [☞ II.2.1] rather than a syllable, and a mora can be, precisely, a vowel, a consonant plus a vowel or iotized diphthong, or the phoneme[25] **n**.

---

[22] In texts before the orthographic reform made after 1945, horizontal writing was also done from right to left.

[23] 仮名 'provisional name'; in reference to the historical origin of these syllabaries that derived from 'provisional' or adapted sound readings for Chinese characters. More information on the chapter dedicated to kanji [☞ III.2].

[24] Unit smaller than a syllable, characteristic of Japanese prosody, see more information in its corresponding section [☞ II.2]

[25] Technically an 'archiphoneme', since it represents different phonetic variations according to its surroundings [☞ II.1.3].

Another thing to note is that the Japanese syllabaries do not represent the phonemes **si**, **ti**, **tu** or **hu**; as these phonemes are not part of Japanese phonology [☞ II]. The following phonemes appear in place of these phonemes: **shi**, **chi**, **tsu** and **fu**. For the same reason, the derived sound phonemes **zi**, **di** or **du** are also not represented, as the phonemes **ji** instead of *zi* or *di* and **zu** instead of *du* take their place.

1.1 Hiragana

Hiragana[26] is composed of 46 characters that phonetically represent the basic morae of the Japanese language, i.e., 5 basic vowels (*a*, *i*, *u*, *e*, *o*), 40 groups of morae composed of a root consonant plus a basic vowel and the nasal consonant *n*. These 46 characters, through the use of graphic modifications or combinations between them, can also represent the syllables with voiced consonants and syllables with long vowels and diphthongs.

The hiragana syllabary comprises 46 fundamental or root morae that are represented by corresponding graphs (letters). Of these 46 graphs, 5 represent the vowels **a**, **i**, **u**, **e** and **o**, and 35 the combinations of these vowels with the consonants **k**, **s**, **t**, **n**, **h**, **m**, and **r**. The semivowels **y** and **w** only have possible combinations with three (*a*, *u*, *o*) and one (*a*) vowels respectively. The last character within the set represents the mora **n**, which can appear after a vowel.

Root Hiragana Syllabary:

The root syllabary is the set of characters from which the entire hiragana syllabary derives. The arrangement of this syllabary is based on the Sanskrit[27] vowel and syllable order, so the vowel order is *a*, *i*, *u*, *e*, *o*, instead of *a*, *e*, *i*, *o*, *u* as in English. The origin of the hiragana root syllable itself is a cursive form of Chinese characters associated with the syllables represented with them.

n ん	A あ	I い	U う	E え	O お
K	ka か	ki き	ku く	ke け	ko こ
S	sa さ	shi し	su す	se せ	so そ
T	ta た	chi ち	tsu つ	te て	to と
N	na な	ni に	nu ぬ	ne ね	no の
H	ha は	hi ひ	fu ふ	he へ	ho ほ
M	ma ま	mi み	mu む	me め	mo も
Y	ya や		yu ゆ		yo よ

---

[26] 平仮名 'even *kana*'.

[27] A classical language of the Indian cultural sphere that became known in Japan—and thus served as an inspiration in the ordering of the hiragana—through the influence of Buddhism.

| R | ra | ら | ri | り | ru | る | re | れ | ro | ろ |
| W | wa | わ | wi | ゐ | | | we | ゑ | (w)o | を |

※ The stand-alone character for the phoneme **n** (ん) only appears at the end of a syllable or word, due to Japanese phonotactic rules.

※ In blue, the phonemes that have a derived, non-intuitive pronunciation.

※ The character **wo** (を) is pronounced as *o* and is only used in contemporary Japanese to represent the accusative particle **o** [☞ VIII.1.1].

※ In a light color, historical phonemes **wi** (ゐ) and **we** (ゑ), currently pronounced as *i* and *e*. These characters are considered historical because they are not used in contemporary Japanese. They were in use normatively before 1945, so it is still possible to find them in old texts and in some proper names.

Derived Hiragana Syllabary:

The voiced derived phonemes [☞ II.1.3] are marked on the syllabary with two quotation marks[28] (゛) written in the upper right corner of the characters representing their voiceless equivalents, while the plosive phoneme **p** is marked with a small circle[29] (゜) in the upper right corner of the characters representing the syllables of *ha, hi, fu, he* or *ho*.

	A		**I**		**U**		**E**		**O**	
G	ga	が	gi	ぎ	gu	ぐ	ge	げ	go	ご
Z	za	ざ	ji	じ	zu	ず	ze	ぜ	zo	ぞ
D	da	だ	dji	ぢ	dzu	づ	de	で	do	ど
H	ba	ば	bi	び	bu	ぶ	be	べ	bo	ぼ
P	pa	ぱ	pi	ぴ	pu	ぷ	pe	ぺ	po	ぽ

※ In blue, the phonemes that have a derived, non-intuitive pronunciation. *Dji* and *dzu* are commonly pronounced as *ji* and *zu* in contemporary Japanese [☞ III.4], but they are represented with a different transliteration in order to maintain coherence with the Japanese orthography.

Double Vowels in Hiragana:

When writing double vowels [☞ II.1.1] in hiragana, it is done by default by doubling the character for each vowel as follows:

---

[28] Called *dakuten* 濁点 ('impurity mark') in Japanese, because in traditional Chinese and Japanese phonology voiced phonemes were called 'impure' as opposed to voiceless phonemes which were called 'pure'.

[29] Called *handakuten* 半濁点 ('half impurity mark').

| aa ああ | ii いい | uu うう | ee ええ | oo おお |

おおい〔多い〕ooi (*many*)

But as we noted previously in the phonetics section [☞ II.1], the double vowels for *e* and *o* admit two distinct spellings ē and ō which are etymological vestiges of an earlier pronunciation. These double vowel variants are written in hiragana as **ei** and **ou** respectively.

| ē (ei) えい | ō (ou) おう |

えいご〔英語〕ēgo (*English*)

When the vowel of a syllable beginning with a consonant is doubled, the character for that vowel a is simply added to that syllable. In the case of the alternative versions of *ee* (**ei** → ē) and *oo* (**ou** → ō), an *i* or *u* is added accordingly:

とおい〔遠い〕tooi (*far*) ; とうじ〔当時〕tōji (*that time*)

Iotized Syllables in Hiragana:

Iotized syllables or diphthongs [☞ II.1.1]—composed of a consonant plus vowel (*a, u* or *o*) —are written with the characters representing syllables beginning with a consonant and i followed by a semivocalic syllable beginning with *y* (*ya, yu* or *yo*), which is written in a smaller size, after the previous character.

The combination of **sh**, **j** or **ch** plus *ya, yu,* or *yo* is possible, but in such combinations, the *y* is assimilated to the preceding consonant and is no longer pronounced.

Below is a sample of the different combinations of iotized diphthongs:

	K	G	SH	J	CH	N	H	B	P	M	R
YA	kya きゃ	gya ぎゃ	sha しゃ	ja じゃ	cha ちゃ	nya にゃ	hya ひゃ	bya びゃ	pya ぴゃ	mya みゃ	rya りゃ
YU	kyu きゅ	gyu ぎゅ	shu しゅ	ju じゅ	chu ちゅ	nyu にゅ	hyu ひゅ	byu びゅ	pyu ピュ	myu みゅ	ryu りゅ
YO	kyo きょ	gyo ぎょ	sho しょ	jo じょ	cho ちょ	nyo にょ	hyo ひょ	byo びょ	pyo ぴょ	myo みょ	ryo りょ

※ In blue, the characters that represent an assimilated phoneme.

These iotized diphthongs can also be extended to voiced derivatives—represented with the characters of the derived syllabary—and to double vowels:

みょう〔妙〕myō (*unusal*) ; じゅう〔十〕juu (*ten*)

Double Consonants in Hiragana:

Double consonants are marked in hiragana with the character of the syllable *tsu* in small size (っ) placed before the character of a syllable beginning with the consonant to be doubled.

$$っ + C \rightarrow CC$$

※ C stands for a consonant

The differentiation of the size of っ is important, because in some cases it is decisive to know whether the character alludes to a double consonant or to the syllable *tsu*:

hatsuka はつか〔二十日〕: 20 days • hakka はっか〔発火〕: combustion

Glottal Stop in Hiragana:

The small *tsu* character (っ) is also used—placed after the last syllable of the sentence—to mark a glottal stop [☞ II.1.2] at the end of a sentence or interjection in some colloquial language transcriptions.

a'! あっ!: ah!

1.2 Katakana

The katakana[30] syllabary is similar in structure and composition to hiragana because, like hiragana, it is composed of characters that represent the morae [☞ II.2.1] phonotactically possible in the Japanese language. It is relatively easy to distinguish this syllabary from hiragana because the appearance of katakana characters is more square than the former.

Katakana thus consists of the same number of characters as hiragana: 46, divided into 5 vowels, 7 consonants combined with these 5 vowels, the semivowel *y* combined with 3 vowels (*a, u, o*), the semivowel *w* combined with the vowel *a* and, finally, the single mora *n* that can appear after a vowel.

Root Katakana Syllabary:

As its hiragana counterpart, the root katakana syllabary is the set of characters from which the entire katakana syllabary derives. The arrangement of this syllabary is the same as in hiragana and its origin is a set of abbreviated forms of Chinese characters associated with the syllables represented with them.

---

30 片仮名 'side *kana*'

n	ン	A	ア	I	イ	U	ウ	E	エ	O	オ
K		ka	カ	ki	キ	ku	ク	ke	ケ	ko	コ
S		sa	サ	shi	シ	su	ス	se	セ	so	ソ
T		ta	タ	chi	チ	tsu	ツ	te	テ	to	ト
N		na	ナ	ni	ニ	nu	ヌ	ne	ネ	no	ノ
H		ha	ハ	hi	ヒ	fu	フ	he	ヘ	ho	ホ
M		ma	マ	mi	ミ	mu	ム	me	メ	mo	モ
Y		ya	ヤ			yu	ユ			yo	ヨ
R		ra	ラ	ri	リ	ru	ル	re	レ	ro	ロ
W		wa	ワ	wi	ヰ			we	エ	(w)o	ヲ

※ The stand-alone character for the phoneme **n** (ン) only appears at the end of a syllable.

※ In blue, the phonemes that have a derived, non-intuitive pronunciation.

※ The character **wo** (ヲ) is pronounced as *o*. This character is hardly used in current Japanese combined texts [☞ III.5], as in transcriptions of foreign words other combinations [☞ III.4] are preferred to represent what would be the sound *wo*. The most likely instance of finding this character is in a katakana full-text, representing, like its hiragana counterpart *wo* (を), the accusative particle *o* [☞ GE:VIII.1.1].

※ In a light color, historical phonemes **wi** (ヰ) and **we** (エ), currently pronounced as *i* and *e*. These historical characters are not used today and can only be found in old texts and, very occasionally, in proper names that use a historical spelling in katakana.

Derived Katakana Syllabary:

As in hiragana, from the katakana root syllabary the voiced phonemes are also derived by adding two "quotation marks" or *dakuten* (゛) to the root characters; while the plosive phoneme **p** is represented by adding a small circle or *handakuten* (゜) to the characters of the h-row.

		A		I		U		E		O
G	ga	ガ	gi	ギ	gu	グ	ge	ゲ	go	ゴ
Z	za	ザ	ji	ジ	zu	ズ	ze	ゼ	zo	ゾ
D	da	ダ	dji	ヂ	dzu	ヅ	de	デ	do	ド
H	ba	バ	bi	ビ	bu	ブ	be	ベ	bo	ボ
P	pa	パ	pi	ピ	pu	プ	pe	ペ	po	ポ

46

※ In blue, the phonemes that have a derived, non-intuitive pronunciation. The pronunciation of *dji* and *dzu* is the same as their hiragana equivalents: *ji* and *zu* respectively.

Double Vowels in Katakana:

In katakana, all double vowels are written by adding a long hyphen (一) to the single vowel.

aa アー	ii イー	uu ウー	ee エー	oo オー

オーブン oobun (*oven*)

When the vowel of a syllable beginning with a consonant is doubled, the character the long hyphen (一) is simply added to that syllable.

ケーキ keeki (*cake*)

The only exception is when an entire text is written in katakana for stylistic reasons, in which case the spelling rules used in hiragana will be followed, but replacing the hiragana characters with katakana characters.

Iotized Syllables in Katakana:

The representation of iotized diphthongs [☞ II.1.1] follows the same rules as in hiragana. A katakana syllable combining consonant plus *i* is taken and one of the three possible combinations *ya*, *yu*, or *yo* is added in reduced size (ャ, ュ, ョ).

	K	G	SH	J	CH	N	H	B	P	M	R
YA	kya キャ	gya ギャ	sha シャ	ja ジャ	cha チャ	nya ニャ	hya ヒャ	bya ビャ	pya ピャ	mya ミャ	rya リャ
YU	kyu キュ	gyu ギュ	shu シュ	ju ジュ	chu チュ	nyu ニュ	hyu ヒュ	byu ビュ	pyu ピュ	myu ミュ	ryu リュ
YO	kyo キョ	gyo ギョ	sho ショ	jo ジョ	cho チョ	nyo ニィ	hyo ヒョ	byo ビョ	pyo ピョ	myo ミョ	ryo リョ

It is also possible to represent an extension of iotized diphthongs with a double vowel by adding a long hyphen (一) to such combinations:

ニュース nyuusu (*news*)

Double Consonants in Katakana:

Double consonants are marked in katakana—as in hiragana—by using the *tsu* syllable character in a small size (ッ) and placing it before the character of a syllable beginning with the consonant to be doubled:

パック pakku (*pack*)

Phonetic Extension in Katakana:

Because katakana is mainly used to represent words of foreign origin, this syllabary makes it possible to display a larger number of syllabic combinations than those that occur in native Japanese phonotactics. In order to represent these new sounds, a number of combinations of full-sized characters with half-sized characters have been developed. The most common phonetic enlargement combinations are shown below:

	A	I	U	E	O
KW	kwa クァ	kwi クィ		kwe クェ	kwo クォ
GW	gwa グァ	gwi グィ		gwe グェ	gwo グォ
SH				she シェ	
SW	swa スァ	swi スィ		swe スェ	swo スォ
J				je ジェ	
T		ti ティ	tu トゥ		
TS	tsa ツァ	tsi ツィ		tsi ツィ	tso ツォ
CH				che チェ	
D		di ディ	du ドゥ		
Y		yi イィ		ye イェ	
F	fa ファ	fi フィ		fe フェ	fo フォ
W		wi ウィ		we ウェ	wo ウォ
V	va ヴァ	vi ヴィ	vu ヴ	ve ヴェ	vo ヴォ

Here are some examples:

フォーク fooku (*fork*); ディスプレイ disupurei (*display*)

2. KANJI

By kanji[31]—'sinogram' in English—we mean the logographic characters of Chinese origin used in the writing system of the Japanese language. The term *logographic* reveals that each character—kanji—refers to a morpheme. In fact, Kanji is used to represent a large number of native morphemes and almost all morphemes imported from classical Chinese. These characters represent not only a meaning but also a phoneme or series of phonemes (sounds). Hence, when a kanji is used in Japanese, it represents both a meaning and a sound associated with that meaning.

2.1 Readings of Kanji

Things get complicated in Japanese when it comes to reading a kanji because, as we have said, each sinogram represents both a meaning and a sound. Once the represented meaning is understood, the problem then lies in establishing the sound associated with that meaning. It poses a problem because each kanji does not have an association with only one sound but usually with two and sometimes multiple different phonetic options.

This is because the Japanese, when they imported the Chinese writing system throughout history, had two options when dealing with the characters: 1. Read the kanji with a phonetic adaptation of its associated Chinese sound; 2. Read the kanji with the native Japanese word equivalent to the meaning represented by that kanji. These two reading methods are still in practice today, and that is why kanji is still used not only for writing words of Chinese origin with their corresponding Sinitic phonemes—reading option number 1—but also for reading the roots of many native Japanese words—reading option number 2. The Sinitic reading (of Chinese origin) is called in Japanese *onyomi*[32] and the native reading is called *kunyomi*[33].

- **Sinitic Reading** (*onyomi*): Phonetic reading of a kanji by means of monosyllabic phonemes of Chinese origin associated with that kanji. It usually appears in combination with other Sinitic morphemes.

- **Native Reading** (*kunyomi*): Semantic reading of a kanji using native Japanese words associated with the meaning of that kanji.

Here is an example of the two possible types of reading:

hito 人: 'person' • ninsē 人生: 'human life'

We see, then, that the character 人, whose meaning is 'person', can be read as hito—native word for 'person'—when it appears alone, as *nin*—synonymous phoneme for the same meaning—when it appears together with another kanji, in this case 生 ('life', whose *onyomi* reading is *sē*).

Most kanji admit one *onyomi* reading and another *kunyomi* reading. However, certain characters also admit several *kunyomi* readings—because they are prone to several

---

31 漢字 'Chinese letter'

32 音読み 'phonetic reading'

33 訓読み 'interpretative reading'

semantic interpretations conveyed by different words of native origin—or several on readings—because Japanese has adopted phonosemantic borrowings from classical Chinese in several eras or waves from different dialects. Let us illustrate this with the second character of the above example 生 ('life'), which is an extreme case of reading variation. This character can be read in the following   ways:

Kunyomi Readings:

生きる ikiru: 'to live'

生む umu: 'to give birth'

生える haeru: 'to grow'

生 nama: 'raw'

Onyomi Readings:

-生- -sē-: 'living' (as part of a compound word) | e.g. 生命 sēmē: 'life'

-生- -shō-: 'living' (as a part of a compound word) | e.g. 生涯 shōgai: 'lifetime'

The student will have no choice but to learn   on the fly the reading associated with each new word written in kanji as he or she encounters it. As a general hint, native readings (*kunyomi*) usually appear alone or followed by particles or grammatical inflections written in hiragana, while Sinitic readings (*onyomi*) usually appear in the form of morphological compounds in words of Chinese origin. This is why as a rough guide, it is usually accurate to interpret a kanji followed by kana as to be read in *kunyomi* and that two or more kanji in a row are to be read in *onyomi*. This pattern, however, is not universal and there are quite a few exceptions.

2.2 Number of Kanji

Because kanji are logograms that can represent all kinds of meanings, one is not wrong to think that the total number of kanji is very large; in fact, there is no agreement on the exact number of extant kanji (it estimated to be around 50,000 units including variants). However, the student of Japanese can be relatively relieved to know that the Japanese Ministry of Education has fixed a limited list of kanji to be used officially in Japanese. This list only includes 2136 kanji, whose knowledge is therefore necessary to be considered completely literate in the language. What this means is that the student of Japanese must know this number of kanji to be able to comfortably read any modern Japanese text.

The learner will have no choice but to memorize this number of sinograms if he or she wants to read Japanese texts fluently. This can be done by using some holistic learning method[34] or by learning them little by little in context.

2.3 Structure of Kanji

Before starting to learn kanji, it is advisable to acquire some knowledge about their structure to facilitate the learning process. It is important to know that each kanji is not independent of the others, but that they are structurally related—which can help to memorize them as a whole. This is because the great bulk of kanji can be divided into two

---

[34] C.f. *The World of Kanji* by Alex Adler.

groups: simple characters—also called 'primitive characters'—and compound characters, the second group being the most numerous by far.

Primitive characters represent an idea by themselves in a more or less pictographic way, and are therefore considered *ideograms*. Below I will show some examples of primitive characters:

人: 'person' • 日: 'sun' • 木: 'tree' • 犬: 'dog' …

Such characters are usually recognizable by their apparent graphic simplicity. Primitive characters generally represent, in addition to their respective Sinoxenic morphemes, native Japanese nouns that do not require additional hiragana characters.

Compound characters, on the other hand, are composed of two or more graphic components. These components can be of two types: 1. Semantic; 2. Phonosemantic.

Semantic components give a semantic clue to the character as a whole and the group of such components is formed by the majority of primitive characters or simplified variants of them. These semantic components are also called *radicals*.

Phonosemantic components give not only a semantic but also a phonetic clue, and the group forming such components consists of some primitive characters and other compound characters that also act as phonosemantic components.

Let us illustrate this with an example:

銘 mē ('inscription'); formed by the primitive semantic component 金 → 釒 (metal), plus the compound phonosemantic component 名 mē ('name'), which, in turn, is made up of the primitive component 夕 ('crescent moon' → 'evening') plus 口 ('mouth'). Thus we have that the character 銘 which means 'inscription' and whose *onyomi* reading is *mē* is composed of 'metal' (金) and 'name' (名), which is also read as *mē*.

In compound kanji, each element or component is placed one next to the other following limited patterns: left-right (◫; ◫); top-bottom (◲; ◲); surrounding-inner (◫) o partially surrounding-inner (◫; ◫; ◫; ◫; ◫).

The structural formation process of Sinitic characters, as you have seen, is complex and self-referential. Besides, many characters have undergone a long process of both graphical and semantic evolution, which sometimes makes their compositional analysis not so easy. Knowing the components and structure is useful, but I reiterate that the student must nevertheless face the learning of kanji as an arduous and conscientious task to be performed in parallel with the learning of the language itself.

3. PUNCTUATION

Japanese punctuation and orthography have some peculiarities that make it quite different from languages written with the Latin alphabet. The most striking feature of the Japanese writing system is the absence of spaces between words. This absence of spaces, which may diminish the readability of a text, is somehow solved by the presence of kanji and katakana, which contrasts prominently with the grammatical endings and particles written in hiragana.

Although there are no spaces in Japanese writing, there are other types of punctuation such as periods and commas, ellipsis, quoting marks and parentheses. Their use, however, differs slightly from the Latin alphabet. Let us see, then, how punctuation is used in Japanese writing.

Dots & Commas:

The end of sentences, as with the Latin alphabet, is marked with a period. However, the appearance of this period is different from that used in the Latin alphabet (.), as it is a small circle instead of a proper dot: 。.

As for commas, their use is more infrequent than in European languages and is not subject to such delimited rules as in those languages. The main differentiation is that the Japanese comma denotes a phonetic pause that can go in the middle of a sentence, before the verb. The comma (,) in Japanese is written in an inverse direction to that of the Latin alphabet: 、.

The three dots in a row, known as ellipsis (...) which in the Latin alphabet are used to mark an unfinished sentence, in Japanese have a broader and less delimited use, as it is sometimes used to mark elongated pauses in speech, an incomplete thought, or a certain degree of hesitation. Although formally the Japanese ellipsis is also marked with three dots, the number of dots may be increased or even reduced at the writer's discretion.

- **Dot** [。]: Used to mark the end of a sentence.

- **Comma** [、]: Mostly used to mark a pause in the middle of a sentence.

- **Ellipsis** [...]: Used to mark an unfinished sentence, hesitation or an incomplete thought. The number of dots used may be subject to variation.

Quotes & Parentheses:

Quotation marks are used and written as follows: 「 and 」 for single quotes and 『 and 』 for double quotes. The parentheses are similar to those of the Latin alphabet: (and).

- **Single Quotes** [「 」]: Used to mark literal quotations and titles.

- **Double Quotes** [『 』]: Used to mark quotations within other quotations.

- **Parentheses** [( )]: Used, as in English, to separate a text within another text for explanatory purposes.

Exclamation & Interrogation:

In Japanese writing, the question mark (?) and exclamation mark (!) also exist, but their use is more limited than in the Latin alphabet and is usually considered informal. This is because the intonations marked by such symbols in Japanese can be implicitly inferred through the interrogative particles [☞ GE:VIII.3.1] or the admirative particle [☞ GE:VIII.3.2].

Separation Marks:

In Japanese punctuation, there are also two commonly used separation marks that do not exist in languages written with the Latin alphabet:

- **Interpunct** [·]: Used as a separator between words. This graph is mainly used when it is necessary to make clear the separation of two words or names when it can be ambiguous due to the absence of spaces. It can also be used, instead of a comma, as a separator between two items in a list.

- **Elongation Mark** [∼]: Mainly used to mark the lengthening of the last syllable of a word, but also to indicate a range between two numbers.

Word Emphasis:

In texts written in the Latin alphabet, the emphasis or highlighting of a word can be marked with the bold type, italics or capitalization of the word. This has to be done differently in Japanese, as there is no orthographic custom of using bold or italics characters and there is no set of capital letters either. Katakana [☞ III.1.2] is sometimes used to emphasize a word, but such usage normally carries semantic or phatic overtones as well. The way to emphasize a word neutrally in Japanese is to place thick black dots[35] (•) over each syllable.

Iteration Marks:

In Japanese, there are certain words that consist of two identical kanji, one after the other. In this case, the second kanji will always be replaced by the following iteration mark: 々.

hitobito 人人 → 人々 : several people

In texts written in 1945, there were also iteration marks for both hiragana and katakana characters.

These symbols were as follows: ゝ in hiragana and ヽ in katakana. These iteration marks are nowadays used only in handwriting or very occasionally in proper names.

Vertical Punctuation:

Some of the punctuation marks described above have equivalent vertical variants for vertical writing, such as the parentheses (⌒ ⌒), the quotation marks (⌐ ; ⌐) or the ellipsis symbol (⋮).

4. TRANSLITERATION

The most widely used **romanization** or transliteration system of Japanese both in Japan and internationally is the Hepburn system. This book uses that system but with some slight variations:

---

[35] Called *bōten* 傍点 in Japanese, meaning 'side dot'.

53

Hepburn	The Book of Japanese Language
じ/ジ ji • ぢ/ヂ ji	じ/ジ ji • ぢ/ヂ dji
ず/ズ zu • づ/ヅ zu	ず/ズ zu • づ/ヅ dzu
ああ/ア— ā	ああ/アア aa
いい/イ— ī	いい/イ— ii
うう/ウ— ū	うう/ウ— uu
ええ/エ— ē • えい ei	ええ/エ— ee • えい ē
おお/オ— ō • おう ou	おお/オ— oo • おう ō*
ん/ン n/n'†	ん/ン n

※ The transliteration ぢ *dji* and づ *dzu* denotes the voiced derivation of ち *chi* and つ *tsu* respectively, which, however, in contemporary Japanese only appears in written compound words with sound changes [☞ II.1.3] and their pronunciation is equivalent to *ji* and *zu*. The Hepburn system represents these sounds phonetically, losing the graphic distinction, while in the distinction is maintained.

※ *The double vowel ō representing the hiragana combination おう (*ou*) will exceptionally be written **ou** in verbs ending in that conversation for morphological purposes and ease of morphological analysis. E.g. おもう [思う] omou.

※ †In Hepburn transliteration, n's that end a syllable which is followed by another syllable beginning in a vowel are written as ***n'***: E.g. げんいん [原因] (cause) → gen'in. In this book, the beginning of a new syllable starting with a vowel after a syllable ending in n is marked with dieresis: E.g. げんいん [原因] (cause) → genïn.

In the transliteration used in this book, Japanese words will be written separated by spaces within sentences in keeping with the Hepburn romanization system. The only word classes [☞ IV.1] that are written attached to other morphemes or words are nominal, numeral, and verbal inflections [☞ GE:I.1.5].

5. COMBINED WRITING

Modern Japanese writing is a mixture of kanji, hiragana and katakana. As a general rule, kanji is used for words of Chinese origin and roots of native words; hiragana is used for words of native origin that do not have an associated kanji, for colloquial expressions and for grammatical particles and suffixes attached to kanji, which are called *okurigana*[36]; and katakana is used for words of foreign origin, a large part of animals and plants, and occasionally to emphasize certain words that would normally be written in kanji or hiragana.

---

[36] 送り仮名 'passing *kana*'

食堂に箸でラーメンを食べます。
A   B C B   D   B E   F

shokudō ni hashi de **ramen** o tabemasu (*I eat ramen with chopsticks in the restaurant*)

※ A: Sino-Japanese compound word in kanji; B: particles in hiragana; C: native word in kanji; D: Foreign word in katakana; E: native root in kanji; F: grammatical suffixes in hiragana (*okurigana*).

Sometimes kanji may be accompanied by hiragana on top when an unusual or unfamiliar reading needs to be indicated. This method of clarification is called *furigana*[37]. *Furigana* is especially common in children's books. In the examples of this book, furigana will also be used.

しょくどう　はし　　　　　　　　た
食堂に箸でラーメンを食べます。

It should also be noted that there is a certain irregularity and freedom in the use of one format or another for certain words, and the choice of one method or the other may affect the nuance that one wants to give to the written word. The general 'feeling' of each type of writing is as follows: words written in kanji have a more formal and serious feel, words written in hiragana have a more familiar and casual feel, and words written in katakana have a more 'punchy' feel.

---

[37] 振り仮名 'swinging *kana*'

IV. LANGUAGE STRUCTURE

The grammar of a language must keep a structure for it to be functional. This structure is mainly based on two principles: word classes and word order within a sentence. In order to study a language in a self-taught way, unless you are completely immersed in a native environment twenty-four hours a day, it is important to know these principles, as this will help you to understand better how the language works so that you can learn it more quickly and effectively.

From now on, we will see the most important types of words in Japanese—**word classes**—and the order in which those words are normally placed within a sentence—**word order**.

1. WORD CLASSES

Each word class is a group of words that share the same grammatical function and syntactic behavior. To understand word classes, we must first clarify the concept of 'word'.

A *word* is the smallest meaningful unit within a language such that it can be understood by itself. There is still a smaller unit, the *morpheme* [☞ I.2], which is the smallest unit with meaning within a word. In Japanese, being an agglutinative language [☞ I.1.1], most words are morphemes as well, but there are also some non-word morphemes that always have to be added to another morpheme (c.f. affixes [☞ GE:I.8]). In Japanese, there are *conjugable* and *non-conjugable* words, as well as *dependent* and *independent* words. Conjugable words refer to terms that can change their meaning or function (conjugate) with the help of new morphemes, while dependent words need to be accompanied by another word when they appear in a sentence.

In English, there are eight main word classes: noun, pronoun, article, verb, adjective, adverb, adverb, preposition, conjunction and interjection. As a general rule, a noun names concepts, objects, people, animals, places, or ideas (e.g. 'house'); a pronoun replaces a noun (e.g. 'you'); an article is a word that identifies a noun by marking it (e.g. 'the'); a verb designates an action or state (e.g. 'to eat'); an adjective qualifies or modifies a noun or pronoun (e.g. 'red'); an adverb modifies a verb, adjective, or another adverb (e.g. 'well'); a preposition establishes a semantic relationship between two nouns or between a noun and a verb (e.g. 'of'); a conjunction establishes a connection between two words or phrases (e.g. 'but'); and an interjection is a word that occurs in isolation to express an emotion or reaction (e.g. 'wow!').

Japanese shares the following categories with English: noun, pronoun, verb, adverb, conjunction and interjection. We see here three English grammatical categories that do not appear in Japanese: the article, the adjective and the preposition.

The article does not exist in Japanese, words like 'the' or 'a' are not used in front of nouns in this language.

The adjective as a word that modifies a noun or pronoun exists functionally but not morphologically. That means that there are words in Japanese that fulfill this function but are not considered as a separate type of word because their main function is another. In

Japanese, adjectives' functionality is fulfilled by the so-called adjectival verbs [☞ GE:I.1.2] and adjectival nouns [☞ GE:I.7.2]. There are, thus, some types of verbs and some types of nouns that specifically supply the functionality of adjectives. This will be explained in more detail in their corresponding sections.

Regarding prepositions, in English, as the name implies (*pre-*), they are placed before the modified word. In Japanese, this type of word does not exist because words that perform the function of linking two nouns or verbs and nouns are placed after the modified noun, so they are technically *postpositions*. In Japanese grammar, however, this type of word is grouped into a broader category called *particles*.

To summarize, let us look at the most important word classes to keep in mind in Japanese.

- **Nominal Words:** Words that name or refer to concepts, objects, people, animals, places or ideas. There are three types of nominals:

  - **Nouns:** Words that refer directly to a concept, object, person, animal, place, or idea. E.g. 'love' (*ai* 愛).

  - **Pronouns:** Words that can replace a noun. E.g. 'you' (*anata* あなた).

  - **Numerals:** Words designating a quantity, i.e. numbers. E.g. 'one' (*ichi* 一).

- **Verbs:** Conjugable words that express a state or action. E.g. 'to eat' (*taberu* 食べる).

- **Adjectival Words:** Words that define a state or condition of an explicit or implicit noun. E.g. 'red' (*akai* 赤い). In Japanese there are no adjectives in terms of their grammatical function as such. Hence, this category is divided into two groups belonging to other word classes:

  - **Adjectival Verbs**[38]: Adjectival words that are conjugated similarly to a verb.

  - **Adjectival Nouns:** Nouns that through the help of the copula (equivalent to the verb 'to be') act as an adjectival word.

- **Adverbs:** Non-conjugable words that modify a verb. E.g. 'well' (*yoku* よく)

- **Particles:** Dependent words that supply various linking functions between a noun and another noun or a verb; or between two phrases. E.g. *no* の (roughly an equivalent to the preposition 'of').

- **Conjunctions:** Words that start a new phrase by linking it to a previous phrase. E.g. 'however' (*shikashi* しかし).

- **Interjections:** Isolated words that act as a sentence with its own meaning. E.g. 'yes' (*hai* はい).

Each word class will be explained in more detail in their corresponding sub-section in the Part of Speech section of Grammatical Explanations [☞ GE:I].

---

[38] Sometimes referred simply as 'adjectives' throughout this book for brevity.

2. WORD ORDER

For the different word classes discussed so far to maintain a comprehensible correlation, they must be subject to a specific order of appearance within a sentence. To understand this properly, the concept of 'sentence' must first be clarified.

A *sentence* is a group of words composed of a *subject* and a *predicate*. The subject is the word or group of words referring to the entity that performs or experiences the action or state marked by a verb or verbal word. The predicate[39] is the part of the sentence consisting of verbal and optional *arguments*[40], i.e. other words that are neither the subject nor the verb. We see, then, that a sentence can be broken down into subject, argument, and verb. In Japanese, the subject can be implied, that is, not mentioned within the sentence but understood through context [☞ I.1.2]. The structure of a sentence, in Japanese, is thus as follows:

$$\text{(Subject +)} \quad \underline{\text{(Arguments +)} \quad \text{Verbal}}$$
$$\text{Predicate}$$

Arguments, on the other hand, can be divided into two categories: *object* and *complement*. An object is an entity formed by a word or group of words that is affected by the action marked by a verb. The complement, on the other hand, is a word or group of words that explains—'complements'—the circumstances in which the action or state of the verb takes place.

Having understood these concepts, we will see that in Japanese, the word order within a sentence is generally as follows:

$$(C + \cdots)\ (S +)\ (C + \cdots)\ (O +)\ (C + \cdots)\ V$$

※ C stands for *complement*; $\cdots$ stands for more possible verbal complements; S for the *subject*; O for *object*; and V for *verbal*. Parentheses stand for optionality.

We find that Japanese has, as we pointed out in the typology sub-section [☞ I.1], a strictly SOV word order, which means that the subject, if it appears, always comes before the verb, which is placed at the end of the sentence, while the object, if there is one, appears typically between the subject and the verb (it can exceptionally appear before the subject for emphasis). Complements can be placed, regardless of their number, anywhere before the verb.

Either the subject, the object, or the complement if it is a functional noun, may have its meaning extended or modified by an additional word—usually an adjectival word—called *nominal modifier*. The part of a modified subject or object that is not the nominal modifier is called the *head*. The order of the Japanese sentence with the extensions provided by optional modifiers will thus be as follows:

---

[39] We take here as a reference the terms used in traditional grammar, since there are other types of modern grammar in which the word 'predicate' has other definitions.

[40] So called because they 'argue' the meaning of the verb or subject.

([M +] C +)	([M +] S +)	([M +] C +)	([M +] O +)	([M +] C +)	V
Complement	*Subject*	*Complement*	*Object*	*Complement*	*Verbal*

※ M stands for *nominal modifier*; C for *complement* S for the *head* of the *subject*; O for the *head* of the *object*; and V for *verbal*. Parentheses and brackets stand for optionality.

Modifiers, optional before a noun, will always be placed to the left of the head word, which identifies Japanese as a 'head final and left branching' language.

In Japanese, there is also the peculiarity of the use of particles to link nouns with verbs or other nouns so that both the head of the subject and the head of the object will almost always[41] be marked with a particle. Nouns and some adverbs acting as complements are also accompanied by particles:

$$([M +] C\{p\}+) ([M +] S\{p\} +) ([M +] C\{p\}+) ([M +] O\{p\} +) ([M +] C\{p\}+) V$$

※ {p} in blue stands for *particle*, {p} in red stands for *particle* as long as the complement (C) is a noun.

Here is an example in practice:

M   S   p   C   p   C   p   M   O   p   V

あの 人 が ｜ 食堂 に ｜ 箸 で ｜ 美味しい ラーメン を ｜ 食べます。

ano hito ga | shokudō ni | hashi de | oishii ramen o | tabemasu

[that person | restaurant in | chopsticks with | delicious ramen | eats]

that person / eats / delicious ramen / with chopsticks / in the restaurant

What has been discussed up to this point is a basic sample of the behavior of words in Japanese when forming sentences. To see this in more detail with respect to the formation of compound sentences or how each type of word acts within the sentence structure, see the Syntax section in Grammar Explanations [☞ GE:II].

3. REGISTER & FORMALITY

As already explained in the section on typology and morphology [☞ I], the Japanese language is strongly regimented grammatically and semantically by different degrees of formality according to the speech register, the gender of the speaker and the social position of the interlocutors. Although a good introduction in this regard has already been given in that section, I find it convenient to summarize here the different registers and formalities according to which Japanese grammar functions, for this will be very relevant throughout the grammatical explanations given in this book.

---

[41] Only in colloquial language the occasional omission of a particle is possible (C.f. Particle Omission [☞ GE:II.3.2]).

3.1 Register

Register in a language is a particular way of speaking in relation to a specific environment or context in which the discourse place. In Japanese, three main registers can be distinguished:

- **Neutral Register**: An unmarked register. If the register is considered neutral, it means that it can occur in both written and spoken language without further distinction. If a neutral register is used in conversation, then formality will be taken into consideration.

- **Coloquial Register** [*col.*]: A specifically conversational manner of speaking, which is rare in written language unless it is a transcription or recreation of a conversation.

- **Literary Register** [*lit.*]: A specifically literary manner of speaking, the occurrence of which is more or less frequent in formal written language such as that used in academics, but rare and considered as whimsical in spoken language unless it is a quotation.

- **Obsolete Register** [*obs.*]: Not used in everyday speech neither colloquially nor literally but sometimes still attested in fossilized expressions or grammatical constructions.

3.2 Formality

Formality designates the manner of speaking depending on the social relationship between the speaker and the listener. Formality takes special consideration in spoken language, as written language tends to be plain since the social position of the "listener" or reader is ambiguous.

Two concepts must be taken into consideration for formality: group and hierarchy. In group relations, we consider the people who belong to the group—*insiders*—and the people who do not—*outsiders*—; the perspective is horizontal. An in-group can be, for example, family, a group of friends of similar ages, or co-workers with the same position in the company. In hierarchical relationships, the participants' social status is taken into account from a vertical perspective, that is, which of the interlocutors is in a *higher* or *lower* social status to the other, or whether they are *equals*. A hierarchical relationship can be, for example, that of a parent and a child, a teacher and a pupil, or an employer and an employee.

Within the parameters outlined so far, we can distinguish five main scales of formality:

- **Plain Formality**: Ambiguous formality, mostly used in impersonal texts or thoughts.

- **Formal Formality** [*for.*]: Manner of speaking carried out between outsiders in formal situations. Commonly seen in business settings or official statements.

- **Familiar Formality** [*fam.*]: Manner of speaking carried out among insiders. or towards people of equal or inferior status. When an outsider, especially if considered socially inferior, speaks in a familiar way, it can be understood as offensive.

- **Polite Formality** [*pol.*]: Manner of speaking carried out among outsiders in conversational environments, or towards people of a higher social status.

- **Humble Formality** [*hum.*]: Manner of speaking carried out by someone of a lower status when talking about him or herself with someone of a higher status. Used to show respect while humbling oneself.

- **Honorific Formality** [*hon.*]: Manner of speaking carried out by someone of a lower status when addressing or talking about someone of a higher status. Used to show respect towards the listener by uplifting him or her.

3.3 Gender

In certain conjugations and expressions, the gender of the speaker can be revealed through the way he or she speaks. In Japanese, there is an inferred gender, which means that there are certain conjugations, expressions and words that tend to be used more by men and others by women. Three main ways of speaking can be distinguished according to gender:

- **Neuter Gender:** Manner of speaking that does not reveal any gender of the speaker. Most conjugations and expressions are naturally of this type.

- **Masculine Gender** [*mas.*]: Manner of speaking mostly used by men or exceptionally by women or characters with a somewhat masculine personality.

- **Feminine Gender** [*fem.*]: A way of speaking mostly used by women or exceptionally by men or characters with a somewhat feminine personality.

VOCABULARY

VOCABULARY

In this part, we present the Japanese words whose knowledge is most relevant for having a fluent Japanese language conversation.

The words presented here are grouped by part of speech, and within this grouping, by semantic fields.

The grouping by parts of speech is as follows:

I. **Pronouns & Prenominals**

II. **Nouns**

III. **Numerals & Classifiers**

IV. **Verbs & Nominal Verbs**

V. **Adjectives & Adjectival Nouns**

VI. **Adverbs & Nominal Adverbs**

VII. **Interjections & Conjunctions**

VIII. **Nominal Affixes**

I. PRONOUNS & PRENOMINALS

Pronouns are a type of nominal word that is used to refer to the participants in speech or to someone or something that has been previously mentioned or can be understood contextually. Like any nominal word, Japanese pronouns can also be modified by a modifying word, unlike English, where pronouns cannot be modified. There are several types of pronouns in Japanese: personal pronouns, interrogative pronouns, indefinite pronouns and demonstrative pronouns.

The word class known as **prenominals** defines morphemes that are placed before a nominal in order to modify it and serve to express a reference to that nominal. It is common in Japanese for a group of pronouns to have a lexically related set of prenominals.

1. PERSONAL PRONOUNS

Personal pronouns are pronouns that refer to one or more persons who can be pointed out within a sentence. The use of personal pronouns in Japanese is restricted by formality and register and, furthermore, it is usually preferred to omit their use whenever possible. Normally one only resorts to the use of personal pronouns when the person or persons one wants to refer to cannot be deciphered by the given context.

It should be taken into account that in Japanese personal pronouns are subject to a more diverse overtone than they are in English, so the use of one pronoun or another, depending on the situation, will affect the semantic sense and feeling of the sentence dramatically.

Like other nominals, personal pronouns may be followed by particles, so in Japanese there is no necessity for possessive pronouns such as ('my', 'your', etc), since the possessive forms are formed by adding the genitive particle *no* ('of') to any personal pronoun.

1.1 First Person Singular

Personal pronouns that refer to one speaker ('I'). In Japanese the use of these pronouns is relegated to the need of making a contrast ('I instead of you') or making clear that the subject of the conversation is oneself when that is not known previously. As it happens with any pronoun in Japanese, with the first person singular pronoun there are several options with different nuances. In this sense, the choice of one pronoun or another will depend on the register in which it is used, the varying in degrees of formality and familiarity with respect to the listener and even gender (whether the speaker is male or female).

Important Words

watashi 私 [*for.*] *I*	boku 僕 [*mas.*] *I*

watákushi 私: [*for.*] **I; me**

O.J. *wa* (I; me) + *takushi*: (I) *takusu* (to entrust) ‖ Originally referring to s.t. concerning to oneself, s.t. 'private'.

❖ U. by both men and women, it is the most pol. first person pronoun. It is m. u. when the listener is in the speaker's out-group and socially higher or equal to him or her.

Ⓕ **watáshi** 私: [*for.*] **I; me**

← *watakushi (I; me)*

❖ U. by both men and women in for. situations. In casual situations it is m. u. only by women.

Ⓕ **atáshi** あたし 〔私〕 : [*fam.*][*fɔm.*] **I; me**

← *watashi (I; me)* ← *watakushi (I; me)*

uchí₁ うち 〔❶ 内/ ❷ 家〕 : ① [*col.*][*fam.*] [*fɔm.*] ① **I; me** ② **our** (house's/family's)

Cognate w. *uchi (inside)*

❖ ❷ In this sense it is u. by both males and females.

Ⓕ **bòku** 僕 Ⓒ : [*mas.*] **I; me**

‖ Originally this Chinese character meant 'servant'.

❖ U. by males as a neutral first person pronoun.

Ⓜ **oré** 俺: [*fam.*][*mas.*] **I; me**

← *ware (I; me)*.

❖ U. by males when the listener is equal or lower than the speaker in age or social status.

wàre 我: [*lit.*][*for.*] **I; me**

O.J. *wa (I; me)* + O.J. suf. *re (thing)*

wàga 我が: [*lit.*] ① **my** ② **our**

O.J. *wa (I; me)* + O.J. possessive p. *ga*

1.2 Second Person Singular

Second person pronouns are those pronouns that refer to the listener ('you'). As with the first person singular pronouns, in Japanese second person pronouns are also generally not used unless strictly necessary when the context requires it.

In most cases the speaker will address the listener without mentioning any pronoun. When it is required to draw the listener's attention, it would be preferred to use his or her professional title in formal contexts (e.g. 'teacher', 'boss', etc), or his or her name accompanied by a personal suffix [☞ VIII. 2.1] in a familiar contexts. If the person's title is not known in a formal register, the demonstrative pronoun *sochira* is often used instead of a second person personal pronoun [☞ I. 3.4].

The second person personal pronouns listed here are mostly only used in informal and familiar contexts, because using them with strangers or in formal situations would sound rude or impolite.

Important Words

anata あなた *you*	kimi 君 [*fam.*] *you*

Ⓕ **anàta** あなた 〔貴方〕 : **you**

← *ano kata (that person)* ‖ Originally u. to indirectly refer to the addressee exactly as the word *sochira (that direction)* is u. nowadays.

❖ Originally u. in for. settings when the listener is equal or lower status, but it is tending to be more u. by females in a rather familiar way.

ànta あなた: [*col.*][*fam.*][*fɔm.*] **you**

← *anata (you)*

❖ M u. by females when the listener is in the speaker's in-group and is socially lower or equal.

Ⓕ **kimí** 君: [*fam.*] **you**

‖ Originally this Chinese character meant 'prince'.

❖ U. when the listener is in the speaker's in-group and equal or lowr in status.

⊕ otáku お宅: [*hon.*] ① **your home**; your family ② **you**

Ⓙ Hon. pre. *o* + Ⓒ *taku* 宅 *(residence)*

❖ ❷ A polite, respectful way of saying 'you' to s.o. of equal status while implying a sense of distance.

Ⓛ omáe お前: [*col.*][*fam.*][*mas.*] **you**

Hon. pre. *o* + *mae (in front of)*

❖ M. u. by males to address s.o. equal or lower social status or age in casual situations. It can be usually considered rude when not u. appropriately.

temáe てまえ〔手前〕: [*mas.*] **you**

te (hand) + *mae (in front of)*

❖ M. seen as rude, u. to people of lower age or status.

kisáma 貴様: [*mas.*] **you** (bastard)

Ⓒ *ki* 貴 *(valuable)* + Ⓙ *hon. suf. sama* ‖ *Originally it was u. to refer respectfully to each other, but later it started to be u. ironically and now is only u. in a pejorative way.*

❖ This pronoun is deliberately u. in a rude and derogatory way.

1.3 Third Person Singular

Third person personal pronouns refer to a person who is neither the speaker nor the listener ('he'; 'she'; 'it'). As with all other personal pronouns in Japanese, third person pronouns also tend to be avoided and the use of the title or name with a personal suffix is often preferred when referring to a particular person. Third person pronouns are only used when it is strictly necessary. In that case, the formulation **ano hito** ('that person') or its polite version **ano kata** are normally preferred. The *kare* ('he'; 'him') or **kanojo** ('she'; 'her') forms are often relegated to the addressing of either distant people or very intimate people. Depending on context, *kare* and *kanojo* can even mean 'boyfriend' and 'girlfriend' respectively.

Important Words

kare 彼 *he*	kanojo 彼女 *she*

- -

Ⓣ karé 彼: ① **he; him** ② boyfriend

O.J. distal pre. ka + *O.J. suf. re (thing)*

Ⓣ kànojo₁ 彼女: ① **she; her** ② girlfriend

Ⓙ *O.J. kano (that)* + Ⓒ *jo* 女 *(woman)*

anò hito あの人〔彼の人〕: **that person; he; she**

ano (that) + *hito (person)*

anó katà あの方〔彼の方〕: [*pol.*] **that person; he; she**

ano (that) + *kata (direction)*

yàtsu₁ やつ〔奴〕: [*col.*][*mas.*] ① thing ② **that guy; that one; that person; he; she**

1.4 Reflexive Pronouns

Reflexive pronouns are those pronouns referring to a person already named in the discourse (they are co-referential). In English these pronouns are 'oneself', 'myself', 'yourself', etc. In Japanese, there is not a reflexive pronoun for each person but rather general reflexive pronouns—*jibun* or the less common **jishin**—that can be used for any person, the person which will normally be indicated in the form of a subject earlier in the speech or text. In the event that the co-referenced person does not appear in the speech, that person will be understood according to the context, although it would normally refer to the first person ('oneself') or to the second person if the sentence is a command or suggestion.

Important Word

jibun 自分 *oneself*

ⓕ **jibún** 自分 Ⓒ (*oneself+dividing*): ① **one**; **oneself**; **myself** ② **own** ③ [*for.*] **I; me**

❖ ❷ Followed by the genitive p. *no.*

❖ ❷ Referring to both abstract things (emotions or thoughts) and concrete things (one's own body).

ⓜ **jìshin** 自身 Ⓒ (*oneself+body*): ① **(by) oneself**; **(one's) self** ② **one's own**

❖ ❶ Attached to other n.s or pronouns.

❖ ❷ Followed by the genitive p. *no.*

❖ Usually referring to actions that are done by 'oneself'.

jibún jìshin 自分自身: ① **oneself; myself; yourself**

Ⓒ *jibun* 自分 (*oneself*) + *jishin* 自身 (*oneself*)

ⓙ **jìko** 自己 Ⓒ (*oneself+self*): ① **oneself; self** ② **one's own**

❖ ❶ Placed before other n.s.

❖ ❷ Followed by the genitive p. *no.*

❖ Referring to abstract things (one's emotions, thoughts or believes).

onóre 己: ① [*lit.*][*mas.*] **oneself; self; own** ② [*hum.*] **I; me** ③ **you**

Obs. *ono* (oneself) + O.J. suf. *re* (thing)

❖ ❷ It can be understood as arrogant due to its use as a sarcasm.

❖ ❸ U. in a disdainful way.

ⓣ **tagái (ni)** 互いに: [*lit.*] **each other; one another**

➤ [*col.*] otágai (ni) お互いに

1.5 Plural Personal Pronouns

Plural personal pronouns refer to two or more people. In Japanese, the plurality in personal pronouns is marked by the addition of a pluralizing suffix (mostly -*tachi* and -*ra*). As with all other personal pronouns, the choice of one or another pronoun next to one or another suffix will depend on the register and formality of the speech.

Important Words

watashitachi 私たち [*for.*] *we*	bokutachi 僕たち [*mas.*] *we*
anatatachi あなたたち *you guys*	kimitachi 君たち [*fam.*] *you guys*
karera 彼ら *they* (male)	kanojotachi 彼女たち *they* (female)

-tachi たち〔達〕: pluralizing suffix

-ra ら〔等〕: pluralizing suffix

　<- O.J. suf. *ra* (abouts)

➤ watakushitachi 私たち: [*for.*] **we; us**

➤ watashitachi 私たち: [*for.*] **we; us**

➤ bokutachi 僕たち: [***mas.***] **we; us**

➤ atashitachi あたしたち: [*fam.*][*f⁈m.*] **we; us**

➤ oretachi 俺たち: [*fam.*][*mas.*] **we; us**

➤ warera 我ら: [*lit.*] **we; us**

➤ bokura 僕ら: [*fam.*][*mas.*] **we; us**

➤ orera 俺ら: [*fam.*][*mas.*] **we; us**

㊤ waréware 我々: [*for.*] **we; us**

ware (I; me) ×2

❖ M. u. when talking about one's group or company.

watákushìdomo 私ども〔私共〕: [***hum.***] [*for.*] **we; us**

watashi (I; me) + obs. hum. pluralizing suf. *domo*

➤ [*col.*][***hum.***] watáshidomo 私ども〔私共〕

➤ anatatachi あなたたち: **you** (guys)

➤ kimitachi 君たち: [*fam.*] **you** (guys)

➤ omaetachi お前たち: [*fam.*][*mas.*] **you** (guys)

anátagata あなた方〔貴方方〕: [*hon.*] **you** (people)

- -

➤ ano hitotachi あの人たち: **those people; they; them**

➤ kanojotachi 彼女たち: **they; them** (female)

➤ karera 彼ら: **they; them** (male)

➤ kanojora 彼女ら: **they; them** (female)

➤ yatsura やつら: [*col.*] **those guys; those people; they; them**

- -

minà 皆: [*for.*] **everyone; everybody**

➤ [*col.*] ㊦ mińnà みんな〔皆〕

➤ [*pol.*] ㊦ minàsan 皆さん: you (plural)

PERSONAL PRONOUNS

	Reg.	Gen.	Singular	Plural	Listener
	Neutral	Either	watashi 私	watashitachi	Anyone
	pol.	Either	[*lit.*] ware 我	wareware	Anyone
				warera	
			watakushi 私	watakushitachi	Higher
1st Person		*f⁈m.*	atashi あたし	atashitachi	Equal / Lower
	fam.		boku 僕	bokutachi	
		mas.		bokura	
			ore 俺	oretachi	
				orera	

69

			anata あなた	anatatachi	Anyone
2nd Person	Plain	Either	kimi 君	kimitachi	Equal / Lower
	pol.	Either	name or title	anatagata	Equal / Higher
	fam.	*fam.*	anta あんた	-	Equal / Lower
		mas.	omae お前	omaetachi	
3rd Person	-	Either	ano hito あの人	ano hitotachi	Anyone
			kare 彼 (*he*)	karera	
			kanojo 彼女 (*she*)	kanojotachi	
				kanojora	

2. INTERROGATIVES & INDEFINITES

Interrogative pronouns are used to ask which thing ('what'), person ('who'), place ('where'), method ('how'), reason ('why'), quantity ('how much') or occasion ('when') the discourse is about.

Indefinite pronouns, on the other hand, answer in a non-specific way to those questions above. Non-specification can be negative ('no'), universal ('every'), exclusive elective ('some') or non-exclusive elective ('any'). Indefinite pronouns are formed from the interrogative pronouns by the addition of particles such as the concessive particles **mo** and **de mo** ('even') or the interrogative particle **ka**.

In Japanese, interrogative and indefinite pronouns are usually morphologically related, as many indefinite pronouns are lexically derived from the interrogatives. Meanwhile, there are a number of prenominals also related to the roots used in those interrogatives pronouns.

2.1 What & Which

Interrogative and indefinite pronouns and prenominals that answer or allude to the questions 'what' and 'which'.

Important Words

nani 何 *what*	dore どれ *which*
donna どんな *what kind of...*	dono どの *which...*

Ⓣ nàni 何: **what**

➢ nan 何: ① **what...** ② many... ③ without any...

❖ ❶ U. before classifiers and before the cop. {D}.

❖ ❷ When u. before classifiers followed by the p. mo.

❖ ❸ When u. before classifiers and followed by the v. adj. **nai**.

naní mo₁ / nàni mo 何も: **nothing**; **anything**; any

nani (what) + thematic-concessive p. *mo*

❖ U. w. neg. f.s of v.s.

Ⓤ **nań de mo₁** / nàn de mo なんでも 〔何でも〕: **anything**; everything; whatever

*nan** + concessive p. *de mo* |* ← *nani (what)*

nàni ka 何か: **something**; anything

nani (what) + interrogative p. *ka*

Ⓤ **nàn ka** なんか 〔何か〕: [*fam.*] ① **something**; anything; any ② **somehow**

*nan** + interrogative p. *ka* |* ← *nani (what)*

❖ ❶ It usually carries a neg. nuance.

- -

Ⓣ **dòre** どれ 〔何れ〕: **which** (one)

Indeterminate pre. *do* + O.J. suf. *re (thing)*

Ⓣ **dòno** どの 〔何の〕: **which…**; what…; what kind of…

Indeterminate pre. *do* + attributive p. *no*

❖ *Prenominal*: Only u. before a n.

Ⓣ **dònna** どんな: ① **what kind** of…; what… ② (no matter) how much…

← *dona*: Indeterminate pre. *do* + copulative-attributive p. *na*

❖ ❶ *Prenominal*: Only u. before a n.

❖ ❷ When u. before an adj.

Ⓦ **dò iu** どういう 〔どう言う〕: **what kind** of…

dō (how) + *iu (to say)*

❖ *Prenominal*: Only u. before a n.

nàn no 何の: ① **what kind** of…; what sort of… ② **any** (kind of)…

nan (what) + genitive p *no (of)*

❖ *Prenominal*: Only u. before a n.

❖ ❷ When u. before a n. followed by the p. **mo**.

dòre mo どれも 〔何れも〕: ① **every**; all; each ② **none**; either

dore (which) + thematic-concessive p. *mo*

❖ ❷ U. w. neg. f.s of v.s.

izúre mo いずれも 〔何れも〕: ① **every**; all ② **none**; either

From the now obs. original meaning of *izure (which)* + thematic-concessive p. *mo*

❖ ❷ U. w. neg. f.s of v.s.

dòre de mo どれでも 〔何れでも〕: **any**; whichever

dore (which) + concessive compound p. *de mo*

dòre ka どれか 〔何れか〕: ① **one of**; any of ② **either of** ③ **which one**

dore (which) + interrogative p. *ka*

❖ ❷ U. w. neg. f.s of v.s.

izúre ka いずれか 〔何れか〕: ① **one of**; any of; whichever ② **either of**

From the now obs. original meaning of *izure (which)* + interrogative p. *ka*

- -

Ⓤ **àru₁** ある 〔或る〕: **a certain…**; **some…**

From the v. *aru (to exist)*

❖ *Prenominal*: Only u. before a n.

Ⓤ **aráyùru** あらゆる 〔凡ゆる〕: **all…**; **every…**

*ara** + O.J. passive suf. *yuru* |*Irrealis f. of v. *aru (to exist)*

❖ *Prenominal*: Only u. before a n.

Ⓤ **iwáyùru** / iwàyuru いわゆる 〔所謂〕: **what is called…**; the **so-called..**; …**as it is called**

*iwa** + O.J. passive suf. *yuru* |*Irrealis f. of v. *iu (to say)*

❖ *Prenominal*: Only u. before a n.

2.2 Who

Interrogative and indefinite pronouns that answer or allude to the questions 'who' and 'which person'.

Important Word

dare 誰 *who*

ⓣ **dàre 誰: who**

← O.J. *tare:* O.J. *ta (who)* + O.J. suf. *re (thing)*

ⓛ **dònata** どなた〔何方〕: [*hon.*] **who**; which person

Indeterminate pre. *do* + suf. *nata (way)* ‖ The original meaning of this pronoun was 'which way', which in turn was u. as an indirect way of asking 'who'.

dòitsu どいつ〔何奴〕: [*col.*][*fam.*] **who**; which guy; which person

← *doyatsu:* indeterminate pre. *do* + fam. *yatsu (person)*

✤ It usually has a derogatory sense.

dàre mo 偽〔誰も〕: ① **everybody**; everyone ② **nobody**; no one

dare (who) + thematic-concessive p. *mo*

✤ ❷ U. w. neg. f.s of v.s.

dàre de mo 誰でも: **anybody**; anyone

dare (who) + concessive compound p. *de mo*

dònata de mo どなたでも〔何方でも〕: [*hon.*] **anybody**; anyone

donata (who) + concessive compound p. *de mo*

ⓛ **dàre ka** 誰か: ① **somebody**; someone ② **anybody**; anyone

dare (who) + interrogative p. *ka*

dònata ka どなたか〔何方か〕: [*hon.*] ① **somebody**; someone ② **anybody**; anyone

donata (who) + interrogative p. *ka*

2.3 Where & Which Way

Interrogative and indefinite pronouns that answer or allude to the questions 'where' and 'which way'.

Important Words

doko どこ *where*	dochira どちら *which way*

ⓣ **dòko** どこ〔何処〕: **where**; which place; which part

Indeterminate pre. *do* + O.J. suf. *ko (place)*

dòko mo どこも〔何処も〕: ① **everywhere** ② **nowhere**

doko (where) + thematic-concessive p. *mo*

✤ ❷ U. w. neg. f.s of v.s.

dòko de mo どこでも〔何処でも〕: **anywhere**; wherever; no matter where

doko (where) + concessive compound p. *de mo*

dòko ka どこか〔何処か〕: ①
somewhere; some place ② **where**

doko (where) + interrogative p. *ka*

- -

⊕ **dòchira** どちら〔何方〕: ① **which way;**
where ② **which** (one) ③ [*pol.*] **who**

Indeterminate pre. *do* + *chi (place)* + suf. *ra (abouts)*

✤ ❶ In for. language it is u. as an indirect way of asking 'where'.

✤ ❷ U. w. the meaning of 'which one' when choosing between two options.

✤ ❸ This pronoun is sometimes u. for asking 'which person' or 'who' in an indirect, polite way.

➢ [*fam.*] **dòcchi** どっち〔何方〕

dòchira mo どちらも〔何方も〕: ① **both;**
either (of two); ② **neither** (of two)

dochira (which way) + thematic-concessive p. *mo*

✤ ❷ U. w. neg. f.s of v.s.

➢ [*fam.*] **dòcchi mo** どっちも〔何方も〕

dòchira de mo どっちも〔何方も〕:
either way; whichever

dochira (which way) + concessive compound p. *de mo*

➢ [*fam.*] **dòcchi de mo** どっちも〔何方も〕

dòchira ka どちらか〔何方か〕: **either**
way; rather

dochira (which way) + interrogative p. *ka*

➢ [*fam.*] **dòcchi ka** どっちか〔何方か〕

2.4 How & Why

Interrogative and indefinite pronouns that answer or allude to the questions 'how' and 'why'.

Important Words

dō どう *how*	dō shite どうして *why*

- -

Ⓣ **dò** どう〔如何〕: **how**; how about

← *dono yō: dono (which)* + *yō (way)*

✤ U. for asking about the state of s.o./s.t. or the way of doing s.t.

✤ Also u. to offer or suggest s.t. to the listener.

⊕ **ikàga** いかが〔如何〕: [*for.*] **how**; how about

O.J. *ika (how)* + nominative p. *ga*

✤ U. for asking about the state of s.o./s.t.

✤ Also u. to offer or suggest s.t. to the listener.

dò yatte どうやって: [*col.*] **how**; in what way; by what means

dō (how) + *yatte*: Gerundive f. of the col. v. *yaru (to do)*

✤ U. for asking about the way of doing s.t.

Ⓣ **dò shite** どうして〔如何して〕: **why**;
what for; how come

dō (how) + *shite*: Gerundive f. of the v. *suru (to do)*

✤ U. for asking for reasons, causes and methods.

ⓔ **nànde** なんで〔何で〕: [*fam.*] **why;** what for; how come

✤ U. for asking for reasons, causes and methods.

nàze なぜ〔何故〕: [*for.*] **why**

✤ U. for asking for reasons and causes. It may sound direct.

dó ka₁ どうか〔如何か〕: **somehow;** anyhow ② [*for.*] **how about;** how about

dō (how) + interrogative p. *ka*

ⓣ **dò mo₁** どうも〔如何も〕: **no matter how; somehow;** quite; howsoever ② **not at all**

dō (how) + thematic-concessive p. *mo*

✤ ❷ U. w. neg. f.s of v.s.

✤ U. to indicate that one cannot make a definite statement about s.t. due to lack of evidence.

ⓔ **dó shitè mo** / dò shite mo どうしても 〔如何しても〕: **no matter what/how**

dō shite (why) + thematic-concessive p. *mo*

dó de mo / dò de mo どうでも〔如何で も〕: **anyhow;** anyway; whatever

dō (how) + concessive compound p. *de mo*

2.5 When & How Much

Interrogative and indefinite pronouns and prenominals that answer or allude to the questions 'when', 'how many' and 'how much'.

Important Words

itsu どこ *when*	ikutsu いくつ *how many*	ikura いくら *how much*

ⓣ **ìtsu** いつ〔何時〕: **when**

➤ ⓣ **ìtsu mo** いつも〔何時も〕: ① **always**; all the time ② **never**

itsu (when) + thematic-concessive p. *mo*

✤ ❷ U. w. neg. f.s of v.s.

➤ **ìtsu de mo** いつでも〔何時でも〕: **anytime**; whenever

itsu (when) + concessive compound p. *de mo*

➤ **ìtsu ka** いつか〔何時か〕: **sometime;** someday; somewhen

itsu (when) + interrogative p. *ka*

iku 幾: **how many...**

✤ *Prenominal*: Only u. before a classifier.

➤ ⓜ **ikutsu** いくつ〔幾つ〕: **how many**

iku (how many) + *tsu (general classifier)* [☞ III. 2.1]

ⓜ **ikura** / ikúra いくら〔幾ら〕: **how much**

iku (how many) + suf. *ra (abouts)*

✤ M. u. for things that have a definite limit.

ⓔ **dònna ni** どんなに: ① **how much; how** ② no matter how; regardless of how much

donna (which) + adverbializing p. *ni*

✤ M. u. for exclamatory statements indicating surprise by the degree to which an action or state takes place.

ikà ni いかに〔如何に〕: [*for.*] ① **how** ② in what way ③ how much

O.J. *ika (how)* + adverbializing suf. *ni*

❖ M. u. for exclamatory statements indicating surprise by the degree to which an action or state takes place.

➤ [*col.*] ikàn いかん〔如何〕

ìkutsu mo いくつも〔幾つも〕: ① **many**; a great number of ② **hardly**

ikutsu (how many) + thematic-concessive p. *mo*

❖ ❷ U. w. neg. f.s of v.s.

ikura mo いくらも〔幾らも〕: ① **much**; a lot ② **not much**; little

ikura (how much) + thematic-concessive p. *mo*

❖ ❷ U. w. neg. f.s of v.s.

ìkutsu de mo いくつでも〔幾つでも〕: **any number of**

ikutsu (how many) + concessive compound p. *de mo*

ikura de mo / ikúra de mò いくらでも〔幾らでも〕: ① **any amount of** ② **no matter how** (much)

ikura (how much) + concessive compound p. *de mo*

ìkutsu ka いくつか〔幾つか〕: **some number of; some**

ikutsu (how many) + interrogative p. *ka*

➤ ìkutsu ka no いくつかの〔幾つかの〕: **some**; few; several

❖ *Prenominal*: Only u. before a n.

ìkura ka / ikúra kà いくらか〔幾らか〕: **some amount of; some**

ikura (how much) + interrogative p. *ka*

INTERROGATIVE & INDEFINITE PRONOUNS

Interrogative Pronouns	Indefinite Pronouns		
	+ **mo** も (*ever.../no...*)	+ **de mo** で (*any...*)	+ **ka** か (*some...*)
nani 何 **what**	nani mo **nothing**	nan de mo **anything**	nan(i) ka **something**
izure いずれ [*obs.*] which	izure mo **every; none**	-	izure ka **either of; any of**
dore どれ **which** (one)	dore mo **every; none**	dore de mo **any one**	dore ka **which one; any of**
dare 誰 **who**	dare mo **everybody; nobody**	dare de mo **anybody**	dare ka **somebody**
donata どなた [*hon.*] **who**	-	donata de mo [*hon.*] **anybody**	donata ka [*hon.*] **somebody**
doko どこ **where**	doko mo **everywhere; nowhere**	doko de mo **anywhere**	doko ka **somewhere**
dochira どちら **which way**	dochira mo **both ways**	dochira de mo **either way**	dochira ka **either way**

docchi どっち	docchi mo	docchi de mo	docchi ka
[*fam.*] **which way**	[*fam.*] **both ways**	[*fam.*] **either way**	[*fam.*] **either way**
dō どう	dō mo	dō de mo	dō ka
how	**no matter how**	**anyhow**	**somehow**
dō shite どうして	dō shite mo	-	-
[*fam.*] **why**; how	**no matter what**		
naze なぜ	-	-	naze ka [*for.*]
[*for.*] **why**			**for some reason**
itsu いつ	itsu mo	itsu de mo	itsu ka
when	**always; never**	**any time**	**sometime**
ikutsu いくつ	ikutsu mo	ikutsu de mo	ikutsu ka
how many	**many; hardly**	**any number of**	**some number of**
ikura いくら	ikura mo	ikura de mo	ikura ka
how much	**much; not much**	**any amount**	**some amount**

3 DEMONSTRATIVES

Demonstrative pronouns and prenominals are used to point out an entity to which the speech refers through context and to distinguish it from other entities.

Japanese demonstratives can answer the questions 'which', 'what kind of', 'where', and 'how' and are divided into three distances: proximal ('this'), medial ('that') and distal ('that over there'). Japanese demonstrative pronouns follow a very clear morphological pattern developed according to these distances: Proximal demonstratives use the morpheme **ko-**, medial demonstratives use the morpheme **so-** and distal demonstratives use the morpheme **a-**.

3.1 Which One

Demonstrative pronouns and prenominals that answer the question 'which'. The pronouns add the suffix -*re* to the root and the prenominals add the suffix -**no**. The suffix -**no** is simply the genitive particle no ('of') added to the root demonstrative morphemes. For this reason, sometimes demonstrative prenominals can also be understood as 'of this/that' as well as 'this/that'.

This group of demonstratives also includes the distributive morphemes[42] that refer to 'each and every'.

Important Words

---

[42] These morphemes are usually considered as prefixes in other grammars, but they are considered demonstrative prenominals in this book because they express a direct reference to the nominal rather than specify one of its characteristics.

kore これ *this one*	sore それ *that one*	are あれ *that one*
kono この *this...*	sono その *that...*	ano あの *that...*
ryō 両 *both...*	mai 毎 *each... (w. time)*	kaku 各 *every...*

Ⓕ koré これ 〔此れ〕: **this** (one)

Proximal pre. *ko* + O.J. suf. *re (thing)*

❖ U. to talk about s.t. that is close to the speaker or s.t. known to him/her.

➤ kore wa → [*col.*] korya こりゃ

➤ korèra これら 〔此れ等〕: **these**

Ⓕ konó この 〔此の〕: **this...**

Proximal pre. *ko* + attributive p. *no*

❖ *Prenominal*: Only u. before a n.

❖ U. to talk about s.t. that is close to the speaker or s.t. known to him/her.

Ⓕ soré それ 〔其れ〕: **that** (one)

Medial pre. *so* + O.J. suf. *re (thing)*

❖ U. to talk about s.t. that is close to the listener or s.t. known to the speaker or listener.

➤ sore wa → [*col.*] sorya そりゃ

➤ sorèra それら 〔其れ等〕: **those**

Ⓕ sonó その 〔其の〕: **that...**

Medial pre. *so* + attributive p. *no*

❖ *Prenominal*: Only u. before a n.

❖ U. to talk about s.t. that is close to the listener or s.t. known to the speaker or listener.

Ⓕ aré あれ 〔彼れ〕: **that** (one over there)

Distal pre. *a* + O.J. suf. *re (thing)*

❖ U. to talk about s.t. that is far from the speaker and the listener or known to both.

➤ are wa → [*col.*] arya ありゃ

➤ arèra それら 〔彼れ等〕: **those** (over there)

Ⓕ anó あの 〔彼の〕: **that** (over there)

Distal pre. *a* + attributive cop. *no*

❖ *Prenominal*: Only u. before a n.

❖ U. to talk about s.t. that is far from the speaker and the listener or known to both.

Ⓛ ryóhò / ryóhō 両方 Ⓒ (*both + direction*): Ⓝ **both** (sides) Ⓐ (no) both

❖ M. u. for non-human objects.

ryò₁ 両 Ⓒ : **both...**

❖ *Prenominal*: Only u. before a n.

---

mài 毎 Ⓒ (*every*): **every...**; **each...**

❖ *Prenominal*: Only u. before a n.

❖ M. u. w. temporal n. adv.s and classifiers (e.g. days, times, etc).

kàku 各 Ⓒ (*each*): **each...**; **every...**

❖ *Prenominal*: Only u. before a n.

❖ M. u. w. non-temporal n.s and classifiers.

sorézòre₁ no それぞれの 〔其々の〕: **each**

*sorezore** + attributive cop. |* ← *soresore*: *sore (that)* ×2

❖ *Prenominal*: Only u. before a n.

❖ M. u. w. non-temporal n.s and classifiers.

3.2 What Kind of

Demonstrative prenominals that answer the question 'what kind of'.

Important Words

konna こんな *this kind of...*	sonna そんな *that kind of...*	anna あんな *that kind of...*

Ⓣ końna こんな: **this kind of...**; such...; like this...

← *kona*: Proximal pre. *ko* + copulative-attributive p. *na*

❖ *Prenominal*: Only u. before a n.

❖ U. to talk about s.t. that is close to the speaker or s.t. known to him/her.

kố iú こういう〔斯う言う〕: **such...; this sort of...**

kō (like this) + iu (to say)

❖ *Prenominal*: Only u. before a n.

kố shita こうした〔斯うした〕: [*lit.*] **such...; this sort of...**

kō (like this) + shita: Perfective f. of the v. *suru (to do)*

❖ *Prenominal*: Only u. before a n.

Ⓣ sońna そんな: **that kind of...**; ...like that; that sort of...; such...

← *sona*: Medial pre. *so* + copulative-attributive p. *na*

❖ *Prenominal*: Only u. before a n.

❖ U. to talk about s.t. that is close to the listener or s.t. known to him/her.

số iú そういう〔然う言う〕: ① **such...; that sort of...**; ② very

sō (like that) + iu (to say)

❖ *Prenominal*: Only u. before a n.

⊕ ańna あんな: **that kind of...**; ...like that; that sort of...; such...

← *ana*: Distal pre. *a* + copulative-attributive p. *na*

❖ *Prenominal*: Only u. before a n.

❖ U. to talk about some place that is far from the speaker and the listener or known to both.

3.3 Where

Demonstrative pronouns that answer the question 'where'.

Important Words

koko ここ *here one*	soko そこ *there*	asoko あそこ *there*

Ⓣ kokó ここ〔此処〕: **here**; this place; this part

Proximal pre. *ko* + O.J. suf. *ko (place)*

❖ U. to talk about somewhere that is close to the speaker or known to him/her.

Ⓣ sokó そこ〔其処〕: **there**; that place; that part

Medial pre. *so* + O.J. suf. *ko (place)*

❖ U. to talk about some place that is close to the listener or known to the speaker or listener.

⊕ asóko あそこ 〔彼処〕 : **there**; that place (over there); that part (over there)

Distal pre. *a* + *soko* (*there*)

❖ U. to talk about some place that is far from the speaker and the listener or known to both.

3.4 Which Way

Demonstrative pronouns that answer the question 'which way'. These pronouns are also used in formal language to indirectly answer the question 'which person' or 'who'.

Important Words

kochira こちら *this way*	sochira そちら *that way*	achira あちら *that way*

Ⓣ kochíra こちら 〔此方〕 : ① **this way**; this thing ② [*for.*][*pol.*] **I**; me; this person

Proximal pre. *ko* + O.J. *chi* (*way*) + suf. *ra* (*abouts*)

❖ U. to talk about some direction that is close to the speaker or known to him/her.

➤ [*fam.*] kocchì こっち 〔何処も〕

⊕ sochíra そちら 〔其方〕 : ① **that way**; this thing ② [*for.*][*pol.*] **that person**; you

Medial pre. *so* + O.J. *chi* (*way*) + suf. *ra* (*abouts*)

❖ U. to talk about some direction that is close to the listener.

➤ [*fam.*] socchì そっち 〔何処も〕

Ⓙ achíra あちら 〔彼方〕 : ① **that way** (over there) ② [*for.*][*pol.*] **that person**; he; she

Distal pre. *a* + O.J. *chi* (*way*) + suf. *ra* (*abouts*)

❖ U. to talk about some direction that is far from the speaker and the listener.

➤ [*fam.*] acchì あっち 〔何処も〕

Ⓙ achìkochi / achíkòchi あちこち 〔彼方此方〕 : **here and there**; all around; everywhere

← *acchikocchi*: *acchi* (*that way*) + *kocchi* (*this way*)

3.5 How

Demonstrative pronouns that answer the question 'how'.

Important Words

kō こう *like this*	sō そう *like that*	aa ああ *like that*

Ⓣ kó こう 〔斯う〕 : **like this**; in this way; so; thus

Ⓣ só そう 〔然う〕 : **like that**; in such a way; so; thus

❖ U. to talk about s.t. that is near the listener or a topic that is known either by the speaker or the listener.

⊕ aá ああ : **like that** (kind of thing); so

Distal pre. *a* ×2

79

❖ U. for s.t. distant from both the speaker   and the listener.

3.6 Which Guy

Demonstrative pronouns that answer the question 'which guy'. These pronouns are almost universally used in a familiar setting and in an informal register.

Important Words

koitsu こいつ *this guy*	soitsu そいつ *that guy*	aitsu あいつ *that guy*

koítsu こいつ 〔此奴〕 : [*col.*][*fam.*] **this guy**; this fellow; this person

← *koyatsu:* Proximal pre. *ko* + Fam. *yatsu (person)*

➤ koítsura こいつら 〔此奴等〕 : **these guys**

soítsu そいつ 〔其奴〕 : [*col.*][*fam.*] **that guy**; that fellow; that person

← *soyatsu:* Medial pre. *so* + fam. *yatsu (person)*

❖ U. for s.o. that is near the speaker or known by either the speaker or the listener.

➤ soítsura そいつら 〔其奴等〕 : **those guys**

aítsu あいつ 〔彼奴〕 : [*col.*][*fam.*] **that guy**; that fellow; that person

← *ayatsu:* Distal pre. *a* + fam. *yatsu (person)*

❖ U. for s.o. distant from both the speaker and the listener.

➤ aítsura あいつら 〔彼奴等〕 : **those guys** (over there)

DEMONSTRATIVE PRONOUNS AND PRENOMINALS

Interrogatives	Demonstratives		
	Proximal (**ko-**)	Medial (**so-**)	Distal (**a-**)
dore どれ which (one)	kore これ **this** (one)	sore それ **that** (one over here)	are あれ **that** (one over there)
dono どの which	kono この **this**	sono その **that** (over here)	ano あの **that** (over there)
donna どんな what kind of	konna こんな **this kind of**	sonna そんな **that kind of**	anna あんな **that kind of**
doko どこ where	koko ここ **here**	soko そこ **there** (near)	asoko あそこ **there** (far)
dochira どちら which way	kochira こちら **this way**	sochira そちら **that way**	achira あちら **that way**
docchi どっち [*fam.*] which way	kocchi こっち [*fam.*] **this way**	socchi そっち [*fam.*] **this way**	acchi あっち [*fam.*] **this way**
dō どう how	kō こう **like this**	sō そう **like that**	aa ああ **like that**
doitsu どいつ [*col.*][*fam.*] who	koitsu こいつ [*col.*][*fam.*] **this person**	soitsu そいつ [*col.*][*fam.*] **that person**	aitsu あいつ [*col.*][*fam.*] **that person**

II. NOUNS

Nouns are a type of nominal word that express a general concept that identifies any kind of abstract or concrete entity (person, place, object or quality).

In Japanese there are three types of nouns:

1. **Proper Nouns**: Apply to a single unit within a group.

2. **Common Nouns**: Apply to a whole class of abstract or concrete entities.

3. **Postpositional Nouns**: Apply to general places where the action of a verb may occur.

Postpositional nouns are semantically equivalent to some of the prepositions or adverbs of place in English ('inside', 'outside', etc.). This type of Japanese words are functionally nouns and need the particle *no* in order to modify other nouns.

As for common nouns, undoubtedly the most abundant type of word in any language, they can be divided in Japanese into three main categories according to their etymology:

1. **Native Nouns**: Purely Japanese nouns.

2. **Sino-Japanese Nouns**: Nouns of Chinese origin.

2. **Foreign Nouns**: Nouns of imported from languages other than Classical Chinese.

This differentiation is relevant because these three types of nouns usually have different nuances. Native nouns tend to be more abundant in colloquial language, and Sino-Japanese nouns, except the very common ones, tend to be relegated to formal language. Many concepts that can be said in Japanese in two ways: through a native noun (more colloquial) or through a Sino-Japanese noun (more formal). Sino-Japanese nouns are mostly made up of two kanji, each with a meaning that, when joined, form a new concept. Native Japanese nouns are usually etymologically compounds too.

Foreign nouns or nouns derived from foreign languages other than classical Chinese are linguistic loans called *gairaigo* (外来語) in Japanese and the overwhelming majority of them are imported directly from English. These words are written in katakana and they are the predominant type of word when talking about objects of Western origin. These words also usually have a more casual and modern overtone. There are many occasions when, despite the existence of a native or Sino-Japanese noun, people tend to use a *gairaigo* equivalent, especially in commercial settings and among young people.

1. POSTPOSITIONAL NOUNS

Postpositional nouns are a purely semantic categorization that, however, helps the foreign student of Japanese better understand how these concepts work in the language. There are a number of English prepositions ('inside', 'outside', 'in the middle', 'between', etc) that in Japanese are not marked by locative particles like other prepositions ('in', 'to', 'from', etc) but by the genitive particle *no* followed by a noun indicating a place.

[*noun*] + ***no*** + [*postpositional noun*]

Important Words

naka 中 *inside*	aida 間 *between*	ue 上 *above*	shita 下 *below*
soba そば *near*	soto 外 *outside*	mae 前 *in front*	ushiro 後ろ *behind*
migi 右 *right*	hidari 左 *left*	saki 先 *ahead*	soto 外 *outside*

Ⓣ naká 中: ① **in; inside;** within ② **among;** out of (e.g. certain number of people) ③ **middle; center** ④ **during;** while

❖ Referring to s.t. positioned within and approximately in the center of a place or object.

Ⓜ uchí₂ 内: ① **in; inside;** within ② **among;** out of (e.g. certain number of people) ③ **during;** while ④ **one's own**

Ⓛ òku 奥: **inside; interior;** inner part

❖ This word puts the focus on an inner and comparatively deep part of an object.

Ⓜ chuúshin 中心 Ⓒ (*middle+heart*): Ⓝ Ⓢ **center; core**

❖ It refers specifically to a concrete and precise centric position.

Ⓛ mańnnaka 真ん中: [*col.*] **middle; center; mid-way**

← *manaka: ma (just) + naka (middle)*

Ⓛ chuúò / chuúō 中央 Ⓒ (*middle+center*): **center; middle**

❖ M. u. fig. rather than physically, but also u. to refer to the central part of big geographical boundaries.

chuúkan 中間 Ⓒ (*middle+interval*): ① **middle; midway** ② interim

❖ Referring to a point wor position around the middle of s.t. that has length.

Ⓜ tochúu 途中 Ⓒ (*route+middle*): ① **on the way;** en route; halfway ② **in the middle of**

Ⓣ aída 間: ① **space;** gap; interval ② **between; among** ③ **meanwhile;** while

---

Ⓣ sòba そば〔側・傍〕: ① **beside;** besides ② **near; close** (to); nearby ③ proximity; vicinity

❖ M. u. in a physical sense.

gawá 側: Ⓝ Ⓢ ① **side** (of s.t. or s.o.); **side part** ② **beside; besides** ③ **near; close** (to); nearby; ④ proximity; vicinity

Ⓜ chikàku / chìkaku 近く: **near; close** (to); nearby ② proximity; vicinity ③ neighborhood

Stem of the adj. *chikai (near)* + adverbializing suf. *ku*

❖ U. both in a physical and fig. way.

Ⓛ àtari あたり〔辺り〕: Ⓝ **vicinity; nearby;** neighborhood; surroundings Ⓢ **around; about;** thereabouts

(I) *ataru (to hit; to be in contact)*

Ⓜ tonári 隣: ① **neighbor** ② **next to;** adjoining; nearby; neighboring ③ **house next door;** next-door neighbor

(I) *tonaru (to neighbor)*

❖ M. u. when talking about two objects of more or less the same category.

Ⓛ yokó 横: ① **horizontal** (thing) ② **side to side** (horizontally); **beside;** sideways ③ **next to** ④ lying down

Ⓛ tàte 縦: ① **vertical** (thing); ② vertically

⑦ ué 上: ① **above**; **up**; **over** ② **top**

⑦ shitá 下: ① **below**; **down**; **under**; beneath; underneath ② **bottom**

⑦ sakí 先: ① **ahead**; hereafter ② the other side ② **previous**; prior; former

⑦ màe₁ 前: ① (in) **front** (of) ② **before**; ago; earlier

⊕ omótè 表: ① **surface** ② **front** (of)

temae 手前: ① **just in front** (of one); just before oneself. ② **you**

te (hand) + mae (in front of)

♣ ❷ U. in a derogatory way.

⊕ ushíro 後ろ: **behind**; **back**; rear

⊕ urà 裏: ① **back** (surface); **reverse side** ② behind

♣ Referring to the opposite side of a surface.

⑦ migí 右: **right**; right hand side

⑦ hidári 左: **left**; left hand side

⑤ mukồ / mukó 向こう: **other side**; **opposite side**; **beyond**; over there

← *mukau (to face)*

⑦ sòto 外: **outside**; exterior

POSTPOSITIONAL NOUNS

Inside	naka 中	uchi 内	oku 奥 *inner part*		
Middle		mannnaka 真ん中 *just in the middle*			
Between	aida 間				
Beside	soba そば	gawa 側 *side*			
Nearby			chikaku 近く *proximity*	tonari 隣 *neighbor*	yoko 横 *sideways*
Next					
Outside	soto 外				

Front	Back	Above	Below	Right	Left	Opposite
mae 前	ushrio 後ろ	ue 上	shita 下	migi 右	hidari 左	mukō 向こう
omote 表 *front surface*	ura 裏 *back surface*					

2. MANKIND

Nouns that refer to concepts related to man, his actions and his interpersonal relationships.

2.1 Human Being & Life

Nouns that refer to concepts related to human typology and human life course.

Important Words

hito 人 *person*	otoko 男 **man**	onna 女 *woman*
akachan 赤ちゃん *baby*	kodomo 子供 *child*	otona 大人 *adult*
	inochi 命 *life*	

Ⓕ hitó 人: **person**

➤ hitòbito 人々: **people**; persons

Ⓔ jìnbutsu 人物 Ⓒ *(person+thing)*: ① (a specific) **person** ② (a) character

Ⓔ katàgata 方々: [*hon.*] (those) **gentlemen**; (those) people; they

kata (way) ×2

Ⓔ niǹgen 人間 Ⓒ *(person+interval)*: **human being**

Ⓔ jińshu 人種 Ⓒ *(person+seed)*: **race** (of people or animals)

mìnzoku 民族 Ⓒ *(common people+tribe)*: ① (a) **people** ② (a) race

⊕ jińkō 人口 Ⓒ *(person+mouth)*: **population**

Ⓔ kòjin 個人 Ⓒ *(individual+person)*: **individual**

- -

Ⓕ otókò 男: **man**

O.J. *oto (young)* + *ko (child)*

❖ Although *otoko* is the plain term for 'man', it can carry a derogatory tone if used in reference to a specific person, especially in conversation.

Ⓕ otóko no hito 男の人: **man**

otoko (man) + genitive p. *no* + *hito (person)*

⊕ dańsē 男性 Ⓒ *(man+disposition)*: **male**; man

- -

Ⓕ ońnà 女: **woman**

← *omina*: O.J. *o (small)* + *mi** + O.J. augmentative suf. *na* |* ← O.J. *me (female)*

❖ Although *onna* is the plain term for 'woman', it can carry a derogatory tone if used in reference to a specific person, especially in conversation.

Ⓕ ońna no hito 女の人: **woman**

onna (woman) + genitive p. *no* + *hito (person)*

⊕ josé 女性 Ⓒ *(woman+disposition)*: **female**; woman

⊕ akánbō 赤ん坊: **baby**

Ⓙ *aka (red)* + *n** + Ⓒ *bō* 坊 *(boy)* |*Genetive p. *no*

⊕ àkachan 赤ちゃん: [*fam.*] **baby**

aka (red) + fam. suf. *chan*

Ⓕ kodómo 子供: **child**

ko (child) + obs. plural suf. *domo*

⊕ kó 子: Ⓝ Ⓢ **child**

❖ R. u. without a modifier, especially in conversation.

Ⓕ otókò no ko 男の子: (little) **boy**

otoko (man) + genitive p. *no* + *ko (child)*

Ⓔ shónen 少年 Ⓒ *(little+year)*: (young) **boy**

Ⓔ dànshi 男子 Ⓒ *(man+child)*: ① **boy** ② young man

Ⓕ onnà no ko 女の子: (little) **girl**

onna (woman) + genitive p. *no* + *ko (child)*

Ⓛ shòjo 少女 Ⓒ (*little+woman*): (young) **girl**

Ⓛ joshí 女子 Ⓒ (*woman+child*): ① **girl** ② young woman

séshònen 青少年: ① **youth** ② **young person** ③ teenager

Ⓒ *sē* 青 (*green*) + *shōnen* 少年 (*boy*)

Ⓕ otóna 大人: **adult** (person)

O.J. *oto (young)* + O.J. augmentative suf. *na*

Ⓛ séjin 成人 Ⓒ (*resulting+person*): **adult** (person)

❖ Legal term to refer to the legal age that one is considered officially as an adult (20 years old in Japan, 18 from the year 2022).

Ⓛ rójin 老人 Ⓒ (*old age+person*): **old person**; senior citizen

sénzo 先祖 Ⓒ (*previous+ancestor*): **ancestor**(s)

- - - - - - - - - - - - - - - - -

Ⓜ sèmē 生命 Ⓒ (*living+fate*): **life**

❖ Word denoting the meaning of 'life' in a biological, physical way.

Ⓜ jìnsē 人生 Ⓒ (*person+living*): (human) **life**

❖ Word u. specifically for human life. Also, the most common term to refer to one's course of 'life'.

Ⓛ ìnochi 命: ① **life** ② lifetime

❖ General, neutral term for 'life'. Also, 'life' understood as the lifespan of a person.

O.J. *i (breath)* + pos. p. *no* + O.J. *chi (way)*

Ⓛ tañjō 誕生 Ⓒ (*nativity+living*): **birth**

shì 死 Ⓒ : **death**

2.2 Language & Thought

Nouns related to words, thought, conversation and knowledge.

Important Words

namae 名前 *name*	kotoba 言葉 *language*	hanashi 話 *talk*
kazu 数 *number*	shitsumon 質問 *question*	mondai 問題 *problem*

- - - - - - - - - - - - - - - - -

Ⓕ namáe お名前: **name** (of a person)

na (name) + O.J. emphatic pol. suf. *mae*

❖ This is the most commonly u. form for the 'name' of a person. In a broader sense, it may mean either 'full name', 'family name' or 'given name'.

➤ shitá no namáe 下の前: **surname**

Ⓛ na 名: **name**

❖ M. u. when referring to the abstract concept of 'name' in a poetic or emotional way.

méshō 名称 Ⓒ (*name+appellation*): **name** (of a thing)

- - - - - - - - - - - - - - - - -

Ⓕ kotóbà 言葉: ① **language** ② **words**

O.J. *koto (word)* + *ba ← ha (edge)*

❖ 'Language' in a more natural sense, as in the everyday's language. Also addresses the concept of 'word(s)'.

Ⓛ gèngo 言語 Ⓒ (*speech+talking*): **language**

❖ Technical and neutral word for the concept of 'language'.

⊕ buńpō 文法 ⓒ (writings+law): **grammar**

⊕ tańgo 単語 ⓒ (simple+talk): **word**

gòi 語彙 ⓒ (talking+same kind): **vocabulary**

kotówaza ことわざ 〔諺〕 ⓔ : **proverb**; **saying**

  O.J. *koto (word)* + *waza (technique)*

nyùansu ニュアンス ⓔ : **nuance**

- -

⊤ hanáshì お話: ① **talk** ② speech

  (I) *hanasu (to talk)*

⊕ monógàtari 物語: **story**; tale

  mono (thing) + *katari*: (I) *kataru (to talk about)*

shińwa 神話 ⓒ (god+talking): **myth**

deńsetsu 伝説 ⓒ (transmitting+explaining): ① **legend** ② folklore

⊕ ùso₁ 嘘: (a) **lie**

⊕ mònku 文句 ⓒ (writing+sentence): ① **complaint** ② phrase

komyúnikèeshon コミュニケーション ⓔ : **communication**

- -

⊕ kańgàe 考え: ① **thought** ② idea

  (I) *kangaeru (to think)*

❖ This word comprises the concept of a sudden or logical 'thought'.

⊕ shisố 思想 ⓒ (thinking+thought): ① **thought** ② **idea**

❖ Word referring to the broad, abstract idea of 'thought' or the concept of a deep, reflected thinking.

⊕ keńkai 見解 ⓒ (looking+loosening): (shared) **opinion**

- -

kójitsu 口実 ⓒ (mouth+reality): **excuse**

❖ 'Excuse' prepared beforehand.

iíwake 言い訳: **excuse**

  *ii** + *wake (reason)* | *(I) iu (to say)*

❖ 'Excuse' said after a deed has been done.

⊕ móshiwake 申し訳: [*pol.*] **excuse**

  *mōshi** + *wake (reason)* |*(I) hon. v. *mōsu (to say)*

⊕ sèshin 精神 ⓒ (pure+god): ① **mind**; psyche; mentality ② **spirit**

❖ This word originally refers to the intangible force that is understood as the source of human thought and activity, a concept normally interpreted as 'spirit' in English. At the same time, however, the most commonly understood meaning of this word in J. nowadays is that of 'mind' or 'psyche', that is, the source of thought.

- -

⊕ mokúteki 目的 ⓒ (eye+aim): **purpose**; **aim**; **goal**; objective

❖ A broad 'objective'.

⊕ mokùhyō 目標 ⓒ (eye+signpost): **target**; **goal**; objective; mark

❖ A finite 'objective'.

⊕ taíshō 対象 ⓒ (opposite+figure): **target**; object (of an action)

dóki 動機 ⓒ (moving+mechanism): **motivation**; motive

⊕ kyòmi 興味 ⓒ (vitalizing+taste): **interest** (in s.t.)

❖ A subjective 'interest' displayed towards one's preferences, m. conveying an emotional affiliation.

⊕ kańshin 関心 ⓒ (related+heart): ① **interest** (in s.t.) ② **concern** ③ attention

❖ A concrete or rational 'interest' towards an object or topic that grabs one's attention.

kókìshin 好奇心 ⓒ (liking+unusual+heart): **curiosity**

⊕ keńtò 見当 ⓒ (looking+hitting): **estimate**; **guess**; **conjecture**

- -

Ⓓ mòji 文字 Ⓒ (writings+letter): ① **letter** (of a writing system) ② (a) **writing**

Ⓜ bùnshō 文章 Ⓒ (writings+chapter): ① **sentence** ② composition; article

❖ ❶ M. u. for written sentences.

Ⓛ bùn 文 Ⓒ (writings): **sentence**

Ⓕ kàzu 数: **number**

❖ This word refers to a 'number' as an abstract concept.

Ⓜ suúji 数字 Ⓒ (number+letter): **number**

❖ This word is u. to identify a specific number in a written form.

Ⓛ bańgǒ 番号 Ⓒ (number in a series+mark): **number** (in a series)

❖ This word is u. to identify the number of s.t. that is part of a series of numbers.

Ⓛ wadái 話題 Ⓒ (talking+topic): **topic**; subject

tèema テーマ Ⓖ [thema]: **theme**; topic

❖ U. to refer to a central matter in relation to a peripheral matter.

gakká 学科 Ⓒ (learning+science): ① **study subject; course of study** ② (university) **department**

Ⓛ gimón 疑問 Ⓒ (questioning+asking): **doubt**

Ⓛ toí 問い: **question**

(I) tou (to ask)

Ⓕ shitsúmon 質問 Ⓒ (matter+asking): **question**

❖ M. referring to broad and general questions, or to academic or philosophical ones.

Ⓜ kotàe 答え: **answer**

(I) kotaeru (to answer)

Ⓕ mońdai 問題 Ⓒ (asking+topic): **problem**; issue

Ⓛ mèwaku 迷惑 Ⓒ (loosing one's way+infatuation): Ⓝ **trouble; annoyance**; inconvenience Ⓐ (na) troublesome Ⓥ (suru) to be troubled by

Ⓛ chiè 知恵 Ⓒ (knowing+blessing): **wisdom**

Ⓛ chìshiki 知識 Ⓒ (knowing+knowledge): **knowledge**

Ⓛ gozónji ご存知: [hon.] **knowing**

Ⓒ Hon. pre. go + zon 存 (existence) + ji 知 (knowing)

❖ U. as an idiomatic expression, accompanied by the cop. in very formal and honorific speech.

Ⓛ jòhō 情報 Ⓒ (emotion+reporting): **information**

Ⓛ kìhon 基本 Ⓒ (base+foundation): **basics**; fundamentals

Ⓛ jóshiki 常識 Ⓒ (usual+knowledge): **common sense**; common knowledge

Ⓜ shikáta 仕方: **method**; way (of doing); means

shi* + kata (direction) |*(I) suru (to do)

❖ This word makes reference to the the action(s) to be taken in order to achieve a certain goal.

Ⓛ shùdan 手段 Ⓒ (hand+steps): **means**; way (of doing)

❖ Specifically referring to what is necessary to do or use in order to make an action.

Ⓛ hóhō 方法 Ⓒ (direction+law): **method**; way (of doing)

❖ Referring to both 'means' and 'actions'.

shuhó 手法 Ⓒ (hand+method): **technique**

Ⓛ sèdo 制度 Ⓒ (system+occasion): ① **system** ② institution

shìsutemu システム Ⓔ : **system**

❖ M. u. in relation to technological or complex systems.

⊕ juń 順 Ⓒ : ⃞N⃞S **order**

jùnjo 順序 Ⓒ (*order+preface*): ① **order** ② **sequence**

juńban 順番 Ⓒ (*order+number in a series*): ① (one's) **turn**; (sequential) **order**

---

rònri 論理 Ⓒ (*argument+reason*): **logic**

mujún 矛盾 Ⓒ (*spear+shield*): **contradiction**; inconsistency

---

⊕ jôdàn 冗談 Ⓒ (*superfluous+discussion*): **joke**; funny story

sharé 洒落: **joke**; pun; jest; wordplay

← (I) r. u. *shareru* (to joke)

⊕ nazó 謎: ① **riddle** ② **puzzle** ③ **mystery**

- -

tegàkari 手がかり: **clue**; key

te (hand) + gakari ← kakari (duty)

susume お勧め: **recommendation**; **suggestion**; **advice**

(I) *susumeru (to suggest)*

2.3 Emotions & Feelings

Nouns related to subjective feelings, emotions and sensations.

Important Words

kimochi 気持ち *feeling*	kibun 気分 *mood*	kanji 話 *sensation*
koe 声 *voice*	oto 音 *sound*	aji 味 *flavor*
nioi 臭い *smell*	kaori 香 *good smell*	yume 夢 *dream*
	ai 愛 *love*	

⊕ kimóchi 気持ち: **feeling**

Ⓒ *ki (mood)* + Ⓙ *mochi ← (I) motsu (to hold)*

❖ M. u. to define a concrete feeling experienced by a person.

⊕ ki 気 Ⓒ (*mood*): ① **feeling** ② **mood**

⊕ kìbun 気分 Ⓒ (*mood+dividing*): ① **feeling** ② **mood**

❖ M. u. to describe the mood of a person.

⊕ kańjō 感情 Ⓒ (*sensation+emotion*): ① **emotion** ② feeling

❖ Word u. to describe the concept of human emotions as an abstract and broad sense.

⊕ kanjí 感じ: ① **feeling** ② **sensation** ③ impression

(I) *kanjiru (to feel)*

❖ M. u. to describe a sensorial perception of an external thing.

⊕ fuńìki 雰囲気 Ⓒ (*atmosphere+surrounding+mood*): ① **mood** ② **atmosphere**; ambience ④ feel

⊕ chóshi 調子 Ⓒ (*tuning+child*): ① **tone**; tune ② **condition**; state of health ③ **mood**; manner

ińsupirèeshon インスピレーション Ⓔ : **inspiration**

Ⓣ kòe 声: **voice**

⊕ otò 音: **sound**

chínmoku 沈黙 ⓒ (*sinking+silent*): **silence**

⊕ ají 味: **flavor**; taste

Ⓛ niòi ❶ 匂い/ ❷ 臭い: ① **smell**; ② bad odor

(I) *niou (to smell)*

Ⓛ kaóri ❶ 香り/ ❷ 薫り: ① **fragrance**; (good) smell ② atmosphere

(I) *kaoru (to be fragrant)*

Ⓛ sékaku 性格 ⓒ (*disposition+form*): **personality**; character

❖ The characteristic temper of a person.

jínkaku 人格 ⓒ (*person+form*): ① **personality**; character ② persona

❖ The acquired 'personality' or 'persona' that a person consciously or unconsciously carries.

Ⓛ hyójò 表情 ⓒ (*revealing+emotion*): **facial expression**

Ⓛ ègao 笑顔: **smile** (smiling face)

e* + gao† | *Stem of the v. *emu (to smile)* |† ← *kao (face)*

Ⓛ tachíbà / tàchiba 立場: **position** (standpoint); **stance**

tachi* + ba (place) | *(I) *tatsu (to stand up)*

⊕ shùmi 趣味 ⓒ (*preference+taste*): ① **hobby**; pastime ② **tastes**; preference; liking

kònomi / konómì 好み: **liking**; **taste**

(I) *konomu (to like)*

Ⓛ ài 愛: **love**

❖ Referring to unconditional love for another's person.

Ⓛ kòi 恋: **love**

(I) *kou (to love)*

❖ M. referring to selfish, conditional love.

nikúshimi 憎しみ: **hatred**

(I) O.J. *nikushimu* → C.J. *nikumu (to hate)*

ikárì 怒り: **anger**

(I) *ikaru (to get angry)*

sutòresu ストレス Ⓔ : **stress**

Ⓛ yorókobi 喜び: **delight**

(I) *yorokobu (to be pleased)*

kanáshimi / kanáshìmi 悲しみ: **sadness**

(I) *kanashimu (to be sad)*

osórè 恐れ: **fear**; dread

(I) *osoreru (to fear)*

shòkku ショック Ⓔ : **shock**

odóroki / odórokì 驚き: **surprise**

(I) *odoroku (to be surprised)*

Ⓛ yùuki 勇気 ⓒ (*courage+mood*): **courage**; bravery; nerve

⊕ yumè 夢: **dream**

yu* + me (eye) | * ← O.J. *i (sleeping)*

àkumu 悪夢 ⓒ (*bad+dream*): **nightmare**

Ⓛ nozómi 望み: **desire**

(I) *nozomu (to desire)*

kokórozashi 志: [*lit.*] ① **will** ② **intention** ③ motive

(I) *kokorozasu (to intend)*: *kokoro (heart)* + *zasu* ← *sasu (to point)*

Ⓛ ìshi ❶ 意思/ ❷ 意志 ⓒ (*idea+knowledge*): ① **intention** ② **will**

❖ 'Intention' understood as a thought about what to do.

īto 意図 [C] (idea+planning): **intention**; aim

❖ 'Intention' understood as a concrete plane.

- -

Ⓛ jishín 自信 [C] (oneself+faith): (self) **confidence**

Ⓛ hokóri 誇り: **pride** (of belonging or achievement)

(I) hokoru (to be proud of)

Ⓛ gàman 我慢 [C] (myself+ridicule): ① **patience**; endurance; tolerance ② self-control

- -

Ⓛ hìgeki 悲劇 [C] (sad+drama): **tragedy**

Ⓛ kìgeki 喜劇 [C] (rejoicing+drama): **comedy**

2.4 Human Body & Health

Nouns related to the body, its parts and their automatic actions, and to health and illness.

Important Words

karada 体 *body*	hone 骨 *bone*	kawa 皮 *skin*	atama 頭 *head*
kami 髪 *hair*	kao 顔 *face*	me 目 *eye*	mimi 耳 *ear*
kuchi 口 *mouth*	kokoro 心 *heart*	hara 腹 *belly*	senaka 背中 *back*
te 手 *hand*	ashi 足 *foot-leg*	chikara 力 *strength*	byōki 病気 *illness*

- -

Ⓕ karáda 体・身体: **body**

Ⓛ shìntai 身体: **body**

❖ M. u. in a physical sense and in technical or academic contexts.

Ⓛ mi 身: ① (one's) **body** ② oneself

❖ U. in several idiomatic expressions and also to refer to one's body in a humble way.

Ⓛ honè 骨: **bone**

Ⓛ kìnniku 筋肉 [C] (sinew+body part): **muscle**

Ⓛ chí 血: **blood**

Cognate with O.J. *chi* (spirit)

Ⓛ kawà ❶ 皮/ ❷ 革: ① **skin** ② leather

❖ U. for any kind of skin.

Ⓛ hàda 肌: (human) **skin**

❖ U. for the surface of the human skin.

Ⓕ atámà / atàma 頭: **head**

*ata** + *ma* (space) |*Irrealis f. of v. O.J. *atsu* (to be right) → C.J. *ataru* (to be right)

nò 脳 [C] : **brain**

Ⓜ ke 毛: ① **hair** ② **fur**

❖ U. for any hair from any part of the body, be it an animal's or a person's one.

Ⓜ kàmi 髪: **hair** (on the head)

Cognate with *kami* (top)

❖ U. specifically for the mass of hair on s.o.'s head.

Ⓛ kàmi no ke 髪の毛: **hair** (on the head)

kami (top/hair) + genitive p. *no* + *ke* (hair)

❖ Most common way to refer to s.o.'s hair on the head.

kamígata 髪型: **hairstyle**

kami (hair) + *gata* ← *kata* (type)

㊤ higé ひげ 〔❶ 髭／ ❷ 鬚／ ❸ 髯〕: ① **mustache** ② beard ③ sideburns

hi* + ge† | ** ← he (place)* | *† ← ke (hair)*

❖ Refers to any kind of facial hair. Usually u. as a suf. in ①, ② or ③.

㊥ kaó 顔: **face**

㊤ hòho / hohó 頬: **cheek**

➤ [*col.*] hòo 頬

hòppeta ほっぺた 〔頬っぺた〕: [*fam.*] **cheek**

← hoobeta: hoo (cheek) + beta ← heta (vicinity)

㊤ hitái ひたい 〔額〕: **forehead**

← hita (straightaway) + hi (sun) ‖ Referring to the place where the sun hits right away.

odèko おでこ 〔お凸〕: [*fam.*] **forehead**

Hon. pre. *o + deko (bump)*

㊦ mè 目: **eye**

màyu 眉: **eyebrow**(s)

O.J. *ma (eye)* + unknown O.J. suf. *yu*

màtsuge まつ毛 〔睫毛〕: **eyelashes**

ma* + O.J. genitive p. tsu + ge ← ke (hair) | ** ← me (eye)*

㊦ mimì 耳: **ear**

㊦ haná 鼻: **nose**

㊦ kuchí 口: **mouth**

㊦ shità 舌: **tongue**

㊦ hà 歯: **tooth**

㊤ nòdo 喉: **throat**

← nondo ← nomido: nomi* + do (door) | **(I) nomu (to drink)*

kuchíbiru 唇: **lips**

kuchi (mouth) + biru ← hiru* ← heri (edge) | **Possibly through as an association with suf. biru (to act like)*

agò あご 〔顎〕: ① **chin** ② jaw

㊤ kubí 首: **neck**

㊤ munè 胸: ① **chest** ② breast

O.J. *mu (body) + ne (root)*

㊤ kokórò / kokòro 心: ① **heart** ② **mind**

koko (here) + O.J. suf. ro (area)

❖ U. for the meaning of 'heart' in a fig. or metaphysical sense, related to the mood or senses, as the word 'mind' would convey.

㊤ shińzō 心臓 ⒸҶ (*heart+organ*): **heart**

❖ U. for the word 'heart' in a strictly physical way.

㊤ ì 胃: **stomach**

㊤ harà 腹: **belly**; abdomen

㊤ onáka お腹: [*pol.*] **belly**; abdomen

Hon. pre. *o +naka (inside)*

㊥ senáka 背中: **back** (of the body)

se (back) + naka (middle)

㊤ koshí 腰: **waist; lower back**; hips

㊤ shirì ぉ尻: **buttocks**

㊦ tè ぉ手: **hand**

㊥ yubì 指: ① **finger** ② toes

← teoyobi: te (hand) + oyobi* | ** (I) oyobu (to extend)*

㊥ udè 腕: **arm**

u* + de† | ** ← ue (over)* | *† ← te (hand)*

㊤ wakì 脇: ① **armpit** ② side (of the body)

(I) *waku (to split)*

㊤ kàta 肩: **shoulder**

hijì 肘: **elbow**

㊤ hizá 膝: **knee**

㊦ ashì ❶ 足／ ❷ 脚: ① **foot** ② **leg**

chìnchin ぉちんちん・ォチンチン: [*col.*] **penis**

mànko ぉまんこ・ォマンコ: [*col.*] **vagina**

tsumé 爪: ① (finger or toe) **nail** ② claw

Ⓔ àse 汗: **sweat**

nìkibi にきび〔面皰〕: **pimple**

shiwá しわ〔皺〕: **wrinkle**

tsùba 唾: ① **saliva** ② spit

← tsubaki: O.J. tsu (spit) + baki*|* ← haki: (I) haku (to vomit)

Ⓔ nàmida 涙: **tear**

← namita: na* + O.J. mi (water) + ta† |*(I) O.J. naru (to result in) |†(I) O.J. taru (to be)

Ⓔ ìki 息: **breath**

(I) ikiru (to live)

akúbi あくび〔欠伸〕: **yawn**

ibiki いびき〔鼾〕: **snore**

hanámizu 鼻水: **snot**

hana (nose) + mizu (water)

gèro ゲロ: [col.] **vomit**

tsùba つば〔唾〕: **spit**

geppú ゲップ: **burp**

onára おなら〔屁〕: **fart**

← onarashi: Hon. p. o + narashi ← (I) narasu (to sound)

daíbèn 大便 Ⓒ (big+convenience): **feces**; poo

kusò クソ〔糞〕: [col.] **shit**

Cognate with kusai (to be stinky)

ùnko うんこ: [fam.] **poop**; shit

ùnchi うんち: [fam.][fam.] **poop**

shóbèn 小便 Ⓒ (small+convenience): ① **urine**; pee

oshìkko おしっこ: [fam.] **pee**

⊕ chikárà 力: ① **force**; **strength** ② **power**

❖ U. both in a physical and fig. sense.

ikíòi 勢い: **force**; **vigor**; energy

iki (breath) + oi: (I) ou (to chase)

❖ M. u. in a physical sense.

Ⓣ byóki 病気 Ⓒ (sickness+mood): **disease**; **illness**; sickness

yàmai 病: [lit.] **disease**; **illness**; sickness

Ⓔ itámì 痛み: **pain**

Nominalization of adj. *itai (to hurt)*

Ⓣ kazé 風邪: (a) **cold**

Cognate with *kaze (wind)*

kushàmi くしゃみ〔嚔〕: **sneeze**

Ⓔ sekì 咳: **cough**

⊕ netsù 熱 Ⓒ: **fever**

uìrusu / ùirusu ウイルス Ⓓ [Virus]: **virus**

memài めまい〔目眩〕: **dizziness**

me (eye) + mai ← (I) mau (to be dizzy)

hakíkè 吐き気: **nausea**

Ⓙ haki* + Ⓒ ke 気 (mood) |*(I) haku (to vomit)

gerí 下痢 Ⓒ (below+diarrhea): **diarrhea**

Ⓔ zutsúu 頭痛 Ⓒ (head+hurting): **headache**

Ⓔ kizú 傷: ① **wound** ② injury

Ⓔ kańja 患者 Ⓒ (suffering+person): (a) **patient**

2.5 Family & Relationships

Nouns related to family, family members and affective relationships.

Considering that Japanese is a language that places special emphasis on register and formality, it should be noted that intra-family relationships play a relevant role within distinct formal singularities. The words used to name one or another member of the family are not generic as in European languages but must be chosen according to who is saying that word and in what context. Therefore, in Japanese, there are usually at least two words for the same member of a family: one word used to refer to a specific member of one's own family and another word to refer to a specific member of a family outside one's own.

Important Words

kazoku 家族 *family*	oya 親 *parent*	okaasan お母さん *mother*	otōsan お父さん *father*
otto 夫 *husband*	tsuma 妻 *wife*	musuko 息子 *son*	musume 娘 *daughter*
imōto 妹 *younger sister*	otōto 弟 *younger brother*	ane 姉 *older sister*	ani 兄 *older brother*
ojisan おじさん *uncle*	obasan おばさん *aunt*	ojiisan お爺さん *grandfather*	obaasan お婆さん *grandmother*
tomodachi 友達 *friend*	koibito 恋人 *lover*	kareshi 彼氏 *boyfriend*	kanojo 彼女 *girlfriend*

Ⓣ kàzoku ご家族 Ⓒ (*house+tribe*): ① **family** ② family member

Ⓤ shìnseki 親戚 Ⓒ (*familiar+kin*): **relative**(s); family member

myòji 名字・苗字 Ⓒ (*name+letter*): **family name; surname**

sè 姓 Ⓒ: [*for.*] **family name; surname**

Ⓣ ryòshin ご両親 Ⓒ (*both+parent*): (both) **parents**

fùbo 父母 Ⓒ (*father+mother*): (both) **parents**; father and mother

Ⓤ oyà 親: ① (any) **parent** ② parents

Cognate with O.J. *oyu (to age)* → C.J. *oiru (to age)*

Ⓣ otòsan お父さん: [*fam.*] **father**; dad

Hon. pre. *o* + *tō** + hon. suf. *san* |* ← *toto* (*father* [children language]) ← *chichi* (*father*)

❖ U. to address s.o.'s father or to talk about one's father within the family.

Ⓤ chichì / chìchi 父: (my) **father**

❖ U. to talk about one's own father when speaking to an outsider.

Ⓤ chichíoya 父親: (my) **father**

chichi (father) + *oya* (parent)

❖ Word u. to refer to one's father when talking to another person.

Ⓣ okàasan お母さん: [*fam.*] **mother**; mum

hon. pre. *o* + *kaa** + hon. suf. *san* |* ← *kaka* (*mother* [children language]) ← *haha* (*mother*)

❖ U. to address s.o.'s mother or to talk about one's mother within the family.

Ⓤ hàha 母: (my) **mother**

Reduplication of O.J. *ha* (mother)

94

❖ U. to talk about one's own mother when speaking to an outsider.

Ⓤ **haháoya** 母親: (my) **mother**

haha (mother) + oya (parent)

❖ Word u. to refer to one's mother when talking to another person.

Ⓜ **ottó** 夫: **husband**

← *ohito:* O.J. *o (male) + hito (person)*

❖ Neutral word to refer to one's own husband or to speak about s.o. else's husband in abstract or legal terms.

dańna 旦那: [*fam.*] **husband**

From Sanskrit *dāna (giving)*

❖ U. to refer to one's husband, but also u. as a casual term to refer to s.o. else's husband.

Ⓕ **òkusan** 奥さん: [*pol.*] **wife**

Ⓒ *oku (interior)* + Ⓙ pol. personal suf. *san*

❖ For. term to refer to s.o. else's wife.

Ⓜ **tsùma** 妻: [*for.*] **wife**

❖ Neutral word to refer to one's own wife or to speak about s.o. else's wife in abstract or legal terms.

Ⓤ **fujín** ご夫人 Ⓒ *(husband+person)*: [*for.*] **wife**

❖ For. term to refer to either one's or s.o. else's wife.

Ⓤ **fuùfu** 夫婦 Ⓒ *(husband+wife)*: **married couple** (husband and wife)

Ⓜ **musúko** 息子: **son**

musu (to beget) + ko (child)

Ⓜ **musúmè** 娘: **daughter**

musu (to beget) + O.J. me (female)

Ⓤ **imótò** 妹: **younger sister**

← *imohito:* O.J. *imo (sister) + hito (person)*

Ⓣ **otótò** 弟: **younger brother**

← *otohito:* O.J. *oto (young) + hito (person)*

Ⓣ **ané** 姉: **older sister**

O.J. *a (I; me) + n* +* O.J. *e (eldest sibling)* | * ← genitive p. *no*

❖ Word u. to talk about one's older sister to an outsider.

onèesan お姉さん: [*pol.*] **older sister**

Hon. pre. *o + nee* +* hon. suf. *san* | * ← *ane (older sister)*

Ⓣ **àni** 兄: **older brother**

Apophonic f. of *ane (older sister)*

❖ Word u. to talk about one's older sister to an outsider.

onìisan お兄さん: [*pol.*] **older brother**

Hon. pre. *o + nii* +* hon. suf. *san* | * ← *ani (older brother)*

Ⓣ **kyòdai** 兄弟 Ⓒ *(elder brother+younger brother)*: ① **sibling** ② brother(s)

❖ Word u. for brothers independently of their age and also for sisters, that is, siblings in generals.

Ⓤ **shimái** 姉妹 Ⓒ *(elder sister+younger sister)*: **sister**(s)

❖ Word u. for sisters independently of their age.

Ⓤ **itòko** いとこ 〔❶ 従兄弟/ ❷ 従姉妹〕: ① **cousin** ② male cousin ③ female cousin

O.J. *ito (young child) + ko (child)*

Ⓣ **ojísan** おじさん 〔❶ 伯父さん/ ❷ 叔父さん〕: ① **uncle** ② older than one's parent ③ younger than one's parent

O.J. *o (small) + ji* +* hon. suf. *san* | * ← *chi* ← *chichi (father)*

Ⓣ **obásan** おばさん 〔❶ 伯母/ ❷ 叔母〕: ① **aunt** ② older than one's parent ③ younger than one's parent

O.J. *o (small) + ba* +* hon. suf. *san* | * ← O.J. *ha (mother)*

Ⓣ **ojìisan** ❶ お祖父さん/ ❷ お爺さん: ① **grandfather** ② old man

Hon. pre. *o* + *jii** + hon. suf. *san* |* ← *jiji* ([fam.] *grandfather*): *derivation of chichi (father)*

ⴲ sòfu 祖父 [c] (*ancestor+father*): **grandfather**

❖ Word u. to talk about one's grandfather to an outsider.

Ⓕ obàasan ❶ お祖母さん/ ❷ お婆さん: ① **grandmother** ② old woman

Hon. pre. *o* + *baa** + hon. suf. *san* |* ← *baba* ([fam.] *grandmother*): *derivation of haha (mother)*

ⴲ sòbo 祖母 [c] (*ancestor+mother*): **grandmother**

❖ Word u. to talk about one's grandmother to an outsider.

Ⓛ magò 孫: **grandchild**

- -

tsunágari 繋がり: ① **relationship** ② connection

(I) *tsunagaru (to connect)*

nàka 仲: **relation**; relationship

Cognate w. *naka (middle)*

❖ M. u. in idioms or in compound words.

Ⓕ tomódachi 友達: [*fam.*] **friend**

O.J. *tomo (friend)* + pluralizing suf. *tachi* ‖ Originally a plural word, now is u. both in a plural and singular sense.

Ⓛ yuújin 友人 [c] (*friend+person*): [*for.*] **friend**

shińyuu 親友 [c] (*familiar+friend*): **close friend**

Ⓛ aítè 相手: ① **partner**; companion ② **opponent** ③ other party

pre. *ai (inter-)* + *te (hand)*

❖ The lit. meaning of this word is 's.o. w. whom one does s.t.'.

Ⓛ tekí 敵 [c] : **enemy**; adversary; rival; foe

katàki 敵・仇: [N][S] **enemy**; adversary; rival; foe

Ⓛ koíbito 恋人: **significant other**; lover

koi (love) + *bito ← hito (person)*

kàreshi 彼氏: **boyfriend**

[J] *kare (he)* + [c] *shi 氏 (mr.)*

ⴲ kànojo₂ 彼女: ① **girlfriend** ② she

[J] O.J. *kano (that)* + [c] *jo 女 (woman)*

ⴲ seńpai 先輩 [c] (*previous+comrade*): **senior** (s.o. older or w. more experience than oneself)

kóhai 後輩 [c] (*later+comrade*): **junior** (s.o. younger or w. less experience than oneself)

shiríai 知り合い: **acquaintance**

*shiri** + *ai†* |*(I) *shiru (to know)* |†(I) *au (to meet)*

2.6 Action & Interaction

Nouns related to human proactive actions and their consequences.

Important Word

jiken 事件 *incident*

- -

Ⓛ tàido 態度 [c] (*condition+occasion*): **attitude**

mìburi 身振り: **gesture**

mi (body) + *buri ← (I) buru (to behave like)*

shisé 姿勢 [c] (*figure+force*): **posture**

Ⓢ shuúkan 習慣 Ⓒ (learning+used to): **habit**; custom

kusè くせ〔癖〕: ① (bad) **habit**; **vice** ② **tendency**; idiosyncrasy

kòi 行為 Ⓒ (going+doing): **deed**; act

⊕ rìsuku リスク Ⓔ: **risk** (possible neg. outcome)

Ⓢ gài 害 Ⓒ: **harm**; **damage**

kigái 危害 Ⓒ (dangerous+harm): ① **harm**; **injury** ② danger

❖ Referring to 'harm' that is dangerous to life or goods.

tasúkè 助け: **help**; aid

(I) tasukeru (to help)

⊕ jìko 事故 Ⓒ (affair+happenstance): **accident**

Ⓢ machígài 間違い: **error**; **mistake**

(I) machigau (to make an error)

ayámari / ayámàri 誤り: [for.] **mistake**; error

(I) ayamaru (to seek forgiveness)

Ⓢ dekìgoto 出来事: **event**; incident; happening

deki* + goto† | *(I) dekiru (to be able) | † ← koto (thing)

Ⓢ jìken 事件 Ⓒ (affair+case): (unfortunate) **event**; **incident**; (criminal) **case**; happening

❖ Referring to particularly problematic 'incidents'.

taísaku 対策 Ⓒ (opposite+scheme): **measure** (action); counter-measure

Ⓢ jikkén 実験 Ⓒ (reality+verification): Ⓝ **experiment** Ⓥ (suru) to do an experiment

shimyúrèeshon シミュレーション Ⓔ: **simulation**

⊕ sensó 戦争 Ⓒ (battle+fighting): **war**

Ⓢ héwa 平和 Ⓒ (flat+peaceful): **peace**

Ⓢ tatákai 戦い: ① **battle**; **fight**; **struggle**; conflict

(I) tatakau (to fight)

ikùsà / ikúsa 戦: [lit.] ① **battle**; fight ② war

arásoi / arásòi 争い Ⓒ (boisterous+noisy): **conflict**; quarrel; dispute

Ⓢ bùki 武器 Ⓒ (military+instrument): **weapon**

Ⓢ gùntai 軍隊 Ⓒ (army+regiment): **army**

Ⓢ kachì 勝ち: **victory**; winning

(I) katsu (to win)

Ⓢ maké 負け: **defeat**; loss

(I) makeru (to lose)

bòryoku 暴力 Ⓒ (violent+strength): **violence**

batsù 罰 Ⓒ: **punishment**

2.7 Society & Activities

Nouns related to social groups, social activities, sports and fields of study.

Important Word
shakai 社会 *society*

97

Ⓛ **shuúdan** 集団 ⓒ (*gathering*+*group*): **group**; mass

❖ A 'group' understood as a mass of people sharing some commonality.

Ⓛ **dańtai** 団体 ⓒ (*group*+*body*): ① **group** ② organization ③ team

❖ A big 'group' of people participating in a formal activity.

Ⓛ **gurùupu** グループ ⓔ : **group**

Ⓛ **chìimu** チーム ⓔ : **team**

❖ A 'group' of people participating in some kind of competition.

hàn 班 ⓒ : ⓃⓈ **group**; team; party; crew

❖ A small 'group' or 'team' of people congregated for work or study.

kumì 組: ⓃⓈ ① **set** ② **group**

(I) *kumu* (to intertwine)

❖ A 'group' of people or things that can be overseen or controlled.

murà 群: ① **flock** ② **group**

Cognate with *mura* (village)

❖ A 'group' of animals. Also, a 'group' of people or things that is object of study.

Ⓜ **shàkai** 社会 ⓒ (*society*+*meeting*): **society**; community

- -

Ⓕ **yasúmì** 休み: ① **rest** ② **holiday**; **vacation**

(I) *yasumu* (to rest)

❖ U. for both long and short periods of recess.

Ⓛ **kyuúka** 休暇 ⓒ (*resting*+*spare time*): ① **holiday**; vacation ② **day off**

❖ U. specifically for the cessation of academic or working activities.

Ⓕ **pàatii** パーティー ⓔ : **party**

Ⓛ **matsúri** 祭り: **festival**

(I) *matsuru* (to enshrine)

Ⓛ **tańjòbi** 誕生日: **birthday**

ⓒ *tanjō* 誕生 (*birth*) + *hi* 日 (*day*)

Ⓜ **okúrimono** 贈り物: (a) **present**; **gift**

okuri* + *mono* (*thing*) | *(I) *okuru* (to send)

Ⓛ **purèzento** プレゼント ⓔ : (a) **present**; **gift**

Ⓜ **ibénto** イベント ⓔ : (planned) **event**

gyòji / *gyóji* 行事 ⓒ (*going*+*affair*): **event**

Ⓜ **kài** 会 ⓒ : ⓃⓈ ① **meeting** ② party; association; assembly; club

Ⓜ **kàigi** / *kaígì* 会議 ⓒ (*meeting*+*deliberation*): ① **meeting**; convention ② **conference**

❖ Referring to a gathering to discuss some topic.

tàyori 便り: **news**; information (about s.o.)

(I) *tayoru* (to rely on)

Ⓛ **kókyō** 公共 ⓒ (*public*+*together*): ① (the) **public** ② (a) **public** (thing) ③ **community**

shìritsu 私立 ⓒ (*private*+*standing*): **private** (establishment)

Ⓜ **nińki** 人気 ⓒ (*person*+*mood*): **popularity**

Ⓛ **ryuúkō** 流行 ⓒ (*flowing*+*going*): **fashion**; **vogue**; fad; trend

- -

Ⓕ **jùgyō** 授業 ⓒ (*granting*+*deal*): ① **lesson** ② class

Ⓛ **kógì** 講義 ⓒ (*lecture*+*righteousness*): **lecture**

Ⓕ **shukúdai** 宿題 ⓒ (*lodging*+*topic*): **homework**

Ⓕ **tèsuto** テスト ⓔ : **test**

⊕ shikén 試験 C (testing+verification): N **examination; test** V (suru) to have a test; to do a test

⊕ fukúshuu 復習 C (again+learning): **review**; revision

ànkeeto / áńkèeto アンケート F [enquête]: **survey**; questionnaire

- -

⊥ bùnya 分野 C (dividing+plains): **field** (of study)

⊕ séji 政治 C (government+governing): **politics**

⊕ kàgaku 科学 C (science+learning): **science**

⊕ suúgaku 数学 C (number+learning): **maths**

kógaku / kògaku 工学 C (craft+learning): **engineering**

⊕ ìgaku 医学 C (doctor+learning): **medicine** (discipline)

⊕ chìri 地理 C (ground+reason): **geography**

⊕ rekíshi 歴史 C (passage+history): **history**

⊕ bùngaku 文学 C (writing+learning): **literature**

⊥ géjutsu 芸術 C (art+technique): (fine) **art**
❖ Word most commonly u. for the high-end fine arts one can find in museums, commercial galleries or art festivals.

bìjutsu 美術 C (beautiful+technique): (visual) **art**
❖ Word u. for visual arts in general, as an activity: painting, drawing, etc.

⊥ kenchiku 建築 C (building+constructing): **architecture**

⊥ tetsùgaku / tetsúgaku 哲学 C (wisdom+learning): **philosophy**

⊤ shìnri 心理 C (heart+reason): **psychology**

hógaku 法学 C (law+learning): **law**

- -

⊤ supòotsu スポーツ E : (competitive) **sport**(s)

⊕ shiái 試合: **match**; game
shi + *ai*† | *(I) suru (to do)* |†*au (to meet)*

⊥ kyògi 競技 C (competing+ability):(sports) **competition; contest**

kòntesuto コンテスト E : **contest**

rèesu レース E : **race** (competition)

⊥ shò 賞 C : N S **prize**; award

⊕ jùudō 柔道 C (pliant+way): **judo**

⊕ suíē 水泳 C (water+swimming): **swimming**

⊥ tozán 登山 C (ascending+mountain): (mountain) **climbing**

⊕ tènisu テニス E : **tennis**

⊕ sàkkaa サッカー E : **soccer**

⊕ yakyúu 野球 C (plains+ball): **baseball**

gòrufu ゴルフ E : **golf**

basúketto bòoru バスケットボール E : **basketball**

sumó 相撲 C (mutual+slap): **sumo wrestling**

tsurí₁ 釣り: **fishing**
(I) *tsuru (to fish)*

⊥ boóru ボール E : (playing) **ball**

⊥ sènshu 選手 C (choosing+hand): (professional) **player**; athlete

shógi 将棋 C (general+chess piece): **shogi** (J. chess)

2.8 Countries & Cultures

Nouns related to cultures, forms of government and countries.

Important Words

bunka 文化 *culture*	kuni 国 *country*	gaikoku 外国 *foreign country*

⊕ bùnka 文化 Ⓒ (*writing+transforming*): **culture**

⊕ shikì / shìki 式 Ⓒ (*style*): ⓃⓈ ①
ceremony ② **style** ③ **formula**

⊕ sutàiru スタイル Ⓔ: **style**

⊕ régì 礼儀 Ⓒ (*courtesy+etiquette*): (good)
manners; etiquette; courtesy

shitsùrē 失礼 Ⓒ (*losing+courtesy*):
discourtesy; impoliteness

fuúsoku 風俗 Ⓒ (*wind+quick*): **customs;
manners (of acting)**

kakúmē 革命 Ⓒ (*modification+orders*):
revolution

⊕ sēyō 西洋 Ⓒ (*west+ocean*): **the West**

tōyō 東洋 Ⓒ (*east+ocean*): **the East**

⊕ afúrika アフリカ Ⓟ: **Africa**

⊕ àjia アジア Ⓟ: **Asia**

⊕ yoóròppa ヨーロッパ Ⓟ [*Europa*]: **Europe**

kitá amerika 北アメリカ: **North America**

  Ⓙ *kita (north)* + Ⓔ *amerika [America]*

minámi amerika 南アメリカ: **South
America**

  Ⓙ *minami (south)* + Ⓔ *amerika [America]*

⊤ kuní 国: **country**

➤ kuníguni 国々: **countries**

⊕ kòkka 国家 Ⓒ (*country+house*): **country;
nation**

⊕ zènkoku 全国 Ⓒ (*whole+country*): **the
whole country**

⊤ gaíkoku 外国 Ⓒ (*outside+country*): ①
foreign country ② **the rest of the world**

⊕ kàigai 海外 Ⓒ (*sea+outside*): **overseas**

⊕ keń / kèn 県 Ⓒ: ⓃⓈ **prefecture;
province**

⊕ amérika アメリカ Ⓔ: **America** (U.S.A.)

⊤ nihón 日本 Ⓒ (*sun+foundation*): **Japan**

⊕ chuúgoku 中国 Ⓒ (*middle+country*): **China**

⊕ kańkoku 韓国 Ⓒ (*Korea+country*): (South)
Korea

⊕ taíwan 台湾 Ⓒ (*podium+golf*): **Taiwan**

⊕ furánsu フランス Ⓕ: **France**

⊕ itária イタリア Ⓘ [*Italia*]: **Italy**

⊕ doítsu ドイツ Ⓓ [*Duits*]: **Germany**

⊕ igírisu イギリス Ⓟ [*inglês*]: **United
Kingdom**

⊕ roshía ロシア Ⓡ [*Rossija*]: **Russia**

⊕ supéin スペイン Ⓔ: **Spain**

⊕ ìndo インド Ⓒ: **India**

⊕ oósutoraria オーストラリア Ⓔ:
Australia

kanàda カナダ Ⓔ: **Canada**

[country name] + jin 人 Ⓒ: **country's
person**

[country name] + go 語 Ⓒ: **country's
language**

⊤ égo 英語 Ⓒ (*England+talking*): **English**

⊕ sèfu 政府 Ⓒ (*government+borough*):
government

mińshushùgi 民主主義: **democracy**

  Ⓒ *minshu* 民主 (*popular sovereignty*) + *shugi*
主義 (*doctrine*)

dokúsai 独裁 Ⓒ (*alone+judging*): **dictatorship**

⊕ ò 王 Ⓒ: **king**

Ⓔ **ŏji** 王子 Ⓒ (*king+child*): **prince**

Ⓔ **ŏjo** 王女 Ⓒ (*king+woman*): **princess**

éyuu 英雄 Ⓒ (*mighty+male*): **hero**

doré 奴隷 Ⓒ (*servant+slave*): **slave**

Ⓔ **gùntai** 軍隊 Ⓒ (*army+regiment*): **soldier**

Ⓔ **shìmin** 市民 Ⓒ (*city+common people*): **citizen**

Ⓔ **kokúmin** 国民 Ⓒ (*country+common people*): **citizen of a country**; (a) **national**

Ⓔ **daítŏryō** 大統領: **president of a country**

> Ⓒ *dai* 大 (*big*) + *tŏryō* 統領 (*ruler*)

Ⓔ **tō** 党 Ⓒ (*faction*): Ⓝ Ⓢ (political) **party**

Ⓕ **hŏ** 法 Ⓒ : Ⓝ Ⓢ ① (a) **law** ② method

Ⓗ **hŏritsu** 法律 Ⓒ (*law+regulation*): (the) **law**

Ⓗ **kisòku** / **kìsoku** 規則 Ⓒ (*norm+rule*): (written) **rule(s)**; **regulation(s)**

Ⓔ **kimári** 決まり: [*fam.*] **rule**

> (I) *kimaru* (to be decided)

rùuru ルール Ⓔ : **rule**; regulation

> ❖ M. u. in sports, games and entities that want to give a modern impression.

kirítsu 規律 Ⓒ (*norm+regulation*): ① **discipline**; observance; order ② **rules**; **regulations**

3. NATURE

Nouns used to express the different aspects of nature and what one can find in it.

3.1 Reality & Spirituality

Nouns related to what is real and true, to the part and the whole, to quantity and measurability, to circumstances, causes and consequences and to the realm of the supernatural and spirituality.

Within this group, two highly important words are widely used in Japanese while also fulfilling grammatical functions beyond their nominal use [☞ GE:I.2]. These nouns are **koto** and **mono**, which serve to designate any perceived or imagined 'thing'. Both nouns can be translated by the word 'thing', but it is important to know from the beginning how different they are. *Koto* is used to designate any abstract and intangible thing and *mono* is used to designate physical and tangible things.

Important Words

koto こと (*non-physical*) ***thing***	mono もの (*physical*) ***thing***
hoka 他 ***other*** (*thing*)	baai 場合 ***situation***
bubun 部分 ***part***	zenbu 全部 ***whole*** (*thing*)
tēdo 程度 ***extent***	ryō 量 ***quantity***
moto 元 ***origin***	wake 訳 ***reason***
un 運 ***luck***	kami 神 ***god***

Ⓣ **kotò** こと〔事〕: ① **thing** ② event

Cognate with O.J. *koto (word)*

❖ M. u. to describe non-physical or intangible 'things', such as events, situations or ideas.

Ⓣ **monò₁** / monó もの〔❶❷ 物/ ❸ 者〕: ① **thing** ② object ③ person

❖ M. u. to refer to physical or tangible 'things' or 'objects'.

❖ ❸ M. u. in idiomatic compounds.

Ⓤ **yàtsu₂** やつ〔奴〕Ⓒ (*making+product*): [*col.*][*mas.*] ① **thing** ② guy; fellow ③ person

---

Ⓤ **geńjitsu** 現実 Ⓒ (*revealed+reality*): (apparent) **reality**

❖ Referring to a view of the world of particular things as the opposite of imagination or ideals.

Ⓤ **jissái** 実際 Ⓒ (*reality+juncture*): ① (objective) **reality** ② practicality ③ actuality

❖ This word refers to the state of being 'real' rather than being imaginary.

Ⓜ **jìjitsu** 事実 Ⓒ (*affair+reality*): ① **fact** ② **truth** ③ reality

❖ It m. refers to subjective ideas considered as being true.

shìnjitsu 真実 Ⓒ (*true+reality*): ① (factual) **truth** ② reality

❖ 'Truth' understood as s.t. that is an actual fact in contrast to fake things or falsehood.

shìnri 真理 Ⓒ (*true+reason*): (ultimate) **truth**

❖ Word m. u. in a philosophical or religious sense, referring to s.t. that is considered to be absolutely right, being a 'truth' that anyone can admit but not necessarily prove.

---

nisé 偽: Ⓝ ① **fake** (thing); **false** (thing) ② **imitation**; counterfeit Ⓟ pseudo-; fake

(I) *niseru (to imitate)*

Ⓣ **hoká₁** 他 Ⓒ (*section+dividing*): ① **other** (place; thing; person) ② **the rest**

Ⓣ **bùbun** 部分 Ⓒ (*section+dividing*): **part**

Ⓜ **zeńtai** 全体 Ⓒ (*whole+body*): ① (the) **totality**; (the) **whole**

Ⓤ **gókē** 合計 Ⓒ (*coming together+reckoning*): **total amount**

Ⓜ **hańbùn** 半分 Ⓒ (*half+dividing*): (the) **half**; half

Ⓤ **daibubun** 大部分: (the) **majority**; (the) **most part**

Ⓒ *dai* 大 (*big*) + *bubun* 部分 (*part*)

Ⓤ **tasùu** 多数 Ⓒ (*many+number*): **majority**; great number; countless

shósùu 少数 Ⓒ (*little+number*): **minority**; small number; few

fukúsùu 複数 Ⓒ (*double+number*): **multiple** (number); **several** (things)

Ⓜ **tédo** / tèdo 程度 Ⓒ (*extent+degree*): Ⓝ Ⓢ ① **degree** ② extent

Ⓤ **hànï** 範囲 Ⓒ (*exemplary+surrounding*): **range**; scope; extent; span

---

Ⓜ **ryò** 量 Ⓒ : Ⓝ Ⓢ **quantity**; **amount**; portion of

❖ U. for things that can be measured (e.g. weight or volume).

Ⓤ **sùu** 数 Ⓒ (*number*): Ⓝ Ⓢ **number of**; **amount**; **quantity**

❖ U. for things that can be counted by numbers.

Ⓤ **waríai** 割合: **rate**; **ratio**; **proportion**; percentage *wari (rate)* + suf. *ai (together)*

Ⓛ **naíyō** 内容 Ⓒ (*inside+container*): **content**

Ⓛ **sògo** 相互 Ⓒ (*mutual+reciprocal*): (a) **mutual** (thing); (a) **reciprocal** (thing)

- -

Ⓣ **baái** 場合: ① **case** ② **situation**

ba (place) + *ai ← (I) au (to meet)*

❖ A particular instance of a situation.

Ⓛ **jókyō** 状況 Ⓒ (*printing+situation*): (objective) **situation; circumstances**; state of things

❖ U. to address conditions that affect things and people.

Ⓛ **jótai** 状態 Ⓒ (*printing+condition*): **state; condition**; (current) situation; circumstances

❖ M. u. to refer to the state or condition of physical things.

Ⓗ **guái** 具合 Ⓒ (*tool+together*): (physical) **condition; state**

❖ M. u. to refer to health conditions.

Ⓛ **yósu** 様子 Ⓒ (*manner+child*): [*fam.*] ① **state**; situation ② **look; appearance**

❖ An informal way to refer to the subjective state or condition of s.t. towards which attention is directed.

Ⓛ **tsugó** 都合 Ⓒ (*metropolis+coming together*): Ⓝ ① **convenient circumstances**; (one's) convenience ② **personal reasons** (circumstances) Ⓥ (suru) to arrange; to manage

- -

Ⓛ **hońshitsu** 本質 Ⓒ (*foundation+quality*): **essence**

Ⓗ **geńin** 原因 Ⓒ (*source+caused*): **cause**; origin; source

❖ Referring to the origination of a causal relationship.

Ⓗ **motò** / motó ❶ 元/ ❷ 本/ ❸ 基: Ⓝ ① **origin**; cause; source ② **root**;

foundation ③ **base**; basis Ⓟ **former**; **original**; ex-; past

❖ Referring to the 'original' state of a thing that develops into another thing.

Ⓗ **riyúu** 理由 Ⓒ (*reason+cause*): **reason**; **motive**; pretext

❖ U. in relation to a cause-and-effect relationship

Ⓗ **wàke** わけ〔訳〕: ① **reason**; **reasoning**; conclusion

(I) *wakeru (to understand)*

❖ U. both in relation to a cause-and-effect relationship and in subjective reasonings.

Ⓛ **kòka** 効果 Ⓒ (*effective+fruit*): **effect**

kekká 結果 Ⓒ (*tying+fruit*): **consequence**; **result**

Ⓛ **kanósē** 可能性: **possibility**

Ⓒ *kanō* 可能 (*possible*) + *sē* 性 (*disposition*)

rèberu レベル Ⓔ: **level**

- -

Ⓛ **rè** 例: **example**

➤ **rè no** 例の: **...in question**

Ⓛ **tatoe** 例え: Ⓝ **example** Ⓑ **even if; no matter (what); supposing**

(I) *tatoeru (to compare)*

- -

Ⓛ **kàmi** 神: **god**

Cognate with *kami (top)*

➤ **kamìgami** 神々: **gods**; deities

Ⓛ **àkuma** 悪魔 Ⓒ (*bad+demon*): (the) **devil**

tèngoku 天国 Ⓒ (*heaven+country*): **heaven**

jigóku / jigókù 地獄 Ⓒ (*ground+prison*): **hell**

Ⓛ **ùn** 運 Ⓒ: **luck**; fortune

ùnmē 運命 Ⓒ (*carrying+fate*): **fate**; destiny

Ⓛ **enèrugii** / enérùgii エネルギー Ⓔ: **energy**

tàmashii 魂: ① **soul** ② spirit

O.J. *tama (soul)* + *shii* ← *sihi*: (I) O.J. *shiu (to compel)* → C.J. *shiiru*

---

yùurē 幽霊 Ⓒ *(confinement+soul)*: **ghost**

❖ The visible form of a departed soul or spirit.

obàke お化け: **ghost**

Hon. pre. *o* + *bake* ← (I) *bakeru (to change)*

❖ Word referring particularly to ghosts that are able to change their visible form.

---

mònsutaa モンスター Ⓔ : **monster**

❖ Neutral word for 'monster' understood as a strange creature, but not necessarily scary.

kaíbutsu 怪物 Ⓒ *(weird+thing)*: **monster**

❖ A dreadfully looking strange creature.

bakémòno / bakémonò 化け物: (evil) **monster**

---

bake* + *mono (thing)* | **(I) bakeru (to change)*

❖ A particularly scary, evil and strange creature.

---

tènshi 天子 Ⓒ *(heaven+child)*: **angel**

mahó 魔法 Ⓒ *(demon+law)*: **magic**

màjo 魔女 Ⓒ *(demon+woman)*: **witch**

inórì 祈り: **prayer**

(I) *inoru (to pray)*

Ⓛ shùukyō 宗教 Ⓒ *(religion+teaching)*: **religion**

kàruto カルト Ⓔ : **cult**

bùkkyō 仏教 Ⓒ *(Buddha+teaching)*: **Buddhism**

shìntō 神道 Ⓒ *(god+way)*: **Shintoism**

kirísutokyō クリスト教: **Christianity**

sèsho 聖書 Ⓒ *(holy+writing)*: **Bible**

bósan 坊さん: (buddhist) **monk**

Ⓒ *bō* 坊 *(boy)* + Ⓙ hon. suf. *san*

3.2 Form & Color

Nouns related to measurable physical qualities: shape, typology, size and color.

Most colors, in Japanese, are grammatically nouns to which the particle *no* can be added in order to function as attributes (adjectives) [☞ V].

Important Words

katachi 形 *form*	sugata 姿 *figure*	imeji イメジ *image*
kata 型 *style*	taipu タイプ *type*	saizu サイズ *size*
ten 店 *point*	sen 線 *line*	iro 色 *color*
kuro 黒 *black*	shiro 白 *white*	ao 青 *blue*
midori 緑 *green*	aka 赤 *red*	kiiro 黄色 *yellow*

Ⓕ katàchi 形・容: [*fam.*] ① **form; shape** ② **figure**

Cognate with *katai (hard)*

❖ Referring to the appearance of a physical thing or object, including also the human body.

kétai 形態 Ⓒ *(shape+condition)*: ① **form; shape** ② **figure**

❖ It refers to the overall appearance of complex things as seen from the outside as a whole.

késhiki 形式 Ⓒ (*shape+style*): ① **form** ② **format** ③ **formality**

❖ 'Form' as opposed to substance. Also, a designed or planned 'form'.

⊕ **sùgata**₁ 姿: ① **figure** ② **appearance**

❖ M. u. to indicate the kind of clothes or style that one is wearing, or the impression one gets from a person's overall appearance. Sometimes also u. fig.

Ⓛ **kakkó**₁ 格好 Ⓒ (*form+liking*): Ⓝ ① **figure** ② **appearance** ③ **shape** ④ **pose** Ⓐ (na/no) suitable; fit

❖ M. u. to describe the shape and condition of the physical appearance of things or people as seen from the outside, often referring to clothing or movements.

Ⓛ **samà**₁ 様: **appearance**; situation; state

O.J. *sa (that)* + *ma (space)*

moyó 模様 Ⓒ (*mold+manner*): **pattern**; design; figure

⊕ **imèeji** / ìmeeji イメージ Ⓔ : ① **image** ② aspect

- -

⊕ **tàipu** タイプ Ⓔ : **type**; kind

❖ Word u. to refer to things that share common distinct characteristics among a broader set of things.

Ⓛ **shùrui** 種類 Ⓒ (*kind+type*): ① **type**; kind; variety; category

❖ Word u. to comprise a set of things that can be classified by definite categories.

Ⓛ **katà** ❶❷ 型/ ❸ 形: Ⓝ Ⓢ ① **type**; style; pattern ② **model**; template; mold ③ (visible) **form**

❖ Word u. to comprise a set of things that can be classified by shape or appearance.

moké 模型 Ⓒ (*mold+model*): **model**; maquette; dummy

bì 美 Ⓒ : **beauty**

- -

sàizu サイズ Ⓔ : **size**

❖ Word commonly u. to refer to the size of retail products such as articles of clothing.

tàkasa 高さ: **height**

Nom. f. of the adj. *takai (tall)*

nàgasa 長さ: **length**

Nom. f. of the adj. *nagai (long)*

Ⓛ **hàba** 幅: **width**

fukàsa / fùkasa 深さ: **depth**; profundity

Nom. f. of the adj. *fukai (deep)*

❖ Vertical distance below a surface.

òkuyuki 奥行き: **depth**; length

oku (inside) + *yuki ← (I) yuku (to go)*

❖ Horizontal distance between the front and the back.

shìryō 資料 Ⓒ (*assets+foodstuff*): **material**

Ⓣ **teń** 点Ⓒ : **point**; dot

⊕ **sèn** 線 Ⓒ : Ⓝ Ⓢ **line**

Ⓛ **ràin** ライン Ⓔ : **line**

gyò 行 Ⓒ (*going*): Ⓝ Ⓒ ① **line** (in a text) ② **row**

rètsu 列 Ⓒ (*array*): ① **column** (in a text) ② **file**; sequence

Ⓛ **marú**₁ 丸: Ⓝ **circle** Ⓟ whole; complete

Stem of the adj. *marui (round)*.

Ⓛ **wà** 輪: ① **ring shape** ② circle

Ⓔ tamà₁ ❶❷ 玉/ ❸ 球/ ❹ 弾: ① **sphere** ② jewel ③ **ball** ④ **bullet**

shikákù 四角 Ⓒ (*four+angle*): ① **square** ② **rectangle**

sànkaku 三角 Ⓒ (*three+angle*): **triangle**

- -

Ⓜ chigái 違い: **difference**

(I) *chigau (to be different)*

Ⓔ sa 差 Ⓒ : (quantitative) **difference**

sài 差異 Ⓒ (*distinction+difference*): [*lit.*] **difference**; disparity

❖ Specifically u. when the 'difference' is between two or more things compared to each other

Ⓔ tokúchō 特徴 Ⓒ (*type+sign*): **feature**; **characteristic**; distinction; trait

❖ A 'characteristic' that stands out in comparison with other people or things.

kózō 構造 Ⓒ (*setting up+creating*): **structure**

kijún 基準 Ⓒ (*base+level*): (a) **standard**

- -

Ⓔ àto ❶❷ 跡/ ❸ 痕: ① **trace**; tracks; remains ② mark ③ **scar**

O.J. *a (foot)* + O.J. *to (place)*

Ⓔ shrúshi 印: **mark**; sign; symbol

(I) *shirusu (to write down)*

geńkai 限界 Ⓒ (*limiting+boundary*): **limit**; boundary

Ⓕ irò 色: **color**

Ⓕ kùro 黒: **black**

Cognate with *kurai (dark)*

Ⓕ shìro 白: **white**

Ⓕ ào 青: ⓃⓅ ① **blue** ② **green**

❖ Word m. u. for 'blue' but also for 'green' when referring to natural green colors and traffic lights.

Ⓕ mìdori 緑: **green**

Ⓕ àka 赤: ⓃⓅ **red**

Cognate with *akaru (to become bright)*

Ⓕ kiíro 黄色: **yellow**

Ⓒ *ki 黄 (yellow)* + Ⓙ *iro (color)*

Ⓕ chaíro 茶色: **brown**

Ⓒ *cha 茶 (tea)* + Ⓙ *iro (color)*

pìnku ピンク Ⓔ : **pink**

orènji オレンジ Ⓔ : **orange** (color)

muràsaki 紫: ① **purple** ② **violet**

mura (gathering) + *saki* ← (I) *saku (to bloom)*

gurèe グレー Ⓔ : **gray**

haíiro 灰色: **gray**

hai (ash) + *iro (color)*

3.3 Land & Sea

Nouns related to the main visible aspects of the physical nature of land and sea.

Important Words

sekai 世界 *world*	shizen 自然 *nature*	tsuchi 土 *land*	ki 木 *tree*
hana 花 *flower*	hi 火 *fire*	ishi 石 *stone*	yama 山 *mountain*
mizu 水 *water*	umi 海 *sea*	shima 島 *island*	kawa 川 *river*

kita 北 *north*	minami 南 *south*	higashi 東 *east*	nishi 西 *west*

tokoro 所 *place*

⊕ sèkai 世界 [c] (*generation+world*): (the) **world**; society

❖ It refers to the place where life is lived (the physical world) but also to the set of people living in that place.

yò / yo 世: [*lit.*] **world; society**

❖ M. u. in idiomatic expressions or otherwise w. religious or spiritual connotations.

➤ yo nò naka 世の中: (the) **world**; **society**

⊥ shizén 自然 [c] (*oneself+thus*): **nature**

⊥ chikyúu 地球 [c] (*ground+ball*): **Earth**

⊕ tsuchì 土: ① **earth** ② **soil**

⊕ chì 地 [c]: [N][S] ① **land** ② (the) **ground** ③ soil

⊥ tochí 土地 [c] (*earth+ground*): **soil; lot; plot of land**

⊕ hen 辺 [c] (*proximity*): (surrounding) **area**; vicinity

⊥ chìiki 地域 [c] (*ground+region*): ① **region** ② **area**

⊤ kì 木: ① **tree** ② wood

➤ kìgi 木々: **trees**

⊥ màtsu 松: **pine** (tree)

také 竹: **bamboo**

⊕ ha 葉: **leaf**

Cognate w. ha*/†/‡ and haeru (to sprout) | *blade and also probably w. †feather, ‡tooth

⊕ edá 枝: **branch**

⊕ morí 森: **forest**

⊥ nè 根: **root**

⊥ tàne 種: **seed**

tsùe 杖: **stick**

⊕ kusà 草: [N] **grass** [P] ① fake; false ② amateur

⊤ hanà 花: **flower**

ha (leaf) + O.J. augmentative suf. na

➤ hanàbana 花々: **flowers**

bará ばら・バラ〔薔薇〕: **rose**

⊥ sakúra 桜: ① **cherry blossom** ② cherry tree

saku (to bloom) + pluralizing suf. ra

⊕ hì 火: **fire**

⊥ hònoo 炎: **flame**

ho* + genitive p. no (of) + o† |* ← hi (fire) |† ← ho (ear of grain)

⊥ kemúri 煙: **smoke**

(I) kemuru (to smoke)

⊥ haí 灰: **ash**

⊕ ishì 石: **stone**

Cognate with *iso (rocky beach)*

⊥ iwà 岩: **rock**

⊕ suná 砂: **sand**

⊥ subáku 砂漠 [c] (*sand+obscure*): **desert**

⊤ mizú お水: **water**

← *miizu*: O.J. *mi (water)* + O.J. *izu (to come out)*

⊕ yù お湯: **hot water**

❖ Term specifically u. when one wants to make a distinction w. respect to cold water.

⑦ ùmi 海: ① **sea** ② beach

O.J. *u (ocean)* + O.J. *mi (water)*

⊕ kaígan 海岸 Ⓒ *(sea+coast)*: **coast**

hamábe / hamábè 浜辺: ① **seashore** ② **beach**

hama (seashore) + be: ← O.J. he (vicinity)

⊥ namì 波: **wave**

The morpheme *mi* probably has a relation with O.J. *mi (water)*

- -

⑦ yamà ₒ山: **mountain**

➤ yamàyama 山々: **mountains**

⊥ oká 丘: **hill**

⊥ tanì 谷: **valley**

⊥ sakà / sàka 坂: **slope**

⊕ shimà 島: **island**

⑦ ikè 池: **pond**

⊕ mizúùmi 湖: **lake**

mizu (water) + umi (sea)

kawà 川: ⎕Ⓢ **river**; stream

⊥ koóri 氷: **ice**

⊥ izúmi 泉: **spring** (natural source)

O.J. *idzu (to come out)* + O.J. *mi (water)*

- -

⑦ tokóro 所: ① **place** ② address

O.J. *to (place)* + O.J. suf. *ko (place)* + O.J. suf. *ro (area)*

❖ General term for 'place', both in a physical and fig. sense. Also widely u. w. the sense of 'address'.

⊕ bashó 場所: **place**; location

Ⓙ *ba (place)* + Ⓒ *sho 所 (place)*

❖ M. u. in relation to the actions or behaviors that are done in that place, or in relation to a space where s.o./s.t. stays.

yosò / yòso よそ〔余所〕Ⓒ *(remaining+place)*: ① **another place**; somewhere else ② outside

⊕ mawári ❶❷ 周り/ ❸ 回り: ① **circumference** ② **surroundings** ③ area around s.t.

(I) *mawaru (to rotate)*

⑦ kàdo 角: (outside) **corner**

⊥ sùmi 隅: ⎕Ⓢ (inside) **corner; nook**

⊥ shógai 障害 Ⓒ *(hindering+harm)*: **obstacle**

⊥ anà 穴: **hole**; opening

- -

⑦ kitá / kità 北: **north**

⑦ minámi 南: **south**

⑦ higáshi / higáshì 東: **east**

← *hingashi* ← O.J. *himukashi*: *hi (sun)* + *mukashi*: *muka** + *shi†* | **Irrealis f. of v. mukasu (to face)* |†(I) O.J. *su (to do)* → C.J. *suru*

⑦ nishí 西: **west**

3.4 Sky & Weather

Nouns related to what is visible in the sky and to the weather.

Important Words

sora 空 *sky*		kaze 風 *wind*		hi 日 *sun*		tsuki 月 *moon*
	tenki 天気 *weather*		ame 雨 *rain*		yuki 雪 *snow*	

Ⓣ sòra 空: ① sky ② heaven

Ⓛ ùchuu 宇宙 Ⓒ (*cosmos+universe*): **universe; cosmos**

Ⓣ kazé 風: **wind**

⊕ kùuki 空気 Ⓒ (*sky+mood*): **air**

⊕ hoshí 星: **star**

⊕ hi 日: ① **sun** ② **day**

❖ ❶ 'Sun' understood as the heavenly body that affects human life, having hence an anthropocentric perspective.

➤ hibí 日々: (several) **days**

Ⓛ taiyō 太陽 Ⓒ (*great+sunshine*): **sun**

❖ 'Sun' understood as an objective, scientific and detached concept.

Ⓛ tsukì 月: ① **moon** ② **month**

Ⓣ tènki お天気 Ⓒ (*heaven+mood*): **weather**

kikő 気候 Ⓒ (*mood+climate*): **climate**

Ⓣ harè 晴れ: **fine weather; good weather**

(I) *hareru (to clear up)*

kaísē 快晴 Ⓒ (*pleasant+sunny*): **clear weather; cloudless weather; good weather**

❖ Word specifically u. for the weather in which there are very few or no clouds in the sky.

Ⓛ òndo 温度 Ⓒ (*warm+degree*): **temperature**

⊕ netsù 熱 Ⓒ : ① **heat** ② fever

àtsusa 暑さ: **hotness; heat (of the weather)**

Nominalization of the adj. *atsui (to be hot)*

sàmusa 寒さ: **cold; coldness**

Nominalization of the adj. *samui (to be cold)*

⊕ kùmo 雲: **cloud**

Ⓣ kumórì 曇り: **cloudy weather**

(I) *kumoru (to become cloudy)*

Ⓣ àme 雨: **rain**

Cognate with the affix *ame (sky)*

Ⓛ kamínàri / kamínarì 兆し: **thunder; lighting**

kami (god/top) + *nari*: (I) *naru (to sound)*

Ⓛ àrashi 嵐: **storm**

(I) *arasu (to destroy)*

Ⓛ kàge ❶❷ 影/ ❸❹ 陰: ① **shadow** ② **silhouette** ③ **shade** ④ background (place where one cannot be seen)

Ⓛ kirí 霧: ① **fog** ② mist

Ⓛ tsùyu / tsuyù 露: **dew**

nijí 虹: **rainbow**

Ⓣ yukì 雪: **snow**

⊕ hikárì 光: **light**

(I) *hikaru (to shine)*

yamì 闇: **darkness**

(I) *yamu (to cease/to be ill)*

Ⓛ kaṅkyō 環境 Ⓒ (*ring+border*): **environment**

Ⓛ jishín 地震 Ⓒ (*ground+shaking*): **earthquake**

saígai 災害 Ⓒ (*disaster+harm*): **disaster; calamity**

3.6 Time & Seasons

Nouns related to the passage of time and its measurement.

Important Words

toki 時 *time*			
jikan 時間 *hour-time*	fun 分 *minute*	byō 秒 *second*	shunkan 瞬間 *moment*
asa 朝 *morning*	gozen 午前 *a.m*	gogo 午後 *p.m.*	toshi 年 *year*
hiru 昼 *daytime*	hi 日 *day-month*	ban 版 *evening*	yoru 夜 *night*
shuu 週 *week*	nichiyōbi 日曜日 *Sunday*	getsuyōbi 月曜日 *Monday*	kayōbi 火曜日 *Tuesday*
suiyōbi 水曜 *Wednesday*	mokuyōbi 木曜日 *Thursday*	kinyōbi 金曜日 *Friday*	doyōbi 土曜日 *Saturday*
haru 春 *spring*	natsu 夏 *summer*	aki 秋 *fall*	fuyu 冬 *winter*
genzai 現在 *present*	kako 過去 *past*	shōrai 将来 *(one's) future*	mirai 未来 *future*

Ⓣ tokì 時: ① **time** ② moment

❖ M. u. in relation to actions that are done in a certain 'time'.

Ⓣ jikán₁ 時間 Ⓒ *(time+interval)*: ① **time** ② **hour**

❖ M. u. to refer to a time span or interval, but can also be u. to express points in time.

Ⓜ jikóku 時刻 Ⓒ *(time+carving)*: ① **time** ② moment; instant

❖ Specifically refers to an exact point in time.

Ⓛ shuńkan 瞬間 Ⓒ *(blinking+interval)*: **moment**; instant

Ⓛ kikài / kikái 機会 Ⓒ *(mechanism+meeting)*: **opportunity**; chance

❖ This word lit. means 'a suitable time to do s.t.'.

Ⓛ chànsu チャンス Ⓔ: **chance**; **opportunity**

kikkáke 切っ掛け: **chance**; **occasion**; motive; excuse

kik* + kake† |*← kiru (to cut) |†(I) kakeru (to hang)

Ⓛ fùn₁ 分 Ⓒ : **minute** (unit of time)

Ⓛ byò 秒 Ⓒ : **second** (unit of time)

hi nó de 日の出: **sunrise**

hi (sun) + genitive p. no + de ← (I) deru (to go out)

Ⓛ yoákè 夜明け: **dawn**; daybreak

affix yo (night) + ake ←(I) akeru (to open)

❖ This word can be u. both physically and fig.

akégata 明け方: **dawn**; daybreak

ake* + gata ← kata (direction) |*(I) akeru (to get bright)

❖ Specifically referring to the time of the day when the night falls.

Ⓣ àsa 朝: **morning**

❖ Word u. specifically to refer to the early morning, from sunrise to midmorning (around 10:00 a.m.).

ⓗ gòzen 午前 ⓒ (noon+before): ① **a.m.** ② **morning**

❖ Period of time between midnight and noon.

ⓛ shògo 正午 ⓒ (correct+noon): **noon**

ⓗ gògo 午後 ⓒ (noon+after): ① **p.m.** ② **afternoon**

❖ Period of time between noon and midnight.

ⓣ hirù 昼: ① **daytime** ② noon; midday

hi (sun) + emphatic suf. ru

➤ hirúma 昼間: **daytime**; during the day

yuúhi 夕日: **sunset**; evening sun

Obs. *yuu (evening) + hi (day)*

❖ Referring to the sun in the evening when it is setting.

hi nó iri 日の入り: **sunset**

hi (sun) + genitive p. no + iri ← (I) iru (to go into)

❖ Referring specifically to the time in which the sun sets.

ⓛ yuúgata 夕方: ① **evening** ② **dusk**

Obs. *yuu (evening) + gata: ← kata (direction)*

❖ Word u. specifically to refer to the period of time that goes from sunset until the sky becomes dark.

yuúbè / yuíube ❶ 夕べ/ ❷ 昨夜: ① **evening** ② **last night**; yesterday evening

Obs. *yuu (evening) + be: ← O.J. he (vicinity)*

ⓣ bań 晩 ⓒ : Ⓝ Ⓒ ① **evening** ② **night**

❖ The period of time just after dusk, an early evening. Also frequently u. to refer to the period that goes from dinner time until bedtime.

ⓣ yòru 夜: ① **night** ② **late evening**

Obs. *yo (night) + emphatic suf. ru*

yonákà 夜中: ① **midnight** ② **at night**; nighttime ③ **all night**

Obs. *yo (night) + naka (middle)*

ⓗ hi 日: ① sun ② **day**

➤ hìbi 日々: **every day**; daily; day after day

ⓛ yóbi 曜日 ⓒ (weekday+day): **day of the week**

➤ nichíyòbi 日曜日: **Sunday**

➤ getsúyòbi 月曜日: **Monday**

➤ kayòbi 火曜日: **Tuesday**

➤ suíyòbi 水曜日: **Wednesday**

➤ mokúyòbi 木曜日: **Thursday**

➤ kińyòbi 金曜日: **Friday**

➤ doyòbi 土曜日: **Saturday**

ⓛ hidzúke 日付: **date**

hi (day) + dzuke ← tsuke (contact)

ⓛ shùu 週 ⓒ : **week**

shuúmatsu 週末 ⓒ (week+ending): **weekend**

ⓛ tsukì 月: ① moon ② **month**

➤ tsukìdzuki / tsukídzuki 月々: **every month**; monthly

[number] + gatsu 月 ⓒ (month): **nth month**

ⓣ toshì 年: **year**

nènnen 年々: **every year**; yearly

ⓛ sèki 世紀 ⓒ (generation+chronicle): **century**

- - - - - - - - - - - - - - - -

ⓗ kisètsu / kìsetsu 季節 ⓒ (season+node): **season** (time of the year)

ⓣ hàru 春: **spring**

ⓣ natsù 夏: **summer**

ⓣ àki 秋: **autumn**

Cognate with *aki (bright/red)*

ⓣ fuyù 冬: **winter**

- - - - - - - - - - - - - - - -

⊕ jidái 時代 Ⓒ (time+superseding): ① **era**; **age** (period of time) ② generation (era)

⊥ kikàn / kìkan 期間 Ⓒ (period of time+interval): ① **period** (of time) ② term

⊤ gènzai 現在 Ⓒ (revealed+being at): **present** (time)

⊥ kàko 過去 Ⓒ (beyond+going away): **past**

⊕ shórai 将来 Ⓒ (will+coming): **future**; prospects

❖ M. u. in relation w. the 'future' activities of people or organizations.

⊥ mìrai 未来 Ⓒ (not yet+coming): **future**

❖ 'Future' understood objectively as the concept describing the time that is ahead

⊥ kìndai 近代 Ⓒ (near+superseding): **modern times**

chùuse 中世 Ⓒ (middle+generation): **middle age**

kòdai 古代 Ⓒ (old+superseding): **ancient times**

⊥ hajíme 初め・始め: **begenning**; **start**

(I) hajimeru (to start)

⊕ owári 終わり: (the) **end**

(I) owaru (to finish)

❖ Word u. to refer to the 'end' of s.t. that has been going for a long time, or to refer to the specific point in which s.t. finishes.

shiágari 仕上がり: **finish**; completion; end

(I) shiagaru (to finish): shi* + agaru (to give) | *(I) suru (to do)

❖ M. u. to refer to a finished state as a result of a process.

kirì 切り: **end**; finish

(I) kiru (to cut)

dańkai 段階 Ⓒ (steps+storey): **phase**; stage; step

katé 過程 Ⓒ (beyond+extent): **process**

3.7 Animals & Insects

Nouns used to name animals and insects. Except for some animals whose mention is quite common, it has been established as a consensus in today's Japanese to write the names of animals in katakana.

Important Words

dōbutsu 動物 *animal*	kemono 獣 *hairy animal*	inu 犬 *dog*	neko 猫 *cat*
ushi 牛 *cow*	uma 馬 *horse*	buta 豚 *pig*	tsubasa 翼 *wing*
tori 鳥 *bird*	niwatori 鶏 *chicken*	sakana 魚 *fish*	mushi 虫 *insect*

⊤ dóbutsu 動物 Ⓒ (moving+thing): **animal**

❖ General term for all types of animals.

kemóno 獣: ① **beast** ② animal

ke (hair) + mono (thing)

❖ U. mainly to refer to animals covered with hair.

osù おす〔雄〕: **male** (animal; plant)

← O.J. o (male)

mesù めす〔雌〕: **female** (animal; plant)

← O.J. *me (female)*

- -

Ⓣ inù 犬: **dog**

Ⓣ nèko 猫: **cat**

Ⓤ ushí 牛: ① **cow** ② **bull** ③ **cattle** ④ ox

Ⓤ umà 馬: **horse**

butá 豚: ① **pig** ② pork

Ⓙ *bu** + Ⓒ *ta* 太 *(fat)* | * ← *buu* ← *buubuu (oink; grunting sound of a pig)*

hitsúji 羊: **sheep**

usági ウサギ〔兎〕: **rabbit**

nezúmi ネズミ〔鼠〕: ① **mouse** ② rat

nezumi ← *nesumi: ne (root)* + *sumi* ← (I) *sumu (to live in)*

kitsúne 狐: **fox**

*kitsu** + *ne (sound)* | * ← *kitsu kitsu (onomatopoeic sound of laughter)*

shiká / shikà 鹿: **deer**

kumà / kùma 熊: **bear**

sàru サル〔猿〕: **monkey**

raíon ライオン Ⓔ : **lion**

torá 虎: **tiger**

zò 象 Ⓒ : **elephant**

tsunò 角: **horn**

ò 尾: **tail**

shippò 尻尾: [*fam.*] **tail**

← *shirio: shiri (buttocks)* + *o (tail)*

Ⓤ tsubása 翼: **wing**

Ⓤ torí 鳥: **bird**

niwátori 鶏: **chicken**

niwa (garden) + *tori (bird)*

kàmo カモ〔鴨〕: **duck**

Probably an alteration of the v. *ukamu (to float)*

hané 羽: ① **feather** ② bird's wings

O.J. *ha (feather)* + *ne (root)*

washí ワシ〔鷲〕: **eagle**

hàto ハト〔鳩〕: **pigeon**

kàrasu カラス〔烏〕: **crow**

kara (onomatopoeic caw of a crow) + O.J. suf. *su (bird)*

Ⓣ sakána 魚: **fish**

*saka** + O.J. *na (vegetables)* | * ← *sake (alcohol)* ‖ This word originally meant a 'side dish', over time, however, *sakana* has become the most common word for both living and cooked fish.

uó 魚: (living) **fish**

O.J. *u (ocean)* + O.J. *o (fish)*

❖ This word is currently m. found in compounds.

magúro マグロ〔鮪〕: **tuna**

sàke 鮭: **salmon**

kujíra クジラ〔鯨〕: **whale**

irúka イルカ〔海豚〕: **dolphin**

samé サメ〔鮫〕: **shark**

toge 刺: **thorn**

tàko タコ〔蛸〕: **octopus**

kaní カニ〔蟹〕: **crab**

*ka** + *ni (vermilion)* | * ← *kara (shell)*

kàki カキ〔牡蠣〕: **oyster**

(I) *kaku (to scratch)*

kaéru カエル〔蛙〕: **frog**

Cognate with kaeru (to hatch)

kàme 亀: **turtle**

wàni ワニ〔鰐〕: **crocodile**

kùmo クモ〔蜘蛛〕: **spider**

Probably an alteration of the v. *kumu* (to
cross together)

hèbi 蛇: **snake**

- -

Ⓒ mushí 虫: ① **insect**; bug ② worm

arí アリ〔蟻〕: **ant**

katàtsumuri カタツムリ〔蝸牛〕: **snail**

kata* + tsumuri† |*Stem of adj. *katai* (hard) |
† ← *tsuburi* (small round thing)

deńdènmushi でんでん虫: [col.] [*fam.*]
snail

hachí ハチ〔蜂〕: ① **bee** ② wasp

haé ハエ〔蠅〕: **fly**

kà 蚊: **mosquito**

chòchō チョウチョウ〔蝶々〕: **butterfly**

3.8 Fruits & Vegetables

Nouns used to name fruits and vegetables. As with animal names, it has been established
as consensus in contemporary Japanese to write the names of fruits and vegetables in
katakana. This custom most likely derives, by analogy, from the fact that many of the
names of fruits and vegetables that were introduced into Japan in later times come directly
from English (hence written in katakana as such).

Important Words

kudamono 果物 *fruit*	yasai 野菜 *vegetables*

- -

Ⓕ kudàmono 果物: (picked) **fruit**

ku* + da† + mono (thing) |* ← *ko* (tree) |†O.J.
possessive marker

❖ Refers to any fruit that is ready to eat,
also when they are found in nature.

furùutsu フルーツ Ⓔ: **fruit**

❖ M. u. when referring to 'fruits' as a
product that is ready for consumption.

kàjitsu 果実 Ⓒ (*fruit+substance*): ① **fruit** ② nut

❖ This word specifically refers to the
fruits growing on trees or plants, not
necessarily ready to eat.

Ⓛ mi 実: ① **fruit** ② nut

❖ This is the general term for the edible
tissues of plants including fruits, nuts and
vegetables.

ringó リンゴ〔林檎〕Ⓒ (*grove+apple*): **apple**

momó モモ〔桃〕: **peach**

nashì / nashí ナシ〔梨〕: **pear**

umé ウメ〔梅〕: **plum**

bànana バナナ Ⓔ: **banana**

sakúranbo サクランボ〔桜んぼ・桜桃〕:
cherry

Ⓙ *sakura* (cherry tree) + *n* + bo†* |* ←
genitive p. *no* |† ← Ⓒ *bō* 坊 (boy)

ichígo / ìchigo イチゴ〔苺〕: **strawberry**

budó ブドウ〔葡萄〕Ⓒ (*grape+grape vine*):
grape

rèmon / remón レモン Ⓔ: **lemon**

orènji オレンジ Ⓔ: **orange** (fruit)

mikán ミカン〔蜜柑〕Ⓒ (*honey+tangerine*):
mandarin orange

mèron メロン Ⓔ: **melon**

suíka スイカ〔西瓜・水瓜〕Ⓒ (*West+gourd*):
watermelon

kakí 柿: **persimmon**

kurì クリ〔栗〕: **chestnut**

- -

Ⓣ yasái 野菜 Ⓒ *(plains+vegetables)*: **vegetables**

nínjin ニンジン〔人参〕: **carrot**

> Ⓒ *nin* 人 *(person)* + *sai* 参 *(to be nonplussed)* ‖ *Term originally u. to refer to ginseng, due to its perplexingly human form.*

kyùuri キュウリ〔胡瓜〕: **cucumber**

> ← *kiuri: ki* 黄* *(yellow)* + *uri* 瓜 *(gourd)* |* → 胡 *(foreign)*

rètasu レタス Ⓔ: **lettuce**

hórènsō ほうれん草〔菠薐草〕: **spinach**

> Ⓒ *hōren* 菠薐 *(spinach)* + *sō* 草 *(grass)*

pìiman ピーマン Ⓕ [*piment*]: **green pepper**

tógàrashi 唐辛子: **chili pepper**

> Ⓒ *tō* 唐 *(China's Tang Dynasty)* + Ⓙ *gara** + Ⓒ *shi* 子 *(child)* |* ← *kara* 辛 *(spicy)*

nínniku ニンニク〔大蒜・蒜・葫〕: **garlic**

> Ⓒ Adoption of the Buddhist term *ninniku* 忍辱 *(forbearance)* as an association with the smell and taste.

tamánègi タマネギ〔玉ねぎ・玉葱〕: **onion**

tama (sphere) + *negi (scallion)*

jagáimo じゃが芋・ジャガイモ: **potato**

> *jaga** + *imo* 芋 *(tuber)* |* ← *jagatara* ← *Jakarta*

satsúmaimo さつま芋・サツマイモ〔薩摩芋〕: **sweet potato**

> *satsuma (Satsuma Province)* + *imo (tuber)*

kabócha カボチャ〔南瓜〕: **pumpkin**

tòmato トマト Ⓔ: **tomato**

kìnoko キノコ〔茸〕: **mushroom**

> *ki (tree)* + genitive p. *no* + *ko (child)*

mamè 豆: **bean**

mìso 味噌 Ⓒ *(taste+boisterous)*: **miso** (bean paste)

tófu / tófù 豆腐 Ⓒ *(bean+decay)*: **tofu** (bean curd)

kaisó 海藻 Ⓒ *(sea+weed)*: **seaweed**

kokùmotsu 穀物 Ⓒ *(cereals+thing)*: **grain**

tómòrokoshi トウモロコシ〔玉蜀黍〕: **corn**

> Ⓒ *tō* 唐* *(China's Tang Dynasty)* + Ⓙ *morokoshi†* *(sorghum)* |* → 玉 *(jewel)* | †*morokoshi* ← *morokoshi‡ kibi (millet)* | ‡*(China): moro (various)* + *koshi (tribe)*

3.8 Food & Drinks

Nouns used to express the different meals taken during the day and the different types of food and drink—other than fruits and vegetables—and also medicines.

Important Words

tabemono 食べ物 *food*	gohan ご飯 *meal*	nomimono 飲み物 *drink*
asagohan 朝ご飯 *breakfast*	hirugohan 朝ご飯 *lunch*	bangohan 晩ご飯 *dinner*
kome 米 *rice*	pan パン *bread*	sandoicchi サンドイッチ *sandwich*
suupu スープ *soup*	sarada サラダ *salad*	niku 肉 *meat*
gyuuniku 牛肉 *beef*	butaniku 豚肉 *pork*	toriniku 鶏肉 *chicken*

tamago 卵 *egg*	shio 塩 *salt*	satō 砂糖 *sugar*
soosu ソース *sauce*	shōyuu しょうゆ *soy sauce*	abura 油 *oil*
kashi 菓子 *sweets*	keeki ケーキ *cake*	sake 酒 *alcohol-sake*
cha 茶 *tea*	kohii コヒー *coffee*	gyuunyuu 牛乳 *milk*
biiru ビール *beer*	tabako タバコ *tobacco*	kusuri 薬 *medicine*

Ⓣ tabémòno / tabèmono 食べ物:
(prepared) **food**

tabe* + mono (thing) |*(I) taberu (to eat)

Ⓤ shokúhin 食品 Ⓒ (*eating+product*):
foodstuff; (sold) food

washóku 和食 Ⓒ (*Japan+eating*): **Japanese food**

yóshoku 洋食 Ⓒ (*western+eating*): **Western food**

chùuka 中華: **Chinese food**

Ⓒ ← *chuuka ryōri:* 中華 (*Chinese*) + *ryōri* 料理 (*cuisine*) |*chuu 中 (*center*) + *ka* 華 (*splendor*)

Ⓤ nàma 生: ⓃⓅ ① **raw** (thing) ② **uncooked** (thing) ③ **natural** (thing) ④ live (broadcasting)

okázu おかず〔お菜〕: [*fam.*] **side dish**

❖ Lit., 'food that is eaten without rice'.

Ⓤ zaíryò 材料 Ⓒ (*material+foodstuff*):
ingredients

Ⓣ gòhan ご飯〔御飯〕 Ⓒ (*honorable+meal*):
[*pol.*] ① **meal** ② (cooked) rice

Ⓤ meshì 飯: [*mas.*] ① **meal** ② (cooked) rice

(I) *mesu (to call)*

❖ Originally refers to the white cooked rice served as staple food in most Japanese dishes. Over time, this term has come to be also understood as any 'meal' in general.

Ⓤ shokúji 食事 Ⓒ (*eating+affair*): Ⓝ **meal** Ⓥ (suru) [*for.*] to have a meal

aságòhan 朝ご飯: **breakfast**

asa (morning) + gohan (meal)

chóshoku 朝食 Ⓒ (*morning+eating*): [*pol.*] **breakfast**

hirúgòhan 昼ご飯: **lunch**

hiru (daytime) + gohan (meal)

ohìru お昼: [*pol.*] **lunch**

Hon. pre. *o + hiru (daytime)*

❖ This word originally means 'daytime' or 'noon'.

chuúshoku 昼食 Ⓒ (*daytime+eating*): [*pol.*] **lunch**

baǹgòhan 晩ご飯: **dinner**

Ⓒ *ban* 晩 (*dusk*) + *gohan (meal)*

yuúshoku 夕食: [*pol.*] **dinner**

Ⓙ *yuu (evening) +* Ⓒ *shoku* 食 (*eating*)

Ⓣ komè お米: (uncooked) **rice**

Ⓣ pàn パン Ⓟ [*paō*]: ① **bread** ② pastry

shokúpan / shokúpàn 食パン: **white bread**

⊕ sàrada サラダ Ⓟ [*salada*]: **salad**

⊕ saǹdoìcchi サンドイッチ Ⓔ: **sandwich**

mèn 麺 Ⓒ: (uncooked) **noodles**

ràmen ラーメン Ⓜ [lamian]: (cooked) **noodles**

Ⓛ sùupu スープ: **soup**

❖ Term u. for western style soups.

shìru 汁: ① **soup** ② **broth**

❖ Term normally u. for the small side soups of Japanese cuisine.

gyóza 餃子 Ⓜ [jiaozi]: **fried dumplings**

teńpura 天ぷら〔天麩羅〕Ⓟ [tempero]: **tempura** (deep fried foods in light batter)

Ⓛ chìizu チーズ Ⓔ: **cheese**

dońburi 丼: **bowl of food**

beńtò お弁当: **lunch box**

- -

Ⓣ nikù 肉 Ⓒ: ① **meat** ② **flesh**

⊕ sutèeki ステーキ Ⓔ: **steak**

yakíniku 焼肉: **grilled meat**

Ⓙ yaki* + Ⓒ niku 肉 (meat) |*(I) yaku (to grill)

tońkatsu トンカツ・とんかつ: **pork cutlet**

Ⓙ Pre. ton (pork) + Ⓔ katsu ← katsuretsu (cutlet)

Ⓣ gyuúniku 牛肉 Ⓒ (cow+meat): **beef**

Ⓣ butániku 豚肉: **pork**

Ⓙ buta (pig) + Ⓒ niku 肉 (meat)

toríniku 鶏肉: **chicken meat**

Ⓙ tori (bird) + Ⓒ niku 肉 (meat)

Ⓣ tamàgo / tamágo ❶ 卵/ ❷ 玉子: ① **egg**(s) ② **cooked eggs**

tama (ball) + go ← ko (small)

hàmu ハム Ⓔ: **ham**

sòoseeji / soósèeji ソーセージ Ⓔ: **sausage**

sushì / sùshi お寿司: **sushi** (vinegar rice served with fish or vegetables)

O.J. sushi → C.J. sui (sour)

sashímì 刺身: **sashimi** (raw sliced fish)

sashi* + mi (body; flesh) |*(I) sasu (to stick into)

- -

Ⓣ shiò 塩: **salt**

Ⓣ satò 砂糖 Ⓒ (sand+sugar): (granulated) **sugar**

sòosu ソース Ⓔ: **sauce**

Ⓣ shóyu しょうゆ〔醤油〕Ⓒ (thick paste+oil): **soy sauce**

Ⓣ karée カレー Ⓔ: **curry**

⊕ koshò コショウ〔胡椒〕Ⓒ (foreign+pepper): **pepper**

Ⓛ abúra ❶ 油/ ❷ 脂: ① **oil** ② **oily fat**

shibō 脂肪 Ⓒ (fat+fatness): **fat**

sù 酢: **vinegar**

wàsabi わさび〔山葵〕: **wasabi**

- -

⊕ dezàato デザート Ⓔ: **dessert**

⊕ kèeki ケーキ Ⓔ: **cake**

Ⓛ aísukurìimu アイスクリーム Ⓔ: **ice-cream**

chokórèeto チョコレート Ⓔ: **chocolate**

Ⓣ kàshi お菓子 Ⓒ (candy+child): ① **sweets** ② **snack**

❖ Word u. for sweet snacks.

sunákku gàshi スナック菓子: **snack**

sunakku* + gashi† |* ← Ⓔ [snack] |† ← kashi (snack)

❖ Word u. for non-sweet snacks (e.g. chip potatoes).

- -

nomímòno / nomìmono 飲み物: **drink; beverage**

nomi* + mono (thing) |*(I) nomu (to drink)

ińryò 飲料 Ⓒ (drinking+foodstuff): **drink; beverage**

✤ Word m. u. in compounds.

arúkooru アルコール D [alcohol]: **alcohol**

Ⓛ saké お酒: ① rice wine (**sake**) ② **alcohol** (alcoholic beverage)

Cognate with *sakae* ← (I) *sakaeru (to flourish)*

Ⓛ wàin ワイン E : **wine**

Ⓛ bìiru ビール D [bier]: **beer**

Ⓕ cha お茶 C : **tea**

Ⓕ koóhìi コーヒー D [koffie]: **coffee**

Ⓛ jùusu ジュース E : **juice**

Ⓕ gyuúnyuu 牛乳 C (cow+milk): (cow's) **milk**

Ⓛ mìruku ミルク E : **milk**

✤ Word m. u. to refer to milk that goes with coffee, tea or desserts.

- -

tabáko たばこ・タバコ P [tabaco]: **tobacco**; cigarettes

Ⓕ kusúri お薬: **medicine**

Ⓛ dokù 毒 C : **poison**

mayáku 麻薬 C (hemp+medicine): (narcotic) **drugs**

pìru ピル E : **pill**

4. MATTER

4.1 House & Furniture

Nouns related to the house as a place to live in, the spaces of which it is composed and the furniture that fills it.

Important Words

ie 家 *house*	heya 部屋 *room*	kabe 壁 *wall*	yuka 床 *floor*
kaidan 階段 *stairs*	doa ドア *door*	mado 窓 *window*	toire トイレ *toilet*
teeburu テーブル *table*	tsukue 机 *desk*	isu 椅子 *chair*	beddo ベッド *bed*

- -

Ⓕ iè 家: ① **house** ② household

←*ihe*: i* + O.J. *he (place)* |*Probably related to *ikiru (to live)* → (I) *iki* → *i*

✤ M. u. for the meaning of 'house' in a physical sense (the building) or as the concept of the traditional family unit (household).

➢ ièie 家々: ① (many) **houses** ② each house

⊕ uchí₂ お家: [*fam.*] ① **house** ② home

Cognate with *uchi (inside)*

✤ U. for the meaning of 'house' as a building but also in a more familiar sense, as 'home', lit. the place where one lives.

⊕ taku お宅: [*hon.*][*for.*] ① **house** ② home

✤ For. term u. to refer to s.o. else's house.

⊕ katé 家庭 C (house+garden): **home**; household; family

Ⓕ apàato アパート E : **apartment**

- -

Ⓣheyàお部屋: **room**

O.J. *he (place)* + affix *ya (salon)*

Ⓛimà 居間: (J. style) **living room**

i* + *ma (space)* | *(I) *iru (to be at)*

ribíngurùumu リビングルーム Ⓔ:
(Western style) **living room**

Ⓣdaídokoro 台所: **kitchen**

Ⓒ *dai* 台 *(podium)* + Ⓙ *dokoro* ← *tokoro (place)*

kìcchin キッチン Ⓔ: **kitchen**

❖ Term most commonly u. for larger, American style kitchens.

shínshitsu 寝室 Ⓒ (*lying down down+room*):
bedroom

Ⓣtòire おトイレ Ⓔ: **toilet**

otèarai お手洗い: [*pol.*] **restroom; bathroom; toilet**

Hon. pref. *o* + *te (hand)* + *arai* ← (I) *arau (to wash)*

yokúshitsu 浴室 Ⓒ (*bathing+room*): **bathroom**

- -

⊕kabé 壁: **wall**

Ⓛyuká 床: **floor**

Irrealis f. of v. *yuku (to go)* 〉 *not going* ‖ Originally meaning 'bed'

Ⓛyàne 屋根: **roof**

Affix *ya (salon)* + *ne (root)*

Ⓛokújō 屋上 Ⓒ (*salon+above*): **rooftop**

tenjó 天井 Ⓒ (*heaven+well*): **ceiling**

hashírà / hashíra 柱: **column**

Ⓣróka 廊下 Ⓒ (*corridor+below*): **corridor**

Ⓛchìka 地下 Ⓒ (*ground+below*): **cellar**

Ⓣkaidán 階段 Ⓒ (*floor+steps*): **stairs**

Ⓣdòa ドア Ⓔ: **door**

❖ General term for doors of one panel through which people can pass (Western style doors).

to 戸: **door**

❖ M. u. to refer to 'doors' that open and close by sliding (J. style doors).

tobíra 扉: **door**

to (J. style door) + *bira* ← *hira (flat thing)*

❖ Referring to 'doors' that have a mechanism that makes them open and close by turning a hinge or the like on an axis.

Ⓣmàdo 窓: **window**

ma* + *do* ← *to (door)* | * ← *me (eye)*

Ⓣniwá 庭: **garden;** yard

sakù 柵 Ⓒ [*palisade*]: **fence**

beránda ベランダ Ⓔ [*veranda*]: **balcony**

éngawa 縁側: (J. style) **porch**

en (verge) + *gawa (side)*

- -

Ⓛkàgu 家具 Ⓒ (*house+tool*): **furniture**

Ⓣteéburu テーブル Ⓔ: **table**

Ⓛshokútaku 食卓 Ⓒ (*eating+table*): **dining table**

Ⓣtsukúe 机: **desk**

Ⓛisú 椅子 Ⓒ (*chair+child*): **chair**

Ⓛsòfaa ソファー Ⓔ: **sofa**

jùutan じゅうたん〔絨毯〕 Ⓒ (*wool cloth+wool rug*): **carpet; rug**

kàapetto / kaápètto カーペット Ⓔ: **carpet**

tatámi 畳: **tatami** (J. style straw floor covering)

(I) *tatamu (to fold)*

Ⓣhòndana 本棚: **bookshelf**

Ⓒ hon 本 (book) + Ⓙ dana* 棚 |* ← tana (shelf)

Ⓣ bèddo ベッド Ⓔ : **bed**

⊕ futón 布団 Ⓒ (cloth+group): **futon** (J. style floor bedding)

⊕ hikídashi 引き出し: **drawer**

hiki* + dashi† |*(I) hiku (to pull) |†Inf. f. of the v. dasu (to take out)

kuròozetto クローゼット Ⓔ : **closet**

tańsu たんす・タンス〔箪笥〕Ⓒ (basket+container): **wardrobe**

4.2 Utensils & Appliances

Nouns denoting objects and materials that are commonly used inside the house.

Important Words

mono 物 *thing*	kagi 鍵 *key*	hako 箱 *box*
sara 皿 *plate*	hashi 箸 *chopsticks*	supuun スプーン *spoon*
fooku フォーク *fork*	naifu ナイフ *knife*	napukin ナプキン *napkin*
kappu カップ *mug*	koppu コップ *drinking glass*	bin 瓶 *bottle*
kagami 鏡 *mirror*	shawaa シャワー *shower*	furo フロ *bathtub*

Ⓣ monò₂ / monó 物: ① **object** ② (physical) **thing**

Ⓔ sakúhin 作品 Ⓒ (making+product): ① (a) **work** ② **production**

Ⓔ shiná 品: ① **article**; item ② goods

❖ Referring to any object intended for consumption.

Ⓔ shòhin 商品 Ⓒ (trading+product): ① **goods** ② **product** ② commodity; article of commerce; merchandise

❖ Any 'product' understood within a market context.

Ⓔ sèhin 製品 Ⓒ (manufacture+product): (manufactured) **product**; manufactured goods

❖ Word u. specifically to refer to manufactured 'products'.

Ⓔ shitsú / shitsù 質 Ⓒ (gold+belonging): ⓃⓈ **quality**

hińshitsu 品質 Ⓒ (product+matter): **quality**

❖ Specifically referring to the material 'quality' of a product.

⊕ garásu ガラス Ⓓ [glas]: **glass** (material)

Ⓔ kìnzoku 金属 Ⓒ (gold+belonging): **metal**

mokùzai / mokúzai 木材 Ⓒ (tree+material): ① **wood** ② timber

purásuchìkku プラスチック Ⓔ : **plastic**

Ⓔ kagì 鍵: **key**

hìita ヒータ Ⓔ : **heater**

eákon エアコン Ⓔ : **air-conditioner**

Ⓔ dènshi 電子 Ⓒ (electricity+child): **electricity**

seńpùuki 扇風機 Ⓒ (fan+wind+mechanism): (electric) **fan**

uchìwa うちわ〔団扇〕: (J. style) **fan**

uchi* + wa† |*(I) utsu (to hit) |† ← O.J. ha (feather)

Ⓣ rézòko 冷蔵庫 Ⓒ (cool+shed+warehouse): **fridge**

rétòko 冷凍庫 Ⓒ (cool+freeze+warehouse): **freezer**

dénshirènji 電子レンジ: **microwave**

> Ⓒ denshi 電子 (electricity) + renji * | ← Ⓔ range

òobun オーブン Ⓔ: **oven**

furáipan フライパン Ⓔ: **frying pan**

Ⓛ nàbe 鍋: **cooking pot**

> O.J. na (vegetables) + be ← O.J. he (place)

suíhànki 炊飯器 Ⓒ (cook+meal+instrument): **rice cooker**

Ⓛ sará お皿: ① **plate** ② **dish**

Ⓛ utsúwa 器: **bowl; vessel;** container

Ⓣ hàshi お箸: **chopsticks**

> Cognate with hashi (tip)

Ⓣ supùun スプーン Ⓔ: **spoon**

Ⓣ fòoku フォーク Ⓔ: **fork**

Ⓣ nàifu ナイフ Ⓔ: **knife**

nàpukin ナプキン Ⓔ: **napkin**

chawán お茶碗 Ⓒ (tea+bowl): (J. style) **bowl**

bòru ボウル Ⓔ [bowl]: **mixing bowl**

Ⓣ kàppu カップ Ⓔ [cup]: **mug**

Ⓣ koppú コップ Ⓓ [kop]: (drinking) **glass**

Ⓛ gùrasu グラス Ⓔ: (drinking) **glass**

❖ U. for drinking glasses that are specifically made of glass.

Ⓛ bìn 瓶 Ⓒ: **bottle**

Ⓛ kań 缶 Ⓓ [kan]: **can** (recipient)

---

màkura 枕: **pillow**

kùsshon クッション Ⓔ: **cushion**

zabùton 座布団: **seating cushion**

> Ⓒ za 座 (sitting) + futon 布団 (futon)

Ⓛ mòfu 毛布 Ⓒ (fur+fabric): **blanket**

shìitsu シーツ Ⓔ [sheet]: **bedsheet**

⊕ kagàmì 鏡: **mirror**

> kaga* + mì† |* ← kage (shadow) |†(I) miru (to see)

⊕ kàaten カーテン Ⓔ: **curtain**

Ⓛ sutándo スタンド Ⓔ [stand]: **table lamp**

rànpu ランプ Ⓔ: **lamp**

Ⓛ hi 灯: (lamp) **light**

> Cognate with hi (sun; fire)

Ⓛ akári 明かり: **light** (bulb)

> From akarui (to be bright)

Ⓣ shàwaa シャワー Ⓔ: **shower**

Ⓛ furò / furó お風呂: ① **bathtub** ② **bathroom** ③ **bath**

> Ⓒ fuu (wind) 風 + ro 呂 ← ro 炉 (hearth)

yokusō 浴槽 Ⓒ (bathing+tub): **bathtub**

❖ Word to specifically refer to the physical bathtub.

Ⓣ sekkén せっけん〔石鹸〕Ⓒ (stone+saltiness): **soap**

supónji スポンジ Ⓔ: **sponge**

Ⓛ tàoru タオル Ⓔ: **towel**

ha bùrashi 歯ブラシ: **toothbrush**

> Ⓙ ha (tooth) + Ⓔ burashi (brush)

hamìgaki 歯磨き: **tooth paste**

> ha (tooth) + migaki ← (I) migaku (to polish)

---

chirígami 塵紙: ① **tissue** ② toilet paper

chiri (dust) + gami ← kami (paper)

❖ Word u. for both wet tissues and toilet paper.

tòirepeepaa トイレペーパー E : **toilet paper**

❖ Word specifically u. for toilet paper.

Ⓛ aíron アイロン E : (electric) **iron**

heá doràiyaa ヘアドライヤー E : **hair dryer**

señtakùki / señtàkuki 洗濯機 C

(wash+rinse+mechanism): **washing machine**

Ⓣ hakó 箱: **box**

kagó かご〔籠〕: **basket**; cage

Ⓛ fukúrò 袋: (plastic/paper) **bag**

Ⓛ gomì ゴミ〔塵〕: **trash**

gomíbàko / gomíbako ゴミ箱〔塵箱〕: **trash bin**

gomi (trash) + bako ← hako (box)

4.3 Clothing & Accessories

Nouns referring to different items of clothing. Most of this group of nouns come from English as they refer to Western-style garments that are now universal in Japan but were once imported as novelties along with a corresponding new vocabulary.

Important Words

fuku 物 *clothes*	bōshi 帽子 *hat*	megane メガネ *glasses*
tokē 時計 *clock*	tebukuro 手袋 *gloves*	shatsu シャツ *shirt*
uwagi 上着 *jumper*	zubon ズボン *pants*	kutsu 靴 *shoes*
saifu 財布 *wallet*	poketto ポケット *pocket*	kaban カバン *bag*

⊕ fukù 服 C : Ⓝ Ⓢ **clothes**

Ⓛ ìfuku 衣服 C (garment+clothing): [lit.] **clothes**

Ⓛ hadáka 裸: **nudity**; nude; bare; naked

← hadaaka: hada (skin) + aka (red)

Ⓣ bóshi 帽子 C (headgear+child): **hat**

kyàppu キャップ E : **cap**

Ⓣ mègane めがね・メガネ〔眼鏡〕: **glasses**

me (eye) + gane ← kane (metal)

sañgùrasu サングラス E : **sunglasses**

ìyaringu イヤリング E : **earring**

nèkkuresu ネックレス E : **necklace**

màfuraa マフラー E [muffler]: **scarf**

Ⓣ toké 時計: **clock**; watch

← tokikē: Ⓙ toki (time) + C kē 計 (measuring)

⊕ yubíwa 指輪: **ring**

yubi (finger) + wa (circle)

⊕ tebùkuro 手袋: **gloves**

te (hand) + bukuro ← fukuro (bag)

nèkutai ネクタイ E : **necktie**

Ⓛ berúto ベルト E : **belt**

ⓉＴ shàtsu シャツ Ⓔ : **shirt**

ti shàtsu Ｔシャツ Ⓔ : **t-shirt**

buràusu ブラウス Ⓔ : **blouse**

jakètto / jàkettok ジャケット Ⓔ : **jacket**

ⓉＴ uwági 上着: **jumper**

uwa* + gi† |* ← ue (above) |† ← ki: (I) kiru (to wear)

ⓉＴ kòoto コート Ⓔ : **coat**

ⓉＴ sèetaa セーター Ⓔ : **sweater**

⊕ shitági 下着: **underwear**

shita (below) + gi ← ki ← (I) kiru (to wear)

bùra ブラ Ⓔ : **bra**

pàntsu パンツ Ⓔ [*pants*]: **underpants**

mizúgi 水着: **swimsuit**

mizu (water) + gi ← ki ← (I) kiru (to wear)

⊕ kimóno 着物: **kimono** (J. style dress)

ki* + mono (thing) |*(I) kiru (to wear)

ⓉＴ yófuku 洋服 Ⓒ [*western+clothing*]: ①
(western style) **clothes** ② **suit** ③ **dress**

⊕ sùutsu スーツ Ⓔ : **suit**

wanpìisu ワンピース Ⓔ [*one piece*]: **dress**

pàjama パジャマ Ⓔ : **pajamas**

ⓉＴ zubòn / zùbon ズボン Ⓕ [*jupon*]: **pants**

hań zùbon 半ズボン: **shorts**

Ⓒ *han* 半 *(half)* + Ⓕ *zubon (pants)*

Ⓛ jìinzu ジーンズ Ⓔ : **jeans**

ⓉＴ sukàato スカート Ⓔ : **skirt**

ⓉＴ kutsù 靴: ① **shoes** ② footwear

ⓉＴ kutsùshita / kutsúshità 靴下: **socks**

kutsu (shoes) + shita (below)

sòkkusu ソックス Ⓔ : **socks**

❖ M. u. for women's or sports socks.

shimí 染み: **stain**

(I) *shimiru (to permeate)*

ⓉＴ saìfu 財布 Ⓒ (*wealth+fabric*): **wallet**

ⓉＴ pokètto / pòketto ポケット Ⓔ : **pocket**

ⓉＴ botán ボタン Ⓔ : **button**

ⓉＴ kabán かばん・カバン〔鞄〕: **bag**

⊕ hańdobàggu ハンドバッグ Ⓔ :
handbag

bakkúpakkù バックパック Ⓔ : **backpack**

ⓉＴ kàsa 傘: **umbrella**

4.4 Work & Leisure

Nouns related to objects normally used in work, academic, communication or entertainment activities.

Important Words

konpyuutaa コンピューター *computer*	intaanetto インターネット *internet*	sumaho スマホ *smartphone*
terebi テレビ *TV*	nyuusu ニュース *news*	shinbun 新聞 *newspaper*
e 絵 *picture*	kamera カメラ *camera*	shashin 写真 *photo*
ega 映画 *movie*	dōga 動画 *video*	geemu ゲーム *game*

omocha おもちゃ *toy*	ongaku 音楽 *music*	hon 本 *book*
jisho 辞書 *dictionary*	boorupen ボールペン *pen*	kami 紙 *paper*
meeru メール *mail*	messeeji メッセージ *message*	karendaa カレンダー *calendar*

⊕ nòryoku 能力 C [capability+strength]: **ability**; capacity

saínō 才能 C [talent+capability]: **talent**

⊕ dógù 道具 C [road-way+tool]: **tool**

⊥ tsùuru ツール E : **tool**

❖ Word especially u. in IT contexts

⊕ gìjutsu 技術 C [ability+technique]: **technology**

⊥ kikài 機械 C [mechanism+appliance]: **machine**

⊥ kìnō 機能 C [mechanism+capability]: **function**

⊕ pasókon パソコン E [personal computer]: (personal) **computer**

❖ Word u. specifically for personal computers such as desktop computers and laptops.

⊕ konpyúùtaa コンピューター E : **computer**

❖ U. for any kind of computer machine, including super computers.

nòoto pishi ノートPC E [notebook+PC]: **laptop**

deńtaku 電卓 C (electricity+table): **calculator**

mezàmashi 目覚まし: **alarm clock**

me (eye) + zamashi ← samashi: (I) samasu (to clear one's mind)

⊕ ińtaanètto インターネット: **internet**

purìntaa /puríntaa プリンター E : **printer**

⊕ kétai 携帯: **cellphone**

← C kētai* (carrying) + denwa (telephone) | *kē (carry) + tai (wear)

sumáho スマホ E : **smartphone**

dìsupurei ディスプレイ E : **display**

botán ボタン E : **button**

dènchi 電池 C (electricity+pond): **battery**

juúdenki 充電器: **charger**

C juuden 充電 (charging) + ki 器 (instrument)

⊤ tèrebi テレビ E : **television**

rimókon リモコン E : **remote control**

⊤ ràjio ラジオ E : **radio**

màiku マイク E : **microphone**

heddóhòn ヘッドホン E : **headphones**

⊤ nyùusu ニュース E : **news**

⊤ shińbun 新聞 C (new+listening): **newspaper**

⊥ kìji 記事 C (writing down+affair): (news) **article**

⊤ è 絵 C : ① (drawn or painted) **picture** ② drawing ③ painting

⊤ kàmera カメラ E : **camera**

⊤ shashín 写真 C (transcribing+true): **photograph**; (photographic) picture

⊕ gazó 画像 C (picture+depiction): (electronic) **image**

⊤ èga / éga 映画 C (reflecting+picture): **movie**

dóga 動画 C (moving+picture): **video**

⊥ eńgeki 演劇 C (performance+drama): ① **theater** ② drama

ⓔ gèemu ラジオ ⓔ : ① **game** ②
videogame

ⓒ omòcha おもちゃ 〔玩具〕: **toy**

Hon. p. o + mocha ← mochiasobi: mochi* +
asobi† | *(I) motsu (to hold) | †(I) asobu (to play)

- -

ⓕ òngaku 音楽 ⓒ (sound+enjoyable): **music**

ⓕ utà 歌: **song**

kyokú / kyòku 曲 ⓒ (bending): N̄C̄ **tune**;
song (piece of music); track (on a
record)

ⓒ kònsaato /końsàato コンサート ⓔ :
concert

ⓔ gakkí 楽器 ⓒ (enjoyable+instrument):
(musical) **instrument**

ⓔ piáno ピアノ ⓔ : **piano**

gìtaa ギター ⓔ : **guitar**

- -

ⓕ hòn 本 ⓒ : **book**

ⓕ peéji ページ ⓔ : **page**

ⓒ shósetsu 小説 ⓒ (small+explaining): **novel**;
written story

ⓒ zasshí 雑誌 ⓒ (miscellaneous+records):
magazine

ⓔ shi 詩 ⓒ : ① **poetry** ② **poem**

ⓔ mańga 漫画 ⓒ (unrestrained+picture):
comics

ⓔ kyókàsho 教科書 ⓒ
(teaching+science+writing): **textbook**

ⓕ jìsho 辞書 ⓒ (terms+writing): **dictionary**

ⓒ jitén 辞典 ⓒ (terms+code): **dictionary**

❖ Word m. u. in dictionary names.

jibíkì 字引: [col.] **dictionary**

ⓒ ji 字 (letter) + biki ← hiki: (I) hiku (to pull)

ⓔ sańkō 参考 ⓒ (nonplussed+pondering):
reference

ⓔ nòoto ノート ⓔ [note book]: **notebook**

ⓒ nikkí 日記 ⓒ (day+writing down): **diary**

ⓔ kiróku 記録 ⓒ (writing down+record): **record**

ⓕ boórupen ボールペン ⓔ [ball pen]: **pen**

ⓕ fudé 筆: (writing) **brush**

← fumite: fumi (writing) + te (hand)

ⓔ eńpitsu 鉛筆 ⓒ (lead+brush): **pencil**

ⓕ kamì 紙: **paper**

ⓔ keshígomu 消しゴム: **eraser**

keshi* + gomu† | *(I) kesu (to erase) |† ← Ⓓ
gom (rubber)

ⓔ hasámì / hasàmi はさみ・ハサミ 〔鋏〕:
scissors

(I) hasamu (to hold between)

- -

ⓔ tegámi 手紙: **letter** (message)

te (hand) + gami ← kami (paper)

ⓕ mèeru / meéru メール ⓔ : **email**

ⓔ mèsseeji メッセージ ⓔ : **message**

- -

ⓕ sakúbun 作文 ⓒ (making+letters): **writing**;
essay; **composition**

ⓔ shorúi 書類 ⓒ (writing+type): **document**

ⓔ ichíran 一覧 ⓒ (one+perusal): **summary**;
list; catalogue

ⓔ rìsuto リスト ⓔ : **list**

ⓔ karèndaa カレンダー ⓔ : **calendar**

- -

ⓔ nawà 縄: **rope**

Irrealis f. of v. nau (to twine)

❖ M. u. for thin ropes.

tsunà 綱: **rope**

❖ M. u. for thick ropes.

ròopu ロープ ⓔ : **rope**

Ⓔ hàri 針: **needle** kugí 釘: **nail**

tsuchì 槌: **hammer; mallet**

4.5 Occupations & Labor

Nouns referring to work as an activity, to the different positions within a hierarchical work system and to the different professions.

Important Words

shigoto 仕事 *work*	sensē 先生 *teacher*	gakusē 学生 *student*
kashu 歌手 *singer*	haiyuu 俳優 *actor*	kaishain 会社員 *employee*

Ⓣ shigóto ⓞ仕事: **work**

shi* + goto† |*(I) suru (to do) |† ← koto (thing)f

Ⓔ arúbàito アルバイト Ⓖ *[arbeit (work)]*: **temporary work**

➤ *[col.]* baíto バイト

Ⓔ shokùgyō 職業 Ⓒ *(employment+deal)*: **occupation**

Ⓣ gìmu 義務 Ⓒ *(righteousness+serving)*: **obligation; duty**; responsibility

❖ 'Obligations' or 'duties' in relation to legal or moral rules and performed in accordance w. the dictates of work or society.

sèkimu 責務 Ⓒ *(obligation+righteousness)*: **obligation**; duty

❖ 'Obligations' understood as tasks that have to be carried out.

Ⓣ sekínin 責任 Ⓒ *(obligation+responsibility)*: **responsibility**; duty

❖ 'Responsibility' referring specifically to the duties that a person has to assume in accordance w. his or her position or task.

Ⓣ yakù 役 Ⓒ *(duty)*: ⓃⓈ **role**

Ⓣ kurái 位: **grade; level; rank; position**

Obs. *kura (seat)* + *i*: Stem of the v. *iru (to be at)*

Ⓣ jókèn 条件 Ⓒ *(close+case)*: ① **condition** ② terms

Ⓣ shōko 証拠 Ⓒ *(proof+basis)*: **evidence; proof**

Ⓣ kóshiki 公式 Ⓒ *(public+style)*: ① **formality** ② (a) **formal** (thing) ③ (an) **official** (thing)

keńryoku 権力 Ⓒ *(authority+strength)*: **authority**; (political) power

kyùuryō 給料 Ⓒ *(bestowed+foodstuff)*: **salary; wage; pay**

Ⓤ hokén 保険 Ⓒ *(protecting+precipitous)*: **insurance**

Ⓣ kóza 口座 Ⓒ *(mouth+sitting)*: (bank) **account**

akàunto アカウント Ⓔ: **account**

méshi 名刺 Ⓒ *(name+piercing)*: **business card**

Ⓣ pùro プロ Ⓔ *[pro]*: (a) **professional**

Ⓣ ishá 医者 Ⓒ *(doctor+person)*: **doctor**

kańgòfu 看護婦: **female nurse**

Ⓒ *kango* 看護 *(nursing)* + *fu* 婦 *(lady)*

kańgòshi 看護師: **nurse**

Ⓒ *kango* 看護 *(nursing)* + *shi* 師 *(teacher)*

Ⓣ **seńsē** 先生 Ⓒ (*previous+living*): ℕ Ⓢ [*pol.*] **teacher**

❖ Word referring to a person that instructs others, but also u. as a title, in a much more general and broad sense, w. people who are at a top level in his or her career.

Ⓤ **kyòshi** 教師 Ⓒ (*teaching+teacher*): **teacher**

❖ Word u. specifically to refer to people whose occupation is teaching.

Ⓜ **kyōju** 教授 Ⓒ (*teaching+granting*): [*for.*] **professor**

Ⓣ **gakúsē** 学生 Ⓒ (*learning+living*): **student**

❖ U. for high school or college 'students'.

Ⓜ **sèto** 生徒 Ⓒ (*living+on foot*): **student**; pupil

❖ U. for elementary, high school or private 'students'.

dókyùusē 同級生 Ⓒ (*same+rank+living*): **classmate**

kurásumèeto クラスメート Ⓔ : [*fam.*] **classmate**

❖ Word most commonly u. to refer to a close classmate.

Ⓤ **kàshu** 歌手 Ⓒ (*singing+son*): **singer**

Ⓤ **haíyuu** 俳優 Ⓒ (*actor+outstripping*): **actor**

Ⓤ **joyúu** 女優 Ⓒ (*woman+outstripping*): **actress**

Ⓤ **shujìnkō** 主人公 Ⓒ (*main+person+public*): **protagonist**

Ⓤ **kańtoku** 監督 Ⓒ (*overseeing+supervision*): (movie) **director**

géjutsuka 芸術家: **artist**

Ⓒ *gējutsu* 芸術 (*art*) + *ka* 家 (*house*)

gaká 画家 Ⓒ (*brush stroke+house*): **painter**

mańgaka 漫画家: **comic artist**

Ⓒ *manga* 漫画 (*comic*) + *ka* 家 (*house*)

Ⓤ **sakká** 作家 Ⓒ (*making+house*): **writer**; author; artist

❖ 'Writer', or sometimes another kind of 'artist', understood as an occupation.

Ⓤ **chòsha** 著者 Ⓒ (*authoring+person*): **author**; writer

séjika 政治家: **politician**

Ⓒ *sēji* 政治 (*politics*) + *ka* 家 (*house*)

késatsùkan / késàtsukan 警察官: **policeman**

Ⓒ *kēsatsu* 警察 (*police*) + *kan* 官 (*bureaucrat*)

➤ Ⓣ [*col.*] **kékan** 警官

doróbō 泥棒: **thief**; robber

❖ Referring to a person who steals other people's money or goods.

gótō 強盗 Ⓒ (*strong+stealing*): ① **robber** ② **robbery**; burglary

❖ Referring to a person who takes another person's property by force and/or intimidation.

saíbànkan 裁判官: **judge**

Ⓒ *saiban* 裁判 (*trial*) + *kan* 官 (*bureaucrat*)

beńgòshi 弁護士: **lawyer**

Ⓒ *bengo* 弁護 (*advocacy*) + *shi* 士 (*gentleman*)

hèshi 兵士 Ⓒ (*soldier+gentleman*): **soldier**

uńtènshu 運転手: (professional) **driver**

Ⓒ *unten* 運転 (*driving*) + *shu* 手 (*hand*)

eńjìnia エンジニア Ⓔ : **engineer**

Ⓤ **kómùin** 公務員: **civil servant**

Ⓒ *kōmu* 公務 (*public business*) + *in* 員 (*employee*)

kàkari 係 Ⓒ (*writings+law*): ① **charge**; duty ② **person in charge**

(I) *kakaru* (to take)

juúgyòin 従業員: ① **employee** ② worker

Ⓒ *juugyō* 従業 (*employment*) + *in* 員 (*employee*)

kyùuji 給仕 ⓒ (*bestowed+working for*): **waiter; waitress**

hìsho / hishò 秘書 ⓒ (*concealing+writing*): **secretary**

---

kaíshàin 会社員: **company employee**

ⓒ *kaisha* 会社 (*company*) + *in* 員 (*employee*)

✤ A person who is employed by a company and is engaged in its business.

sarárìiman サラリーマン Ⓔ [*salaried man*]: **office worker**; company employee

✤ Word lit. referring to a person who works for a salary.

⊕ shachó 社長 ⓒ (*society+long*): **president of a company**

⊥ kaichó 会長 ⓒ (*meeting+long*): **president** (of a society); **chairman**

⊥ buchó 部長 ⓒ (*section+long*): **chief of department**; director of department

⊥ kachó 課長 ⓒ (*lesson+long*): **section manager**

jòshi 上司 ⓒ (*above+governing*): **boss**

⊥ shàin 社員 ⓒ (*society+employee*): **company employee**

dóryō 同僚 ⓒ (*same+colleague*): **colleague; coworker**

rìidaa リーダー Ⓔ: **leader**

kanémòchi 金持ち: **rich person**; wealthy person

kane (money) + *mochi* ← (I) *motsu* (to hold)

seńmonka 専門家 ⓒ (*above+governing*): **expert**

ⓒ *senmon* 専門 (*speciality*) + *ka* 家 (*house*)

teńsai 天才 ⓒ (*heaven+talent*): **genius**

4.6 Trade & Commerce

Nouns related to business, commercial activities and buying and selling in general.

Important Words

kane 金 *money*	en 円 *yen (J. currency)*	nedan 値段 *price*

⊕ gyòmu 業務 ⓒ (*deal+serving*): **business** (operation); work

✤ 'Business' understood as a job or as an occupation that is performed on an ongoing basis.

⊥ kìgyō 企業 ⓒ (*undertaking+deal*): **business** (enterprise); enterprise

✤ 'Business' understood from the perspective of a company that develops it.

jìgyō 事業 ⓒ (*affair+deal*): **business** (project); service

✤ Term referring to any economic activity that is done for profit.

⊕ kèzai 経済 ⓒ (*lapsing+concluding*): **economics; economy**

⊕ sańgyō 産業 ⓒ (*producing+deal*): **industry**

baibai 売買 ⓒ (*selling+buying*): ① **trade** ② buying and selling

⊥ shìjō 市場 ⓒ (*market+place*): (the) **market**

⊤ kané お(❶)金: ① **money** ② **gold**

gìn 銀 ⓒ: **silver**

⊤ èn 円: **yen** (J. currency)

dòru ドル Ⓔ: **dollar**

yùuro ユーロ Ⓔ: **euro**

kŏka 硬貨 [C] (*hard+goods*): **coin**; hard currency

❖ Word u. specifically for hard currency.

kòin コイン [E] : **coin**

❖ Word u. col. for hard currency, but also for any kind of token that resembles a coin.

shìhē 紙幣 [C] (*paper+cash*): **banknote**; bill; note

Ⓙ geńkìn 現金 [C] (*revealed+gold*): **cash**

Ⓙ kàado カード [E] : (credit or debit) **card**

tsurí₂ おつり〔釣り〕: (money) **change** (for a purchase)

(I) *tsuru (to fish)*

- -

⊕ ne 値: ① **value** ② **price**

⊕ atái ❶ 値/ ❷ 価: ① (mathematical) **value** ② price; cost

❖ Word u. specifically for numerical 'value'. Occasionally, it appears in idioms w. the meaning of 'price'.

⊕ kachì 価値 [C] (*price+value*): **value; worth**

❖ A 'value' that doest not necessarily have a limit. Also fig. and subjective 'value'.

⊕ kakáku / kàkaku 価格 [C] (*price+form*): **price**

Ⓙ nedán 値段: [*col.*] **price**

Ⓙ *ne (price)* + [C] *dan 段 (steps)*

Ⓙ bukká 物価 [C] (*thing+price*): ① **prices** ② cost of living

Ⓙ hìyō 費用 [C] (*spending+using*): **cost; expense**

waríbiki 割引: **discount**

(I) *waribiku (to discount)*

òpushon オプション [E] : **option**

kaúntaa カウンター [E] : ① **counter** ② cashier

reshìito レシート [E] : **receipt**

sàimu 債務 [C] (*bond+serving*): **debt**

bakkín 罰金 [C] (*punishment+gold*): (a) **fine**

Ⓙ zékin 税金 [C] (*tax+gold*): **tax**

Ⓙ zè 税 [C] : [N][S] **tax**

❖ M. u. in compounds.

- -

Ⓣ fuútō 封筒 [C] (*enclosure+cylinder*): **envelope**

pàkku パック [E] : **pack**

pàkkeeji パッケージ [E] : **package**

Ⓙ sàabisu サービス [E] [*service*]: **free extra product**

Ⓙ chuúko 中古:(s.t. that is) **second hand**; (s.t. that is) **used**

- -

⊕ kyakú 客 [C] (*guest*): ① **guest; visitor** ② **customer; client**

4.7 Transportation & Travel

Nouns referring to different means of transport and travel.

Important Words

kuruma 車 *car*	basu バス *bus*	jitensha 自転車 *bicycle*
densha 電車 *train*	chikatetsu 地下鉄 *subway*	takushii タクシー *taxi*
hikōki 飛行機 *plane*	fune 船 *boat*	tabi 旅 *travel*

ⓟ **norimono** 乗り物: **vehicle**

nori* + mono (thing) | *(1) noru (to get on; to board)

ⓕ **kurúma** 車: **car**

kuru (to spin) + ma (space)

ⓕ **bàsu** バス Ⓔ: **bus**

ⓤ **toràkku** トラック Ⓔ: **truck**

ⓕ **jitènsha** / jiténsha 自転車: **bicycle**

Ⓒ *jiten (rotation) 自転 + sha 車 (car)*

ⓤ **bàiku** バイク Ⓔ [*bike*]: **motorbike**

ⓕ **deńsha** / dènsha 電車 Ⓒ *(electricity+car)*: **train**

ⓕ **chikátetsu** 地下鉄: **subway**

Ⓒ *chika 地下 (underground) + tetsu 鉄 (iron)*

ⓕ **tàkushii** タクシー Ⓔ: **taxi**

ⓟ **kótsuu** 交通 Ⓒ *(mingling+through)*: **traffic**

ⓤ **ènjin** エンジン Ⓔ: **engine**

ⓟ **gàsu** ガス Ⓔ: **gas**

sharín 車輪 Ⓒ *(car+wheel)*: **wheel**

ⓕ **hikòki** 飛行機: **plane**

Ⓒ *hikō 飛行 (flying) + ki 機 (mechanism)*

ⓤ **fùne** ❶ 船/ ❷ 舟: ① (small) **boat** ② (large) **ship**

⸻

ⓤ **tabì** 旅: **travel**; trip; journey

Cognate w. *tabi (time when s.t. happens)*

ⓤ **kańkō** 観光 Ⓒ *(view+light)*: ① **sightseeing** ② **tourism**

ⓤ **miyáge** ぉ土産: ① **souvenir** ② gift

miya (shrine) + ge ← ke (small jar)

ⓕ **chìzu** 地図 Ⓒ *(ground+diagram)*: **map**

ⓤ **ańnài** 案内 Ⓒ *(guidance+inside)*: ① guidance ② information

ⓤ **pasúpòoto** パスポート Ⓔ: **passport**

ⓤ **chikètto** / chiketto チケット Ⓔ: **ticket**

❖ 'Tickets' u. in events or shows that are understood to be influenced by or derived from Western culture.

kippú 切符: **ticket**

Ⓙ *ki* +* Ⓒ *fu 符 (token) | * ← kiru (to cut)*

❖ 'Tickets' u. for transportation.

ⓤ **ken** 券 Ⓒ: ⓃⓈ **ticket**; certificate; coupon

❖ M. u. in compounds.

⸻

ⓟ **sèki** 席 Ⓒ: **seat**; position

❖ This word refers to a place to sit, but not necessarily a chair or other similar object. Also u. in a fig. sense for locations.

ⓤ **zaséki** 座席 Ⓒ *(sitting+seat)*: **seat**

❖ Referring to the specific object on which one seats.

⸻

ⓟ **hó** 方 Ⓒ: **direction**; way; side

ⓤ **hókō** 方向 Ⓒ *(direction+facing)*: **direction**

❖ Usually related to movement.

hómèn 方面 Ⓒ *(direction+face)*: ① **direction** (place of destination) ② destination

❖ Direction towards a destination.

ikísaki 行き先: **destination**

iki* + saki (ahead) | *(1) iku (to go)

❖ Also u. in a fig. sense.

noríkae 乗り換え: **transfer**

nori* + kae† | *(1) noru (to embark) | †Inf. f. of the v. kaeru (to change)

sènro 線路 Ⓒ *(line+path)*: (railway) **track**

katámichi 片道: **one-way trip**

kata (one piece) + michi (road)

Ⓔ sòkudo 速度 Ⓒ (*quick+degree*): **speed**; velocity

Ⓕ nìmotsu 荷物: **baggage**

Ⓙ *ni (load)* + Ⓒ *motsu* 物 *(thing)*

4.8 City & Countryside

Nouns that refer to cities, towns and the countryside and the different places and establishments you can find in them.

Important Words

toshi 都市 *city*	mura 村 *village*	machi 街 *downtown*
michi 道 *road-street*	tatemono 建物 *building*	eki 駅 *station*
hoteru ホテル *hotel*	byōin 病院 *hospital*	ginkō 銀行 *bank*
gakkō 学校 *school*	daigaku 大学 *university*	kōen 公園 *park*
kaisha 会社 *company*	resutoran レストラン *restaurant*	baa バー *bar*
mise 店 *shop*	ichiba 市場 *market palce*	konbini コンビニ *convenience store*
jinja 神社 *shrine*	tera 寺 *temple*	inaka 田舎 *countryside*

Ⓜ tòshi 都市 Ⓒ (*metropolis+city*): ① **city**; town ② metropolitan area

❖ Word m. u. in an objective sense, referring to a 'city' as a physical location where social and economic activities are performed. M. u. in compounds.

Ⓜ shì 市 Ⓒ : NS ① **city** ② municipality

❖ M. u. in compounds.

Ⓔ tokái 都会 Ⓒ (*metropolis+meeting*): (big) **city**

❖ Often u. in relation to a subjective context.

shìgai 市街 Ⓒ (*city+street*): ① **urban area**; downtown; the streets

Ⓜ kògai 郊外 Ⓒ (*outskirts+outside*): **suburbs**

Ⓜ shùto / shutò 首都 Ⓒ (*head+metropolis*): **capital city**

Ⓕ murà 村: **village**

Cognate with *mura (gathering)*

furùsato ふるさと〔故郷〕: **home town**; birthplace; one's old home

furu* + r. u. *sato (village)* |*Stem of the adj. furui (old)*

Ⓕ machì ❶ 町/ ❷❸ 街: ① **town** ② (main) **street** ③ downtown area

Ⓕ michí 道: ① **road** ② street

O.J. hon. pre. *mi* + O.J. *chi (way)*

Ⓜ toórì 通り: ① **street** ② way

(I) *tooru (to go by)*

Ⓜ kìnjo 近所 Ⓒ (*near+place*): **neighborhood**; vicinity

Ⓔ shìngo 信号 Ⓒ (*faith+mark*): **traffic lights**

Ⓔ hodó 歩道 Ⓒ (*step-road-way*): **sidewalk**

Ⓣ ódan hòdō 横断歩道: **crosswalk**

  Ⓒ *ōdan* 横断 *(crossing)* + *hodō* 歩道 *(walkway)*

Ⓗ jùusho 住所 Ⓒ *(dwelling+place)*: **address**

- -

Ⓣ tatèmono / tatémòno 建物: **building**

tate* + *mono (thing)* | **(I) tateru (to build)*

Ⓗ bìru ビル: **building**

❖ Word u. for medium to tall height modern buildings made of concrete.

← Ⓔ *birudingu (building)*

kàoku 家屋 Ⓒ *(house+salon)*: **house** (building)

Ⓣ erébèetaa エレベーター Ⓔ: **elevator**

Ⓣ hashì 橋: **bridge**

Cognate with *hasamu (to hold between)* and *hosoi (slender)*

Ⓗ kuúkō 空港 Ⓒ *(sky+harbor)*: **airport**

Ⓗ mináto 港: **port**

O.J. *mi (water)* + O.J. genitive p. *na (of)* + *to (gate)*

Ⓣ èki 駅 Ⓒ: (train) **station**

basú tàaminaru バスターミナル Ⓔ: **bus terminal**

basútē バス停: **bus stop**

  Ⓔ *basu [bus]* + Ⓒ *tē* 停 *(halt)*

chuúshajō 駐車場: **parking lot**

  Ⓒ *chuusha* 駐車 *(parking)* + *jō* 場 *(site)*

yuúbìnkyoku 郵便局: **post office**

  Ⓒ *yuubin* 郵便 *(mail)* + *kyoku* 局 *(bureau)*

Ⓣ hòteru ホテル Ⓔ: **hotel**

Ⓗ ryokán 旅館 Ⓒ *(travel+building)*: (J. style) **hotel**

Ⓣ byóin 病院 Ⓒ *(sickness+institution)*: **hospital**

yakkyóku 薬局 Ⓒ *(medicine+bureau)*: **pharmacy**

Ⓣ gińkō 銀行 Ⓒ *(silver+going)*: **bank**

eétiièmu ATM Ⓔ: **ATM**

yóchìen 幼稚園: **kindergarten**

  Ⓒ *yōchi* 幼稚 *(infancy)* + *en* 園 *(park)*

Ⓣ gakkố 学校 Ⓒ *(learning+school)*: **school**

Ⓣ daígaku 大学 Ⓒ *(big+learning)*: **university**

Ⓣ kyóshitsu 教室 Ⓒ *(teaching+room)*: **classroom**

ryồ 寮 Ⓒ: **dormitory**

Ⓣ toshòkan 図書館: **library**

  Ⓒ *tosho* 図書 *(books)* + *kan* 館 *(building)*

Ⓣ ēgákàn 映画館: **movie theater**

  Ⓒ *ēga* 映画 *(movie)* + *kan* 館 *(building)*

Ⓗ bijútsùkan 美術館: **art museum**

  Ⓒ *bijutsu* 美術 *(fine arts)* + *kan* 館 *(building)*

Ⓛ hakúbutsùkan 博物館: **museum**

  Ⓒ *hakubutsu* 博物 *(broad area of learning)* + *kan* 館 *(building)*

teńji 展示 Ⓒ *(exhibition+showing)*: **exhibition**

Ⓣ kốen 公園 Ⓒ *(public+park)*: **park**

fuńsui 噴水 Ⓒ *(spouting+water)*: **fountain**

hìroba 広場: **public square**

  Affix *hiro (wide)* + *ba (place)*

Ⓛ ońsen 温泉 Ⓒ *(warm+fountain)*: ① **hot spring** ② **public bath**

Ⓣ taíshìkan 大使館: **embassy**

  Ⓒ *taishi* 大使 *(ambassador)* + *kan* 館 *(building)*

Ⓗ jimùsho 事務所: **office**

  Ⓒ *jiju* 事務 *(clerical work)* + *sho* 所 *(place)*

Ⓣ kaísha 会社 Ⓒ *(meeting+society)*: **company** (corporation)

Ⓛ kikàn / kìkan 機関 Ⓒ *(mechanism+related)*: (an) **organization; agency**

Ⓣ kốban 交番 Ⓒ *(interchanging+number)*: **police station**

⊕ késatsu 警察 C (admonition+observation):
police

kangoku 監獄 C (overseeing+prison): ① **prison**
② jail

⊤ rèsutoran レストラン E : **restaurant**

⊕ bàa バー E : **bar**

izákaya / izákàya 居酒屋: (J. style) **bar**

> *i* + zaka† + affix ya (salon) |*(I) iru (to be at) |† ← saka ← sake (alcohol)*

koóhii shòppu コーヒーショップ E :
coffee shop

kissátèn / kissáten 喫茶店: ① (traditional)
coffee shop ② tea room

> C *kissa 喫茶 (tea drinking) + ten 店 (shop)*

końdate 献立: **menu**

> C *kon 献 (offer) + J date ← tate:*
> Continuative f. of the v. *tatsu (to stand up)*

mènyuu メニュー E : **menu**

⊤ misé 店: ① **shop**

> ← *misedana: mise* + dana† |*mise: (I) miseru (to show) |† ← tana (shelf)*

⊕ ìchiba 市場: **market** (place)

> *ichi (market) + ba (place)*

⊕ màaketto /maákètto マーケット E :
(outdoors) **market**

⊕ sùupaa スーパー E : **supermarket**

⊕ depàato デパート E : **department store**

końbini コンビニ E : **convenience store**

biyòin 美容院: **hair salon**

> C *biyō 美容 (beauty of figure) + in 院 (institution)*

hońya 本屋: **bookshop**

> C *hon 本 (book) + J affix ya (salon)*

sòko 倉庫 C (storehouse+warehouse): ①
warehouse ② storehouse

bochí 墓地 C (tomb+ground): **cemetery**

⊥ hakà お墓: **grave** (tomb)

⊕ kójò 工場 C (craft+site): **factory**

kańban 看板 C (observation+board): **signboard**

iríguchi 入り口: **entrance**

> *iri* + guchi† |*(I) iru (to enter) |† ← kuchi (mouth)*

dèguchi 出口: **exit**

> *de* + guchi† |*(I) deru (to exit) |† ← kuchi (mouth)*

⊕ jìnja 神社 C (god+society): (shintoist)
shrine

⊕ terà / terá 寺: (buddhist) **temple**

kyókai 協会 C (cooperation+meeting): **church**

⊥ shiró 城: **castle**

⊥ tó 塔 C : N S **tower**

kyuúden 宮殿 C (royal residence+palace): **palace**

⊕ ináka 田舎: **countryside**

> *ina* + ka (house) |* ← ine (rice plant)*

nójò / nójò 農場 C (agriculture+site): **farm**

⊥ hatàke / hàtake 畑 C (agriculture+site): N S
field; cultivated land

⊥ nò 野: N P ① (the) **wild** ③ plains

> *hata* + suf. ke (house) |*ha† + ta (rice field) | †O.J. ha (fire)*

ìdo 井戸: (water) **well**

> *i (well) + do ← to (door)*

III. NUMERALS & CLASSIFIERS

Numerals are words used specifically to designate numbers. In Indo-European languages, numerals are grammatically simple words that work like any other adjective. In Japanese, however, numerals are placed grammatically within the nominals and are marked by a number of peculiarities that clearly distinguish them from other types of nominals.

The most important of these peculiarities are:

1. There are two systems of numerals: one native and one Sino-Japanese.

2. When 'counting' things, numerals must be followed by a **classifier** [☞ III. 2], that is, a counting suffix.

In order to understand the whole number system in Japanese, numerals must necessarily be grouped with classifiers.

1. NUMERALS

Numerals—words that refer to a specific number—morphologically are of only one type in Japanese: cardinal numerals, that is, numerals that are used when counting something within a series.

1.1 Cardinal Numerals

In Japanese, there are two cardinal number groups: Sino-Japanese numbers and native numbers.

Native cardinals are only limited to the first ten numbers (from 1 to 10) and other than in fossilized expressions, they are exclusively used when followed by a handful of specific native classifiers [☞ III. 2]. This is why the most widely used type of numbers are undoubtedly the Sino-Japanese.

Cardinal numerals of any type obligatorily have to be followed by a classifier whenever an object or concept is being counted. Sino-Japanese cardinal numerals can only be used independently when counting consecutively (one, two, three...) or when reading or thinking about a numerical figure on its own.

The basic numerical lexemes[43] in Japanese are the following:

ichi 一 *1*	ni 二 *2*	san 三 *3*	yon 四 *4*
go 五 *5*	roku 六 *6*	nana 七 *7*	hachi 八 *8*
kyuu 九 *9*	juu 十 *10*	hyaku 百 *100*	sen 千 *1000*
	man 万 *10,000*	oku 億 *100,00,000*	

---

[43] Lexemes on which new numbers are constructed. Also referred as *base numbers*.

As you have seen, in addition to the base numbers equivalent to those in English, in Japanese, there are also lexemes for the numbers 10,000 (*man*) and 100,000,000 (*oku*). This is important to keep in mind because when counting numbers higher than 10,000, such base morpheme will always be needed, and the same applies to numbers higher than 100,000,000.

Within this system, there are some cases when two alternatives exist for the same number, albeit one of these alternatives is always more common than the other. The number 'zero' can be pronounced *zero* (preferred form, borrowed from English) or *re* (borrowed from Chinese). The number 'four' can be pronounced **yon** (preferred form, actually borrowed from the native system) or **shi**[44] (borrowed from Chinese). The number 'seven' can be pronounced *nana* (preferred form, borrowed from the native system) or **shichi**[45] (borrowed from Chinese). The number 'nine' can be pronounced **kyuu** (preferred form) or **ku** and the number 'ten' can be pronounced **juu** (preferred form) or **ju**.

1.2 Number Formation

Number formation in Japanese is relatively simple as it is done through the combination of base numbers and there are not too many phonetic changes and those that are present follow a simple pattern.

In order to make teens, the desired unit base number[46] has to be added to the morpheme *juu* (10). On the other hand, to form tens of 10, 20, 30, etc, the morpheme *juu* (10) is added to the corresponding unit base number. To form hundreds, thousands and ten thousands, the same thing is done: the corresponding basic numeral morpheme (*hyaku* for hundreds, *sen* for thousands and *man* for ten thousands) has to be added to the corresponding unit base number.

Teens: juu + [*base number*]

Tens: [*base number*] + juu

Hundreds: [*base number*] + hyaku

Thousands: [*base number*] + sen

Ten Thousands: [*base number*] + man

When pronouncing the numbers 100 and 1,000 in particular, it can be done in two different ways: 1. Saying only the base number (*hyaku* and *sen* respectively); 2. Saying *ichi* (1) followed by the base number, in which case phonetic assimilation is produced: **ippyaku** (*ichi* + *hyaku*) for 100 and **issen** (*ichi* + *sen*) for 1,000. The numbers 10,000 and 100,000,000 are always pronounced **ichi man** and **ichi oku** respectively.

Below there is a table summarizing the Japanese cardinal number system:

CARDINAL NUMERALS

---

[44] The phoneme *shi* is also used to refer to the meaning of 'death', so popular usage has ended up preferring the use of the native form *yon*, which sounds less dramatic.

[45] Probably to avoid confusion among *shichi* ('seven') and *ichi* ('one').

[46] Unit Base Number: A number from 1 to 9.

Number	Preferred Reading	Alternative Reading	Native System
0	zero ゼロ	rē 零	
1	ichi 一		hito-
2	ni 二		futa-
3	san 三		mit-
4	yon 四	shi 四	yot-
5	go 五		itsu-
6	roku 六		mut-
7	nana 七	shichi 七	nana-
8	hachi 八		yat-
9	kyuu 九	ku 九	kokono-
10	juu 十	ju 十	too
11	juu ichi 十一		
20	ni juu 二十		
100	hyaku 百	ippyaku 一百	
200	ni hyaku 二百		
1,000	sen 千	issen 一百	
2,000	ni sen 二千		
10,000	ichi man 一万		
20,000	ni man 二万		
100,000,000	ichi oku 億		

Number formation is subject to a few and comprehensible phonetic changes that are the result of assimilation produced by the conjunction of a consonant followed by *h* or a consonant followed by *s*. These phonetic changes are illustrated in the following table:

VOICED COMBINATIONS OF CARDINAL NUMERALS

300	3,000	600	800	8,000
sanbyaku	sanzen	roppyaku	happyaku	hassen

2. CLASSIFIERS

When it comes to counting any kind of object or abstraction in Japanese, it must be done by combining a cardinal numeral and a specific counting suffix for the thing that is being counted. These counting suffixes are called classifiers because they actually "classify" the object being counted within a specific semantic category.

Classifiers are, then, a type of nominal suffix that is added to a numeral in order to count things. On some occasions, a classifier lexeme can also act as an independent noun.

The choice of an appropriate classifier for a word is customarily fixed, but it is usually based on semantic analogy, as classifiers are mostly derived from Sino-Japanese morphemes with a specific meaning, so a noun will be counted with a classifier with meaning according to the semantic class to which that noun belongs.

It is clear, then, that when counting or expressing "a number of something" it has to be done with the help of a classifier, however, there are three basic grammatical forms in which one can do so. If the classifier is self-explanatory, it is enough to mention the number followed by the classifier. However, if it is necessary to specify the type of thing counted (beyond the information provided by the classifier), this can be done by the formula noun (N) + number (Num.) + *no* + classifier (C) or by the formula noun + number + classifier.

Number & Classifier constructions:

Num. + C	**[Num. + C] + *no* + N**
	N + [Num. + C]

Classifiers can also be used as adverbs with the following formula (V stands for 'verb'):

$$N\{p\} + [Num. + C] + V$$

When you want to ask "how much of something" it is done through construction:

$$nan + C$$

2.1 Universal Classifier

Although most classifiers are of Chinese origin, there is a very widely used native classifier that, of course, is used along with the native cardinal system. This is the universal classifier *-tsu*. This classifier works as a "wildcard" classifier that can be used for any semantic class of noun. It is certainly the most widely used classifier, but since the native system is limited to the numbers 1-10, this classifier is restricted to these numbers too.

Since this classifier is limited to ten numbers, and native cardinals cannot be used, except in fossilized expressions, without a classifier, it is most practical to learn this list of native numbers followed by the *-tsu* classifier as a fixed list. This list of numbers (number + classifier) is the way of counting that the student will use most often in colloquial conversation, because these native numbers plus universal classifier can be used when counting anything except people and animals. Overusing this classifier, however, can make the speaker seem somewhat uneducated and lacking in vocabulary. This classifier is also used by young children when telling their age.

This list has only one exceptional feature: the number-classifier for 10 is simply the native cardinal *too* (without the *-tsu* suffix).

When asking "how much of" this classifier is an exception, since it does not take the interrogative *nan-* [☞ III. 2] but the prenominal *iku*, forming the *ikutsu* construction [☞ I. 2.5].

Ⓣ hitòtsu₁ 一つ: **one** (thing; piece)

Ⓣ futátsù 二つ: **two** (things; pieces)

Ⓣ mittsù 三つ: **three** (things; pieces)

Ⓣ yottsù 四つ: **four** (things; pieces)

Ⓣ itsùtsu 五つ: **five** (things; pieces)

Ⓣ muttsù 六つ: **six** (things; pieces)

Ⓣ nanàtsu 七つ: **seven** (things; pieces)

Ⓣ yattsù 八つ: **eight** (things; pieces)

Ⓣ kokònotsu 九つ: **nine** (things; pieces)

Ⓣ tòo 十: **ten** (things; pieces)

2.2 People & Animals

People and animals always need to be counted with their specific classifiers, as the universal classifier *-tsu* cannot be used with animated things.

In classifiers for people, there is a particularity, and that is that when counting a person or two people there are two corresponding fossilized expressions coming from an old native classifier for people (*-tari*): **hitori** ('one person') *and* **futari** ('two people').

Ⓣ hitòri₁ 一人: **one person**

hito (one) + O.J. -tari (classifier for people)

Ⓣ futárì 二人: **two people**; two persons

← *futatari: futa (two) + O.J. -tari (classifier for people)*

Ⓣ -nin 人 [c] : **person**

-mē 名 [c] *(name)*: [*pol.*] **people**

- -

Ⓙ -hiki 匹: **small animal**; fish; insect

Ⓙ -tō 頭 [c] *(head)*: **big animal**

Ⓙ -wa 羽: ① **bird** ② rabbit

Cognate w. O.J. ha (feather)

2.3 Matter

This section lists classifiers that are added to numerals when counting physical objects.

There is also a generic Sino-Japanese classifier that is used to refer to single articles within a group. This classifier is the morpheme *-ko*, which can be roughly translated with the word 'unit' or 'article'. Although this classifier is not semantically the same as the universal classifier *-tsu* [☞ III. 2.1], it is also sometimes used in a general way when the speaker cannot remember a more specific classifier, although it is nevertheless restricted to physical things.

Most Common

-ko 個 *generic classifier*	-hon 本 *long things*	-mai 枚 *flat things*	-dai 台 *platforms*
-men 面 *broad things*	-en 円 *yens (J. currency)*	-kire 切れ *slices*	-kai 階 *floors*

Ⓕ -ko 個 Ⓒ (*individual*): **generic classifier** (pieces)

Ⓜ -hon 本 Ⓒ : **long, thin thing**

♣ Also u. fig. (for counting things such as phone calls, movies, etc).

Ⓜ -mai 枚 Ⓒ : **flat, thin thing**

Ⓛ meń₁ 面 Ⓒ (*face*): Ⓝ ① **face** ② mask Ⓒ ① **broad, flat thing** ② stages

Ⓜ daí / dài 台 Ⓒ (*podium*): Ⓝ **platform**; podium; stand Ⓒ ① **machine**; electronic device ② **vehicle** (on the road) ③ **stand**; pedestal; furniture

-ryō₂ 両 Ⓒ (*both*): **train**; carriage

-seki 隻 Ⓒ (*single vessel*): **boat**; ship

Ⓛ -satsu 冊 Ⓒ : **book**

Ⓕ èn 円: ⓃⒸ **yen** (J. currency)

Ⓛ shiná 品: ⓃⒸ **article**; item

Ⓛ -hin 品 Ⓒ (*product*): **article of food**; course (food)

Ⓛ sará 皿: ⓃⒸ **plate**; dish

Ⓛ kań 缶 Ⓓ [*kan*]: ⓃⒸ **can** (recipient); tin

kuchí 口: Ⓝ **mouth** Ⓒ **bite**; mouthful

♣ U. w. traditional numerals.

-hai 杯 Ⓒ (*cup*): **drink**; cup; glass; container with liquid inside

zeń 膳 Ⓒ : Ⓝ **dining tray** Ⓒ ① **bowl of rice** ② **pair of chopsticks**

-ninmae 人前 Ⓒ (*person+in front*): **portion of food**; food ration

Ⓛ kirè 切れ: ⓃⒸ **slice**; strip; piece

(I) *kireru (to be cut)*

tsùbu 粒: Ⓝ **grain**; bead; drop Ⓒ **tiny piece**; small object

tamà₂ 玉: ⓃⒸ **ball**

Ⓛ hakó 箱: Ⓝ **box** Ⓒ **box**; pack

♣ U. w. traditional numerals.

Ⓛ fukúrò 袋: ⓃⒸ (plastic/paper) **bag**

fusà 房: Ⓝ **tuft**; tassel Ⓒ **bunch**; cluster

tàba 束: ⓃⒸ **bundle**; bunch

Ⓛ sètto セット Ⓔ : ⓃⒸ **set**

Ⓛ kài 階 Ⓒ : ⓃⒸ **floor**; storey

-jō 畳 Ⓒ : **tatami mat**

♣ Specially as a measure of room size (around 1.5 m²)

-sèki 席 Ⓒ : ⓃⒸ **seat**

kàsho 箇所・カ所・ヶ所 Ⓒ (*article of+place*): ⓃⒸ **place**; spot; part

Ⓛ kèn 軒 Ⓒ (*eaves*): Ⓝ **eaves** Ⓒ **building**; house; shop

-kàkoku ヶ国〔箇国〕 Ⓒ (*article of+country*): **country**

-chaku 着 Ⓒ (*wearing*): **suit of clothing**

-soku 足 Ⓒ (*foot*): **pair of shoes**; pair of socks

keń 件 Ⓒ : ⓃⒸ **matter**; case; affair; subject

Ⓛ mòji 文字 Ⓒ (*writings+letter*): ⓃⒸ **letter** (of a writing)

Ⓛ -go 語 Ⓒ : **word**

-tsuu 通 Ⓒ (*passing through*): ① **document** ② **message**

kyokú / kyòku 曲 Ⓒ (*bending*): ⓃⒸ **composition**; song (piece of music); track (on a record)

-wa 話 Ⓒ (*speaking*): ① **story** ② **episode**

2.4 Time & Extent

Listed here are classifiers used to measure time, extent or degree. Days are listed apart in the following subsection due to the particularities of the words related to them.

Most Common

-nen 年 *years*	-sai 歳 *years old*	-kagetsu ヶ月 *months*
-shuu 週 *weeks*	-ban 晩 *nights*	-ji 時 *hour*
-jikan 時間 *hours*	-fun 分 *minutes*	-byō 秒 *seconds*
	-kai 回 *times*	

-dai 代 Ⓒ (*era*): **generation; era**

Ⓣ -nen 年 Ⓒ : **year**

Ⓣ -sai 歳・才 Ⓒ : **years old**

➤ hatàchi 二十歳: **twenty years old**

   ← *hatatoshi*: O.J. *hata* (twenty) + *toshi* (year)

Ⓔ neńdai 年代: Ⓝ **age; era; period** Ⓢ **-ies** (indicates decades)

-nensē 年生: ① **born in the year...** ② **student of the year...** (course of the year...); nth year student

Ⓔ tsukì 月: Ⓝ ① **moon** ② **month** Ⓒ **month**

   ❖ U. w. native numerals.

-gatsu 月 Ⓒ (*month*): **month of the year**

-kagetsu ヶ月〔箇月〕Ⓒ (*article+month*): **month-long period**

Ⓔ shùu 週 Ⓒ : ⓃⒸ **week**

Ⓔ bań 晩 Ⓒ : ⓃⒸ **night; evening**

-haku 泊 Ⓒ (*lodging*): **night of a stay**

Ⓜ -ji 時 Ⓒ (*time*): **hour** (o'clock)

Ⓔ fùn2 分 Ⓒ (*dividing*): Ⓝ Ⓒ **minute** (unit of time)

Ⓔ byǒ 秒 Ⓒ : Ⓝ Ⓒ **second** (unit of time)

-kan 間 Ⓒ (*interval*): **period of time**

   ❖ Also added to the irregular day-classifiers [☞ III. 2.5].

➤ -funkan 分間: **minute-long period**

➤ Ⓔ jikán2 時間 Ⓒ (*time+interval*): Ⓝ **hour; time** Ⓒ **hour-long period**

➤ -shuukan 分間: **week-long period**

➤ -kagetsukan ヶ月間: **month-long period**

➤ -nenkan 年間: **year-long period**

Ⓜ kài 回 Ⓒ (*times*): Ⓝ Ⓒ **time (instance); number of times; occurrence**

Ⓔ do 度 Ⓒ (*degree*): Ⓝ **degree; extent** Ⓒ **number of times; occurrence**

Ⓜ baí 倍 Ⓒ (*double*): Ⓝ **double** Ⓒ **multiple (-fold); times**

Ⓔ dàn 段 Ⓒ (*step*): Ⓝ **step** (on a sequence) Ⓒ **rank; grade; level**

-tō 等 Ⓒ (*equivalent*): **class; order; rank**

(上) bùn 分 [c] (*dividing*): $\boxed{N}\boxed{C}$ **part** (as a partition); **segment**

bù / bu 部 [c] (*section*): $\boxed{N}\boxed{C}$ **part** (as a component)

(中) teń 点 [c] : $\boxed{N}\boxed{C}$ **point; dot; mark**

hò 步 [c] : $\boxed{N}\boxed{C}$ (foot)**step; stride**

-hatsu 発 [c] : **launch; shot**

2.5 Days & Days of the Month

To count days either cardinally (how many days) or ordinally (which day of the month) the native classifier -*ka* is used, which is logically added to the numbers of the native system. That this classifier requires a separate section is due to the fact that the native numbers, affected by this classifier, have been affected phonetically in a considerable way, so it becomes necessary to learn these new formations separately.

In addition, when counting a single day or mentioning the first day of the month, two different forms are used: *ichi nichi* (Sino-Japanese rendering) for 'one day' and ***tsuitachi*** (special native lexeme) for the first day of the month. When counting twenty days, there is also an exception, since a unique lexeme is used: ***hatsuka***, which is formed with a fossilized form of the old native number for 'twenty'.

(下) ichínichì 一日 [c] (*one+day*): **one day**

ichi (one) + nichi (day)

(下) tsuítachì 一日: **1st day of the month.**

← *tsukitachi: tsuki (month) + tachi: (1) tatsu (to stand)*

(下) futsúka 二日: ① **two days** ② **2nd day of the month**

← *futaka: futa (two) + ka (classifier for days)*

(下) mikká 三日: ① **three days** ② **3rd day of the month**

(下) yokká 四日: ① **four days** ② **4th day of the month**

(下) ìtsuka 五日: ① **five days** ② **5th day of the month**

(下) muíka 六日: ① **six days** ② **6th day of the month**

← *mukka: O.J. mut (six) + ka (classifier for days)*

(下) nanóka 七日: ① **seven days** ② **7th day of the month**

← *nanaka: nana (seven) + ka (classifier for days)*

(下) yóka 八日: ① **eight days** ② **8th day of the month**

← *yakka: O.J. yat (eight) + ka (classifier for days)*

(下) kokónokà 九日: ① **nine days** ② **9th day of the month**

(下) toóka 十日: ① **ten days** ② **10th day of the month**

(中) hatsúka 二十日: ① **twenty days** ② **20th day of the month**

← *hataka: O.J. hata (twenty) + ka (classifier for days)*

2.6 Ordinal Markers

As it was said at the beginning of this section [☞ III. 1.1], in Japanese there are only proper lexemes for cardinal numerals. As there are no separate ordinal lexemes as in English (first, second, etc.), ordinals, that is, numbers defined as a position within a series, are marked in Japanese by means of ordinal suffixes or markers.

The most common ordinal marker is the native suffix *-me*. Somewhat colloquial in nature, it is mostly used attached to the native universal qualifier *-tsu* [☞ III. 2.1]. Then, there is the ordinal Sino-Japanese classifier *-ban*, which actually means 'number within a series', so the formation x-*ban* can be translated as 'the number x'. From the combination of this classifier with the above-mentioned suffix *-me*, the *-banme* formation is obtained, which now can be added directly to a number and thus functions as another ordinal marker complementary to the *-tsume* formation, but whose literal translation would be 'the x-th number'. Finally, there is a purely Sinitic ordinal marker, ***dai-***, which is a prefix preceding a number followed in turn by a specific classifier. This marker is usually reserved for written language or formal language.

Formation of ordinal constructions:

[**Num. + C**] + *-me* ➤ [**Num.**] + *-banme*	*dai-* + [**Num. + C**]

- -

Ⓛ -me 目: Ⓢ **position in an ordinal sequence** (-th)

❖ Added to classifiers.

Ⓛ -bàn 番 ⒸcⒸ **①number in a series ② turn**

➤ -banme 番目: **number position in an ordinal sequence** (number -th)

ban (number) + me (ordinal number)

dai- 第: [*for.*] Ⓟ **position in an ordinal sequence** (-th)

❖ Placed before a number that is followed by a classifier.

-ji 次: Ⓒ **position in an ordinal sequence**

❖ Placed after a number that is preceded by the pre. *dai* 第.

2.7 Euphonic Changes

When a numeral is combined with a classifier, in many cases a phonetic change is produced by assimilation. Although there are some exceptions and variations, these changes mostly follow a set pattern as shown in the table below:

	-k	① -s ② -sh	① -t ② -ch	-h	-f	-p	-w
ichi	ikk-	❶ iss- ❷ issh-	❶ itt- ❷ icch-	ipp-			
san				sanb-	sanp-		sanb-
yon				yonp-			yonb-
roku	rokk-			ropp-			
hachi	hakk-	❶ hass- ❷ hassh-	❶ hatt- ❷ hacch-	happ-			
juu	jukk-	❶ juss- ❷ jussh-	❶ jutt- ❷ jucch-	jupp-			
hyaku	hyakk-			hyapp			
sen				senb-	senp-		
man				manb-	manp-		
nan				nanb-	nanp-		

IV. VERBS & NOMINAL VERBS

Verbs are independent conjugable words that express a state or action and function as the main endowment of meaning in the sentence, so it is undoubtedly the most important kind of word in any language.

Semantically, verbs can be separated into two groups: static verbs, which refer to a passive state that occurs or affects a subject; and active verbs, which refer to an action done by a subject.

It should also be mentioned that, etymologically, as with nouns, there are two main types of verbs: native verbs and Sino-Japanese verbs. In this case, the typology also carries a morphological distinction: for native verbs only function as verbs, while Sino-Japanese verbs are actually Sino-Japanese nouns to which the native verb *suru* (to make) has to be added to make them function as verbs. These Sino-Japanese nouns which admit the verb suru in order to act as verbs can also be called nominal verbs. This set of verbs and nominal verbs can be grouped, then, under the broad category of verbals.

In this section of the book, the verbs will be listed in the dictionary form (realis form), which is the one used for expressing the imperfective aspect and the indicative mood of the verbs (equivalent to the present indicative in English).

1. STATIVE VERBALS

Static verbals are verbs and nominal verbs that express a particular state of being. This state can be continuous—that is, occurring at the moment of speech—or transformative—that is, at changing or transforming into a new state at the moment of speech. In addition, there is the copula (equivalent to the English verb 'to be') which, although semantically it could be considered as a continuous state, needs a separate classification due to its grammatical peculiarities.

1.1 The Copula

The notion of 'being' in Japanese is not defined by a verb per se but by a type of word with a distinct grammatical function: the copula. The Copula, defined by its function, is a word that links the subject of the sentence with the complement (A *is* B), either explicitly or implicitly. The Copula as such in English corresponds to the verb 'to be'.

Copula in Japanese, grammatically speaking, is not exactly a verb since, unlike verbs, it cannot be used independently, as it always has to be accompanied by at least one subject or complement.

The Japanese copula, albeit not being able to be used independently like verbs, is subject, like them, to different conjugations of mood and aspect [☞ GE:I.1.3]. In this section, only the indicative imperfective forms will be listed.

+ *More information in Grammar Explanations* [☞ GE:I.3].

Most Common Forms (Imperfective Indicative)

da だ [*fam.*] to *be*	desu です [*pol.*] to *be*

Ⓣ da だ ①: [*fam.*] to **be**

✤ Cop., a particular verbal f. with the special grammatical rule that dictates that it has to be always attached to a n. or an adj.

Ⓣ dèsu です ①: [*pol.*] to **be**

✤ Pol. f. of the cop. *da*.

Ⓤ de gozáimàsu でございます 〔で御座います〕: [*for.*][*hon.*][*pol.*] to **be**

de* + hon. v. *gozaimasu (to exist)* | **Gerundive f. of the cop. *da*

✤ Hon. f. of the cop. *da*. The *gozaimasu* part of this construction is conjugated as the hon. v. *gozaimasu (to exist)*.

✤ M. u. in very formal situations such as vendor-customer relationships.

de àru である: [*lit.*] to **be**

de* + *aru (to exist)* | **Gerundive f. of the cop. *da*

✤ Lit. f. of the cop. *da*. The *aru* part of this construction is conjugated as the v. *aru (to exist)*.

1.2 Continuous States

Continuous states denote a state that at the time of speech is understood as going on indefinitely.

Within continuous states, the most significant and the one that is most often expressed in language is the existential continuous state, that is, 'to be there' or 'to exist', which in English sometimes overlaps with the verb 'to be'. In Japanese, these states are grammatically distinct from the copula because they do not necessarily link a subject with a complement.

Important Words

aru ある *to be at*; *to exist* (inanimate)	iru いる *to be at*; *to exist* (animate)
sumu 住む *to live at*	ikiru 生きる *to be living*
dekiru できる *to be able*	okoru 起る *to happen*
niru 似る *to be alike*	chigau 違う *to be different*
tsudzukeru 続ける *to continue*	nokoru 残る *to remain*

Ⓣ àru₂ ある 〔❶❷ 在る/ ❸ 有る〕: Ⓥ ① to **be** (at) ② to **exist** ③ to **have** (possession) Ⓢ *to have ~*

✤ ❶❷ U. w. inanimate things.

✤ ❸ The possessed thing is marked w. the p. **ga** and the subject may be followed by the particle **ni**.

✤ The neg. f. of this v. is irregular: nai [☞ Ⅴ 2.5].

Ⓣ irú いる 〔居る〕 Ⓢ: ① to **be** (at) ② to **exist** Ⓢ *to be ~*

✤ U. w. animate beings.

Ⓤ irásshàru いらっしゃる: [*hon.*] ① to **be** ② to go ③ to come

← O.J. *iraseraru: ira** + *seraru†* | **Irrealis f. of v. *iru (to enter)* |†O.J. hon. f. of the v. *suru (to do)*

145

oíde ni nàru おいでになる〔お出にな る〕: [*hon.*] ① to **be** ② to go ③ to come

hon. pre. *o* + *ide** + lative p. *ni* + *naru (to become)* |*(I) r. u. hon. v. *ideru (to go; to come)* ‖ This whole construction is actually the redundant hon. f. of the r. u. hon. v. *ideru*.

Ⓔ **òru** おる〔居る〕: [*hum.*] ① to **be** ② to **exist**

❖ ❶❷ U. w. animate things.

gozáimàsu ございます〔御座います〕: [*hum.*][*pol.*] ① to **be** (at) ② to **exist**

← O.J. *gozaru*: hum. f. of the v. *aru (to be; to exist)*

❖ ❶❷ U. for both animate and inanimate things.

Ⓔ **sońzai** (suru) 存在する ⒸⒸ *(existence+being)*: Ⓝ **existence** Ⓥ to **exist**

Ⓔ **ìchi** (suru) 位置する ⒸⒸ *(position+putting)*: Ⓝ **position**; location Ⓥ to **be located** (at)

Ⓕ **sùmu** 住む: to **live** (**at**); to **reside** (at)

❖ In a present state this v. uses the progressive f. *sunde iru*.

- -

⊕ **ikìru** 生きる Ⓢ: to **live**; to be alive

❖ Referring to the state of preserving life and functioning as an organism, also in a fig. sense.

Ⓔ **kurásu** 暮らす: ① to **live** (one's daily existence); to spend (time); to get along; to lead a life ② to make one's living

⊕ **sékatsu** (suru) 生活する ⒸⒸ *(living+life)*: Ⓝ **livelihood**; living Ⓥ ① to **live** (one's daily existence) ② to make one's living

❖ Referring to the way in which people live their lives, e.g. 'lifestyle' or 'livelihood'.

- -

Ⓕ **dekíru** できる〔出来る〕Ⓢ: ① to **be possible**; to **be able**; **can** ② to be ready (to function).

← *dekuru* ← *deku* ← *ideku: ide** + O.J. *ku (to come)* → C.J. *kuru* |*(I) O.J. *idzu (to come out)*

‖ This v. originally meant 'to come out'. Afterwards the meaning shifted to '*to appear*' and finally it adopted the current meaning of 'to be able to do'.

⊕ **okòru₁** 起こる: Ⓘ to **occur**; to **happen**

hasśé (suru) 発生する Ⓒ *(launch+born)*: Ⓝ **occurrence** Ⓥ to **occur**

- -

⊕ **nirú** 似る Ⓢ: ① to **resemble**; to look alike ② to be similar; to be like; to be alike

❖ Most of the time this v. is u. in the progressive f. *nite iru*.

ruíji (suru) 類似する Ⓒ *(type+resembling)*: Ⓝ **similarity**; resemblance Ⓥ to **be similar**; to be alike

Ⓔ **niàu** 似合う: to **suit**; to **match**; to be like

ni* + *au (to come together)* |*(I) *niru (to resemble)*

Ⓔ **sótō₁** (suru) 相当する Ⓒ *(mutual+hit)*: Ⓝ **correspondence**; **equivalence** Ⓥ to **be corresponding** (to); to **be equivalent** (to)

Ⓔ **kańren** (suru) 関連する Ⓢ Ⓒ *(related+along)*: Ⓝ **relation** Ⓥ to **be related** (with)

- -

Ⓕ **chigáu** 違う: ① to **be different**; to differ (from) ② to **not match** (the correct answer); to not be

❖ ❷ This expression is u. in conversational language when one wants to negate the other persons' stance, as one would say 'no' in English.

⊕ **kotónàru** 異なる: to **differ**; to **vary**

koto (difference) + *naru (to become)*

Ⓔ **sugúrèru** 優れる Ⓢ: ① to **be superior** (to) ② to **excel**

otóru / otòru 劣る: ① to be **inferior** (to) ② to **fall behind**

- -

Ⓑ tàtsu₁ 経つ: to **pass** (time); to elapse

Ⓒ tsudzúku 続く: Ⓘ ① to **continue** ② to **last**

Ⓒ tsudzúkeru 続ける Ⓢ: Ⓣ to **continue** Ⓐ to keep on ~

Ⓒ nokòru 残る: Ⓘ to **remain**; to be **left** Ⓐ to be left un-~

Ⓒ nokòsu 残す: Ⓣ to **leave behind**; to save; to bequeath Ⓐ to leave s.t. un-~

amàru 余る: Ⓘ ① to **remain**; to be left over ② to be too many; to be in excess

❖ This v. refers to that which remains in excess, exceeding a limit or capacity.

hayàru 流行る: ① to be **prevalent**; to **thrive**; to be popular (s.t.) ② to spread widely; to come into fashion

- -

Ⓑ hikàru 光る: to **shine**; to be bright

Probably related to hi (sun)

❖ U. to describe things that appear brighter by themselves while emitting or reflecting light. Also u. in a fig. sense.

kagáyàku 輝く: to **shine**; to glitter; to sparkle

❖ U. to describe things that emit a dazzling amount of light in all directions. Usually, it has pos. connotations.

ukábu 浮かぶ: ① to **float**; to be floating ② to come to mind

Cognate w. uku (to float upwards)

1.3 Transformative States

Transformative states refer to a state in which the subject is in the process of transformation or change at the moment of speech.

Important Words

naru なる to **become**	umareru 生まれる to be **born**
kieru 消える to **disappear**	shinu 死ぬ to **die**
kawaru 変わる to **change**	kaeru 変える to **change** s.t.

Ⓣ nàru なる〔成る〕: ① to **become** ② to **achieve**; to complete ③ to be composed of; to consist of

❖ ❶ After the p. **ni**.

❖ ❸ After the p. **kara**.

Ⓑ aráwàsu ❶ 現す/❷❸ 表す: f ① to **show**; to reveal; to **display** ② to **represent**; to signify ③ to express

From adj. arawa (to be exposed) + O.J. su (to do) → C.J. suru

Ⓑ aráwarèru 現れる Ⓢ: Ⓘ ① to **appear** ② to be expressed

nińshin (suru) 妊娠する Ⓒ (pregnant+pregnancy): Ⓝ **pregnancy** Ⓥ to **become pregnant**

umú ❶ 生む/❷ 産む: Ⓘ ① to **give birth** ② to **produce**

Ⓣ umáreru 生まれる Ⓢ: Ⓘ ① to **be born**

⊕ **utsùsu** 写す・移す: ① to **reproduce** ② to **duplicate** ③ to **transcribe** ④ to **substitute**

- -

⊤ **kesú** 消す: ⊤ to **erase**; to **delete** 🅐 *to deny by ~*

⊤ **kiéru** 消える ⑤: Ⓘ to **disappear**; to **vanish**

⊤ **shinú** 死ぬ: to **die**

  Ⓒ *shi* 死 *(death)* + Ⓙ O.J. dep. v. *nu (to complete)*

  ❖ U. for people, animals and also abstract things in a fig. way.

⊕ **shibô** (suru) 死亡する Ⓒ *(dying+perishing)*: Ⓝ **death** Ⓥ to **die**; to pass away

  ❖ M. u. only for humans.

⊕ **nakúnaru** 亡くなる: [*pol.*] to **pass away**; to **die**

  naku* + naru (to become) |*(I) *nai (not being)*

⊕ **kusàru** 腐る: to **rot**; to **decay**; to go bad

shibómu 萎む: ① to **wither** ② to **fade** (away)

magireru 紛れる ⑤: Ⓘ ① to **disappear into** ② to **be diverted from**

- -

⊕ **kawáru** ❶❷ 変わる/ ❸ 換わる/ ❹ 替わる・代わる: Ⓘ ① to **change** ② to be **transformed** ③ to be **exchanged** ④ to be **replaced**

⊕ **kaéru** ❶❷ 変える/ ❸ 換える/ ❹ 替える・代える ⑤: Ⓣ ① to **change** ② to **transform** ③ to **exchange** ④ to **replace** 🅐 *to renew by ~*

⊕ **hènka** (suru) 変化する Ⓒ *(changing+transforming)*: Ⓝ ① **change**; alteration ② **transformation** Ⓥ ① to **change** ② to **transform**

⊕ **heńkō** (suru) 変更する Ⓒ *(changing+renewal)*: Ⓝ ① **change**;

modification; alteration ② **revision** Ⓥ ① to **change** ② to **revise**

  ❖ Specifically u. for planned changes.

⊕ **arátamèru** 改める ⑤: Ⓣ ① to **change**; to alter ② to **reform**; to **renew**; to improve

  ← *aratamu*: Verbalized f. of the adj. *arata (new)*

  ❖ U. for a 'change' of an old thing for the better.

shìnka (suru) 進化する Ⓒ *(advancing+transforming)*: Ⓝ **evolution** Ⓥ to **evolve**

⊕ **shòri** (suru) 処理する Ⓒ *(location+reason)*: Ⓝ ① **process** ② processing Ⓥ to **process**

teńkai (suru) 展開する Ⓒ *(exhibition+opening)*: Ⓝ **development** Ⓥ to **develop**

- -

yòku surú 良くする: Ⓣ to **improve**

  yoku* + suru (to do) |*Adv. f. of the adj. *yoi (good)*

yòku nàru 良くなる: Ⓘ to **get better**

  yoku* + naru (to become) |*Adv. f. of the adj. *yoi (good)*

---

warùku surú 悪くする: to **worsen**

  waruku* + suru (to do) |*Adv. f. of adj. *warui (bad)*

warùku nàru 悪くなる: to **get worse**

  waruku* + naru (to become) |*Adv. f. of adj. *warui (bad)*

- -

kôshin (suru) 更新する Ⓒ *(renewal+new)*: Ⓝ ① **renewal** ② **update** Ⓥ ① to **renew** ② to **update**

kaíkaku (suru) 改革する Ⓒ *(reforming+modification)*: Ⓝ **reform**; reformation Ⓥ to **reform**

fukúgen (suru) 復元する Ⓒ *(time and again+origin)*: Ⓝ **restoration** (to original state); **reconstruction** Ⓥ to **restore**; to reconstruct

---

Ⓛ **nobìru** ❶❷ 伸びる/ ❸❹ 延びる Ⓢ: Ⓘ ① to **extend**; to stretch ② to lengthen ③ to make progress ④ to be postponed; to be prolonged

Ⓛ **nobàsu** ❶❷ 伸ばす/ ❸ 延ばす: Ⓣ ① to **extend** ② to **expand** ③ to prolong; to postpone

Ⓛ **hirógaru** 広がる: Ⓘ ① to **spread** (out) ② to **extend** ③ to stretch

Intransitive f. of the O.J. v. *hirogu** *(to spread)* |**Stem of adj. hiroi (to be spread) + derivative suf. gu*

hirógeru 広げる Ⓢ: Ⓣ ① to **spread** ② to **extend** ③ to stretch

fukúreru 膨れる Ⓢ: Ⓘ ① to **swell** ② to expand

---

chidjímu 縮む: Ⓘ to **shrink**; to **contract**; to become smaller

chidjímeru 縮める Ⓢ: Ⓣ ① to **shorten** ② to **shrink**

Ⓜ **sukú** 空く: Ⓘ to **get empty**

Ⓛ **futòru** 太る: to **gain weight**; to become fat; to get weight

futo* + verbal suf. *ru* |**Stem of the adj. futoi (to be fat)*

Ⓛ **yaséru** 痩せる: to **lose weight**; to become thin; to reduce (one's) weight

---

Ⓛ **kawàku** ❶ 乾く/ ❷ 渇く: Ⓘ ① to (get) **dry** ② to **be thirsty**

kawákasù 乾かす: Ⓣ to (make) **dry**

Ⓛ **nuréru** 濡れる Ⓢ: Ⓘ to **get wet**

nurásu 濡らす: Ⓣ to **wet**

Ⓛ **harèru** 晴れる Ⓢ: Ⓘ to **clear up**; to clear away; to be cleared

Ⓜ **kuréru** 暮れる Ⓢ: Ⓘ to **get dark**

Ⓜ **wakú** 沸く: Ⓘ to **boil**; to get boiled

Ⓜ **wakásu** 沸かす: Ⓣ to **boil**

Ⓜ **yakú** 焼く: Ⓣ ① to **burn** ② to **roast** ③ to **heat** (up)

Ⓜ **yakéru** 焼ける Ⓢ: Ⓘ ① to **burn** ② to be **heated** ③ to be roasted

Ⓛ **moéru** 燃える Ⓢ: Ⓘ to **burn**

❖ This word is m. u. in a fig. way.

---

atátamèru 温める Ⓢ: Ⓣ ① to **warm** ② to **heat**

← *atatamu*: Verbal f. of the adj. *atatai (warm)*

nessúru / nessùru 熱する: Ⓣ to **heat** (up)

Ⓒ *nes** + Ⓙ *suru (to do)* |** ← netsu 熱 (heat)*

Ⓛ **hièru** 冷える: Ⓘ to **cool down**; to get chilly

hiyàsu 冷やす: Ⓣ to **cool** (s.t.)

Ⓛ **koóru** 凍る: Ⓘ to **freeze**

tokèru 溶ける: Ⓘ to **melt**; to dissolve

katámaru 固まる: Ⓘ to **harden**; to **solidify**

Ⓛ **akìru** 飽きる: to **get tired of**; to have enough; to lose interest in

uńzàri (suru) うんざりする [ideophone]: to be **fed up with**; to be tired of; to be boring

❖ This word usually has neg. connotations.

2. ACTIVE VERBALS

Active verbals are verbs and nominal verbs that denote an action performed by someone or something. Active verbs are by far the most abundant type of verb in any language.

2.1 Speech

Verbals related to speech and to what is said.

Important Words

hanasu 話す	iu 言う	tsutaeru 伝える
to speak; *to talk*	*to say; to tell*	*to communicate*

Ⓣ hanàsu 話す: ① to **speak** ② to **talk** (with)

❖ Referring to the fact of having a conversation with another person or the fact of 'speaking' a language.

Ⓛ shabèru しゃべる〔喋る〕Ⓦ: [*col.*] ① to **talk**; to chat ② to **speak**

❖ Col. word u. when talking about light things w. another person. Also u. col. w. the meaning of to 'speak' a language (❷).

Ⓛ katáru 語る: ① to **talk about**; to **speak of** ② to **tell**

❖ U. to refer to having a conversation w. another person or when telling or narrating a story to a listener in a coherent way.

Ⓣ iú 言う: ① to **say** ② to **tell**

❖ Referring to the expression of thoughts through words.

➤ [*col.*] yuú 言う

⊕ mòsu 申す: [*hum.*] ① to **say** ② to **tell**

⊕ móshiagèru / moshíageru 申し上げる Ⓢ: [*hum.*] ① to **say** ② to **tell**

mōshi* + *ageru* ([*pol.*] *to give*) | *(I) *mōsu* ([*hum.*] *to say*)

osshàru おっしゃる〔仰る〕: [*hon.*] to **say**

tsugéru 告げる Ⓢ: Ⓣ ① to **tell** ② to **inform**

❖ Referring to the clear expression of one's feelings.

Ⓛ nobèru 述べる Ⓢ: ① to **state**; to express ② to **mention**

Cognate w. *noberu (to expand)*, a transitive f. of the v. *nobiru (to become longer)*

❖ Specially u. in reference to s.t. that is or has been expressed in writing.

Ⓛ hyógèn (suru) 表現する Ⓒ (*displaying+revealed*): Ⓝ **expression** Ⓥ to **express**

❖ Referring to the fact of describing subjective feelings or thoughts.

hatsúgen (suru) 発言する Ⓒ (*launch+saying*): Ⓝ **statement; remark** Ⓥ to **state**; to **utter**

❖ Referring to the expression of opinions in formal settings.

⊕ hatsúon (suru) 発音する Ⓒ (*launch+sound*): Ⓝ **pronunciation** Ⓥ to **pronounce**

Ⓣ ìmi (suru) 意味する Ⓒ (*idea+taste*): Ⓝ **meaning** Ⓥ to **mean**

⊕ setsùmē (suru) 説明する ⓒ
(*explaining+clear*): Ⓝ **explanation** Ⓥ to
explain; to make clear

yakùsu 訳す: ① to **translate** ② to
interpret

- -

⊕ tsutáeru 伝える Ⓢ: Ⓣ ① to **convey**; to
communicate ② to transmit ③ to tell

Transitive f. of the currently r. u. v. *tsutau (to
follow)*

❖ U. when s.o. says s.t. clearly in order
to be understood.

⊕ tsutáwaru 伝わる: Ⓘ ① to **be informed**
② to be transmitted ③ to be told

⊕ tsuúshin (suru) 通信する ⓒ (*going
through+faith*): Ⓝ **communication** Ⓥ to
communicate; to transmit

⊕ hókoku (suru) 報告する ⓒ
(*reporting+announcing*): Ⓝ (a) **report** Ⓥ to
report; to inform

hódō (suru) 報道する ⓒ (*reporting+road-way*):
Ⓝ **report** Ⓥ to **report**; to inform

❖ U. when informing about s.t. to the
public at large.

⊕ happyó (suru) 発表する ⓒ
(*launch+revealing*): Ⓝ **announcement**;
statement Ⓥ to **announce**

kokúhaku (suru) 告白する ⓒ
(*announcing+white*): Ⓝ **confession**;
acknowledgment Ⓥ ① to **confess** ② to
declare one's love

- -

⊕ sakèbu 叫ぶ: Ⓘ to **scream**; to **shout**

chikáu / chikàu 誓う: to **swear**; to vow

⊕ inòru 祈る: to **pray**

- -

⊕ damàru 黙る: to **be silent**; to **say
nothing**

2.2 Conversation & Argument

Verbals related to conversation, debate and word exchange.

Important Words

yobu 呼ぶ to **call** (out)	kaiwa suru 会話する to **converse**	denwa 電話 to **phone**	yakusoku (suru) 約束する to **promise**

- -

⊕ yobú 呼ぶ: to **call**; to call out

⊕ kaíwa (suru) 会話する ⓒ (*meeting+talking*):
Ⓝ **conversation** Ⓥ to **have a
conversation**; to talk about s.t.

❖ Referring to two or more people
exchanging words when talking about
the same topic.

taíwa (suru) 対話する ⓒ (*opposite+talking*): Ⓝ
① **conversation** ② dialogue ③ argument

Ⓥ ① to **have a dialogue** (with); to have
a conversation ② to talk

❖ Referring to open discussions between
a large number of people.

⊕ denwá (suru) 電話する ⓒ (*electricity+talk*):
Ⓝ ① **telephone** ② telephone call Ⓥ to
call (by phone); to phone

Ⓔ **gìron** (suru) 議論する Ⓒ

(*deliberation+argument*): Ⓝ **discussion**; debate; argument Ⓥ to **discuss**; to argue

❖ Referring to an exchange of opinions over a wide variety of matters.

hanáshiàu 話し合う: to **discuss**; to talk together

hanashi* + au (to meet) |*(I) hanasu (to talk)

❖ Referring to an exchange of views on a problem done in order to resolve an issue or reach a certain agreement.

---

tògi (suru) 討議する Ⓒ (*subduing+deliberation*): Ⓝ **debate** Ⓥ to **discuss**; to **debate**

❖ A discussion as an attempt to come to a conclusion or resolution by exchanging opinions.

tòron (suru) 討論する Ⓒ (*subduing+argument*): to **discuss**; to **debate**

❖ A quarrel over each other's opinions and arguments.

- - - - - - - - - - -

⊕ **yakúsoku** (suru) 約束する Ⓒ

(*promise+bundle*): Ⓝ **promise** Ⓥ to **promise**; to make a promise

dói (suru) 同意する Ⓒ (*same+idea*): Ⓝ **agreement** Ⓥ to **agree**

kochó (suru) 誇張する Ⓒ (*boasting+extending*): Ⓝ **exaggeration** Ⓥ to **exaggerate**

- - - - - - - - - - -

Ⓔ **mònku** (o) iú 文句を言う: to **complain**

Ⓒ *monku* 文句 (*complain*) + Ⓙ accusative p. *o + iu (to say)*

Ⓔ **uttàeru** 訴える Ⓢ: Ⓘ ① to **complain** ② to **sue**

❖ To tell s.o. about a demand or complaint when there is an intention to solve things relying on it.

boyàku ぼやく: Ⓘ to **complain**; to **whine**; to grumble

❖ M. referring to personal complaints done individually.

Ⓔ **hihán** (suru) 批判する Ⓒ

(*criticism+judgement*): Ⓝ ① **criticism** ② judgement Ⓥ to **criticize**

Ⓔ **shikáru** / shikàru 叱る: to **scold**

bujóku (suru) 侮辱する Ⓒ

(*disdaining+disgracing*): Ⓝ **insult** Ⓥ to **insult**

donàru 怒鳴る: Ⓘ ① to **curse** ② to **swear** ③ to **shout** (in anger)

Ⓒ *do* 怒 (*angry*) + Ⓙ *naru (to sound)*

2.3 Asking & Answering

Verbals related to questions, suggestions, orders and answers.

Important Words

kiku 聞く *to ask; to listen*	shitsumon (suru) 質問する *to ask*	tanomu 頼む *to request*	kotaeru 答える *to answer*

- - - - - - - - - - -

Ⓣ **kikú**₁ ❶❷ 聞く/ ❸ 訊く: ① to **ask** ② to listen ③ to search for an answer

❖ Word w. the implication that the subject will listen attentively to the

answer, since the original meaning of this word is 'to listen'.

Ⓣ **shitsúmon** (suru) 質問する Ⓒ

(*matter+asking*): Ⓝ **question** Ⓥ to **ask**; to pose a question

❖ M. referring to broad and general 'questions', such as academic or philosophical ones.

⊕ tazúnèru₁ 尋ねる Ⓢ: [*for.*] ① to **ask**; to inquire

❖ To 'ask' s.o. about s.t. you are not sure about.

ukágau₁ 伺う: [*hum.*] to ask; to inquire

❖ U. when asking s.t. to a superior.

toú / tòu 問う: [*lit.*] to **ask**

❖ Word u. in a situation where one is looking for the answer to a concrete, usually abstract problem.

─────────────

Ⓣ tanòmu 頼む: to **ask** (s.o. to do s.t.); to **request**

Ⓛ yókyuu (suru) 要求する Ⓒ (*needing+pursuing*): Ⓝ **demand**; **request** Ⓥ to **require**; to demand

❖ It can be also u. when there is a physiological need.

Ⓛ sódan (suru) 相談する Ⓒ (*mutual+discussion*): Ⓝ **consultation** Ⓥ to **consult**

⊕ méjiru / méjìru 命じる Ⓢ: to **order** (s.o. to do s.t.); to command

Ⓒ mē 命 (*orders*) + Ⓙ jiru ← zuru ← suru (*to do*)

Ⓛ mézuru / mézùru 命ずる: [*lit.*] to **order** (s.o. to do s.t.)

Ⓒ mē 命 (*orders*) + Ⓙ zuru ← suru (*to do*)

Ⓛ mérē (suru) 命令する Ⓒ (*orders+command*): Ⓝ **order** (command); **command** Ⓥ to **give an order**; to order; to command

─────────────

Ⓣ kotáèru / kotàeru ❶答える/❷応える Ⓢ: ① to **answer**; to reply ② to respond (in kind)

⊕ heńjì (suru) 返事する Ⓒ (*turning+affair*): Ⓝ **reply**; answer; response Ⓥ to **reply**; to respond; to answer

❖ Referring to verbal 'responses' but also to responses to another people's actions.

Ⓛ kaítō (suru) 回答する Ⓒ (*revolving+answering*): Ⓝ (specific) **answer**; reply Ⓥ [*for.*] to **answer**; to reply

❖ A return of specific words in response to a question or request w. specific content.

2.4 Thought

Verbals related to thought, memory, imagination, choice, opinion and decision-making.

Important Words

kangaeru 考える to **think** (objectively)	omou 思う to **think** (subjectively)	shinjiru 信じる to **believe**
shuuchuu (suru) 集中する to **concentrate**	shinpai (suru) 心配する to **worry**	ki ni suru 気にする to **worry**; to **mind**
oboeru 覚える to **memorize**	omoidasu 思い出す to **remember**; to **recall**	wasureru 忘れる to **forget**
kuraberu 比べる to **compare**	kimeru 決める to **decide**	erabu 選ぶ to **choose**

Ⓣ **kańgaèru** / kańgàeru 考える Ⓢ: to **think** (about); to **consider**

❖ 'Thinking' as a means to make logical and objective decisions.

Ⓣ **omòu** 思う: to **think** (subjectively)

❖ 'Thinking' as using the mind subjectively and emotionally.

Ⓛ **shikó** (suru) 思考する Ⓒ (*thinking+pondering*): Ⓝ **thought** Ⓥ to **think**; to consider

❖ Referring to objective 'thinking' that follows a single line of reasoning.

zońjìru / zońjiru 存じる Ⓢ: [*hum.*] ① to **consider** ② to think

Ⓒ *zon* 存 *(existence)* + Ⓙ *jiru ← zuru ← suru (to do)*

Ⓜ **shuúchuu** (suru) 集中する Ⓒ (*gathering+middle*): Ⓝ **concentration**; focusing Ⓥ to **concentrate**; to focus

---

Ⓜ **shinpái** (suru) 心配する Ⓒ (*heart+distributing*): Ⓝ **worry** Ⓥ to **worry**; to concern; to care Ⓐ (na) concerning

❖ M. u. in relation to things or situations.

Ⓛ **kamàu** 構う: to **care about**; to care for; to be concerned about; to mind

❖ M. u. in relation to people.

Ⓛ **kí ni surú** 気にする: Ⓣ to **worry**; to **mind**; to care about;

Ⓒ *ki* 気 *(mood)* + Ⓙ lative p. *ni* + *suru (to do)*

❖ The thing that is the object which one 'cares about' is grammatically a subject, so it takes the nominative p. **ga**.

kí ni nàru 気になる: Ⓘ ① to **care about**; to be concerned ② to be **interested in**

Ⓒ *ki* 気 *(mood)* + Ⓙ lative p. *ni* + *suru (to do)*

❖ The thing that is the object of 'care' or 'interest' is grammatically a subject, so it takes the nominative p. **ga**.

Ⓛ **kurùu** 狂う: to **go mad**; to **go crazy**; to go insane; to lose one's mind

---

Ⓜ **shińjiru** 信じる Ⓢ: to **believe**

Ⓒ *shin* 信 *(faith)* + Ⓙ *jiru ← zuru ← suru (to do)*

shińzùru 信ずる: [*lit.*] to **believe** (in); to have faith

Ⓒ *shin* 信 *(faith)* + Ⓙ *zuru ← suru (to do)*

Ⓜ **shińrai** (suru) 信頼する Ⓒ (*faith+relying*): Ⓝ **trust**; **confidence**; reliance; Ⓥ to **trust**; to have confidence in

❖ To rely on other people's abilities.

Ⓛ **shińyō** (suru) 信用する Ⓒ (*faith+using*): Ⓝ **credit**; **confidence** Ⓥ to **have confidence** (in); to **have faith** (in); to believe (in)

❖ To 'believe' and not doubt about what s.o. says.

shińkō (suru) 信仰する Ⓒ (*faith+looking up at*): Ⓝ **faith**; (religious) belief Ⓥ ① to **believe** (in) ② to have faith (in)

❖ U. in religious contexts, but also fig. in other areas w. the sense of 'having faith' in s.t.

kakúshin (suru) 確信する Ⓒ (*assurance+faith*): Ⓝ **conviction**; belief Ⓥ to be **convinced** (about); to believe (in)

❖ To have a very strong 'belief'.

Ⓛ **kakúnin** (suru) 確認する Ⓒ (*assurance+recognizing*): Ⓝ **confirmation** Ⓥ to **confirm**

Ⓛ **tashíkamèru** 確かめる: to **confirm**; to **check**

tashika (sure) + *transitive suf. meru*

Ⓛ **sańsē** (suru) 賛成する Ⓒ (*approval+resulting*): Ⓝ **approval** Ⓥ ① to **approve** ② to support

（上） yosóku (suru) 予測する ⓒ (beforehand+fathoming)： Ⓝ **prediction** Ⓥ to **predict**

（中） ìken (suru) 意見する ⓒ (idea+looking)： Ⓝ (personal) **opinion** Ⓥ to **have an opinion**

（上） shuchó (suru) 主張する ⓒ (main+extending)： Ⓝ **claim**; **assertion** Ⓥ ① to **assert** ② to **insist** ③ to **claim**

（上） kyōchō (suru) 強調する ⓒ (strong+tuning)： Ⓝ **highlight**; **emphasis** Ⓥ to **highlight**; to **stress**

- -

（上） sózō (suru) 想像する ⓒ (thought+depiction)： Ⓝ **imagination** Ⓥ ① to **imagine** ② to **guess**

❖ M. u. when the imagined thing is realistic.

kuúsō (suru) 空想する ⓒ (sky+thought)： Ⓝ **fantasy** Ⓥ ① to **fancy**; to **daydream**; to **imagine**

❖ M. u. when imaging unrealistic things.

suísoku (suru) 推測する ⓒ (supporting+measuring)： Ⓝ ① **guess** ② **conjecture** Ⓥ to **guess**

mésō (suru) 瞑想する ⓒ (closed eyes+thought)： Ⓝ **meditation** Ⓥ to **meditate**

- -

（中） obóeru 覚える Ⓢ： ① to **remember** ② to **memorize** ③ to **learn**

❖ ❶ Only u. in the sense of remember s.t. that has been actively memorized.

（中） omóidàsu / omóidasu 思い出す： to **remember**; to **recall**

omoi* + dasu (to get out) | *(1) omou (to think)

❖ To bring back to mind an event that has happened before or s.t. that had been forgotten.

（中） kióku (suru) 記憶する ⓒ (writing down+recollection)： Ⓝ ① **memory** ② **recollection** Ⓥ to **remember**; to **recall**

ańki (suru) 暗記する ⓒ (dark+writing down)： Ⓝ **memorization** Ⓥ to **memorize**

（下） wasúreru 忘れる Ⓢ： to **forget** Ⓐ to *forget to ~*

- -

（中） kuráberu 比べる Ⓢ： to **compare**

（上） hikáku (suru) 比較する ⓒ (comparing+contrast)： Ⓝ **comparison** Ⓥ [for.] to **compare**; to make a comparison

tatóèru 例える： Ⓣ to **compare** (s.t.) to; to **liken**

（上） hyòka (suru) 評価する ⓒ (evaluation+price)： Ⓝ **evaluation** Ⓥ to **evaluate**

（上） hàndan (suru) 判断する ⓒ (judgement+severing)： Ⓝ ① **judgement** ② **decision** Ⓥ to **judge**

（上） sàbetsu (suru) 差別する ⓒ (distinction+separating)： Ⓝ **discrimination**; **differentiation** Ⓥ to **discriminate**

（上） homèru 褒める Ⓢ： ① to **praise** ② to **admire**

ⓒ ho 褒 (exalting) + Ⓙ transitive suf. meru: Analogy of the transitive f. of the verbalized f.s of adj.s.

- -

（中） kiméru 決める Ⓢ： Ⓣ to **decide**; to **determine**

❖ U. to refer to decisions by either groups or individuals.

（中） kimáru 決まる： Ⓘ to **be decided**

（中） ketté (suru) 決定する ⓒ (deciding+settling)： Ⓝ **decision** Ⓥ to **decide**

❖ U. when a person reachers a certain conclusion w. a strong will and makes a decision upon it.

kessùru / kessúru 決する： [lit.] to **determine**; to **decide**

← ketsu suru: ⓒ ketsu 決 (deciding) + Ⓙ suru (to do)

sadámèru 定める: to **determine**; to decide; to establish

❖ U. specifically when talking about the will of an organization or group.

⊕ eràbu 選ぶ: to **choose**; to **select**

⊕ seńtaku (suru) 選択する Ⓒ

(*choosing+selection*): Ⓝ **selection; choice**; **option** Ⓥ [*pol.*] to **select**; to **choose**

⊕ kaíketsu (suru) 解決する Ⓒ

(*loosening+deciding*): Ⓝ **solution** Ⓥ ① to **solve**

⊕ yoté (suru) 予定する Ⓒ

(*beforehand+establishing*): Ⓝ ① **plan**(s) ② **schedule** Ⓥ to **plan**; to **program**; to **expect**

❖ Referring to s.t. that has been decided in advance.

⊕ kékaku (suru) 計画する Ⓒ

(*measuring+picture*): Ⓝ **plan** Ⓥ to **plan**; to **program**

❖ Referring to a general idea or set of procedures that are to be u. in order to do s.t.

2.5 Knowledge & Learning

Verbals expressing actions related to comprehension, learning and knowledge.

Important Words

wakaru 分かる	oshieru 教える	shiru 知る
to *und*ə*rstand*	to *t*ə*ach*	to *know*
manabu 学ぶ	narau 習う	benkyō (suru) 勉強する
to *l*ə*arn (deliberately)*	to *l*ə*arn (by repetition)*	to *study*

⊤ wakàru 分かる: Ⓘ to **understand**; to **be understood**; to figure out; to be comprehensible

Intransitive f. of the v. *wakeru (to divide)* ‖ Etymologically this word had the meaning of 'to be divided into parts', notion from which derives the current meaning of 'understand'.

❖ Being this v. intransitive, the equivalent of the direct object of the v. in English is marked in J. with the nominative p. *ga*, which morphologically marks the subject.

❖ The lit. meaning of this word is 'to be or become clear (to s.o.)'.

⊕ rìkai (suru) 理解する Ⓒ (*reason+loosening*): Ⓝ **understanding; comprehension** Ⓥ [*for.*] to **understand**; to comprehend

nińshiki (suru) 認識する Ⓒ

(*recognizing+knowledge*): Ⓝ **recognition** Ⓥ to **recognize**

⊤ oshíeru 教える Ⓢ: ① to **teach** ② to show (how s.t. works; how s.t. is)

⊕ manábu / manàbu 学ぶ: to **learn**

❖ To 'learn' s.t. w. an intention of obtaining a good result from that learning. M. implying a deliberate effort.

⊕ gakúshuu (suru) 学習する Ⓒ

(*learning+learning from*): Ⓝ **learning** Ⓥ to **learn**

❖ In reference to repeated 'learning' done in order to acquire knowledge and skills.

⊕ naràu 習う: ① to **learn** ② to be taught

✦ ❶ To 'learn' s.t. by repeated practice.

⊕ beńkyō (suru) 勉強する ⓒ (*studious+forcing*):
Ⓝ **study** Ⓥ to **study**

✦ Referring to the proactive effort of 'learning' s.t. through study. U. both in a theoretical and in a practical sense.

⊥ buńseki (suru) 分析する ⓒ (*dividing+chop*):
Ⓝ **analysis** Ⓥ to **analyze**

✦ To break down a thing in order to reveal its overall structure and nature.

kaíseki (suru) 解析する ⓒ (*loosening+chop*): Ⓝ
analysis Ⓥ to **analyze**

✦ Referring to the study of things in detail.

Ⓣ shirú 知る Ⓦ: to **know**; to understand

✦ The lit. meaning of this word is 'to get to know'.

✦ In imperfective, affirmative sentences the progressive f. shitte iru is u. In neg. sentences, however, the neg. indicative f. shiranai is preferred.

⊕ shiráseru 知らせる Ⓢ: to **inform**; to let know; to notify

zońjìru / zońjiru 存じる: [*hum.*] to **know**

⊥ utágau 疑う: to **doubt**

końdō (suru) 混同する ⓒ (*mixing+same*): Ⓝ
confusion Ⓥ to **confuse**

2.6 Emotion & Needs

Verbals related to emotions, feelings, hopes and human needs.

Important Words

kitai (suru) 期待する to *expect*	kibō (suru) 希望する to *hope*	nozomu 望む to *desire*
iru 要る to *need*	naku 泣く to *cry*	warau 笑う to *laugh*
okoru 怒る to *get angry*	odoroku 驚く to *be surprised*	osoreru 恐る to *fear*

In Japanese, the notions of 'liking' (*suki*) and 'disliking' (*kirai*), as well as 'wanting' (*hoshii*), 'being afraid' (*kowai*) and 'being embarrassed' (*hazukashii*) are expressed with adjectives rather than verbs [☞ V. 2.1; 2.5].

Ⓣ ài (suru) 愛する ⓒ (*love*): Ⓝ **love** Ⓥ [*lit.*] to **love**

✦ When u. as a v., it is usually done in the progressive f. ai shite iru, or in its col. variant ai shiteru.

✦ Referring to unconditional love for another's person.

⊥ kòi (suru) 恋する: Ⓝ ① **love** ②
endearment Ⓥ to **love**

✦ M. referring to selfish, conditional love.

⊥ ki ni irú 気に入る Ⓦ: Ⓘ to **like**; to be pleased with

ⓒ ki 気 (*mood*) + Ⓙ lative p. ni + iru (to enter)

✦ U. when the object of the liking is experienced for the first time.

❖ The thing that is the object that one 'likes' is grammatically a subject, so it takes the nominative p. **ga**.

konòmu 好む: T to **prefer**; to **like**

❖ Referring to a reasoned liking.

Ⓔ **kańshin** (suru) 感心する C

(*sensation+heart*): N **admiration** V to **admire**

kańshō (suru) 鑑賞する C (*heeding+reward*): N **appreciation** V to **appreciate**

- -

kiráu 嫌う: to **dislike**

nikùmu 憎む: to **hate**; to **detest**

uráyàmu 羨む: to **envy**

netàmu 妬む: to **be jealous of**

❖ M. u. in a neg. sense.

shittó / shìtto (suru) 嫉妬する C

(*jealousy+jealous*): N **jealousy** V to **be jealous** (of)

❖ Frequently u. in the sense of being 'jealous' w. a lover.

- -

Ⓗ yorókòbu 喜ぶ: to **be pleased**; to be delighted; to be glad

❖ M. u. when talking about s.o. else's feelings.

Ⓔ **kańdō** (suru) 感動する C (*sensation+moving*): N ① **excitement**; (deep) **emotion** ② (strong) **impression** V to **be moved** (emotionally); to **be excited**; to be impressed

❖ Usually focuses on a shared feeling or impression.

kańgeki (suru) 感激する C (*sensation+violent*): N ① **impression**; (deep) **emotion** ② inspiration V to **be moved** (emotionally); to be **impressed**; to be **inspired**

❖ Usually focuses on a personal feeling or impression.

Ⓔ **ińshō** (suru) 印象する C (*mark+figure*): N **impression** V to **impress**

- -

Ⓔ **jimán** (suru) 自慢する C (*oneself+ridicule*): N **pride** V to **have pride** (in); to **boast**; to brag

❖ 'Pride' about s.t. related to oneself that it is not necessarily considered to be worthwhile. It is usually understood as an egotistical 'pride'.

hokòru 誇る: to **be proud** (of); to boast

❖ 'Pride' about s.t. that is considered to be worthwhile in the eyes of others.

- -

Ⓗ **kitái** (suru) 期待する C (*period+waiting*): N **expectation** V to **expect**; to **hope**; to **anticipate**

❖ An 'expectation' about s.t. that one wants to see fulfilled when there are high probabilities to that to be fulfilled.

Ⓔ **yosó** (suru) 予想する C (*beforehand+thought*): N **forecast**; **prediction**; expectation; conjecture V to **expect**; to forecast; to predict

❖ To make an 'estimate' of what will happen in advance.

mikómu / mikòmu 見込む: to **expect**; to estimate; to anticipate

*mi** + *kosu (to remain)* |*(I) miru (to see)*

❖ A reasoned 'expectation'.

- -

Ⓗ **kibó** (suru) 希望する C (*exceptional+wish*): N **hope** V ① to **hope** ② to **wish**

❖ Subjective expectation for s.t. that may happen but does not depend on oneself.

Ⓗ **negàu** 願う: ① to **hope** ② to **wish**; to desire

❖ U. specially when making a request to another person or when praying to a god.

Ⓔ **nozómu** / nozòmu 望む: to **desire**; to wish; to expect

✣ Referring to one's own desire or to a request to another person. M. u. when the expectations are not necessarily very realistic.

hossúru / hossúrù 欲する: to **want**

㊦ **irú** いる〔要る〕Ⓦ: Ⓘ to be **needed**; to **need**

❖ This v, being intransitive, marks the thing 'needed' w. the nominative p. **ga** and the person that needs the thing w. the thematic p. **wa**.

izón (suru) 依存する Ⓒ (reliant+existence): Ⓝ **dependency** Ⓥ to **depend** (on)

tayòru 頼る: to **rely on**; to **depend on**

ta* + yoru (to approach) |* ← te (hand)

➤ **tàyori ni surú** 頼りにする: to **rely on**

chùudoku (suru) 中毒する Ⓒ (middle+poison): Ⓝ **addiction** Ⓥ to **be addicted** (to)

- -

㊉ **ańshin** (suru) 安心する Ⓒ (safe+heart): Ⓝ **relief** Ⓥ to **relieve**

❖ Referring to an enduring sense of 'relief'.

hottó / hòtto (suru) ほっと・ホットする [ideophone]: to **relieve**; to **feel relief**

❖ Referring to a brief mental 'relief'.

nagúsamèru 慰める: to **console**; to comfort; to amuse

- -

㊉ **nakú** ❶ 泣く / ❷ 鳴く: ① to **cry**; to weep ② to sing (birds)

na* + O.J. ku (to come) |*← O.J. ne (sound)

- -

㊤ **hohóèmu** 微笑む: to **smile**

hoho (cheek) + currently r. u. emu (to smile)

bishó (suru) 微笑する Ⓒ (faint+smiling): Ⓝ **smile** Ⓥ [lit.] to **smile**

㊉ **waráu** 笑う: to **laugh**

wara* + reiterative suf. u |* waru (to slash)

㊤ **okòru₂** 怒る: ① to **get angry**; to get mad ② to scold; to tell s.o. off; to get angry at

❖ ❷ It is u. as an intransitive v., hence it marks the 'scolded' person w. the dative p. *ni*.

❖ To express the idea that s.o. is angry, it is most frequently u. w. the progressive f. okotte iru.

ikàru 怒る: [lit.] to **get angry**; to get mad

harà (ga) **tàtsu** 腹が立つ: [col.] to **get angry**

hara (belly) + tatsu (to stand up)

ìraira₁ (suru) イライラする〔苛々〕 [ideophone]: to **get annoyed**; to **get irritated**; to lose patience

kòkai (suru) 後悔する Ⓒ (later+regretful): Ⓝ **regret** Ⓥ to **regret**

- -

㊉ **chùui** (suru) 注意する Ⓒ (pouring+idea): Ⓝ **attention**; **caution** Ⓥ ① to **pay attention** ② to **be careful**

kí o tsukèru 気をつける〔気を付ける〕: Ⓘ ① to **take care** ② to **be careful**

ki (mood) + dative p. ni + tsukeru (to attach)

❖ As an intransitive v. it uses the p. **ni** instead of *o* attached to the object.

- -

㊉ **odóròku** 驚く: Ⓘ to **be surprised**

Cognate with *todoroku* (to roar) and also probably a cognate with *odokasu* (to scare) and *odosu* (to threaten).

odórokàsu 驚かす: Ⓣ to **surprise**; to frighten

- -

㊤ **kyòfu** / kyófu (suru) 恐怖する Ⓒ (dreadful+fearful): Ⓝ **fear**; **terror** Ⓥ to **fear**; to dread; to panic

❖ Word that refers to a specific deep fear for s.t. which consequences or results are yet unknown.

osórèru 恐れる Ⓢ: Ⓣ to **fear**; to **be afraid** (of)

Transitive f. of O.J. *osoru (to be afraid)*

❖ It usually implies some worry or concern.

kowágàru 怖がる: Ⓘ to **fear**; to **be afraid** (of)

*kowa** + *garu*† |*(1) *kowai (scary)* | †Experimental p. *garu*

❖ It refers to a rather mild 'fear'.

odósu / odòsu 脅す: Ⓣ to **threaten**; to menace; to frighten; to scare

Probably a cognate with *odoroku (to be surprised)*

❖ This word implies that the 'threat' provokes fear.

odókasu / odókàsu 脅かす Ⓢ: Ⓣ to **threaten**; to menace; to scare

kyóhaku (suru) 脅迫する Ⓒ

(threatening+imminent): Ⓝ **threat**; **coercion** Ⓥ to **threat**; to coerce; to menace

2.7 Sensation & Feelings

Verbals related to physical sensations perceived through the five senses.

Important Words

kanjiru 感じる to *feel*	miru 見る to *see; to look*	kiku 聞く to **hear**	sawaru 触る to **touch**
mieru 見える to *be seen*	**miseru** 見せる to **show**	**kidzuku** 気づく to **notice**	**tsukareru** 疲れる to *get tired*

The most common word used to describe the sensation of 'hurting' in Japanese is an adjective (*itai*) rather than a verb [☞ V. 2.3].

Ⓣ kańjiru 感じる Ⓢ: to **feel**

Ⓒ *kan* 感 (sensation) + Ⓙ *jiru ← zuru ← suru (to do)*

⊕ surú₁ する Ⓘ: to **feel**; to smell; to hear

❖ Only when the felt, smelled or heard thing takes the nominative p. **ga**.

Ⓛ kańkaku (suru) 感覚する Ⓒ

(sensation+awareness): Ⓝ **sense**; feeling; sensation Ⓥ to **sense**; to **feel**

❖ Referring to what is felt through the five senses.

Ⓛ kéken (suru) 経験する Ⓒ

(lapsing+verification): Ⓝ **experience** Ⓥ to **experience**

taíken (suru) 体験する Ⓒ *(body+verification)*: Ⓝ **experience** Ⓥ to **experience**

❖ U. when the experience is particularly related to the five senses.

Ⓣ mìru ❶❷ 見る/ ❸ 観る/ ❹ 診る Ⓢ: Ⓣ ① to **see** ② to **look** (at) ③ to watch ④ to examine Ⓢ to *try ~*

Cognate with *me (eye)*

Ⓣ miérù 見える Ⓢ: Ⓘ ① to **be seen**; to be visible ② to **seem**

Ⓛ gorán ni nàru ご覧になる〔御覧になる〕: [hon.] Ⓣ ① to **see** ② to **look** (at)

Ⓒ *goran* 御覧 (look) + Ⓙ *ni naru (to become)*

Ⓣ **misèru** 見せる Ⓢ: to **show**; to display Ⓢ ① *to definitely* ~ ② *to be determined to* ~

❖ Literal term m. u. when s.o. shows s.t. visibly to another person.

⊕ **shimèsu** 示す: to **indicate**; to **show**; to point out

❖ To 'show' s.t. in order to make people understand.

⊕ **mitómeru** 認める Ⓢ: Ⓣ ① to **recognize**; to **acknowledge** ② to **accept** ③ to **admit**

mi* + tomeru (to stop) | *(I) miru (to see)

mikákeru 見かける 〔見掛ける〕Ⓢ: to **notice**

mi* + kakeru (to hang) | *(I) miru (to see)

miúkeru / **miúkèru** 見受ける Ⓢ: to **observe**

mi* + ukeru (to be given) | *(I) miru (to see)

hyóji / **hyòji** (suru) 表示する Ⓒ (*surface+showing*): Ⓝ ① **indication** ② **expression** Ⓥ ① to **indicate** ② to **express** ③ to **display**

shitéki (suru) 指摘する Ⓒ (*pointing+plucking*): Ⓝ **identification** Ⓥ to **point out**; to **identify**

Ⓤ **ìshiki** (suru) 意識する Ⓒ (*idea+knowledge*): Ⓝ **consciousness** Ⓥ to **be aware** (of)

❖ Understood in the sense of directing one's feelings or senses towards a particular thing.

⊕ **kidzùku** 気づく 〔気付く〕: Ⓘ ① to **notice**; to perceive ② to **realize**; to become aware; to recognize

← *ki ga tsuku (to notice)*

❖ As an intransitive v. it uses the p. **ni** instead of *o* attached to the object.

Ⓤ **kí ga tsùku** 気がつく 〔気が付く〕: Ⓘ ① to **notice** ② to **realize**; to become aware

ki (mood) + nom. p. ga + tsuku (to be attached)

❖ As an intransitive v. it uses the p. **ni** instead of *o* attached to the object.

satóru / **satòru** 悟る: ① to **realize**; to become aware ② to perceive

❖ To detect and grasp things that are originally hidden or difficult to see.

shóchō (suru) 象徴する Ⓒ (*figure+sign*): Ⓝ **symbol** Ⓥ to **symbolize**

- -

Ⓣ **kikú₂** ❶ 聞く / ❷ 聴く: Ⓣ ① to **listen** ② to **hear**

⊕ **kikóeru** 聞こえる Ⓢ: Ⓘ ① to **be heard** ② to be audible

mimì ni surú 耳にする: [*col.*] to **hear**

mimi (ear) + lative p. ni (to) + suru (to do)

Ⓤ **narú** 鳴る: Ⓣ ① to **sound** ② to ring

narásu 鳴らす: Ⓘ ① to **sound** ② to ring

- -

kagú 嗅ぐ: Ⓣ to **smell**; to sniff

niòu ❶ 匂う / ❷ 臭う: Ⓘ ① to **smell** (① good/ ② bad)

❖ Also u. in a fig. sense when talking about s.t. suspicious.

kaóru 香る: Ⓘ to **smell** (good); to be fragrant

---

ajíwàu / **ajíwau** 味わう: Ⓣ ① to **taste**

aji (taste) + derivative suf. wau

---

onáka (ga) **sukú** お腹が空く: to **be hungry**

onaka (belly) + suku (to be empty)

harà (ga) **herú** 腹減る: [*fam.*][*mas.*] [*col.*] to **be hungry**

col. hara (belly) + heru (to decrease)

---

nòdo (ga) **kawàku** 喉が渇く: to **be thirsty**

nodo (throat) + *kawaku (to get dry)*

yòu 酔う: to **get drunk**; to feel sick

➤ yoppárau / yoppáràu 酔っ払う: to **get** (very) **drunk**

- -

⊕ furéru 触れる ⑤: Ⓘ ① to **touch** ② to come in contact with

✤ As an intransitive v. it uses the p. **ni** instead of *o* attached to the object.

✤ It usually has the nuance of a 'gentle' or 'light' touch. It also can be u. in a metaphorical sense. This word can also be u. to imply that the touching is accidental.

⊥ sawáru 触る: Ⓣ Ⓘ to **touch**; to feel (by touch)

✤ It usually implies that the touching is willful. It can be also u. fig.

- -

⊥ shigéki (suru) 刺激する Ⓒ *(piercing+violent)*: Ⓝ **stimulus** Ⓥ to **be stimulated**; to **be excited**; to be motivated; to be aroused

✤ Referring to a force that causes s.o./s.t. to become physically or mentally aroused.

kófun (suru) 興奮する Ⓒ *(vitalizing+rousing)*: Ⓝ **excitement**; stimulation; arousal Ⓥ to **be excited**; to be stimulated; to be aroused

✤ It refers to a heightened sense of emotion.

⊕ tanóshìmu 楽しむ: Ⓘ ① to **enjoy** (oneself)

Verbalization of the v. *tanoshii (to have fun)*

nadèru 撫でる: ① to **stroke** ② to **caress**

- -

⊥ kegà (suru) 怪我する Ⓒ *(weird+myself)*: Ⓝ **injury** Ⓥ to **hurt** (s.o. physically); to injure

itàmu ❶ 痛む/ ❷ 傷む: Ⓘ ① to **hurt** (to feel pain) ② to be injured; to be spoiled

Verbalization of the adj. *itai (to be hurt)*

itámèru 痛める ⑤: Ⓣ ① to **hurt** ② to **injure**

- -

⊕ komàru 困る: Ⓘ to be **troubled**; to be embarrassed; to be at a loss; to be worried

✤ M. u. to talk about psychological or emotional suffering.

⊥ kurúshìmu 苦しむ ⑤: Ⓘ to **suffer**

Verbalization of the adj. *kurushii (painful)*

✤ M. u. to describe a feeling of mental or physical hardship.

kurúshimèru 苦しめる ⑤: Ⓣ to **bother**; to harass

- -

⊥ ijímeru いじめる〔苛める〕⑤: to **torment**; to tease; to bully; to be tough on

jamá (suru) 邪魔する Ⓒ *(injustice+demon)*: Ⓝ **obstacle**; hindrance; nuisance Ⓥ to **disturb**; to hinder; to cause a nuisance Ⓐ (na) troublesome

taèru ❶❷❸ 耐える/ ❹ 堪える ⑤: Ⓘ to **bear**; to **endure**; to withstand; to put up with

fután (suru) 負担する Ⓒ *(carrying+carrying)*: Ⓝ **burden** Ⓥ to **be a burden**; to **bear** (a responsibility)

⊤ tsukárèru 疲れる ⑤: Ⓘ to **get tired**; to **be tired**

✤ M. u. in the perfective f. tsukareta when saying casually that one is tired.

- -

⊥ baránsu (suru) バランスする Ⓔ: Ⓝ **balance** Ⓥ to **balance**

✤ M. u. when talking about movements.

kíṅkō (suru) 均衡する Ⓒ *(leveling+balance)*: Ⓝ **balance**; equilibrium Ⓥ to **balance**

ⓔ ańtē (suru) 安定する: Ⓝ **stability** Ⓥ to **be stable**

2.8 General Actions

Verbals related to general actions done or performed by a subject, and to the use of tools in order to perform those actions.

Important Words

suru する *to do*	okonau 行う *to perform*	tsukuru 作る *to make*	tsukau 使う *to use*

ⓕ surú₂ する ①: to **do**

❖ The verb *suru* has the following extended meanings: *to cost*; *to wear* (accessories); *to be sensed*; *to be* (occupatin/role); *to have* (appearance); *to play* (sport/game).

⊕ itàsu いたす〔致す〕: [*hum.*] to **do**

Causative f. of the v. *itaru (to lead to)*

❖ Normally u. in the pol. f. itashimasu.

⊕ nasàru なさる〔為さる〕: [*hon.*] to **do**

Causative f. of the v. *nasu (to accomplish)*

yarú₁ やる〔遣る〕: [*fam.*][*col.*] ① to **do** ② to undertake ③ to have sex Ⓢ *to ~ (unwillingly)*

ⓕ okónau 行う: [*for.*] Ⓣ to **perform**; to **do**; to conduct; to carry out

⊕ nàsu なす〔❶ 為す /❷ 成す〕: [*lit.*] ① to **do**; to perform ② to **form** ③ to **accomplish**; to achieve

❖ M. u. in idioms.

hastàsu 果たす: ① to **accomplish**; to **achieve**; to carry out ② to perform

ⓕ katsúdō (suru) 活動する Ⓒ (*living+moving*): Ⓝ **activity** Ⓥ to **be active**

⊕ kódō (suru) 行動する Ⓒ (*going+moving*): Ⓝ ① **action** ② behavior Ⓥ to **act**

ⓔ narèru 慣れる: **to get used to**; to become familiar w. Ⓐ to get used to ~

ⓔ hańnō (suru) 反応する Ⓒ (*opposition+responding*): Ⓝ **reaction** Ⓥ to **react**

ⓕ tsukùru ❶ 作る/ ❷ 造る/ ❸ 創る: ① to **make** ② to manufacture ③ to create (s.t. original)

⊕ sésan (suru) 生産する Ⓒ (*born+producing*): Ⓝ **product** Ⓥ to **produce**; to **manufacture**

setté (suru) 設定する Ⓒ (*establishing+settling*): Ⓝ **setup; establishment;** configuration Ⓥ to **establish**; to **set**

mókèru 設ける (Ⓢ): ① to **establish**; to create; to set up ② to prepare (ahead of time)

⊕ jùnbi (suru) 準備する Ⓒ (*level+ready*): Ⓝ **preparation;** setup Ⓥ to **get ready**; to prepare

⊕ yòi (suru) 用意する Ⓒ (*using+idea*): Ⓝ **provision;** preparation Ⓥ to **get ready**; to prepare; to lay out

❖ This word puts an emphasis on 'preparing' things in advance so that they can be u. when the time comes.

ⓔ kùmu 組む (Ⓢ): ① to **put together**; to assemble ② to **construct**; to build; to produce ③ to set ④ to intertwine

Ⓛ **jitsúgen** (suru) 実現する Ⓒ
(*reality+revealing*): Ⓝ ① **materialization** ②
implementation Ⓥ ① to **implement** ②
to materialize

---

tàtsu₂ 建つ: Ⓘ to **be built**

Cognate with *tatsu (to stand up)*

tatèru₂ 建てる Ⓢ: Ⓣ to **build**

❖ Specifically u. for the 'building' of
buildings (houses, apartments, etc)

Ⓛ **keńsetsu** (suru) 建設する Ⓒ (*profit+using*):
Ⓝ **construction** Ⓥ to **build**; to
construct.

❖ U. for the 'construction' or 'building' of
big structures.

Ⓛ **sózō** (suru) 創造する Ⓒ (*preparing+creating*):
Ⓝ **creation** Ⓥ to **create**

Ⓛ **hakái** (suru) 破壊する Ⓒ (*ripping+destroying*):
Ⓝ **destruction** Ⓥ to **destroy**

- -

Ⓛ **tamèsu** 試す: to **try** (out); to attempt;
to test

❖ To perform an action in order to see if
it works.

kokóromìru 試みる Ⓢ: ① to **try**; to test

kokoro (heart) + miru (to see)

❖ To 'test' and see if one can do an
action.

yatté miru やってみる Ⓢ: [*col.*] to **try**; to
have a go

Tentative f. of the fam. v. *yaru (to do)*

hakàru₁ 図る: ① to **plan**; to devise; to plot
② to **attempt**; to aim for

❖ To try to do s.t. having an intention in
mind.

Ⓕ **reńshuu** (suru) 練習する Ⓒ
(*elaborating+learning*): Ⓝ **practice** Ⓥ to
practice

Ⓛ **gańbàru** 頑張る: Ⓘ to **persevere**; to
persist; to keep at

- -

Ⓕ **tsukáu** ❶ 使う/ ❷ 遣う: ① to **use**; to
make use of ② to **spend**; to consume

Ⓗ **mochíru** / mochíiru 用いる Ⓢ: [*lit.*] to
use; to utilize; to make use of

mochi* + iru (to get in) | **(I) motsu (to hold)*

Ⓕ **riyó** (suru) 利用する Ⓒ (*profit+using*): Ⓝ
use Ⓥ to **use**; to utilize; to make use of

❖ Referring to the 'use' of s.t. or s.o. for
benefit of the user.

Ⓕ **shiyó** (suru) 使用する Ⓒ (*profit+using*): Ⓝ
use Ⓥ to **use**; to utilize

❖ To 'use' s.t. for a specific purpose.

Ⓛ **katsúyō** (suru) 活用する Ⓒ (*living+using*):
Ⓝ **application**; practical use Ⓥ to **apply**;
to use

❖ To 'use' s.t. more effectively in order to
achieve one's goal.

- -

morú 盛る: Ⓣ ① to **fill** (s.t. w. s.t.) ② **to
pile** up ③ to serve (a dish) ④ to
exaggerate

---

sosógu / sosògu 注ぐ: Ⓣ to **pour**

tsugú 注ぐ: Ⓣ to **pour**

---

tsukéru 漬ける: Ⓣ ① to **soak** (in); to dip
② to **immerse**

shikú 敷く: Ⓣ ① to **lay out** ② to spread
(out)

Ⓛ **sàsu** ❶ 指す/ ❷❸ 刺す: ① to **point** ② to
stick ③ to **stab**

kosùru こする 〔擦る〕: ① to **rub** ② to
scrub

Ⓛ **hikù** 弾く: to **play** (a keyboard or a
stringed instrument)

- -

Ⓗ **chósen** (suru) 挑戦する Ⓒ
(*challenging+battle*): Ⓝ **challenge** Ⓥ to
challenge

Ⓔ **bóken** (suru) 冒険する Ⓒ
(*risking*+*precipitous*): Ⓝ **adventure** Ⓥ ① to **have an adventure**

- -

midàsu 乱す: Ⓣ to **disturb**; to **disarrange**; to throw out of order

midárèru 乱れる Ⓢ: Ⓘ to **be disturbed**; to **be disordered**; to get confused

soròu そろう〔揃う〕: Ⓘ to **be in order**; to be uniform

soróèru そろえる〔揃える〕Ⓢ: Ⓣ to **arrange**; to **put in order**; to make uniform

❖ It implies a unification of disparate things in order to make them 'uniform'.

totónòu ❶ 整う/ ❷ 調う: Ⓘ ① to **be put in order**; to be in order; to be arranged ② to **be prepared**

totónòeru ❶ 整える/ ❷ 調える Ⓢ: Ⓣ ① to **arrange**; to **put in order** ② to **prepare**

❖ It implies an improvement of the arranged result in comparison to its previous state.

⊕ **sòshiki** (suru) 組織する Ⓒ
(*assembling*+*weave*): Ⓝ **organization** Ⓥ to **organize**

⊕ **narábu** 並ぶ: Ⓘ to **line up**; to stand in a line

Ⓔ **naráberu** 並べる: Ⓣ to **form a line**; to **line up**; to stand in a line

kanèru かねる〔兼ねる〕Ⓢ: to serve several functions Ⓐ ① *to cannot* ~ ② *to not be able to* ~

sokónàu 損なう: Ⓘ to **spoil** Ⓐ *to fail to* ~

Ⓔ **machígàu** 間違う: Ⓘ ① to **be wrong** ② to **make a mistake**

ma (just) + chigau (to be different)

Ⓔ **machígaèru** / machígàeru 間違える: Ⓣ ① to **make a mistake**; to commit an error ② to **confuse**

2.9 Actions of the Body

Verbals related to conscious and unconscious actions performed with the body.

Important Words

aruku 歩く *to **walk***	hashiru 走る *to **run***	matsu 待つ *to **wait***
suwaru 座る *to **sit down***	tatsu 立つ *to **stand up***	neru 寝る *to **lie down***
yasumu 休む *to **rest***	nemuru 眠る *to **sleep***	okiru 起きる *to **wake up***
	taberu 食べる *to **eat***	nomu 飲む *to **drink***

- -

Ⓕ **arùku** 歩く: to **walk**

Ⓕ **sanpo** (suru) 散歩する Ⓒ (*scattering*+*step*): Ⓝ (a) **walk**; **stroll** Ⓥ to **stroll**; to take a walk

Ⓕ **hashìru** 走る: to **run**

Ⓔ **oyògu** 泳ぐ: to **swim**

hàu 這う: ① to **crawl** ② to **creep**

kakèru 駆ける: to **dash**

⊕ **undó** (suru) 運動する Ⓒ (*carrying*+*moving*): Ⓝ ① (physical) **exercise** ② sport ③ active movement Ⓥ to **do exercise**; to **work out**

meshi* + ageru (to give) | **(I) O.J. mesu (to see)*

ⓉⒺ tàtsu₃ 立つ: Ⓘ to **stand** (up)

Cognate w. *tatsu (to be built)*

Ⓣ tatèru₁ 立てる: Ⓣ ① to **stand** (up) ② to put up; to set up

Ⓣ suwáru ❶座る/ ❷据わる: ① to **sit** (down) ② to hold still

koshíkakèru 腰掛ける: to **sit** (on an object)

koshi (waist) + kakeru (to hang)

Ⓣ nerú 寝る Ⓢ: ① to **lie down** ② to **go to bed** ③ to **sleep** (lying down)

ⓉⒺ nemúru 眠る Ⓢ: to **sleep**; to fall asleep

Ⓔ nebō (suru) 寝坊する: Ⓝ **oversleeping** Ⓥ to **sleep late**; to oversleep

Ⓙ *ne** + Ⓒ *bō 坊 (boy)* |**(I) neru (to sleep lying down)*

Ⓔ tetsúya (suru) 徹夜する: to **stay up all night**

Ⓒ *tetsu 徹 (thoroughness)* + Ⓙ *ya ← obs. yo (night)*

yumé (o) mìru / yumè (o) miru 夢見る: to **dream**

Ⓙ *yume (dream) + miru (to see)*

ⓉⒺ okìru 起きる Ⓢ: Ⓘ to **rise up**; to **get up**; to **wake up**

ⓉⒺ yasùmu 休む: to **rest**

Ⓣ màtsu 待つ: to **wait**

kizétsu (suru) 気絶する Ⓒ *(mood+dying out)*: to **faint**

Ⓣ tabèru 食べる Ⓢ: to **eat**

Ⓔ kùu 食う: [*mas.*] to **eat**

❖ This word is preferred when the sense of 'eating' is fig.

Ⓔ meshíagaru / meshíagàru 召し上がる: [*hon.*] ① to **eat** ② to **drink**

Ⓔ nòmu 飲む: to **drink**

Ⓔ kàmu 噛む・咬む: to **bite**

Ⓔ suú 吸う: ① to **suck** ② to **inhale**

namèru 舐める Ⓢ: Ⓣ ① to **lick**

ⓉⒺ fùku / fukù ❶❷吹く/ ❸噴く: ⓉⒾ ① to **blow** ② to emit (smoke) ② to spout (gas or liquid)

Ⓔ hàku / hakù 吐く: ① to **vomit**; to throw up ② to **spit**

➤ tsùba o hàku 唾を吐く: to **spit**

tsùku / tsukù 吐く: to **breathe out**

sekì (ga) deru 咳が出る Ⓢ: to **cough**

Ⓒ *seki 咳 (cough) + deru (to exit)*

Ⓔ kokyúu (suru) 呼吸する Ⓒ *(calling+sucking)*: Ⓝ **breathing**; **breath** Ⓥ to **breathe**

ìki (o) surú 息をする: to **breathe**

iki (breath) + suru (to do)

❖ M. u. for humans.

àkubi / akùbi (o) surú あくび〔欠伸〕: to **yawn**

akubi (yawn) + suru (to do)

ibíkì (o) kàku いびきをかく〔鼾をかく〕: to **snore**

ibiki (snore) + kaku (to crack)

onára (o) surú オナラをする〔屁をする〕: to **fart**

onara (fart) + suru (to do)

---

daíbèn (o) surú 大便をする Ⓒ *(big+convenience)*: to **defecate**

daiben (breath) + suru (to do)

kusò (o) surú クソをする Ⓒ *(big+convenience)*: [*col.*] to **shit**

daiben (breath) + suru (to do)

ùnko (o) surú うんこをする [c]

(*big+convenience*): [*fam.*] to **poo**

daiben (breath) + suru (to do)

ùnchi (o) surú うんちをする [c]

(*big+convenience*): [*fam.*][*fam.*] to **poo**

daiben (breath) + suru (to do)

shóbèn (o) surú 小便をする [c]

(*big+convenience*): to **urinate**

daiben (breath) + suru (to do)

oshìkko (o) surú おしっこをする [c]

(*big+convenience*): [*fam.*] to **pee**

daiben (breath) + suru (to do)

2.10 General Movement

Verbals related to the movement of people and objects, either linear (from point a to point b) or stationary (on-site).

Important Words

iku 行く *to go*	kuru 来る *to come*	tobu 飛ぶ *to fly*
kaeru 帰る *to go back*	mawaru 回る *to turn*	nagareru 流れる *to flow*
noru 乗る *to ride*	tsuku 着く *to arrive*	shitagau 従う *to follow*
tooru 通る *to go through*	sugiru 過ぎる *to pass*	ugoku 動く *to move*
ryokō (suru) 旅行する *to travel*	nigeru 逃げる *to escape*	

ⓣ ikú 行く ①: to **go** Ⓢ *to ~ and go*

❖ It expresses that s.o./s.t. moves in a direction away from the speaker or from the speaker's viewpoint.

ⓛ mukú₁ 向く: Ⓘ to **go towards**; to **face**

ⓛ mukéru 向ける Ⓢ: Ⓣ to **point towards**

mezàsu 目指す: ① to **aim to**; to have an eye on ② to **head for**

me (eye) + zasu ← sasu (to point)

ⓣ kurù 来る ①: to **come** Ⓢ *to have been ~*

❖ M. referring to a movement done towards the speaker.

ⓣ kaéru ❶❷ 返る/ ❸ 帰る Ⓦ: Ⓘ ① to **return**; to go back ② to go back home

Cognate with *kaeru (to change)*

❖ The general sense of this v. is that of 'going or coming back to the place where one belongs'.

ⓣ kàesu ❶❷ 返す/ ❸ 帰す: Ⓣ ① to **return** (s.t.) ② to **repay** ③ to send s.o. back (home) Ⓐ *to ~ again*

⊕ modòru 戻る: Ⓘ to **return**; to go back; to turn back; to recover

❖ Specifically u. to point out that s.o./s.t. returns to the place where he/she/it has come from.

ⓛ modòsu 戻す: Ⓣ to **restore**; to put back ② to **vomit** Ⓐ *to ~ back*

torímodòsu / torímodosu 取り戻す: Ⓣ ① to **get back** ② to **recover**; to regain

ⓛ màiru 参る Ⓦ: [*hum.*] ① to **go** ② to **come**

kayóu 通う: to **commute**; to go back and forth; to attend (a place); to go to (school; work; etc)

⊕ hakóbu 運ぶ: Ⓣ to **transport**; to **carry**

⊥ tsuréru 連れる Ⓢ: Ⓣ to **take** (s.o. w. oneself); to bring along; to go with; to be accompanied by

> Probably derived from *tsuru (to hang; suspend; pull)*

⊤ norú ❶ 乗る/ ❷ 載る: ① to **ride** ② to be **loaded** (placing on top)

⊥ noséru ❶ 乗せる/ ❷ 載せる: ① to **give** (s.o.) **a ride**; to place on ② to **load** (luggage); to carry; to take on board

⊥ uńten (suru) 運転する Ⓒ (*carrying+rotating*): Ⓝ **driving** Ⓥ to **drive**

⊤ ryokó (suru) 旅行する Ⓒ (*travel+going*): Ⓝ ① **travel** ② tour Ⓥ to **travel**

❖ Word only u. for human 'travel'.

ófuku (suru) 往復する Ⓒ (*journey+again*): Ⓝ **round trip** Ⓥ to **make a round trip**

⊥ keńbutsu (suru) 見物する Ⓒ (*seeing+thing*): Ⓝ **sightseeing** Ⓥ to **do visit** (as a tourist)

⊕ tsùku / tsukù 着く: to **arrive** (at); to **reach**

❖ U. when s.t. or s.o. reaches a certain place by itself.

⊥ itàru 至る: [*lit.*] ① to **arrive** ② **lead to** (a place); to **get** to; to **reach** (a point)

❖ U. when s.t. or s.o. reaches a certain place by itself.

⊥ tóchaku (suru) 到着する Ⓒ (*arrival+reaching*): Ⓝ **arrival** Ⓥ to **arrive**

❖ U. when s.t. or s.o. gets to a target location or planned destination.

⊕ ma ni àu 間に合う: **be in time** (for)

ma (just) + lative p. *ni (to)* + v. *au (to meet)*

⊕ todòku 届く: Ⓘ ① to **reach** ② to arrive; to get at

❖ U. when s.t. that been delivered reaches its destination. Also u. fig. when talking about thoughts or opinions.

⊥ todókeru 届ける Ⓢ: Ⓣ to **deliver**

⊥ tassúru 達する: to **reach** (a goal); to get to

❖ M. u. with abstract or fig. concepts rather than physical places.

oyóbu / oyòbu 及ぶ: ① to **reach** ② to span; to amount to

❖ M. u. fig.

⊥ yorú 寄る: Ⓣ to **approach**; to draw near

⊥ tsuújiru 通じる Ⓢ: Ⓘ ① to **lead to**; ② to **flow**; to pass ③ to understand; to comprehend

Ⓒ *tsuu* 通 (*passing through*) + *jiru ← zuru ← suru (to do)*

⊥ mawáru 回る: Ⓘ ① to **turn** ② to revolve; to rotate ③ to go around Ⓢ *to go around ~*

⊥ mawásu 回す: Ⓣ to **turn** (s.t.)

---

megúru 巡る: to **go around**

kakómu 囲む: to **surround**; to **enclose**; to encircle

⊕ tòoru 通る: Ⓘ to **go through**; to **pass through**; to get across; to connect

❖ To go from one side to the other side according to a certain path. Also u. in a fig. way.

⊕ tòosu 通す: Ⓣ ① to **let** s.t. **through**; to **allow through**; to let pass ② to persist; to continue Ⓢ *to ~ through*

⊕ sugìru 過ぎる: Ⓘ ① to **pass through**; to pass by ② to **go beyond**; to be too much Ⓐ *to ~ too much*

❖ Understood as surpassing the established limit of space or time.

㊤ **sugòsu** 過ごす: ⊤ ① to overdo ② to **pass** (time); to spend

---

⊕ **watáru** 渡る: Ⅰ ① to **go across**; to cross over ② to go over; to extend; to span

❖ M. u. when referring to the crossing of a river or a sea.

⊕ **watásu₁** 渡す: ⊤ ① to **carry across**; to **traverse**; to pass ② to **hand over**; to transfer

❖ To move s.t. from one side to the other, also u. fig.

㊤ **kosú** 超す: ① to **cross over**; to surpass ② to pass time

---

chirú 散る: Ⅰ to **be scattered**; to **be dispersed**; to scatter; to dissolve

chirásu 散らす: ⊤ to **scatter**; to **disperse**

- -

⊕ **ùgoku** 動く: Ⅰ to **move**

㊤ **ugókàsu** 動く: ⊤ to **move** (s.t.)

㊤ **idó** (suru) 移動する ⒞ (*relocating+moving*): Ⓝ **relocation**; **movement** (from one point to another) Ⓥ Ⅰ to **relocate**; to **move** (from one point to another)

❖ M. understood in a physical sense.

㊤ **utsùru** 移る: **to move** (from one point to another); to transfer

❖ Also broadly u. in a fig. sense.

hikkòsu 引っ越す: **to move** (house); to change residence

hik* + kosu (to cross over) |* ← hiku (to pull)

㊤ **yuréru** 揺れる Ⓢ: Ⅰ to **shake**; to sway

❖ Referring to a wobbling, continuous motion.

㊤ **furú** 振る: ⊤ to **shake** (s.t.); to **swing**; to wave

㊤ **furúeru** 震える Ⓢ: Ⅰ to **shake**; to shiver; to tremble; to quake

❖ M. referring to s.t. that 'shakes' from a fixed point.

shińdō (suru) 振動する ⒞ (*wielding+moving*): Ⓝ **vibration** Ⓥ to **vibrate**

- -

㊤ **isògu** 急ぐ: to **hurry**

⊕ **tobú** ❶ 飛ぶ/ ❷❸ 跳ぶ: ① to **fly** ② to **leap**; to jump

⊕ **jànpu** (suru) ジャンプする Ⓔ : Ⓝ **jump** ② to **jump**

⊕ **nagáreru** 流れる Ⓢ: Ⅰ to **flow**

Potential f. of the O.J. v. *nagaru** (*to calm down*) |*Intransitive f. of the r. u. v. *nagu (to mow down)*

㊤ **nagàsu** 流す Ⓢ: ⊤ to **make flow**; to distribute; to pour; to shed

- -

⊕ **nigèru₁** 逃げる Ⓢ: ⊤ to **escape**; to run away

nigàsu₁ 逃がす: ⊤ to **let escape**; to set free; to let loose

❖ To let go s.t. that has been caught.

nogàsu 逃す: ⊤ ① to **let escape**; to let go; to set free ② to **miss** 🅐 *to fail to ~*

❖ M. u. fig.

nogáreru 逃れる Ⓢ: Ⅰ to **escape**

❖ To move away from things both before those things have reached the subject or after they have reached it.

---

hanàtsu 放つ: ① to **release**; to free; to let go ② to emit; to hit

kaíhō (suru) 解放する ⒞ (*loosening+releasing*): Ⓝ **release**; liberation Ⓥ to **release**; to liberate

❖ Meaning 'to break free from bondage', specifically referring to human beings.

Ⓔ **shitágau** / shitágàu 従う: Ⓘ ① to **follow** ② to obey

❖ M. u. w. the sense of following s.o. else's instructions or actions.

Ⓔ **oú** 追う: Ⓣ to **chase**; to **pursue**; to run after; to follow

❖ To 'follow' the movement of a target in order to catch it. Also u. fig.

tomónàu 伴う: Ⓘ to **accompany** Ⓣ to be **accompanied by**

tsùite kùru ついてくる〔付いてくる〕Ⓘ: to **follow**; to accompany

tsuite* + kuru (to come) |*Gerundive f. of the v. tsugu (to follow)*

❖ To go together w. another person or thing. Also u. fig.

soú / sòu 添う: Ⓘ ① to **follow along**; to accompany ② to satisfy

❖ M. u. fig.

tsugu ❶ 継ぐ/ ❷ 次ぐ: Ⓣ ① to **succeed; follow up** ② to come after

❖ 'Following' in the sense that s.t. comes or goes after another.

2.11 Up & Down

Verbs that specifically describe upward and downward movements.

Important Words

agaru 上がる *to go up*	noboru 上る *to to go up (by oneself)*
kudáru 下る *to go down*	oriru 下りる *to go down (by oneself)*
ochiru 落ちる *to fall*	furu 降る *to fall (from above)*

Ⓜ **agáru** 上がる: Ⓘ to **go up**; to **rise** Ⓐ *to ~ thoroughly*

❖ Referring to s.t. that goes up w. no own input. It describes the upward movement proper. Also u. fig.

Ⓔ **agéru** ❶ 上げる/ ❷ 挙げる/ ❸ 揚げる Ⓢ: Ⓣ ① to **raise**; to elevate ② to **lift** ③ to fry

mochíageru 持ち上げる Ⓢ: Ⓣ to **lift up**; to raise

mochi* + ageru (to lift) |*(1) motsu (to take)*

❖ To raise s.t. w. one's hands, but also u. fig.

Ⓔ **nobóru** ❶ 登る/ ❷ 上る/ ❸ 昇る: Ⓘ ① to **climb** (up) ② to go up ③ to **ascend**; to raise

❖ This v., being intransitive, marks the object that is being climbed w. the dative p. *ni*

❖ Referring to s.t. or s.o. that goes up by its own means.

Ⓜ **okìru** 起きる Ⓢ: Ⓘ ① to **get up**; to rise ② to wake up

okòsu 起こす: Ⓣ ① to **get** (s.o./s.t.) **up**; to rise ② to **waken**

Ⓔ **kudáru** 下る: Ⓘ ① to **climb down**; to **descend** ② to go down

❖ Focused on the process of descending.

ⓔ kudásu 下す: Ⓣ ① to **lower** (s.t.); to drop (s.t.); to unload ② to **make a decision**

❖ M. u. fig.

ⓒ orìru ❶ 下りる/ ❷ 降りる Ⓢ: Ⓘ ① to **descend**; to go down ② to **get off**

❖ Referring to s.t. or s.o. that moves down by its own means.

ⓔ oròsu 降ろす・下ろす: Ⓣ ① to **lower** ② to drop off; to unload

❖ To move s.t. from the top to the bottom, changing its position.

ⓔ sagèru 下げる Ⓢ: Ⓣ ① to **lower**; to **reduce** ② to **suspend**; to hang Ⓐ *to ~ down*

❖ M. u. when the end of the object is fixed while the other end is moved down.

ⓔ sagàru 下がる: Ⓘ ① to **go down**; to fall ② to decrease

❖ Referring to s.t. that moves from a certain position towards a lower position w. no own input.

ⓒ ochìru 落ちる Ⓢ: Ⓘ ① to **fall** (down); to drop ② to decrease

❖ U. when s.t. or s.o. changes drastically its position from top to bottom.

ⓔ otòsu 落とす: Ⓣ to **drop** (s.t.); to let fall

ⓔ taórèru 倒れる: Ⓘ to **fall** (over/down); to **collapse**

❖ U. when s.t. or s.o. that is upright (standing) tilts and ends up lying down.

taòsu 倒す: Ⓣ to **make fall**; to **overthrow**; to bring down; to defeat

ⓔ koróbu 転ぶ: Ⓘ to **fall** (over/down)

❖ U. specifically for animated objects that fall down while in motion. Sometimes also u. fig.

ⓒ fùru 降る: to **fall**

❖ U. when s.t. falls from above over a wide area.

➤ àme (ga) fùru 雨が降る: to **rain**

➤ yukì (ga) fùru 雪が降る: to **snow**

- -

ⓔ ukú 浮く: to **float**

❖ U. in the sense of 'floating' while moving upwards.

ⓔ shizùmu 沈む: Ⓘ to **sink**; to descend; to submerge; to go under

2.12 In & Out

Verbs that specifically describe inward and outward movements.

Important Words

deru 出る *to go out*	dasu 出す *to take out*	hiku 引く *to pull*
hairu 入る *to go in*	ireru 入れる *to put in*	osu 押す *to push*
	okuru 送る *to send*	

ⓣ dèru 出る Ⓢ: Ⓘ ① to **go out**; to exit; to leave; to get out ② to **depart**

ⓣ dàsu 出す: Ⓣ to **take out**; to get out Ⓐ ① *to ~ out* ② *to start ~*

㊥ **dekákeru** 出かける〔出掛ける〕Ⓢ: Ⓘ
① to **go out**; to **leave** ② to **depart**

de* + kakeru (to hang) |*(I) deru (to go out)

❖ U. when a person is leaving the place where he or she is in order to do some errand.

㊤ **shuppátsu (suru)** 出発する Ⓒ (*out+launch*):
Ⓝ **departure** Ⓥ to **depart**

㊤ **sàru** 去る: to **leave**; to **go away**

hanásu 離す: Ⓣ to **separate**; to **divide**; to keep apart

㊤ **hanáreru** 離れる Ⓢ: Ⓘ ① to **leave**; to go away ② to **be separated**; to be apart

- -

㊦ **hairú** 入る Ⓦ: Ⓘ to **enter**; to **go into**; to get into

hai* + iru (to enter) |*(I) hau (to crawl)

㊦ **iréru** 入れる Ⓢ: Ⓣ to **put in**; to insert

haméru はめる〔c〕Ⓢ: Ⓣ ① to **insert**; to **put in** ② [*col.*] to have sex

❖ To put s.t. in some place so that it fits perfectly.

hamáru はまる〔嵌まる〕: ① to **fit into**; to go into; to fall into; to get stuck ② to be **addicted to**; to be crazy about ③ to be deceived

- -

㊥ **osú** 押す: ① to **push** ② to **press**

osáeru / osàeru ❶ 押さえる/ ❷ 抑える: ① to **hold back**; to **suppress** ② to **restrain**

㊥ **hikú** 引く: to **pull**; to drag

㊥ **okúru** 送る: ① to **send**; to dispatch ② to **spend** (time)

2.13 Wearing Clothes & Accessories

Verbs used to denote the actions of dressing, undressing and wearing clothes and accessories. In Japanese, not a single verb is used to say that someone puts on a garment ('to wear' in English), rather, one verb or another is used depending on the type of garment the subject wears.

Important Words

kaburu 被る to *wear* (on the head)	kiru 着る to *wear* (upper body)	haku 履く to *wear* (lower body)

- -

㊦ **kirú** 着る Ⓢ: ① to **wear** (from the shoulders down) ② to **put on** (from the shoulders down)

㊤ **hakú** 履く: ① to **wear** (clothes for the lower-body or feet) ② to **put on** (clothes for the lower-body or feet)

㊤ **kabùru** かぶる〔被る〕: ① to **wear** (on the head) ② to **put on** (the head)

haméru はめる〔嵌める〕Ⓢ: ① to **put on** (on the hand)

㊤ **sàsu** 差す: to **carry** (under one's arm)

㊥ **nùgu** 脱ぐ: to **take off** (clothes); to **undress**

- -

㊤ **keshò (suru)** 化粧する ⓒ
(*transformed+cosmetics*): Ⓝ **makeup**; cosmetics Ⓥ to **makeup**

soméru 染める: to **dye**

to **wear** on a specific body part	
kaburu 被る	Head
kiru 着る	Upper body
sasu 差す	Under the arm
hameru はめる	Hands & fingers
haku 履く	Legs or feet

to **wear** a specific object	
suru する *to do*	Accessories
tsukeru 付ける *to attach*	
shimeru 締める *to tie*	Neckties, belts...
kakeru かける *to hang*	Glasses

2.14 Open & Close

Verbs used to designate the specific physical or metaphorical movements of opening and closing.

Important Words

akeru 開ける *to open*	shimeru 閉める *to close*

Ⓕ akú ❶ 開く・明く／❷ 空く：Ⅰ ① to **open**; to be open ② to **be empty**

❖ This word expresses the process of 'opening' as an action that unblocks a blocked space.

Ⓜ akéru ❶ 開ける／❷ 空ける／❸❹ 明ける Ⓢ：Ⓣ ① to **open** (s.t.) ② to **empty** Ⅰ ③ to **get bright** ④ to dawn

Ⓕ hiràku 開く：ⓉⅠ ① to **open** ② to bloom

❖ The 'opening' process represented by this word symbolizes an opening that is made from a shrunken gesture to an expanded gesture, usually leaving s.t. exposed. This word can also be u. fig. to

indicate when s.t. is opened to the public, as s.t. is left exposed.

Ⓜ shimàru ❶ 閉まる／❷ 締まる：Ⅰ ① to **close**; to be closed ② to be tightened

Ⓕ shimèru ❶ 閉める／❷ 締める Ⓢ：Ⓣ ① to **close** (s.t.); to shut ② to **tie**; to fasten

❖ To cover an open space by a linear movement such as up and down, left and right or back and forth.

Ⓛ tojìru 閉じる Ⓢ：ⓉⅠ to **close**; to **shut**

❖ To 'close' a space not only w. linear movements but also w. arc-like movements (like a book). Also u. fig.

Intransitive	Transitive	Meaning
aku 開く	akeru 開ける	to **open**
hiraku 開く		to **open** / to **bloom**

173

tojiru 閉じる		to **close**
shimaru 閉まる	shimeru 締める	to **close** / to **tie**

2.15 Start & Finish

Verbals that refer to the actions of starting and finishing something.

Important Words

hajimeru 始める *to **start***	shimau しまう *to **finish***	owaru しまう *to **end***
susumu 進む to **advance**	tomaru 止める to **stop** (moving)	yameru やめる to **stop** (an activity)

Ⓕ hajímaru 始まる: Ⓘ to **start**; to **begin**; to be started

Ⓕ hajímeru 始める Ⓢ: Ⓣ to **start** (s.t.); to **begin**; to initiate 🅰 *to start ~*; *to begin to ~*

⊕ kaíshi (suru) 開始する ⓒ (*opening+starting*): Ⓝ **beginning** (of an event); **start** Ⓥ to **begin**; to **start**

sutàato / sutáato (suru) スタートする Ⓔ: Ⓝ **start** Ⓥ to **start**

- -

⊕ shimáu しまう 〔仕舞う〕: Ⓣ to **finish** (s.t.); to **end** (s.t.); to complete 🆂 *to ~ completely*

Cognate w. *shimaru (to be closed)*

Ⓔ sùmu 済む: Ⓘ to **finish**; to be **completed** 🅰 *~ without any problem*

❖ U. exclusively to express the completion of human actions.

⊕ owáru 終わる: ⓉⒾ to **finish**; to **end** 🅰 *to finish ~*

❖ U. when s.t. stops being as it was.

Ⓔ oeru 終える Ⓢ: Ⓣ to **finish** (s.t.); to **end**; to conclude

Probably cognate w. *ou (to follow)*

shiágèru 仕上げる Ⓢ: Ⓣ to **complete** (s.t.); to **finish up** (s.t.)

shi* + ageru (to rise) | **(I) suru (to do)*

shiágàru 仕上がる: Ⓘ to **be completed**; to **be done**; to be finished; to end

shi* + agaru (to go up) | **(I) suru (to do)*

Ⓔ kańsē (suru) 完成する ⓒ
(*completion+resulting*): Ⓝ ① **completion** ② **perfection** Ⓥ to **complete**; to accomplish

❖ M. u. in relation to the 'completion' of a tangible thing or product.

Ⓔ kańryō (suru) 完了する ⓒ
(*completion+realization*): Ⓝ **completion**; **conclusion** Ⓥ to **complete**; to **finish**

❖ M. u. in relation to the 'completion' of a task.

shuúryō (suru) 終了する ⓒ (*ending+realization*): Ⓝ **end**; termination; closure Ⓥ to **end**

❖ Referring to the 'end' of anything that has started.

- -

⊕ susúmu 進む: Ⓘ ① to **advance**; to **progress** ② to improve

ⓗ susúmeru₁ 進める ⑤: Ⓣ ① to **advance** (on s.t.); to **make progress** (w.) ② to pursue

shìnpo (suru) 進歩する ⓒ (*advancing+step*): Ⓝ **progress**; development; advance Ⓥ to **progress**; to develop; to advance; to improve

ⓕ tomáru ❶ 止まる/ ❷ 留まる/ ❸ 泊まる: Ⓘ ① to **stop** (moving) ② to **stop** (becoming fixed in place) ③ to stay (overnight)

ⓗ toméru ❶ 止める/ 停める/ ❸ 留める ⑤: Ⓣ ① to **stop** (movement) ② to **turn off** ③ to **fix** (in place)

ⓗ yaméru やめる〔❶❷ 止める/ ❸ 辞める〕⑤: Ⓣ ① to **stop** (an activity); to **cease** ② to terminate ③ to quit

ⓛ yòsu よす〔止す〕: Ⓣ ① to **cease**; to **quit**; to desist

ⓗ kuríkàesu / kuríkaesu 繰り返す: to **repeat**

kuri* + kaesu (to return) |*(l) *kuru (to spin)*

todómàru 留まる: Ⓘ to **stay**

todómèru 留める ⑤: Ⓣ to **retain**; to **keep** (in place)

ⓛ koté (suru) 固定する ⓒ (*solid+establishing*): Ⓝ **fix** Ⓥ to **fix**

tsuku つく〔点く〕: Ⓘ ① to **be lit** ② to be **turned on**

tsukèru つける〔点ける〕⑤: Ⓣ to **turn on**; to **switch on**

ⓛ sakú 咲く: to **bloom**

Intransitive	Transitive	Meaning
hajimaru 始まる	hajimeru 始める	to **start** / to **begin**
sumu 済む	shimau しまう	to **finish** / to **complete**
owaru 終わる	oeru 終える	to **finish** / to **end**
tomaru 止まる	tomeru 止める	to **stop**
	yameru やめる	to **stop** / to **cease**

2.16 Give & Get

Verbals referring to the actions of giving and receiving.

In Japanese, the action of giving and receiving is closely linked to the sense of formality and the honorific system by which the speaker has to become aware of what his or her position is with respect to the listener or the person being spoken of. In Japanese, the verbs 'to give' and 'to receive' are expressed differently depending on who the giving person is and who the recipient is. In addition, there is a verb to indicate that one is given something ('to be given'), which has a different connotation from the verb 'to receive'. This notion is important because these verbs are restrictive, meaning that the verbs for 'to give' (such as *ageru*), cannot be used when the person to whom something is given is oneself, thus making the verb with the meaning of 'to be given' (i.e. *kureru*) necessary.

Important Words

ageru 上げる	sashiageru 差し上げる
to *give* (to s.o. equal or lower)	to *give* (to s.o. higher)
kureru くれる	kudasaru 下さる
to *be given* (from s.o. equal or lower)	to *be given* (from s.o. higher)
morau もらう	ukeru 受ける
to *receive* (from s.o. equal or lower)	to *receive* (from s.o. higher)

⊕ **agéru** あげる 〔上げる〕 Ⓢ: ① to **give** ② to **offer** Ⓢ *to do ~ for s.o.*

Cognate w. *ageru (to raise)*

❖ U. when the receiver is of equal or lower status than the giver (the subject).

⊕ **sashíageru** / sashíagèru 差し上げる Ⓢ: [*hum.*] ① to **give** ② to **offer**

sashi* + pol. v. ageru (to give) |*(I) sasu (to shine)

❖ U. when the receiver is of higher status than the giver.

⊕ **atáeru** 与える Ⓢ: [*for.*] to **give**

Potential f. of the O.J. v. atau* (to be able) | *Derivation of the O.J. v. atsu → C.J. ateru (to hit)

❖ U. when the receiver is of lower status than the giver, and also when the given thing is detrimental for the receiver.

yarú₂ やる 〔遣る〕: [*fam.*] to **give**

❖ U. when the receiver is a nonhuman, a person of lower status or s.o. of equal status very close to the giver.

⊕ **kuréru** くれる 〔呉れる〕 Ⓢ: to **be given**; to give Ⓢ *to be done the favor of ~*

❖ U. when the receiver is the speaker, s.o. close to the speaker or s.o. of equal status to the speaker.

⊕ **kudásàru** 下さる: [*hon.*] ① to **be given**; to give ② to confer Ⓢ *to be done the favor of ~*

Shift to weak conjugation from the strong v. *kudasareru:* hon. f. of the v. *kudasu (to lower)*

❖ U. when the receiver is the speaker or s.o. close to the speaker, while the giver is s.o. of higher status than the speaker.

⊕ **watásu₂** 渡す: ① to **hand over**; to transfer ② to give

⊕ **purèzento** (suru) プレゼントする Ⓔ: Ⓝ (a) **present**; gift Ⓥ to **give a present**; to present

okúru 贈る: [*pol.*] to **give** (as a present or gift); to **confer**; to present

⊕ **moráu** もらう 〔貰う〕: to **receive**; to take Ⓢ *to get s.o. to ~*

❖ U. when the receiver is the speaker or s.o. close to the speaker, while the giver is s.o. of equal status. This v. has the nuance that the receiving person is somewhat happy about what he or she has received.

⊕ **ukèru** 受ける Ⓢ: to **receive**; to **get**

❖ U. when s.o. receives s.t. from a person of higher status.

⊕ **ukétoru** / ukétòru 受け取る: ① to **receive**; to **get** ② to accept

uke* + toru (to take) |*(I) ukeru (to receive)

⊕ **itadáku** いただく 〔頂く〕: [*hum.*] ① to **receive**; to get ② to accept ③ to eat

❖ U. when the receiver (the subject) is of lower status than the giver.

❖ The original meaning of this word, still u. from time to time, was that of 'to place s.t. above one's head', which suggests the metaphorical connotation of receiving s.t.

while lowering oneself (with the head down).

❖ M. u. in the pol. f. itadakimasu.

- -

Ⓔ **shónin** (suru) 承認する Ⓒ
(*accepting+recognizing*): N **approval**;
agreement; recognition V to **approve**;
to **agree**; to recognize; to consent

Ⓔ **shóchi** (suru) 承知する Ⓒ
(*accepting+knowing*): N **consent**; **agreement**;
acceptance V to **consent**; to **admit**; to
accept

❖ U. when the 'agreement' or
'acceptance' implies an understanding of
what has been agreed upon.

Ⓔ **nattóku** (suru) 納得する Ⓒ (*fitting+gaining*):
N ① **understanding**; comprehension ②
agreement ③ consent V ① to **consent**;
to **agree**; to **assent**; to grasp

❖ Referring to the 'comprehension' and
'acceptance' of other people's ideas.

Ⓔ **ukéireru** / ukéirèru 受け入れる: to
accept

uke + *ireru (to put in)* | *(I) ukeru (to
receive)*

Ⓔ **kotówàru** 断る: to **refuse**; to **decline**;
to reject

O.J. *koto (word)* + *waru (to split)*

kyòhi (suru) 拒否する Ⓒ (*refusing+no*): N
refusal; **rejection**; denial V to **refuse**;
to **reject**; to **deny**

❖ Referring to a strong 'rejection' of a
wish, request or decision.

kyozétsu (suru) 拒絶する Ⓒ (*refusing+dying
out*): N **refusal**; **rejection** V to **refuse**; to
reject

❖ Referring to an unwillingness to
comply w. a request or wish.

uchíkesu / uchíkèsu 打ち消す: to **deny**; to
negate

uchi + *kesu (to erase)* | *(I) utsu (to hit)*

Reg.	Verb	Action	Giver	Receiver
-	ageru 上げる	to **give** *us to others*	Me / Insider	Equal / Lower
hum.	sashiageru 差し上げる			Higher
for.	ataeru 与える	to **give** *anyone*	Anyone	Lower / Insider
fam.	yaru やる			
-	kureru くれる	to **be given** *others to us*	Equal / Lower	Me / Insider
hon.	kudasaru 下さる		Higher	
-	ukeru 受ける	to **receive**	Higher	Anyone
-	morau もらう		Equal / Lower	Me / Insider
hum.	itadaku いただく		Higher	

2.17 Take & Toss

Verbals related to the action of taking something and also to the action of leaving something somewhere or throwing it away.

Important Words

motsu 持つ *to **hold***	toru 取る *to **take***	oku 置く *to **put***
nageru 投げる *to **throw** (s.t. forward)*	suteru 下さる *to **throw away***	kakeru 掛ける *to **take** (time & money)*

ⓉⒺ **mòtsu** 持つ: Ⓣ Ⓘ ① to **hold** ② to **take**; to get ③ to **have**; to **own**; to posses

❖ It lit. means 'to hold in one's hand'. It also carries the connotation of 'having' or 'possessing'.

➤ **mòtte irú** 持っている Ⓢ: Ⓣ to **have**; to posses

➤ **mòtte ikú** 持っていく: Ⓣ to **take** (away); to **carry** (away)

➤ **mòtte kùru** 持ってくる: Ⓣ to **bring** (an object or a person)

ⓉⒺ **tòru** ❶取る/ ❷捕る/ ❸摂る ❹撮る/ ❺採る: Ⓣ ① to **take** ② to **catch**; to capture ③ to **ingest** ④ to take a picture or video ⑤ to **harvest** Ⓐ ~ *and hold*

❖ This v. means to 'grab' s.t. in order to do a specific action w. it

Ⓔ **torèru** ❶取れる/ ❷捕れる/ ❸摂れる/ ❹撮れる Ⓢ: Ⓘ ① to **be taken** ② to **be caught** ③ to **be ingested** ④ to be taken (picture or video)

toráeru 捉える・捕らえる Ⓢ: Ⓣ to **capture**; to seize; to grasp; to catch

❖ To 'catch' s.t. and hold it tightly in order to not let it escape. Also u. in a fig. sense.

tsukàmu つかむ〔掴む〕: Ⓣ to **grab**; to grip

❖ To 'hold' s.t. firmly w. one's hand. Also u. in a fig. sense.

Ⓔ **tsukámaeru** 捕まえる Ⓢ: Ⓣ ① to **catch**; to seize; to capture ② to **arrest**

❖ To 'catch' s.t. and hold it tightly in order to not let it escape.

nigíru 握る: Ⓣ to **grip**; to grasp; to clutch

❖ To 'grab and hold' an object firmly, wrapping w. the palm and fingers of one's hand.

Ⓔ **shoyúu** (suru) 所有する Ⓒ *(place+having)*: Ⓝ **ownership**; one's possesions Ⓥ to **own**; to posses

tamòtsu 保つ: Ⓣ to **keep**; to **mantain**; to retain

ta* + motsu (to hold) | ** ← te (hand)*

Ⓔ **kakáeru** 抱える: ① to **hold under the arms** ② to **have** (problems) ③ to **employ**; to **hire**

Ⓔ **sasáeru** / sasàeru 支える Ⓢ: to **sustain**; to **support**

Ⓔ **kagìru** 限る Ⓦ: to **limit**; to restrict

Ⓔ **hiróu** 拾う: to **pick up**

Ⓔ **nukú** 抜く: Ⓣ to **take out**; to **extract** Ⓐ *to ~ through*

Ⓔ **nukéru** 抜ける Ⓢ: Ⓘ ① to **be extracted** ② to **come out** Ⓐ *to ~ through*

torídàsu / torídasu 取り出す: Ⓣ ① to **take out**

⎯ *tori* + dasu (to take out)* |**(1) toru (to take)*

Ⓣ okú 置く: Ⓣ to **put**; to **place** Ⓢ ① *to leave ~* ② *to ~ in advance*

Ⓣ kakèru かける〔掛ける〕Ⓢ: Ⓣ ① to **hang** ② to **take** (time or money) Ⓐ *to be about to ~*

⊕ kakàru かかる〔掛かる〕: Ⓘ ① to **be hanging** ② to **take** (a resource; time); to **cost** (money) Ⓐ *to have just ~*

⊕ nagèru 投げる Ⓢ: to **throw**

❖ U. in the sense of 'throwing' s.t. somewhere with a target in mind. Also u. fig.

hóru 放る: ① to **toss**; to throw away ② to let go; to abandon; to discard

❖ U. when the thing that has been thrown doesn't have any specific target. Also u. fig.

⊕ sutéru 捨てる Ⓢ: ① to **throw away**; to discard ② to **abandon**; to forsake; to resign

❖ U. w. the sense of 'discarding' s.t. or getting rid of it. Also u. fig. in the sense of giving up s.t. that one has loved or giving up one's effort.

hazúsu 外す: to **remove**; to **disconnect**; to take off; to leave

nokéru 退ける Ⓢ: to **remove**; to take away

Ⓔ ubàu / ubáu 奪う: to **snatch away**; to **take away**; to steal

2.18 Search & Find

Verbals related to the actions of hiding, seeking and finding.

Important Words

kakusu 隠す *to **hide***	oou 覆う *to **cover***
motomeru 求める *to **seek***	sagasu 探す *to **search for***
	mitsukeru 見つける *to **find***

Ⓔ kakùsu 隠す: Ⓣ to **hide**

Ⓔ kakúrèru 隠れる Ⓢ: Ⓘ to **hide**; to be hidden

himèru 秘める Ⓢ: Ⓣ to **hide**

❖ U. when talking about 'hiding' s.o.'s feelings.

Ⓔ oóu / oòu 覆う: Ⓣ ① to **cover** (up) ② to **conceal**; to hide

❖ It refers to a 'covering' that results in complete hiding of the covered object.

Ⓔ kabùru 被る: Ⓘ to **be covered**

kabúsèru 被せる: Ⓣ to **cover**

❖ To put s.t. on top of another thing. Also u. fig.

Ⓣ motómèru 求める Ⓢ: to **seek**; to **pursue**; to search for; to want

❖ Specifically. u. for abstract things when s.o. 'pursues' s.t. that he or she wants.

179

⊕ sagásu ❶ 探す/ ❷ 捜す: to **search** (for); to **search** (for); to seek

❖ U. in the sense of 'searching' for s.t. that one wants to get or to see (❶), or 'searching' for s.t. that has gone of out of sight (❷).

⊕ keńsaku (suru) 検索する [C] (*examination+search*): $\boxed{\text{N}}$ **search** $\boxed{\text{V}}$ to **search for**; to look up

❖ U. specifically w. the sense of 'searching' for data.

⊕ mitsúkeru 見つける〔見付ける〕Ⓢ: $\boxed{\text{T}}$ ① to **find** (out); to locate ② to **discover**

mi* + tsukeru (to attach) |*(I) miru (to see)

❖ M. u. for physical things.

⊕ mitsúkaru 見つかる〔見付かる〕: $\boxed{\text{I}}$ ① to **be found** ② to be discovered

mi* + tsukaru (to be attached) |*(I) miru (to see)

⊕ hakkén (suru) 発見する [C] (*launch+looking*): $\boxed{\text{N}}$ **discovery** $\boxed{\text{V}}$ to **discover**; to find

❖ U. for both concrete and abstract things.

midásu / midásù 見出す: $\boxed{\text{T}}$ to **find out**; to discover; to detect

mi* + dasu (to get out) |*(I) miru (to see)

miátaru 見当たる: $\boxed{\text{I}}$ to **be found**

mi* + ataru (to hit) |*(I) miru (to see)

2.19 Social Deeds

Verbals used to refer to actions that have to do with social relations and interactions.

Important Words

au 会う *to meet*	yurusu 許す *to allow*	ayamaru 謝る *to apologize*

⊤ àu₁ 会う: $\boxed{\text{I}}$ ① to **meet** ② to **come across**; to encounter $\boxed{\text{A}}$ ① *to ~ together* ② *to ~ to each other*

❖ This v., being intransitive, marks the person or thing that is being 'met' w. the dative p. *ni*.

⊕ deàu 出会う: $\boxed{\text{I}}$ to **meet** (by chance); to **come across**; to **encounter**

de* + au (to meet) |*(I) deru (to come out)

⊤ shókai (suru) 紹介する [C] (*introduction+jam*): $\boxed{\text{N}}$ **introduction** $\boxed{\text{V}}$ to **introduce**

⊕ àisatsu (suru) 挨拶する [C] (*sequential+approach*): $\boxed{\text{N}}$ **greetings** $\boxed{\text{V}}$ to **greet**; to say hi

⊕ àkushu (suru) 握手する [C] (*taking hold of+hand*): $\boxed{\text{N}}$ **handshake** $\boxed{\text{V}}$ to **shake hands**

meńsetsu (suru) 面接する [C] (*face+contact*): $\boxed{\text{N}}$ (job) **interview** $\boxed{\text{V}}$ to **have an interview**

⊕ kańkē (suru) 関係する [C] (*related+correlation*): $\boxed{\text{N}}$ **relationship**; relation $\boxed{\text{V}}$ to **have a relationship**

⊕ reńraku (suru) 連絡する [C] (*along+entangling*): $\boxed{\text{N}}$ **contact** (communication between people) $\boxed{\text{V}}$ to **contact**; to **get in touch**

⊕ dèeto (suru) デートする Ⓔ [*date*]: $\boxed{\text{N}}$ **date** (with s.o.) $\boxed{\text{V}}$ to **date** (with s.o.)

kìsu (suru) キスする Ⓔ: $\boxed{\text{N}}$ **kiss** $\boxed{\text{V}}$ to **kiss**

hàgu (suru) ハグする Ⓔ: $\boxed{\text{N}}$ **hug** $\boxed{\text{V}}$ to **hug**

⊕ idàku 抱く: ① to **embrace** ② to hug

❖ Also u. in a fig. sense.

sèkkusu (o) (suru) セックスする E [*sex*]: N
sex V to **have sex**

ècchi (suru) エッチする E [*aitch*]: N **sex** V
to **have sex**

⊕ **kekkón** (suru) 結婚する C (*tying+marriage*):
N **marriage** V to **marry**

❖ This word, when acting as a *suru* v.
marks the married or to-be-married
person w. the comitative p. *to (with)*.

uwáki (suru) 浮気する C (*taking hold of+hand*):
N extramarital sex; (love) affair;
infidelity V to **cheat on** (a significant
other); to be unfaithful (to a significant
other)

uwa* + ki (feeling) |*ue (over)

- -

⊕ **sańka** (suru) 参加する C
(*participating+adding*): N **participation** V to
participate

⊕ **kesséki** (suru) 欠席する C (*lacking+seat*):
N **absence** V to **be absent**; to miss
(school)

⊕ **yoyáku** (suru) 予約する C (*beforehand+promise*):
N **reservation** V to **reserve**

kyànseru (suru) キャンセルする E [*cancel*]:
N **cancellation** V to **cancel**

- -

⊥ **manèku** 招く: to **invite**

❖ U. in a physical sense but also u. in the
sense of 'inviting' or 'encouraging' s.o. to
do s.t.

⊥ **shòtai** (suru) 招待する C
(*beckoning+waiting*): N **invitation** V [*for*.]
to **invite**

❖ Strictly u. in a physical sense, as in 'to
invite' s.o. to some place or event.

⊥ **sasóu** 誘う: to **invite** s.o. to do s.t.; to
ask s.o. to do s.t.

chódài (suru) 頂戴する C (*top+coronation*):
[*hum.*] N **receiving**; **reception** V ① to
be presented with ② to **receive**

⊕ **tazúnèru₂** 訪ねる S: [*for.*] to **visit**

⊥ **ukágau₂** 伺う: [*hum.*] to **visit**

⊥ **mukáeru** 迎える S: ① to **go out to
meet** ② to **welcome**; to **greet** ③ to
receive; to **accept**

⊥ **atsúkau** / atsúkàu 扱う: to **deal with**; to
treat; to handle

kókai (suru) 公開する C (*public+opening*): N
opening to the public V ① to **open** (to
the public) ② to **exhibit**

kaísai (suru) 開催する C (*opening+signs*): N ①
hosting (of an event) ② opening V to
hold (an event); to **host** (an event)

moyóòsu / moyóosu 催す: T ① to **hold** (an
event); to throw (a celebration) ② to
show signs of; to arouse (emotions)

- -

⊕ **yurùsu** 許す: ① to **permit**; to **allow** ②
to **forgive**

⊥ **kyòka** (suru) 許可する C (*permitting+able*):
N **permission** V to **permit**; to
authorize

❖ M. u. in the sense of a planned or well
thought 'permission'.

⊥ **ayámàru** 謝る: I to **apologize**; to seek
forgiveness

⊥ **kànsha** 感謝する C (*sensation+apologizing*): N
thanks V to **thank**

⊕ **saséru** させる S: to **make** s.o. do s.t.

Causative f. of the v. *suru (to do)*

⊥ **kíńshi** (suru) 禁止する C
(*prohibition+stopping*): N **ban**; **prohibition** V
to **forbid**

- -

⊕ **kańri** (suru) 管理する C (*tube+reason*): N
control; management V to **control**; to
manage

✣ Understood in the sense of taking care of procedures or people's activities.

Ⓛ **shìhai** (suru) 支配する Ⓒ (*sustaining+distributing*): Ⓝ **control**; rule; direction ② dominance Ⓥ ① to **control**; to rule ② to **dominate**

✣ M. u. w. the sense of 'controlling' big groups of people.

Ⓛ **koǹtoròoru** (suru) コントロールする Ⓔ: Ⓝ **control** Ⓥ to **control**

✣ U. w. the sense of 'controlling' the functions of a machine or mechanism or the movements or actions of people.

Ⓛ **kaǹtoku** (suru) 監督する Ⓒ (*overseeing+coach*): Ⓝ ① **supervision** ② control Ⓥ ① to **supervise**; to oversee ② to **control**

kaǹshi (suru) 監視する Ⓒ (*overseeing+sight*): Ⓝ ① **observation** ② **surveillance** Ⓥ ① to **observe** ② to **watch** (over)

⊕ **ēkyó** (suru) 影響する Ⓢ Ⓒ (*shadow+echo*): Ⓝ **influence** Ⓥ to **influence**

Ⓛ **jisshí** (suru) 実施する Ⓒ (*reality+performing*): Ⓝ **enforcement** Ⓥ to **enforce**

shiìru 強いる: to **coerce**; to force (to do)

kyósē (suru) 強制する Ⓒ (*strong+system*): Ⓝ **coercion** Ⓥ to **force** (to do)

bassúru / bassùru 罰する: to **punish**

⊕ **daíhyō** (suru) 代表する Ⓒ (*superseding+revealing*): Ⓝ **representation** Ⓥ to **represent**

mohó (suru) 模倣する Ⓒ (*mold+emulating*): Ⓝ **imitation** Ⓥ to **imitate**

⊕ **kyóiku** (suru) 教育する Ⓒ (*teaching+bringing up*): Ⓝ **education** Ⓥ to **educate**

Ⓛ **sodàtsu** 育つ: to **grow up**; to be brought up; to be raised (as a child)

⊕ **sodáteru** 育てる: Ⓣ to **raise**; to **bring up**; to **rear**

⊕ **nyuúgaku** (suru) 入学する Ⓒ (*entering+learning*): Ⓝ **admission to school**; **enrollment** Ⓥ to **enroll** (in school)

⊕ **sotsúgyō** (suru) 卒業する Ⓒ (*finish+deal*): Ⓝ **graduation** Ⓥ to **graduate**

⊕ **kinén** (suru) 記念する Ⓒ (*writing down+sense*): Ⓝ **commemoration** Ⓥ to **commemorate**

sakúsē (suru) 作成する Ⓒ (*making+resulting*): Ⓝ **writing** (a document) Ⓥ to **fill** (a document)

⊕ **keńkyuu** (suru) 研究する Ⓒ (*sharpening+researching*): Ⓝ **research** Ⓥ to **do a research**

Ⓛ **chòsa** (suru) 調査する Ⓒ (*order+revision*): Ⓝ ① **investigation** ② **survey** Ⓥ ① to **make a survey** ② to investigate

⊕ **shirábeeru** 調べる Ⓢ: Ⓣ to **examine**; to investigate; to search

Ⓛ **hattén** (suru) 発展する Ⓒ (*launch+exhibition*): Ⓝ **development** (creation) Ⓥ to **develop**; to make progress

✣ 'Development' through growth m. in regards to prosperity. Also u. in a fig. sense.

Ⓛ **hattátsu** (suru) 発達する Ⓒ (*launch+exhibition*): Ⓝ **development**; growth (creation) Ⓥ to **develop**; to grow

✣ 'Development' m. understood in the sense of a 'growth' in sophistication or complexity.

Ⓛ **kaíhatsu** (suru) 開発する Ⓒ (*opening+launch*): Ⓝ ① **development** ② exploitation Ⓥ ① to **develop** ② to exploit

✣ U. w. the sense of 'developing' s.t. through the exploitation of resources.

Ⓔ sènkyo (suru) 選挙する Ⓒ (choosing+elevating): Ⓝ elections Ⓥ to have elections

hósō (suru) 放送する Ⓒ (releasing+sending): Ⓝ broadcast Ⓥ to broadcast

2.20 Work & Leisure

Verbals related to physical and mental work and leisure activities.

Important Words

hataraku 働く to **work**	asobu 遊ぶ to **play**	arau 洗う to **wash**
utau 歌う to **sing**	odoru 踊る to **dance**	ryōri (suru) 料理する to **cook**
	kaku 書く to **write**	yomu 読む to **read**

Ⓣ határaku 働く: to **work**

❖ Referring to any use of the body or mind in order to perform a profitable task.

Ⓣ shigóto (suru) 仕事する Ⓒ (making+deal): Ⓝ ① work ② job ③ occupation Ⓥ to **work**

shi* + goto ← koto (thing) |*(I) *suru (to do)*

❖ Focused on 'work' as a means to earn a living.

Ⓔ sàgyō (suru) 作業する Ⓒ (making+deal): Ⓝ ① work ② operation; procedure Ⓥ to **work** (at s.t.)

❖ Focused on the realization of a task.

Ⓔ tsutómèru ❶ f 作る/ ❷ 務める/ ❸ 努める Ⓢ: ① to **work for** ② to **work as** ③ to **put effort** (in)

❖ U. when one becomes a member of an organization to do a fixed job in order to get money.

Ⓔ ródō (suru) 労働する Ⓒ (labor+working): Ⓝ labor Ⓥ to **work**

❖ Referring to the use of physical or intellectual strength to work in order to earn an income. Most frequently u. w. the sense of manual 'labor'.

kìnmu (suru) 勤務する Ⓒ (employed+serving): Ⓝ ① (office) work ② service Ⓥ to **work** (in an office)

❖ U. w. the sense of working in a place where people are employed.

Ⓔ kikú₃ ❶ 効く/ ❷ 効く: ① to **be effective** ② to **work** (function)

Ⓔ doryoku (suru) 努力する Ⓒ (striving+strength): Ⓝ effort; hard work Ⓥ to **strive**

Ⓔ tsurú 釣る: to **fish**

karú / kàru 狩る: to **hunt**

Ⓔ kéyaku (suru) 契約する Ⓒ (pledging+promise): Ⓝ contract Ⓥ to **make a contract**

Ⓔ sàin (suru) サインする Ⓔ (sign): Ⓝ signature; autograph Ⓥ to **sign**

Ⓔ shomé (suru) 署名する Ⓒ (police station+name): Ⓝ signature Ⓥ to **sign**

tóroku (suru) 登録する Ⓒ (ascending+record): Ⓝ registration Ⓥ to **register**

tójō (suru) 登場する Ⓒ (ascending+site): Ⓝ entry; appearance (on stage or screen)

Ⓥ to **enter** (a market); to appear (on stage or screen)

❖ Lit. u. for the concept of 'entering in' or 'ascending to' a stage, which is extended to the appearance on screen. Also u. fig. for the entry in an economic market.

- -

Ⓣ asóbu 遊ぶ: ① to **play** ② to **enjoy oneself**; to have a good time

❖ This word refers to the fact of carrying out any kind of idle activity either by children or by adults.

kakèru 賭ける Ⓢ: ① to **bet**; to wager ② to **gamble**

fuzákèru ふざける 〔巫山戯る〕 Ⓢ: to **joke**

Ⓣ utáu 歌う: to **sing**

uta (song) + reiterative suf. *u*

┌─────────────────────────────┐
Ⓤ odóru 踊る: to **dance**

maú / màu 舞う: to **dance**

❖ M. referring to artistic, slow dances.
└─────────────────────────────┘

- -

┌─────────────────────────────┐
Ⓣ yòmu 読む: to **read**

dòkusho 読書 Ⓒ (*reading+writing*): Ⓝ **reading** Ⓥ to **read**
└─────────────────────────────┘

Ⓣ kàku ❶ 書く / ❷❸ 描く: ① to **write** ② to **draw** ③ to paint

Cognate w. kaku (to scratch)

shìrusu 記す: to **write down**

Ⓤ egàku 描く: to **draw** ② to **paint**

e (picture) + gaku ← kaku (to draw)

Ⓙ nurú 塗る: to **paint**

Ⓙ kazáru 飾る: to **decorate**

Ⓙ shuppán (suru) 出版する Ⓒ (*out+printing*): Ⓝ **publication** Ⓥ to **publish**

heńshuu (suru) 編集する Ⓒ (*compiling+gathering*): Ⓝ **editing** Ⓥ to **edit**

Ⓤ hońyaku (suru) 翻訳する Ⓒ (*turning over+translation*): Ⓝ **translation** Ⓥ to **translate**

tsùuyaku (suru) 通訳する Ⓒ (*compiling+translation*): Ⓝ **interpretation** (oral translation) Ⓥ to **translate** (orally)

- -

yogòsu / yogósu 汚す: Ⓣ to **make dirty**; to stain

Ⓙ yogórèru / yogóreru 汚れる Ⓢ: Ⓘ to **get dirty**

Ⓤ sóji (suru) 掃除する Ⓒ (*sweeping+removing*): Ⓝ **cleaning** Ⓥ to **clean**

- -

Ⓣ aráu 洗う: to **wash**

Ⓙ seńtaku (suru) 洗濯する Ⓒ (*washing+rinse*): Ⓝ **washing**; **laundry** Ⓥ to **wash** (clothes)

- -

Ⓙ abíru 浴びる: ① to **bathe in** ② to **take a bath/shower**

Ⓤ migáku 磨く: ① to **polish** ② to **brush** (one's teeth)

Ⓙ katádzukèru 片付ける Ⓢ: Ⓣ to **tidy up**; to **put in order**

kata (one piece) + dzukeru ← tsukeru (to attach)

Ⓙ sèri (suru) 整理する Ⓒ (*order+reason*): Ⓝ **sorting**; **arrangement** Ⓥ ① to **sort** (out); to **arrange**; to **put in order**

- -

Ⓣ ryóri (suru) 料理する Ⓒ (*foodstuff+reason*): Ⓝ ① **cooking** ② **cuisine** ③ (a) dish Ⓥ to **cook**

Ⓙ tsutsùmu 包む: ① to **wrap up** ② to **pack**

makú 巻く: ① to **roll**; to wrap (around) ② to **envelop** ③ to **wear** (a wrapping thing such a scarf)

Ⓙ uéru 植える: to **plant**; to **grow** (a plant; vegetable)

← O.J. *uu (to plant)*

hṓmùru 葬る: to **bury**

2.21 Help & Harm

Verbals that refer to actions of aid and cooperation and also to actions of competition and conflict.

Important Words

tetsudau 手伝う to **help** (with s.t.)	tasukeru 助ける to **help**	susumeru 進める to **recommend**
naosu 直す to **fix**	tatakau 闘う to **fight**	korosu 殺す to **kill**

Ⓔ tetsúdàu 手伝う: to **help**; to aid; to assist

te (hand) + tsudau* | ← Currently r. u. *tsutau (to follow)*

❖ M. u. in a situation when s.o. helps another person w. work or some task.

Ⓔ tasúkèru 助ける Ⓢ: Ⓣ ① to **help** ② to **save** (rescue)

❖ M. u. when s.o. is helped in order to escape from a bad situation.

tasúkàru 助かる: Ⓘ ① to **be saved**; to be rescued; to escape harm; to survive

Ⓔ kyùjo (suru) 救助する Ⓒ (*saving+assisting*): Ⓝ **rescue** Ⓥ to **rescue**; to save (s.o. from s.t.)

shién (suru) 支援する Ⓒ (*sustaining+assistance*): Ⓝ **support**; backing; aid Ⓥ to **support**; to back

❖ Referring to an indirect type of help.

shìji (suru) 支持する Ⓒ (*sustaining+holding*): Ⓝ **support**; backing Ⓥ to **support**; to back

❖ Referring to the support and recognition of other people's opinions or actions.

Ⓔ kyóryoku (suru) 協力する Ⓒ (*cooperation+strength*): Ⓝ **cooperation**; collaboration Ⓥ to **cooperate**

❖ Referring to the act of helping each other in other to perform a task.

Ⓔ kyōdō (suru) 共同する Ⓒ (*together+same*): Ⓝ **collaboration**; cooperation Ⓥ to **do together** (as equals); to share work

❖ Referring to deliberate joint effort.

Ⓔ susúmeru₂ ❶ 勧める/ ❷ 薦める Ⓢ: ① to **encourage**; to **recommend** (s.o. to do s.t.); to **advise** ② to **recommend** (s.t.)

Cognate w. *susumeru (to advance)*

❖ Referring to the act of telling s.o. what one thinks he or she should do (❶), or to tell s.o. about s.t. one thinks he or she should adopt (❷).

Ⓔ suísen (suru) 推薦する Ⓒ (*supporting+encouraging*): Ⓝ **recommendation** Ⓥ to **recommend**

❖ To 'recommend' s.t. that is considered good for others.

jogén (suru) 助言する Ⓒ (*assisting+saying*): Ⓝ **advice**; **suggestion** Ⓥ to **advise**; to **suggest**

❖ Referring to the act of helping another person by offering useful words.

Ⓔ kékoku (suru) 警告する Ⓒ (*admonition+announcing*): Ⓝ ① **warning** ② **advice** Ⓥ to **warn**

❖ An encouragement to take precautions.

ańji (suru) 暗示する C (*dark+showing*): N ① **hint** ② **suggestion** V to **suggest**

❖ An implication to make another person's mind reach a particular knowledge.

Ⓛ **téan** (suru) 提案する C (*along+proposal*): N **proposal** V to **propose**

Ⓛ **shidó** (suru) 指導する C (*pointing+guiding*): N ① **guidance** ② **leadership** V ① to **guide** ② to **lead**

⊕ **naòsu** ❶ 直す/ ❷ 治す: T ① to **fix**; to **repair** ② to **cure**; to heal Ⓐ to ~ *again*

Verbalization of the adj. *nao (straight)*

❖ The lit. meaning of this word is 'to make s.t. right'.

Ⓛ **naoru** ❶ 直る/ ❷ 治る: I ① to be **mended**; to be **repaired** ② to be **cured**; to be **healed**

tsukúròu 繕う: T to **mend**; to **fix**; to **repair**

← *tsukurau ← tsukura** + reiterative suf. *u* | **Irrealis f. of v. tsukuru (to make)*

❖ U. specifically for the action of returning s.t. to its original state or improving its appearance. M. u. when referring to physical objects.

Ⓛ **shùuri** (suru) 修理 C (*mastering+reason*): N **repair**; fix V to **repair**

❖ M. u. when the repairing process involves complicated procedures.

Ⓛ **chiryó** (suru) 治療する C (*healing+cure*): N **treatment**; cure V to **treat**

Ⓛ **shùjutsu** (suru) 手術する C (*hand+technique*): N **surgery**; (surgical) operation V to **perform a surgery**

Ⓛ **mamòru** 守る: ① to **protect**; to guard; to keep ② to **defend**

ma* + *moru†* (*to put into*) |*← *me (eye)* | †Cognate w. *miru (to see)*

❖ ❶ U. in the sense of 'keeping' s.t. as it is.

bóē (suru) 防衛する C (*defending+protection*): N **defense** V ① to **defend** ② to protect

hògo (suru) 保護する C (*protecting+defense*): N ① **protection**; safeguard ② preservation V ① to **protect** ② to preserve

---

fusègu 防ぐ: ① to **prevent** ② to defend (against); to **defend** (against)

samátagèru 妨げる S: ① to **prevent** ② to **hinder**; to obstruct

❖ M. referring to abstract things.

habàmu 阻む: ① to **prevent**; to hinder; to thwart; to obstruct ② to **oppose**

❖ M. referring to physical things.

⊕ **kyósō** (suru) 競争する C (*competing+fight*): N **competition** V to **compete**

arásòu 争う: ① to **compete** ② to **argue**; to quarrel ③ to fight against

---

semèru ❶ 攻める/ ❷❸ 責める S: ① to **attack** ② to **blame**; to accuse ③ to **criticize**

Ⓛ **kógeki** (suru) 攻撃する C (*attacking+beating*): N ① **attack** ② condemnation; denunciation V ① to **attack** ② to denounce

---

Ⓛ **keńka** (suru) 喧嘩する C (*boisterous+noisy*): N **fight**; **quarrel**; argument V to **fight**; to **quarrel**; to argue

❖ M. u. for physical or verbal 'fights' among two people.

Ⓛ **tatákau** ❶ 戦う/ ❷ 闘う: ① to **fight**; to combat ② to fight an obstacle; to struggle

tataka* + reiterative suf. *u* | **Irrealis f. of v. tataku (to strike)*

❖ M. u. in relation to battles or wars.

seńtō (suru) 戦闘する Ⓒ (battle+contending): Ⓝ combat; battle; fight Ⓥ ① to combat ② to fight

❖ M. u. in the sense of 'fighting' w. weapons, such as in the context of war.

Ⓔ korósu 殺す: to kill

Ⓔ urágìru 裏切る Ⓦ: to betray

ura (behind) + giru ← kiru (to cut)

Ⓔ bakúhatsu (suru) 爆発する Ⓒ (explosion+launch): Ⓝ explosion Ⓥ to explode

okàsu / okásu ❶❷ 犯す/ ❸ 侵す: ① to commit (a crime); to break (the law) ② to invade

Cognate w. *okosu (to rise)*

gómon (suru) 拷問する Ⓒ (torture+asking): Ⓝ torture Ⓥ to torture

yuúkai (suru) 誘拐する Ⓒ (persuading+kidnapping): Ⓝ kidnapping; abduction Ⓥ to kidnap

fukúshuu (suru) 復讐する Ⓒ (again+enemy): Ⓝ revenge Ⓥ to revenge

Ⓔ nusùmu 盗む: to steal

damàsu 騙す: to deceive; to cheat; to trick

Ⓔ osén (suru) 汚染する Ⓒ (dirty+dying): Ⓝ pollution Ⓥ to pollute

- - - - - - - - - - - - - - - - - -

Ⓜ hantai (suru) 反対する Ⓒ (reverse+opposite): Ⓝ ① opposition ② resistance Ⓥ to oppose

❖ M. u. for abstract things.

hań sùru 反する: to be contrary to; to oppose; to go against; to transgress

Ⓒ *han 反 (reverse) + suru (to do)*

❖ M. referring to the fact of disobeying or 'opposing' s.o.'s intentions, orders or rules.

Ⓔ sakáràu 逆らう: ① to go against; to oppose ② to defy

❖ U. for both physical things (directions) and abstract things.

2.22 Gain & Loss

Verbals related to the notions of obtaining something and losing it.

Important Words

eru 得る *to get*		katsu 勝つ *to win*	makeru 負ける *to lose*
	ushinau 失う *to lose (s.t.)*	nakusu なくす *to lose (misplace)*	

Ⓕ èru 得る Ⓢ: Ⓣ to get; to obtain; to gain Ⓐ ① to be possible to ~ ② to be ~able

❖ M. u. for things that affect oneself.

Ⓔ kasègu 稼ぐ: to earn (an income); to make a living

Ⓔ rìeki (suru) 利益する Ⓒ (profit+benefit): Ⓝ ① profit; gains ② advantage Ⓥ to profit

Ⓔ osámèru 収める・納める Ⓢ: Ⓣ ① to supply ② to achieve

osámàru 収まる・納まる: Ⓘ to settle down; to be settled

- - - - - - - - - - - - - - - - - -

Ⓜ kàtsu 勝つ: Ⓘ to win

✤ M. u. for personal and everyday matters.

Ⓛ shòri (suru) 勝利する Ⓒ (winning+profit): Ⓝ **victory** Ⓥ to **win**

✤ M. u. for big events.

---

makásu 負かす: Ⓣ to **defeat**; to win (against s.o.)

⊕ makéru 負ける Ⓢ: Ⓘ to **lose**; to be defeated

⊕ ushínau 失う: Ⓣ to **lose** (s.t.)

✤ Referring specifically to the 'loss' of s.t., tangible or intangible, due to external factors. M. understood w. the sense that the lost will be hard to be taken back later.

⊕ nakúsu なくす〔❶ 無くす/❸ 亡くす〕: Ⓣ ① to **lose** (s.t.); to misplace ② to get ride of ③ to lose s.o. (through death)

✤ ❶ M. referring to the 'loss' of tangible things that can be later somehow taken back.

Ⓛ nakúnaru なくなる〔無くなる〕: Ⓘ to **be lost**; to be missing; to disappear

naku + *naru (to become)* |*Adverbial f. of the adj. *nai (not to be)*

---

nigàsu₂ 逃がす: Ⓣ to **let go**; to **miss** (fail to get)

Ⓛ nigèru₂ 逃げる Ⓢ: Ⓘ to get **away**; to **escape**

Ⓛ shóhi / shòhi (suru) 消費する Ⓒ (*disappearing+spending*): Ⓝ **consumption** Ⓥ to **consume**

⊕ sékō (suru) 成功する Ⓒ (*resulting+success*): Ⓝ **success** Ⓥ ① to be **successful**

⊕ shippái (suru) 失敗する Ⓒ (*losing+failing*): Ⓝ ① **failure** Ⓥ to **fail**

2.23 Add & Subtract

Verbals related to the union and accumulation of things and also to their separation and reduction.

Important Words

tsukeru 付ける *to attach*	au 合う *to unite*	mazeru 混ぜる *to mix*
wakeru 分ける *to split*	tasu 足す *to add*	atsumeru 集める *to gather*

Ⓣ tsùku / tsukù つく〔付く〕: Ⓘ to **be attached**; to **stick**; to adhere

Ⓣ tsukèru つける〔付ける〕Ⓢ: Ⓣ ① to **attach** ② to join ③ to add Ⓐ ① *to become used to ~* ② *to usually ~* ③ *to ~ vigorously*

⊕ àu₂ 合う Ⓢ: Ⓘ to **come together**; to **merge**; to unite; to meet Ⓐ *to ~ together*

Cognate w. *au (to meet)*

Ⓛ awásèru 合わせる Ⓢ: Ⓣ ① to **match** ② to **join** (together) ③ to combine

awasaru 合わさる: Ⓘ to **match**

---

mazèru 混ぜる Ⓢ: Ⓣ to **mix**; to blend

mazàru 交ざる・混ざる: Ⓘ to **be mixed**; to mingle with

majìru 混じる Ⓢ: 🄸 ① to **mingle with**; to blend with; to be mixed with; to intermingle ② to associate with

✤ To be 'mixed' into a large quantity.

㊤ **wakèru** 分ける Ⓢ: 🅃 ① to **separate**; to **split**; to divide ② to **distribute**; to share 🅰 *the proper way to ~*

✤ ❶ To 'divide' one thing, or several things that come together to form one united entity, into multiple groups.

㊤ **wakárèru** ❶ 分かれる/ ❷ 別れる Ⓢ: 🄸 ① to **be divided**; to be split ② to be separated (from another person)

㊤ **warú** 割る: 🅃 ① to **divide**; to **split** ② to **break**; to rip

✤ M. u. for the division of physical things.

waréru 割れる Ⓢ: 🄸 to **be divided**; to **be split**

㊤ **buńri** (suru) 分離する 🄲 (*dividing+leaving*): 🄽 **separation**; isolation 🅅 to **separate**; to detach

✤ 'Separation' in the sense of breaking apart things that have been united into one. Also u. w. the sense of keeping things 'separate' without being united.

㊥ **tasú** 足す: 🅃 ① to **add** (sum)

✤ Referring to the 'addition' of things of the same type. Also u. w. mathematical operations.

㊤ **kuwáeru** / kuwáèru 加える Ⓢ: 🅃 to **add**; to sum (up)

✤ It refers to an increase in the number of both different things and the same type of things.

㊤ **kuwáwaru** / kuwáwàru 加わる: 🄸 ① to **be added** ② to **join in** ③ to participate ④ to increase

---

tsumú 積む: 🅃 to **pile up**; to **stack**

✤ Lit., to 'pile' one thing on top of another.

tsumòru / tsumóru 積もる: 🄸 ① to **pile up**; to **accumulate** ② to **estimate**

✤ M. u. when the accumulation is excessive.

tsumèru 詰める Ⓢ : 🅃 to **pack**; to jam; to stuff into

✤ Also u. fig.

tsumàru 詰まる: 🄸 ① to **be packed** (with); to **be full** (space) ② to be blocked ③ to be settled

✤ Referring to the state of being 'full' of things.

㊥ **atsúmèru** 集める Ⓢ: 🅃 to **collect**; to **gather**

← aitsumeru: ai + tsumeru (to stuff into)* | *(I) *au (to meet)*

㊥ **atsúmàru** 集まる: 🄸 ① to **gather** ② to **come together**

shuúshuu (suru) 収集する 🄲 (*yielding+gathering*): 🄽 **collection** 🅅 **to collect**; to gather

✤ M. u. w. the sense of 'collecting' goods or items for study or as a hobby.

---

taméru ためる〔❶ 溜める/ ❷ 貯める〕: 🅃 ① to **store** ② to **save** (money)

tamáru たまる〔❶ 溜める/ ❷ 貯める〕: 🄸 ① to **be stored** ② to **be saved up** (money)

㊤ **chokín** (suru) 貯金する 🄲 (*savings+money*): 🄽 **savings** 🅅 to **save** (money); to put money aside.

㊤ **gőkei** (suru) 合計する 🄲 (*together+measuring*): 🄽 (the) **total** (amount) 🅅 to **sum** (up)

ⓒ fuèru 増える・殖える Ⓢ: Ⓘ to **increase**

ⓑ fuyàsu 増やす: Ⓣ to **increase**

❖ M. u. for an 'increase' of quantity.

ⓑ masú 増す: Ⓣ to **increase**; to **grow**

❖ M. u. for an 'increase' of degree.

ⓑ zóka (suru) 増加する Ⓒ (*increasing+adding*): Ⓝ ① **increase**; rise ③ **growth** Ⓥ ① to **increase** ② to **grow**

❖ M. u. for an 'increase' of quantity.

ⓑ séchō (suru) 成長する Ⓒ (*resulting+long*): Ⓝ **growth** Ⓥ to **grow**

❖ Only u. to refer to the growth of persons or things but not to the increment in the number of things.

ⓑ kakúdai (suru) 拡大する Ⓒ (*extension+big*): Ⓝ **enlargement** Ⓥ to **enlarge**

ⓒ kakèru 掛ける Ⓢ: ① to **multiply**

Cognate w. *kakeru (to hang)*

ⓒ hikú 引く: ① to **subtract**

Cognate w. *hiku (to drag)*

ⓑ herú 減る Ⓦ: Ⓘ to **decrease**; to **be reduced**

ⓑ herásu 減らす: Ⓣ to **decrease**; to **diminish**; to **reduce**; to **shorten**

2.24 Count & Measure

Verbals related to quantity and measurement.

Important Words

kazoeru 数える *to* **count**	tariru 足りる *to be enough*	kakeru 欠ける *insufficient*

ⓑ kazóèru 数える Ⓢ: to **count**

ⓑ hakàru₂ ❶❷ 測る/ ❸ 計る: ① to **measure** ② to **weigh** ③ to **count** (time or numbers)

Cognate w. *hakaru (to plan)*

ⓑ késan (suru) 計算する Ⓒ (*reckoning+calculation*): Ⓝ **calculation** Ⓥ ① to **reckon** ② to **count**

tarú 足る: [*lit.*] to **be enough**; to **suffice**

Cognate w. *tasu (to add)*

taríru 足りる Ⓢ: to **be enough**; to be **sufficient**

michìru 満ちる Ⓢ: Ⓘ to **be full**

mitàsu 満たす: Ⓣ ① to **fill** (up) ② to **satisfy**; to **fulfill**

kòmu 込む: Ⓘ ① to **become crowded**; to **get packed** Ⓐ to ~ *thoroughly*

komèru 込める Ⓢ: Ⓣ ① to **include** ② to **load**

ⓑ koéru ❶ 超える/ ❷ 越える: ① to **pass** (through); to **surpass** ② to **exceed**; to be **more than**

kakú 欠く: Ⓘ to **lack**

ⓑ kakéru 欠ける: Ⓘ ① to be **insufficient**; to be **short** (of) ② to **wane**

2.25 Trade & Exchange

Verbs and verbal nouns related to buying, selling, lending and economic transactions in general.

Important Words

uru 売る *to sell*	kau 買う *to buy*	kasu 貸す *to lend*	kariru 借りる *to borrow*

下 urú 売る: T to **sell**

Cognate w. O.J. *uru (to get)* → C.J. *eru*

❖ Also u. fig.

上 uréru 売れる S: I to **sell** (well); to be sold

haṅbai (suru) 販売する c (*sale+selling*): N **sales**; selling V to **sell**

❖ M. u. in business environments, under the context of regulated trade.

下 kaú 買う: to **buy**

中 haràu 払う: ① to **pay** ② to give away

tsuíyàsu 費やす: to **spend**; to **expend**

中 kasú 貸す: to **lend**

中 karíru 借りる S: ① to **borrow** ② to **rent** (from s.o.) ③ to owe

上 ryṓgae (suru) 両替する c (*both+exchanging*): N **money exchange** V to **exchange money**

中 ḗgyō (suru) 営業する c (*conducting+deal*): N **business** (activity) V to **trade**

❖ Term referring to 'business' as the activity or work that is required in order to maintain a business operation.

中 kēḗ (suru) 経営する c (*lapsing+conducting*): N **management**; administration V to **manage** (a business); to run (a business)

中 kṓkoku (suru) 広告する c (*wide+announcing*): N **advertisement** V to **advertise**

上 tṓshi / tòshi (suru) 投資する c (*throwing+assets*): N **investment** V to **invest**

上 tḗkyō (suru) 提供する c (*along+providing*): N **offer** V to **make an offer**

上 chuúmon (suru) 注文する c (*pouring+writings*): N **order** (for an item) V to **order** (an item)

上 yushútsu (suru) 輸出する c (*transport+going out*): N **export** V to **export**

上 yunyúu (suru) 輸入する c (*transport+entering*): N **import** V to **import**

2.26 Hit & Break

Verbs related to hitting, bending and breaking.

Important Words

utsu 打つ *to hit*	ataru 当たる *to be hit*	kowasu 壊す *to break*	kiru 切る *to cut*

⊕ ùtsu ❶ 打つ/ ❷ 撃つ / ❸ 討つ: ① to **hit**; to **beat**; **to strike** ② to **shoot** ③ to attack an opponent

❖ U. for both intentional and unintentional 'hits', m. while using a tool or weapon.

bùtsu ぶつ〔打つ〕: to **strike**; to beat

❖ U. specifically for hits to animate things.

nagùru 殴る: to **hit**; to **strike**; to punch

Cognate w. *nageru (to throw)*

❖ It m. refers to a violent 'hit' w. the hand or w. a weapon.

tatàku 叩く: ① to **strike**; to **beat** ② to **clap**

❖ U. specifically when s.o. 'hits' a target (m. an inanimate object) w. bare hands, implying a repetition of 'strikes'. Also u. fig. It doesn't necessarily imply a violent action.

⊥ atéru 当てる Ⓢ: Ⓣ to **hit**

❖ The focus of this v. is on the 'hit' itself (the result or the receiving part), rather than the action of 'hitting' itself (the process or the proactive part).

❖ This v. is highly u. in a fig. sense.

⊕ atáru 当たる: Ⓘ ① to (be) **hit**

tsukú / tsùku 突く: ① to **poke** ② to **stab**

- -

magáru 曲がる: Ⓘ ① to **bend** ② to turn

magéru 曲がる Ⓢ: Ⓣ to **bend**

⊥ òru 折る: Ⓣ ① to **bend** ② to **fold** ③ **to break** (off); to snap (off)

❖ It implies a bending at a right angle that usually ends up in a break or snap of the object.

---

orèru 折れる Ⓢ: Ⓘ ① to **break** ② to **snap**

⊥ kowàsu 壊す: Ⓣ ① to **break** ② to **wreck**; to destroy ③ to ruin

❖ Normally u. when some object's function stops working.

kowáreru 壊れる Ⓢ: Ⓘ to **break**; to be broken

kuzùsu 崩す: Ⓣ ① to **destroy** ② to **demolish**; to tear down

❖ It refers to the sense of losing the unity of things.

---

tsubúsu 潰す: Ⓣ to **smash**; to crush

tsubúreru 潰れる: Ⓘ ① to **be smashed** ② to **become ruined**

⊥ yabùru 破る: Ⓣ ① to **tear** ② to **smash**; to **destroy** ③ to **defeat**

❖ M. u. w. big objects.

sàku ❶ 裂く/ ❷ 割く: Ⓘ ① to **tear** ② to **spare** (time or money)

⊥ sakèru ❶ 避ける/ ❷ 裂ける: Ⓣ ① to **avoid** ② to **tear** (s.t.); to split

❖ ❷ M. u. w. thin objects.

Ⓕ kirú ❶❷ 切る/ ❸ 斬る Ⓦ: Ⓣ ① to **cut** ② to turn off (power or light) ③ to **slice** Ⓐ *to ~ completely*

karú 刈る: to **cut** (grass; hair); to **reap**; to clip; to trim

---

sòru 剃る: to **shave** (body hair)

mukú₂ むく〔剥く〕: to **peel**; to skin

➤ kawa (o) mukú 皮をむく〔皮お剥く〕

hòru 掘る: to **dig**

2.27 Connect & Disconnect

Verbals related to union and disunion.

Important Words

tsunagu	musubu	hodoku	toku
繋ぐ *to fasten*	結ぶ *to tie*	解く *to unfasten*	解く *to untie*

tsunágu つなぐ〔繋ぐ〕: Ⓣ ① to **tie** ② to **fasten** ③ **to connect**

tsuna (rope) + derivative suf. *gu*

Ⓤ tsunágaru つなげる〔繋がる〕: Ⓘ ① to **connect**; to **be connected**; to **be linked** ② to be tied together ③ to be fastened

Ⓤ musúbu 結ぶ: Ⓣ ① to **tie**; to **bind** ② to **link**

❖ U. for the 'tying' of slender things such as strings or laces. Also u. fig.

shibàru 縛る: Ⓣ to **bind**; to tie

❖ U. specifically for the 'binding' of things with ropes, although it can be also u. fig.

Ⓤ hodòku ほどく〔解く〕: Ⓣ ① to **untie** ② to unfasten

Ⓤ hodókèru ほどける〔解ける〕 Ⓢ: Ⓘ ① to **be untied** ② to be unfastened

Ⓤ tòku ❶❷❸ 解く / ❹ 説く: Ⓣ ① to **untie** ② to **solve** ③ to relieve ④ to explain

❖ Also u. fig.

Ⓤ tokèru 解ける Ⓢ: Ⓘ ① to **untie** ② to **be solved** ③ to be relieved

Ⓤ tóitsu (suru) 統一する Ⓒ *(supervising+one)*: Ⓝ **unification**; unity Ⓥ to **unify**

3. HONORIFIC VERBS

List of verbs that have different humble and honorific versions.

The humble versions of the verbs are used when the subject of the action is oneself and one wants to show respect to the listener, while the honorific versions are used when one wants to show respect to the subject of the action.

plain verb	meaning	*humble*	*honorific*
aru ある	to **be** (inanimate)	[*pol.*] gozaimasu ございます	irassharu いらっしゃる
iru いる	to **be** (animate)	oru おる	
iku 行く	to **go**	mairu 参る	
kuru 来る	to **come**		
suru する	to **do**	itasu 致す	nasaru なさる
iu 言う	to **say**	mōsu 申す ——— mōshiageru 申し上げる	ossharu おっしゃる
shiru 知る	to **know**	zonjiru 存じる	gozonji ご存知
[*pol.*] ageru 上げる	to **give**	sashiageru 差し上げる	-
kureru くれる	to **be given**	-	kudasaru 下さる
morau もらう	to **receive**	itadaku いただく	-
taberu 食べる	to **eat**		meshiagaru 召し上がる
nomu 飲む	to **drink**		
miru 見る	to **see**		goran ni naru ご覧になる
kiku 聞く	to **ask**	ukagau 伺う	-
[*for.*] tazuneru 尋ねる			
[*for.*] tazuneru 訪ねる	to **visit**		

4. HOMOPHONE VERBS

Here are listed the homophone verbs appearing in this section, that is, the verbs that with the same phonemes designate different concepts. There are multiple—homophones with more than two different meanings—and double—homophones with substantially two different meanings.

4.1 Multiple Homophone Verbs

akeru	開ける to **open**	明ける to **get bright**	空ける to **empty**		
kaeru	返る to **return**	帰る to **go back**	変える to **change**	換える to **exchange**	替える to **replace**
kakeru	書ける to **be written**	描ける to **be drawn**	欠ける to **be insufficient**		
	かける to **take**	掛ける to **hang**	駆ける to **dash**	賭ける to **bet**	
kaku	書く to **write**	描く to **draw**	欠く to **lack**		
kiku	聞く to **hear**	聴く to **listen**	訊く to **ask**	効く to **function**	
saku	咲く to **bloom**	裂く to **tear**	割く to **spare**		
sasu	指す to **point**	刺す to **stab**	差す to **wear**		
tatsu	立つ to **stand**	建つ to **build**	経つ to **elapse**		
tsukeru	付ける to **be attached**	点ける to **turn on**	漬ける to **soak**		
tsuku	付く to **attach**	着く to **arrive**	突く to **poke**	吐く to **breath out**	点く to **be lit**

4.2 Double Homophone Verbs

ageru	上げる to **rise**	上げる to **give**
aku	開く to **be open**	空く to **be empty**
furu	降る to **go down**	振る to **shake**
hakaru	図る to **plan**	測る to **measure**
haku	吐く to **vomit**	履く to **wear** (lower body)
hanasu	話す to **talk**	離す to **separate**
hiku	引く to **pull**	弾く to **play** (an instrument)
iru	いる to **be** (at)	要る to **need**
karu	刈る to **clip**	狩る to **hunt**
kiru	Ⓦ 切る to **cut**	Ⓢ 着る to **wear** (upper body)
kureru	くれる to **give**	暮れる to **get dark**
muku	向く to **face**	剥く to **peel**
naru	なる to **become**	鳴る to **sound**
okasu	犯す to **commit** (a crime)	侵す to **invade**
okoru	起こる to **happen**	怒る to **get angry**
okuru	送る to **send**	贈る to **confer**
oru	おる [*hum.*] to **be**	折る to **break**
shimeru	閉める to **close**	締める to **tie**
sumu	住む to **live at**	済む to **be complete**
susumeru	進める to **advance**	勧める to **suggest**
tazuneru	尋ねる [*for.*] to **ask**	訪ねる [*for.*] to **visit**
toku	解く to **loosen**	説く to **explain**
tsugu	注ぐ to **pour**	継ぐ to **come after**
ukagau	伺う [*hum.*] to **ask**	伺う [*hum.*] to **visit**
yaru	やる [*fam.*][*col.*] to **give**	やる [*fam.*][*col.*] to **do**

V. ADJECTIVES & ADJECTIVAL NOUNS

An adjective is a type of word that modifies a noun or a noun phrase by changing the information about that noun. In English, adjectives are non conjugable in their attributive form (modifying directly the noun, prefixed to it), while in their predicative form (describing a characteristic, placed at the end of the sentence), they require the verb 'to be'. Thus, it is easy to categorize adjectives as a separate part of speech with a specific grammatical function. In Japanese, on the other hand, there is no such type of word grammatically, so to modify a noun, other types of words are used:

1. **Adjectival Verbs**: A specific type of conjugable verb that can act both in an attributive and predicative way. Sometimes referred here simply as 'adjectives' for brevity.

2. **Adjectival Nouns**: Nouns that with the help of a copular verb adequately conjugated can act in an attributive or predicative way.

Adjectival verbs are technically a special category of verbs with a different ending than the active or static verbals [☞ IV], which ends in -*i* instead of -*u*. Adjectival verbs, called sometimes 'adjectives' in this book for convenience and linguistic economy, can be conjugated in mood and aspect like other verbs but require a different inflection from them and can also act in an attributive manner when they are placed before a noun [☞ GE:II.1.3]. In turn, this type of adjectival verbs, being verbs, do not need a copula [☞ IV. 1.1] when acting in a predicative way. This type of verb-adjective is reduced in number compared to other types of words in Japanese and it is also a closed class, that is, it does not admit new words within the category.

As for adjectival nouns, there are three types according to the copular form they use to act in an attributive way (when modifying another noun):

1. *Na* **Adjectival Nouns**: A noun that can act as an attribute placed before another noun when it has the morpheme *na*[47] attached to it.

2. *No* **Adjectival Nouns**: A noun that can act as an attribute placed before another noun when it §has the morpheme *no*[48] attached to it.

3. **Versatile Adjectival Nouns**: A noun that can act as an attribute placed before another noun when either the morpheme *no* or *no* attached to it.

When acting in a predicative way, any type of adjectival noun need the copula conjugated in a predicative form like any other noun. It is also worth saying that there are some adjectival nouns (mostly of the *na* type) whose functioning as nouns is very scarce or virtually non-existent due to their semantic quality.

Na adjectival nouns are, like adjectival verbs, a closed class word but larger in number than those, although less common in everyday use. Versatile (*na/no*) adjectival

---

[47] The default attributive form of the copula *da*.

[48] A modified form of the attributive form of the copula (*na*) only used with some adjectival nouns. Probably a cognate of the genitive particle *no* ('of').

nouns are, on the other hand, an open class. *No* adjectives mostly derive from adverbs or nominal adverbs [☞ VI] that can be used also as adjectival nouns.

1. OBJECTIVE CHARACTERISTICS

Adjectives and adjectival nouns that describe characteristics that can be measured in some way.

1.1 Size & Shape

Adjectives and adjectival nouns that refer to the size and shape of things.

Important Words

ookii 大きい *big*	chiisai 小さい *small*	hiro 広い *wide*	futoi 太い *fat*
atsui 厚い *thick*	hosoi 細い *thin (& long)*	usui 薄い *thin (& broad)*	semai 狭い *narrow*
takai 高い *tall*	nagai 長い *long*	hikui 低い *low*	mijikai 短い *short (thing)*
omoi 重い *heavy*	karui 軽い *light*	fukai 深い *deep*	asai 浅い *shallow*
onaji 同じ *same*	ippan (na/no) 一般 *na/no* *general*	kanzen (na/no) 完 全 *na/no* *perfect*	marui 丸い *round*

- -

Ⓣ oókìi 大きい: ① **big** ② large

Cognate w. the adj. *ooi (many)*

Ⓣ òokina 大きな ①: ① **big** ② large

❖ *Prenominal:* Only u. before a n.

Ⓣ chiísài 小さい: **small**; little (size); tiny

O.J. affix *chi (small)* + adjectivizing suf. *i* + nominalizing suf. *sa* + adjectivizing suf. *i* ‖ Cognate w. *chotto (a little bit)*, w. r. u. *chitto (a little bit)* and w. O.J. *chiisa (baby)*

Ⓣ chìisana 小さな ①: **small**; little (size); tiny

O.J. *chisa (baby)* + attributive p. *na*

❖ *Prenominal:* Only u. before a n.

Ⓤ kyodái (na) 巨大 *na* Ⓒ *(huge+big)*: **gigantic**; colossal; huge

dekài でかい: [*col.*] ① **huge** ② big

← *doikai*: Intensifier pre. *do* + *ikai (brave)*

Ⓥ hiròi 広い: **wide**; broad

Ⓦ futòi 太い: ① **thick** ② fat

❖ U. for long, cylindrical things.

➤ futòtte irú 太っている: to be **fat** (u. for animate things)

Ⓦ atsúi 厚い: **thick**

❖ U. for spread things.

Ⓢ hosòi 細い: **thin**; **fine**; slender

❖ U. for long things or people.

Ⓢ usúi / usùi 薄い: **thin**; light

❖ U. for spread things.

Ⓢ semài 狭い: **narrow**

Ⓢ komákài 細かい: **minute** (detailed); **fine**; small

- -

Ⓣ takài₁ 高い: ① **high**; **tall** ② expensive

➤ se ga takài 背が高い: **tall** (stature)

Ⓣ nagài ❶ 長い/ ❷ 永い: ① **long** (length) ② eternal

Ⓣ hikùi 低い: **low**

➤ se ga hikùi 背が低い: **short** (stature)

Ⓣ mijíkài 短い: **short** (length); brief

- -

Ⓣ omói 重い: **heavy**

Ⓣ karúi 軽い: **light** (weight)

- -

Ⓢ fukài 深い: **deep**; profound

Ⓢ asái / asài 浅い: **shallow**; superficial

Ⓢ gyakú₁ (na/no) 逆な/の Ⓒ (going against): Ⓝ (the) **reverse**; (the) **other way around** Ⓐ **reverse**; opposite

sakásama (na/no) 逆さまな/の 〔逆様〕: Ⓝ **inverted** (thing); inversion Ⓐ ① **inverted**; **upside down**; **reversed**; back to front

Pre. saka (inverse) + sama (situation)

Ⓣ onáji 同じ (①): (the) **same**; **similar**; alike; identical

❖ This adj. does not need the *na* ending when acting as an attribute (before the modified n.).

1.2 **Quantity**

Ⓤ dóyō (na/no) 同様な/の Ⓒ (same+manner): **same**; **similar**; equal; identical

❖ U. when there are similar characteristics between two or more things.

Ⓤ hitóshìi 等しい: **equal**; **equivalent**; (the) same

❖ U. when there is no difference at all between two or more things.

Ⓤ byódō (na/no) 平等な/の Ⓒ (flat+equivalent): Ⓝ **equality** Ⓐ **equal**; even

❖ Referring to the absence of discrimination and the existence of uniform equality. M. u. abstractly.

Ⓢ ippán (na/no) 一般な/の Ⓒ (one+generic): **general**; ordinary; universal; average

Ⓤ kyótsuu (na/no) 共通な/の Ⓒ (together+passing through): ① **common** (to) ② mutual

Ⓢ hijó₁ (na/no) 非常な/の Ⓒ (negation+usual): Ⓝ **emergency** Ⓐ **extraordinary**; **unusual**

Ⓢ tokúbetsu (na/no) 特別な/の Ⓒ (special+separating): Ⓝ **exception** Ⓐ ① **special**; particular

Ⓤ betsú₁ (na/no) 別な/の Ⓒ (separating): Ⓝ ① **distinction**; **difference** ② exception Ⓐ ① **separate** ② **different** ③ **another**

Ⓤ dokútoku (na/no) 独特な/の Ⓒ (alone+special): Ⓝ ① **uniqueness** ② peculiarity Ⓐ ① **unique** ② (one's) **own**

yunìiku (na) ユニークな Ⓔ : ① **unique** ② individual ③ original

Ⓢ kańzen (na/no) 完全な/の Ⓒ (completion+whole): Ⓝ **perfection** Ⓐ ① **perfect** ② **complete** ③ total

Ⓤ marúi / marùi ❶❷ 丸い/ ❸❹ 円い: ① **round** ② spherical ③ circular ④ complete

Adjectives and adjectival nouns related to quantity.

This category of adjectival words that designate the concept of 'much' (*ooi*) and 'few' (*sukunai*) are not grammatically totally equivalent to the English words of the same meaning, since in this sense, they can only be used as a predicate (placed at the end of the sentence).

Important Words

ooi 多い *many*	sukunai 少ない *few*	iroiro 色々 *various*	juubun な (na) 十分 *enough*
saikō (na/no) 最高 な/の *most*	saitē (na/no) 最低 な/の *least*	takai 高い *expensive*	yasui 安い *cheap*

Ⓕ **òoi** / oòi 多い: (there are) **many**; **numerous**; (there is) much; plenty

❖ This adj. cannot be u. to mean 'many' or 'much' when functioning as an attribute (before a n.). As an attribute, it means 'with many', which usually needs another modifier before (X + *no*[A] + *ooi*[B] + Y = Y [B]*having many* [A]*of X*).

❖ This word has, aside from the meaning of 'a lot', the implication of 'a large proportion' in comparison to some previous standard.

➤ kazú (ga) òoi 数多い: **many**

➤ òoku no 多くの: **many...**

Ⓕ oózè (no) 大勢の: **many people**

Ⓕ **sukúnài** 少ない: (there are) **few**; (there is) **little**; (there are) not many; scarce

❖ This adj. cannot be u. to mean 'little' or 'few' when functioning as an attribute (before a n.). As an attribute it means 'with few', which usually needs another modifier before (X + *no*[1] + *sukunai*[2] + Y = Y [2]*having few* [1]*of X*).

❖ This word has, aside of the meaning of 'few', the implication of 'small quantity in proportion' in comparison to some previous standard.

➤ kazúsukùnai 数くない: **few (in number)**

Ⓙ **wàzuka**[1] (na) わずかな〔僅か〕: (a) **little; few**

Ⓕ **iróiro** (na) いろいろな〔色々〕: **various**

iro (color) ×2

➤ [col.] **irónna** いろんな〔色んな〕

❖ This col. f. of the adj. can only be u. as an attribute.

⊕ **samàzama** (na) 様々な: [for.] ① **various** ② varied

sama (situation) ×2 → *sama + zama ← sama*

⊕ **juúbùn**[1] (na) 十分な Ⓒ (*ten+division*): **enough; sufficient**

Ⓙ **yùtaka** (na) 豊かな: ① **abundant** ② **wealthy**; rich ③ plentiful

mazúshìi 貧しい: ① **poor** ② scanty

bìnbō (na) 貧乏な Ⓒ (*poor+limited*):: **poor** (person w. no money); destitute

yoké (na) 余計な Ⓒ (*remaining+reckoning*): **too many; too much; excessive;** unnecessary

❖ M. u. in a fig. way.

⊕ **saíkō** (na/no) 最高な/の Ⓒ (*utmost+high*): ① **most** ② **best** ③ **supreme** ④ highest

Ⓙ **saítē** (na/no) 最低な/の Ⓒ (*utmost+low*): ① **least** ② **worst** ③ lowest

saíaku (na/no) 最悪な/の Ⓒ (*utmost+bad*): ① **worst** ② **horrible; awful; terrible**

kìtte no 切っての: **the most...** (of all)

Ⓣ takài₂ 高い: ① **expensive** ② **high; tall** (height)

Ⓣ yasùi 安い: **cheap**

1.3 Color & Temperature

Adjectives and adjectival nouns used to designate the different colors and temperatures.

Most colors in Japanese are nouns that can take the particle *no* to become adjectives [☞ II 3.2]. The most prominent colors, however, also have a purely adjectival form (adjectival verb). These adjectival verbs are the ones listed here.

Important Words

kuroi 黒い *black*	shiroi 白い *white*	aoi 青い *blue-green*	akai 赤い *red*
atatakai 暖かい *warm*	atsui 暑い *hot*	samui 寒い *cold (temp.)*	tsumetai 冷たい *cold (thing)*

Ⓣ kuròi 黒い: **black**

Cognate w. kurai (dark)

Ⓣ shiròi 白い: **white**

Ⓣ aòi 青い: ① **blue** ② **green** (vegetation)

Ⓣ akái 赤い: **red**

Cognate w. akarui (bright) and aku (open)

tómē (na) 透明な Ⓒ (*showing through+clear*): **transparent**

kòi 濃い: **dark** (tone); dense; deep (color); strong (flavor; smell)

Ⓣ atátakài ❶ 暖かい/ ❷ 温かい: ① **warm** (temperature) ② **warm** (thing)

➤ [*col.*] attákài あったかい

Ⓣ atsùi ❶ 暑い/ ❷ 熱い: ① **hot** (temperature) ② **hot** (thing)

Ⓜ nurùi ぬるい 〔温い〕: ① **lukewarm** ② half-hearted

✧ ❶ M. u. in the sense of 'not hot enough' or 'not cold enough'.

Ⓣ samùi 寒い: **cold** (temperature)

Ⓣ tsúmetai 冷たい: **cold** (thing)

Ⓜ suzúshìi 涼しい: **cool** (temperature)

1.4 Taste & Smell

Adjectives and adjectival nouns related to tastes and smells.

Important Words

oishii 美味しい *tasty*	amai 甘い *sweet*	karai 辛い *spicy*	shiokarai 塩辛い *salty*

Ⓣ **oíshii** / oíshìi おいしい 〔美味しい〕: **tasty; delicious**

Hon. pre. *o* + *ishii* ← O.J. *tsukushii* → C.J. *utsukushii (beautiful)*: Cognate w. *itsukushimu (affectionate)*

Ⓜ **ùmai** / umái うまい 〔❶ 美味い/ ❷ 旨い/ ❸ 上手い〕: [*mas.*] [*col.*] ① **delicious**; tasty; yummy ② **wise** ③ skillful

*uma** + adjectivizing suf. *i* |*Cognate w. *umu*[12] (¹to be ripe, ²to give birth)

Ⓔ **mazùi** まずい 〔不味い〕: **unappetizing; tasteless; disgusting**

ma (just) + *zui* ← *sui (sour)*

❖ Also u. fig.

Ⓜ **amái** 甘い: **sweet** (flavor)

Ⓔ **karài** 辛い: ① **spicy**; hot (flavor) ② harsh; severe; painful

nigài 苦い: **bitter**

shiókarài 塩辛い: **salty**

shio (salt) + *karai (spicy)*

shóppài しょっぱい 〔塩っぱい〕: [*col.*] ① **salty** ② harsh ③ unpleasant

shitsúkòi しつこい 〔執拗い〕: ① **greasy**; fatty ② insistent; persistent

Ⓔ **kusài**₁ 臭い: **stinking; smelly**

1.5 Distance & Time

Adjectives and adjectival nouns related to physical and temporal distances.

Important Words

chikai 近い *near*	tooi 遠い *far*	hayai 早い *fast*	osoi 遅い *slow*
wakai 若い *young*	atarshii 新しい *new*	furui 古い *old*	

Ⓣ **chikài** 近い: **near; close**

Ⓣ **toói** 遠い: **far; distant**

Ⓣ **hayài** ❶ 早い/ ❷ 速い: ① **early** ② **fast**; quick

Ⓔ **kósoku** (na/no) 高速な/の: Ⓒ *(high+quick)* Ⓝ **high-speed** Ⓐ **express** (fast)

Ⓣ **osói** / osòi 遅い: ① **late** ② **slow**

Ⓔ **kyuú** (na) 急な Ⓒ *(urging)*: ① **sudden**; abrupt ② **unexpected**

Ⓣ **wakái** 若い: **young**

Ⓣ **atárashìi** 新しい: **new**

← O.J. *aratashi*

Ⓜ **àratana** 新たな: [*lit.*] **new**

❖ *Prenominal*: Only u. before a n.

Ⓔ **shińsen** (na) 新鮮な Ⓒ *(new+fresh)*: **fresh**

Ⓣ **furùi** 古い: **old** (thing)

Ⓜ **saíshuu** (no) 最終の Ⓒ *(utmost+ending)*: Ⓝ (the) **last** (thing) Ⓐ **final**; closing

Ⓔ **éen** (na/no) 永遠な/の Ⓒ *(perpetual+far)*: Ⓝ **eternity** (infinity of time) Ⓐ **eternal**

mugén (na/no) 無限な/の Ⓒ *(not being+limit)*: Ⓝ **infinity** (of size or quantity) Ⓐ **infinite; unlimited**

2. SUBJECTIVE CHARACTERISTICS

Adjectives and adjectival nouns related to characteristics that cannot be measured objectively but are perceived subjectively.

2.1 Good & Bad

Adjectives and adjectival nouns that relate to what is considered good or convenient and what is bad or inconvenient.

Important Words

yoi 良い *good*	ii いい [*col.*] *good*	daijobu (na) 大丈夫な *alright*	warui 悪い *bad*
suki (na) 好きな *liked*	kirai 嫌い *disliked*	iya (na) 嫌な *disagreable*	dame (na) だめな *no good*
nikui 憎い *hated*	kekkō (na) 結構 *nice*	sugoi すごい *amazing*	hidoi ひどい *awful*

	tadashii 正しい *correct*	benri (na) 便利な *comfortable*	fuben (na) 不便な *unhandy*

In Japanese, the concepts of 'liking' (*suki*), 'disliking' (*kirai*) or 'hating' (*nikui*), unlike in English, are expressed by means of adjectives (adjectival verbs) whose subject is not the person speaking but the thing liked or disliked.

Ⓕ yòi ❶ 良い/ ❷ 善い: ① **good** (favorable); nice ② **good** (virtuous) Ⓐ
easy to ~

Ⓕ ii いい 〔良い〕①: [*col.*] ① **good** ② nice

← *ē* ← *yoi* (good)

✤ This col. f. of the adj. *yoi* does not inflect, that is, it is only u. in the realis f. (present indicative). For the rest of tenses, the f. *yoi* is u.

Ⓣ daíjòbu₁ (na) 大丈夫な Ⓒ

(*big*+*length*+*husband*): **alright**; fine

This word originally meant 'gentleman' or 'man of character'. That sense later evolved into the meaning of 's.o. w. good health', and ultimately into the meaning of ' being alright'.

yoróshìi / yoróshii よろしい 〔よろし い〕: [*pol.*] **fine**; all right; good

Ⓕ warùi 悪い: ① **bad** ② wicked; evil

Ⓕ sukì (na) 好きな: ① **liked**; to **like** ② loved

✤ This adj.'s lit. meaning is that of 'likable' or 'liked', but it can be more conveniently translated as 'to like', since its usage is equivalent to said v. in English.

✤ Referring to the previous note, it has to be taken into account that the liked thing grammatically acts as the subject, hence taking the nominative p. **ga**.

konómashìi 好ましい: ① **likable** ② desirable ③ nice

203

konoma* + qualificative suf. shii |*Irrealis f. of v. konomu (to like)

natsúkashìi 懐かしい: **dear**; fondly-remembered; nostalgic; missed

natsuka* + qualificative suf. shii |*Irrealis f. of v. <u>natsuku</u> (to become emotionally attached)

koíshìi 恋しい: **missed**; longed for

koi + qualificative suf. shii

mashí (na) ましな〔増し〕: ① **preferable** ② better

(I) *masu (to increase; to grow)*

❖ Only u. when there are two not-so-good options to be chosen from.

Ⓛ sakán (na) 盛んな: **popular**; **prosperous**; thriving

← *sakari*: (I) *sakaru (to prosper)* ← *sakaeru (to prosper)* ← *saku (to bloom)*

Ⓣ kirái (na) 嫌いな: ① **disliked**; to **dislike** ② hated; to hate

Cognate w. *kirau (to dislike)*

❖ This adj.'s lit. meaning is that of 'disliked', but it can be more conveniently translated as 'to dislike' or 'to like not', since its usage is equivalent to said v. in English.

❖ Referring to the previous note, it has to be taken into account that the object which is disliked grammatically acts as the subject (requiring the p. **ga** or **wa**).

❖ This word implies that one holds a bad impression of s.t.

Ⓣ iyà (na) 嫌な: ① **disagreeable** ② **detestable**; **unpleasant**

❖ M. u. in situations when one finds some situation or attitude disagreeable and he or she is not willing to accept it.

Ⓛ damè₁ (na) だめな〔駄目〕 Ⓒ *(packhorse+eye)*: ① **no good** ② wasted; useless ③ cannot; not allowed

❖ U. when talking about s.t. that s.o. strongly rejects, implying non-allowance or uselessness.

⊕ nikùi にくい〔❶ 憎い/ ❷ 難い〕: ① **hateful**; detestable ② Ⓐ *difficult to ~*; *hard to ~*

Cognate w. v. *nikumu (to hate)*

⊕ kèkkō₁ (na) 結構な Ⓒ *(tying+setting up)*: **nice**; fine (mood); well enough

Ⓛ rippá (na) 立派な: **splendid**; **fine**; prominent; magnificent

erài えらい〔偉い〕: ① **great**; excellent ② [*col.*] terrible; terribly; very

⊕ tadáshìi 正しい: ① **correct**; **right** ② proper ③ straight

tada (straightforward) + qualificative suf. shii

Ⓛ sékaku (na) 正確な Ⓒ *(correct+assurance)*: **accurate**; exact; veracious

Ⓛ kuwáshìi 詳しい: **detailed**; full; accurate

⊕ sótō₂ (na/no) 相当な/の Ⓒ *(mutual+hitting)*: **considerable**; proportionate

Ⓛ fusáwashìi ふさわしい〔相応しい〕: **appropriate**; suitable; adequate

Ⓛ tekítō (na) 適当な Ⓒ *(aptness+hitting)*: **appropriate**; **suitable**; proper; adequate

Ⓛ kakkő₂ (na/no) 格好な/の Ⓒ *(form+liking)*: **suitable**; fit; reasonable

Ⓛ chokúsetsu (na/no) 直接な/の Ⓒ *(straight+contact)*: Ⓝ directness Ⓐ **direct**; immediate; firsthand Ⓑ **directly**

mottáinài もったいない〔勿体無い〕: **unworthy** (of); too good for; wasteful

Ⓒ R. u. *mottai* 勿体 *(air of importance)* + Ⓙ *nai (to not be)*

⊕ sugòi₁ すごい〔凄い〕: ① **terrible** ② **amazing**

❖ Having originally the neg. connotation of 'terrible' or 'dreadful', this word is currently, in a col. reg., more commonly

u. w. the sarcastic sense of 'amazing'. Nevertheless this adj. always has the implication of some degree of astonishment.

㊤ hidòi ひどい 〔酷い〕: ① **terrible**; awful ② **harsh**; hard ③ **cruel**

[C] hidō* 非道 (unjust) + [J] adjectivizing suf. i | *hi 非 (negation) + 道 (way)

❖ Referring to s.t. that is undesirable.

yabài やばい: [col.] ① **awful** ② **crazy**

Probably a cognate w. the v. ayabumu (to fear s.t.)

- -

㊤ tsùmi (na/no) 罪な/の: [N] ① **offence** ② **sin** ③ wrongdoing [A] ① **culpable** ② **sinful** ③ criminal

uráyamashìi 羨ましい: **envious; jealous**; to **envy**; to be jealous of

urayama* + qualificative suf. shii | *Irrealis f. of v. urayamu (to envy)

❖ When the subject is other than the speaker, this adj. must be followed by a semblative ending [☞ EY:VI.2.2].

❖ This adj.'s lit. meaning is that of 'provoking envy', but it can be more conveniently translated as 'to be jealous' or 'to envy', since its usage is equivalent to said v. in English.

- -

㊤ yakù ni tàtsu 役に立つ: to **be useful**; to **be helpful**

[C] yaku 役 (role) + [J] lative p. ni (to) + tatsu (to stand up)

mudá (na) 無駄な: **useless**; no good

Probably a cognate of munashii (void)

㊥ bènri (na) 便利な [C] (convenience+profit): **convenient; handy; useful**

㊤ fùben (na) 不便な [C] (convenience+profit): [N] **inconvenience; unhandiness** [A] **inconvenient; unhandy**

- -

kóhē (na) 公平な [C] (public+flat): [N] **fairness; impartiality** [A] **fair**

fukòhē (na) 不公平な: [N] **injustice; unfairness** [A] **unfair**; unjust

[C] fu 不 (no) + kōhē 公平 (fair)

kakkánteki (na) 客観的な: **objective** (thing)

[C] kyakkan 客観 (objectivity) + adjectivizing suf. teki 的

shukánteki (na) 主観的な: **subjective**

[C] shukan 主観 (subjectivity) + adjectivizing suf. teki 的

kisókuteki (na) 規則的な: **regular; systematic**

[C] kisoku 規則 (regulation) + adjectivizing suf. teki 的

fukìsoku / fukísòku (na) 不規則な: [N] **irregularity** [A] **irregular**

[C] fu 不 (no) + kisoku 規則 (regulation)

kótēteki (na) 肯定的な: **affirmative**

[C] hitē 否定 (affirmation) + adjectivizing suf. teki 的

hitéteki (na) 否定的な: **negative**

[C] hitē 否定 (negation) + adjectivizing suf. teki 的

2.2 Looks & Impressions

Adjectives and nouns related to appearances.

Important Words

kawaii	utsukushii	kirē (na)
可愛い *cute*	美しい *beautiful*	綺麗な *clean-pretty*

subarashii 素晴らしい *splendid*	fushigi (na) 不思議な *wonderful*	suteki (na) 素敵な [*fam.*] *great*
minikui 醜い *ugly*	kitanai 汚い *dirty*	hen (na) 変な *strange*
akiraka (na) 明らかな *clear*	abunai 危ない *dangerous*	kowai 怖い *sacary*

Ⓣ **kawáìi** かわいい 〔可愛い〕: **cute**; **adorable**; pretty

← O.J. kawayui ← O.J. kawahayushi* (evoking compassion) |*kawa† + O.J. hayushi (flushed) |† ← O.J. kawo (face) → C.J. kao ‖ The meaning of 'evoking compassion' later evolved into the meaning of 'being lovable'.

⊕ **utsúkushìi** 美しい: **beautiful**

utsuku* + qualificative suf. shii |* ← itsuku (to worship): Cognate w. itsukumu (affectionate)

❖ Describing s.t. that is pleasing to the eye, ear or the emotions.

⊕ **kìrē** (na) きれいな 〔綺麗〕 Ⓒ (*elegant+magnificent*): ① **clean**; clear ② [*fam.*] **beautiful**; lovely; pretty

❖ U. for both an objective (hygienic) 'cleanness' and a subjective 'cleanings' referring to s.t. looking good or 'pretty'.

Ⓛ **séketsu** (na) 清潔な Ⓒ (*pure+unsullied*): **clean**

❖ M. referring to an objective, sanitary sense of 'cleanness'.

juńsui (na/no) 純粋な/の Ⓒ (*sheer+refined*): ① **pure** ② **genuine** ③ unmixed

Ⓛ **bimyő** (na) 微妙な Ⓒ (*faint+exquisite*): ① **subtle**; delicate ② difficult; tricky

⊕ **subárashìi** 素晴らしい: ① **wonderful**; splendid ② terrific

subara* + qualificative suf. shii |*Irrealis f. of v. O.J. subaru (to shrink) → C.J. subomaru ‖ Originally this word had a neg. connotation translatable to the words 'extreme' or

'terrible'. The meaning later evolved into an ironic pos. sense such as the word 'terrific' in English.

❖ Referring to s.t. impressive from a rather objective point of view.

⊕ **fushígi** (na) 不思議な: Ⓝ ① **wonder** ② **mystery** Ⓐ **wonderful**; amazing; marvelous; mysterious

← Ⓒ fuskashigi* 不可思議 (unfathomable) |* fu 不 (no) + ka 可 (able) + shi 思 (thinking) + gi 議 (deliberation)

❖ M. u. to refer to s.t. that cannot be interpreted by one's own knowledge or reason.

Ⓛ **sutéki** (na) 素敵な: [*fam.*] **great**; lovely; fantastic

Ⓙ *su* + Ⓒ adjectivizing suf. teki 的 |* ← subarashii (wonderful)*

yùuga (na) 優雅な Ⓒ (*tender+elegant*): Ⓝ elegance; refinement Ⓐ **elegant**

kakkóìi かっこいい 〔格好いい〕: [*col.*] **attractive**; good-looking; cool (looking)

Ⓒ *kakkō 格好 (figure) +* Ⓙ *ii (good)*

Ⓛ **miníkùi** 醜い: **ugly**

mi* + nikui (difficult to) |*(I) miru (to look)

dasài ダサい: [*col.*] **uncool**; **lame**; unfashionable

Ⓒ *Adjectivization of dasaku 駄作 (poor piece of work)*

Ⓛ **kitánài** 汚い: **dirty**

⊕ **hèn** (na) 変な Ⓒ (*changing*): **strange;** **weird;** curious; funny

❖ Often u. in the sense of 'funny'.

Ⓔ **mezúrashìi** 珍しい: **unusual; rare;** curious

mezura* + qualificative suf. *shii |* ← medzura:* Irrealis f. of v. O.J. *medzuru (to admire)* → C.J. *mederu*

❖ U. when a person feels newly interested or surprised by s.t. that rarely happens.

Ⓔ **kìmyō** (na) 奇妙な Ⓒ (*unusual+exquisite*): **strange;** unusual; odd

❖ U. for things that are rarely seen.

Ⓔ **myò̀** (na) 妙な Ⓒ (*exquisite*): **strange;** unusual; odd

Ⓔ **himítsu** (na/no) 秘密な/の Ⓒ (*concealing+secrecy*): Ⓝ (a) **secret** Ⓐ **secret**

shìnpi (na/no) 神秘な/の Ⓒ (*god+concealing*): Ⓝ **mystery** Ⓐ **mysterious**

aímai (na) 曖昧な Ⓒ (*not clear+unclear*): **ambiguous; vague**

yayákoshìi ややこしい: **confusing;** puzzling; complicated

⊕ **akìraka** (na) 明らかな: ① **clear** ② **obvious;** evident

aki* + O.J. adjectivizing suf. *raka |*(I) aku (to be open)*

fumé (na/no) 不明な/の Ⓒ (*god+concealing*): **unclear; unknown;** uncertain; obscure

⊕ **ańzen** (na) 安全な Ⓒ (*safe+whole*): Ⓝ **safety** Ⓐ **safe**

❖ U. w. the sense that there is no fear of harm or damage.

Ⓔ **bují** (na/no) 無事な/の Ⓒ (*not being+affair*): Ⓝ **safety;** without damage Ⓐ ① **safe** ② **without problem**(s); all right

❖ This word refers to the absence of any neg. upheavals in some particular situation.

⊕ **abúnai** / abúnài 危ない: **dangerous**

⊕ **kikén** (na) 危険な Ⓒ (*dangerous+precipitous*): Ⓝ **danger;** risk Ⓐ ① **dangerous;** risky

igái / ìgai (na) 意外な Ⓒ (*idea+outside*): **surprising; unexpected**

⊕ **kowài** 怖い・恐い: **scary;** frightening

Ⓔ **osóroshìi** ❶❷ 恐ろしな/ ❶ 怖ろしいな: ① **terrifying; frightening; terrible** ② **tremendous;** amazing

Cognate w. *osoreru (to fear)*

kóun (na) 幸運な Ⓒ (*dangerous+precipitous*): Ⓝ **good luck; fortune** Ⓐ **fortunate**

ràkkii (na) ラッキーな Ⓔ : [*col.*] **lucky**

ùn (ga) **ii** 運がいい: **lucky**

Ⓒ *un* 運 *(luck)* + Ⓙ *ii (good)*

2.3 Sensation

Adjectives and adjectival nouns related to what is perceptible with the physical senses.

Important Words

katai 硬い *hard*	yawarakai 柔らかい *soft*	akarui 明るい *bright*	kurai 暗い *dark*

tsuyoi	yowai	genki (na)	itai
強い *strong*	弱い *weak*	元気な *good*	痛い *painful*

⊕ katái / katài ❶ 硬い / ❷ 堅い / ❸ 固い: ① **hard** ② **solid** ③ **firm**

⊕ yawárakài ❶ 柔らかい / ❷ 軟らかい: ① **soft** (texture) ② **soft** (without resistance)

nibúi / nibùi 鈍い: **dull**; blunt

namèraka (na) 滑らかな: **smooth**

- -

⊕ akárui / akárùi 明るい: **bright**; light; luminous; well-lit

Cognate w. aku (to open)

⊕ kurái 暗い: ① **dark** ② gloomy

Cognate w. kuroi (black)

- -

⊤ tsuyòi 強い: **strong**

⊤ yowài 弱い: **weak**

⊤ géńki (na) 元気な ⓒ (*origin+mood*): **good** (health); vigorous; healthy; energetic

❖ This word has a subjective, abstract connotation, m. referring to a 'good spirit' or 'good mood'.

⊕ keńkō (na) 健康な ⓒ (*healthy+ease*): Ⓝ **health** Ⓐ **healthy**

❖ This word focuses on physical 'health'.

⊥ jòbu (na) 丈夫な: **robust**; **strong**; **healthy**

❖ Referring to a lasting 'healthy' physical makeup rather than one's temporary physical state.

⊕ itài 痛い: **painful**; sore; to hurt

❖ M. u. for physical 'pain'. A common translation to this adj. is 'to hurt', rather than 'painful', since its usage is similar to said v. in English.

kurúshìi 苦しい: **painful**; unpleasant; difficult

❖ M. referring to a long-term 'pain', be it physical or emotional.

kutsúu (na/no) 苦痛な/の ⓒ (*bitter+hurting*): Ⓝ **pain** Ⓐ **painful**

❖ U. for both mental and physical 'pain'.

⊥ tsurái / tsurài つらい〔辛い〕: ① **painful** (emotionally); bitter; hard to bear ② **tough** (situation); difficult

❖ M. u. for mental or psychological 'pain'.

⊥ rakú (na) 楽な ⓒ (*enjoyable*): ① **comfortable** (situation) ② **easy**; **simple** (circumstances)

⊥ kaíteki (na) 快適な ⓒ (*pleasant+aptness*): ① **pleasant**; agreeable ② **comfortable**

❖ M. u. to describe the absence of anything unpleasant.

kokóroyòi 快い: **pleasant**; agreeable

kokoro (heart) + yoi (good)

❖ U. to describe a good sensory feeling.

2.4 Emotions & Feelings

Adjectives and adjectival nouns that describe human emotions and feelings.

In Japanese, the words describing the action of 'wanting' (*hoshii*) and 'needing' (*hitsuyō na*), unlike in English, are adjectives (adjectival verbs), so the subject of the sentence is not the person speaking but the thing 'wanted' or 'needed'.

Important Words

tanoshii 楽しい *fun*	omoshiroi 面白い *interesting*	tsumaranai つまらない *boring*
hoshii 欲しい *wanted*	histsuyō (na) 必要な *needed*	okashii おかしい *funny*
ureshii 嬉しい *happy*	kanashii 悲しい *sad*	nemui 眠い *sleepy*

Ⓣ tanóshìi 楽しい: ① **fun; enjoyable** ②
happy

❖ When the subject is other than the
speaker, this adj. must be followed by a
semblative ending [☞ EY:VI.2.2].

❖ ❷ When referring to a long, sustained
state of 'happiness' derived from one's
own experience.

Ⓣ omóshiròi 面白い: **interesting**;
amusing; funny

Ⓒ tsumàranai つまらない〔詰まらな
い〕: **boring**; dull; uninteresting

Neg. f. of the v. tsumaru (to be settled)

➢ [*col.*] tsumànnai つまんない

Ⓣ mànzoku (na) 満足な Ⓒ *(fulfilling+foot)*: Ⓝ
satisfaction Ⓐ ① **sufficient; enough** ②
satisfying

Ⓣ hoshìi 欲しい: **wanted; to want**

*ho + qualificative suf. shii | *(I) O.J. horu (to
want): Cognate w. horu (to dig)*

❖ The wanted thing acts as the subject of
the sentence, hence it is marked w. the
nominative p. **ga**.

❖ This word's lit. meaning is that of s.t.
that is 'wanted', but it can be more
conveniently translated as 'to want' when
u. w. the first person.

Ⓣ hitsúyō (na) 必要な Ⓒ *(necessarily+necessary)*:
Ⓝ **need** Ⓐ **needed; necessary**

meǹdò (na) 面倒な Ⓒ *(face+falling down)*: Ⓝ
trouble; difficulty Ⓐ **bothersome**;
inconvenient

➢ [*fam.*] meǹdōkusài 面倒くさい〔面
倒臭い〕

➢ [*col.*] meǹdòi 面倒い

yakkái (na) 厄介な Ⓒ *(misfortune+jam)*: Ⓝ
nuisance; trouble; burden Ⓐ
troublesome; bothersome

kuyáshìi 悔しい: **frustrating**; annoying;
regrettable; mortifying

Ⓒ okáshìi おかしい〔可笑しい〕: ①
funny; strange; odd; laughable

➢atámà (ga) okáshìi 頭がおかしい:
crazy; insane; nuts

Ⓒ uréshìi 嬉しい: ① **happy; glad** ②
pleased; delighted

❖ When the subject is other than the
speaker, this adj. must be followed by a
semblative ending [☞ EY:VI.2.2].

❖ Referring to a cheerful and pleasant
feeling for things that turn out as one
desires, m. implying a momentary state
of joy.

Ⓒ shiáwase (na) 幸せな: Ⓝ ① **happiness**
② good fortune Ⓐ ① **happy** ② **lucky**

Subjunctive f. of the O.J. v. shiawasu (to
put together well) |* ← shi† + awasu (to
join together) |†(I) suru (to do)*

❖ Referring to a somewhat subjective
and long-term state of satisfaction
derived from things that are turning out
as one desires.

Ⓔ saíwai (na) 幸いな: Ⓝ ① **happiness** ②
good fortune Ⓐ ① **happy** ② **lucky**

← sachiwai ← (I) O.J. sachiwau* (to prosper) |* ← sachihau ← sachi (fortune) + hau (to spread out)

❖ This word is u. when one judges, rather objectively, s.t. that is convenient for oneself.

Ⓔ **kófuku** (na) 幸福な Ⓒ (fortune+blessing): Ⓝ ① **happiness**; joy ② well-being Ⓐ **happy**

❖ Referring to a somewhat long-term state of mental or material well-being.

medétài めでたい 〔目出度い〕: **happy**; joyous; auspicious

← medeitai: mede* + itai (painful) |*(I) mederu (to cherish)

Ⓔ **héwa** (na) 平和な Ⓒ (flat+peaceful): Ⓝ **peace** Ⓐ **peaceful**

Ⓔ **muchúu** (na/no) 夢中な/の Ⓒ (dream+middle): **absorbed in**; **immersed in**; crazy about; obsessed with

Ⓟ **kanáshii** / kanáshìi 悲しい・哀しい: **sad**

❖ When the subject of this word is a person other than the speaker, this adj. must be followed by a semblative ending [☞ EY:VI.2.2].

Ⓔ **sabíshìi** 寂しい・淋しい: **lonely**

❖ When the subject is other than the speaker, this adj. must be followed by a semblative ending [☞ EY:VI.2.2].

Ⓟ **fuán** (na) 不安な Ⓒ (no+safe): Ⓝ **anxiety** Ⓐ **anxious**; **nervous**; **worried**

Ⓟ **zańnèn** (na) 残念な Ⓒ (leftover+sense): Ⓝ **regret** Ⓐ ① **regrettable**; **unfortunate**; **sorry** ② **pity**

❖ This word refers to a lingering sense of sorrowful dissatisfaction in the mind of s.o. that has made s.t. against his or her wishes, hence it is not related to the concept of guilt.

oshìi 惜しい: ① **regrettable**; **disappointing**; to be a pity; unfortunate ② **precious**

❖ This word has the connotation of s.t. that feels sad or disappointing as a consequence of a neg. result or as a consequence of s.t. or s.o. that has been lost.

Ⓔ **tamáranai** たまらない 〔堪らない〕: **intolerable**; unbearable

Neg. f. of the r. u. v. tamaru (to bear)

Ⓔ **nemúi** / nemùi 眠い: **sleepy**

Cognate w. the v. nemuru (to sleep)

pèkopeko (na) ペコペコな [ideophone]: **very hungry**

2.5 Character & Nature

Adjectives and adjectival nouns related to different characteristics of things beyond good and bad, appearances, sensations or emotions.

Important Words

kanō (na) 可能な *possible*	fukanō (na) 不可能な *impossible*	nai ない *not being*
hontō (na/no) 本当な/の *true*	tashika (na) 確かな *sure*	taisetsu (na) 大切な *funny*
taihen (na) 大変な *serious*	yasashii 優しい *easy*	muzukashii 難しい *difficult*

jōzu (na) 上手な *good at*	heta (na) 下手な *bad at*	shizuka (na) 静かな *quiet*
urusai うるさい *loud*	kashikoi 賢い *smart*	baka (na) ばかな *stupid*
muri (na/no) 無理な/の *loud*	isogashii 忙しい *loud*	yuumē (na) 有名な *loud*

It is worth mentioning here the adjectival verb *nai* ('not to be') which has no equivalent in English, for it is the word used as the negative form of the verb *aru* ('to be there') [☞ IV 1.2].

- -

Ⓣ **kanō** (na) 可能な Ⓒ (*able+capability*): Ⓝ **possibility** Ⓐ **possible**

Ⓛ **fukànō** (na) 不可能な Ⓒ (*no+able+capability*): Ⓝ **impossibility** Ⓐ **impossible**

Ⓣ **nài** ない 〔無い〕: **not being** (there); nonexistent

❖ This adj. is u. when one wants to say that 'there is *no* s.t.'.

❖ This is the plain neg. f. of the irregular v. *aru (to be)*.

Ⓦ **hońtō₁** (na/no) 本当な/の Ⓒ (*foundation+hit*): Ⓝ ① **truth** ② **reality** Ⓐ ① **true** ② **real**

rìaru (na) リアルな Ⓔ: [*col.*] ① **real** ② realistic ③ **true**

Ⓦ **tàshika₁** (na) 確かな: ① **certain; clear; sure;** without a doubt ② **reliable**

tashi* + O.J. adjectivizing suf. か *|*(I) tasu (to add)*

Ⓛ **kakújitsu** (na) 確実な Ⓒ (*assurance+real*): Ⓝ certainty; reliability Ⓐ ① **certain** ② **reliable**

Ⓦ **tózen** (na/no) 当然な/の Ⓒ (*hit+thus*): ① **natural** ② (as a matter) **of course** ③ reasonable

Ⓛ **shizén** (na) 自然な Ⓒ (*oneself+thus*): Ⓝ **nature** Ⓐ **natural**

Ⓛ **atárimae** (na/no) 当たり前な/の: ① **natural** ② **reasonable** ③ **usual;** ordinary ④ **obvious**

atari* + mae (before) |*(I) ataru (to hit)

hiníku (na/no) 皮肉な/の Ⓒ (*skin+meat*): Ⓝ **irony; sarcasm** Ⓐ ① **ironic; sarcastic** ② unexpected

Ⓦ **jiyùu** (na) 自由な Ⓒ (*oneself+cause*): Ⓝ **freedom** Ⓐ **free**

- -

Ⓣ **taisetsu** (na) 大切な Ⓒ (*heavy+needing*): ① **important** ② valuable

❖ Specially u. for sentimental things.

Ⓦ **dàiji** / daíjì / Ⓐ daíji (na) 大事な Ⓒ (*big+affair*): Ⓝ **serious matter** Ⓐ **important;** serious; valuable

❖ Specially u. when there is a sense of urgency in what it is referred to.

Ⓦ **juúyō** (na) 重要な Ⓒ (*heavy+needing*): ① **important** ② essential

❖ U. when the 'important' thing is 'important' in relation to the function or role that the referred thing partakes on.

Ⓦ **kibíshìi** 厳しい: **strict; severe;** rigid; stern

Ⓤ **hagéshìi** 激しい: ① **intense**; violent; extreme

kitsúi / kitsùi きつい: ① **tight**; hard; severe ② intense

Ⓕ **taíhen₁** (na) 大変な ⓒ *(big+changing)*: Ⓝ **serious thing** Ⓑ ① **serious; grave**; difficult ② **immense** ③ **terrible**

❖ Referring to 'serious' things in the sense of urgency implying some neg. connotations.

Ⓤ **juúdai** (na) 重大な ⓒ *(heavy+big)*: **serious**; **significant; grave**

❖ Referring to 'serious' things in the sense of urgency implying some neg. connotations.

Ⓤ **shínkoku** (na) 深刻な ⓒ *(deep+carving)*: Ⓝ **seriousness** Ⓐ **serious; severe**; deep

❖ Referring to the deepness or high degree of importance of the subject matter one is talking about.

Ⓤ **shínken** (na) 真剣な ⓒ *(true+sword)*: Ⓝ ① **seriousness** ② **earnestness** Ⓐ ① **serious** ② **earnest**

❖ Referring to the expression of weighty things w. an avoidance of humor.

Ⓤ **majíme** (na) 真面目な: ① **serious** ② **earnest**; diligent

ⓒ *shin* 真 *(true)* + *menboku* 面目 *(honor)*

❖ Referring to the expression of weighty things w. an avoidance of humor.

➤ [*col.*] **màji** (na) マジな:

Ⓜ **shójiki** / shójikì (na) 正直な ⓒ *(correct+straight)*: ① **honest**; frank ② **straightforward** Ⓑ **honestly**; frankly

tanómoshìi 頼もしい: **reliable**; **trustworthy**

zurùi ずるい〔狡い〕: **dishonest**; sly; cunning; unfair

Ⓕ **yasáshii** / yasáshìi やさしい〔❶ 易しい/ ❷ 優しい〕: ① **easy; simple** ② **kind; gentle**; tender

❖ Usually u. in the frame of a subjective opinion.

Ⓜ **kañtan** (na) 簡単な ⓒ *(brief+simple)*: **simple; easy**

❖ Referring to an objective kind of simplicity and brevity.

Ⓕ **muzúkashìi** / muzúkashii 難しい: **difficult**; **hard; complicated**

❖ Usually u. in the frame of a subjective opinion.

➤ [*col.*] **muzùi** むずい

Ⓜ **fukúzatsu** (na) 複雑な ⓒ *(double fold+miscellaneous)*: **complicated; complex**

❖ Referring to an objective kind of complexity.

Ⓤ **kònnan** (na) 困難な ⓒ *(bothered+difficult)*: Ⓝ ① **difficulty** ② **distress** Ⓐ **difficult**; troublesome; hard

❖ U. both for 'difficulty' on procedures and 'difficulty' as a hardship or distress for a person's mental or emotional state.

Ⓜ **józu** (na) 上手な ⓒ *(above+hand)*: **good at**

❖ U. after a n. followed by the p. **ga**.

Ⓜ **hetá** (na) 下手な ⓒ *(below+hand)*: **bad at**; poor at

❖ U. after a n. followed by the p. **ga**.

Ⓜ **hazúkashìi** 恥ずかしい: ① **shy** ② **embarrassed**; ashamed

sùnao (na) 素直な: **obedient; docile**

Ⓜ **shitáshìi** 親しい: **familiar; close** (relationship); **friendly**; intimate

Ⓤ **shìnsetsu** (na) 親切な ⓒ *(familiar+cutting)*: ① **kind; gentle**

⊕ **shìzuka** (na) 静かな: **quiet**; calm; peaceful; gentle

Cognate w. the v. *shizumu (to sink)*

❖ M. u. when talking about the environment.

Ⓔ **odàyaka** (na) 穏やかな: **calm** ; **quiet**; **gentle**; peaceful

❖ M. u. when talking about behaviors or situations.

Ⓔ **urúsài** うるさい〔煩い〕: **noisy**; **loud**; annoying

➤ [*col.*] **uzài** ウザイ

- -

Ⓔ **kashíkòi** 賢い: **wise**; **smart**; clever; intelligent

Ⓔ **rikṓ** (na) 利口な Ⓒ (*profit+mouth*): **intelligent**; **smart**; clever; wise

atàma (ga) **ìi** 頭がいい: [*col.*] **intelligent**; **clever**

atama (head) + ii (good)

Ⓔ **bàka** (na) ばかな〔馬鹿〕: [*col.*] **fool**; **stupid**; foolish; idiot

❖ M. u. when referring to people.

òroka (na) 愚かな: **foolish**; **stupid**

❖ M. u. when referring to actions or situations.

atàma (ga) **warùi** 頭が悪い: [*col.*] **dumb**; **stupid**

atama (head) + warui (bad)

⊕ **mùri**₁ (na/no) 無理な/の Ⓒ (*not being+reason*): **unreasonable**; **nonsense**; **excessive**; **impossible**

nìnï / **niní** (na/no) 任意な/の Ⓒ (*responsibility+idea*): ① **optional**; voluntary ② **arbitrary**; **random**

ràndamu (na) ランダムな Ⓔ : **random**

- -

Ⓣ **isógashìi** 忙しい: **busy** (person)

isoga* + qualificative suf. shii |*Irrealis f. of v. isogu (to hurry)

❖ U. when an individual has many things to do.

Ⓔ **nigìyaka** (na) 賑やかな: **lively**; busy

❖ U. to describe a situation in which many people are doing some activity somewhere at some place. This word can also be u. to describe a person as 'lively' and talkative.

Ⓔ **himá** (na) 暇な: Ⓝ **spare time** Ⓐ **free** (time); **idle**; inactive

- -

Ⓔ **tènē** (na) 丁寧な Ⓒ (*block+composure*): **polite**; courteous

kańdai (na) 寛大な Ⓒ (*leniency+big*): ① **generous** ② tolerant

Ⓣ **yuúmē** (na) 有名な Ⓒ (*having+name*): **famous**

yuúkan (na) 勇敢な Ⓒ (*person+mood*): **brave**; heroic

- -

gutáiteki (na) 具体的な: **concrete**; **specific**; **definite**

Ⓒ *gutai* 具体 (concrete) + adjectivizing suf. *teki* 的

chuúshōteki (na) 抽象的な: **abstract**

Ⓒ *chuushō* 抽象 (abstract) + *adjectivizing suf. teki*

VI. ADVERBS & NOMINAL ADVERBS

Adverbs are non-conjugable, dependent words that are used to modify verbs, adjectives, clauses, phrases or other adverbs.

Although there are a certain number of pure adverbs in Japanese, it is important to note that there are many nominal adverbs, that is nouns or adjectival nouns that are also used as adverbs. Many of these nouns can be used as adverbs through the addition of the adverbializing suffix *ni* or, occasionally, through the adjunctive particles such as *de*. Apart from this, any adjectival verb can be converted into an adverb by means of its stem plus the inflection *-ku* [☞ GE:X.3] and some verbs can also be adverbialized by means of their gerund form ending in *-te* [☞ GE:III.3.2].

Many pure adverbs—adverbs that act exclusively as adverbs and fulfill no other functionality—are etymologically *ideophones* [☞ GE:IX.1.1], i.e. words that phatically express an imitative or imaginary sound.

In this section, the most relevant adverbs will be listed regardless of whether they are pure adverbs or adverbs formed in the ways previously mentioned.

1. GRADE & QUANTITY

Adverbs that refer to measurable quantity and extent.

1.1 Few & Little

Adverbs related to what is considered a small amount.

Important Words

chotto ちょっと *a little*	sukoshi 少し *a few*	tada (ni) ただに *only*
amari (ni) あまりに *not very (much)*	hotondo ほとんど *almost*	hobo ほぼ *almost*

Ⓣ **chòtto₁** / chottó ちょっと 〔一寸〕:
[*col.*] ① **just a little** ② **somewhat** ③ just a minute

← R. u. chitto (*a little*): O.J. affix *chi* (*small*) + O.J. adverbial p. *to*

❖ This adv. is also u. to state that s.t. is inconvenient for the speaker when he or she is being invited to do s.t.

Ⓣ **sukòshi** 少し: Ⓝ small quantity Ⓑ [*for.*] ① **little; a few**; a little bit ② **a little while**

➤ **sukòshi mo** / sukóshi mo 少しも: **not a bit**

Ⓛ **shòshō** 少々 Ⓒ (*little×2*): Ⓝ small quantity Ⓑ [*for.*] **just a minute**

Ⓛ **yàya** やや 〔稍〕 [ideophone]: ① **slightly; a little** (bit) ② **somewhat** ③ a little while

Ⓣ hitòtsu₂ ひとつ 〔一つ〕: **a little bit; just**

← classifier *hitotsu (one thing)*

❖ M. u. before a sentence when the speaker makes an invitation to do s.t. or asks s.o. a favor.

Ⓣ tàda₁ (ni) ただに 〔只 〕: **only; merely; simply** Ⓐ (no) **ordinary; common**

Ⓛ tattá たった:**only; merely**

← *tada (only)*

Ⓛ wàzuka₂ (ni) わずかに 〔僅か〕: Ⓝ small quantity Ⓑ ① (a) **little** ② **only; merely**

Ⓛ tàn ni 単に Ⓒ *(simple)*: **simply; only; merely; solely**

Ⓛ yùiitsu 唯一 Ⓒ *(only+one)*: Ⓑ **only** Ⓐ (no) **only; sole; unique**

Ⓣ amári₁ (ni) あまりに 〔余り〕: Ⓝ remainder Ⓑ ① **not very (much)**; not **too much**; not (very) often ② **too much**

(1) *amaru (to be left over)*

❖ ❶ U. w. neg. f.s of v.s.

❖ ❷ U. in dependent clauses.

➤ [*col.*] ańmari₁ (ni) あんまりに

Ⓛ tashő 多少 Ⓒ *(many+little)*: Ⓝ amount Ⓑ **somewhat; more or less; a little; some**

Ⓣ hotòndo ほとんど 〔殆ど〕: Ⓝ most Ⓑ **almost; mostly; nearly**

⊕ hòbo ほぼ 〔略〕: ① **almost; roughly** ② **approximately**

❖ This adv. cannot be u. w. neg. sentences.

1.2 Much & Many

Adverbs related to what is considered a large quantity.

Important Words

totemo とても *very*	taihen 大変 *very*	ooku 多く *many*
takusan たくさん *a lot*	motto もっと *more*	mō もう *more*
sarani さらに *furthermore*	ichiban 一番 *(the) most*	mottomo 最も *(the) most*

Ⓣ totémo とても 〔迚も〕: ① **very** ② exceedingly ③ (not) **at all; by no means**

❖ ❸ When u. w. neg. f.s of v.s.

➤ [*col.*] tottémo とっても 〔迚も〕

Ⓣ taíhen₂ 大変 Ⓒ *(big+changing)*: Ⓝ serious thing Ⓑ [*for.*] **very; greatly**

nań to mo / nàn to mo 何とも: ① **very**; extremely; really; quite ② **not at all**; not a bit

nan* + comitative-cumulative p. *to mo* |** ← nani (what)*

❖ ❷ When u. w. neg. f.s of v.s.

yohódo よほど 〔余程〕: Ⓑ **very; much; greatly; quite** Ⓐ (na/no) extraordinary; unusual

215

C *yo* 余 *(remaining)* + J upper limitative p. *hodo (as much as)*

yoppódo よっぽど: [*col.*] B **very**; **much**; greatly; quite A (na/no) extraordinary; unusual

← adv. *yohodo (very)*

sugóku すごく〔凄く〕: [*col.*] ① **very**; immensely; extremely ② **awfully**

Adverbial f. of the adj. *sugoi (terrible)*

mèccha めっちゃ〔目茶〕: [*col.*][*fam.*] ① **very** ② extremely; excessively

Emphatic f. of the adj. *mecha (excessive)*

mechákucha めちゃくちゃ〔目茶苦茶〕: [*col.*] ① **incredibly** ② really ③ super

---

⊕ **hijó₂** (ni) 非常に C *(only+one)*: N emergency B [*for.*] ① **extremely**; very; extraordinarily

❖ U. when one is describing a degree of being beyond normal.

Ⓛ **kiwàmete** 極めて: **extremely**; **exceedingly**

Gerundive f. of the v. *kiwameru (to carry to extremes)*

❖ U. when s.o. talks about s.t. that is so 'extreme' that it makes it very unusual.

Ⓣ **òoku** 多く: ① **many**; much; a lot ② mostly; largely; abundantly

Adverbial f. of the adj. *ooi (to be much)*

❖ This word has, aside from the meaning of 'a lot', the implication of 'a large proportion' in comparison to some previous standard.

⊕ **takúsàn** たくさん〔沢山〕: N a large number or amount B **a lot** (of); **much**; **many**; a great deal A (na/no) many; lots of

- -

Ⓣ **mòtto** もっと: **more**; further; longer

❖ Not u. before numerals or before neg. v.s.

Ⓣ **mò** もう: ① **more** (u. w. small amounts) ② **anymore**; any more; no more

❖ ❶ Only u. before numerals followed by classifiers.

❖ ❷ When u. w. neg. f.s of v.s.

yorí より: **more**

❖ Only u. before adj.s or adv.s. when they are being implicitly or explicitly compared [☞ GE:XIV.2.1].

Ⓣ **ìjō** 以上 C *(by means of+above)*: B **beyond**; **further** S **not less than...**; **over...**; **more than...** N above-mentioned

---

⊕ **sàrani₁** さらに〔更に〕: **furthermore**; moreover; even more; more and more

Ⓛ **masùmasu** ますます〔益々〕: ① **increasingly**; **more and more** ② decreasingly; less and less

masu (to increase) ×2

issó いっそう〔一層〕 C *(one+stratum)*: **much more**; still more; more than ever

- -

⊕ **dańdàn** / **dańdan** だんだん〔段々〕 C *(steps×2)*: ① **gradually**; little by little; step by step

shidái (ni) 次第に: B ① **in turn**; in order; in sequence ② **gradually** (progressing into a state) N order

C *shidai* 次第 *(order)* + adverbializing p. *ni*

- -

Ⓣ **ichìban** 一番 C *(one+number in a series)*: N ① **number one** ② first B ① (the) **most** ② (the) best

⊕ **mottòmo₁** 最も: ① (the) **most** ② extremely; so much

motto (more) + concessive p. *mo*

Ⓔ **taíhan** / taíhàn 大半 Ⓒ (*big+half*): Ⓝ **majority**; most (of) Ⓑ **mostly**; **mainly**; largely

yoké (ni) 余計に Ⓒ (*remaining+reckoning*): Ⓑ ① **abundantly** ② **excessively** ③ needlessly Ⓐ (na) extra

Ⓔ **oózèi** (de) 大勢で Ⓒ (*big+force*): Ⓝ (a) **crowd**; a large number of people Ⓑ **in a crowd**; as a crowd

1.3 Quite

Adverbs that denote quantities that are neither too big nor too small.

Important Words

kanari かなり *quite*	kekkō 結構 *quite*	juubun (ni) 十分に *sufficiently*

Ⓜ **kànari** かなり〔可也〕: **quite**; **considerably**; fairly; pretty much

Ⓒ *ka* 可 (*able*) + Ⓙ *O.J. nari* (*to be*)

❖ U. when the degree matches one's expectations and surpasses them a little.

Ⓜ **kèkkō₂** けっこう〔結構〕Ⓒ (*tying+setting up*): Ⓑ ① nicely ② **quite**; rather; fairly; pretty Ⓐ (na) nice

❖ U. when talking about a degree that is considerably less than expected. M. affecting adj.s and v.s w. pos. meanings.

❖ This adv. cannot be u. w. neg. f.s.

Ⓔ **nakánaka** なかなか〔中々〕: ① **quite**; **rather**; fairly; very ② by no means

naka (inside) ×2

❖ ❷ When u. w. neg. f.s of v.s.

❖ U. when talking about a degree that is considerably better than expected.

Ⓔ **sótō₃** 相当 Ⓒ (*mutual+hit*): **considerably**

Ⓔ **daíbu** だいぶ〔大分〕Ⓒ (*only+one*): ① **considerably**; greatly; fairly ② (quite) a lot

❖ U. when talking about a degree a little bit greater than expected.

zùibun ずいぶん〔随分〕Ⓒ (*only+one*): ① **very**; considerably ② **extremely**

❖ U. when talking about a degree or quantity that is considerably greater than expected.

Ⓜ **juúbùn₂** (ni) 十分に Ⓒ (*ten+dividing*): Ⓑ ① **sufficiently** ② **fully**; thoroughly Ⓐ (na) enough; sufficient Ⓝ ten minutes

---

Ⓔ **sukúnakù to mo** 少なくとも: **at least**

(I) *sukunai (to be few)* + comitative-cumulative p. *to mo*

❖ Specifically u. when talking objectively, about quantities or numbers.

sèmete せめて: **at least**

❖ M. u. when one is talking about s.t. subjectively.

Ⓔ **sèzē** せいぜい〔精々〕Ⓒ (*fine*×2): **at (the) most**; **at best**; as much/far as possible

1.4 Whole & Part

Adverbs related to the whole and the parts.

Important Words

zenbu 全部 *everything*	subete 全て *all*	mattaku 全く *completely*
zenzen 全然 *completely (not)*	chittomo ちっとも *not at all*	ippai いっぱい *all (of)*

⊕ zènbu 全部 |c| (*whole+section*): |N| **everything**; the whole thing |B| **entirely**; all

⊕ sùbete 全て: [*for.*] |N| **everything** |B| ① **all**; the whole ② **entirely**; wholly

Gerundive f. of the O.J. v. *subu (to combine)* → r. u. C.J. *suberu*

⊕ mattáku 全く: |B| ① **completely**; **absolutely**; **entirely**; wholly ② indeed ③ (not) at all |A| (no) absolute

❖ ❸ When u. w. neg. f.s of v.s

⊕ sukkárì すっかり [ideophone]: **completely**; entirely; thoroughly

❖ M. u. to describe actions that are done to their fullest.

⊕ zeńzen 全然 |c| (*whole+thus*): ① **completely** (not); (not) **at all** ② [*col.*] totally; very

❖ ❶ U. w. neg. f.s of v.s.

⊕ chittómò ちっとも 〔些とも〕: [*col.*] [*fam.*] **not at all**; not in the least

R. u. *chitto (a little)* + concessive p. *mo*

❖ U. w. neg. f.s of v.s.

sappárì さっぱり [ideophone]: **completely** (not); (not) **at all**

❖ U. w. neg. f.s of v.s.

❖ M. u. w. an emotional overtone.

marúkkiri まるっきり 〔丸っ切り〕: ① **totally**; **completely** ② **not at all**

pre. *maru (whole)* + *kkiri* ← *kiri*: (1) *kiru (to cut)*

❖ ❷ U. w. neg. f.s of v.s.

ìssai (ni) 一切に: |N| **everything**; without exception |B| **not at all**; **absolutely not**; entirely not; whatsoever

❖ |B| U. w. neg. f.s of v.s.

❖ M. u. in an emphatic way, making an emphasis on the totality or lack thereof.

naní mo₂ / nàni mo 何も: **in any way**; not at all; whatsoever

← Indefinite pronoun *nani mo (aything)*

❖ U. w. neg. f.s of v.s.

nànra / nańra 何ら: [*for.*] **in any way not** ; at all; whatsoever

← *nanira: nani (what)* + suf. *ra (abotus)*

❖ U. w. neg. f.s of v.s.

⊕ ippái いっぱい 〔一杯〕 |c| (*one+cup*): |N| ① **all** (of) ② amount necessary to fill a container |B| ① **fully**; to capacity ② a lot; much

⊕ tappùri たっぷり [ideophone]: **fully; in plenty**

⊕ nakábà₁ / nakàba 半ば: |N| **middle** (part) |B| **half; semi-**

naka (middle) + suf. ba (place)

tòtō 等々 c (equivalent): [for.] **and so on; etcetera;** and the others

---

2. CERTAINTY & PROBABILITY

Adverbs related to the probability of things.

2.1 Certainly & Generally

Adverbs related to the certainty and degree of normality of things.

Important Words

mochiron もちろん *of course*	hontō (ni) 本当に *really*	kitto きっと *surely*
tashika (ni) 確かに *certainly*	kanarazu 必ず *necessarily*	zettai (ni) 絶対に *absolutely*
kesshite 決して *no way*	tsumari つまり *namely*	yaku 約 *approximately*
futsuu (ni) 普通に *normally*	toku (ni) 特に *especially*	betsu (ni) 別に *not really*

Ⓣ **mochìron** もちろん〔勿論〕c

(*not+argument*): ① **of course;** certainly ② let alone; not only

---

⊕ **hontō**₂ (ni) 本当に c (*foundation+hitting*): Ⓝ truth Ⓑ **really;** truly

❖ M. understood in a subjective sense.

Ⓔ **jitsù** (ni) 実に c (*real*): Ⓝ reality Ⓑ **actually;** really; truly

❖ M. understood in an objective sense.

makóto (ni) 誠に: Ⓝ truth; reality Ⓑ **indeed; really;** truly; very

ma (just) + koto (thing)

ikà ni mo いかにも〔如何にも〕: **really; truly;** indeed

ika ni (how) + concessive p. mo

sàmo さも〔然も〕: [*lit.*] **really; truly;** evidently

⊕ **kìtto** きっと〔屹度〕 [ideophone]: **surely; certainly;** definitely

❖ Often u. for subjective judgments. It implies a high probability of what one affirms.

⊕ **tàshika**₂ (ni) 確かに: Ⓐ (na) sure; certain Ⓑ ① **certainly; surely** ② [*col.*] if I remember correctly

❖ ❷ U. without the p. *ni*.

Ⓔ **màsani** まさに〔正に〕: **exactly; certainly;** surely

Obs. *masa (exact)* + adverbializing p. *ni*

tekkiri てっきり: **surely; certainly;** without a doubt

Ⓔ **zèhi** ぜひ〔是非〕 c (*being+negation*): Ⓝ right and wrong Ⓑ **by all means;** at any cost; without fail; surely

❖ Only u. w. pos. sentences.

❖ This adv. implies a strong volition about an action that is going to be done.

⊕ kanárazu 必ず: **necessarily**; invariably; without fail; absolutely

← karinarazu: pre. kari (temporary) + narazu* | Neg. continuative f. of the v. naru (to become)

❖ Only u. w. pos. sentences.

❖ Often u. for objective judgments. It implies a complete assurance about what one affirms.

⊕ zettái (ni) 絶対に c (dying out+opposite): N (an) absolute B ① **absolutely**; **definitely** ② no way; by no means.

❖ ❷ When u. w. neg. sentences.

❖ Often u. for objective judgments.

⊥ nań de mo₂ / nàn de mo なんでも〔何でも〕: I don't know for sure but…

← Interrogative pronoun nan de mo (anything)

⊥ kanárazù shi mo 必ずしも: **not always**; **not necessarily**

kanarazu (necessarily) + shi* + concessive p. mo |*(I) suru (to do)

❖ U. w. neg. f.s of v.s.

⊕ kesshíte 決して: **by no means**; **in no way**; **never**; not in the least

Gerundive f. of the v. kessuru (to determine)

❖ U. w. neg. f.s of v.s.

dó ni mo どうにも〔如何にも〕: (not) in **any way**; **in no way**; **at all**

dō (how) + dative p. ni (to) + thematic concessive p. mo (even)

❖ U. w. neg. f.s of v.s.

⊕ tsùmari つまり〔詰まり〕: ① **that is**; **namely**; I mean; basically ② **to sum up**; in short

(I) tsumaru (to be settled)

⊥ sunàwachi すなわち〔即ち〕: **that is**; **namely**

⊥ yósùru ni 要するに: **in short**; in a word; to sum up

v. yōsuru* (to need) + adverbialization marker ni |*c yō 要 (needing) + J suru (to do)

---

kàette かえって: **on the contrary**; **rather**

Gerundive f. of the v. kaeru (to change)

⊕ yàku 約 c (approximately): [for.] **approximately**; **about**; around

❖ U. before numbers.

⊥ oyóso およそ〔凡そ〕: [for.] ① **approximately**; around; about ② **generally**; commonly

❖ U. before numbers

⊕ dáitai だいたい〔大体〕 c (big+body): N ① outline ② main point B ① **approximately**; substantially; about ② **usually**; mostly A (no) general

---

⊥ taítē たいてい〔大抵〕 c (big+resistance): B ① **mostly** ② **usually**; generally A (no) most

❖ This word m. implies objective views.

⊕ futsúu (ni) 普通に c (regular+passing through): B **normally**; **generally**; **usually**; ordinarily A (no) **normal**; common; general

❖ This word m. implies objective views.

⊥ tsuújō 通常 c (passing through+usual): [for.] B **usually**; **commonly**; normally; generally A **usual**; common; ordinary

⊥ fudàn 普段 c (regular+steps): [for.] **usually**; **normally**; generally; regularly

❖ It implies a temporal connotation, having the meaning of 'most of the time'.

⊤ tòku (ni) 特に c (special): **especially**; **particularly**

220

❖ M. u. subjectively.

Ⓕ **betsú**₂ (ni) 別に Ⓒ (*separating*): **not especially**; **not really**; not particularly

❖ U. w. neg. f.s of v.s.

toríwake とりわけ〔取り分け〕: [*for.*] **above all**; **especially**; particularly

tori* + wake (reasoning) | *(I) toru (to take)

mìrukara (ni) 見るからに: ① **at a glance** ② **obviously**

Ⓕ **hoká**₂ (ni) 他に: Ⓝ **other** (thing) Ⓑ ① **besides**; **in addition** Ⓐ (no) **other**; another

ichíō 一応 Ⓒ (*one+responding*): ① **just in case**; **tentatively**; technically; for the most part ② **more or less**; **pretty much**; roughly

òmo (ni) 主に: Ⓑ **mainly**; primarily Ⓐ (no) **main**; **chief**; principal

2.2 Expectedly & Unexpectedly

Adverbs related to what can and cannot be expected.

Important Words

yappari やっぱり *as expected*	tabun (ni) 多分に *perhaps*	bikkuri びっくり *surprisedly*
kyuu (ni) 急に *suddenly*	masaka まさか *unexpectedly*	gyaku (ni) 逆に *conversely*

⊕ **yahàri** やはり〔矢張り〕: [*for.*] ① **as expected** ② **after all** ③ **still** (the same); sure enough

❖ M. u. when the expectation was done regarding one option as the most probable among many.

➤ [*col.*] ⊕ **yappárì** やっぱり〔矢っ張り〕

Ⓛ **sasúga** (ni) さすがに〔流石〕: ① **as expected** ② **after all** ③ **still** (the same) ④ **even** (as)

❖ M. u. when the expectation was good.

hatàshite 果たして: [*lit.*] ① **as expected** ② **indeed** ③ lo and behold

Gerundive f. of the v. hata suru (to accomplish; to achieve)

Ⓕ **tàbun** (ni) 多分に Ⓒ (*many+dividing*): **maybe**; **perhaps**; **probably**

Ⓛ **osòraku** おそらく〔恐らく〕: [*for.*] **perhaps**; **likely**; **probably**

← Obs. osoraku wa: osoraku* + thematic p. wa |* ← osoru† (to fear) + O.J. adverbializing suf. aku |† → C.J. osoreru ‖ The semantic derivation of this adv. is similar to the English expression 'I'm afraid that...' when expressing a sense of probability.

⊕ **kyuú** (ni) 急に Ⓒ (*urging*): ① Ⓝ **urgency**; **suddenness** Ⓑ **suddenly**; abruptly ② **unexpectedly**

❖ This word also implies some sense of 'urgency'.

Ⓛ **totsúzen** (ni) 突然に Ⓒ (*poking+thus*): Ⓑ ① **suddenly**; all of a sudden; abruptly ② **unexpectedly** Ⓐ (no) **sudden**; **unexpected**; abrupt dòyara どうやら: **apparently; seemingly;** it seems like; it appears that

dō (how) + yara: Irrealis f. of v. yaru (to do)

---

futò ふと 〔不図〕: [*col.*] **suddenly; accidentally;** unexpectedly

ikínari いきなり 〔行き成り〕: [*col.*] **suddenly;** all of a sudden; abruptly

iki* + nari: (I) naru (to become) | *(I) iku (to go)

battàri ばったり [ideophone]: [*col.*] **suddenly; unexpectedly; abruptly**

Ⓔ bikkúrì びっくり 〔吃驚〕 [ideophone]: [*col.*] Ⓑ **surprisedly;** abruptly Ⓥ (suru) to be surprised

Ⓔ màsaka₁ まさか: Ⓑ **unexpectedly** Ⓝ emergency

Obs. *masa (exact)* + interrogative p. *ka*

❖ This adv. expresses that the speaker has a strong belief that s.t. is not expected to happen.

Ⓔ gyakú₂ (ni) 逆に Ⓒ (*going against*): Ⓝ the reverse; the contrary Ⓑ **contrary to one's expectation; conversely**

Ⓔ guúzen (ni) 偶然に Ⓒ (*unexpected+thus*): Ⓝ chance Ⓑ **by chance;** by coincidence; unexpectedly

Ⓔ tamàtama たたまた 〔偶々〕: **by chance;** accidentally; unexpectedly

tama (occasionally) ×2

❖ U. when the speaker is not particularly surprised by what happened.

3. METHOD & QUALITY

Adverbs related to the methods of doing things and the quality in which those things are done.

3.1 Method

Adverbs related to the method of doing things.

Important Words

issho (ni) 一緒に *together*	betsu (ni) 別に *separately*	chanto ちゃんと *properly*
toninaku とになく *anyhow*	hayaku 早く *fast*	yukkuri ゆっくり *slowly*
hitori (de) ひとりで *alone*	sorezore それぞれ *respectively*	mēmē めいめい *individually*

Ⓣ isshó (ni) 一緒に Ⓒ (*one+twine*): Ⓝ **same** (thing); identical (thing) Ⓑ **together**

❖ ❶ Usually preceded w. the comitative p. **to**.

❖ Ⓑ Referring to the fact of doing s.t. 'together' at the same time and location.

tomó / tòmo (ni) ともに 〔共〕: [*for.*] Ⓝ same (thing) Ⓑ ① **together; jointly; with** ② **at the same time** Ⓢ **both** comitative-cumulative p. *to mo (and)* + adverbializing p. *ni*

kotógòtoku ことごとく〔悉く・尽く〕: ①
altogether ② entirely

koto (thing) + *dep. adv. gotoku (to be like)*

Ⓣ **betsú₃ (ni)** 別に ⓒ *(separating)*: Ⓝ
distinction Ⓑ **separately**; differently

jìkani 直に: **directly**; **in person**; **firsthand**

⊕ **chańto** ちゃんと [ideophone]: [*col.*]
properly; perfectly; exactly

Ⓔ **kichìnto** きちんと [ideophone]: ①
accurately; precisely ② **neatly**

Ⓔ **chódo** ちょうど〔丁度〕ⓒ
(block+occasion): **just**; **exactly**; precisely

❖ Referring to s.t. that exactly matches some requirements.

sokkùri そっくり [ideophone]: **exactly like**; **just like**

⊕ **shikkàri** しっかり〔確り〕 [ideophone]: ①
firmly; tightly ② **reliable**

❖ Referring to stability or certainty.

pittàri ぴったり [ideophone]: ① **exactly**; **precisely** ② **tightly**; closely

❖ Referring to an absence or a situation in which the required conditions are met to a very high degree.

sappàri さっぱり [ideophone]: ①
refreshingly; with relief ② **neatly**; **cleanly** ③ **not at all**; not in the least

❖ ❸ U. w. neg. f.s of v.s.

❖ M. u. to refer to s.t. physically 'clean' that produces a 'refreshing' feeling.

sukkìri すっきり [ideophone]: ① with
refreshingly; with relief ② **neatly**; cleanly

❖ Referring to a subjective 'refreshing' feeling that gives a pleasant or carefree mood.

Ⓔ **sekkáku** せっかく〔折角〕ⓒ
(breaking+angle): Ⓑ **with effort** Ⓐ (no) precious; valuable

Ⓔ **wàzato** わざと〔態と〕: **on purpose**

waza (intent) + comitative p. *to (with)*

wàzawaza わざわざ〔態々〕: **expressly**; especially

waza (intent) ×2

Ⓔ **narúbeku** / narúbèku なるべく〔成るべ
く〕: **if possible**; as much as possible

naru (to become) + suf. *beku (in order to)*

àete あえて〔敢えて〕: ① **dare** (to do s.t.); **daringly**; boldly; on purpose ② **not necessarily**; not particularly; definitely not

❖ ❷ U. w. neg. f.s of v.s.

mùri₂ (ni) 無理に ⓒ *(not being+reason)*: Ⓝ
unreasonableness Ⓑ **by force**; forcibly
Ⓐ (na/no) unreasonable

shìite 強いて: **by force**

Gerundive f. of the v. *shiiru (to force)*

Ⓔ **tsùi₁** つい: ① **unintentionally**; **by mistake** ② **just**; only

❖ ❶ Referring specifically to actions that cannot be controlled.

omòwazu 思わず: ① **unintentionally**; **involuntarily** ② **spontaneously**

Lit. neg. f. of the v. omou (to think)

ukkari うっかり [ideophone]: **carelessly**; thoughtlessly

ùrouro うろうろ [ideophone]: **aimlessly**; restlessly

VOCABULARY

àkumade mo / akùmade mo あくまでも 〔飽くまでも〕: **to the last; to the end; consistently**; persistently

O.J. aku (to tire of) + limitative p. made (until) + concessive p. mo

---

tònikaku とにかく 〔兎に角〕: **anyhow; anyway; at any rate; anyway; in any case**

O.J. to (place) + locative p. ni (in) + kaku (like this)

tòmokaku ともかく 〔兎も角〕: ① **anyhow; anyway; at any rate; anyway; in any case**

O.J. to (place) + concessive p. mo (even) + kaku (like this)

nàni shiro 何しろ: ① **anyhow; anyway**; whatsoever; at any rate ② **as a matter of fact; no matter what; believe it or not**

nani (what) + shiro: Imperative f. of the v. suru (to do)

dóse どうせ: **after all**; in any case; anyhow

dō (how) + se: imperative f. of suru (to do)

❖ M. u. subjectively, implying a degree of uncertainty, or in other cases a neg. sense of resignation or ridicule, indicating that no matter what one does, the situation will not change.

---

nàn to ka なんとか 〔何とか〕: **somehow; one way or another**

nan (what) + composite inexhaustive enumerative p. to ka (and)

dò ni ka どうにか 〔如何にか〕: **somehow; one way or another**

dō (how) + composite inexhaustive enumerative p. to ka (and)

---

hàyaku 早く: ① **fast**; quickly ② **early**; soon

(I) hayai (fast)

dòndon どんどん [ideophone]: ① **banging**; stamping ② **rapidly; quickly**; steadily

suttó / sùtto すっと [ideophone]: ① **quickly** ② **straight** (away); **directly**; right away

yukkúrì ゆっくり [ideophone]: ① **slowly** ② at ease

❖ This word has the connotation of 'in a relaxed, leisurely manner'.

jittó じっと 〔凝乎と〕 [ideophone]: **quietly**; motionlessly; still

sòrosoro₁ そろそろ [ideophone]: **quietly**; steadily

---

sottó そっと [ideophone]: ① **softly**; gently ② **secretly**

tsùrutsuru つるつる [ideophone]: **smoothly**; softly

---

jikkúrì じっくり: **carefully**; thoroughly

nòńbìri のんびり [ideophone]: **carefree**; at leisure; in a relaxed manner

---

hitòri₂ (de) ひとりで 〔独り・一人〕: Ⓝ one person Ⓑ ① **by oneself**; on one's own; alone

Cognate w. *hitori₁ (one person)*

---

sorèzore₂ / sorézòre それぞれ 〔其々〕: Ⓑ **respectively; each**; each and every Ⓐ (no) **each**

← *soresore: sore (that) ×2*

mémè めいめい 〔銘々〕 ⓒ *(inscription×2)*: Ⓝ **each one** Ⓑ **each one** (individually) Ⓐ (no) **each**

❖ Only u. for people.

onòono 各々 ⓒ *(inscription×2)*: **each one**; each person

❖ Only u. for people.

3.2 Quality

Adverbs related to the quality in which things or actions are performed.

Important Words

yoku よく *well*	hidoku 酷く *badly*	mushiro むしろ *rather*	maamaa まあまあ *so-so*	hakkiri はっきり *clearly*

Ⓣ yòku₁ よく〔良く〕: ① **good**; **well**; properly ② often; frequently

(I) *yoi (good)*

❖ ❶ Not u. w. the sense of 'skillfully'

yoròshiku / yoróshiku よろしく〔宜しく〕: [*for.*] **well**; properly

Stem of the adj. *yoroshii (good)* + adverbializing suf. *ku*

❖ This word is m. u. w. pol. set expressions.

Ⓔ hìdoku ひどく〔酷く〕: **badly**; in a bad manner

(I) *hidoi (terrible)*

rokú ni ろくに〔禄に〕: **not well**; not enough

Ⓒ *roku 禄 (happiness)* + Ⓙ *adverbializing suf. ni*

❖ U. w. neg. f.s of v.s.

Ⓗ mushírò むしろ〔寧ろ〕 Ⓒ (*writings+law*): **rather**; **instead**; **preferably**; better

màamaa まあまあ: **so-so**; passable

maa (well) ×2

Ⓔ marú₂ de まるで〔丸〕: Ⓝ circle Ⓑ **completely**; **at all**

maru* + ablative p. de | *Stem of the adj. marui (round; complete)

❖ ❶ U. w. neg. f.s of v.s.

❖ ❷ Usually u. before expressions that are followed by semblative p.s such as *yō* or *mitai*.

❖ ❶ It implies a neg. judgment by the speaker.

Ⓗ hakkìri はっきり [ideophone]: **clearly**; distinctly

dòkidoki ドキドキ [ideophone]: **with a fast beat**

❖ U. to talk about situations in which one's heart would beat.

pìkapika ピカピカ [ideophone]: **with a glitter; with a sparkle**

bùtsubutsu ブツブツ [ideophone]: **grunting; grumbling**

nìkoniko ニコニコ [ideophone]: **with a smile**

wàkuwaku ワクワク [ideophone]: ① **trembling** ② **thrilled**

Ⓔ ìraira₂ イライラ〔苛々〕 [ideophone]: **annoyingly**

gòrogoro ゴロゴロ [ideophone]: ① **thundering** ② **idling around**

hàrahara ハラハラ [ideophone]: **anxiously; nervously**

4. TIME

Adverbs related to what happens along the timeline. Most Japanese time adverbs are actually nouns (temporal nouns) that can be used as adverbs.

4.1 Now

Adverbs and nominal adverbs related to the present time.

Important Words

ima 今 *now*	mō もう *already*	kyō 今日 *today*
saikin (ni) 最近に *nowadays*	kekkyoku 結局 *eventually*	yatto やっと *finally*

Ⓣ ìma 今: ⓃⒷ **now** Ⓐ (no) present; current

➤ Ⓛ ìma ni 今に: ① **before long** ② **even now**

➤ Ⓛ ìma ni mo 今にも: **at any moment**

⊕ kòndo 今度 Ⓒ *(now+occasion)*: ① **this time**; now ② **next time**; soon

⊕ kònkai 今回 Ⓒ *(now+times)*: ① **this time**; now

- -

⊕ koré karà / korékara これから: **from now on**; after this

kore (this) + egressive p. kara (from)

⊕ końgo / kòngo 今後 Ⓒ *(now+later)*: **from now on**; after this; right now

- -

Ⓛ ìrai 以来 Ⓒ *(by means of+coming)*: **since**; henceforth

✤ Meaning from a point in the past to the present.

ìgo 以後 Ⓒ *(by means of+later)*: **since** (then); thereafter; after that

✤ This word means both from a point in the past or from a point in the future.

Ⓛ ìzen 以前 Ⓒ *(by means of+before)*: **before**; previous; since; ago

tokkúnì とっくに〔突くに〕: **long ago**; a **long time ago**; already

- -

Ⓣ mő もう: ① **already** ② **shortly** (already the time to do s.t.)

✤ Referring, rather subjectively, to s.t. unexpected that has just happened or has just been accomplished.

Ⓛ sùdeni すでに〔既に〕: **already**; previously

✤ Objectively referring to s.t. that has been accomplished or occurred at some point in the past.

mòhaya 最早: ① **already**; now ② **no longer**; not anymore

← motto haya: adv. motto (more) + adv. haya (already) ← adj. hayai (early)

✤ ❷ U. w. neg. f.s of v.s.

- -

Ⓣ kyồ 今日 Ⓒ *(now+day)*: **today**

- -

Ⓛ konban 今晩 Ⓒ *(now+dusk)*: **this evening**; **tonight**

Ⓤ **kònya** 今夜 Ⓒ (*now+night*): **tonight**

Ⓤ **kèsa** 今朝 Ⓒ (*now+morning*): **this morning**

← *keasa*: O.J. *ke* (*this*) + *asa* (*morning*)

Ⓤ **kònshuu** 今週 Ⓒ (*now+week*): **this week**

Ⓤ **kòngetsu** 今月 Ⓒ (*now+month*): **this month**

Ⓤ **kotóshi** 今年: **this year**/ temp. n.

← *kontoshi* ← *konotoshi*: Ⓒ *kon* (*this*) + Ⓙ *toshi* (*year*)

konógoro この頃 〔此の頃〕: **these days**; nowadays; at present; recently

kono (*this*) + approximate p. *goro* (*around*)

Ⓤ **saíkin** (ni) 最近に Ⓒ (*utmost+near*): **lately**; **recently**; nowadays

❖ Referring to either a current state that has continued since a recent point in time or an event that occurred at a recent point in time.

- -

Ⓤ **kekkyóku** 結局 Ⓒ (*tying+bureau*): **after all**; **eventually**; in the end

❖ Referring to a conclusion or result that has been reached after various steps have been taken.

Ⓤ **tòtō** とうとう 〔到頭〕 Ⓒ (*arrival+head*): **finally**; **at last**; after all

❖ U. when s.t. eventually materializes or fails to do so after a long process.

Ⓤ **tsùi₂ ni** ついに 〔遂に〕: **finally**; **at last**; in the end

❖ U. when initial expectations 'finally' come true.

Ⓤ **yattó** やっと [ideophone]: **at last**; **finally**

❖ This word indicates that a desirable situation will 'finally' occur in the future.

yóyaku ようやく 〔漸く〕: ① **at last**; **finally** ② **barely**; narrowly

Ⓤ **tàdachini** 直ちに: **at once**; **immediately**; directly

iki (*breath*) + *oi*: (I) *ou* (*to chase*)

sòku 即 Ⓒ (*immediate*): Ⓑ **immediately**; **instantly** Ⓟ immediate; instant

4.2 Earlier & Later

Adverbs and nominal adverbs related to what happened in the past and will happen in the future.

Important Words

mada まだ *yet*	mae (ni) 前に *before*	mazu まず *first*	saisho (ni) 最初に *at first*
saigo (ni) 最後に *at last*	toriaezu とりあえず *for now*	sugu (ni) すぐに *right away*	mō sugu もうすぐ *soon*
ato (ni/de) 後に/で *later*	mata また *again*	tsugi (ni) 次に *next*	honrai 本来 *originally*

	mukashi 昔 *formerly*	kinō 昨日 *yesterday*	ashita 明日 *tomorrow*	

- -

Ⓣ **màda** まだ: **yet**; **still**

❖ This word indicates that no change has

taken place 'yet'. In affirmative sentences, this word corresponds w. the English word 'still' and in neg. sentences it corresponds w. '(not) yet'.

ⓉⓂ màe₂ (ni) 前に: Ⓝ the front Ⓑ ① before; ago; earlier ② ahead ③ in front (of)

← *mahe*: *ma** + O.J. *he (place)* | * ← *me (eye)*

Ⓣ sakí₂ (ni) 先に: ① before; earlier; previously ② ahead

Cognate w. *saki (river delta)*

❖ The original sense of this word is directional, meaning 'towards the front'. When using this word, then, the focus is put on the future action.

Ⓜ tòji 当時 Ⓒ *(hitting+time)*: during that time; in those days

❖ Referring to a period of time in the distant past (a number of years ago).

arákajime あらかじめ〔予め〕: beforehand; in advance; previously

sàkihodo 先ほど: ① a short while ago; a moment ago; some time ago ② just now

saki (previously) + upper limitative p. *hodo (as much as)*

➤ Ⓜ [col.] sàkki さっき〔先〕

- -

Ⓣ màzu まず〔先ず〕: ① first (of all) ② not really

❖ ❷ U. w. neg. f.s of v.s.

Ⓜ saísho (ni) 最初に Ⓒ *(utmost+beginning)*: Ⓝ (the) first (thing); onset; beginning Ⓑ at first

Ⓜ sàigo (ni) 最後に Ⓒ *(utmost+later)*: Ⓝ ① last ② end ③ conclusion Ⓑ ① finally; at the end ② at last

❖ This word refers to a thing that has been done for the 'last' time and is not going to be done again.

Ⓛ zènkai / zeńkai 前回 Ⓒ *(before+times)*: Ⓝ previous time; last time Ⓑ previously Ⓐ (no) last; previous

---

Ⓜ toríàezu / toríaèzu とりあえず〔取りあえず〕: ① for now; for the time being; first (of all) ③ at once

*tori** + *aezu†* |*(I) *toru (to take)* |†Obs. variant. f. of the adv. *aete (purposely)*

Ⓜ sùgu (ni) すぐに〔直ぐ〕: ① immediately; right away ② soon

Cognate w. *sugiru (to pass)*

➤ Ⓛ massúgù (ni) まっすぐに〔真っ直ぐ〕: straight; direct; right

➤ mò sugu もうすぐ〔もう直ぐ〕: soon

Ⓛ sòrosoro₂ そろそろ [ideophone]: before long; soon; shortly

Ⓛ yagáte やがて〔軈て〕: ① before long; soon; soon ② eventually; finally

mamònaku まもなく〔間も無く〕: [for.] soon; before long; in a short time

ma (just) + concessive p. *mo* + *naku*: Infinitive f. of adj. v. *nai (to be not)*

Ⓜ ichídò (ni) 一度に Ⓒ *(one+occasion)*: ① once; one-time; on one occasion; all at once ② temporarily; for a moment

❖ Specifically u. to say that s.t. occurs 'one time' or in 'one occasion'.

Ⓛ kàtsute かつて〔嘗て〕: ① once; one time ② before; formerly

❖ Referring to s.t. that has occurred 'once' in the past.

ittán いったん〔一旦〕 Ⓒ *(one+daybreak)*: for a/the moment; once; temporarily; now

❖ Referring to s.t. that occurs for a brief time.

Ⓣ àto (ni/de) 後に/で: ① later ② after; afterward; ③ behind

Cognate w. *ato (trace*

nochì/ nochí (ni) のちに〔後〕: [for.] later (on); after; afterwards

Ⓛ izúre いずれ〔何れ〕: **eventually**; sooner or later; someday

> Interrogative pre. *izu* + O.J. suf. *re (thing)* ‖ Originally this adverbial pronoun meant 'which' or 'any'. Over time the meaning shifted to 'at any point in time' up to the current meaning of 'eventually'.

Ⓕ matà₁ また〔又〕: **again**

➤ matámata / matàmata またまた 〔又々〕: **again and again**; repeatedly; once again

Ⓛ futátabi 再び: [*for.*] **again**; once more

> *futa (two) + tabi (times)*

arátàmete 改めて: [*for.*] **another time**; **again**; over again; once again

> Gerundive f. of the v. *aratameru (to change)*

Ⓛ jìkai / jikái 次回 ⒸⒸ (*subsequent+times*): **next time** (occasion)

Ⓕ tsugì (ni) 次に: **next; following**; as follows

> (1) *tsugu (to follow up)*

Ⓜ hònrai 本来 Ⓒ (*foundation+coming*): Ⓑ **originally**; essentially Ⓐ (no) originally

❖ M. referring to s.t. that is inherent to its nature.

Ⓛ motómoto もともと〔元々〕: **originally**; by nature; from the start

> *moto (origin)* ×2

❖ Referring specifically to a result that is identical to the previous state.

Ⓜ mukáshi 昔: Ⓑ **in the old times**; **formerly**; (in the) past Ⓐ (no) **ancient**; past

> *muka** + O.J. nominalizing suf. *shi* |*Irrealis f. of v. *muku (to go towards)*

Ⓛ senjitsu 先日 Ⓒ (*previous+day*): **the other day**; a few days ago

Ⓜ kinò 昨日: **yesterday**

Ⓛ otótoì 一昨日: the **day before yesterday**; two days ago

> ← *ototsuhi:* O.J. *oto (past)* + O.J. genitive p. *tsu (of)* + *hi (day)*

Ⓜ ashítà 明日: **tomorrow**

> Cognate w. *asa (morning)*

asù 明日: [*for.*] **tomorrow**

yokújitsu 翌日 Ⓒ (*the following+day*): (the) **next day**; (the) following day

Ⓛ asàtte 明後日: the **day after tomorrow**

> ← *asasatte: asa (morning)* + *satte*: Gerundive f. of the v. *saru (to pass)*

Ⓛ sènshuu 先週 Ⓒ (*previous+week*): **last week**; the week before

Ⓛ ràishuu 来週 Ⓒ (*coming+week*): **next week**

Ⓛ sèngetsu 先月 Ⓒ (*previous+month*): **last month**

Ⓛ ràigetsu 来月 Ⓒ (*coming+month*): **next month**

Ⓛ kyònen 去年 Ⓒ (*going+year*): **last year**

Ⓛ raínen 来年 Ⓒ (*coming+year*): **next year**

4.3 While & Ever

Adverbs and nominal adverbs related to what is perpetuated in time.

Important Words

zutto ずっと *continuously*	yoku よく *often*	amari あまり *not often*

shibaraku しばらく *for a while*	tokidoki 時々 *sometimes*	tamani たまに *occasionally*
mainichi 毎日 *every day*	kinō 昨日 *yesterday*	ashita 明日 *tomorrow*
	nichiō 日常 *regularly*	mainichi 毎日 *every day*

⊕ zuttó ずっと: **continuously**; throughout; all along; the whole time

Ⓣ yòku₂ よく 〔良く〕: ① **often**; frequently ② good; well; properly

(I) *yoi (good)*

❖ Only u. w. pos. sentences.

Ⓔ shìbashiba しばしば 〔屡々〕: **often**; frequently; repeatedly; again and again

shiba* ×2 |*Irrealis f. of v. shibaru (to tie)

❖ Only u. w. pos. sentences.

tabítabi たびたび 〔度々〕: **often**; **frequently**; again and again; repeatedly

tabi (number of times) ×2

❖ Only u. w. pos. sentences.

Ⓣ amári₂ あまり 〔余り〕: Ⓝ remainder Ⓑ ① **not often**; not very often **(much)** ② not much; not too much

(I) *amaru (to be left over)*

❖ ❶ Only u. w. neg. sentences.

➢ [*col.*] ańmari₂ あんまり

mèttani 滅多に Ⓒ *(ruined+many)*: **seldom**; **rarely**; **not** (too) **much**; hardly

❖ U. w. neg. f.s of v.s.

⊕ shibàraku しばらく 〔暫く〕: **for a while**; for a moment; temporarily

← *shibaruaku: shibaru (to tie)* + O.J. adverbializing suf. *aku*

⊕ tokídoki 時々: **sometimes**

← tokitoki: *toki (time) ×2*

Ⓔ tamàni たまに 〔偶に〕: **occasionally**; once in a while

màru ichi nichi 丸一日: **the whole day**; a whole day

maru (round; whole) + *ichi nichi (one day)*

ichínichìjuu 一日中: **all day long**

Ⓒ *ichinichi 一日 (one day)* + *juu 中 (middle)*

⊕ nichíjō 日常 Ⓒ *(day+usual)*: **everyday**; regularly; usually

❖ Meaning 'in a regular basis'.

⊕ màinichi 毎日 Ⓒ *(every+day)*: **every day**

Ⓔ màiasa / maíasa 毎朝: **every morning**

Ⓒ *mai 毎 (every)* + Ⓙ *asa (morning)*

Ⓔ màiban / maíban 毎晩 Ⓒ *(every+dusk)*: **every night**

Ⓔ maíshuu 毎週 Ⓒ *(every+week)*: **every week**

Ⓔ maítsuki 毎月: **every month**; each month; monthly

Ⓒ *mai 毎 (every)* + Ⓙ *tsuki (moon)*

Ⓔ maítoshi 毎年: **every year**; each year; yearly

Ⓒ *mai 毎 (every)* + Ⓙ *toshi (year)*

ìtsu made mo いつまでも 〔何時までも〕: **forever**; for good

itsu (when) + limitative p. *made (until)* + concessive p. *mo (even if)*

aíkawarazu 相変わらず: **as always**; **as ever**; **as usual**

Pre. *ai (together)* + *wakarazu*: Obs. neg. f. of the v. *wakaru (to know)*

Ⓔ isshó 一生 Ⓒ *(one+living)*: **a lifetime**; a **whole life**; all through life dàidai 代々 [c] *(superseding×2)*: **for generations**; generation after generation

VII. INTERJECTIONS & CONJUNCTIONS

Within this section, interjections and conjunctions, two types of words that appear between sentences, are grouped together. Interjections, on the one hand, express meaning by themselves, being a type of phrase on their own. Conjunctions, on the other hand, are used to bind two different phrases while filling gaps in their interpretation.

1. INTERJECTIONS

Interjections are independent words or expressions that carry meaning and appear in isolation. In most cases, interjections also convey a certain degree of emotionality.

1.1 Affirmation & Negation

Expressions used to express affirmation or negation.

Important Words

hai はい *yes*	sō そう *right*	naruhodo なるほど *I see*
mochiron もちろん *of course*	daijobu 大丈夫 *it's alright*	iie いいえ *no*

In Japanese, there are two basic words that are translated as 'yes' and 'no': *hai* and *iie* respectively. These words, however, do not correspond exactly to the English ones, since the Japanese word *hai* ('yes') is actually an interjection that emphatically indicates that the speaker has heard and understood what has been said, rather than a demonstration of affirmation or assertion. The word *iie* ('no'), on the other hand, carries an emphasis on negation that does not exist in the corresponding English word. This is why in Japanese such words are not used as much as the respective English words. Rather, one resorts to other formulas such as the repetition of the verb either in the affirmative or in the negative form. Especially in the case of negative answers, other indirect formulas are used, such as saying 'it's different' (*chigaimasu*) or expressions such as *dekimasen* ('I can't') or *muzukashii* ('it's difficult') when refusing offers. In addition to this, it should be taken into consideration that such affirmative and negative interjections (*hai* and *iie*) are actually formal and have other more familiar versions.

Another thing to keep in mind when the speaker is confronted with yes or no questions in Japanese is that when a negative question is asked, the negation is affirmed with an affirmative expression, contrary to English.

Ⓕ hài はい: [*for.*][*pol.*] **yes**; okay; got it

Probably from Ⓒ hai 拝 (*paying homage*)

✦ The exact nuance of this word is that of 'that is correct' or 'that's right'.

Ⓕ èe ええ: [*col.*][*for.*] ① **yes**; yeah; that's right ② **hum**; hmm; er ③ **huh?**

⊕ ùn うん: [*fam.*] ① **yes; yeah; uh-huh**

➤ [*col.*] ん ん

⊕ sǒ {D} そう 〔然う〕: ① **uh-huh; I see**
② **really?** ③ **right; yes**

From the adv. sō (*like that*)

❖ U. specifically when the speaker wants
to show that is paying attention.

➤ ❶ [*fam.*] sǒ da そうだ

➤ ❶ [*pol.*] sǒ désu ne そうですね

➤ ❶ [*pol.*] sǒ désu ka そうですか

➤ ❷ sǒ ka そうか

➤ ❷ [*fam.*] sǒ ka na そうかな

⊕ narúhodo なるほど 〔成る程〕: **I see;
indeed; uh-huh**

*naru (to become) + upper limitative p. hodo (as
much as)*

---

sòsō そうそう 〔然う然う〕: **oh yeah!;
that's right; indeed**

sòno toóri その通り 〔其の通り〕: **I
agree; that's right! indeed**; quite so

sono (that) + toori (way)

Ⓔ mochìron {D} もちろん 〔勿論〕 ⒸC
(*not+argument*): **of course**; certainly

⊕ daíjòbu₂ {D} 大丈夫: **it's all right; it's
okay; no problem**

From adj. daijōbu (to be fine)

❖ U. either to ask if s.o./s.t. is alright or
to indirectly rejecting an offering.

yòshi よし 〔良し〕: **all right; alright;
okay; good**

*Fossilized O.J. predicative f. of the C.J. adj. yoi
(good)*

nàisu ナイス ⒺE (*nice*): [*col.*][*fam.*] **nice!;
good!**

Ⓕ iíè いいえ 〔否〕: [*pol.*] ① **no** ② no
problem; you are welcome

← iya* (no) ← O.J. ina (no) |*Cognate w. iya
(disagreeable)

❖ The exact nuance of this word is that
of 'that is not correct'. The use of this
word may be considered overly direct.

❖ ❷ This sense is taken when responding
to the thanks given.

➤ [*col.*] iè いえ

chigáimasu 違います: [*pol.*] ① **to be
different** ② **no; that is not right**

❖ This expression, meaning 'it's different'
is more commonly u. to say that s.o. is
not correct while not sounding too direct.

uùn ううん: [*fam.*] **no; nope;** nuh-uh

ìya いや 〔否〕: **no**

Cognate w. adj. iya (disagreeable)

❖ M. u. in a sense of dislike.

yàda やだ: [*fam.*][*fᵃm.*] **no; nuh-uh**

← iya (no) + da (to be)

❖ M. u. in a sense of dislike.

	Polite	Plain	Casual
Yes	hai	ee	un
No	iie		uun

---

shikáta (ga) nài 仕方がない 〔仕方無い〕:
it can't be helped; there's no remedy;
nothing can be done

shi* + kata (method) + nai (not be) |*(I)
suru (to do)

shǒ ga nài しょうがない: [*col.*] **it can't be
helped**; there's no remedy; nothing can be
done

← shiyō* + nominative p. ga + nai (not be)
|*shi† + ⒸC yō† 様 (way) |†(I) suru (to do)

1.2 Addressing & Greetings

Different formulas and expressions used for greetings. Like many other aspects of the Japanese language, greetings are also subject to certain degrees of formality and not all of them can be used universally.

Important Words

ohayō おはよう *good morning*	konnichiwa こんにちは *good afternoon*	konbanwa 今晩は *good evening*
moshimoshi もしもし *hello (on phone)*	irasshai いらっしゃい *welcome in*	sayōnara さようなら *farewell*
tadaima ただいま *I'm home*	okaeri おかえり *welcome home*	hisashiburi 久しぶり *long time no see*

Ⓣ ohárō gozaimàsu おはようございます〔お早う御座います〕: [*pol.*] **good morning**

Hon. pre. o + hayō* + pol. gozaimasu (to be) | *← hayau ← hayaku (early)

➤ [*fam.*] ohárō

Ⓣ końnichiwà こんにちは〔今日は〕: **hello; good afternoon**; good day

Obs. konnichi (this day) + thematic p. wa ‖ A shortened version of longer pol. obs. expressions such as 'konnichi wa gokigen ikaga desu ka' (how are you doing today?).

Ⓣ końbanwà こんばんは〔今晩は〕: **good evening**

konban (this evening) + thematic p. wa

nèe ねえ: [*fam.*][*fam.*] **hey!**

← Emphatic p. *ne*

nà な: [*fam.*][*mas.*] ① **hey!; look!**

òssu おっす〔押忍〕: [*col.*][*fam.*][*mas.*] **hi!; hello!**

← *ohayōgozaimasu (good morning)*

❖ U. informally among close friends.

yàhhoo ヤッホー: [*col.*][*fam.*][*fam.*] **hey!; yoo-hoo!**

yò よう: [*col.*][*fam.*][*mas.*] **hey!; yo!**

yàa やあ: [*col.*][*fam.*][*mas.*] **hey!; yo!; hi!**

òi おい: [*col.*][*mas.*] **hey!; oi!**

kòra こら: **hey!; yo!**

From obs. *kora (children; child)*

❖ Frequently u. towards children. Many times also u. to scold or reprove s.o.

hòra ほら: **hey!; look!**

Ⓜ mòshimoshi もしもし: ① **hello (on the phone)** ② **excuse me!**

moshi* ×2 | *← mōshi: (1) Hum. mōsu (to say)

❖ U. when answering the phone or to confirm that s.o. is listening.

Ⓔ irásshài いらっしゃい: **come in; welcome in**

Hon. imperative f. of the v. irassharu (to go; to come)

❖ U. to welcome s.o.'s visit while inviting him or her to enter.

➤ [*pol.*] irásshaimasè いらっしゃいませ

yòkoso ようこそ: **welcome!; nice to see you!**

← *yokukoso: yoku (well) + emphatic p. koso*

❖ Greeting given upon s.o.'s arrival.

Ⓔ **sayónàra** / sayónarà さようなら〔左様なら〕: [*for.*] **farewell; goodbye**

← *Obs. sayŏ* (like that) + provisional p. nara (if)* | * → *C.J. sŏ* ‖ *The lit. meaning of this word is 'if so'.*

❖ This term implies some closure or termination, so it's not u. when departing a place unless there is no plan to return to it in the recent future.

➤ [*col.*] **sayónàra** / sayónarà さよなら

de wa matá でわまた〔でわ又〕: [*col.*] **see you later**; see you again; bye

de wa (well then) + mata (again)

➤ [*col.*] **ja matá**

matáne またね〔又ね〕: [*col.*] **see you later**; bye

mata (again) + emphatic-inquisitive p. ne

jàane じゃあね: [*col.*][*fam.*] **see you (then); bye**

jaa (well then) + emphatic-inquisitive p. ne

bàibai バイバイ Ⓔ (*bye-bye*): [*col.*][*fam.*] **bye-bye**

odàijini お大事に: **take care of yourself; get well soon**

Ⓙ *Hon. pre. o +* Ⓒ *daiji (important) +* Ⓙ *lative p. ni (towards)* ‖ *A shortened version of longer pol. expressions such as 'odaijini nasatte kudasai' (please take care of yourself).*

- -

⊕ **tadáimà** ただいま〔只今〕: **I'm home!; here I am!; hello!**

← *tadaima* kaerimashita† |*tada (just) + ima (now)* |†*Past pol. f. of the v. kaeru (to come back)*

❖ U. by a person who comes back home.

⊕ **okáerinasài** お帰りなさい: [*pol.*] **welcome home**

Hon. pol. imperative f. of the v. kaeru (to come)

❖ Told to a person who comes back home.

➤ [*fam.*] **okáeri** お帰り

ittékuru 行って来る: [*fam.*] **I'm off; see you later**

itte* + kuru (to come) |**Gerundive f. of the v. iku (to go)*

❖ U. by a person who is leaving.

➤ [*pol.*] **ittékimasu** 行って来ます

ittérasshai いってらっしゃい〔行ってらっしゃい〕: [*pol.*] **have a good day**; see you later; see you later

itte* + rasshai† |*Gerundive f. of the v. iku (to go) |† ← *irasshai: Hon. imperative f. of the v. irassharu (to go; to come)* ‖ *The lit. meaning of this expression is 'please go and come'.*

❖ U. by a person who is staying to a person who is leaving.

	Statement	Response
Arriving	tadaima	okaeri
Departing	ittekimasu	itterasshai

- -

oyásuminasài お休みなさい: **good night; sleep well**

Hon. pol. imperative f. of the v. yasumu (to rest)

❖ Only u. before s.o. goes to bed.

➤ [*fam.*] **oyásumi** お休み

⊕ **hisáshiburi** / hisáshiburì {D} 久しぶり〔久し振り〕: **long time no see**; it's been a while

hajímemàshite 初めまして: [*pol.*] **pleased to meet you; nice to meet you**

Pol. gerundive f. of the v. hajimeru (to start)

- -

gènki {D} 元気 Ⓔ (*origin-mood*): [*fam.*] **I'm fine; I'm good**; I'm okay

➤ [*pol.*] **gènki desu** 元気です

➤ [*pol.*] ogènki desu ka 元気ですか: **how are you?**

➤ [*pol.*] ogènki de お元気で: take care; good-bye; be well

chóshi (wa) dò? 調子はどう: [*fam.*] **how are you doing?**

> Ⓒ *chōshi (condition)* + Ⓙ *dō (how)*

1.3 Etiquette

Certain formulas used to express formality and politeness.

Many of the words and expressions of formality presented here are not grammatically or semantically equivalent to the English equivalents, so careful attention should be paid to each of them. Notably, requests and suggestions are linked to a particular grammar that has no equivalent in English [☞ EY:VI.5].

Important Words

arigatō ありがとう *thank you*	dōmo どうも *thanks*	sumimasen すみません *excuse me*
gomen nasai ごめんんさい *I'm sorry*	kudasai ください *please*	dō zo どうぞ *please*
omedetō おめでとう *congratulations*	kanpai 乾杯 *bottoms-up!*	ganbatte 頑張って *do your best!*

Ⓣ arìgatō ありがとう〔有り難う〕: **thank you; thanks**

> ← arigatau ← *arigataku*: Adverbial f. of the adj. *arigatai* (grateful)* |*arì†+*gatai*‡ |†(I) *aru (to be)* |‡← *katai (hard)*

➤ dòmo arìgatō どうもありがと: thank you very much

➤ [*pol.*] arìgatō gozáimàsu ありがとうございます

⊕ dòmo₂ どうも: [*fam.*] ① **thank you; thanks**

> ← *dōmo arigatō (thank you very much)*

otsúkaresama deshita お疲れ様でした: **I appreciate that; thank you very much** (for your efforts); good work

> Hon. pre. *o* + *tsukare* (tiredness)* + hon. suf. *sama* + *deshita*† |*(I) *tsukareru (to be tired)* | †Perfective f. of the pol. cop. *desu (to be)*

❖ Usually politely said to s.o. after he or she has completed a job or service.

➤ [*fam.*] otsúkaresama お疲れ様

⊥ tońdemo nài とんでもない〔とんでも無い〕: [*fam.*] ① **don't mention it; you're welcome** ② **no way!; not at all!; far from it; impossible!**

> ← *to de mo nai*: Ⓒ *to* 途 *(route)* + Ⓙ composite concessive p. *de mo* + *nai (to not be)*

➤ [*pol.*] tońdemo àrimasen とんでもありません

➤ [*pol.*] tońdemo gozáimàsen とんでもございません

dò itàshimashite どういたしまして〔どう致しまして〕: [*pol.*] **you are welcome; my pleasure; no problem**

> *dō (how)* + gerundive p. f. of the hum. v. *itasu (to do)*

❖ This is m. u. in very formal or official occasions.

kochírakoso arìgatō こちらこそありがとう〔此方こそ有難う〕: **you are welcome**; my pleasure

kochira (this way) + emphatic p. *koso* + *arigatō (thank you)* ‖ Lit. 'thank you too on my behalf'

❖ This is a form to respond to the thanks given saying 'thank you' again.

➤ [*fam.*] **kochírakòso** こちらこそ

➤ [*pol.*] **kochírakòso arìgatō gozáimàsu** こちらこそありがとうございます

Ⓔ **itádakimasu** いただきます〔頂きおます〕: [*pol.*] **thank you for the meal served**

Pol. f. of the hum. v. itadaku (to receive)

❖ U. before starting to eat a served meal.

gochísōsama dèshita ごちそうさまでした〔御馳走様でした〕: [*pol.*] **thank you for the meal** (I've finished)

Ⓒ *Hon. pre. go* 御 + *chisō* 馳走 *(feast)* + *hon. suf. sama* + *deshita: Perfective f. of the pol. cop. desu (to be)*

❖ U. after a served meal has been eaten.

➤ [*fam.*] **gochísōsama** ごちそうさま

Ⓜ **sumímasèn** すみません〔済みません〕: ① **excuse me** ② **pardon me; I'm sorry** ③ thank you

Neg. pol. f. of the v. sumu (to be completed)

❖ ❸ Sometimes u. as a form to say 'thank you' when s.o. has gone to the trouble of doing s.t. for you.

➤ [*fam.*] **sumánai** すまない

➤ [*col.*][*fam.*] **sumán** すまん

shitsùrē shimasu 失礼します: [*pol.*] **excuse me**; I'm sorry

Ⓒ *shiturē* 失礼 *(impoliteness)* + *shimasu: Pol. f. of the v. suru (to do)*

Ⓔ **gomén nasài** ごめんなさい〔御免為さい〕: **sorry**; excuse me

Ⓒ hon. pre. 御 *go* + *men (avoiding)* + imperative f. of the *hon. v. nasaru (to do)*

❖ U. by the speaker when he or she has done s.t. inappropriate.

➤ [*fam.*] **gomén** ごめん

móshiagè gozáimàsen 申し訳ございます: [*pol.*] **I'm so sorry**

mōshiage (excuse) + neg. f. of the pol. v. *gozaimasu (to be)*

❖ M. u. in very formal or official occasions.

➤ [*pol.*] **móshiagè arímasèn** 申し上げありません

- -

Ⓕ **kudásài** ください〔下さい〕: [*pol.*] **please** (give me s.t.)

Imperative f. of the hon. v. kudasaru (to give)

❖ U. after the accusative p. *o* when requesting an object or thing.

❖ U. after the gerundive f. of the v.s when requesting an action or a favor to be performed.

chódài 頂戴 Ⓒ *(top+coronation)*: [*fam.*][*fam.*] **please**

❖ U. after the accusative p. *o* when requesting an object or thing.

❖ U. after the gerundive f. of the v.s when requesting an action or a favor to be performed.

Ⓔ **yoróshiku onégai shimásu** よろしくお願いします: [*hum.*][*pol.*] **please**

yoroshiku (well) + hon pre. *o* + *negai** + *shimasu†* |**(I) negau (to hope)* |†Pol. f. of the v. *suru (to do)*

❖ The nuance of this expression is s.t. of the sort of 'I hope that everything goes well' or 'I hope that I/you/we can perform the task properly', hence it can be u. to emphasize a request but also it can be said on an introduction or before some ceremony or tasks is going to start.

➤ [*hum.*][*pol.*] **onégai shimásu** お願いします

➤ [*hum.*][*fam.*] **onégai** お願い

➤ [*col.*][*fam.*] yoròshiku / yoróshiku よろしく

dồ zo どうぞ: **please** (be it); go ahead; you may (do it)

dō (how) + emphatic-inquisitive p. *zo* ‖ Lit. meaning 'however it be'.

❖ U. to express a strong desire for s.t. to occur or for s.o. to do s.t.

➤ [*pol.*] dồ zo onégai shimásu どうぞお願いします

dố ka₂ どうか: [*pol.*] **please**

dō (how) + interrogative p. *ka*

❖ It indicates a strong request or plea.

Ⓔ omédetō おめでとうと〔お目出度う〕: **congratulations**

← *omedetau* ← *omedetaku*: Hon. pre. *o* + *medetaku*: Adverbial f. of the adj. *medetai (auspicious)*

➤ [*pol.*] omédetō gozáimàsu おめでとうございます

kaṅpai 乾杯 Ⓒ *(dry+cup)*: **cheers!**; bottoms-up!

❖ U. before sharing an alcoholic drink.

baṅzài 万歳 Ⓒ *(ten thousand+years old)*: **long live…!**

yattà やった: [*col.*][*fam.*] **yay!**; hooray!; whee!

Perfective f. of the v. yaru (to do)

❖ U. when the speaker is happy or glad about some achievement or some unexpected event.

gaṅbàre がんばれ〔頑張れ〕: **go for it!**; **keep at it!**; **do your best!**

Imperative f. of the v. ganbaru (to persist)

❖ U. for encouragement or wishing good fortune on a task. It can, however, be considered rude in some contexts – specially when said to a single person– due to its imperative nature. This form is m. u. in order to cheer up groups or teams.

gaṅbàtte がんばって〔頑張って〕: [*fam.*] **go for it!**; **keep at it!**; **do your best**

Gerundive f. of the v. ganbaru (to persist)

❖ U. for encouragement or wishing good fortune on a task. M. u. towards a single person in a familiar way.

➤ [*pol.*] gaṅbàtte kudásài 頑張ってください

1.4 Doubt & Fillers

Expressions used to fill in the sentence when the speaker needs a pause to think.

Important Words

saa さあ *well…*	ja じゃ *so…*	maa まあ *hum…*
ano あの *um…*	etto えっと *er…*	chotto ちょっと *well…*

Ⓣ sàa さあ: ① **come on** ② **well…**; **hmm**; **uh**; let's see…

Ⓣ jà じゃ: **then**; **well…**; **so…**; well then

← Conjunction *de wa (then)*

➤ jàa₁ じゃあ

Ⓔ anó あの: **well…**; **um**; **er**; **uh**

From pronoun *ano (that)*

➤ anó あのう

Ⓔ màa まあ: ① **well…**; **I guess so…** ② **oh!**; **wow!** ③ **hum**

← *ma (just)*

❖ U. to either express partial agreement (**❶**), surprise (**❷**) or hesitation (**❸**).

ettó えっと: **er**; **uh**; **well**; **let me see**...

➤ eétto ええっと

Ⓛ sàte さて〔偖〕: **well**...; **now**...; then...; so...

❖ U. to introduce a new topic.

hàte はて: **well**...; **let me see**...; now...

Ⓣ chòtto₂ / chottó ちょっと〔一寸〕: ① **well**... ② **excuse me**

From adv. *chotto (a little bit)*

❖ Actually an adv. w. the meaning 'a little bit', but frequently u. as an interjection to show hesitation to an offer (**❶**) or to ask for attention (**❷**).

1.5 Surprise & Bewilderment

Expressions used to express surprise or disbelief.

Important Words

a あ *oh!*	haa はあ *what?*	e え *huh?*
hontō 本当 *really?*	sugoi すごい *wow!*	uso 嘘 *no way!*

⊕ à' あっ: **ah!**; **oh!**

aá ああ〔嗚呼〕: ① **ah!**; **oh!** ② [*col.*] **yes**; **indeed**; **that's correct**

àra / ará あら: [*fam.*] **oh!**; **ah!**

wàa わあ: **wow!**; **oh!**

oyà / òya おや: **oh!**; **oh my!**

Ⓛ hàa はあ: **what?**; **huh?**

àre / aré あれ: **eh?**; **huh?**; **what?**

From pronoun *are (that)*

è え: **eh?**; **really?**

➤ [*fam.*] hèe へえ:

Ⓣ hòntō₃ (ni) 本当に: ① **really?** ② **really**

From n. *hontō (truth)*

➤ [*col.*] hònto ほんと

màjide マジで: [*col.*] **seriously?**; **really?**

← *maji (serious)* + *de*: Gerundive f. of the cop. *da (to be)*

nàn to 何と: ① **what** ... ? ② **how** ... !: what (a/an) ... !; so ... !

nan (what) + quotative p. *to*

➤ [*col.*] nàn te なんて

⊕ sugòi₂ すごい〔凄い〕: **amazing!**; **great!**; awesome!

From adj. *sugoi (terrific)*

➤ [*col.*][*mas.*] sugè すげい

⊕ ùso₂ 嘘: ① **lie** ② **no way!**; **I don't believe that**

Ⓛ màsaka₂ まさか〔真逆〕: **no way!**; **that's not possible!**; you don't say!

From adv. *masaka (unexpectedly)*

Ⓛ tóndemo nài とんでもない〔とんでも無い〕: **absolutely not!**; **not at all!**; far from it!; impossible!

← *to de mo nai*: Ⓒ *to* 途 (route) + composite concessive p. *de mo* + *nai* (not to be)

kyàa きゃあ: [*fam.*] ① **yikes!** ② eek!

gè' ゲツ: **yuck!**; **ack!**; gross!

òtto おっと : **oops**; uh-oh

itàch' 痛っ : **ouch!**; that hurt!

← *itai (hurtful)*

yòisho よいしょ : hop (u. when sitting down or picking up s.t. heavy)

1.6 Swearing & Coercing

Expressions that express disgust and anger.

Important Words

kuso くそ *damn!*	dame だめ *stop it!*	urusai うるさい *shut up*

chikúshò ちくしょう 〔畜生〕: **damn it!**; fuck; shit

From n. *chikushō (beast)*

shimàtta ちくしょう : **damn it!**

Perfective f. of the v. *shimau (to finish)* ‖ Lit. 'it's finished'.

kusò くそ 〔糞〕: ① **shit** ② **damn!**

damè₂ ダメ 〔駄目〕: **no!**; stop it!

From adj. dame (no good)

urúsài うるさい 〔煩い〕: ① **noisy**; loud ② **shut up!**; be quiet!

damàre だまれ 〔黙れ〕: **shut up!**

Imperative f. of the v. damaru (to be silent)

2. CONJUNCTIONS

The agglutinative nature and SOV order of the Japanese language means that in most cases, the connective functions between verbs and, therefore, clauses, are done through various particles and endings that are added to verb conjugations, adjectives and nouns. These endings and particles usually replace in Japanese the role that conjunctions have in English [☞ GE:I.5]. However, this does not mean that there is not also a series of sentence-initial conjunctions in Japanese.

In contrast to connector particles, sentence-initial conjunctions also serve as a somewhat emphasized introduction to the newly connected clause. It is for this reason that Japanese conjunctions are usually followed by a pause (represented in the written language by a comma).

As a matter of fact, most Japanese conjunctions, etymologically, are not pure conjunctions but are usually conjugative derivations of verbs and adjectival verbs, or nouns and adverbs used as conjunctions with the help or not of some particle.

2.1 Consecutive & Enumerative

Consecutive conjunctions introduce a clause that is a consequence of the previous one, while enumerative conjunctions are used to list clauses

Important Words

sō shite そうして *and*	dakara だから *so*	sore de それで *and*

㊥ só shité 〔然うして〕: ① **and**; and then ② like that

sō (that way) + *shite*: Gerundive f. of the v. *suru (to do)*.

❖ It connects two parallel events, that is, events that are somehow related.

➤ ㊤ soshíte そして 〔然して〕: ① **and**; and then; and now ② **thus**; like that

㊥ soré kará それから 〔其れから〕: **and then** ② **after that**; since then

sore (that) + causal p. *kara (since; because)*

❖ It indicates that the content of the later sentence follows in time the preceding one.

㊥ dà kara だから: **so; therefore**

Cop. *da (to be)* + causal p. *kara (since; because)*

㊤ shitágatte したがって 〔従って〕: [*for.*] **therefore**; consequently; accordingly

Gerundive f. of the v. *shitagau (to follow)*

yuèni ゆえに 〔故に〕: [*lit.*] **therefore**; consequently

yue (reason) + punctual p. *ni (in)*

㊥ soré dé それで 〔其れで〕: **and**; **because of that**; thereupon

sore (that) + gerundive f. of the cop. *da (to be)*

❖ This word indicates objectively that the previous sentence is a reason or cause for the following one.

㊤ sokó dé そこで 〔其処で〕: **therefore**; then; so; accordingly; now

soko (there) + locative p. *de (in)*

❖ It describes a situation that leads naturally to another situation.

㊤ surú tó すると: **thereupon; hereupon**

suru (to do) + *conjunctive p. to (and)*

2.2 Cumulative & Disjunctive

Cumulative conjunctions introduce a clause whose meaning adds weight or entity to the preceding clause, while disjunctive conjunctions serve to give a new option over the preceding clause.

Important Words

mata また *also*	mata wa または *or*

㊥ matá₂ また 〔又〕: ① **also** ② **and**

From adv. mata (again)

㊥ soré ní それに 〔其れに〕: **besides**; moreover

sore (that) + locative p. *ni (on)*

❖ It introduces new information w. no emotional or subjective judgment.

㊤ shikà mo しかも 〔然も〕: **moreover**; furthermore; and yet

O.J. *shika (like that)* + thematic-concessive p. *mo (even)*

❖ It introduces new information w. a subjective judgment, sometimes indicating also that what is being expressed is an irony or a paradox.

ⓊⒷ sàrani₂ 更に: **moreover**; furthermore; again; even more

From adv. *sarani (more and more)*

❖ It indicates that a situation changes into an upper level.

ⓊⒷ nào なお 〔尚〕: [*for.*] **in addition**; **furthermore**; still (more); yet

➤ naó sàra なおさら 〔尚更〕: [*for.*] **still more**; **even more**

sonó ué その上〔其の上〕: **in addition**; furthermore; on top of that

sono (that) + ue (on top; above)

kuwáete 加えて: **in addition**; additionally

Gerundive f. of the v. *kuwaeru (to add)*

soré mó それも〔其れも〕: **in addition to that**; what's more

sore (that) + cumulative p. *mo (also)*

màshite まして〔況して〕: **let alone**; not to mention; to say nothing of; still more

➤ [*lit.*] màshiteya ましてや〔況してや〕

- -

oyóbi / òyobi および〔及び〕: [*lit.*] ① **as well as** ② **and** (also)

(I) *oyobu (to reach; to extend)*

❖ U. in order to conclude a complex list of things.

narábi ní 並びに: [*lit.*] ① **as well as**; ② **and** (also)

(I) *narabu (to form a line)*

❖ U. in order to conclude a complex list of things; appearing before the last n. on a list.

kàtsu 且つ: [*lit.*] [*for.*] **and**; **as well as**; besides

❖ M. u. after continuative f.s.

sonò ta その他〔其の他〕: **otherwise**; besides; in addition (to that); other than that

sono (that) + ta (other)

sonò hoka その他〔其の他〕: **otherwise**; besides; in addition (to that); other than that

sono (that) + hoka (other)

- -

Ⓜ matà₂ (wa) または〔又は〕: **or**; otherwise

mata (again; also) + thematic p. *wa*

ⓊⒷ soré tò mo それとも〔其れ共〕: **or else**; **or**

sore (that) + composite comitative-cumulative p. *to mo (and)*

❖ U. when choosing from what is contained in a question.

ⓊⒷ arùiwa あるいは〔或いは〕: [*for.*] ① **or**; either ② perhaps

aru (to be; to exist) + O.J. nominalizing suf. i + thematic p. *wa*

❖ U. when one can choose between two things and it is also possible to choose both of them at the same time.

mòshiku wa もしくは〔若しくは〕: [*lit.*] **or**; otherwise

Con. *moshi (if) +* adverbializing suf. *ku +* thematic p. *wa*

2.3 Adversative & Concessive

Adversative conjunctions are used to specify that the new clause added is somewhat contradictory to the previous one, while concessive conjunctions are used to contrast one idea with another where one piece of information appears to be surprising or unexpected.

Important Words

demo でも *but*	shikashi しかし *however*	da ga だが *but*

Ⓔ **dèmo** でも: [*fam.*] **but**; however; though; even so

Gerundive f. of the cop. *de* + concessive p. *mo (even)*

❖ This word can also be u. as a solicitation or an expression of intent or hope.

Ⓔ **shikàshi** しかし〔然し〕: [*for.*] **however; but**

O.J. *shika (like that)* + *shi:* (I) *suru (to do)*

❖ Referring to a situation or event that is contrary to the possible consequences from the previous sentences.

Ⓔ **dà ga** だが: **but**; however; nevertheless

Cop. *da (to be)* + pol. adversative p. *ga (but)*

❖ Word u. when there is a gap in the flow of content between the first and second sentence.

➤ [*fam.*][*col.*] **dà ga ne** だがね

➤ [*for.*] **dèsu ga** ですが

Ⓔ **kèredomo** けれども: [*lit.*] **however; but**; although

Ⓔ **dà kedo** だけど: [*col.*] **however; but**

Cop. *da (to be)* + col. adversative p. *kedo (but)* ← *keredomo (but)*

Ⓔ **tàda₂** ただ〔只〕: **however; but**; nevertheless

From adv. *tada₁ (only)*

Ⓔ **tàdashi** ただし〔但し〕: [*for.*] **however; but**; provided that

tada (only) + *shi:* (I) *suru (to do)*

❖ This word is u. to add conditions, restrictions or exceptions to the preceding statement.

Ⓔ **dàtte** だって: [*col.*] ① **but** ② **after all** ③ because

From concessive copular p. *datte (even)*

Ⓔ **mottòmo₂** もっとも〔尤も〕: **although**; though; but; yet

motto (more) + concessive p. *mo*

Ⓔ **soré dè mo** それでも〔其れでも〕: **nevertheless**; even so

sore (that) + composite concessive p. *de mo (even)*

Ⓔ **tokórogà** ところが〔所が〕: **even so**; **even though**; still; however

tokoro (place) + nominative p. *ga₂*

❖ Word u. when the content of the later sentence differs substantially from the result inferred from the earlier sentence, usually inferring a subjective point of view.

soré tó それと〔其れと〕: **even so; and then**

sore (that) + conjunctive p. *to (and)*

2.4 Explanative & Conditional

Conjunctions used to indicate that the subsequent sentence is an explanation or a condition of the previous sentence.

Important Words

de wa では *then*...	moshi もし *if*	marude まるで *as if*

	chinamini ちなみに *by the way*	tatoeba 例えば *for example*

Ⓛ **soré dè wa** それでは〔其れでは〕: **well then...; in that case...**

sore (that) + de wa (then)

❖ U. for a definite event without room for hypotheses.

➤ [*col.*] sore jaa それじゃあ〔其れじゃあ〕

Ⓛ **dè wa** では: **then...; well..; so; well then...**

➤ [*col.*] jàa₂ じゃあ

soré nàra それなら〔其れなら〕: **in that case; if that's the case; if so**

sore (that) + nara: Conditional f. of the attributive cop. *na (is)*

❖ U. for an event introduced as a hypothesis or assumption.

➤ [*col.*] sonnara そんなら

Ⓛ **nàze nara** なぜなら〔何故なら〕: [*for.*] **because; the reason is**

naze (why) + provisional p. nara (if)

❖ The verbal f. of the sentence will always have to be followed by a causal p.

➤ **nàze naraba** なぜならば: = **naze nara**

Ⓛ **datte** だって: [*col.*][*fam.*] ① **because** ② **but**

cop. *da (to be)* + col. quotative p. *tte (say that)*

sonó tame そのため〔その為〕: **hence; for that reason**

sono (that) + causal p. *tame (because)*

okáge de おかげで〔お陰で〕: **thankfully; thank God**

Hon pre. o + kage (shade) + locative p. de (in)

Ⓒ **mòshi (mo)** もし: **if; in case** (that); **supposing**

❖ The verbal f. of the sentence will also always be in conditional f. when used with this con.

tatóe / tatòe たとえ〔例え〕: **even if**

(I) *tatoeru (to compare)*

Ⓛ **marú₃ de** まるで〔丸〕: Ⓝ circle Ⓑ **as if; as though**

atakamo あたかも〔恰も〕: **as if; as though**

Ⓒ **chinámini** / chinàmini ちなみに〔因みに〕: **by the way; incidentally**

chinami* + adverbializing p. *ni* |*(I) *chinamu (to be connected with)*

❖ This word is u. to introduce a topic that is somehow connected to what was talked about.

Ⓛ **tokóròde** ところで〔所で〕: **by the way; incidentally**

tokoro (place) + locative p. *de (in)*

❖ U. in order to bring a completely new topic into the conversation.

Ⓒ **jitsù wa** 実は: **as a matter of fact; to tell the truth; by the way**

Ⓒ *jitsu* 実 (reality) + thematic p. *wa*

karíni 仮に: **supposing** (that); **even if**

pre. kari (provisional) + adverbializing p. *ni*

Ⓛ **ippò** (de wa) 一方 Ⓒ (one+direction): ① **on the one hand; on the other hand**; ② **whereas**

hańmèn / hańmen

反面 ⓒ (*reverse+face*): **on the other hand**

tahồ (de wa) 他方 ⓒ (*other+direction*): **on the other hand**

sòre dokóro ka それどころか〔其れ所か〕: **on the contrary**; far from that

sore (that) + deflective-neg. p. dokoroka (not just)

- -

⊕ tatòeba 例えば: **for example; for instance**

Conditional f. of the v. tatoeru (to compare)

⊕ ìwaba / iwàba いわば〔言わば〕: **so to speak…**; so to call it…

O.J. provisional f. of the v. iu (to say)

VIII. NOMINAL AFFIXES

Nominal affixes are non-conjugable, dependent morphemes that are added to a nominal—whether it is before (prefix) or after (suffix)—in order to change its meaning.

1. PREFIXES

Affixes that are placed in front of nouns. Prefixes are functionally similar to adjectives but, unlike adjectives, they cannot be used alone without the noun they modify. Unlike prenominals [☞ I]—morphemes which, like prefixes, are placed before nouns in order to modify them—prefixes do not directly refer to the following noun but simply specify a characteristic of it.

1.1 Honorific Prefixes

Prefixes that "honor" nouns—make them honorific. There is a native (*o-*) and a Sino-Japanese (*go-*) honorific prefix. Theoretically, the native prefix goes with native words and the Sino-Japanese prefix goes with Sino-Japanese words, but there are numerous exceptions to this rule. In any case, the most common honorific prefix is undoubtedly the native *o-*. Both prefixes could be translated literally as 'honorable'. These prefixes are used to show respect for an object used by or offered to someone respectable or with whom one wants to show a certain degree of formality. There are some nouns whose appearance along with an honorific prefix is so common that they have almost become a fossilized expression that seldom appears without such a prefix.

Ⓔ **o-** お〔御〕: honorific noun

❖ M. u. w. Japonic words in order to make those words honorific. It usually also implies that the mentioned thing belongs or is related to the listener as opposed to the speaker.

Ⓔ **go-** ご〔御〕 Ⓒ (*honorable*): honorific noun

❖ M. u. w. Sinitic words in order to make those words honorific. It usually also implies that the mentioned thing belongs or is related to the listener as opposed to the speaker.

1.2 Quantitative Prefixes

Prefixes that modify a noun to indicate an approximate amount related to that noun.

Ⓔ **suu-₁** 数 Ⓒ (*number*): **several**; a number of

sho- 諸 Ⓒ (*various*): **various; several**

ta- 多 Ⓒ (*many*): **many; multi-**; multiple; various

zen- 全 Ⓒ (*whole*): ① **all; whole; pan-**; **omni-** ② in total [2: u. w. numbers]

❖ ❷ Before a number followed by a classifier.

han- 汎 Ⓒ (*all-inclusive*): **pan-**

ⓉＬ hàn- 半 ⓒ (*half*): **half; semi-**   bō- 某: (a) **certain**

1.3 Qualificative Prefixes

Prefixes that modify a noun to indicate a quality of that noun.

Important Lexemes

dai- 大 *big*	shō- 小 *small*	chuu- 中 *medium*
fu- 不 *negation*	hi- 非 *negation*	mu- 無 *negation*

dài 大 ⓒ (*big*): **big; large; great**

oo- 大: **big; large**

chō- 超 ⓒ (*transcending*): [*col.*] **super-; ultra-; extra-; very**

ⓉＬ shō 小 ⓒ (*each*): **small; little**

ko- 小: **little; small**

ⓉＬ chuu- 中 ⓒ (*middle*): **medium; average; middle**

shin- 新 ⓒ (*new*): **new; neo-**

dō- 同 ⓒ : **same**

fuku- 副 ⓒ (*supplemental*): **sub-; vice-; additional; supplemental**

ma- 真っ: **just; right; true; real**

➢ ma'- 真っ

ⓉＬ fu- 不 ⓒ (*no*): **negation** (un-; non-; in-)

hi- 非・否 ⓒ : **negation** (in-; non-; un-)

ⓉＬ mu- 無 ⓒ (*not being*): **non-; un-**

mō- 猛 ⓒ (*ferociousness*): ① **wild; ferocious** ② **extreme; intense**

ko- 故 ⓒ (*happenstance*): [*lit.*] **the deceased; late**

❖ U. before a proper n.

da'- 脱 ⓒ (*undressing*): **de-** (removal or reversal)

han- 反 ⓒ (*reverse*): **anti-**

1.4 Temporal & Locative Prefixes

Prefixes that refer to characteristics of the noun that have to do with time or location.

Important Lexemes

kyuu- 旧 *ex-*	mi- 未 *not yet...*	sai- 再 *re-*

ⓉＬ kyuu- 旧 ⓒ (*old times*): **old; previous; former; ex-**

zen- 前 ⓒ (*before*): **the last; the previous; pre-**

karí- 仮: **temporary** (thing); **provisional** (thing)

ki- 既 ⓒ (*already*): **already; previously**

mi- 未 ⓒ : **not yet** (un-; in-)

ⓉＬ rai- 来 ⓒ (*coming*): **next; coming**

❖ U. w. temporal n.s.

sai- 再 ⓒ (*one more time*): **re-; again; newly**

zai- 在 ⓒ (*being at*): **residing in**; situated in

247

❖ U. w. place names.

2. SUFFIXES

Affixes that are placed after nominals to modify their meaning.

Exceptionally, there are some suffixes that are originally nouns that can act as suffixes with another meaning.

2.1 Personal Suffixes

In Japanese, when referring to the listener or other people, one should take into consideration the formality and the level of respect to be shown to such people. As a general rule, it is impolite in any register to refer to a particular person by their name alone. The resource to be used to maintain good manners in speech is the addition of a series of personal suffixes to the first or last name of the person in question. The suffix to be chosen will depend on the degree of honorability of the person and his social position with respect to the speaker.

In professional relationships, the addition of a professional title (e.g. *sensē* in the case of educators) to the name is often preferred to the personal suffixes listed here.

-sama$_2$ 様: [*hon.*][*pol.*] honorific marker

← N. *sama (appearance)*

❖ Suf. attached to the job titles or names of people to show respect and formality towards them.

❖ U. when the listener is in a higher social position than the speaker. Frequently u. in business settings.

-san さん: [*hon.*][*pol.*] honorific marker

← Hon. suf. *sama*

❖ Suf. attached to the job titles, personal names or family names of people to show respect and formality towards them.

❖ U. neutrally to address s.o. of equal or lower status than the speaker while showing respect.

-chan ちゃん: [*hon.*][*fam.*] honorific marker

← Hon. suf. *san*

❖ Suf. attached to women's or children's personal names.

❖ M. u. when the listener is of a lower or equal social status than the speaker.

-kun 君 Ⓒ (*mister*): [*hon.*][*fam.*] honorific marker

❖ Suf. attached to male's personal or family names.

❖ M. u. when the listener is of a lower or equal social status than the speaker.

-shi 氏 Ⓒ (*surname*): [*pol.*] **Mr.; Ms.**

❖ Suf. attached to names of people to show formality towards them.

❖ M. u. in official documents.

Reg.	Hon.	Listener	Gen.
[*pol.*]	sama	Higher	Anyone
	san	Equal / Lower	
[*fam.*]	chan	Lower	Female
	kun	Equal / Lower	Male

248

2.2 Pluralizing Suffixes

Although grammatical plurality does not exist in Japanese, it is possible to mark the semantic plurality of some nouns by means of the pluralizing suffixes listed here. In any case, these suffixes cannot be added to all types of nouns but only to those nouns related to people.

-tachi たち〔達〕: plural marker

❖ Added to personal pronouns or n.s referring to animate things, m. people, when the plurality needs to be specified.

❖ It can be u. w. personal names when that person is representing a whole group (e.g. スミスたち: 'Smith and company').

-ra ら〔等〕: [*fam.*] plural marker

❖ Added to personal, demonstrative pronouns or n.s referring to animate things, m. people, when the plurality needs to be specified. Although the tone of this suf. is familiar, it can also sound deprecating depending on the context or on the word it is added to.

-gata 方: [*hon.*] plural marker

❖ Added to personal, demonstrative pronouns or n.s referring to people when the plurality needs to be specified and the referent is in a high social position (e.g. 'teachers' → *sensēgata*).

2.3 Qualificative Suffixes

Suffixes that serve to provide a qualitative description of the noun to which they are added.

Important Lexemes

-teki 的 *adjectivizing suf.*	-sē 性 *qualifying suf.* (-ness)	-ka 化 -*ization*

Ⓔ -teki 的 Ⓒ (*aim*): adjectivizing suffix (-**ive**; -**like**; -**ish**; -**ic**; -**ical**; -**y**)

❖ It makes adj.s out of n.s.

➤ -teki na 的な: adjectivizing suffix in its attributive f.

➤ -teki ni 的に: adverbialized form of the adjectivizing suffix → adverbializing composite suffix

-sē 性 Ⓒ (*disposition*): qualifying suffix (-**ity**; -**ness**)

❖ It indicates a quality or condition related to the n. to which it is attached.

-ka 化 Ⓒ (*transformed*): **change into** (-**ization**; -**ification**)

-zumi 済み: **finished**; completed

← *sumi*: (I) *sumu (to finish)*

-kan 観 Ⓒ (*view*): **view of**

-kan 感 Ⓒ (*sensation*): **sense of**; feeling of

-ryoku 力 Ⓒ (*strength*): **power of**; ability of; skill of

-men₂ 面 Ⓒ (*face*): **aspect of**; side of

-gokochi 心地: **feeling of**

← n. *kokochi (feeling)*: Ⓙ *koko** + Ⓒ *suf. chi* 地 *(area)* | *← kokoro (heart)*

-betsu₄ (ni) 別に Ⓒ (*separating*): **classified by**

Ⓔ -darake だらけ: **filled with**; full of

(I) *darakeru (to be lazy/slack)*

❖ Usually it has neg. connotations.

-mamire 塗れ: **covered with**; stained with

(I) *mamireru (to be smeared)*

-zukume ずくめ〔尽くめ〕: **full of**; swathed in; completely

(I) *mamireru (to be smeared)*

-sugata₂ 姿: **dressed in; wearing**

-tsuki 付き: **including; equipped with**

(I) *tsuku (to be attached)*

-tomo とも〔共〕: **all of; including**

-kusai₂ 臭い: **smelling like; reeking of**

❖ Also u. in a fig. way w. the sense of 'having an air of'.

2.4 People & Society

Suffixes that add meanings concerning to people, actions and social relationships.

Important Lexems

-sha 者 *s.o. who does s.t.*	-shugi 主義 *-ism*
-jin 人 *person*	-go 語 *language*

-jin 人 c (*person*): ① **person; people** (from a country; place; group...) ② **-er**

-in 員 c (*employee*): **member**

Ⓔ -sha 者 c : **s.o. who does s.t.**

-ka 家 c (*house*): **expert; professional;** performer; specialist

-kai 会 c : **meeting;** party

tsukái 使い: N ① use; usage ② errand; mission ③ messenger S **user of; manipulator of** (-er; -ist; -ator)

(I) *tsukau (to use)*

-i 位 c (*position*): ① **rank** ② **place**

Ⓔ -go 語 c (*talking*): ① **language of; -ese** ② word

-ben 弁 c (*delivery*): **dialect**

Ⓔ gakú 学 c (*learning*): N **learning** S **-ology; -ics; study of**

Ⓔ shùgi 主義 c (*main+righteousness*): N **doctrine; principle** S **-ism**

-sē 制 c (*system*): **system;** organization

-tai 体 c (*body*): **group of; body of;** organization of

-ha 派 c (*faction*): **group; (political) faction;** wing; sect

dòji 同士 c (*same+gentleman*): N **companion; fellow** S **each other; together**

-ha 権 c : **rights**

-ron 論 c (*arguments*): **theory;** arguments

-shō 症 c (*symptoms*): **illness (-pathy; -ism)**

-byō 病 c (*sickness*): **disease;** illness; **-athy**

2.5 Time & Partition

Suffixes related to the division of time and things.

Ⓔ -bun 分 c (*dividing*): **part; segment; share**

-ki 期 c : **period of time;** season

Ⓕ -han₂ 半 c (*half*): **and a half;** half-past

Ⓔ -nakaba₂ 半ば: **mid;** middle of

naka (middle) + suf. *ba (place)*

❖ Only u. w. age and periods of time.

-gurumi 版: **the whole; the entire;** -wide

← *kurumi:* (I) *kurumu (to wrap up)*

- -

Ⓛ -ka 課 Ⓒ *(lesson)*: ① **section; department** ② **lesson**

-ka 科 Ⓒ *(science)*: ① **faculty;** school; department; section ② **specialization;** branch of study ③ **taxonomical family**

-bu 部 Ⓒ *(section)*: ① **division; department;** bureau ② **category**

-han 版 Ⓒ *(printing)*: **edition;** version

tànï 単位 Ⓒ *(simple+position)*: Ⓝ Ⓢ **unit(s)** (of)

Ⓛ rìtsu 率 Ⓒ : Ⓝ Ⓢ **ratio** (of); **rate** (of); **proportion** (of)

warí 割り/割: Ⓝ Ⓢ **ratio** (of); **rate** (of); **proportion** (of)

(I) *waru (to divide)*

- -

-go 後 Ⓒ *(later)*: **after; post-**

-zen 前 Ⓒ *(before)*: **before; pre-**

-sugi 過ぎ: **past;** after

(I) *sugiru (to pass)*

❖ Only u. w. hours and minutes.

2.6 Things & Places

Suffixes related to the physical places.

- -
- -

⊕ yồ 用 Ⓒ *(using)*: Ⓝ **use; purpose** Ⓢ **for the use of; for the purpose** of

-kē ❶❷ 型/ ❷ 形 Ⓒ : ① **style** ② **shape; form**

-gata 形: ① **shape; form** ② **type**

-gō 号 Ⓒ *(sign)*: **number**

chò 著 Ⓒ *(authoring)*: Ⓝ **book;** (written) **work** Ⓢ **written by** (the author of a book)

-sē 製 Ⓒ *(manufacture)*: ① **made in** ② **made of**

-hi 費 Ⓒ *(spending)*: **cost; expense**

-kin 金 Ⓒ *(money)*: **money;** fee; fare; cost

materiality of things and

-jo 所 Ⓒ : **place**

-ba 場: **place**

-kan 館 Ⓒ *(building)*: **hall; building;** house

Ⓛ -kyoku 局 Ⓒ *(bureau)*: **office; bureau**

-chō 庁 Ⓒ : **government office;** agency

-ten 店 Ⓒ *(disposition)*: **shop;** store

-ya 屋 Ⓒ *(salon)*: ① **shop** ② **seller**

-shitsu 室 Ⓒ : **room**

-en 園 Ⓒ : **park**

-chi 地 Ⓒ *(land)*: **area for**

GRAMMAR EXPLANATIONS

GRAMMAR EXPLANATIONS

In this part, the grammatical forms necessary to speak and understand Japanese comfortably are explained in a detailed, progressive manner and with examples.

The different sections through which Japanese grammar is explained are as follows:

I. **Parts of Speech:** A detailed explanation of the different word classes.

II. **Syntax:** Explanations of the syntactic rules of Japanese.

III. **Verbal Inflection:** Explanations of the most important verbal inflections.

IV. **Nominals & Adjectival Nouns:** Brief description of the syntactic behavior of nouns and adjectival nouns.

V. **Copular Inflection:** Inflections of copulative verbs.

VI. **Extensive Verbal Inflection:** More verbal inflections.

VII. **Verbal Inflection Addenda:** Additional details concerning verbs.

VIII. **Particles:** Presentation of the most important particles.

IX. **Adverbs & Conjunctions:** Brief description of the syntactic behavior and peculiar characteristics of adverbs and conjunctions.

X. **Word and Phrase Class Transformation:** Presentation of the different ways of changing one word or phrase class into another class.

XI. **Verbal Compounds:** Presentation of the most important verbal compounds.

XII. **Verbal Forms Extensions:** Description of combinations of verbal forms with particles.

XIII. **Particle Extensions:** Particles in combination with nouns or other particles.

XIV. **Correlative Constructions:** Complex phrasal structures.

XV. **Formality:** Grammatical peculiarities in relation to formality in the language.

I. PARTS OF SPEECH

In the preliminaries part, we already saw an introduction to the word classes that exist in Japanese [☞ PR:IV.1], and we also saw that these do not correspond exactly to those in English. In this chapter, we will discuss a concept closely related to word classes: parts of speech.

Parts of speech refer to the functionality of words and morphemes in general, since parts of speech also take into account the conjugation or variability of words.

There are conjugable words (which can vary through inflections) and non-conjugable or invariable words. We will find that nominals are non-conjugable words (invariable) and verbs are conjugable words.

There are also dependent and independent morphemes. Independent morphemes do not need other morphemes or words to function within a sentence, while dependent morphemes always need to be linked to other words or morphemes.

- **Independent Words**: Words that do not need other words to convey meaning.

- **Dependent Words**: Words that need another word to convey meaning.

- **Non-Conjugable Words**: Words whose form does not vary. Also called invariable or uninflected words.

- **Conjugable Words**: Lexemes formed by a root that use different inflections to acquire meaning. Also called inflected words.

By separating the words into the two groups of categories of non-conjugable and conjugable words and independent and dependent words, we can better understand word classes in Japanese, which we will now analyze according to their category.

Independent Conjugable Words:

1. **Verbals**: Express actions or states. Verbs and verbal adjectives belong to this group.

Independent Non-Conjugable Words:

2. **Nominals**: They name concepts, people, animals, objects, places or ideas. To this group belong nouns, pronouns and numerals.

Dependent Conjugable Words:

3. **Copula**: Lexeme that acts as a linking verb between a subject and a nominal element defining existence or being.

4. **Coverbs**: Verbs that attach to another verb to modify its meaning.

Dependent Non-Conjugable Words:

5. **Phrasal Nexus**: Words or morphemes that modify either a verb or a noun to either functionally or semantically link them to the rest of a sentence or to another sentence.

6. **Verbal Modifiers**: Words that modify the meaning or nuance of a noun or verb. Adverbs belong to this group.

7. **Nominal Modifiers**: Words that modify the meaning or nuance of a noun or verb. Adverbs belong to this group.

8. **Affixes**: Morphemes that are attached to a nominal to modify its meaning or grammatical function.

Non-Conjugable Isolated Words:

9. **Interjections**: Isolated words that denote surprise or emotion and act as a sentence by themselves.

In this chapter, we will proceed to explain each word class according to the categories above. The terminology introduced from now on will help to understand all the explanations given throughout the book.

1. VERBALS

Verbals are independent conjugable words that describe an action or state. Verbals are always composed of an invariable root morpheme that cannot stand alone plus variable suffixes called inflections [☞ I.5].

1.1 Verbs

Verbs are verbal words that describe actions or states and are composed of a lexemic root and conjugable inflections of their own, which use the final morpheme -*u* in their dictionary form [☞ III.2.1]. Verbs can be classified according to their meaning—semantically—or according to their formation—morphologically.

Semantic Categorization

- **Stative Verbs**: Verbs that describe a state that develops or occurs at the time of speech.

  いる: 'to be at'; 済む: 'to live at'

- **Active Verbs**: Verbs that describe an action.

  食べる: 'to eat'; 歩く : 'to walk'

Morphological Categorization

- **Pure Verbs:** The lexemic root is of native origin and must always be linked to an inflection.

  いる: 'to be at'; 話<ruby>話<rt>はな</rt></ruby>す: 'to speak'

- **Nominal Verbs:** Nominal verbs are nouns that, with the help of the verb *suru* ('to do'), act as verbs. Almost all of these verbs are of Sino-Japanese origin.

  勉強: 'study' → 勉強する: 'to study'

+ More information in Vocabulary [☞ VO:IV].

^{1.2} Adjectival Verbs

Adjectival verbs are verbal words that describe states defining characteristics and are composed of a lexemic root and a set of inflections different from those of stative or active verbs. Verbal adjectives are mostly of native origin and all of them end in -**i** (namely -**ii**, -**ai**, -**oi** or -**ui**) in their dictionary form [☞ III.2.1].

高い: 'to be high'; 優しい: 'to be happy'

The fact that adjectival verbs define characteristics makes them semantically equivalent to adjectives in English. However, since these types of words are conjugable in Japanese, they do not need an equivalent to the verb 'to be' to say that something is *x*, *x* being a characteristic.

高い Ø: "it is high"

+ More information in Vocabulary [☞ VO:V].

^{1.3} Verbal Functions

Verbals are conjugated according to two grammatical categories: aspect and mood.

- **Aspect:** Expresses the time in which the action or state indicated by the verbal occurs. Aspects in Japanese can be grouped into the following groups:
  - **Imperfective Aspects:** Express that an action or event has not ended. It is equivalent to the present tense in English and sometimes also to the future tense. E.g. 'speaks' (*hanasu* 話す).
  - **Perfective Aspects:** Express that an action or event has ended. Equivalent to the past tense in English. E.g. 'spoke' (*hanashita* 話した).
  - **Continuos Aspects:** Express that an action takes place over a long period of time. E.g. 'is speaking' (*hanashite iru* 話している).
  - **Non-Continuous Aspects:** Express that an action or event occurs at a particular time. E.g. 'while speaking' (*hanashi nagara* 話しながら).

- **Inchoative Aspects**: Express that an action or event starts. E.g. 'start speaking' (*hanashi hajimeru* 話し始める).

- **Cessative Aspects**: Express that an action or event is finished at the time of speaking. E.g. 'finish speaking' (*hanashi owaru* 話し終わる).

+ More information in Expressing Yourself in Japanese [☞ EY:I].

- **Mood**: Expresses the speaker's attitude inferentially or deliberately with respect to the action or state indicated by the verbal. In Japanese, the number of moods is even greater than that of aspects. The main moods can be separated into different categories or modalities:

  - **Realis Modality**: Alludes to actions regarded as real and verifiable. E.g. 'speaks' (*hanasu* 話す).

  - **Pseudo-Realis Modality**: Alludes to actions that are subjectively understood as real or potential. E.g. 'can speak' (*hanaseru* 話せる).

  - **Irrealis Modality**: Alludes to actions or states whose occurrence is possible or probable but not assured. E.g. 'want to speak' (*hanashitai* 話したい).

  + More information in Expressing Yourself in Japanese [☞ EY:VI].

1.4 Verbal Polarity

Just as verbs can be conjugated according to their mood and aspect, they can also be conjugated according to their polarity, that is, to whether they affirm or deny an action or state. In English this is marked by auxiliary verbs ('don't', 'doesn't', etc.). In Japanese, however, this is done by conjugation.

- **Affirmative Polarity:** Affirms the occurrence of an action or state. E.g. 'speaks' (*hanasu* 話す).

- **Negative Polarity:** Denies the occurrence of an action or state. E.g. 'doesn't speak' (*hanasanai* 話さない).

1.5 Verbal Parts

Every verbal is composed, morphologically, of two fundamental parts: root and inflection.

- **Verbal Root:** Verbal roots are the fundamental part with lexemic meaning of every verbal. Verbal roots never appear alone but are accompanied by verbal suffixes called inflections. The verbal root on which certain verbal suffixes or inflections are added is called *stem* [☞ III.1.5].

- **Verbal Inflection:** Suffixes added to stems to determine the mood, aspect, and polarity of a verbal.

+ More information in Verbal Inflection [☞ III].

2. NOMINALS

Nominals are independent non-conjugable words that name concepts, objects, people, animals, places or ideas. Within nominals we can distinguish three groups: Nouns, Pronouns and Numerals.

2.1 Nouns

Nouns are nominals that are a signifier by themselves with a concrete definition and can be modified by an affix, modifier, or particle. In Japanese, unlike English, nouns have neither gender nor number.

Nouns can be categorized mainly in two ways: semantic—according to their meaning; and morphological—according to their composition.

Semantic Categorization

- **Proper Nouns**: Designate a single and unique entity.

  日本: 'Japan'; 東京: 'Tokyo'

- **Common Nouns**: Designate a general class of abstract or concrete entities.

  本: 'book'; 愛: 'love'

- **Postpositional Nouns[49]**: Designate a non-specific, relative point in space where an action or state occurs, equivalent to some spatial English prepositions. Postpositional nouns can also act as common nouns.

  上: 'above'; 中: 'middle'

Morphological Categorization

- **Simple Nouns**: Nouns consisting of a single morpheme.[50]

  家: 'house'; 楽: 'comfort'

- **Compound Nouns**: Nouns formed by two or more morphemes. There are three types:

  - **Nominal Compound Nouns**: Formed by two or more morphemes of Chinese or native origin. Nominal compounds of native origin are subordinate, which means that the final element is modified by the first. In compounds of Sinitic origin, the

---

[49] It is not a category with a specific grammatical function, but it is separated in this manual to facilitate learning because of its equivalence to English prepositions.

[50] Contemporary Japanese words that are considered as a single morpheme actually etymologically derive from several morphemes. E.g. *michi* ('road') ← honorific prefix *mi* + Old Japanese n. *chi* ('way'). This is usually the case in multisyllabic morphemes.

order is reversed, so the modified element appears at the beginning. There are also some Sintic compounds that are coordinates (*x* and *y*).

- *Native compound*: 指: 'finger' + 輪: 'circle' → 指輪: 'ring'
- *Sinitic Compound*: 漢-: 'Chinese' + -字: 'letter' → 漢字: 'Chinese letters (kanji)'

- **Verbal Compound Nouns**: Consist of a noun followed or preceded by an adjectival verb stem [☞ III.1.5] or the infinitive form [☞ III.2.3] of a verb. Verb compounds are, like native nominative compounds, subordinate in such a way that the final element is modified by the first.

  乗る: 'to ride' + 物: 'thing' → 乗り物: 'vehicle'

- **Derivative Nouns**: Nouns that derive from words with another functionality [☞ X.1].

  楽しい: 'to be fun' → 楽しみ: 'enjoyment'

+ More information in Vocabulary [☞ VO:II].

Pluralization

Japanese nouns have no grammatical number, yet when strictly necessary, the plurality of nouns can be indicated by specific suffixes [☞ VO:VIII.2.2].

子供: 'child' → 子供たち: 'children'

There is also pluralization by means of reduplication, i.e. the repetition of a morpheme (subject to some voicing rules [☞ PR:II.1.3]). However, this type of pluralization is rather a collectivization, not so much signifying a number of two or greater but the idea of 'several'.

人: 'person' → 人々: 'people'

2.2 Pronouns

Pronouns are nominals capable of formally replacing a noun previously mentioned or implicitly understood by the context. Pronouns in Japanese function syntactically like nouns. There are three types of pronouns:

- **Personal Pronouns**: They stand in for nouns that define one or more persons.

  私: 'I'; あなた: 'you'

- **Interrogative Pronouns**: Used to ask what thing, person, place, method, reason, amount, or occasion the verb of an interrogative sentence is concerned about.

  何: 'what'; 誰: 'who'

- **Indefinite Pronouns**: They indefinitely (non-specifically) respond to a question asked by an interrogative pronoun.

  何か: 'something'/'anything'; 誰か: 'somebody'/'anybody'

- **Demonstrative Pronouns**: They point to an entity inferred through the context in a way that distinguishes it from other entities.

  これ: 'this'; こう: 'this way'

+ *More information in Vocabulary* [☞ VO:I].

2.3 Numerals

Numerals are nominals that designate numbers in a grammatically specific way. There is only one type of numerals: cardinal numerals, which are used to count a series of numbers or to name a number alone. In order to count things within a sentence, numerals have to be used together with classifiers [☞ VO:III.2].

一: 'one'; 二: 'two'

+ *More information in Vocabulary* [☞ VO:III].

3. COPULA

Copulae or copular verbs are dependent verb-like words that describe an intrinsic characteristic or state of being of an entity defined by an explicit or implicit subject. In the structure "A *is* B", 'is' is the copular verb while *A* is the subject and *B* is the subject complement.

In Japanese, copular verbs are dependent words, as they necessarily appear attached to the noun they refer to. The structure "A *is* B" becomes "A B *is*" in Japanese.

車が乗り物だ [car vehicle is]: "A car is a vehicle"

3.1 Bound Copula

The Japanese copula, which defines a state of being, equivalent to the English verb 'to be', must always be linked to a noun or adjectival noun, making it a dependent, bound copula. The Japanese copula is considered a separate grammatical category because, in addition to being dependent, its conjugation is somewhat different from that of independent verbals.

だ: imperfective copula (*am/are/is*) → 人だ [人 (*person*) + だ]: "is a person".

The Japanese copula is also relevant in relation to adjectival nouns. These, being technically nouns, are not conjugated like adjectival verbs, but need to be linked to the subject by the copula.

綺麗: 'beautiful (thing)' → 綺麗だ: "is beautiful"

+ *More information in Copular Inflection* [☞ V].

3.2 Phrasal Copula

In addition to the bound copula, other Japanese verbs can occasionally fulfill the function of a copular verb (defining the existence or state of a nominal as a link to a subject) without being specifically dependent verb-like words. These copular verbs use, on the other hand, particles for this purpose.

人: 'person' → 人に見える [人 + に {particle} + 見える {verbal: 'to be seen'}]: "looks like a person"

4. COVERBS

Coverbs are dependent verbals that act together with a pure verb to specify or change its meaning, mood or aspect. Most coverbs can also act as independent verbals, but some of them are actually *dependent verbs* because they cannot act independently. There are two types of coverbs according to their syntactic behavior:

- **Auxiliary Verbs:** Coverbs that are added to the infinitive form [☞ III.2.3] of a verbal to change its meaning.

  過ぎる: 'to pass' → 食べ過ぎる [食べ (infinitive form of the verb 'to eat') + 過ぎる]: 'to eat to much'

- **Subsidiary Verbs:** Coverbs that are added to the gerundive form [☞ III.3.2] of a verbal to change its mood or aspect.

  いる: 'to be' → 食べている [食べて (gerundive form of the verb 'to eat') + いる]: 'to be eating'

+ *More information in Verbal Compounds* [☞ XI].

5. PHRASAL NEXUS

The phrasal nexus serves as a link between two words or phrases within a clause or between two different clauses. It can thus serve as an internal link (within the same clause) or as an external link (one clause with another). The internal nexus can be made between two nominal phrases or between a verbal phrase and another nominal phrase.

There are two types of phrasal nexus: particles and conjunctions.

5.1 **Particles**

Particles are dependent non-conjugable word-morphemes that can be added to a nominal to link it to another nominal or verbal, to a verbal to link it to another clause, or at the end of a phrase to give it an emphatic nuance.

Particles that connect two nominals or a nominal and a verbal (case particles) mark what is known linguistically as *case* [☞ II.1.6], that is, the syntactic or semantic relationship established between two members of a clause, which in languages such as Latin or German are marked by declensions. In some instances these types of particles can be translated in English by prepositions (e.g. 'in', 'of', 'from', etc.).

Particles that serve as a link between a verbal and another clause or phrase (phrasal particles) serve as coordinators or subordinators—they coordinate or subordinate clauses [☞ II.2.2], linking them in a semantic correlation. The function performed by this type of particles is usually realized in English by conjunctions (e.g. 'and', 'but', 'if', etc.).

Particles that are placed at the end of sentences provide a new tone or nuance to the sentence that it would not have without it, thus changing its mood. The equivalent function of this type of word in English is realized, much more occasionally than in Japanese, with final interjections such as '...right?', '...huh?' or others.

Initially, we can categorize particles according to their morphological composition or according to their syntactic function.

Morphological Categorization

- **Simple Particles**: Particles that are a single morpheme.

  - **Pure Particles**: Morphemes with an etymological origin that is lost in time and are only functionally recognized as particles.

    の: genitive particle (*of*); から: ablative particle (*from*)

  - **Nominal Particles**: Particles that can functionally behave in the same way as nouns do. Nominal particles are derived from nouns. Some of these nouns still continue to work as nouns, while others, the so-called *dependent nouns*, only act in contemporary Japanese as nominal particles.

    ため: '(for the) sake (of)'; 時: '(at the) time (when)'

  - **Adverbial Particles**: Adverbs acting as particles.

    前: 'before'; ほか: 'other' → 'except (for)'

  - **Copulative Particles**: Particles derived from different forms of the copula.

    だろう: presumptive form of the copula (*may be*) → 'probably will...'

- **Compound Particles**: Particles that are composed of a pure particle plus another morpheme or morphemes.

  について [に (*at*) + ついて (*assuming*)]: 'about'

Syntactic Categorization

- **Case Particles**: Particles that mark a case [☞ II.1.6].

- **Aspectual & Modal Particles**: Particles used as inflection extensions in order to modify the aspect or mood of a verbal.

- **Phrasal Particles**: Particles used to join two clauses to form a compound sentence [☞ II.2].

+ *More information in Particles* [☞ VIII].

5.2 Conjunctions

Conjunctions are dependent non-conjugable words that are placed at the beginning of a clause to connect it to an explicit or implicit preceding clause. They differ from particles that link verbals to another clause in their position within the sentence, as particles attach to the verb of the predecessor clause while conjunctions begin the new clause.

そうして: 'and (then)'; また: 'also'

+ *More information in Vocabulary* [☞ VO:VII].

6. VERBAL MODIFIERS

Verbal modifiers are words that modify a verb as a verbal complement. This group includes only adverbs.

6.1 Adverbs

Adverbs are verbal modifiers that can be placed anywhere in the sentence before the verbal and function as a verbal complement by semantically expanding or specifying the action or state defined by the verbal. Four types of adverbs can be morphologically distinguished: pure, nominal, adjectival and verbal.

- **Pure Adverbs**: Adverbs that do not fulfill any other function than that of an adverb. Many of these adverbs are *ideophones*, words that subjectively express an imitative or imaginary sound.

    とても: 'very'; ちゃんと: 'properly'

- **Nominal Adverbs**: Nouns or adjectival nouns that act as adverbs, usually when the particles *ni* ('in') or *de* ('by') are added to them. Some of these types of adverbs do not need any particles to function as adverbs.

    本当: 'truth' → 本当に: 'really'

- **Adjectival Adverbs**: Adjectival verbs that act as adverbs when they take the inflection *-ku* [☞ X.3].

  良^よい: 'good' → 良^よく: 'well'

- **Verbal Adverbs**: Adverbs that derive from contemporary or old verbs in their gerundive form ending in *-te* [☞ III.3.2].

  全^{すべ}て: 'entirely'; やがて: 'eventually'

+ *More information in Vocabulary* [☞ VO:VI].

7. NOMINAL MODIFIERS

Modifiers are dependent non-conjugable words that modify the meaning or nuance of a noun acting as nominal modifiers in a sentence. There are two types: Prenominals and Adjectival Nouns.

7.1 Prenominals

Prenominals are morphemes placed exclusively before a nominal (hence the name) to define a characteristic of the noun or make a reference to it. Prenominals are a sparse[51], closed word class. There are prenominals of three types:

- **Indefinite Prenominals**: They refer to nouns by giving an indefinite response to an interrogative pronoun.

  どの: 'which...'; どんな: 'what kind of...'

- **Demonstrative Prenominals**: They refer to nouns by giving a response to an interrogative pronoun in a way that distinguishes them from other implied nouns.

  この: 'this...'; こんな: 'this kind of...'

- **Adjectival Prenominals**: Prenominals that act just like the attributive form [☞ II.1.3] of a nominal adjective but do not admit a predicative form [☞ II.1.3].

  大^{おお}きな: 'big...'; 小^{ちい}さな: 'small...'

+ *More information in Vocabulary* [☞ VO:I].

---

[51] Only about fifty prenominals are counted in the entire Japanese vocabulary corpus.

7.2 Adjectival Nouns

Adjectival nouns are nouns that, with the help of a properly conjugated copula, act as a word that modifies another noun implicitly or explicitly by describing the properties or qualities of that noun. Adjectives can be grouped according to a morphological categorization and an etymological categorization.

Morphological Categorization

- *Na* **Adjectival Nouns:** Adjectival nouns to which the morpheme *na* [☞ V.1.1] is added in their attributive form (when they come before another noun) [☞ II.1.3]. Most of these adjectival nouns are of Sino-Japanese origin, but there are also those of native origin.

  便利: 'convenience' → 便利な: 'convenient...'

- *No* **Adjectival Nouns:** Adjectival nouns to which the morpheme *no* [☞ V.1.1] is added in their attributive form. These adjectival nouns derive from pure adverbs or nominals.

  それぞれ: 'respectively' → それぞれの: 'each...'

- **Versatile Adjectival Nouns:** Adjectival nouns to which both of the morphemes *na* or *no* can be added in their attributive form. Most adjectival nouns within this group are commonly used as nouns as well, as opposed to *na* only adjectives (mostly used as adjectival nouns) or *no* only adjectives (used also as adverbs).

  完全: 'perfection' → 完全な/の: 'perfect...'

Etymological Categorization

- **Sino-Japanese Adjectival Nouns:** Adjectival nouns derived from nouns of Chinese origin. These constitute the vast majority of the bulk of Japanese adjectival nouns.

  綺麗(な): 'beautiful'; 本当(な/の): 'true'

- **Native Adjectival Nouns:** Adjectival nouns of native origin, usually formed through a morphological derivation of a noun plus the addition of Old Japanese adjectivizing suffixes such as -*ka*; -*yaka*; or -*raka*., which generally denote unmeasurable characteristics. The number of this type of adjectival nouns is quite small compared to Sino-Japanese adjectival nouns.

  静か(な): 'true'; 明らか(な): 'clear'

- **Foreign Adjectival Nouns:** Adjectival nouns derived from adjectives of foreign origin, mostly from English, that only take the attributive copula -*na*. The number of this type of adjectival nouns is quite scarce and they are usually relegated to colloquial usage.

  リアル(な): 'true'; ユニーク(な): 'unique'

+ *More information in Vocabulary* [☞ VO:V].

8. AFFIXES

Affixes are dependent non-conjugable morphemes that are attached directly to a nominal, numeral or, exceptionally, other affixes, to modify their meaning or grammatical function. There are three types of affixes: Nominal Affixes, Numeral Affixes and Verbal Affixes.

8.1 Nominal Affixes

Nominal affixes are affixes attached directly before or after a nominal. There are three types:

- **Prefixes**: Affixes placed directly before a noun.

  全-: 'all' → 全日本 [全 + 日本 (*Japan*)]: 'all Japan'

- **Suffixes**: Affixes placed directly after a nominal or other suffixes. Some suffixes also act as nouns.

  -人: 'person' → 日本人 [日本 (*Japan*) + 人]: 'Japan person' → 'Japanese'

- **Classifiers**: Suffixes placed directly after a numeral in order to count a number of things marked with that numeral. Classifiers semantically specify the type of thing being counted. There are some classifiers that also act as nouns.

  -年: 'year' → 一年 [一 (*one*) + 年]: 'one year'

+ *More information in Vocabulary* [☞ VO:VIII].

8.2 Verbal Affixes

Verbal affixes are suffixes placed after a verbal lexeme. There is only one type:

- **Inflections**: Suffixes that are placed after the stem of a verbal or to other inflections to modify the mood, aspect, or grammatical function of the verbal.

  -た: perfective inflection (-*ed*) → 食べた [食べ (stem of *to eat*) + た]: 'ate'

+ *More information in Verbal Inflection* [☞ III].

9. INTERJECTIONS

Interjections are isolated non-conjugable words that act as a phrase by themselves and express an emotion or reaction.

はい: 'yes'; よし: 'alright!'

+ *More information in Vocabulary* [☞ VO:VII].

10. PARTS OF SPEECH SUMMARY

Dependency	Morphology	Use	Word Class		
Independent	Conjugable	*expressing actions or states*	Verbals	Verbs	
				Adjectival Verbs	
	Non-Conjugable	*expressing concepts*	Nominals	Nouns	
				Pronouns	
				Numerals	
Dependent	Conjugable	*expressing a state of being*	Copula	Bound Copula	
				Phrasal Copula	
		amplifying verbs' meanings	Coverbs	Auxiliary Verbs	
				Subsidiary Verbs	
	Non-Conjugable	*linking words and phrases*	Phrasal Nexus	Particles	
				Conjunctions	
		complementing verbs	Verbal Modifiers	Adverbs	
		complementing nouns	Nominal Modifiers	Prenominals	
				Adjectival Nouns	
		amplifying nouns' meanings	Affixes	Nominal Affixes	Prefixes
					Suffixes
					Classifiers
				Verbal Affixes	Inflections
Isolated	Non-Conjugable	*convey emotion*	Interjections		

II. SYNTAX

To understand the grammatical explanations given in this section of the book, it is advisable to have a basic knowledge of syntax. Syntax is the branch of linguistics that explains the arrangement of words and phrases to form sentences in a given language. Much of the behavior of grammatical functions is developed on the basis of syntax.

Seeing, then, that syntax deals with phrases and sentences, we have to first understand what we mean by the term 'sentence'.

- **Sentence**: A series of words consisting of an implicit or explicit subject and a predicate:

  - **Subject**: A word or group of words indicating the entity that performs an action or experiences a state marked by a verb.

  - **Predicate**: Part of a sentence formed by a finite verbal (indicating a conclusive statement) and, optionally, its arguments.

    - **Argument**: Word or words within a sentence that extend the meaning of the verb.

There are two types of sentences: **simple sentences** and **compound sentences**. Simple sentences are composed of only one clause, while compound sentences are composed of two or more clauses. Let us see, then, what we mean by the term 'clause':

- **Clause**: A verbal or a verbal optionally complemented by arguments and a subject. If the verbal is finite, the clause would be equivalent to a simple sentence (e.g. 'I eat apples'). The term clause becomes relevant in compound sentences since a compound sentence is composed of two or more clauses, sometimes one of them having a nonfinite verb that is dependent on the other clause (e.g. 'eating apples...').

1. SIMPLE SENTENCES

As described above, a simple sentence consists of a single clause with a finite verbal. A sentence with a finite verb, in addition to the verb, can contain a subject and arguments. Arguments are those words that extend the meaning of the verb.

1.1 Verbal Correlation

Both the subject and the arguments have a *verbal correlation* since they affect the verb. Arguments can be an object or a verbal complement.

In Japanese, in addition to the subject and arguments, there is another syntactic entity not extant in English called *topic* or *theme*, which indicates the discourse's topic, which sometimes coincides with the subject but sometimes does not.

Verbal correlation, then, is expressed in Japanese through the following elements:

- **Topic**: Topic of the sentence. E.g. 'As for me' in 'As for me, I study Japanese in the morning'.

- **Subject**: Element that performs or experiences the action or state of the verbal. E.g. 'I' in 'I study Japanese in the morning'.

  ❖ The subject is marked in Japanese with the nominative particle **ga** [☞ VIII.1.1] or with the thematic particle **wa** [☞ VIII.1.3] if the subject is the main topic of the discourse.

- **Object**: Element that is affected by the action of the verb. There are two types of object:

  - **Direct Object**: Object that receives the action of the verb. E.g. 'Japanese' in 'I study Japanese in the morning'.

    ❖ The direct object is marked in Japanese with the accusative particle **o** [☞ VIII.1.1].

  - **Indirect Object**: It refers to the target of the direct object, which appears explicitly or is implicitly left out. E.g. 'Japanese' in 'As for me, I study Japanese in the morning'.

    ❖ The indirect object is marked in Japanese with the dative particle **ni** [☞ VIII.1.1].

- **Verbal Complement**: An element that extends the meaning of the verb. E.g. 'in the morning' in 'I study Japanese in the morning'.

  ❖ Verbal complements are marked in Japanese with different particles [☞ VIII.1.5] depending on the syntactic or semantic nature of said complements.

In Japanese, the topic, the subject, the object, and usually also the complement, must be accompanied by a particle indicating their verbal correlation.

Let us illustrate this with an example:

ぼく 僕は	あさ 朝に	にっぽん ご 日本語を	べんきょう 勉強する
[as for me / I	in the morning	Japanese	study]
topic & subject	complement	object	verb

"I study Japanese in the morning"

The arguments of the sentence can and do appear anywhere in the sentence except at the end; nevertheless, there is a certain degree of preference:

1	2	3	4	5	6	7	8
Time	Place	Subject	Indirect Object	Instrument	Origin	Direction	Direct Object

1.2 Complementation

Both the subject, the topic and the arguments, as long as they are nouns, can be complemented or extended, in turn, by other words. This phenomenon is called *nominal complementation.*

Nominal complements, also called *modifiers*, are usually adjectival words that define the quality of the noun they modify (e.g. 'red' in 'a red house'), or also words that establish a dependency relationship with that noun (e.g. 'man's' in 'the man's house').

家 (*house*) → 赤い家 [赤い (*red*) + 家 (*house*)]: 'red house'
家 (*house*) → 男の家 [男の (*of the man*) + 家 (*house*)]: 'man's house'

When the subject, topic or argument is accompanied by a modifier, that subject, topic or argument will become a series of words called a *phrase*. The part of a phrase that is not a modifier is called a *head*. Phrases within a sentence that function as a noun are called nominal phrases, while phrases that act as adverbs are called adverbial phrases.

1.3 Functional Distribution

Each word class has a predetermined function which, however, can change in relation to its position in the sentence.

Nouns are ambivalent, since, aided by any particle, they can act as argument (verbal complement or object), subject, subject or modifier (nominal complement).

Adverbs will always act as verbal complements.

Verbals can act as a finite verb if they are placed at the end of a clause or as a nominal complement or modifier if they are placed before a noun. If placed at the end of a clause, the verbal will be *predicative*; if placed before a noun, the verbal acts in an *attributive* way. There is also a specific functional distribution called *copulative* form, which in Japanese is performed by the copula.

- **Predicative Form**: Verb or adjectival verb defining an action or state at the end of a clause. E.g. 'walks' in "a man walks".

  人が歩く : "the person walks".

- **Attributive Form**: Verbal or adjectival noun placed before a noun to complement it. E.g. 'walking' in "walking person" or 'who walks' in "the person who walks". The second example is technically analyzed as an attributive subordinate clause [☞ II.2.2].

  歩く人: "a walking person / a person who walks".

- **Copulative Form**: Verb-like form—in the case of Japanese copular verbs—that defines the state of being of a noun.

  歩く人だ: "is a person who walks".

We see, then, that some word classes can act differently according to their position in the phrase or according to their morphological derivation. Let us see, then, a summary of this functional variability:

Functional Distribution Chart

	Predicative Verbal	Verbal Modifier	Nominal Modifier
Verb:	V $\parallel$	$\emptyset$	V[1] N
Adjectival Verb:	V $\parallel$	$\emptyset$	V N
Noun:	N {D} $\parallel$	N {p}	N {p}/{a} N
Adjectival Noun:	n {D} $\parallel$	$\emptyset$	n {a} N
Adverb:	$\emptyset$	ADV	$\emptyset$

※ V stands for verbal; N stands for nominal; n stands for adjectival noun; ADV stands for adverb; Ø stands for impossibility (without word class transformation); $\parallel$ stands for end of a clause; {D} stands for a copula in a predicative form; {p} stands for a particle; {a} stands for an attributive form of the copula.; N stands for a following modified noun.

※ [1]Technically considered as a subordinate clause [☞ II.2.2].

1.4 Verbal Voice

'Voice' describes the relationship established between the action marked by the verb and the subject. In Japanese, three main voices are marked:

- **Active Voice**: It indicates that the subject of the sentence performs the action of the verb. E.g. In "You eat apples" the subject 'you' is an *agent*, so the sentence is in the active voice.

- **Passive Voice**: It indicates that the subject is the one who experiences or receives, as a *patient*, the action of the verb. In passive sentences, the subject is therefore the patient, and the entity performing the action is not considered the subject but an agent complement of the subject. E.g. In the sentence "Apples are eaten by you", the subject 'apples' is patient and 'you' is the agent, so this sentence is passive.

- **Causative Voice**: It indicates that an agent subject causes a patient complement to perform an action. E.g. The sentence "I make you eat apples" in English is analyzed as active, but in Japanese such a statement is constructed with a causative conjugation in which 'I' would be the causative agent and 'you' the patient subject.

In the active voice, the subject is an agent, while in the passive voice the subject is a patient —it experiences the action performed by the *agent* complement.

+ *More information in Extensive Verbal Inflection* [☞ VI.2] *and Expressing Yourself in Japanese* [☞ EY:II].

1.5 Verbal Valency

The verb can be categorized into two types according to its valency, that is, the number of types of arguments it can take. In Japanese there are two types:

- **Transitive Verb**: It can take two types of arguments: an object and one or more optional verbal complements. E.g. In the sentence "I eat apples in this room" the verb 'eat' is transitive as it necessarily takes the direct object ('apples').

- **Intransitive Verb**: It can only take one type of argument: verbal complements, in other words. it cannot take an object. E.g. In the sentence "I play in the room" the verb 'play' is intransitive as it does not take an object.

Normally in English, the same verb can be both transitive and intransitive (e.g. 'open' in "I open the door" or 'opens' in "the door opens"). In Japanese, on the contrary, there are generally verbs that act only transitively and other verbs that act only intransitively (e.g. 開ける *akeru* 'to open s.t.', transitive; 開く *aku* 'to open', intransitive).

1.6 **Case**

The word 'case' defines the type of correlation that a noun maintains with a verb or other noun. In Japanese, cases are marked by case particles, and can be grouped under six categories or 'alignments' according to their function within a clause:

- **Syntactical Alignment**: Cases that mark a noun in relation to the verb insofar as it takes on a syntactic function of the subject, agent, direct object, or indirect object. The cases within this alignment are the following:

  - **Nominative Case**: It marks the subject of the sentence. E.g. 'I' in "I think" is the subject and therefore marked as nominative case in Japanese. It is marked with the nominative particle ga.
    僕が考える [I NOM think]: "I think".

  - **Accusative Case**: It marks the subject of the sentence. E.g. 'this book' in "I read this book" is the direct object and therefore marked as accusative case in Japanese. It is marked with the accusative particle o.
    この本を読む [this book ACC read]: "I read this book".

  - **Dative Case**: It marks the indirect object of the sentence. E.g. 'me' in "He gave me this book" is the indirect object and therefore marked as dative case in Japanese. It is marked with the dative particle ni.
    彼がこの本を僕にくれた [he {nom.} this book {acc.} I DAT(*to*) gave]: "He gave me this book".

  - **Agentive Case**: It marks the agent complement of the sentence. E.g. 'a dog' in "that person was bitten by a dog". It is marked with the dative particle ni.

272

その人は犬に噛まれた [that person {nom.} dog AGENT(*by*) was-bitten]: "That person was bitten by a dog".

- **Complementary Alignment**: Cases that mark a noun as a modifying nominal complement of another noun. The cases within the complementary alignment are the following:

  - **Genitive Case**: It marks a noun or nominal phrase as a modifier—nominal complement—of another juxtaposed noun. E.g. 'of my friend' in "the car of my friend". It is marked with the genitive particle **no**.

    友達の車 [friend GEN(*of*) car]: "The car of my friend".

  - **Comitative Case**: It marks a noun as a simultaneous addition to another explicit or implicit noun. E.g. 'with my friend' in "I go with my friend". It is marked with the nominative particle **to**.

    友達と行く [friend COM(*with*) go]: "I go with my friend". 52

  - **Privative Case**: Cases that mark a noun as a subtraction to a set formed by another explicit or implicit noun. It is marked with the privative particle **nashi**, among others.

    友達なし行く [friend PRIV(*without*) go]: "I go without my friend". 53

- **Focal Alignment**: Cases that mark a noun as the topic of a sentence. There are several focal cases Japanese ([☞ VIII.1.3]), but the most relevant one is undoubtedly the following:

  - **Thematic Case**: It marks the main topic of the discourse as an introduction or contrast. This form of case marking is extremely common in Japanese but has no English equivalent. A more or less reliable translation would be formulas such as "as for...", "as far as ... is concerned" or "regarding...". Although these formulas are used more in formal English language, in Japanese, the thematic case is commonplace. See more information in the corresponding section in Case Particles [☞ VIII.1]. E.g. 'I' (understood as 'as for me') in "I live in Japan". It is marked with the thematic particle **wa** (written as *ha*).

    僕は日本で住んでいる [I TOP Japan-in am-living]: "I live in Japan".

- **Conjunctive Alignment**: Cases that join two or more nouns consecutively in a non-dependent manner.

- **Adjunctive Alignment**: Cases that mark a noun as a verbal complement in which extra information is added.

---

52 In this sentence, the noun in the comitative case (*tomodachi*; 'friend') accompanies—complements—the subject 'I', which in Japanese is implied, that is, it does not appear in the sentence.

53 In this sentence the complemented noun is also the implied subject 'I'.

- **Delimitative Alignment**: Cases marking a noun as a verbal complement that establishes a quantitative limit.

+ *More information in Particles* [☞ VIII] *and Expressing Yourself in Japanese* [☞ EY:VII].

2. COMPOUND SENTENCES

Compound sentences in Japanese are composed of two or more clauses of which only the last one contains a finite verb. There are two types of compound sentences: coordinated and subordinate.

2.1 Coordination

Coordinated sentences join two clauses consecutively without the union modifying the meaning of the clauses, which will remain independent in each of them. There are four types of coordination:

- **Conjunctive Coordination**: Union of two clauses consecutively without added nuances. E.g. 'and I think' in "I read and I think".

  読んで考える: "I read and I think".

- **Cumulative Coordination**: Union of two clauses with the nuance of simultaneity. E.g. 'I also think' in "I read and I also think".

  読んで考えもする: "I read and I also think".

- **Adversative Coordination**: Union of two clauses implying that one of them is contrasted with the other. E.g. 'but I don't think' in "I read but I don't think".

  読むが考えない: "I read but I don't think".

- **Disjunctive Coordination**: Union of two clauses of which only one is considered as possible. E.g. 'or think' in "I (either) read or think".

  読むか考えるか: "I either read or think".

In Japanese, coordination is marked with the conjugation of the verb of the first clause or with the help of particles.

+ *More information in Expressing Yourself in Japanese* [☞ EY:III].

2.2 Subordination

Subordinate phrases join two clauses or phrases in such a way that one of them is dependent on the other to form a complete meaning. There are five types of subordination:

- **Attributive Subordination**: Refers to verbal phrases that act as a modifier of a noun. E.g. 'who is reading' in the clause "a person who is reading". Attributive subordination is realized by placing the *realis form* [☞ III.2.1] of the verbals before the noun. Clauses that function as attributive subordinate clauses are also called relative clauses.

  読んでいる人: "a person who is reading".

- **Interrogative Subordination**: Refers to direct or indirect questions within a sentence signaled by an implicit or explicit verb. E.g. 'if that person is reading' in the sentence "I don't know if that person is reading".

  あの人は読んでいるかどうか分からない: "I don't know if that person is reading (or not)".

- **Quotative Subordination**: Refers to quotations within the discourse of something that someone—the speaker or someone else—has said, thought or heard. E.g. 'that person is reading' in "I think that that person is reading".

  あの人は読んでいると思う: "I think that that person is reading".

- **Comparative Subordination**: Refers to verb clauses that compare with each other. E.g. 'than working' in "Playing is more fun than working".

  働くより遊ぶ方が楽しい: "Playing is more fun than working".

- **Limitative Subordination**: Refers to verb clauses that are understood as a quantitative limit for another verb. E.g. 'the more I study' in "the more I study the more I learn".

  勉強すればするほど学ぶ: "The more I study, the more I learn".

In Japanese, attributive subordination is not inflectionally marked, but it is conditioned by the position of the verbal before the nominal. The other types of subordination are marked by the phrasal particles [☞ VIII.4]. A fundamental syntactic rule regarding subordination in Japanese is that the modifying word or phrase always precedes the modified word or phrase.

Subordination Chart

Subordination Type:	Usual Verbs	In English:		In Japanese	
		Main Clause	Dependent Clause	Dependent Clause	Main Clause
Attributive	Multiple	N	*who/that* V	V	N
Interrogative	*ask; know*	V	*if/whether* P	P {p}	V
Quotative	*say; think*	V	*that* P	P {p}	V
Comparative	*to be more...*	V_1	*than* V_2	V_2 {p}	V_1
Limitative	Multiple	V_1	*as much as* V_2	V_2 {p}	V_1

※ N stands for nominal; V stands for verbal; P stands for phrase; {p} stands for particle.

+ *More information in Expressing Yourself in Japanese* [☞ EY:IV].

3. INVERSION & OMISSION

In the colloquial and informal register, it is quite common for two phenomena to occur that break some of the syntactic rules seen so far: the inversion and omission of some parts of speech when they are implied in the sentence and can be deduced from the context.

Omission phenomena in particular are very common since Japanese, as already explained a bit in the preliminaries section [☞ PR:I.1.2], is a language prone to leave things to be interpreted by the context (pro-drop language).

3.1 Verbal Inversion

Verbal inversion is the phenomenon in which sometimes the verb or predicate appears at the beginning of a sentence—before the subject or arguments—as an independent clause, which is then followed by another explanatory clause.

今授業に行く [now class-to go] → 今行く、授業に [now go, class-to]: "I'll go to class now".

This only occurs in speech that reflects the speaker's thought as it appears in a carefree manner. In poetic language, inversion is also sometimes used for impact.

3.2 Particle Omission

The phenomenon of particle omission or "particle dropping" refers to the dropping or omission of nominative, thematic and accusative—and more occasionally lative—case particles in colloquial language. This phenomenon, although considered to be informal, is widespread.

友達が来た [friend NOM came] → 友達∅来た [friend ∅ came]: "My friend came".

3.3 Subject & Object Omission

It is important to note that in Japanese, the subject of the sentence is typically omitted, that is, it is left to the inference of the context whenever possible unless its appearance is strictly necessary or given for contrast.

コーヒーを飲んでいる [coffee ACC am-drinking]: "I'm drinking a coffee".

Likewise, the direct object of a sentence is left implied whenever it is not strictly necessary to name it, so it is not marked with a pronoun as in English.

昨日買った [yesterday bought]: "I bought it yesterday".

3.4 Verbal Omission

It is also possible, in colloquial speech to omit the final verb of the sentence when it can be inferred. This occurs mostly when answering questions, just as it does in English.

A. どこに行く? [where to go]: "Where do you go?".

B. 学校に Ø [school to ø]: "(I go) to school".

The verb's omission also happens sometimes for the verb of the last clause in some compound sentences. This phenomenon has no parallel in English.

来るって Ø [came-that]: "He told me that he would come".

This phenomenon is closely related to the concept of *aposiopesis* explained in Preliminaries [☞ PR:I.1.5].

III. VERBAL INFLECTION

The inflections of the Japanese verb are highly regular; there are only two strictly irregular verbs and very few inflectional exceptions in the regular conjugations. The Japanese verbal inflection does not directly express person or number, but it does represent perfective (past) and imperfective (present) aspects and a variety of moods. These inflections are constructed by adding several endings to an invariable stem to provide the verb with different modalities and aspects. The main verbal forms obtained from stem extension are of two types: **root forms** and **derivative forms**. Besides, the **negative forms** of the verbs are formed by a special derived conjugation.

- **Root Forms**: Verbal forms on which all verb endings are ultimately based.

- **Derivative Forms**: Verbal forms derived from the root forms.

- **Negative Forms**: A special set of derivative forms that can be further conjugated.

Both root forms and derivative forms allow a series of extensions consisting of attached suffixes or particles that add new meanings to the verbal expression.

The endings added to the verbal stem used to build the root forms vary depending on the verbal conjugation, that is, the type of verb to be modified. In Japanese, there are three regular conjugations: strong verbs, weak verbs, adjectival verbs and, finally, a very reduced set of irregular verbs.

1. VERBAL CONJUGATION

Japanese verbals can be divided into four groups of conjugations:

1.1 **Strong Verbs**: Characterized by keeping its unmodified stem as the basis of most of its root forms, i.e. they keep their stem "strong" because they don't require extensions.

1.2 **Weak Verbs**: Characterized by having its stem accompanied by an extra vowel in the root forms, that is to say, the stem is "weak" because it has to be extended or supported by additional phonemes.

1.3 **Irregular Verbs**: Two pure verbs that have some forms inflected in a way that do not follow the patterns of either strong or weak verbs.

1.4 **Adjectival Verbs**: Conjugation used with adjectival verbs[54]. Adjectival verbs are used to describe characteristics as opposed to common verbs that describe actions and states. They are equivalent to the English constructions of the verb 'to be' plus an adjective.

---

[54] Also called adjectival verbs, static verbs or -i adjectives in other grammars.

1.1 Strong Verbs

(S) = Verb of the Strong Conjugation

❖ The lemma or dictionary form[55] of strong verbs ends in -iru -いる or -eru -える.

❖ All but one of their root forms [☞ III.2] are equivalent to the stem of the verb.

Examples

(S) -iru		(S) -eru	
irú いる	mìru 見る	tabèru 食べる	hajímeru 始める
to be (at)	*to look (at)*	*to eat*	*to start*
ikìru 生きる	dekíru できる	kańgaèru 考える	kiméru 決める
to live	*to be able (to do)*	*to think*	*to decide*

1.2 Weak Verbs

(W) = Verb of the Weak Conjugation

❖ The lemma of weak verbs ends in -u -う

- More specifically: **vowel+u**; **-ku**; **-gu**; **-su**; **-tsu**; **-bu**; **-mu**; or **-ru**.

- There is only a single verb ending in **-nu**: *shinu* 死ぬ (*to die*).

- Only the *sandhi*, apocopated versions of the verb *suru* する (*to do*) end in **-zu**: *suru* →
  zuru → *zu*. This particular version of the verb always appears attached to a noun.

Examples

vowel+u	-ku	-gu	-su
iú いう	kàku 書く	kasègu 稼ぐ	hanàsu 話す
to say	*to write*	*to earn*	*to speak*
-tsu	-bu	-mu	-nu
mòtsu 持つ	manàbu 学ぶ	sumú 住む	shinú 死ぬ
to take	*to learn*	*to live (at)*	*to die*
-aru	-uru	-oru	

---

[55] The term *dictionary form* or *lemma* is a means to describe the plain imperfective indicative form of verbs, which is the one used to list them in Japanese dictionaries.

wakàru 分かる	tsukùru 作る	odóru 踊る	
to understand	*to make*	*to dance*	

❖ Weak verbs ending in **-ru** usually have that syllable preceded by the vowels **a, o** and **u** (-**aru; -oru; -uru**), thus differing from strong verbs which end in **-iru** or **-eru**. However, there is also a series of weak verbs that end, as their strong counterparts, in **-iru** or **-eru**. This list is not very long but every time you come across a weak verb ending in **-i/e-ru**, you have to memorize that it is not a strong verb. Some of the most common weak verbs ending in **-i/e-ru** are the following:

Ⓦ -iru		Ⓦ -eru	
hàiru 入る	irú 要る	kaéru 帰る	shabèru 喋る
to enter	*to need*	*to return*	*to talk*
shirú 知る	hashìru 走る	kèru 蹴る	subèru 滑る
to know	*to run*	*to kick*	*to slide*

1.3 Irregular Verbs

Ⓘ = Irregular verb.

❖ The only two strictly non-subsidiary irregular verbs, that is, the only two verbs that have root forms with a morphology considerably different from that of strong or weak verbs, are the following:

• **surú** する (*to do*) • **kùru** 来る (*to come*).

❖ The following verbs have irregularities in the euphonic sound change of the gerundive [☞ III.3.2] and perfective forms [☞ III.3.3]:

• **ikú** 行く (*to go*) • **toú** 問う (*to ask*) • **kòu** 請う (*to request*).

❖ The verb **àru** ある (*to be at*) has the irregular negative form [☞ III.4] **nai**.

❖ The equivalent to the English verb *to be*, the copula, could be considered an irregular verb, but it is rather designed in Japanese as a different part of speech altogether.

Irregular Verbs

Fully Irregular		Irregular Gerundive & Perfective			Irr. Negative
surú する	kùru 来る	ikú 行く	toú 問う	kòu 請う	àru ある
to do	*to come*	*to go*	*to ask*	*to request*	*to be at*

+ *More information in Irregular Inflections* [☞ III.6]

1.4 Adjectival Verbs

Ⓐ = Adjectival Verb

❖ Adjectival verbs are verbal words that define a characteristic of the subject and can function in both an attributive and a predicative way.

❖ Adjectival verbs may vary in aspect or mood, which are indicated by inflections. Adjectival verbs, therefore, behave technically as verbs.

❖ The conjugation of adjectival verbs, like that of verbs, is made upon different root forms, although their morphology differs slightly from the latter.

❖ The lemma of adjectival verbs always ends in **vowel**+i -い.

• More specifically: -**ai**; -**ii**; -**ui** or -**oi** (never -ei).

• Adjectives ending in -**shii** indicate that the degree of the defining characteristic cannot be objectively measured.

Examples

-ii	-ai	-oi	-ui	-shii
ìi* いい *to be good*	yabài やばい *to be awful*	sugòi すごい *to be amazing*	warùi 悪い *to be bad*	subárashìi 素晴らしい *to be wonderful*
kawáii かわいい *to be cute*	umài うまい *to be delicious*	omóshiròi 面白い *to be fun*	nemùi 眠い *to be sleepy*	utsúkushìi 美しい *to be beautiful*

*Conjugates as *yoi*.

❖ There is only one irregular adjective, **yòi** 良い (*to be good*), which can take the form **ii** いい for the realis inflection (lemma) [☞ III.2.1] but conjugates the rest of the forms as **yòi**. The adjective **kakkóìi** かっこういい (*to be good looking*) is conjugated like **ii** (with the form **yòi**) because it is a noun-adjective compound (**kakkó** + **ìi**).

1.5 Verbal Stem

S = Stem of a Verb
s = Stem of an Adjectival Verb

	Form			Symbols	
Stem	Strong Verbs	Weak Verbs	Adj. Verbs	Verbs	Adj. Verbs
	(–ru)*	(–u)*	(–i)*	**S**	**s**

*Elements subtracted to the lemma

The standard way of listing Japanese verbs is by their imperfective indicative form—the so-called lemma—by which states are declared in a non-past aspect. This indicative form or *realis form* [☞ III.2.1] is characterized by always ending in *-ru* in strong verbs, in *-u* in weak verbs and in *-i* in adjectival verbs. In order to obtain the stem of any of these verbal forms, it is only necessary to remove its characteristic ending, **-ru** (in strong verbs), **-u** (in weak verbs) or **-i** (in adjectival verbs).

The verbal stem is the basis upon which all the root forms, and consequently, all the inflections of Japanese verbs, are formed.

Formation of the Verbal Stem:

✤ Ⓥ **Stem of a Verb**: The form of the verb without the following lemma endings:

- Ⓢ –ru (for the strong conjugation)
- Ⓦ –u (for the Weak conjugation)

✤ Ⓐ **Stem of an Adjectival Verb**: The form of the adjective without the lemma ending -i

- Ⓐ –i

Functions of the Verbal Stem:

✤ Ⓐ **Fossilized Nominalization**: Sometimes, the stem of an adjectival verb can act as a noun. This way of adjectival nominalization is no longer productive and it remains most widely used within colors.

くろ
黒: 'Black color'. *kuro*: Stem of *kuroi* 黒い (*to be black*).

✤ Ⓐ **Fossilized Attributive Prefix**: The stem of adjectival verbs is used as an attributive prefix in a set of compound nouns or adjectives. This is typically seen in place names.

ひろしま
広島: 'Hiroshima'. *hiro*: Stem of *hiroi* 広い (*to be wide*) + *shima* 島 (*island*).

Paradigm

	Ⓢ Strong Verb	Ⓦ Weak Verb	Ⓐ Adjectival Verb
Lemma	irú いる *to be (at)*	iú いう *to say*	umài うまい *to be delicious*
Stem	ir-	i-	uma-

2. ROOT FORMS

The Japanese inflection is made up of four basic forms, or *root forms*, which are so called because they are the forms upon which all verbal aspects and moods are built.

To express new aspects and moods through the verb, a series of particles or verbal endings (inflections) have to be added, once again, to one of the root forms. Originally, the addition of these particles or endings is done in such a way that neither the root form nor the ending itself is modified in an agglutinative way. However, in many constructions, the prolonged use has developed processes of phonetic assimilation that make the original form of the endings obscured. The root form, nevertheless, remains unchanged. The only case in which any phoneme of the root form changes is when, due to the addition of a **u** or **i** to a **t**, it produces **tsu** and **chi** respectively due to the absence of the sounds *tu* and *ti* in the Japanese language.

The four root forms are the following:

2.1. Realis Forms: Used to indicate factual expressions.

2.2. Irrealis Forms: Used to express situations or actions whose realization is uncertain.

2.3. Infinitive Forms: Mostly used to conjoin phrases.

2.4 Subjunctive Form: Used to subjectively refer to a possible realization of an action or state.

ROOT FORMS	Form			Symbols	
	Strong Verbs	Weak Verbs	Adj. Verbs	Verbs	Adj. Verbs
Realis	S-ru	S-u	s-i	U	i
Irrealis		S-a	s-ka	A	ka
Infinitive	S	S-i	s-ku	I	ku
Subjunctive		S-e	s-ke	E	ke

2.1 Realis Form

U = Realis Form of Verbs
i = Realis Form of Adjectival Verbs

Ⓢ Strong Verbs	Ⓦ Weak Verbs	Ⓐ Adjectival Verbs
S+ru	S+u	s+i

The realis form[56] of the verb is used to convey information in an indicative way, that is, by understanding the facts or actions expressed by the verb as *real* and occurring in either the present or future time (imperfective or non-past aspect). This form is used in Japanese dictionaries and word lists as headwords, hence it is also called the lemma or dictionary form.

Formation of the Realis Form:

This form is made by adding to the stem the endings **-ru** in strong verbs, **-u** in weak verbs and in **-i** in adjectival verbs.

Functions of the Realis Form:

❖ **Dictionary Form (Lemma):** The realis form of verbs and adjectival verbs is the one used to search for this type of words in Japanese dictionaries.

❖ [*fam.*] **Imperfective Aspect & Indicative Mood:** It describes a factual action or state that occurs in the present or future time, i.e. not in the past. When this form is used to end a sentence, it implies a familiar register in conversational language. However, it can also sometimes be interpreted as neutral in written language or as dependent clauses.

Ⓥ 子供が遊ぶ: "The kids play". / "The kids will play".

Ⓐ その建物は美しい: "That building is beautiful".

❖ **Imperfective Aspect & Attributive Subordination:** It acts as an attribute that modifies a noun referring to an action or state occurring in the present or future.

Ⓥ 遊ぶ時間がある [play time NOM there-is]: "There is time to play".

Ⓐ この道で美しい建物がある [this street-in beautiful buildings there-are]: "There are beautiful buildings in this street".

Etymology:

Ⓥ Some of the strong conjugation verbs, in Classical Japanese, had an additional predicative form that differed from the attributive form, ending in -u or -ri. With time this form disappeared, and the predicative form eventually merged with the attributive, as it already happened with the weak conjugation forms.

E.g. Originally: *taberu hito* (*eating person*) & *kono hito ga tabu* (*this person eats*) → *taberu hito* (*eating person*) & *kono hito ga taberu* (*this person eats*).

---

56 In traditional Japanese grammar, the realis form is named *izenkē* (已然形), which can be translated roughly as 'true (real) form'. When this form is used as an indicative expression in a predicative form, it gets, in traditional grammar, the name *shuushikē* (終止形), which means 'terminal form'. When it is used as an attributive, it takes the name *rentaikē* (連体形), 'attributive form'; and when it is used as lemma, it gets the name *jishokē* (辞書形), 'dictionary form'.

Ⓐ The realis form of adjectival verbs with the ending in -i actually comes from the Classical Japanese ending -**ki**, analogous to the rest of root forms of adjectival verbs, which are conjugated by the addition of a letter **k** plus a vowel to the stem.

2.2 Irrealis Form

A = Irrealis Form of Verbs
ka = Irrealis Form of Adjectival Verbs

Ⓢ Strong Verbs	Ⓦ Weak Verbs	Ⓐ Adjectival Verbs
S	S+a*	s+ka

* +wa for verbs whose lemma ends in vowel+u

The irrealis form[57] is an inflection that is used to indicate, helped by other endings, facts or states whose realization is not confirmed, events that have not (yet) happened, that are *not real* yet. This form is the basis upon which, for example, the negative forms of the verbs are built.

The irrealis form has no isolated functions whatsoever.

Formation of the Irrealis Form:

In the strong conjugation, this form is equivalent to the stem. In the weak conjugation, -a is added to the stem, and in the adjectival verbs, the ending -**ka** is added to it.

❖ Ⓦ Verbs' lemma ending in **vowel+u** → S+wa

2.3 Infinitive Form

I = Infinitive Form of Verbs
ku = Infinitive Form of Adjectival Verbs

Ⓢ Strong Verbs	Ⓦ Weak Verbs	Ⓐ Adjectival Verbs
S	S+i	s+ku

The infinitive form[58] is used mainly to form verbal compounds, and it is also one of the most used forms in agglutinative derivations.

---

[57] In traditional Japanese grammar, the irrealis form is called *mizenkē* (未然形), which can be translated as 'not-yet true form'.

[58] In traditional Japanese grammar, the infinitive form is called *renyōkē* (連用形), which means 'continuous form', a name obtained from the conjunctive function of the inflection.

Formation of the Infinitive Form:

In the strong conjugation, this form is equivalent to the stem. In the weak conjugation, **-i** is added to the stem and in the adjectival verbs, the ending **-ku** is added to it.

❖ Verbal stems ending in **-s**: **S-s+i** → **-shi**

❖ Verbal stems ending in **-ts**: **S-ts+i** → **-chi**

Functions of the Infinitive Form:

❖ **Conjunctive Coordinator:** The infinitive form can act as a coordinator conjoining a clause to another.

Ⓥ 君が歌い、僕は踊る: "You sing (and), I dance".

Ⓐ 雲が黒く、雨がひどい: "The clouds are black (and), the rain is violent".

❖ Ⓥ **Fossilized Nominalization:** The infinitive form of some verbs makes them act as nouns, but this is a residue of Classical Japanese and this form of nominalization is no longer productive.

分かり: 'Understanding'. From *wakaru* 分かる (*to understand*).

❖ Ⓥ **Fossilized Nominal Prefix:** The infinitive form of some verbs can sometimes act as a nominal prefix to a noun. This use is no longer productive.

着物: 'Japanese clothes'. *Ki*: (Ⅰ) *kiru* 着る (*to wear*) + *mono* 物 (*thing*).

❖ Ⓐ **Adverbialization:** The infinitive form of the adjectival verb when it appears on its own indicates that said adjective has taken on the function of an adverb.

早く !: 'Quick(ly)!'. From *hayai* 早い (*fast; quick; early*).

2.4 Subjunctive Form

E = Subjunctive Form of Verbs

ke = Subjunctive Form of Adjectival Verbs

Ⓢ Strong Verbs	Ⓦ Weak Verbs	Ⓐ Adjectival Verbs
S	S+e	s+ke

This inflection marks imagined, desired, or possible actions, that is, actions or states that have not yet occurred but are being considered as feasible. This subjunctive form[59] has no isolated functions, meaning that it must always be followed by another ending, although in

---

[59] In traditional Japanese grammar this form is called *katēkē* (仮定形), which means 'suppositive form'.

the weak conjugation the imperative form [☞ III.3.5] is morphologically identical to this form.

Formation of the Subjunctive Form:

In the strong conjugation, this form is equivalent to the stem. In the weak conjugation, -e is added to the stem and in the adjectival verbs, the ending -ke is added to it.

2.5 Root Forms Paradigm

	Strong Verb	Weak Verb	Adjectival Verb
	mìru 見る *see*	wakàru 分かる *understand*	tanóshìi 楽しい *fun*
Stem	mi-	wakar-	tanoshi-
Realis	miru	wakaru	tanoshii
Irrealis		wakara-	tanoshika-
Infinitive	mi-	wakari	tanoshiku
Subjunctive		wakare-	tanoshike-

3. DERIVATIVE FORMS

The derivative forms are inflections that are made through the addition of some simple ending to the root forms, and they specify the mood or aspect of the verb. What characterizes these derivative endings as opposed to other types of endings is that these forms can also serve as a basis for new endings through particles or auxiliary verbs.

There are two derivative forms based on the infinitive root form, two derivative forms based on the subjunctive root form, and one derivative form based on the irrealis root form. The realis root form has no linked derivative form whatsoever.

The resulting derivative forms are as follows:

3.1. **Presumptive Form**: Used to state assumptions.

3.2. **Gerundive Form**: Used to indicate clause conjunction.

3.3. **Perfective Form**: Used to indicate the perfective aspect.

3.4. **Provisional Form**: Used to express provisions.

3.5. **Imperative Form**: Used to express commands.

DERIVATIVE FORMS		Form			Symbol
		Strong Verbs	Weak Verbs	Adj. Verbs	
Irrealis:	**Presumptive**	S-yō	S-ō	ka-rō	Ō
Infinitive:	**Gerundive**	I-te*		ku-te	TE
	Perfective	I-ta*		ku-atta	TA
Subjunctive:	**Provisional**	E-reba	E-ba	ke-reba	BA
	Imperative	E-ro / E-yo	E	ke-are	

*Subject to phonetic changes

3.1 Presumptive Form

Ō = Presumptive Form of Verbs and Adjectival Verbs

Ⓢ Strong Verbs	Ⓦ Weak Verbs	Ⓐ Adjectival Verbs
S+yō	S+ō	ka+rō

The presumptive mood, in general terms, is used to express a probable conjecture when one refers to third persons; or to indicate a kind suggestion when speaking in the first person. The term *presumptive* refers to the pre-assumption that is made about the action or state indicated by the verb.

Formation of the Presumptive Form:

The presumptive form was originally built upon the irrealis form [**A/ka**], however, over time, the endings contracted so much that they resulted in the forms -**yō** in strong verbs and -**ō** in weak verbs attached directly to the stem (see *Etymology* below).

❖ Ⓐ -**ka**+rō = s+karō

Functions of the Presumptive Form:

❖ Ⓥ **Presumptive Mood:** The presumptive mood represented by this form originally denotes some degree of conjecture about the realization of the action signified by the verb marked with this inflection, a sense that somehow is still preserved in literary language. In contemporary, conversational Japanese, this form mostly indicates that the performance of the action marked by the verb is quite possible (*it's probably the case that* ~), but the usage of the presumptive mood is nowadays mostly relegated to the copula or stative verbs. | ≈ darō [☞ VIII.3.4]

288

A. この家で本がある？ [this house–in book NOM are?]: "Are there books in this house?".

B. あろう: "I believe there are".

❖ Ⓐ [*lit.*][*for.*] **Presumptive Mood:** In the case of adjectival verbs, the modality marked by the presumptive form is only of conjecture (*must be ~; probably is ~*), but this form for adjectival verbs is usually confined to the literary or very formal language. | ≈ darō [☞ VIII.3.4]

遅かろう: "It must be late".

❖ Ⓥ [*fam.*] **Hortative Mood:** It denotes the proposal to carry out an action (*let's ~*) spoken in a familiar way.

行こう: "Let's go".

Etymology:

> Ⓥ The presumptive mood ending of Classical Japanese was -mu[60], which was added to the irrealis form of the verbs (A). The resulting ending -**amu** underwent many phonetic changes throughout history, developing into the present form **S+ō** through the following process: A+mu → -amu → -anu → -au → -ō. In the weak conjugation, the process was the following: S(e/i)+mu → -enu/-inu → -eu/-iu → iō (by analogy) → -yō.

> Ⓐ Irrealis f. -**ka** + **arō*** → -**kaarō** → -**karō** | *Presumptive f. of the v. *aru (to be there)*: arō ← arau ← aranu ← aramu.

3.2 Gerundive Form

TE = Gerundive Form of Verbs and Adjectival Verbs

Ⓢ Strong Verbs	Ⓦ Weak Verbs	Ⓐ Adjectival Verbs
I+te		ku+te

The gerundive form, made by the addition of the inflection -**te** to the infinitive form, designates that the verb thus inflected functions in conjunction with another verb. This means that a verb in the gerundive form will normally be followed explicitly or implicitly by another verb, thus entailing a concurrence or continuation of actions or states.

Formation of the Gerundive Form:

---

[60] It can be hypothesized that this presumptive ending of Classical Japanese might have a relationship to the *mi*- root of the verb *miru* ('to see'), thus implying that a reference is being made by this presumptive mood to some action or state that may be (presumably) seen in advance.

The gerundive form of the strong verbs and adjectival verbs is done by adding the suffix -te to the infinitive form [I/ku].

❖ Ⓦ The union of the infinitive form of the weak verbs with the ending -te undergoes a euphonic process of vowel assimilation described in the following list:

- -ite / -chite / -rite → -tte
- -nite / -mite / -bite → -nde
- -kite → -ite
- -gite → -ide

Paradigm

Strong Verb	Weak Verbs					Adj. Verbs
-ru	-u /-tsu/-ru	-nu/-mu/-bu	-ku	-gu		-i
irú いる *to be (at)*	iú いう *to say*	asobú 遊ぶ *to play*	kàku 書く *to write*	kasègu 稼ぐ *to earn*		umài うまい *to be delicious*
ite	itte	asonde	kaite	kaseide		umakute

❖ The gerundive form of the verb **iku** 行く (*to go*) is **itte** 行って.

❖ The gerundive form of the verb **tou** 問う and **kou** 請う (*to ask*) is **tōte** 問うて and **kōte** 請うて.

Functions of the Gerundive Form:

❖ **Conjunctive Coordinator:** The basic function of the Japanese Gerundive Form is to connect the verbal with another verbal, implying a consecutive succession of actions (~ *and* ...), thus forming a conjunction of phrases.

Ⓥ どこへ行ってきた？ [where–to go-and come?]: "Where has (he) been to?".

Ⓐ 広くて明るい: "It's spacious and light".

❖ Ⓥ **Gerund:** When this verbal form is in conjunction with so-called subsidiary verbs, it can be understood, rather than as a conjunctive coordinator, as a gerund (hence the name of the form), that is, a verb that acts as a noun for the subsidiary verb that follows it. For more information, see Gerundive Verbal Compounds [☞ [☞ XI.1].

行ってしまった [going finished]: "(He) went away".

❖ Ⓥ **Causal Mood:** As a derivation of the conjunctive sense, this form can also express a reason or cause that introduces a consequence, usually when referring to consequences related to feelings or emotions.

滑って膝を打ったんです: "I slipped and hit my knee." / "I hit my knee because I slipped".

❖ Ⓥ [*fam.*] **Directive Mood**: It expresses a light command within a familiar verbal register. This form of expression results from a hackneyed use of the aposiopesis (phrasal omission), producing a subtle command originally leaving the phrase unfinished. Nowadays, nevertheless, this form is directly understood as a light imperative.

食べって: "(Please) eat".

❖ Ⓥ **Fossilized Adverbialization**: Some adverbs –verbal adverbs– are derived from the gerundive form of a verb. This method of adverbialization is no longer productive.

果たす: 'to accomplish' → 果たして: 'as expected'

Etymology:

> The ending -te comes from the infinitive form of the Classical Japanese dependent verb *tsu* which denotes completeness.

3.3 Perfective Form

TA = Perfective Form of Verbs and Adjectival Verbs

Ⓢ Strong Verbs	Ⓦ Weak Verbs	Ⓐ Adjectival Verbs
I+ta		kʉ+atta

The Perfective Form, in general terms, serves to indicate the perfect aspect, that is, to express actions or states that occurred in the past.

Formation of the Perfective Form:

The perfective form is constructed by adding the suffix -ta to the infinitive form [I]. Still, as in the gerundive form, this inflection within the weak conjugation undergoes a slight euphonic transformation:

❖ Ⓦ TE{–e}+a. Inflections get contracted as in the gerundive form [☞ III.3.2], which can be taken as a model in which the -e ending of said form is replaced by -a in order to make the perfective form.

❖ Ⓐ -kʉ+atta → -katta = s+katta

Paradigm

Strong Verbs	Weak Verbs				Adj. Verbs
-ru	-u /-tsu/-ru	-nu/-mu/-bu	-ku	-gu	-i
irú いる *to be (at)*	iú いう *to say*	asobú 遊ぶ *to play*	kàku 書く *to write*	kasègu 稼ぐ *to earn*	umài うまい *to be delicious*
ita	itta	asonda	kaita	kaseda	umakuta

Functions of the Perfective Form:

✤ [*fam.*] **Perfective Aspect & Indicative Mood**: Expresses an action or state that took place in the past. It is semantically equivalent to the English past tense. This form is used in a familiar register, but also can be considered as neutral in some written settings or as dependent clauses.

Ⓥ 東京へ行った [Tokyo-to went]: "(I/you/he/she/we/they) went to Tokyo" / "(I/you/he/she/we/they) have/has gone to Tokyo"

Ⓐ 面白かった: "It was interesting".

✤ **Perfective Aspect & Attributive Subordination**: As it occurs with the imperfective aspect expressed by the realis form, the perfective form can also be used as an attribute modifying a noun, but in this case, the attribute is understood as having taken place in the past.

Ⓥ 僕が買った本はここにある [I NOM bought book TOP here–in there-is]: "The book I bought is here".

Ⓐ 楽しかったあのゲームをもう一度をしたい [was-fun that game ACC more one-time do–want]: "I want to play again that game that was (so) good".

✤ The perfective aspect is sometimes used in Japanese where in English the present is preferred:

分かりました [understood]: "(I) understand". / "Alright".

Etymology:

Ⓥ Gerundive f. **-te** + v. **aru** *(to be there)* → **-tearu** → **-taru** → **-ta**.

Ⓐ Infinitive f. **-ku** + **atta*** → **-kuatta** → **-katta** | *(I) aru (to be there)*: **atta** ← **arita**.

3.4 Provisional Form

BA = Provisional Form of Verbs and Adjectival Verbs

Ⓢ Strong Verbs	Ⓦ Weak Verbs	Ⓐ Adjectival Verbs
E+reba	E+ba	ke+reba

The provisional form is used to indicate the possibility of the realization of an event or state, taking into account a previous *provision*, thus indicating a result depending on the previous clause. This form can sometimes be equivalent to the conditional clauses expressed in English stated by the conjunction *if*.

Formation of the Provisional Form:

The provisional form is constructed by adding, to the subjunctive form [**E/ke**], the inflection -**reba** in the strong conjugation and adjectival verbs, and the inflection -**ba** in the weak conjugation.

❖ Ⓐ -**ke**+reba = **s**+kereba

Functions of the Provisional Form:

❖ **Provisional Mood:** It expresses a hypothetical provision necessary for developing a subsequent action, i.e. a precondition for something to happen (*if* ~; *when* ~). This implies that the emphasis is on the provision rather than on the outcome.

Ⓥ 時間があれば行こう: "Let's go if you have time".

Ⓐ 天気が良ければ行く [weather NOM good–if go]: "(I'll) go if the weather is good".

Etymology:

Ⓐ Subjunctive f. -**ke** + **areba*** → -**keareba** → -**kereba** | *Provisional f. of the v. *aru (to be there).*

3.5 Imperative Form

Ⓢ Strong Verbs	Ⓦ Weak Verbs	Ⓐ Adjectival Verbs
E+ro [*lit.*] E+yo	E	ke+are

The imperative form is used to give direct orders, so it is often rude when used outright.

Formation of the Imperative Form:

This form is constructed by using the unmodified subjunctive form (**E**) in the weak conjugation and by adding -**ro** or -**yo** to that form in the strong conjugation.

❖ Ⓢ The ending **-ro** is, nowadays, considered the standard form. **-yo,** on the other hand, is now usually confined to the literary language.

❖ Ⓐ ke+are = s-kare. This form is extremely rare in modern Japanese, thus considered obsolete.

Functions of the Imperative Form:

❖ **Imperative Mood:** The Imperative Mood turns verbs into commands or orders. The usage of this form is relegated to:

- **Familiar Register:** Used to insiders or people of lower status than the speaker.

  あっちへ行け: "Go away!".

- **Impersonal Information:** Used as an impersonal command in some sign or instruction.

  止まれ: "Stop".

- **Motivational Speech:** Used with positive commands in order to cheer somebody up.

  がんばれ!: "Cheer up!".

Etymology:

Ⓐ Subjunctive f. **-ke** + **are*** → **-keare** → **-kare** | *Imperative f. of the v. *aru (to be there)*.

3.6 Derivate Forms Paradigm

	Strong Verb	Weak Verb	Verbal Adj.
	miru 見る	wakaru 分かる	tanoshii 楽しい
	see	*understand*	*fun*
Presumptive	miyō	wakarō	tanosikarō
Gerundive	mite	wakatte	tanosikute
Perfective	mita	wakatta	tanosikatta
Provisional	mireba	wakareba	tanosikereba
Imperative	miro / miyo	wakare	tanosikare

4. NEGATIVE FORMS

We have seen that some of the root and derivative forms represent moods and aspects. In the forms seen so far, these moods and aspects appear in affirmative polarity, meaning that the sentences are affirmative when these forms are used. In Japanese, the adjectival verb

nai ('not be')—which is the negative form of the stative verb *aru* ('to be there') [☞ VII.3.1] —added verbals to turn a positive sentence into a negative one.

The adjectival verb *nai* can be conjugated—in the same manner as any adjectival verb —for the realis and infinitive root forms, and for the presumptive, gerundive, perfective and provisional derivative forms. These conjugated forms are added to the irrealis form in verbs and to the infinitive form in adjectival verbs in order to build their corresponding negative forms.

NEGATIVE FORMS		Verbs	Adjectival Verbs
Root Forms:	Realis	**A-**nai	**ku-**nai
	Infinitive	**A-**naku	**ku-**naku
Derivative Forms:	Presumptive	**A-**nakarō	**ku-**nakarō
	Gerundive	**A-**nakute	**ku-**nakute
	Perfective	**A-**nakatta	**ku-**nakatta
	Provisional	**A-**nakereba	**ku-**nakereba

4.1 Negative Realis Form

Ⓥ Verbs	Ⓐ Adjectival Verbs
A+nai	**ku+**nai

The negative irrealis form is similar to the irrealis form in its functionality but making the phrase negative, being somewhat equivalent to the English expressions *don't* or *doesn't*.

The negative irrealis form is then taken to build the rest of the derived negative forms.

Formation of the Negative Realis Form:

This form is constructed by adding the adjectival verb *nai* ('not be') in its realis form [**nai**] to the irrealis form in verbs [**S+a**] and to the infinitive form in adjectival verbs [**s+ku**].

Adjectival verbs also admit a colloquial negative realis form in which one simply adds the contracted phoneme -**n**[61] to the irrealis form [**S+a**]. However, this colloquial form is only used as a sentence ender (as a finite verb), while the standard form (Ⓘ) can be used both in an attributive form and as a base for the rest of the negative conjugations.

Functions of the Negative Realis Form:

---

[61] Originally contracted from the obsolete negative inflection -**nu** [☞ XII.1.2].

✤ [*fam.*] **Negative Imperfective Aspect & Indicative Mood:** It describes a factual action or state that occurs in the present or future time, i.e. not in the past.

Ⓥ まだ帰^からないよ [yet come-back-not {assertive}]: "I'm not going home yet".

Ⓐ 思^{おも}ったほどよくない [thought as-much-as good–not]: "It's not as good as I thought".

✤ **Negative Imperfective Aspect & Attributive Subordination:** As with the positive realis form, the negative realis form can act as an attribute modifying a noun if it is placed before it, indicating that the noun does not perform the action or is not in the state indicated by the verbal.

Ⓥ これは使^つわないことだ: [that TOP use-not thing be]: "That's something that I don't use".

Ⓐ 美味^{お い}しくないケーキだ! [delicious-not cake is]: "It's a cake that is not delicious" / "That's not a good cake!".

4.2 Negative Infinitive Form

Ⓥ Verbs	Ⓐ Adjectival Verbs
A+naku	**ku**+naku

The negative infinitive form of verbals, derived from the infinitive form of the adjectival verb *nai* ('not be'), has a limited function in contemporary Japanese, as it is mostly used just to serve as the base of the negative gerundive form [☞ III.4.4].

Formation of the Negative Infinitive Form:

The negative infinitive form is constructed by adding the infinitive form of the adjectival verb *nai* ('not be') [naku] to the irrealis form in verbs [**S**+**a**], and to the infinitive form in verbal adjectives [**s**+**ku**], but only the adjectival form has a standalone function in contemporary Japanese.

Functions of the Negative Infinitive Form:

✤ Ⓐ [*lit.*] **Negative Conjunctive Coordinator:** The only independent functionality of this form is to act as a negative conjunctive coordinator—conjoining two clauses while negating one of them—in the written language, but only in the case of adjectival verbs. | ≈ nakute [☞ III.4.4]; ≈ nai de [☞ VIII.4.1]

映画^{えいが}はあまり面白^{おもしろ}くなく、途中^{とちゅう}で寝^ねてしまった: "The movie wasn't that fun and I slept in the middle".

4.3 Negative Presumptive Form

Ⓥ Verbs	Ⓐ Adjectival Verbs
A+nakarō	ku+nakarō

The presumptive negative form of verbals turns a sentence in the presumptive mood in the negative polarity. Nowadays, this form is confined to the written language.

Formation of the Negative Presumptive Form:

The negative presumptive form is constructed by adding the presumptive form of the adjectival verb *nai* ('not be') [**nakarō**], to the irrealis form in verbs [**S+a**] and to the infinitive form in adjectival verbs [**s+ku**], although as of today only the form in adjectival verbs is relevant in contemporary Japanese.

Functions of the Negative Presumptive Form:

✤ Ⓐ [*lit.*][*for.*] **Negative Presumptive Mood:** The negative presumptive form turns the presumptive mood into a negation, referring to something that probably is not or does not happen (*probably won't* ~). As with its positive variant [☞ III.3.1], this form is only used, occasionally, in written and formal language and only with adjectival verbs. The corresponding form in verbs is now obsolete. || ≈ nai darō [☞ VIII.3.5]

あの二人の関係は親しくなかろう: "The relationship between the two is probably not close".

4.4 Negative Gerundive Form

Ⓥ Verbs	Ⓐ Adjectival Verbs
A+nakute	ku+nakute

The negative gerundive form is equivalent to the gerundive form but in negative polarity.

Formation of the Negative Gerundive Form

The negative gerundive form is constructed by adding the gerundive form of the adjectival verb *nai* ('not be') [**nakute**] to the irrealis form in verbs [**S+a**] or to the infinitive form in adjectival verbs [**s+ku**].

Functions of the Negative Gerundive Form

❖ **Negative Conjunctive Coordinator**: It joins two clauses in such a way that the first clause is negative and serves as a cause or condition for the following clause. | Ⓥ ≈ nai de [☞ VIII.4.1]

Ⓥ 説明が分からなくて困った: "I didn't understand the explanation and I felt embarrassed".

Ⓐ この本はあまり長くなくて楽しいよ: "This book is not very long and it's fun".

4.5 Negative Perfective Form

Ⓥ Verbs	Ⓐ Adjectival Verbs
A+nakatta	ku+nakatta

The negative perfective form turns the perfective form of verbals into negative polarity, thus negating a past action or state, being somewhat equivalent to the English expression *didn't*.

Formation of the Negative Perfective Form:

The perfective negative form is built by adding the perfective form of the adjectival verb *nai* ('not be') [**nakatta**] to the irrealis form in verbs [**S+a**] and to the infinitive form in adjectival verbs [**s+ku**].

Functions of the Negative Perfective Form:

❖ [*fam.*] **Negative Perfective Aspect & Indicative Mood**: It expresses an action or state that did not take place in the past. This form is used in a familiar register, but also can be considered as neutral in some written settings or as dependent clauses.

Ⓥ それは見なかった: "I didn't see it".

Ⓐ 実はその小説はあまりよくなかった: "Actually, that novel wasn't that good".

❖ **Negative Perfective Aspect & Attributive Subordination**: The negative perfective form can also be used as an attribute modifying a noun, expressing that that noun is not or did not do the state or action marked by the verbal.

Ⓥ これは知らなかったことだ: [this TOP know-not-did thing is] "This is something that I didn't know".

Ⓐ 買った時にそんなに小さくなかったワンピースだ: "It's a dress that wasn't that small when I bought it".

4.6 Negative Provisional Form

Ⓥ Verbs	Ⓐ Adjectival Verbs
A+nakareba	**ku+nakareba**

The provisional negative form negates a provision, that is, it indicates that the state or action of the first clause is something that should not occur for the state or action of the following clause to happen, being somewhat equivalent to the English negative conditional structure *if not*.

Formation of the Negative Provisional Form:

The provisional form of the adjectival verb *nai* ('not be') [**nakereba**] is added to the irrealis form of verbs [**S+a**] or the infinitive form of adjectival verbs [**s+ku**].

Functions of the Negative Provisional Form:

❖ **Negative Provisional Mood**: It expresses a hypothetical negative provision necessary for the development of a subsequent action, indicating that something should not happen in order to something else to happen (*if not ~*). This implies that the emphasis is on the negative provision rather than on the outcome.

Ⓥ 走らなければ間に合わない: "If you don't run you won't be on time".

Ⓐ 面白くなければ読まない: "If it's not interesting I won't read it".

4.7 Negative Forms Paradigm

	Strong Verb	Weak Verb	Adjectival Verb
	mìru 見る	wakàru 分かる	tanóshìi 楽しい
	see	*understand*	*fun*
Realis	minai	wakaranai	tanoshikunai
Infinitive	minaku	wakaranaku	tanoshikunaku
Presumptive	minakarō	wakaranakarō	tanoshikunakarō
Gerundive	minakute	wakaranakute	tanoshikunakute
Perfective	minakatta	wakaranakatta	tanoshikunakatta
Provisional	minakereba	wakaranakereba	tanoshikunakereba

5. COLLOQUIAL FORMS

The colloquial Japanese language occasionally admits shortened variants for some forms. Among the forms seen so far, the provisional form, the negative provisional form and the negative realis form in its indicative mood admit colloquial abbreviations or shortenings.

	Strong Verbs	Weak Verbs	Adjectival Verbs
Provisional	S-reba	S-eba	s-kereba
Col. Provisional	S-rya	S-ya	s-kerya
Neg. Provisional	A-nakereba		ku-nakereba
Col. Neg. Provisional	A-nakerya / A-nakya		ku-nakerya / ku-nakya
Neg. Indicative	A-nai		ku-nai
Col. Neg. Indicative	A-n		-

5.1 Colloquial Provisional Forms

Provisional forms may undergo colloquial shortening as follows:

❖ [*col.*] **Provisional Form:** The series of phonemes **eba** of the provisional form [**BA**] is transformed into **ya**.

- Ⓢ **E-reba [S+reba]** → **S-rya**
- Ⓦ **E-ba [S+eba]** → **S-ya**
- Ⓐ **ke-reba [s+kereba]** → **s-kerya**

Ⓥ 見りゃ分かるよ: "If you see it you'll understand".

Ⓐ 欲しけりゃやる [be-wanted–if do]: "If you want it go for it".

❖ [*col.*] **Negative Provisional Form:** The colloquial shortened form of the negative provisional form is built in the same way as the positive form, i.e. by transforming the phonemes **eba** into **ya**, in this case from the negative provisional form of the adjectival verb *nai* [**nakereba**]. The contracted form, however, still admits one more shortening, turning the already shortened form **nakerya** into **nakya**.

- **A/ku-nakereba** → ❶ **A/ku-nakerya*** → ❷ **A/ku-nakya**

① 要求を入れなけりゃ僕はよす [demand ACC put-in-not-if I TOP leave]: "If they don't comply with my demands I'll leave".

② 英語話者に通じなきゃ意味がない: "It doesn't mean anything if English speakers don't understand".

❖ *The intermediate colloquial negative provisional form (②) is considered somewhat old-fashioned today.

5.2 Colloquial Negative Realis Form

The negative realis form can also be contracted, but the contracted form only occurs for the indicative mood in predicative phrases. This contracted form is used within a colloquial and familiar context, usually by men (masculine language).

✦ Ⓥ [*col.*][*fam.*][*mas.*] **Imperfective Aspect & Indicative Mood:** This colloquial form is realized by adding the phoneme -**n** to the irrealis form of verbs [**S**+**a**].

- **A-nai → A-n**

  分からん！: "I don't know!".

Etymology:

> The colloquial shortening of the negative realis form does not derive from the negative form built with the adjectival verb *nai* (*not be*). Rather, it is actually the shortening of the archaic negative ending-**nu** [☞ XII.1.2], relegated today to literary language.

5.3 Colloquial Forms Paradigm

	Strong Verb	Weak Verb	Adjectival Verb
	mìru 見る *see*	wakàru 分かる *understand*	tanóshìi 楽しい *fun*
Provisional	mireba	wakareba	tanoshikereba
Col. Provisional	mirya	wakarya	tanoshikerya
Neg. Provisional	minakereba	wakaranakereba	tanishikunakereba
Col. Neg. Provisional	minakerya	wakaranakerya wakaranakya	tanoshikunakerya tanoshikunakya
Neg. Indicative	minai	wakaranai	tanoshikunai
Col. Neg. Indicative	min	wakaran	-

6. IRREGULAR INFLECTIONS

In Japanese, there are mainly two irregular verbs: **suru** する ('to do') and **kuru** 来る ('to come'). These verbs are considered irregular because two of their root forms—the irrealis and the infinitive—are not constructed in the same way as the rest of the verbs. This means that most of their derivational forms are not morphologically equivalent to those of the other verbs either.

In addition to the two irregular verbs mentioned above, there is a third pseudo-irregular verb, the verb **aru** ある ('to be there'), whose root forms are regular but has a feature that makes it unique: its negative form is different, for it is the **nai** form, which is actually an adjectival verb with the meaning of 'not to be'. This irregular negative form is, in fact, the one used to make the negative forms of other verbs, as we saw in previous sections [☞ III.4].

	Irregular Verbs		Pseudo Irregular
	Ⓢ surú する	Ⓢ kùru 来る	Ⓦ àru ある
Realis (U)	**suru**	**kuru**	aru
Irrealis (A)	sa- / shi- / se-*	ko-	ara-†
Infinitive (I)	shi	ki	ari-
Subjunctive (E)	**su-**	**ku-**	ar-
Presumptive (Ō)	**shiyō** [*col.*] **sō**	**koyō**	arō
Gerundive (TE)	**shite**	**kite**	atte
Perfective (TA)	**shita**	**kita**	atta
Provisional (BA)	sureba	kureba	areba
Imperative	**shiro** [*lit.*] **seyo**	**koi**	are
Negative	shinai	konai	nai

* -**sa** for the translative forms [☞ VI.2]; -**shi** for the negative forms; -**se** for the archaic negative ending -**n**

† Only used for the archaic negative ending -**zu** [☞ XII.1.2]

In addition to the verbs mentioned above, there is also a minimal irregularity in three different verbals:

❖ The verbal adjective *ii* いい (*good*) conjugates all its forms except the imperfective indicative with the form **yoi** よい.

ゲームはいい: "The game is good" • ゲームは良かった: "The game was good".

❖ The verb *iku* 行く (*to go*) has its gerundive form as **itte** instead the expected *iite, and its perfective form as **itta** instead of *itta.

学校に行った: "I went to school".

❖ The realis form of the verb *iu* 言う (*to say*) is pronounced as **yuu**.

おれは言う: "Says I..."

6.1 Nominal Verbs

Nominal verbs, which, as explained in the Parts of Speech section [☞ I], are formed by adding the irregular verb **suru** ('to do') to a Sino-Japanese noun.

販売 (a sell) → 販売する (*to sell*)

It is also possible to make verbs from Japanese nouns by using the verb *suru*, but in this case, the accusative particle **o** must be added between the noun and the verb *suru*.

息 (*breath*) → 息をする (*to breath*)

IV. NOMINALS & ADJECTIVAL NOUNS

From a grammatical point of view, nominals and adjectival nouns share the characteristic of being linked to a subject with the copula, but they have semantic and functional differences.

    1. **Nominals**: Denote an abstract or concrete entity.

    2. **Adjectival Nouns**: Express a characteristic associated with an entity.

1. NOMINALS

N = Nominal

Syntactically, nominals can appear in the sentence in different ways: as a subject, as a topic, as a verbal complement, as a nominal complement or as a subject complement.

❖ If the nominal appears as subject, topic, verbal complement or nominal complement, it must be accompanied by a particle[62].

    N{p}

    ※ **N** stands for nominal and **{p}** for any particle.

❖ If the nominal appears as a subject complement, the noun will be accompanied by a copula.

    N{D}

    ※ **N** stands for nominal and **{D}** for a form of the copula.

+ *More information about nominals in Vocabulary* [☞ VO:II].

2. ADJECTIVAL NOUNS

n = Adjectival Noun

Adjectival nouns can appear in the sentence only as a nominal complement or as a subject complement.

❖ Adjectival nouns must always be accompanied by a copulative form [☞ V].

---

[62] Except, sometimes, in familiar, colloquial register, where some particles may be omitted [☞ II.3.2].

- If the adjectival noun appears as a nominal complement modifying a nominal, it will be accompanied by an attributive copulative form.

n{a} N

※ **n** stands for adjectival noun; {a} for an attributive form of the copula and **N** for a modified noun.

- If the adjectival noun appears as a subject complement indicating a characteristic of the subject, it will be accompanied by a predicative copulative form.

(N{p}) n{D}

※ **N** stands for a nominal or nominal phrase; {p} for a particle; **n** for an adjectival noun, and {D} for a predicative form of the copula. Parenthesis denote optionality.

+ *More information about adjectival nouns in Vocabulary* [☞ VO:V].

V. COPULAR INFLECTION

As already explained in the Parts of Speech section [☞ I], the copula, in grammatical terms, is a conjugable morpheme that links a nominal to the implicit or explicit subject of the sentence. The concept of copula in Japanese is relevant because it is this word class that defines the state of being of things, which in English is expressed through the verb 'to be'.

❖ The copula is always attached to a nominal [**N**], an adjectival noun [**n**], or exceptionally some particle, so it cannot appear independently.

❖ The nominal to which the copula is attached is thus linked to a subject, that is, marked by the nominative particle **ga** or the thematic particle **wa**.

❖ The copula can be conjugated through inflections that make different **copulative forms**.

Any copulative form appears within the sentence as follows:

Japanese	English
(A{p}) **B** {D}	A be **B**

※ A stands for a noun or nominal phrase acting as a subject; {p} stands for particle (wa/ga); **B** stands for a nominal, adjectival noun or nominal phrase in Japanese or for a noun or adjective in English; {D} stands for any form of the copula; be stands for any conjugated form of the verb 'to be'. Parentheses stand for optionality.

Let's illustrate this with an example:

僕	は	学生	だ
A	{p}	**B**	{D}
I	TOP	student	be

"I'm a student"

The subject in Japanese is often left out [☞ I.3.3]. Let us see how would look that sentence with subject omission:

僕は学生だ "I'm a student" → ∅ 学生だ "I'm/He's/You're... a student"

1. COPULATIVE FORMS

> {D} = Copula (in any form)[63]

As with verbals, there are different forms or conjugations of the copula depending on aspect, mood and register. The copula can be conjugated in the realis form—using a special attributive form in the plain register—and in the presumptive, gerundive, perfective, provisional and imperative derivative forms and their negative counterparts.

COPULA	Literary	Plain	Lit. Negative	Col. Negative
Imperfective		N/n-da		
Imperfective Attributive	N/n-de aru	N/n-no n-na	N/n-de wa nai	N/n-ja nai
Infinitive	N/n-de ari		N/n-de (wa) naku	
Presumptive	N/n-de arō	N/n-darō	N/n-de wa nakarō	
Gerundive	N/n-de atte	N/n-de	N/n-de wa nakute	N/n-ja nakute
Perfective	N/n-de atta	N/n-datta	N/n-de wa nakatta	N/n-ja nakatta
Provisional	N/n-de areba	N/n-nara(ba)	N/n-de nakereba	
Imperative	N/n-de are			

1.1 Realis Copulae

	Literary	Plain	Lit. Negative	Col. Negative
Predicative		N/n+da		
Attributive	N/n+de aru	N(p)/n+no n+na	N/n+de wa nai	N/n+ja nai

Most of the different conjugations of the Japanese copula are constructed from the literary realis form **de aru**, which is composed of the essive particle *de* ('in'; 'at') [☞ VII.3.1] and the stative verb *aru* ('to be there'). The verbal part *aru* is conjugated identically to that verb in order to make all the literary copulative forms. The realis form has the literary version now described, also a plain or neutral version, as well as negative literary and negative colloquial derivations.

---

[63] Symbolized as D because most forms of the copula start with the phoneme *d*.

The realis copulae are used to mark the copula in an imperfective aspect (present) both in a predicative (indicative mood) and attributive manner.

➤ **N/n-de aru** である: [*lit.*][*for.*] ❶ Imperfective Copula | *am/are/is* ‖ ❷ [*lit.*][*for.*] Imperfective Attributive Copula | *that are/is* ~

❖ Mostly used in written or very formal language to give explanations or introduce topics as general facts.

① 神<ruby>神<rt>かみ</rt></ruby>かみは愛<ruby>愛<rt>あい</rt></ruby>である: "God is love".

② 彼<ruby>彼<rt>かれ</rt></ruby>が良<ruby>良<rt>よ</rt></ruby>い作家<ruby>作家<rt>さっか</rt></ruby>であることは事実<ruby>事実<rt>じじつ</rt></ruby>だ [he NOM good author is thing TOP reality is]: "That he is a good author is a fact". / "It's a fact that he's a good actor".

➤ **N/n-de {p} aru**: = N/n-**de aru**

❖ Variation of the imperfective copula **de aru**, where {p} can be any focal particle (*wa, mo, sae,* etc) [☞ ☞ VIII.1.3]. This form is practically only used in compound coordinated sentences.

学生<ruby>学生<rt>がくせい</rt></ruby>ではあるが勉強<ruby>勉強<rt>べんきょう</rt></ruby>していない: "He is a student, but he doesn't study".

➤ **N/n-da** だ: [*fam.*] Imperfective Copula | *am/is/are* ~

❖ This form primarily replaces the **de aru** form in the written language since it is less pompous than the strictly literary version. In the colloquial language, this form is only used in the familiar register.

僕<ruby>僕<rt>ぼく</rt></ruby>が学生<ruby>学生<rt>がくせい</rt></ruby>だ [I NOM student is]: "I am a student".

➤ **N/n-no** の: Imperfective Attributive Copula | *that/who/which am/is/are* ~

❖ Used only with nouns, no adjectival nouns or versatile adjectival nouns.

こちらが友達<ruby>友達<rt>ともだち</rt></ruby>の明<ruby>明<rt>あきら</rt></ruby>だ [over-here NOM friend that-is Akira be]: "This is Akira, (who is) my friend". / "This is my friend Akira".

➤ **N(p*)-no** の: = N/n-**no**

❖ ***No** can follow the case particles **to**, **e**, **kara** and **made**.

友達<ruby>友達<rt>ともだち</rt></ruby>からのメッセージを読<ruby>読<rt>よ</rt></ruby>んだ: "I read the message from my friend". (Lit. "I read the message that is from my friend".)

➤ **N/n-na** な: Imperfective Attributive Copula | *that am/is/are* ~

❖ Used only with nouns, *na* adjectival nouns or versatile adjectival nouns.

静<ruby>静<rt>しず</rt></ruby>かな部屋<ruby>部屋<rt>へや</rt></ruby>だ [quiet that-is room is]: "It is a room that is quiet". / "It is a quiet room".

➤ **N/n-de wa nai** ではない: [*lit.*] ❶ Negative Imperfective Copula | *am/are/is not ~* ‖ ❷ [*lit.*] Negative Attributive Copula | *that are/is not ~*

① 今日は水曜日ではない: "Today is not Wednesday".

② 今日は水曜日ではないことに今気がついた: "I've just realized that today is not Wednesday".

➤ **N/n-ja nai** じゃない: [*col.*][*fam.*] = N/n-**de wa nai**

田中さんは先生じゃない: "Mr. Tanaka is not a teacher".

1.2 Infinitive Copulae

Literary	Literary Negative
N/n+de ari	**N/n**+de (wa) naku

The infinitive forms of the copula are mainly used as a basis for other forms, but occasionally they can also appear in literary language as a conjunctive coordinator [☞ VIII.4.1].

➤ **N/n-de ari** であり: [*lit.*] Conjunctive Copula | *being ~; be ~ and*

彼は給仕であり俳優でもある: "He is a waiter and also an actor".

➤ **N/n-de naku** でなく: [*lit.*] Negative Conjunctive Copula | *not being ~ and; be not ~ but*

❖ Mostly used in established expressions or idioms.

言葉でなく行為をして: "Not words but deeds". / "Do deeds, not words".

➤ **N/n-de wa naku** ではなく: [*lit.*][*for.*] = N/n-**de naku**

日本人ではなく、アメリカ人だった: "He was not Japanese but American".

1.3 Presumptive Copulae

Literary	Plain	Literary Negative
N/n+de arō	**N/n**+darō	**N/n**+de wa nakarō

The presumptive copulae express the presumptive mood of the copula, referring to something that "could be" (*wold be*; *will be*).

➤ **N/n-de arō** であろう: [*lit.*][*for.*] Presumptive Copula | *(probably) would be ~*

これは本当に事実であろうか [that TOP really real be-would {interrogative}]: "I wonder if that's real".

➤ **N/n-darō** だろう: [*fam.*] Presumptive Copula | *(probably) would be ~*

❖ Used in familiar spoken language or plain written language.

あの人が新しい先生だろう: "That person probably is the new teacher".

➤ **N/n-de wa nakarō** ではなかろう: [*lit.*][*obs.*] Negative Presumptive Copula | *(probably) would not be ~*

❖ This form is only encountered residually in very formal written language.

1.4 Gerundive Copulae

Literary	Plain	Literary Negative	Colloquial Neg.
N/n+de atte	**N/n**+de	**N/n**+de wa nakute	**N/n**+ja nakute

The gerundive forms of the copula are used to join a sentence that ends in a copula with another consecutive sentence.

➤ **N/n-de atte** であって: [*lit.*] Conjunctive Copula | *be ~ and; being ~*

普通であって、あまり優雅ではない: "It is ordinary and not very elegant".

➤ **N/n-de** で: Conjunctive Copula | *be ~ and; being ~*

このアパートは静かでいい: "This apartment is quiet and good".

➤ **N/n-de wa nakute** ではなくて: [*lit.*] Negative Conjunctive Copula | *be ~ and; being ~*

大事なのは量ではなくて質である: "What counts is quality and not quantity".

➤ **N/n-ja nakute** ではなく: [*col.*] = N/n-**de wa nakute**

厳しい先生じゃなくてよかった: "He was not a strict and was a good teacher".

1.5 Perfective Copulae

Literary	Plain	Literary Negative	Colloquial Neg.

N/n+de atta	N/n+datta	N/n+de wa nakatta	N/n+ja nakatta

The perfective forms of the copula are used to mark the copula in a perfective aspect both in the indicative mood (*was/were ~*) and as an attributive subordinator modifying a noun (*that was/were ~*).

➤ **N/n-de atta** であった: ❶ [*lit.*] Perfective Copula | *was/were ~* ‖ ❷ Perfective Attributive Copula | *that was/were ~*

① 21 歳であった: "He/She was 21 years old".

② 姉妹であった二人: "Two people who were sisters".

➤ **N/n-datta** だった: ❶ [*fam.*] Perfective Copula | *was/were ~* ‖ ❷ Perfective Attributive Copula | *that was/were ~*

① 夜だった: "It was night".

② その学校の元生徒だった男性だ: "It is a man who was a former pupil of this school".

➤ **N/n-de wa nakatta** ではなかった: ❶ [*lit.*] Negative Perfective Copula | *was/were not ~* ‖ ❷ [*lit.*] Negative Perfective Attributive Copula | *that was/were not ~*

① 昨日は休みではなかった: "Yesterday was not a day off".

② それらは清潔ではなかった服だ: "Those are the clothes that weren't clean".

➤ **N/n-ja nakatta** じゃなかった: [*col.*][*fam.*] = N/n-**de wa nakatta**

それは簡単じゃなかった: "That wasn't easy".

1.6 Provisional Copulae

Literary	Plain	Literary Negative
N/n+de areba	**N/n+nara**(ba)	**N/n+de nakareba**

The provisional copula marks the provisional mood for the copula, expressing that the "state of being" of the marked nominal or adjectival noun is a provision for a consecutive sentence (*if am/are/is/was/were ~*).

➤ **N/n-de areba** であれば: [*lit.*][*for.*] Provisional Copula | *if be ~*

必要であれば言って下さい: "Tell me if it is necessary".

> **N/n-nara** なら: Provisional Copula | *if be* ~

暇なら映画に行こう [free-time is–if movie to go-let's]: "If you are free let's go to the movies".

> **N/n-naraba** ならば: [*for.*] Provisional Copula | *if be* ~

私ならばできる: "If it's me I can do it".

> **N/n-de nakereba** でなければ: [*lit.*][*for.*] Negative Provisional Copula | *if don't/ doesn't* ~ | ≈ nai nara [☞ VIII.3.7]

この本でなければだめだ: "If it's not (with) this book there's no way".

1.7 Infinitive Copula

It indicates the command to the listener to "be" what is marked by the nominal or adjectival noun.

This imperative copula is only literary or formal, so in everyday speech it is not used. Instead, the causative structure **ni shite** [☞ EY:VI.5.5] is preferred.

> **N/n-de are** であれ: [*lit.*][*for.*] Imperative Copula | *be* ~ | ≈ ni shite [☞ EY:VI.5.5]

うそをつくな、正直であれ: "Don't tell lies, be honest".

1.8 Copula Omission

In the colloquial language in a familiar register, it is very common for the familiar copula (**da**) to be omitted—left unsaid—in the imperfective aspect and indicative mood.

この車は便利だ → この車は便利 Ø: "This car is convenient".

VI. EXTENSIVE VERBAL INFLECTION

Verbals, in addition to the root, derivative and negative forms, have more conjugable forms with different functions that have a more complex grammatical derivation than those, but which are essential to know because they are commonly used:

1. **Polite Forms:** Used to indicate a polite register.

2. **Translative Forms:** Used to transform (translate) the voice of a verb.

3. **Potential Forms:** Used to turn the verb into the potential mood.

1. POLITE FORMS

We have seen so far versions for a plain, colloquial, literary, familiar or formal register in many verbal and copulative conjugations. We have yet to see also verbals and copulae conjugated in the polite register, which indicates certain deference, as a sign of respect, on the part of the speaker towards the listener. In this sense, the polite register is contrasted with the familiar register since the former is generally used with strangers or people in a higher social position as opposed to the latter. Polite forms vary depending on whether they are used with verbs, adjectival verbs, or copulae.

	Verbs	For. Copula	Col. Copula	Adj. Verb
Imperfective	I-masu	N/n-de arimasu	N/n-desu	i desu
Presumptive	I-mashō	N/n-de arimashō	N/n-deshō	
Gerundive	I-mashite	N/n-de arimashite	N/n-deshite	
Perfective	I-mashita	N/n-de arimashtia	N/n-deshita	ku-atta desu
Imperative	I-mase*			
Neg. Indicative	I-masen	N/n-de wa arimasen	N/n-ja arimasen	ku arimasen
		N/n-de wa nai desu	N/n-ja nai desu	ku-nai desu

Neg. Perfective	I-masen deshita	N/n-de wa arimasen deshita	N/n-ja arimasen deshita	ku arimasen deshita
		N/n-de wa nakatta desu	N/n-ja nakatta desu	ku-nakatta desu

1.1 Polite Verbs Conjugation

Imperfective	Presumptive	Conjunctive	Perfective	Imperative
I+masu	I+mashō	I+mashite	I+mashita	I+mase

The polite form of verbs is constructed by adding the dependent verb -**masu** to the irrealis form [**I**]. The dependent verb *masu* can be conjugated for the various roots and derivative forms as a regular verb.

➤ **I-masu** ます: [*pol.*] Imperfective Aspect & Indicative Mood

ご飯を食べます: "I eat the meal".

➤ **I-mashō** ましょう: [*pol.*] Presumptive Mood | *let us ~*

踊りましょう: "Let's dance".

➤ **I-mashite** まして: [*pol.*] Conjunctive Coordinator | *~ and; ~ing*

❖ Used in formulaic expressions when talking about a respected person.

初めまして: "(It's a) starting" → "Nice to meet you".

➤ **I-mashita** ました: [*pol.*] Perfective Aspect & Indicative Mood | *~ed*

見つけました: "I found it".

➤ **I-mase** ませ: [*for.*][*pol.*] Imperative Mood | *be ~* | ≈ ni shite [☞ EY:VI.5.5]

❖ This form is almost exclusively used, formulaically, with honorific verbs [☞ VO:IV.3].

ご確認くださいませ: "Please confirm".

1.2 Negative Polite Verbs Conjugation

Negative Imperfective	Negative Imperfective
I+masen	I+masen deshita

Negative polite imperfective forms of verbs are constructed by adding the ending -**masen** to the realis form. The -**masen** form is an archaic negative conjugation (**E+n**) of the dependent verb *masu*.

The negative perfective form is constructed by adding the perfective polite copula **deshita** to the ending -**masen**.

➤ **I-masen** ません: [*pol.*] Negative Imperfective Aspect | *don't/doesn't* ~

私は知りません: "I don't know".

➤ **I-masen deshita** ませんでじた: [*pol.*] Negative Perfective Aspect | *didn't* ~

知りませんでした: "I didn't know".

1.3 Polite Copula Conjugations

Imperfective	Presumptive	Gerundive	Perfective
N/n-desu	N/n-deshō	N/n-deshite	N/n-deshita

The polite form of the copula has two versions: a formal one—derived from the literary copula—and a colloquial one derived from the formal version. The positive formal form is not used anymore, it has become obsolete, since in the written language, the forms of the copula of the plain register are preferred. However, it is not irrelevant to have an idea of the positive formal polite forms in order to have a consistent grasp of how the rest of the polite copula forms have been formed. This formal form is simply the polite version of the literary copula **de aru**, which becomes **de arimasu**. From this form derive the rest of the polite conjugation, for the colloquial forms are its phonetic contractions of these forms.

The colloquial polite forms sometimes also appear even in the written language and are considered as the standard polite forms.

Obsolete Formal Polite Copulae:

➤ **N/n**-de arimasu であります: [*for.*][*pol.*][*obs.*] Imperfective Copula | *am/are/is* ~

➤ **N/n**-de arimashō でありましょう: [*for.*][*pol.*][*obs.*] Presumptive Copula | *would be* ~

➤ **N/n**-de arimashite でありまして: [*for.*][*pol.*][*obs.*] Conjunctive Copula | *be* ~ *and; being* ~

➤ **N/n**-de arimashita でありました: [*for.*][*pol.*][*obs.*] Perfective Copula | *was/were* ~

Plain Polite Copulae:

➤ **N/n**-desu です: [*pol.*] Imperfective Copula | *am/are/is* ~

これは私(わたし)のペンです: "This is my pen".

➤ **N/n-deshō** でしょう: [*pol.*] Presumptive Copula | *would be ~*

簡単(かんたん)でしょう: "Probably it's simple". / "It's simple, right?".

➤ **N/n-deshite** でして: [*pol.*] Conjunctive Copula | *be ~ and; being ~*

❖ Mostly used formally to finish a sentence in an inconclusive manner.

少々(しょうしょう) 内気(うちき)でしてね: "She/He's a little bit shy…".

➤ **N/n-deshita** でした: [*pol.*] Perfective Copula | *was/were ~*

いい旅(たび)でした: "It was a nice trip".

1.4 Negative Polite Copula Conjugations

Negative Imperfective	Negative Perfective
N/n-de wa arimasen [*col.*] **N/n-**ja arimasen	**N/n-**de wa arimasen deshita [*col.*] **N/n-**ja arimasen deshita
N/n-de wa nai desu [*col.*] **N/n-**ja nai desu	**N/n-**de wa nakatta desu [*col.*] **N/n-**ja nakatta desu

The negative forms of the polite copula are constructed by conjugating the polite literary form **de wa nai**, which gives the formal polite form of **de wa arimasen**. Colloquial forms are constructed by contracting the phonemes **de wa** into **ja**.

Another optional negative form is constructed by adding the polite verb **desu** to the negative form of **de wa nai**.

➤ **N/n-de wa arimasen** ではありません: [*for.*][*pol.*] Negative Imperfective Copula | *am/are/is not ~*

彼(かれ)は歌手(かしゅ)ではありません: "He's not a **singer**".

➤ **N/n-ja arimasen** じゃありません: [*col.*][*pol.*] Negative Imperfective Copula | *am/are/is not ~*

それは間違(まちが)いじゃありません: "That's not a mistake".

➤ **N/n-de wa nai desu** ではないです: [*for.*][*pol.*] = N/n-de (wa) **arimasen**

彼女(かのじょ)はお医者(いしゃ)ではないです: "She's not a doctor".

➤ **N/n-ja nai desu** じゃないです: [*col.*][*pol.*] = N/n-ja **arimasen**

それは嘘じゃないです: "That's not a lie".

➤ **N/n-de wa arimasen deshita** ではありませんでした: [*for.*][*pol.*] Negative Imperfective Copula | *was/were not ~*

手紙ではありませんでした: "It isn't a letter".

　➤ **N/n-ja arimasen deshita** じゃありませんでした: [*col.*][*pol.*] Negative Imperfective Copula | *was/were not ~*

　　それはコーヒーじゃありませんでした: "That wasn't coffee".

➤ **N/n-de wa nakatta desu** ではなかったです: [*for.*][*pol.*] = N/n-**de** (wa) **arimasen deshita**

昨日は土曜日ではなかったです: "Yesterday wasn't Saturday".

　➤ **N/n-ja nakatta desu** じゃなかったです: [*col.*][*pol.*] = N/n-**ja arimasen deshita**

　　冗談じゃなかったです: "It wasn't a joke".

Etymology:

> The colloquial shortening of the negative realis form does not derive from the negative form built with the adjectival verb **nai** (*not be*). Rather, it is actually the shortening of the archaic negative ending -**nu** [☞ XII.1.2], relegated today to literary language.

1.5 Polite Adjectival Verbs Conjugation

Imperfective	Perfective
i desu	k~~u~~-atta desu

The polite forms of adjectival verbs are constructed by adding the polite form of the copula, **desu,** to the imperfective and perfective forms.

➤ **i desu** です: [*pol.*] Imperfective Aspect & Indicative Mood | *am/are/is ~*

美しいです: "It's beautiful".

➤ **k~~u~~-atta desu** です: [*pol.*] Perfective Aspect & Indicative Mood | *was/were ~*

美味しかったです: "It was delicious".

1.6 Negative Polite Adjectival Verbs Conjugation

Negative Imperfective	Negative Perfective

ku arimasen	ku arimasen deshita
ku nai desu	ku nakatta desu

The negative polite forms of adjectival verbs are constructed by adding the **arimasen** form to the infinitive form of adjectival verbs.

Another optional negative form is constructed by adding the polite copula **desu** to the negative ending **nai**.

➤ **ku** arimasen ありません: [*pol.*] Negative Imperfective Aspect | *am/are/is not* ~

この時計は高くありません: "This watch is not expensive".

➤ **ku** nai desu ないです: [*pol.*] = ku **arimasen**

今日は寒くないです: "Today it's not cold".

➤ **ku** arimasen deshita ありませんでした: [*pol.*] Negative Perfective Aspect | *am/are/is not* ~

昨日は忙しくありませんでした: "Yesterday I was not busy".

➤ **ku**-nakatta desu なかったです: [*pol.*] = ku **arimasen deshita**

このケーキは美味しくなかったです: "This cake was not tasty".

2. TRANSLATIVE FORMS

The so-called translative forms are specific conjugations that change the voice of verbs.

There are two main verbal voices and one combined voice:

- **Active Voice**: Standard verb voice, indicating that the subject of the sentence is the one who performs the action marked by the verb.
- **Passive Voice**: It indicates that the patient subject of the sentence is the one who receives the action marked by the verb performed by an agent complement.
- **Causative Voice**: It indicates that a patient complement is forced by an agent subject to perform the action marked by the verb.
- **Causative-Passive Voice**: It indicates that a patient subject is forced to perform the action of the verb passively by an agent complement.

The translative forms are constructed by adding a number of different endings to the irrealis form of the strong and weak verbs and using a different form for the irregular verb *suru*.

❖ The resulting translative forms can be conjugated as a strong verb.

318

VOICE & POTENTIALITY	Strong Verbs	Weak Verbs	*Suru*
Passive	**A**-rareru	**A**-reru	sareru
Causative	**A**-saseru **A**-sasu	**A**-seru **A**-su	saseru sasu
Causative-Passive	**A**-saseraru	**A**-serareru	-

2.1 Passive Form

Strong Verbs	Weak Verbs	*Suru*
A-rareru	**A**-reru	sareru

Formation of the Passive Form:

The passive form is constructed by adding the ending -**rareru** to the irrealis form [**A**] of a strong verb and the ending -**reru** to the irrealis form of a weak verb.

❖ The irregular verb **suru** takes the form sareru.

Functions of the Passive Form:

❖ **Passive Voice:** It indicates that the verb has a patient subject receiving the action performed by an agent complement.

- The patient subject is marked with the nominative particle ga or the thematic particle wa.

- The agent complement is marked with the agentive particle ni, or optionally with the ablative particle kara.

　Ⓢ 虫はクモに食られた: "The worm was eaten by the spider".

　Ⓦ 私は先生に褒められた: "I was praised by the teacher".

　Ⓘ 証拠が確認された: "The proof was confirmed".

Etymology:

Ending probably formed as a transitive transformation of the verb **aru** (*to be*) → -**areru**.

2.2 Causative Form

Strong Verbs	Weak Verbs	*Suru*
A-saseru	**A**-seru	saseru
A-sasu	**A**-su	sasu

Formation of the Causative Form:

The passive form is constructed by adding the ending -**saseru** to the irrealis form [**A**] of a strong verb and the ending -**seru** to the irrealis form of a weak verb.

❖ These two endings admit the variants -**sasu** for strong verbs and -**su** for weak verbs. These forms are less common, dialectal or even sometimes considered vulgar; but they can also sometimes define the transitive form of an originally intransitive verb.

❖ The irregular verb **suru** takes the form sareru or the less common form sasu; forms which are identical to the causative ending added to the form irrealis strong verbs.

Functions of the Causative Form:

❖ **Causative Voice:** It indicates that a patient complement is forced to make an action by an agent subject.

• The patient complement is marked with the accusative particle o (for unintentional actions) or the dative particle ni (for intentional actions) with intransitive verbs. With transitive verbs, the particle **ni** is always used.

Ⓢ 彼に果物を食べさせる: "I make him eat fruit".

Ⓦ 風が木を揺らせた: "The wind made the tree shake".

Ⓘ 公園に犬を散歩させます: "I make the dog walk in the park". / "I walk the dog in the park".

❖ **Permissive Mood:** It indicates that the agent subject allows the patient complement to perform the action marked by the verb.

• The agent subject is marked with the accusative particle o or the dative particle ni. With transitive verbs, the particle ni is always used.

Ⓢ 子供達にアイスクリームを食べさせた: "He let his children eat ice-cream".

Ⓦ 私はむすこに好きなだけ泳がせた: "I let my son swim as much as he wants".

Ⓘ この部屋で勉強させた: "I let him study in this room".

Etymology:

The ending for strong verbs is derived directly from the causative form of the verb **suru** (*to do*): **saseru**. The causative form of *suru*, **saseru**, is ultimately an augmentation of the form **seru** (form added to weak verbs to make them causative), an intransitive variation of the O.J. verb **su**; the archaic form of the contemporary *suru*.

2.3 Causative-Passive Form

Strong Verbs	Weak Verbs	*Suru*
A-saserareru	**A**-serareru	saserareru

Formation of the Causative-Passive Form:

The causative-passive form is constructed by adding the ending -**saserareru** to the irrealis form [**A**] of strong verbs and the ending -**serareru** to the irrealis form of weak verbs.

❖ The irregular verb **suru** takes the form saserareru; which is identical to the causative ending added to the irrealis form of strong verbs.

Functions of the Causative-Passive Form:

❖ **Causative-Passive Voice:** It indicates that a patient subject is forced by an agent complement to perform the action marked by the verb.

• As in standard passive sentences, the patient subject (the one who is made to perform the action) is marked with the nominative particle ga or the thematic particle wa, while the agent complement is marked with the agentive particle ni.

Ⓢ その映画は考えさせられる: "One is made to think by that movie". / "That movie makes you think".

Ⓦ 子供は喋らせられた: "The kid was made to talk".

Ⓘ 彼にはイライラさせられる: "I'm annoyed by that". / "That annoys me".

Etymology:

Conjugation of the passive form of the causative endings in strong verbs: -**saseru** → -**saserareru**; which ultimately is an identical form to the causative-passive form of the verb *suru* (to do): **saserareru**. The ending for weak verbs (*serareru*) is a contraction of the ending for strong verbs: -**saserareru** → -**serareru**

2.4 Translative Forms Paradigm

	Strong Verb	Weak Verb	Irregular Verb
	mìru 見る	wakàru 分かる	surú する
	see	*understand*	*do*

Passive	mirareru	wakarareru	sareru
Causative	misaseru misasu	wakaraseru wakarasu	saseru sasu
Passive- Causative	misaseraru	wakaraserareru [*col.*] wakarasareru	

3. POTENTIAL FORM

Strong Verbs	Weak Verbs	*Suru*
E-rareru [*col.*] **E-reru**	**E-ru**	dekiru

In Japanese, there is a special potential form that is constructed by adding a conjugable ending to the subjunctive form of verbs. This potential form indicates that the marked verb 'can' be done, that is, that there is a possibility of realization.

❖ The resulting potential forms can be conjugated as a strong verb.

Formation of the Causative-Passive Form:

The potential form is constructed by adding the ending -**rareru** to the subjunctive form [E] of strong verbs and the ending -**ru** to the subjunctive form of weak verbs. The ending -**rareru** (which is identical to the ending of the passive translative form for strong verbs) admits the colloquial variant -**reru**.

❖ The irregular verb **suru** takes a completely different potential form dekiru.

❖ Some intransitive verbs that do not show any kind of will do not admit a potential form.

Functions of the Passive Form:

❖ **Potential Mood:** It indicates that the marked verb can be performed.

• The direct object of potential verbs can be marked with the accusative particle o or the nominative particle ga. The form **dekiru** always takes the particle **ga**.

　Ⓢ あの人は寿司が食べられない: "That person can't eat sushi".

　Ⓦ 私は日本語が読めます: "I can read Japanese".

　Ⓘ 運転できるよ: "I can drive".

• Ⓢ [*col.*] **Causative Voice**

古い服を着れた: "I was able to wear my old clothes".

Etymology:

Borrowing of the passive form Ⓢ -**rareru** added to the subjunctive form (which denotes possibility) instead of the irrealis form.

3.1 Potential Forms Paradigm

	Strong Verb	Weak Verb	Irregular Verb
	mìru 見る	wakàru 分かる	surú する
	see	*understand*	*do*
Potential	mirerareru mireru	wakareru	dekiru

VII. VERBAL INFLECTION ADDENDA

In this section, we explain different aspects of verbals that have been left out of the two previous sections corresponding to the verbal inflection:

1. **Attributive Forms:** Verbal forms that can modify a nominal or nominal phrase.

2. **Verbal Valency:** Regarding the transitivity or intransitive of a verb.

3. **Special Verbal Usage:** Verbals whose grammatical behaviors are non-intuitive for the English speakers.

4. **Conjugation Summaries:** A summary of all the inflections and forms seen so far.

1. ATTRIBUTIVE FORMS

Throughout the various subsections within the Verbal Inflection section [☞ III], we have encountered various attributive forms, that is, verbal forms that are capable of modifying a nominal when placed in front of it.

Here we present a summary of those forms:

	Verbs	Adj. Verbs	Adjectival Nouns	Nominals
Imperfective	U ⟨N⟩	i ⟨N⟩	n-no ⟨N⟩ n-na ⟨N⟩ [*lit.*] [*for.*] N/n-de aru ⟨N⟩	N-no ⟨N⟩
Neg. Imperfective	A-nai ⟨N⟩	ku-nai ⟨N⟩	[*lit.*] N/n-de wa nai ⟨N⟩ [*col.*] [*fam.*] N/n-ja nai ⟨N⟩	
Perfective	TA ⟨N⟩		N/n-datta ⟨N⟩ [*lit.*] [*for.*] N/n-de atta ⟨N⟩	
Neg. Perfective	A-nakatta ⟨N⟩	ku-nakatta ⟨N⟩	[*lit.*] N/n-de wa nakatta ⟨N⟩ [*col.*] [*fam.*] N/n-ja nakatta ⟨N⟩	

※ ⟨N⟩ stands for modified nominal.

It should be noted that polite forms do not have an attributive form. In the polite register, plain forms are used as attributive subordinators.

2. VERBAL VALENCY

Verbal valency, i.e. verbs' transitivity (admitting a direct object) or intransitivity (not admitting direct object), is marked in Japanese by a specific transformation of the realis or lemma endings of the verbs. This transformation, however, is very inconsistent, so although there are distinguishable patterns, they are not always useful for either telling apart the transitivity of the verbs or to guess how they can change their valency. The usefulness of the patterns presented here simply lies in being able to have a hunch, as a mnemonic device, of the transitivity or intransitivity of the verbs already learned.

2.1 Valency Mark

Although there is no regular pattern, there are certain endings that are exclusive to one valency or another:

❖ Verbs ending in -**su** are always transitive.

出す *(to take out)* ; 溶かす *(to melt)*

❖ Verbs ending in -**aru** always intransitive.

変わる *(to change [on its own])* ; 極まる *(to reach an extreme)*

Etymology:

> The transitive endings in -**su** most probably derive from the verb **suru** (*to do*), the most widespread active and transitive verb; while the intransitive endings in -**aru** probably derive from the verb **aru** (*to be there*), the most widespread stative and intransitive verb.

2.2 Valency Transformation

The transformation of the valency of a verb follows a pattern according to its endings. Still, these patterns are intermingled between transitivity and intransitivity, so it is not possible to establish which verb is transitive or intransitive according to those patterns.

What can be done is to deduce how to change the valency of the verb depending on its ending:

❖ Transitive verbs ending in -**asu** can be made intransitive by changing this ending for -**eru** and vice versa.

増やす *(to increase s.t.)* → 増える *(to grow)*

❖ Transitive verbs ending in -**su** become transitive by transforming that ending into ❶ -**ru** or ❷ -**reru** and vice versa.

① 返す *(to return s.t.)* → 帰る *(to come back)*

② 壊す (*to damage*) → 壊れる (*to break*)

✤ Weak transitive verbs ending in **-ru** become intransitive by changing that ending to ❶ **-reru** or ❷ **-seru** and vice versa.

① 売る (*to sell s.t.*) → 売れる (*to sell [as in to sell well]*)

② 乗る (*to ride s.t.*) → 乗せる (*to be given a ride*)

✤ Weak transitive verbs ending in **-u** can be made intransitive by changing this ending for **-eru** and vice versa.

② 従う (*to follow s.t.*) → 従えるう (*to be accompanied*)

✤ Weak intransitive verbs ending in **-u** can be transformed into transitive by changing that ending to ❶ **-asu** or ❷ **-eru** and vice versa.

① 動く (*to move [on its own]*) → 動かす (*to move s.t.*)

② 建つ (*to be built*) → 建てる (*to build s.t.*)

✤ Intransitive verbs ending in **-aru** become transitive by changing this ending to **-eru** and vice versa.

始まる (*to begin*) → 始める (*to start s.t.*)

✤ Intransitive verbs ending in **-iru** become transitive by changing that ending to ❶ **-osu** or ❷ **-asu** and vice versa.

① 起きる (*to get up*) → 起こす (*to awaken*)

② 生きる (*to live*) → 生かす (*to keep alive*)

We have just seen the different patterns of valency change in Japanese. It should be noted, however, that these patterns are tentative because it only gives a general idea for the majority of the verbs, but it should not be forgotten that there are also some verbs that do not fit into those patterns in spite of having corresponding endings.

Below is a table showing these tentative patterns as a general guideline:

TRANSITIVE	INTRANSITIVE
Ⓦ -u	Ⓢ -eru
-asu	
	Ⓦ -u
Ⓢ -eru	
	-aru

Ⓦ -ru	-seru
	-reru
-su	
	Ⓦ -ru
-osu	Ⓢ -iru
-asu	

3. SPECIAL VERBAL USAGE

There are a number of basic English verbs whose meaning in Japanese is not expressed by simple verbs but by other word classes such as copulae, adjectival verbs or verbs with other meanings. In this subsection, we will look at these verbs whose translation into Japanese is not intuitive.

3.1 Being

The notion of "being" can be expressed in the following ways:

❖ By means of the copulative forms [☞ V] (**da**, **desu**, etc).

事務所はいいところです: "The office is a good place".

❖ By means of the stative verbs **aru** and **iru**, which are used precisely to indicate that something 'is' in a place ('to be at').

• aru ある: Used for inanimate entities such as objects.

財布はテーブルの上にある: "The wallet is on the table".

❖ The negative form of **aru** is nai (adjectival verb).

• iru いる: Used for animated entities such as people or animals.

猫が家にいる: "The cat is in the house".

3.2 Having

The notion of "having" can be expressed in Japanese in two main ways:

❖ By means of the stative verbs **aru** (with inanimate entities) and **iru** (with animate entities) when what is possessed is held or exists for someone temporarily (❶) or non-voluntarily (❷).

• The subject is marked with the thematic particle **wa** or the compound particle **ni wa** and the object which is "had" with the subject particle **ga**.

① あの人は問題がある [that person TOP problem NOM be-there]: "That person has a problem".

② 私には三人の姉妹がいます: "I have three sisters".

✤ By means of the verb **motsu** 持つ (*to hold*) conjugated in the gerundive form **motte iru** when what is held is possessed for an indefinite time.

私はペンを持っている: "I have a pen".

3.3 Wanting

The notion of "wanting something" can be expressed in two ways:

✤ By means of the adjectival verb **hoshii** 欲しい (*be wanted*) when the wanted thing is an object.

hoshii 欲しい: to **be wanted**

- The wanted thing is marked by the nominative particle **ga** since it is grammatically a subject.

車が欲しい: "I want a car".

✤ When someone "wants to do something", a particular grammatical form is used: **I-tai** [☞ XII.1.3].

✤ When someone "wants someone to do something", another grammatical form is used: **TE hoshii** [☞ XII.2.2].

13.4 Knowing

The fact of "knowing something" can be expressed in two ways:

✤ By means of the verb **shiru** 知る (**to know**) always in the gerundive form **shitte iru** when used in positive indicative sentences in the imperfective aspect.

君の名前は知っている: "I know your name".

✤ By the verb **wakaru** 知る (*to understand*) when something is "known" so that the meaning can be replaced by "understanding" (❶) or when talking about "knowing something" in a general and imprecise way (❷).

① フランス語が分かりません: "I don't know French".

② 全く分からなかった: "I didn't know at all". / "I had no idea".

13.5 Liking & Disliking

The notions of "liking" or "disliking" something are expressed in Japanese as follows:

❖ The notion of "liking" is expressed by the adjectival noun **suki** 好き (*to be liked*) (❶). The notion of "loving" is expressed by the adjectival noun **daisuki** 大好き (*to like a lot; to love*).

• The liked or loved thing is marked by the nominative particle **ga** since it is grammatically a subject.

① いちごが好き: "I like strawberries".

② いちごが大好き: "I love strawberries".

❖ The notion of "not liking" can be expressed by the negative form of the adjectival noun *suki*, by the adjectival noun **kirai** (❶) or, in a more colloquial or familiar way, with the adjectival noun **yada** (❷).

① 悪い人が嫌いです: "I don't like bad people".

② そのゲームはやだ: "I don't like that game".

13.6 Giving & Receiving

In Japanese, the concepts of 'giving' and 'receiving' are expressed by a series of verbs whose usage is strictly linked to the register and the social position of the speakers.

Giving:

❖ The concept of 'giving' can be expressed by the verbs **ageru**, **sashiageru** and **yaru**, depending on the register and the social position of the speakers (see below).

❖ In sentences with these verbs, the subject—the *giver*—is marked with the thematic particle **wa** or the nominative particle **ga**; the indirect complement—the *receiver*—is marked with the dative particle **ni**; and the direct complement—the given thing—is marked with the accusative particle **o**.

(A wa/ga) **B** ni **C** o ageru/ashiageru/yaru

A *gives* **C** *to* **B**

❖ With these verbs, we can express that the first person (*I/we*) gives something to the second person (*you*) or third person (*him/her/it/them*); that the second person (*you*) gives something to the third person (*him/her/it/them*) or that the third person (*he/she/it/they*) gives something to another third person (*him/her/it/them*).

1st person *gives to* 2nd person / 3rd person
2nd person *gives to* 3rd person
3rd person *gives to* 3rd person

ageru あげる Ⓢ: to **give**

❖ It is used when the subject gives something to someone of equal or lower social status.

マリアさんに何<ruby>何<rt>なに</rt></ruby>をあげた？: "What did you give to Maria?".

sashiageru 差し上げる Ⓢ: [*hum.*] to **give**

❖ It is used when the subject gives something to someone of higher age or social position.

山田先生<ruby>山田先生<rt>やまだせんせい</rt></ruby>に本<ruby>本<rt>ほん</rt></ruby>を差<ruby>差<rt>さ</rt></ruby>し上<ruby>上<rt>あ</rt></ruby>げました: "I gave a book to Dr. Yamada".

yaru やる: [*fam.*] to **give**

❖ It is used, in a familiar context, when the subject gives something to someone of lower age or social position, or to an animal, plant or object.

弟<ruby>弟<rt>おとうと</rt></ruby>に辞書<ruby>辞書<rt>じしょ</rt></ruby>をやった: "I gave my brother a dictionary".

❖ There is another group of verbs in Japanese that express the concept of 'giving' (**kureru** and **kudasaru**), which are used when it is the second or third person who gives something to the first person or someone who is part of the first person's in-group. For ease of understanding, these verbs can also be translated by the passive form "to be given".

2nd person / 3rd person *gives to* 1st person / 1st person's in-group

kureru くれる Ⓢ: to **give**; to **be given**

❖ It is used when someone of equal or lower status than the receiving person (indirect complement) gives something to the first person (*me/us*) or someone from his or her in-group.

田中<ruby>田中<rt>たなか</rt></ruby>さんは私<ruby>私<rt>わたし</rt></ruby>にお土産<ruby>土産<rt>みやげ</rt></ruby>をくれました: "Tanaka gave me a gift".

kudasaru 下さる: [*hon.*] to **give**; to **be given**

❖ It is used when someone of higher status than the receiving person (indirect complement) gives something to the first person (*me/us*) or someone in his or her in-group.

山田先生<ruby>山田先生<rt>やまだせんせい</rt></ruby>は弟<ruby>弟<rt>おとうと</rt></ruby>にボールペンをくださいました: "Dr. Yamada gave my brother a ballpoint pen".

➤ **N o kudasai をください**: [*pol.*] (please) **give me**

❖ Used to ask for something [N] in a polite way.

ハンバーガーとコーラをください: "I'll have a hamburger and a coke, please".

Receiving:

❖ The concept of 'receiving' can be expressed by the verbs **morau** and **itadaku** depending on the social relationship between the interlocutors (see below).

❖ In sentences with these verbs, the subject—the *receiver*—is marked with the thematic particle **wa** or the nominative particle **ga**; the agent complement—the *giver*—is marked with the dative particle **ni** (*to*) or the ablative particle **kara** (*from*); and the direct complement—the *received thing*—is marked with the accusative particle **o**.

(A wa/ga) **B** ni/kara **C** o morau/itadaku

A *receives* **C** *from* **B**

❖ With these verbs, we can express that the first person (*I/we*) receives something from the second person (*you*) or third person (*him/her/it/them*); that the second person (*you*) receives something from the third person (*him/her/it/them*) or that the third person (*he/she/it/they*) receives something from another third person (*him/her/it/them*).

1st person *receives from* 2nd person / 3rd person
2nd person *receives from* 3rd person
3rd person *receives from* 3rd person

morau もらう Ⓢ: to **receive**

❖ It is used when the subject receives something from someone of equal or lower social status or someone of his or her in-group.

父から自転車をもらった: "I received a bicycle from my father". / "My father gave me a bicycle".

itadaku いただく: [*hum.*] to **receive**

❖ It is used when the subject receives something from someone of higher age or social status.

山田先生に三島の小説をいただきました: "I received a Mishima's novel from Dr. Yamada". / "Dr. Yamada gave me a copy of Mishima's novel".

Giving & Receiving

Verb	Register	S.	Meaning	C.	Social Status
ageru	-	1st p. 2nd p. 3rd p.	**give** *to*	2nd p. 3rd p.	receiver is equal / inferior
sashiageru	[*hum.*]				receiver is superior
yaru	[*fam.*]				receiver is inferior
kureru	-	2nd p. 3rd p.	**give** *to*	1st p.	giver is equal / inferior
kudasaru	[*hon.*]			1st p.'s in-group	giver is superior
morau	-	1st p. 2nd p. 3rd p.	**receive** *from*	2nd p. 3rd p.	giver is equal / inferior
itadaku	[*hum.*]				giver is superior

※ S. stands for *subject*; C. stands for *complement* and p. stands for *person*.

4. CONJUGATION SUMMARIES

4.1 Summary of the Verb Inflection

	Plain	Polite	Plain Neg.	Polite Neg.
Imperfective	U	I-masu	A-nai	I-masen A-nai desu
Perfective	TA	I-mashita	A-nakatta	I-masen deshita A-nakatta desu
Gerundive	TE		A-nakute	
Provisional	Ⓢ E-reba Ⓦ E-ba		A-nakereba	
Presumptive	Ō	I-mashō	A-nakarō	
Imperative	Ⓢ E-ro / Ⓢ E-yo Ⓦ E			

	Strong Verbs	Weak Verbs	*Suru*
Passive	A-rareru	A-reru	sareru
Causative	A-saseru A-sasu	A-seru A-su	saseru sasu
Causative- Passive	A-saseraru	A-serareru	-
Potential	E-rareru [*col.*] E-reru	E-ru	dekiru

4.2 Summary of the Adjectival Verb Inflection

	Plain	Polite	Plain Neg.	Polite Neg.
Imperfective	s-i	s-i desu	s-ku nai	s-ku nai desu
				s-ku (wa) arimasen
Perfective	s-katta	s-katta desu	s-ku nakatta	s-ku nakatta desu
				s-ku (wa) arimasen deshita

Gerundive	s-kute	s-ku nakute
Provisional	s-kereba	s-ku nakereba
Presumptive	s-karō	.

4.3 Summary of the Copula Inflection

	Literary	Plain	Pol. Copula
Imperfective		N/n-da	N/n-desu
Imperfective Attributive	N/n-de aru		N/n-no n-na
Infinitive	N/n-de ari		
Presumptive	N/n-de arō	N/n-darō	N/n-deshō
Gerundive	N/n-de atte	N/n-de	N/n-deshite
Perfective	N/n-de atta	N/n-datta	N/n-deshita
Provisional	N/n-de areba	N/n-nara(ba)	
Imperative	N/n-de are		
Negative Imperfective	N/n-de wa nai		N/n-de wa arimasen [*col.*] N/n-ja arimasen
			N/n-de wa nai desu [*col.*] N/n-ja nai desu
Negative Infinitive	N/n-de (wa) naku		
Negative Gerundive	N/n-de wa nakute [*col.*] N/n-ja nakute		
Neg. Perfective	N/n-de wa nakatta [*col.*] N/n-ja nakatta		N/n-de wa arimasen deshita N/n-ja arimasen deshita
			N/n-de wa nakatta desu N/n-ja nakatta desu

VIII. PARTICLES

In this section, we will list the particles used in Japanese and explain their various functions. The types of particles presented here are as follows:

1. **Case Particles**: Particles marking the case of a noun.

2. **Aspectual Particles**: Particles marking the aspect of a verbal in subordinate sentences.

3. **Modal Particles**: Particles marking the mood of a verb or noun in a copulative manner.

4. **Phrasal Particles**: Particles linking two clauses.

1. CASE PARTICLES

Case particles mark the grammatical case of a noun.

1.1 Syntactic Particles

Syntactic particles mark a noun in relation to the verb insofar as it takes on a syntactic function of subject, agent, direct object, or indirect object.

➤ **N ga が**: Nominative Case

❖ Sometimes pronounced as *nga* (with a nasal *n*).

❖ It marks the subject of a sentence when the subject is introduced for the first time.

あそこに本があります [there in book NOM be-there]: "There's a book over there".

❖ It marks the interrogative pronouns when they are the subject of the sentence (as they are understood as new information).

誰が来た?: "Who came?".

❖ It marks the syntactic subject in adjectival verbs and nouns whose meaning is translated in English by verbs and, therefore, the subject would be an object in that language [☞ VII.3-5].

• The most common adjectival verbs of this nature are the following: **ooi** (*to be many*); **sukunai** (*to be few*); **kowai** (*to be afraid*); **urayamashii** (*to envy*) and **hoshii** (*to want*).

車が欲しい [car NOM be-wanted]: "I want a car".

• The most common adjectival nouns of this nature are the following: **suki** (*to like*); **kirai** (*to dislike*); **joozu** (*to be good at*); **heta** (*to be bad at*) and **hitsuyō** (*to need*).

時間が必要です: "I need time".

❖ It also marks the patient subject in some passive intransitive verbs whose meaning is translated in English by active verbs.

• The most common verbs of this nature are the following: **wakaru** (*to understand*) and **iru** (*to need*).

マリアは日本語が分かります: "Maria understands Japanese". (Lit. "Japanese is understood by Maria".)

❖ It marks the subject of a subordinate clause when it is not the main topic of the whole sentence.

私は友達が来たときラーメンを作ります: "I make ramen when my friends come".

➤ **N o を: ❶** Accusative Case ‖ **❷** Prolative Case | *through ~; by ~* ‖ **❸** Elative Case | *out of ~; from ~*

❖ Written as *wo* を but pronounced **o**.

❖ **❶** It marks the direct object of a clause.

ニュースを読まなかった [news ACC read–did-not]: "I didn't read the news".

❖ **❷** It marks a place through which one passes. The particle **o**, in this case, is actually marking a syntactic direct object, but semantically it is interpreted as prolative case (*through*) [☞ EY:VII.5.6].

• The most common verbs with which this usage appears are the following movement verbs: **aruku** (*to walk*); **hasiru** (*to run*); **tooru** (*to pass*); **iku** (*to to go*); **kuru** (*to come*) and **kaeru** (*to go back home*) and **sanpo suru** (*to take a walk*).

公園を通って帰りましょう: "Let's go back through the park".

❖ **❸** It indicates that the subject leaves the marked place. The particle **o** in this case is actually marking a syntactic direct object, but semantically it is interpreted as elative case (*out of*) [☞ EY:VII.5.4].

• The most common verbs with which this usage appears are the following movement verbs: **deru** (*to go out*) and **shuppatsu suru** (*to leave*).

マリアさんは家を出ました: "Maria left the house". / "Maria got out of the house".

➤ **N ni₁ に: ❶** Dative Case | *to ~* ‖ **❷** Lative Case | *to ~* ‖ **❸** Agentive Case | *by ~*

❖ **❶** It marks the indirect object of the sentence.

友達にメッセージを書いた: "I wrote a message to my friend".

❖ **❷** With a syntactic sense similar to the indirect complement (*to ~*), it marks a place toward which the movement indicated by the verb is directed or oriented, thus marking what is semantically considered as the lative case (*to ~; toward ~*).

今日は早く事務所に行きます: "I'm going to the office early today".

✤ ❷ It marks the resultant object toward or into which transits the action indicated by a transformative stative verb [☞ VO:IV.1.3] such as **naru** (*to become*) or **kawaru** (*to change*).

信号が青に変わりました: "The traffic lights turned green".

✤ ❸ It marks the agent complement of a passive or causative-passive sentence.

その子はお母さんに叱られました: "That child was scolded by his mother".

✤ ❸ Semantically, the agentive particle **ni** can indicate a "cause" when the verbal is an intransitive verb.

大きな音に驚いた: "The loud noise startled me". (Lit. "I was surprised by a big noise".)

1.2 Complementary Particles

Complementary particles mark a noun as a modifying nominal complement of another noun.

➤ **N no₁** の: ❶ Genitive Case | *of ~; ~'s* ‖ ❷ Relative Nominative Case

✤ ❶ It marks a nominal complement, establishing a syntactic and semantic relationship between the marked nominal and a preceding nominal which it modifies or qualifies. The order is always **A *no* B** insofar as the modified element is **A** and the modifying element is **B**, which in English would be repositioned as B *of* A or A's B.

桜の花です [cherry-tree GEN flower is]: "It is a cherry blossom".

✤ ❶ The particle **no** can be omitted between two Sino-Japanese nouns when the relationship is obvious.

時計の時刻を直した → 時計時刻を直した [Watch GEN/ø time ACC fixed]: "I fixed the time on the watch".

✤ ❶ The element B in the structure **A *no* B** can be omitted when it can be inferred by the context.

これは私のカバンです [this TOP I of bag is]: "This is my bag" → これは私のøです [this TOP I of ø is]: "This one is mine".

✤ ❷ In compound sentences, the subject of the subordinate clause can be marked with the particle **no** instead of the nominative particle *ga*.

これは私の作ったケーキです [this TOP I NOM made cake is]: "This is the cake that I made".

➤ **N to₁** と: Comitative Case | *with ~*

❖ It establishes a bidirectional, reciprocal relationship of the marked noun with the subject of the sentence.

• It may indicate a sense of 'companionship' with respect to the subject.

田中さんは原さんと踊っている: "Tanaka is dancing with Hara".

• Or it may indicate a sense of 'comparison' with respect to the subject.

このカバンは僕の車と同じです: "This bag is the same as mine".

➤ **N nashi** なし: Privative Case | *without ~; no ~*

❖ It indicates the absence of the marked element.

それなしには生きていられない: "I can't live without it".

1.3 Focal Particles

Focal particles put the focus of the sentence on the marked noun.

➤ **N(p*) wa** は: ❶ Thematic Case ‖ ❷ Contrastive Thematic Case

❖ Written as *ha* は but pronounced **wa**.

❖ ❶ It introduces a new topic to the discourse.

夏は日が長いです: "In summer the days are long".

❖ ❶ *The topic of the sentence can be already marked by another particle. In that case, **wa** sometimes replaces some particles or be added to other particles. This is done when the topic is already known by the interlocutors.

• It replaces the nominative particle **ga** or the accusative particle **o**.

映画はあまり見ません: "I don't usually watch movies".

• It gets added to case particles other than *ga* or *o*.

そこには花がたくさんあります: "There are lots of flowers over there".

❖ ❶ The topic can be, then, the subject or object of the sentence (replacing the nominative particle **ga** or accusative particle **o**) if that topic is already known by the interlocutors.

A. あそこに本がある: "There's a book over there".

B. 本は日本語の教科書です: "The book is a textbook of Japanese" / "It is a book of Japanese".

❖ ❷ It marks two contrasting elements within a sentence.

魚は好きですが、肉は好きではありません: "I like fish but not meat".

➤ **N(p*) mo** も: ❶ Cumulative Case | *~ too; also ~* ‖ ❷ Concessive Case | *(not) even ~*

♣ ❶ It indicates that the marked noun is a new element that shares a syntactic function with a topic-element already expressed before.

リンゴも好き: "I like apples too".

♣ ❶ *Depending on the case in which the element referenced before is found and which mo incorporates, this particle may replace or be added to the particle marking that case.

- It replaces the nominative particle **ga**, the accusative particle **o** or the thematic case particle **wa**.

  それも本です: "That is a book too".

- It gets added to the particles **ni**, **e**, **de**, **to**, **kara** and **made**.

  大阪へも行きました: "I also went to Osaka".

♣ ❷ It emphasizes the marked nominal, inferring that such emphasis is not expected under normal circumstances.

マリアさんは日本語の新聞も読める: "Maria can even read Japanese newspapers".

➤ **N made₁** まで: Concessive Case | *even ~; not even ~*

♣ It indicates that the marked element is something not expected under normal circumstances.

子供までその仕事ができるよ: "Even kids can do that job".

➤ **N(p*) sae** さえ: Concessive Case | *even ~; not even ~*

♣ It points to an element that is understood as an extreme example of what is expressed in the predicate.

♣ *The particle **sae** replaces the particles **ga** and **o** and is added to the particles **e**, **ni**, **de**, **to**, **kara** or **made**.

それは専門家でさえ知らないでしょう: "Not even the experts would know that".

➤ **N(p*) koso** こそ: Emphatic Case | *(the) very ~; precisely ~*

♣ It emphasizes the marked element.

♣ *The particle **koso** replaces the particles **ga** and **o** and is added to the particles **e**, **ni**, **de**, **to**, **kara** or **made**.

今年こそニューヨークに行こうと思います: "I'm going to New York this (very) year!".

➤ **N nado** など: Enunciative Case | *such as ~; ~ and so on; ~ and the like*

❖ It presents a noun as a representative example within a category of things that usually acts as the topic of the sentence.

たばこなど不要だ: "You don't need tobacco (or such things)".

➢ **N nante** なんて: Emphatic Enunciative Case | *things like ~; even ~*

❖ It presents a noun as a representative example within a category of things while providing an emotional nuance to it.

金の生る木なんてない: "Money doesn't grow on (things like) trees". (Lit. "There are no such trees that bear money".)

1.4 Conjunctive Particles

Conjunctive particles join two or more nouns consecutively in a non-dependent manner.

➢ **N to₁** と: Conjunctive Case | *~ and*

❖ It joins two nouns that constitute the same subject, object or complement.

私は英語と日本語を話す: "I speak English and Japanese".

➢ **N oyobi** および: [*lit.*][*for.*] Conjunctive Case | *~ and; as well as ~*

ここは工業および商業の中心です: "This is the core of industry and commerce".

- -

➢ **N mata wa** または: Alternative Case | *~ or*

❖ It presents an alternative between two elements.

お箸またはフォークで食べてください: "Eat with chopsticks or a fork".

➢ **N ka₁** か: Alternative Enumerative Case | *or (something like) ~*

❖ It presents an element as a possible alternative within an implicit or explicit list of things.

僕は家か喫茶店で朝ご飯を食べる: "I have breakfast at home or in a coffee shop".

- -

➢ **N ya** や: Enumerative Case | *(such as) ~ and*

❖ It joins two nouns that constitute the same subject, object or complement within an inexhaustive (incomplete) list.

田中さんや原さんが来た: "Tanaka, Hara, and others came".

➢ **N to ka** とか: Enumerative Case | *(such as) ~ and*

❖ Combination of the conjunctive particle **to** (*and*) and the alternative enumerative particle **ka** (*or something like*), a construction that can be literally translated as "X and/or something like Y".

❖ It usually appears in pairs.

今朝スーパーでコーヒーとか水とかを買った: "This morning I bought coffee, water, and other things in the supermarket".

➤ **N yara {p}** やら: [*fam.*] Enumerative Case | (*such as*) ~ *and*

❖ Usually appearing in pairs.

風やら雨やらで旅行は台無しだった: "The wind and rain and everything else ruined the trip".

1.5 Adjunctive Particles

Adjunctive particles mark a noun as a verbal complement in which extra information is added.

➤ **N/C de** で: ❶ Essive Case | *in/on/at* ~ ‖ ❷ Instrumental Case | *with* ~ ‖ ❸ Causal Case | *because of* ~; *by* ~

❖ ❶ It indicates the place where the action expressed by the verb occurs.

彼女は喫茶店でジュースを飲んでいます: "She's having a juice in the coffee shop".

❖ ❶ It indicates the amount of time it takes to do the action of the verb.

この仕事はご一時間でできます: "This job can be done in an hour".

❖ ❶ It marks the domain in which a superlative structure [☞ XIV.3.1] takes place.

マリアさんはクラスで一番背が高い人です: "Maria is the tallest person in the class".

❖ ❷ It indicates an instrument or means through which the action expressed by the verb is performed.

天ぷらは魚と野菜で作ります: "Tempura is made with fish and vegetables".

❖ ❸ It indicates a reason or cause that can also be understood as a means (instrumental case) through which—because of which—something happens.

風邪で窓が閉まった: "The window has been closed by the wind".

➤ **N/C ni₂** に: ❶ Essive Case | *in/on/at* ~

❖ It marks a point in space or time in which the action indicated by the verb occurs.

9月に東京へ行きます: "I'll go to Tokyo in September".

❖ It marks a time interval in which the action indicated by the verb occurs.

一週間に一度映画に行く: "I go to the movies once a week".

❖ It marks a place in which a continuous stative verb [☞ VO:IV.1.2] such as **aru** (*to be at*), **iru** (*to be at*) or **sumu** (*to live*) takes place.

教室に先生がいます: "The teacher is in the classroom".

> **N e へ**: Lative Case | *to ~; towards ~*

❖ Written as *he* へ but pronounced **e**.

❖ It indicates the direction toward which the subject of the sentence is moving.

何時に学校へ来る？: "What time are you coming to school?".

❖ It marks the indirect complement when followed by the attributive form **no**.

田中さんへの荷物は重いです: "Tanaka's package is heavy". (Lit. "The package that is for Tanaka is heavy".)

> **N kara から**: ❶ Ablative Case | *from ~; since ~* ‖ ❷ Elative Case | *out of ~*

❖ ❶ It indicates a point in space or time from which the action marked by the verb begins.

子供は学校から家まで走りました: "The kids ran from school to his house".

❖ ❶ It can mark the agent complement of a passive sentence.

私は田中さんから本をもらいました: "I got the book from Mr. Tanaka".

❖ ❷ It indicates the origin, source or cause of something from which an action is performed.

豆腐は大豆から作ります: "Tofu is made from/out of soybeans".

> **N yori より**: [*for.*] Ablative Case | *from ~*

首相会談は３月十三一より東京において行われます: "The Prime Minister's meeting will take place in Tokyo from/starting March 13".

1.6 Delimitative Particles

Adjunctive particles mark a noun as a verbal complement that establishes a quantitative limit.

> **N/C made₂ まで**: Limitative Case | *until ~*

❖ It indicates a temporal or spatial limit that establishes an endpoint to the action or state marked by the verb.

原さんは午後四時まで仕事をします: "Hara works until 4 p.m".

> **N hodo ほど**: Upper Limitative Case | *as much as ~*

❖ Used with verbs in negative forms, it expresses an unattained comparative degree. C.f. Comparison [☞ XIV.2].

武君は健君ほど早く走れない: "Takeshi can't run as fast as Ken".

➤ **N(p*)/C dake (p*)** だけ: Lower Limitative Case | *only ~; just ~*

❖ It expresses a limitation between quantities or implied alternatives.

❖ *The particle **dake** replaces the particles **ga** and o **and** can be placed before or after the particles **e**, **ni**, **de**, **to**, **kara** and **made**.

今朝郵便教区だけへ行った: "I only went to the post office this morning".

➤ **N(p*) bakari** ばかり: Lower Limitative Case | *only ~; just ~*

❖ *The particle **bakari** replaces the particles **ga** and **o** and can be placed after the particles **e**, **ni**, **de**, **to**, **kara** and **made**.

❖ This particle usually has negative or criticizing connotations.

武君、漫画ばかり読んでいる: "Takeshi, you just read manga".

➤ **N(p*)/C shika** しか: Exclusive Lower Limitative Case | *nothing but ~; only ~*

❖ It indicates that the marked element or quantity exists exclusively.

❖ This particle is only used with verbs in negative forms.

❖ *The particle **shika** replaces the particles **ga** and **o** and can be placed after the particles **e**, **ni**, **de**, **to**, **kara** and **made**.

今日は五時間しか働きませんでした: "I only worked five hours today". (Lit. "I didn't work but five hours today".)

➤ **N*/C kurai** くらい: Approximative Case | *approximately/about/around ~*

❖ It indicates an approximate quantity or number.

❖ *Only demonstrative pronouns.

あそこに人が三十人くらいいます: "There are about thirty people over there".

➤ **N*/C gurai** ぐらい: = **kurai**

➤ **N/C goro** ごろ: Approximative Case | *approximately/about/around ~*

❖ It indicates an approximate amount of time.

八時ごろ家へ帰った: "I got home around eight o'clock".

➤ **N/C koro** ころ: = **goro**

➤ **C bakari** ばかり: Approximative Case | *approximately/about/around ~*

田中さんは原さんに二千円ばかり貸した: "Tanaka lent Hara about 2,000 yen".

➤ **C hodo** ほど: [*for.*] Approximative Case | *approximately/about/around* ~

去年日本に三週間ほどいました: "I spent about three weeks in Japan last year".

+ *Exhaustive list of case particles in Expressing Yourself in Japanese* [☞ EY:VII]

2. ASPECTUAL PARTICLES

Aspectual particles indicate aspects of verbs in such a way that they introduce a following clause.

Aspect-marking particles, unlike specific verbal forms or extensions of verbal forms, have the particularity of being able to be added to different verbal forms and sometimes also nominals.

2.1 Punctual & Durative Particles

Particles indicating a punctual aspect refer to a specific time in which two actions or states occur, whereas particles indicating a durative aspect refer to actions or states that are performed specifically at the same time.

➤ **V/na/no/i toki** (ni) ときに: Punctual Aspect | *when* ~

❖ It indicates an action or state whose course is taken as a time reference for the action or state expressed in the following clause.

❖ The aspectual form of the verb of the first clause determines whether the action of the following clause is simultaneous, precedes or follows the action of that first clause.

京都へ行くとき富士山を見た: "I saw Mt. Fuji when I went to Kyoto".

➤ **U/na/no/i aida** (ni)* 間に: Durative Aspect | *while* ~; *during* (*the time when*) ~

❖ It indicates that the action of the first clause takes place during the course of time in which the action of the following clause occurs.

マリアさんは朝の間洗濯をしていました: "Maria had been doing laundry during the morning".

❖ *If the particle ni does not appear, it usually indicates that both the preceding and the following action last for a similar period of time.

日本にいる間日本語を勉強していました: "I studied Japanese while I was in Japan".

➤ **U*/na/no/i uchi ni** うちに: Durative Aspect | *while* ~

❖ It denotes that the action of the predicate occurs during the time that the marked action is performed.

❖ *Usually the progressive form **TE iru**.

❖ Normally, it refers to a period of time that is understood as not lasting for long and hence one should make use of it.

若いうちに遊びなさい: "Have fun while you're young".

❖ It can also indicate that something happens spontaneously while the marked action or state is occurring.

音楽を聞いているうちに寝てしまった: "I fell asleep (while) listening to the music".

➤ **U tabi ni たびに**: Distributive Durative Aspect | *each time ~; whenever ~*

❖ It expresses that the action of the predicate is performed each time the marked action is done.

大坂に行くたびにお寺を訪れる: "Each time I go to Osaka I visit a temple".

2.2 Antessive & Postessive Particles

Particles that indicate an antessive aspect refer to an action or state that occurs before another, while particles that indicate a postessive aspect refer to an action or state that occurs after another.

➤ **U/C/no mae ni 前に**: Antessive Aspect & Case | *before ~*

❖ It expresses that the action of the predicate occurs before the marked clause begins.

私は朝ごはんを食べる前に部屋を片付けます: "I clean up my room before I eat breakfast".

❖ Used after time quantities (marked with a classifier [☞ VO:III.2]), it can be translated by the expression "ago".

ジョンさんは三年前に日本へ行きました: "John went to Japan three years ago".

➤ **A-nai uchi ni ないうちに**: Antessive Aspect | *before ~*

❖ It expresses that the marked action is not controllable and that the action in the following clause must be performed before the action of the first clause begins.

忘れないうちにメモを取っておこう: "I'll make a note of that before I forget".

➤ **TA/C/no ato de/ni* 後で/に**: Postessive Aspect & Case | *after ~*

❖It expresses that the action of the predicate occurs after the marked clause ends.

授業の後でコーヒーを飲もうか: "Let's have coffee after class".

❖ Used after time quantities (marked with a classifier [☞ VO:III.2]), it can be translated with the expression "in".

一時間後に僕を起こしな: "Wake me up in an hour".

❖ *Usually **de** after a verb or noun (**N+no**); and **ni** after a classifier.

2.4 Resultative Particles

Particles indicating a resultative aspect indicate that an action or state has come to take place after a temporal progression.

➤ **U yō ni naru** ようになる: Resultative Aspect | *come to ~; get ~ed*

❖ It indicates that there has been a gradual change resulting in an outcome.

毎日遅くまで仕事をするようになりました: "I got used to work late every day". / "I've reached the point where I work late every day".

➤ **ku naru** になる: Resultative Aspect | *to become ~*

部屋が明るくなった: "The room became brighter".

➤ **N/n/C ni naru** になる: Resultative Copula | *to become ~*

田中さんはお金持ちになりました: "Mr. Tanaka became rich".

+ *Exhaustive list of aspectual particles in Expressing Yourself in Japanese* [☞ EY:I]

3. MODAL PARTICLES

Modal particles are particles used to express various verbal moods.

Mood-marking particles, unlike specific verbal forms or extensions of verbal forms, have the particularity of being able to be added to different verbal forms and sometimes also to nominals.

3.1 Interrogative & Inquisitive Particles

Interrogative particles turn a declarative sentence into an interrogative one, that is, they turn a sentence into a question.

In the formal and polite register, it is obligatory to use the interrogative particle **ka**. In the familiar register, the use of interrogative particles is optional. Sentences with interrogative particles other than the particle **no** do not require the question mark (?) in the written language.

Inquisitive particles express a question asked not to seek an answer but to await affirmation or confirmation from the listener.

➤ **N/n/V/i ka₂ か**: Interrogative Mood | *~?*

❖ Used for both open and closed (yes-no) questions.

• [*for.*] Always used in questions in the formal and polite registers.

夕べパーティーへ行きましたか: "Did you go to the party last night?".

• [*fam.*][*mas.*] Optionally used in a masculine and familiar register, but it cannot follow the informal copula **da**.

行くか: "Are you going?".

➤ **V/na*/i no の**: [*fam.*] Interrogative Mood | *~?*

どうしたの？: "What happened?".

• *After a noun [**N**] and an adjectival noun [**n**], the attributive copula **na** has to be added before the particle **no**.

これはあなたの傘なの?: "Is this your umbrella?".

➤ **N/n/V/i kai かい**: [*fam.*][*mas.*] Interrogative Mood | *~?*

❖ Only used with closed (yes-no) questions.

これは君の車かい: "Is this your car?".

➤ **N/n dai だい**: [*fam.*][*mas.*] Interrogative Mood | *~?*

❖ Only used with questions that have interrogative pronouns and only after nominals.

これ何かい: "What is this?".

....

➤ **N/n/V/i ne ね**: Inquisitive Mood | *~right?; isn't it?*

❖ It expresses that the speaker utters an interrogation in search of an implicit confirmation from the listener.

分かったね: "You got it (right?)".

❖ It indicates that the speaker expects his or her interlocutor to feel the same way.

いいですね: "That's nice (isn't it?)".

3.2 Admirative & Assertive Particles

Admirative and assertive particles turn sentences into moods that convey, respectively, a specific tone of surprise or assertion on the part of the speaker. These particles always appear at the end of a sentence.

➤ **N/n/V/i na な**: [*fam.*] Admirative Mood | *how ~!; what ~!; ~!*

❖ It expresses emotion in an exclamatory manner.

分かった<ruby>分<rt>わ</rt></ruby>かったな: "You got it!".

....

➤ **N/n/V/i yo** よ: Assertive Mood | *~you know*

❖ Particle used to inform the listener of something in an emphatic way.

<ruby>私<rt>わたし</rt></ruby>も<ruby>行<rt>い</rt></ruby>きますよ: "I'll go too". / "I'm coming with you".

➤ **N/n/V/i sa** さ: [*col.*][*fam.*][*mas.*] Assertive Mood | *~you know; sure*

<ruby>人生<rt>じんせい</rt></ruby>とはこんなものさ: "That's life, you know".

➤ **N/n/V/i zo** ぞ: [*col.*][*fam.*][*mas.*] Assertive Mood | *~you know*

❖ Particle used to call someone's attention or give information.

<ruby>急<rt>いそ</rt></ruby>げ！<ruby>電車<rt>でんしゃ</rt></ruby>が<ruby>来<rt>く</rt></ruby>るぞ!: "Hurry up! There's a train coming!".

➤ **N/n/V/i ze** ぜ: [*col.*][*fam.*][*mas.*] Assertive Mood | *~you know*

おい、もう<ruby>帰<rt>かえ</rt></ruby>るぜ: "Hey, I'm leaving!".

➤ **N/n/V/i wa** わ: [*col.*][*fam.*][*fem.*] Assertive Mood | *~you know*

<ruby>私<rt>あたし</rt></ruby><ruby>行<rt>い</rt></ruby>きたくないわ: "I don't want to go!".

3.3 Causal & Final Particles

The causal mood indicated by causal particles expresses that the action or state that the marked verb expresses is the cause for the predicate.

Final moods express an objective or purpose for which the action of the predicate is carried out.

Clauses following causative particles can be predicted by consecutive [☞ VO:VII.2.1] or explanative [☞ VO:VII.2.4] conjunctions.

➤ **V/i kara** から: Causal Mood | *because/since ~; ~ so*

❖ It indicates a cause or reason that leads the speaker to have an opinion or carry out a decision.

<ruby>病気<rt>びょうき</rt></ruby>でしたから<ruby>学校<rt>がっこう</rt></ruby>をお<ruby>休<rt>やす</rt></ruby>みました: "I was sick, so I took a break from school".

➤ **N/n {D} kara** だ/ですから: Causal Mood | *because/since it is ~*

➤ **V/i kara ({D})** からだ/です: Causal Copula | *it is because ~*

あまり<ruby>好<rt>す</rt></ruby>きじゃないからです: "(That's) because I don't like it much".

➤ **V/na/i no de** ので: Causal Mood | *because/since ~; ~ so*

❖ It expresses the cause of a state or action that occurred spontaneously.

天気が悪いので出掛けない: "I'm not going out because the weather is bad".

➤ **V/na/no/i tame (ni) ために**: [*lit.*][*for.*] Causal Mood | *because/since ~; due to ~*

❖ It denotes, in a formal or written context, the natural cause of a state or action that occurred spontaneously.

停電のために授業が中止になりました: "Classes were canceled due to power outage".

➤ **VN/I ni に**: Final Mood | *for ~; to ~*

❖ It indicates a purpose for which one is going or returning from somewhere.

❖ Only before verbs of motion such as **iku** (*to go*), **kuru** (*to come*) or **kaeru** (*to go back home*).

新宿へ映画を見に行った: "I went to Shinjuku to see a movie".

➤ **U/no tame ni ために**: ❶ Final Mood & Case | *for ~; (in order) to ~* ‖ ❷ Benefactive Case | *for (the benefit of) ~*

❖ ❶ It indicates that the marked action or element is controlled by the subject and is also a purpose for which the action expressed in the following clause is carried out.

車を買うためにアルバイトをしている: "I'm working part-time to buy a car".

❖ ❷ It indicates an element or person that benefits from the action expressed by the following clause.

❖ ❷ Only used after nouns (**N+no**).

友達のマリアさんのために辞典を買った: "I bought a dictionary for my friend Maria".

➤ **U/no tame no 〈N〉 ための**: Final Mood & Attributive Copula| *that is for ~*

これは外国人のための文法書だ: "This is a grammar book for foreigners".

➤ **U* yō ni ように**: Final Mood | *for (being able to) ~; so that ~*

❖ *If the subject is the first person, the verb has to be in the potential or negative forms of the verbs.

❖ It indicates actions or states beyond the control of the subject, which are a purpose or hope understood as an objective for which the action of the following clause is performed.

• In positive sentences, the marked verb is in the potential form.

読めるように綺麗に書いてください: "Please write neatly so that I can read it".

• In negative sentences, the marked verb does not have to be in the potential form.

風が入らないように窓を閉めてください: "Close the windows so the wind can't get in".

❖ It indicates that the subject wants a third person to do something.

先生は学生が楽しく勉強するように面白いクラスをします: "The teacher makes the class interesting so that students enjoy studying".

➤ **U no ni** のに: Final Mood | *for ~; to ~*

❖ It indicates an objective or purpose for which the subject goes through a process developed through a medium, instrument or period of time.

作文を書くのに辞書を引きます: "I use a dictionary to write my essays".

➤ **VN/U** (no) **ni wa** のには: Final Mood | *for ~; to ~*

❖ It expresses an objective or purpose for which the subject goes through a process developed through a means, instrument or space of time, while also inferring a moral or practical judgment in the predicate.

このかばんは旅行{する}には重すぎる: "This bag is too heavy to travel with".

3.4 Presumptive & Assumptive Particles

The presumptive and assumptive moods indicate a supposition or conjecture subjectively made by the speaker, not necessarily based on verifiable facts.

➤ **N/n/V/i darō** だろう: Presumptive Mood | *will (probably) ~*

❖ The particle **darō**, which is actually the presumptive form of the copula, added to a verbal or nominal, indicates that the speaker assumes something subjectively.

このハンドバッグは高いだろう: "This bag probably is expensive". / "This bag must be expensive".

➤ **N/n/V/i deshō** でしょう: [*pol.*] Presumptive Mood | *will (probably) ~*

明日雨が降るでしょう: "It's (probably) going to rain tomorrow".

➤ **TA/na/i tsumori {D}** つもりだ/です: Assumptive Mood | *be convinced that ~; believe (that) ~; feel sure that ~*

❖ It expresses the conviction of the occurrence of the marked state or action even if it does not correspond to reality.

私は親切なつもりです: "I'm convinced I'm nice".

3.5 Evidential & Inferential Particles

The evidential mood expresses that the speaker makes a conjecture about a fact based on direct visual evidence or intuitive observation of a circumstance. The inferential mood indicates, on the other hand, that the conveyed information has been obtained from a particular source.

These moods are expressed in Japanese by adding the demonstrative pronoun sō ('like that') to different verbal and nominal forms.

The use of evidential and inferential expressions in Japanese is much more frequent than in English. In English, the speaker usually makes affirmative, declarative statements even when the information is inferred or based on opinion, but in Japanese, it is usual to speak more indirectly, making clear that what is said "seems" and not necessarily "is".

➤ **I/n/s sō ({D})** そう だ/です: Evidential Semblative Copula | *look(s) like ~; seem to/ that ~*

❖ It denotes a conjecture made on the basis of physical or psychological observations.

❖ This copulative form is placed at the end of a sentence.

今日は誰かお客さんが来そうです: "It seems that we're going to have some visitors today". / "I think we're going to have some visitors today".

➤ **I/n/s sō na ⟨N⟩** そうな: Evidential Semblative Attributive Copula | *... that seems ~*

❖ This attributive form is placed before a noun, modifying it.

田中さんは偉そうな顔をしている: "(It seems that) Tanaka has a great look on his face". (Lit. "Tanaka has a face that seems that is great".)

➤ **I/n/s sō ni** そうに: Evidential Mood| *looks like ~; seems like ~*

❖ This adverbial form is placed in the middle of a clause, modifying the verb.

子供は楽しそうに遊んでいる: "(It looks like) the kids are playing happily".

➤ **A nasa sō ({D})** なさそう だ/です: Negative Evidential Semblative Copula| *doesn't look like ~; doesn't seem that ~*

この辺にコーヒーシャップはなさそう: "There doesn't seem to be any coffee shacks around here".

➤ **I/n/s sō ni/mo nai** そう{に/も}ない: Negative Evidential Semblative Copula| *doesn't look like ~; doesn't seem that ~*

この問題はあまり難し君そうもない: "This problem doesn't look too difficult".

- -

➤ **V/i sō ({D})** そう だ/です: Inferential Mood | *I heard (that) ~; apparently ~*

❖ It indicates that the marked clause has been heard or that it is said by someone other than the subject.

山田<ruby>やまだ</ruby>さんは来週<ruby>らいしゅう</ruby>日本<ruby>にほん</ruby>へ帰<ruby>かえ</ruby>るそうです: "(I heard that) Yamada is going back to Japan next week".

➤ **N/n {D} sō ({D})** そう*だ/*です: Inferential Mood | *heard (that) is ~; apparently is ~*

ジョンさんは英語<ruby>えいご</ruby>の先生<ruby>せんせい</ruby>だそうだ: "I heard John is an English teacher".

3.6 Semblative & Expectative Particles

The semblative mood denotes a hypothesis deduced through a similarity established between two elements or facts, made on the basis of direct observation or experience. The expectative mood expresses that the realization of an action or occurrence of an event is understood as a logical deduction or something foreseen and expected.

➤ **V/na/no/i yō {D}** よう*だ/*です: Semblative Copula | *be like ~; seem(s) (that) ~*

❖ It denotes a hypothesis deduced from observation.

このアプリの使<ruby>つか</ruby>い方<ruby>かた</ruby>は簡単<ruby>かんたん</ruby>なようだ: "Seems like this app is easy to use".

❖ It indicates similarity to an element.

この子供<ruby>こども</ruby>の話<ruby>はな</ruby>し方<ruby>かた</ruby>は大人<ruby>おとな</ruby>のようです: "This kid talks like an adult".

➤ **V/na/no/i yō na ⟨N⟩** ような: Semblative Attributive Copula | *... that is like ~*

❖ This attributive form is placed before a noun, modifying it.

マリアさんは疲<ruby>つか</ruby>れたような顔<ruby>かお</ruby>をしている: "Maria looks tired".

➤ **V/na/no/i yō ni** ように: Semblative Mood | *like (~ing); as (if) ~*

❖ This adverbial form is placed in the middle of a clause, modifying the verb.

昨日<ruby>きのう</ruby>のことのように覚<ruby>おぼ</ruby>えている: "I remember it like it was yesterday".

➤ **N/n/V/i mitai ({D})** みたい*だ/*です: Semblative Copula | *be like ~; seem(s) (that) ~*

❖ It denotes a hypothesis deduced from observation.

これは学生<ruby>がくせい</ruby>にはわかりにくいみたい: "This seems to be difficult for students to understand".

❖ It indicates a resemblance to an element.

春<ruby>はる</ruby>みたい: "It's like spring".

❖ This form also admits attributive (**mitai na**) and adverbial (**mitai ni**) variants.

➤ **N/n/V/i rashii** らしい: Approximative Semblative Copula | *~ish; ~ful; ~like*

❖ This auxiliary adjective verb expresses a conjecture based on information that has been read, heard or seen.

351

来年ジョンさんが日本へ来るらしいです: "Apparently John is coming to Japan next year".

❖ It expresses an approximate comparison deduced from more or less objective observations, showing that the subject has similar characteristics to the compared element.

あの人は日本人らしい: "That man is like a Japanese".

❖ It indicates that something is characteristic of (or meets the characteristics of) the marked element.

これは本当に君らしい: "This is really (like) you".

➤ **N/n/s ppoi っぽい**: Approximative Semblative Copula | *~ish; ~ful; ~like*

❖ It indicates that the subject is more or less similar to the marked element or shares a degree of the marked characteristic.

あの人は女っぽい: "That person is quite feminine". (Lit. "That person is somewhat like a girl".)

➤ **U/na/no/i hazu {D} はずだ/です**: Expectative Copula | *expect to ~; no wonder ~*

❖ It indicates that the occurrence of the marked action or state is a logical deduction based on an objective fact.

武君のカバンとコートはここにあるのでまだ学校にいるはずだ: "Takeshi's bag and coat are here, so he should still be at school".

❖ It expresses a forecast or deduction about a future event.

明日出発するはずです: "They are leaving tomorrow".

➤ **N/n/V/i hazu no ⟨N⟩ はずの**: Expectative Attributive Copula | *that is expected to ~*

誰もいないはずの建物からガサガサと音がする: "There's a rustling sound coming from a building that should be empty".

➤ **A/ku nai hazu {D} ないはずだ/です**: Negative Expectative Copula| *it's not expected that ~*

ジョンさんはアメリカへ帰らないはずです: "John is not going back to the States".

➤ **U/i hazu ga/wa nai はず{が/は}ない**: Negative Expectative Copula| *it's not expected that ~*

ジョンさんはアメリカへ帰るはずわありません: "John is not going back to the States".

3.7 Provisional Particle

There is a provisional particle derived directly from the provisional copula **nara** [☞ V.1.6] which, when used with verbals, indicates that the marked clause is an actual or hypothetical provision in terms of which the following clause is developed.

➤ **V/i** (no) **nara** のなら: Provisional Mood | *if ~; provided that ~*

❖ It expresses that the marked clause is a provision based on information known beforehand by both the speaker and the listener.

あの部屋が明るいのなら借りますよ: "If that room is bright enough, I'll rent it".

+ *Exhaustive list of modal particles in Expressing Yourself in Japanese* [☞ EY:VI]

4. PHRASAL PARTICLES

Phrasal particles join two phrases or clauses without indicating any mood or aspect.

There are two types of phrasal particles: Coordinating particles (coordinators) and subordinating particles (subordinators). Coordinators join two phrases or clauses in consecution or contrast without altering their meaning. Subordinators establish the subordinate relationship between two clauses insofar as they are syntactically codependent on each other.

4.1 Coordinators

Coordinators are particles or verbal forms that link two clauses, either conjunctively ('and'), disjunctively ('or'), enumeratively ('and things like'), adversatively ('but') or concessively ('even').

Clauses following coordinators may be predicted by different conjunctions [☞ VO:VII.2].

The infinitive and gerundive root forms of verbals can also act as conjunctive coordinators.

➤ **TE ø**: Conjunctive Coordinator | *~ and*

❖ The main function of the gerundive form [☞ III.3.2] is to join two consecutively occurring clauses.

Ⓥ 朝ご飯を食べて学校へ行く: "I eat breakfast and go to school".

Ⓐ あの部屋は広くて明るいです: "That room is big and bright".

➤ **N/n de** で: Conjunctive Coordinator | *be ~ and*

山田さんは先生で大学で教えています: "Mr. Yamada is a teacher and teaches at a university".

➤ **I ø**: Conjunctive Coordinator | ~ *and*

❖ One of the functions of the infinitive form [☞ III.2.3] is to join two clauses that syntactically follow one after the other, but do not necessarily do so temporally.

毎朝七時に起き散歩に行く: "I get up at seven every morning and go for a walk".

➤ **V/i shi し**: Conjunctive Coordinator | ~ *and (also)*

❖ It joins two clauses by putting the emphasis on the conjunction itself.

昨日雨も降ったし風邪も吹いた: "It rained yesterday and it was also windy".

➤ **N/n {D} shi し**: Conjunctive Coordinator | *be* ~ *and*

このアパートは奇麗だし、安い: "This apartment is clean and cheap".

➤ **A-nai de ないで**: ❶ Negative Conjunctive Coordinator | ~ *and not; without* ~*ing* ‖ ❷ [*fam.*] Privative Coordinator | *without* ~*ing*

❖ ❶ It indicates that an action occurs after the non-performance of the marked action.

武君はお風呂に入らないで寝た: "Takeru went to bed without taking a bath". / "Takeshi didn't take a bath and went to bed".

❖ ❷ It indicates that although the action of the marked verb is not performed, the action of the following clause takes place contrary to what is expected.

辞書を見ないで作文を書きなさい: "Write an essay without looking at the dictionary".

➤ **A-zu ni ずに**: Privative Coordinator | ~ *and not; without* ~*ing*

勉強せずに試験に受かった: "I took the exam without studying".

➤ **N/n/V/i ka₂ か**: Disjunctive Coordinator | *(either)* ~ *or ...*

❖ It presents a clause as an alternative to choose between two or more options.

❖ It usually appears twice in a set of two alternative clauses.

私と一緒に来ますか、それともここにいますか: "Will you go with me or will you stay here?".

➤ **N/na/U/ku mata wa または**: [*lit.*][*for.*] Disjunctive Coordinator | ~ *or*

上げるまたは持ち上げること: "Raise or lift".

➤ **N/U to ka とか**: Enumerative Case & Coordinator | *(do) things such as* ~ *and*

❖ It indicates that the marked actions are part of a non-exhaustive list of possible actions.

❖ It usually appears in pairs. C.f. Correlative Constructions [☞ XIV].

週末はレストランに行く<ruby>とか<rt>しゅうまつ</rt></ruby>友達会うとか: "On weekends I go to a restaurant, meet with friends…".

➤ **N/na/U/i yara** やら: [*fam.*] Enumerative Case & Coordinator | *(do) things such as ~ and*

❖ It usually appears in pairs. C.f. Correlative Constructions [☞ XIV].

石を投げるやら大声で叫ぶやら大変な騒ぎだった: "There was a lot of throwing of rocks and (things like) shouting".

➤ **V/i ga** が: Adversative Coordinator | *~ but*

❖ It links two clauses by indicating a contrast, opposition or contradiction between them.

田中さんは来ましたが山田さんは来ませんでした: "Tanaka came, but Yamada didn't".

➤ **N/n {D} ga** が: Adversative Coordinator | *~ but*

猫は大好きですが犬はあまり好きじゃありません: "I love cats, but I don't really like dogs".

➤ **V/i keredomo** けれども: [*for.*] Adversative Coordinator | *~ but*

あのレストランは高いけれどもおいしくないですう: "That restaurant is expensive but (the food) is not tasty".

➤ **V/i keredo** けれど: Adversative Coordinator | *~ but*

陽は出ていたけれど、寒かった: "The sun was out, but it was cold".

➤ **V/i kedo** けど: Adversative Coordinator | *~ but*

あのズボンは高いけど買うよ: "Those pants are expensive, but I'll buy them".

➤ **V/na/i no ni** のに: Concessive Coordinator | *even though ~*

❖ It links two clauses indicating a contrast, opposition or contradiction between them while expressing an attitude of surprise, dissatisfaction or disbelief on the speaker's part.

❖ Normally used when talking about known and contrasted facts (not hypothetical).

武君は病気なのに学校へ行った: "Takeshi went to school even though he was sick".

+ *Exhaustive list of coordinators in Expressing Yourself in Japanese* [☞ EY:III]

4.2 **Subordinators**

Subordinative particles establish a relation of syntactic dependence between two clauses, meaning that a clause marked with a subordinator particle cannot appear on its own without another clause.[64]

➢ **P* to₂** と: Quotative Subordinator | *that ~*

✤ It indicates that the marked clause is a direct quotation of something that has been said, heard, written or thought.

- Usually followed by verbs related to speech, hearing or thinking such as **iu** (*to say*); **omou** (*to think*); **kaku** (*to write*) or **kiku** (*to hear*). More info in Subordinators Extensions [☞ XIII.3.1].

<ruby>建物<rt>たてもの</rt></ruby>

あの建物が大変綺麗だと思います: "I think that that building is beautiful".

- It may indicate a quotation in direct style, in which what someone else has said is repeated verbatim. In this case, the quote is transcribed as it was said, usually written between single quotes (「」).

原さんは「暑いですね」と言った: "Hara said: 'It's hot'".

- It can also indicate a quotation in indirect style, expressing what has been said but not literally. The indirect style is reflected in Japanese simply in that the repeated saying is conveyed in the plain register instead of any other register that the original speaker may have used.

原さんは暑いと言った: "Hara said (that) it was hot".

✤ *Any sentence in the direct speech. In the indirect speech, usually **N/n/V/i**.

➢ **N/n/V/i ka₂** か: Interrogative Subordinator | *whether/if/what/ ~*

✤ It indicates that the marked clause is interrogative within a compound sentence.

原さんがいつ来るか分からない: "I don't know when Hara comes".

➢ **N*/n/V/i ka to** かと: Interrogative Quotative Subordinator | *whether ~; if ~*

✤ This combined particle indicates a quotation of a question in indirect style.

- Followed by verbs related to asking such as **kiku** (*to ask*) or **tazuneru** (*to ask*); or related to doubt and knowledge such as **wakaru** (*to understand*); **shiru** (*to know*) or **oboeru** (*to remember*).

山田さんは原さんに田中さんがいつ来たかと聞きました: "Yamada asked Hara when did Tanaka arrive".

----

[64] Unlike some aspectual or modal particles which, although they also appear in combined subordinate sentences, they may appear in stand-alone clauses in certain circumstances, such as the answer to a question.

❖ *Only indefinite pronouns.

❖ In the direct style, the quotation of the question is constructed by adding the particle **to** to the interrogative phrase, whether that sentence already had the particle interrogative particle **ka** or not.

山田さんは原さんに「田中さんはいつ来ましたか」と聞きました: "Yamada asked Hara: 'When did Tanka arrive?'".

➤ **N/na/V/i yori** より: Comparative Subordinator | *compared to ~; as opposed to ~; rather than ~*

❖ It establishes that the marked element is compared with the following clause.

❖ Only used with verbs in the positive polarity.

僕は出かけるより家にいたい: "I'd rather stay home than go out".

➤ **U/na/i hodo** ほど: Upper Limitative Subordinator | *as much as ~; so much that ~*

❖ It indicates that an action is marked as a limit toward which the action or state marked by the following clause is comparatively derived.

動けないほどたくさん食べた: "I ate so much I can't move".

➤ **U/na/i kurai** くらい: Upper Limitative Subordinator | *as much as ~; so much that ~*

もう歩けないくらい疲れている: "I'm so tired I can't walk anymore".

➤ **U/na/i gurai** くらい: = kurai

+ *Exhaustive list of subordinators in Expressing Yourself in Japanese* [☞ EY:IV]

IX. ADVERBS & CONJUNCTIONS

In this section, we will look at the specific grammatical characteristics of two types of non-conjugable words:

1. **Adverbs**: Non-conjugable dependent words that modify a verbal or another adverb.

2. **Conjunctions**: Non-conjugable dependent words that link clauses.

1. ADVERBS

Adverbs are non-conjugable dependent words that modify a verb or another adverb.

❖ In Japanese, adverbs always precede the verb or adverb they modify.

• Adverbs are usually placed immediately before the verb.

山田は先生は早く話します: "Professor Yamada speaks quickly".

• Or between other verbal complements and the verb.

よく宿題をしてください: "Do your homework well".

❖ In Japanese, there are many nouns that can also act as adverbs, thus being nominal adverbs [☞ X.3].

• Adverbialized nouns [☞ X.3] by means of the suffix **ni**.

田中さんは実に親切です: "Mr. Tanaka is really kind". (実: *reality*)

• Nouns and pronouns of place adverbialized by means of adjunctive particles such as **de** or **ni**. This group also includes propositional nouns [☞ VO:II.1].

ここで待っていてください: "Wait for me here".

• Nouns of time that do not require any particle or suffix to act adverbially.

夕方家へ帰ります: "I'll be home in the evening".

❖ Certain constructions with the gerundive form [**TE**] [☞ III.3.2] can also be used adverbially.

注意して車を運転してください: "Drive your car with caution/cautiously".

+ *More information on adverbs in Vocabulary* [☞ VO:VI]

1.1 Ideophones

In Japanese, there is a very distinct type of pure adverb that has no equivalent in the English language. These types of adverbs are the so-called ideophones[65], which are adverbs that imitate sounds or express subjective phonemes representative of an emotional, psychological or physical state of a person. Most of these adverbs consist of a repeated phoneme (E.g. *pikapika*, 'brightly').

❖ Most of the time, the translation of these adverbs into English can be done smoothly using semantically equivalent adverbs or adjectives.

彼はイライラしている: "He's annoyed". (Lit. "He's doing annoyingly".)

❖ Occasionally, however, especially when it comes to ideophones imitating a sound, the translation has to be more elaborate since a literal translation would denote a somewhat childish language in English.

雨がポタポタ落ちている: "The rain is falling in puddles." (Lit. "The rain is falling doing pop-pop".)

2. CONJUNCTIONS

Conjunctions are non-conjugable dependent words that link two clauses. Functionally they are similar to phrasal particles, but syntactically they behave differently, because instead of being placed after a clause linking it directly to a new clause, they are placed at the beginning of a new sentence made after a pause, introducing it into the discourse.

Conjunction Syntax:	Particle Syntax:
P_1 • CON P_2	P1{p} P_2

※ **P** stands for phrase (a clause in this instance); **CON** stands for conjunction; and **{p}** for any particle.

+ *More information about conjunctions in Vocabulary* [☞ VO:VII.2]

2.1 Special Conjunction Usage

In Japanese, certain modal phrases are formed by using particles and conjunctions at the same time. Here we will list the most common of these constructions:

❖ **Conditional mood** [*if*]: The conjunction moshi can precede sentences in the conditional mood [☞ EY:VI.2.6].

もしお金があったら家を建てるでしょう: "If I had the money, I'd build a house".

❖ **Concessive Provisional mood** [*even if*]: The conjunction tatoe can precede sentences in the concessive provisional mood [☞ EY:VI.2.5].

---

[65] Literally: "idea-sound".

たとえ山田さんが手伝ってくれるとしても明日までにこの仕事はできないでしょう: "Even if Mr. Yamada helps us, we won't be able to do this job by tomorrow".

✤ **Semblative mood** [*as if*]: The conjunction maru de can precede sentences in the semblative mood [☞ EY:VI.2.3-4].

まるで夢を見ているようだ: "It's like I'm dreaming".

X. WORD & PHRASE CLASS TRANSFORMATION

In this section, we display how to change one word class into another. There are in total four ways to transform the class of one word into another:

1. **Nominalization:** Turning into a noun.

2. **Adjectivalization:** Turning into an adjective.

3. **Adverbialziation:** Turning into an adverb.

4. **Verbalization:** Turning into a verb.

1. NOMINALIZATION

Nominalization refers to the transformation of a non-nominal word into a noun. Both verbs and verbal adjectives can be nominalized.

1.1 Verbal Nominalization

Here are the different ways of transforming a verb into a noun:

➤ **I ø**

❖ The infinitive form of the verb [☞ III.2.3] can sometimes make for a syntactical and semantical nominal.

動く (*to move*) → 動き (*movement*)

➤ **I mono 物**

❖ Fossilized, no longer productive way of nominalization.

買う (*to buy*) → 買い物 (*shopping*)

➤ **VN ø**

❖ Most Sino-Japanese nominal verbs are themselves nouns when they are not attached to the verb *suru* [☞ X.4].

理解する (*to comprehend*) → 理解 Ø (*comprehension*)

❖ Virtually all verbals can also be syntactically nominalized through the phrasal nominalization particles *no*, *koto* and *mono* [☞ X.1.3].

1.2 Adjectival Nominalization

Adjectival nouns and verbs can be transformed into nouns in the following ways:

➤ **n ∅**: Adjectival Noun

❖ Many adjectival nouns are themselves nouns when they are not linked to a copula.

➤ **n*/s-sa さ**: Nominalization Marker

❖ It expresses a degree or quality.

高い (*be high*) → 高さ (*height*)

❖ *Some adjectival nouns of Sino-Japanese origin can modify their meaning (expressing degree) by means of the nominalizing suffix **sa**.

便利 (*convenient*) → 便利さ (*convenience*)

➤ **s-mi み**: Nominalization Marker

❖ It expresses a tinge or trace of a quality or the quality itself.

楽しい (*be fun*) → 楽しみ (*enjoyment; the fun*)

1.3 Phrasal Nominalization

Nominalizing particles turn a verbal phrase into a noun phrase that functions grammatically as a noun to which a particle or a copula shall be added.

➤ **V/na*/i no₂ の**: Nominalization Marker | *that ~; to ~; ~ing; ~ one*

❖ It transforms a clause into a noun phrase, that is, it converts clauses ending with verbals or copulae into phrases that act as nouns.

❖ The nominalization marker **no** nominalizes verbals that express phenomena that are perceptible or realizable by humans.

外国語を覚えるのは難しいです: "It's difficult to learn a foreign language".

❖ Some noun phrases built with the nominal particle **no** are translated in English with the relative pronoun *one*.

僕が作ったのはこれだ: "This is the one I made".

❖ *After a noun or adjectival noun, the attributive copulative form **na**, or the literary form **de aru** must be added before the nominalizing marker **no**.

小さなのが欲しいです: "I want the one that is small"/ "I want the small one".

➤ **V/na/i koto こと**: Nominalization Marker | *that ~; to ~; ~ing*

❖ The nominalizer **koto** indicates a certain distance of the speaker from the content of the nominalized phrase or is linked to verbals expressing an abstract or intellectual phenomenon.

私の趣味はチェスをすることです: "My hobby is playing chess".

➤ **V/na/i mono** もの: Nominalization Marker | *that which ~; something ~*

❖ Nominalizer typically used to give explanations or definitions.

愛は重要なものです: "Love is (an) important (thing)".

2. ADJECTIVALIZATION

Many Sino-Japanese nouns can be transformed into adjectival nouns by adding the following suffix:

➤ **N-teki** 的: Adjectival Noun

哲学 (*philosophy*) → 哲学的 (*philosophical*)

❖ There is no way to turn any word into an adjectival verb because this word class is closed (no longer productive) in contemporary Japanese.

3. ADVERBIALIZATION

The transformation of adjectival nouns and verbs into adverbs can be done by adding certain suffixes to their roots.

➤ **s-ku** く : Adverbialization Marker | *~ly*

❖ It transforms an adjectival verb into an adverb.

早い (*fast; quick*) → 早く (*quickly*)

➤ **n-ni** に: Adverbialization Marker | *~ly*

❖ It transforms an adjectival noun into an adverb.

綺麗 (*beautiful*) → 綺麗に (*beautifully*)

➤ **N-teki ni** 的に: Adverbialization Marker | *~ly*

❖ It transforms a noun into an adverb, passing through the previous step of transforming the noun into an adjectival noun.

哲学 (*philosophy*) → 哲学的 (*philosophical*) → 哲学的に (*philosophically*)

4. **VERBALIZATION**

The only still productive way of turning nouns into verbs is adding the verb **suru** to a Sino-Japanese noun:

➤ **N-suru**: Verbalization

料理 (*cuisine*) → 料理する (*to cook*)

❖ Very occasionally, some non-Chinese borrowing is turned into a verb by adding the suffix **-ru**, but these neologisms are considered colloquial or slang.

メモ (*note; memo*) → メモる (*to make a memo*)

XI. VERBAL COMPOUNDS

Verb compounds are a fairly common phenomenon in Japanese that involves joining two verbs to create a new meaning or modify an aspect or mood.

There are two types of compound verbs according to their formative process:

1. **Gerundive Verbal Compounds**: Composed by means of the gerundive form of verbs.

2. **Infinitive Verbal Compounds**: Constructed by means of the infinitive form of verbs.

1. GERUNDIVE VERBAL COMPOUNDS

Gerundive verb compounds are constructions made by the gerundive verbal forms to which a subsidiary verbal is added to transform the aspect or mood of the modified verb.

A subsidiary verbal is a verb or adjectival verb which has a specific meaning on its own but which, if added to the gerundive form of a verb, is used to change that verb's aspect or mood.

1.1 Aspectual Compounds

Gerundive compounds are used to change the aspect of the marked verb.

➤ **TE iru** いる: ❶ Progressive Aspect | *be ~ing* ‖ ❷ Continuous Stative Aspect | *have/ has ~ed; be ~ed*

❖ ❶ It expresses an action that progresses at the moment of speech.

子供は庭で遊んでいます: "The kids are playing in the yard".

❖ ❷ It expresses a continuous state in which the subject of the sentence is.

とても疲れている: "I'm very tired".

❖ This form has a colloquial variant in which the vowel **i** of the verb **iru** is omitted.

愛してる: "I love you". (Lit. I'm loving you".)

➤ **TE aru** ある: Stative Aspect | *have/has been ~; be ~ed; be ~ing*

❖ It expresses the state resulting from an action.

壁に絵がかけてあります: "There is a picture hanging on the wall".

➤ **TE oku** おく: ❶ Preparatory Perfective Aspect | *~ in advance; ~ beforehand; ~ ahead* ‖ ❷ Preparatory Stative Aspect | *leave ~ed*

❖ ❶ It expresses that an action has been carried out in advance.

昼ごはんの料理をしておきました: "I've prepared lunch (in advance)".

❖ ❷ It expresses that a state or action is deliberately (in advance) left to continue.

ドアを開けておいてください: "Please leave the door open".

❖ This form has a colloquial variant in which the vowel **e** of the gerundive form [TE] is omitted.

この書類を読んどこう: "I'll read this document beforehand". (Lit. "I'll leave this document read".)

➤ **TE shimau** しまう: Complete Terminative Aspect | *to finish ~ (up)*

❖ It expresses that an action is completely finished, inferring that such completion was perhaps somewhat unexpected.

夕べケーキを全部食べてしまった: "I ate all the cake last night".

❖ This form has a colloquial variant in which the form **TE**+**shimau** gets contracted into chau in verbs whose gerundive form ends in -**te**, and contracted to jau in verbs whose gerundive form ends in -**de**.

まあ、これ、壊れちゃったわ: "Oh, it broke!".

➤ **TE kuru** くる: ❶ Translative Progressive Aspect | *come (about) to ~* ‖ ❷ Resultative Inceptive Aspect | *been ~ing up to now; get ~ed* ‖ ❸ Connective Regressive Motion marker | *to ~ and come back*

❖ ❶ With involuntary verbs, it expresses a progressive change of state or situation which has been operating from a moment in the past and has continued up to the present.

気温がだんだん高くなってきました: "The temperature is getting warmer and warmer". (Lit. "The temperature has come to get higher step by step".)

❖ ❷ Also with involuntary verbs, it expresses a mental process that has resulted in a present result.

日本の生活に慣れてきた: "I'm getting used to life in Japan".

❖ ❸ With verbs of will, it expresses that the subject performs the marked action and returns to the place where he or she was.

図書館へ行ってきます: "I'm going to the library (and I'll come back)".

➤ **TE iku** 行く: ❶ Continuous Progressive Aspect | *go/goes on ~ing; continue(s) to ~* ‖ ❷ Connective Egressive Motion marker | *go as ~; ~ and go*

❖ ❶ It expresses that a situation or state has been or will be changing from a specific point in time.

これから暑くなっていくでしょうね: "It's going to get hotter from now on".

♣ ❷ It expresses that after performing the marked action something else is going to be done.

お茶を飲んでいきましょう: "Let's have some tea (and go)".

1.2 Modal Compounds

Modal compounds are used to change the mood of the marked verb.

➤ **TE miru** みる: Probationary Mood | *try to ~; try ~ing*

♣ It expresses that the speaker intends to perform the action marked by the verb.

日本語の新聞を読んでみよう: "I'll try to read Japanese newspapers".

➤ **TE ageru** あげるう: Active Benefactive Mood | *to ~ for the sake of s.o.*

♣ It expresses that the subject performs an action as a favor to the indirect object, which is a second or third person.

❖ The indirect object is someone of equal or inferior status to the subject or someone belonging to the subject's in-group.

私は田中さんにセーターを編んであげるつもりです: "I'm going to knit a sweater for Mr. Tanaka".

➤ **TE sashiageru** 差し上げる: [*hum.*] Active Benefactive Mood | *~ for s.o.*

❖ Used when the indirect object is someone of higher status than the subject.

➤ **TE yaru** やる: [*fam.*] Active Benefactive Mood | *~ for s.o.*

❖ Used, in a familiar register, when the indirect object is someone of equal or lower status than the subject.

➤ **TE kureru** くれる: Active Benefactive Mood | *~ for s.o.*

♣ It expresses that the subject, which is a second or third person, does something for the benefit of the indirect object, which is a first person or someone from the speaker's in-group.

❖ Used when the subject is the first person or someone from his in-group and the one performing the action is someone of equal or lower status than him.

マリアさんは僕の英語の宿題を直してくれました: "Maria revised my English homework (for me)".

➤ **TE kudasaru** 下さる: [*hon.*] Active Benefactive Mood | *~ for s.o.*

❖ Used when the subject is the first person or someone from his in-group and the one who performs the action is someone of higher status than him.

367

> **TE morau もらう**: Passive Benefactive Mood | *~ for s.o.*

❖ It expresses that the subject benefits from an action that the agent complement performs in its favor.

❖ Used when the agent complement is someone of equal or lower status than the subject or someone belonging to the subject's in-group.

あなたはマリアさんにパーティに招待してもらいましたか: "Did Maria invited you to her party?". / "Were you invited to the party by Maria?".

> **TE itadaku いただく**: [*hum.*] Passive Benefactive Mood | *~ for s.o.*

❖ Used when the agent complement is someone of higher status than the subject.

> **TE kudasai 下さる**: [*pol.*] Directive Mood | *please ~*

❖ It expresses a polite request made to someone to do something.

窓を開けてください: "Open the window, please".

> > **TE ø**: [*fam.*] Directive Mood | *please ~*

明日早く来てね: "Come early tomorrow, okay?".

> ~ **A nai de kudasai**: Negative Directive Mood | *please don't ~*

この紙を折らないでください: "Please do not fold this paper".

> > **A nai de**: [*fam.*] Negative Directive Mood | *please don't ~*

この雑誌を持って帰れないで: "Don't take this magazine home".

> **TE kure くれ**: [*fam.*][*mas.*] Directive Mood | *~*

買い物に行って来てくれ: "Go do some shopping".

> **TE chōdai ちょうだい**: [*fam.*][*fem.*] Directive Mood | *please ~*

全部食べてちょうだい: "Eat it all, please".

> **TE hoshii 欲しい**: Patient Volitive Mood | *want (s.o.) to ~*

❖ It denotes that the subject wants a second or third person—the indirect object —to perform the marked action.

❖ Used with people of equal or lower status than the speaker.

金田さんに郵便教区へ行って欲しい: "I want you (Mr. Kaneda) to go to the post office".

> ~ **A nai de hoshii**: Negative Patient Volitive Mood | *don't want (s.o.) to ~*

台所を汚さないで欲しい: "I don't want you messing up my kitchen".

➤ **TE moraitai** もらいたい: [*pol.*] Patient Volitive Mood | *want (s.o.) to ~*

田中さんにあの本を送ってもらいたいです: "I want you (Mr. Tanaka) to send me that book".

↝ **A nai de moraitai**: [*pol.*] Negative Patient Volitive Mood | *don't want (s.o.) to ~*

私の日記を読まないでもらいたい: "I don't want you to read my journal".

➤ **TE itadakitai** もらいたい: [*hum.*] Patient Volitive Mood | *want (s.o.) to ~*

❖ Used with people of higher status than the speaker.

先生に作文を読んでいただきたいです: "I want you (teacher) to read my essay".

2. INFINITIVE VERBAL COMPOUNDS

Infinitive verb compounds are constructions made with the infinitive forms of a verb to which another auxiliary verbal is added to change or specify the meaning of the first verb. In some cases, the change of meaning also involves a change of verbal aspect.

An auxiliary verb is a verb or adjectival verb with a specific meaning that serves to specify or modify the meaning of the verb to which it is added. The number of auxiliary verbs that form infinitive compound verbs is very large. Here we will list the most common ones according to their semantic use.

2.1 Temporal Progression

Auxiliary verbs that express a specific temporal aspect.

➤ **I tsudzukeru** 続ける: Continuative Aspect | *to keep on ~; to continue ~*

❖ It expresses that the marked action continues.

日本語を勉強をし続けるつもりです: "I'm going to keep studying Japanese".

➤ **I hajimeru** 始める: Inceptive Aspect | *to begin/start (to) ~*

❖ It expresses the beginning of an action or state.

作文を書き始めた: "I started writing my essay".

➤ **I dasu** 出す: Non-Intentional Inceptive Aspect | *to begin/start (to) ~*

❖ It indicates that an action begins without the agency of a subject or the will of a person.

雨が降り出した: "It started to rain".

➤ I kakeru かける: ❶ Deflective Terminative Aspect | *start to ~ (and not finish)* ‖ ❷ Deflective Inceptive Aspect | *almost ~*

♣ ❶ It indicates that an action has started but has been left unfinished.

本を読みかけたらすぐに寝てしまった: "I started to read a book, but soon fell asleep".

♣ ❷ It indicates that an action is about to begin.

彼女は死にかけた: "She almost died".

➤ I owaru 終わる: Terminative Aspect | *to finish/end ~*

♣ It expresses that an action has been carried out to completion.

やっと作文を書き終わった: "I finally finished writing my essay".

➤ I naosu 直す: Iterative Aspect | *to ~ again; to ~ over*

♣ It expresses that the marked action is redone.

計画を練り直した: "I reworked the plan".

➤ I nareru 慣れる: *to get used to ~*

この街には住み慣れました: "I'm used to living in this city".

2.2 Degree

Auxiliary verbs that express a quantitative degree to which an action is performed.

➤ I komu 込む: *into ~; ~ deeply*

♣ It expresses that the marked action is performed inwards.

冷たい空気が流れ込んでいます: "There's a cold air flowing in".

♣ Also used metaphorically to express that something is made "thoroughly" giving a sense of completeness.

知らない間に眠り込んでいた: "I fell (fully) asleep before I knew it".

➤ I sugiru すぎる: *too ~; ~ too much*

♣ It expresses that an action is performed too much.

食べすぎた: "I ate too much".

➤ I kiru 切る: *~ fully; ~ completely*

♣ It expresses that the marked action is done completely, utterly or resolutely.

彼がプールの距離を泳ぎ切りました: "He swam the entire distance of the pool".

3.1 Difficulty

Auxiliary verbs that express ease or difficulty in performing an action.

➤ I yasui やすい: *easy to ~*

❖ It expresses that something is easy to do.

自分の言語は一番読みやすいでしょう: "Your own language will be the easiest to read".

➤ I nikui にくい: *difficult/hard to ~*

❖ It expresses that something is difficult to do.

食堂の食べ物は食べにくい: "Food in the cafeteria is hard to eat".

➤ I dzurai づらい: *difficult/hard to ~*

言いづらいことだ: "It's hard to say".

➤ I gatai がたい: [*for.*] *very difficult/hard to ~; unable to ~*

❖ It expresses that something is very difficult or almost impossible to do.

彼女はその職の適任者とは言いがたい: "She's hardly the right person for the job". (Lit. "It's hard to say that she's a candidate for that job".)

XII. VERBAL FORMS EXTENSIONS

Extensions of root or derivational forms are particles added to a root or derivational form to specify a mood or aspect. The difference, in this case, between a particle and an inflectional extension is that the particle can usually be added to a verbal form regardless of the verbal conjugation type, while inflections are added differently depending on the conjugation.

The particles used for verbal forms extensions differ from other particles in that they are only added to a particular verbal form rather than to nominals or several possible verb forms at the same time.

1. ROOT FORMS EXTENSIONS

Particles added to root forms, which are the realis, irrealis and infinitive forms.

1.1 Realis Form Extensions

Root Form:	Extension:	Function:	Rough Translation:
U/i	+to	Conditional Mood	*if ~*
U	+na	Prohibitive Mood	*don't (you) ~*
	+mai	Negative Presumptive Mood	*probably won't ~*
	+beku	Final Mood	*in order to ~*
	+tokoro	Prospective Aspect	*be about to ~*
	+tsumori	Intentional Mood	*plan to ~*

➤ **U/i to₃** と: Conditional Mood | *if ~; when ~*

❖ It expresses that the marked clause is a necessary, inevitable and non-hypothetical condition for the following consequence that occurs in a direct and consecutive way.

部屋がうるさいと勉強ができない: "If it's noisy in the room I can't study".

❖ It indicates an event or action after which another consecutive event or action is naturally triggered.

秋になるとこの葉が落ちます: "When fall comes, leaves will fall" / "In fall the leaves fall off".

➤ **N/n {D} to** だ/です と: Conditional Mood | *if is ~*

学生だと割引があります: "If you're a student there's a discount".

➤ **U na な**: [*mas.*] Prohibitive Mood

✣ It expresses a prohibition in a strong and direct manner.

泣くな: "Don't cry!".

➤ **U mai まい**: [*for.*] Negative Presumptive Mood | *probably won't* ~

✣ It indicates that the speaker believes that an action or state is probably not such.

それは今我々には必要ではあるまい: "That's not (probably) what we need right now".

➤ **ku wa aru mai はあるまい**: [*for.*] Negative Presumptive Mood | *probably isn't* ~

この問題はこの学校の学生にはそれほど難しくはあるまい: "This problem shouldn't be too difficult for students of this school".

➤ **N/n de wa aru mai ではあるまい**: [*for.*] Negative Presumptive Copula | *probably isn't* ~

これは何かの間違いではあるまいか: "This must be some kind of mistake".

➤ **U beku べく**: [*lit.*][*for.*] Final Mood | *in order to* ~

✣ It expresses that the marked action is a purpose for which the action of the predicate is done.

彼は芸術家になるべく生まれてきた: "He was born to be an artist".

➤ **U tokoro {D} ところだ/です**: ❶ Prospective Aspect | *be about to* ~ ‖ ❷ Durative Progressive Aspect | *be in the midst of ~ing*

✣ ❶ It indicates that an action is about to begin.

家を出るところだ: "I'm about to leave home". / "I'm leaving home".

✣ ❷ With a verb in the progressive form **TE iru**, it indicates that one is in the process of doing an action.

メールを書いているところです: "I'm writing an email".

➤ **U tsumori {D} つもりだ/です**: Intentional Mood | *plan/intend to* ~

✣ It indicates that there is a plan to carry out the marked action.

海へ行くつもりです: "I plan to go to the beach". / "I'm going to the beach".

1.2 Irrealis Form Extensions

Root Form:	Extension:	Function:	Rough Translation:
A	+nu	Negative Polarity	*don't/doesn't ~*
	+zu	Negative Gerundive	*don't/doesn't ~ and*

➤ **A nu** ぬ: [*lit.*][*obs.*] ❶ Negative Imperfective Aspect | *don't/doesn't ~* ‖ ❷ Attributive Negative Imperfective Aspect | *that does/doesn't ~*

❖ Archaic negative form mostly used today in idioms, although sometimes it is also used more widely in literary or stiff language.

日本語が話せる者はこの辺にはおらぬ: "There is no one around here who speaks Japanese".

➤ **A zu** ず: Privative Coordinator | *without ~ing*

❖ It indicates that the action of the predicate is done without the marked action being performed.

❖ Generally followed by the particle ni.

何も食べずに一日過ごす: "I spend the day without eating anything".

1.3 Infinitive Form Extensions

Root Form:	Extension:	Function:	Rough Translation:
I	+tai	Volitive Mood	*want to ~*
	+tagaru		
	+nasai	Directive Mood	*please (do) ~*
	+na		
	+nagara	Simultaneous Durative a.	*while ~; as ~*
	+tsutsu	Simultaneous Progressive a.	*~ing while*
	+ppanashi	Egressive Progressive a.	*remain ~ing*
	+ppa		
	+ni	Final Mood	*to ~; in order to ~*

➤ **I tai** たい: Volitive Mood | *want to ~*

❖ This auxiliary dependent adjectival verb indicates that someone wants to do the action marked by the verb.

❖ Used only with the first person or with the second person in a question.

海へ行きたいです: "I want to go to the beach".

❖ With transitive verbs, the direct object can be marked either with the particle **ga** or with the particle **o** if the direct object is juxtaposed to the extended verb form.

コーヒー{を/が}飲みたい: "I want (to drink) coffee".

➢ I tagaru たがる: Volitive Mood | *want to* ~

❖ Auxiliary dependent verb indicating that it appears that someone wants to perform the action expressed by the verb.

❖ Used only with the second or third person.

山田さんは泳ぎたがっています: "(It seems that) Mr. Yamada wants to swim".

➢ I nasai なさい: [*pol.*] Directive Mood | *please* ~; *do* ~

❖ This form indicates a command expressed in a polite way.

❖ Used when the listener is someone of equal or lower status than the speaker.

もっと食べなさい: "(You should) eat more".

　➢ I na な: [*col.*] Directive Mood | *please* ~; *do* ~

　酒をあまり飲むな: "Don't drink too much sake".

➢ I nagara (ni) ながらに: Simultaneous Durative Aspect | *at the same time as* ~; *as* ~; *while* ~

❖ It indicates that the marked action is done simultaneously with the action of the following clause, which receives the focus.

❖ The subject of both clauses has to be the same.

原さんは音楽を聞きながら宿題をしている: "Hara is doing his homework while listening to music".

➢ I tsutsu つつ: [*for.*] Simultaneous Progressive Aspect | *~ing while*

❖ It expresses that an action is being performed progressively at the same time as another action is being performed.

悪いことと知りつつ友達に嘘をついてしまった: "I lied to my friends, knowing it was wrong".

　➢ I tsutsu aru つつある: [*for.*] Progressive Aspect | *be ~ing*

❖ It expresses an action that is in progress and not yet finished.

❖ This structure is not used with transitive verbs that define everyday actions.

今家に帰りつつあります: "He's going home now" / "He's on his way home now".

➤ **I ppanashi {D}** っぱなし: Egressive Progressive Aspect | *have been ~ing; remain ~ing; leave ~ing*

❖ It expresses that an action or state has been left to progress indefinitely without completion.

彼はずっとしゃべりっぱなしだ: "He's been talking the whole time (without stopping)".

➤ **I ni** に: Final Mood | *to ~; in order to ~*

❖ It indicates the purpose for which one goes to a place indicated by a motion verb such as **iku** (*to go*), **kuru** (*to come*) or **kaeru** (*to go back*).

デパートへセーターを買いに行った: "She went to the mall to buy a sweater".

2. DERIVATIVE FORMS EXTENSIONS

Particles added to derivative forms, which are the presumptive, gerundive, perfective and provisional forms.

2.1 Presumptive Form Extensions

Root Form:	Extension:	Function:	Rough Translation:
Ō	+ka	Propositive Mood	*shall we ~?*

➤ **Ō ka** か: Propositive Mood | *shall we ~?; let's ~*

❖ It indicates that it is proposed to the listener to perform an action or to receive the benefit of the action performed by the subject.

その件はまた後で話し合おうか: "We'll talk about it later, okay?". / "Let's talk about it later".

2.2 Gerundive Form Extensions

Root Form:	Extension:	Function:	Rough Translation:
TE	+kara	Postessive Aspect	*after ~*
	+mo	Concessive Provisional Mood	*even if ~*
	+wa	Thematic Conditional Mood	*if (it is the case that) ~*

➤ **TE kara** から: ❶ Postessive Aspect | *after ~* ‖ ❷ Egressive Aspect | *since ~*

❖ ❶ It indicates that after the occurrence of what is expressed by the marked clause, the action or state of the following clause takes place.

仕事が終わってから家へ帰った: "I went home after work".

❖ ❷ It introduces the time elapsed from the occurrence of the marked action until the action or state of the following clause occurs.

日本に来てから３年になった: "It's been three years since I came to Japan".

- -

➤ **TE mo** も: Concessive Provisional Mood | *even if/though ~*

❖ It indicates that the marked clause is a state or action that is a disadvantage for what is expressed in the following clause in normal circumstances but not in this case.

明日天気が悪くてもハイキングに行きます: "I'll go hiking tomorrow even if the weather is bad".

➤ **N/n de mo** でも: Concessive Provisional Mood | *even if ~*

明日病気でも山田さんは働くでしょう: "Even if he's sick tomorrow, Yamada will go to work".

➤ **TE mo ii** もいい: Permissive Mood | *can/may ~*

❖ It expresses consent to perform an action.

Ⓥ もう帰ってもいいですよ: "You can go home now".

Ⓐ 短くてもいいですか: "Could it be short?" / "Can I make it short?".

Ⓝ 明後日でもいいですか: "Can it be the day after tomorrow?" / "Can I do it the day after tomorrow?".

➤ **TE mo yoroshii** もよろしい: [*for.*] Permissive Mood | *can/may ~*

➤ **TE mo kamawanai** もかまわない: Permissive Mood | *can/may ~; it's okay if ~*

Ⓥ ここに座ってもかまいませんか: "Can I sit here?". / "Do you mind if I sit here?".

377

Ⓝ 下手でもかまいませんか: "Is it okay if I'm not good at this?" / "Do you mind if I'm not very good at this?".

··

➤ **TE wa**: Thematic Conditional Mood | *if ~; when ~; if it is the case that ~*

❖ It presents an action or state as a topic about which a negative comment is given.

こんなに寒くては外出できません: "I can't go out when it's this cold".

➤ **TE wa ikenai**: Prohibitive Mood | *don't ~*

タバコを吸ってはいけません: "Don't smoke".

➤ **TE wa dame {D}**: Prohibitive Mood | *don't ~*

悪いことしてはだめですよ: "Don't do anything bad".

2.3 Perfective Form Extensions

Derivative Form:	Extension:	Function:	Rough Translation:
TA	+ra	Conditional Mood	*if ~; when ~*
	+ri	Enumerative Coordinator	*things like ~ and*
	+rō	Perfective Presumptive Mood	*will have ~ed*
	+tokoro	Recent Perfective Aspect	*have just ~*
	+bakari		

➤ **TA ra** ら: Conditional Mood | *if ~; when ~; after ~*

❖ It introduces actions as conditions, hypothetical or not, without which the following clause could not occur.

❖ The actions or states marked by this form occur without the input of the subject.

❖ This form implies a succession of actions.

Ⓥ 着いたら電話してください: "Please, call me when you arrive".

Ⓐ 良かったら買うよ: "If it's good I'll buy it".

➤ **N/n datta ra** だったら: Conditional Mood | *if is ~*

あなただったらそのことはしない: "If I were you I wouldn't do it".

➤ **TA ra dō** らどう: Propositive Mood | *shall we ~?; why don't you ~?*

言ってみたらどう?: "Why don't you tell me?".

➤ **TA ra dō desu ka** らどうですか: [*pol.*] Propositive Mood | *shall we ~?; why don't you ~?*

辞書を引いたらどうですか: "Why don't you consult a dictionary?".

➤ **TA ri** り: Enumerative Coordinator

❖ This form lists an implicit list of actions as partial examples.

❖ This form usually appears twice within a clause.

➤ **TA ri ⟨TA⟩ ri** (suru):

Ⓥ この雨が降ったり止んだりする天気は気に入らない [this rain NOM fall-and stop-and doing weather TOP like-not (energy-in enter-not)]: "I don't like this weather when it's raining on and off".

Ⓐ その映画は楽しかったり悲しかったり…: "That movie is sometimes fun but also sometimes sad".

➤ **TA rō** ろう: Perfective Presumptive Mood | *probably will have ~*

❖ It refers to a hypothesis or presumption about an event that would have occurred in the future.

❖ This form is hardly used today except in archaic literary language, and in that case, it is only used with verbs and not with verbal adjectives or copulative forms.

着いたろうか: "Will have he arrived?".

➤ **TA tokoro {D}** ところだ/です: Recent Perfective Aspect | *have just ~; just ~(-ed)*

❖ It indicates that an action has just been performed.

家に帰ったところだ: "I just got home".

➤ **TA bakari {D}** だけ: Recent Perfective Aspect | *have just ~(ed); just ~(ed)*

❖ It expresses that the action was performed a very short time ago.

作文を書いたばかりです: "I just wrote the essay".

2.4 Provisional Form Extensions

Root Form:	Extension:	Function:	Rough Translation:
BA	+ii	Propositive Mood	*would be good if ~*

➤ **BA ii** いい: Desiderative Mood | *it would be good if ~; I wish ~*

✤ It expresses that the speaker considers that it would be good and would like to perform the marked action.

もっと若ければいい: "I wish I was younger".

3. NEGATIVE FORMS EXTENSIONS

Extensions made to the negative forms of the verbs, which are mainly used to construct the obligative forms.

3.1 Obligative Forms

Obligative forms express the obligation or duty to perform an action.

These forms are not intuitive to the English speaker, as in Japanese, which are conveyed indirectly by provisional negative constructions ("if not") plus the auxiliary verbals **naranai** ('cannot help') or **ikenai** ('be no good for'). In Japanese, obligation is thus expressed by the literal phrase "if not ~ couldn't do" or "if not ~ cannot help". However, in practice, these forms should simply be translated by the expressions 'have to ~', 'must ~' or 'should ~'.

Japanese obligative expressions admit several variants, but here we will list the most common ones. For an exhaustive list, see Expressing Yourself in Japanese [☞ EY:VI.5.1].

A quick summary of the most common obligative forms is as follows:

	nakereba	
Ⓥ A-	nakya	naranai
Ⓐ ku-	nakute wa	*or*
Ⓝ N/n de	nakucha	ikenai
	nai to	

➤ Ⓥ A-**nakereba** naranai なければならない: Obligative Mood | *should ~; have to ~; must ~*

✤ It points to a general obligation dictated by logic or common sense.

和室に入る時靴を脱がなければなりません: "You have to take off your shoes to enter the Japanese-style room".

➤ Ⓐ ku-**nakereba** naranai なければならない: Obligative Mood | *should ~; have to ~; must ~*

アパートは明るくなければならない: "The apartment has to be bright".

➤ Ⓝ **N/n-de nakereba naranai** なければならない: Obligative Mood | *should ~; have to ~; must ~*

秘書が一人必要ですが英語が上手でなければなりません: "We need a secretary but she has to be good at English". / "We need a secretary but she must speak good English".

  ➤ **-nakya naranai** なきゃならない: [*col.*] Obligative Mood | *should ~; have to ~; must ~*

  明日仕事でパリへ行かなきゃならない: "I have to go to Paris for work tomorrow".

    ➤ **-nakya** なきゃ: [*col.*] Obligative Mood | *should ~; have to ~; must ~*

    今日試験を受けなきゃ: "I have to take the test today".

➤ **A/ku-nakute wa naranai** なくてはならない: Obligative Mood | *should ~; have to ~; must ~*

ご飯を食べてから歯を磨かなくてはならない: "You have to brush your teeth after you eat".

➤ **A/ku-nakereba ikenai** なければいけない: Obligative Mood | *should ~; have to ~; must ~*

❖ It indicates that the subject has a particular obligation according to his or her circumstances.

夜早く寝なければいけない: "You should go to bed early at night".

➤ **A/ku-nakute wa ikenai** なくてはいけない: Obligative Mood | *should ~; have to ~; must ~*

おじいちゃんに電話しなくてはいけないよ: "You have to call grandpa".

  ➤ **-nakucha ikenai** なくちゃならない: [*col.*] Obligative Mood | *should ~; have to ~; must ~*

  作文を書かなくちゃいけないんです: "I have to write an essay".

    ➤ **-nakucha** なくちゃ: [*col.*] Obligative Mood | *should ~; have to ~; must ~*

    スマホン買わなくちゃ: "I have to buy a cell phone".

➤ **A/ku-nai to ikenai** ないといけない: Obligative Mood | *should ~; have to ~; must ~*

もっと勉強しないといけない: "You have to study more".

3.2 Negative Obligative Forms

The negation of an obligation, indicating that "it is not necessary to do something", is done by adding the adjectival verb **ii** ('to be good') to the provisional negative concessive form (**A-nakute mo**), a construction whose literal translation is "it is good even if you don't...".

➤ Ⓥ **A-nakute mo ii** なくてもいい: Negative Obligative Mood | *don't have to ~*

来なくてもいい: "You don't have to come".

➤ Ⓐ **ku-nakute mo ii** なくてもいい: Negative Obligative Mood | *don't have to ~*

アパートは新しくなくてもいいですか: "Does the apartment need to be new?".

➤ Ⓝ **N/n de wa nakute mo ii** ではなくてもいい: Negative Obligative Mood | *don't have to be ~*

上手ではなくてもいいです: "You don't have to be good at it".

➤ **N/n ja nakute mo ii** じゃなくてもいい: [*col.*] Negative Obligative | *don't have to ~*

返事今日じゃなくてもいいからね: "You don't have to answer today". / "The answer doesn't have to be today".

4. POLITE FORMS EXTENSIONS

Extensions of some polite forms of verbs used to form polite propositive moods.

➤ **I-mashō ka** ましょうか: [*pol.*] Propositive Mood | *shall (I/we) ~?*

❖ Used by the speaker to propose the realization of an action for the benefit of the listener.

その荷物を持ちしましょうか: "Shall I take that package for you?".

➤ **I-masen ka** ませんか: [*pol.*] Propositive Mood | *shall (I/we) ~?*

❖ Used by the speaker to propose the litsener to make an action.

一緒に映画を見に行きませんか: "Let's go see a movie together".

XIII. PARTICLE EXTENSIONS

Particle extensions are derivations of simple particles made through the combination of various particles or the addition of a conjugated verbal form (usually in the gerundive form) to a simple particle.

In this section, we will list some of the most relevant combined particles and particle extensions in Japanese.

1. CASE PARTICLES EXTENSIONS

Derivations of case particles [☞ VIII.1].

1.1 Syntactic Particles Extensions

➤ **N ni wa** には: Thematic Dative Case | *to ~; for ~*
　この問題は子供には難しすぎる: "This problem is too difficult for a child".

➤ **N ni totte** にとって: Thematic Dative Case | *to ~; for ~*
　外国人にとって漢字を覚えることは大変なことだ: "It's hard for a foreigner to learn Chinese characters".

➤ **N ni tsuite** について: Correlative Case | *about ~*
　社長が言ったことについて意見がありますか: "Do you have an opinion about what the president said?".

➤ **N ni kan shite** に関して: [*for.*] Correlative Case | *about ~; related to ~; concerning ~*
　このテーマに関する意見を聞かせてください: "Please, let me know what you think about this topic".

➤ **N ni tai shite** に対して: Correlative Case | *in regards to ~; with respect to ~*
　政府のやり方に対して色々反対意見がある: "There's a lot of opposition with respect to the government's approach".

➤ **N ni shitagatte** に従って: Perlative Correlative Case | *following ~; in accordance with ~; according to ~*
　民主主義では全て多数の意見に従って決定される: "In a democracy, all decisions are made according to the opinion of the majority".

➤ **N ni kurabete** に比べて: Contrastive Dative Case | *compared with/to ~*

この事故は昨日のに比べて大したことはない: "This accident is nothing compared to yesterday's".

➤ **N ni shite wa** にしては: Contrastive Concessive Case | *for ~; considering that (is) ~*

田中さんは日本人にしては背が高いです: "Tanaka is tall for a Japanese".

➤ **N ni yotte** によって: ❶ Dependent Correlative Case | *depending on ~* ‖ ❷ Agentive Case | *by ~* ‖ ❸ Quotative Correlative Case | *according to ~*

❖ ❷ When the subject of the sentence is a creation, invention, or discovery made by the agent complement.

① 値段によって買うか買わないか決めます: "I'll decide whether to buy or not depending on the price".

② ゲルニカはピカソによってかかれた: "Guernica was painted by Picasso".

➤ **N ni yoru to** によると: Quotative Correlative Case | *according to ~*

天気予報によると明日雨が降るそうです: "According to the weather forecast, it's going to rain tomorrow".

1.2 Complementary Particles Extensions

➤ **N ni oite** において: [*for.*] Thematic Essive Case | *in/on/at ~*

会議は東京において開催されます: "The conference will be held in Tokyo".

➤ **N ni kawatte** に変わって: Substitutive Essive Case | *in place of ~; on behalf of ~; instead of ~*

田中さんに変わって原さんが講演しました: "Mr. Hara gave the lecture instead of Mr. Tanaka".

➤ **N ni mo kakawarazu** に関わらず: [*for.*] Negative Dependent Correlative Case | *regardless of ~; in spite of ~*

5年も中国にいたにも関わらず中国語が話せない: "He can't speak Chinese in spite of having been in China for five years".

➤ **N ni moto dzuite** に基づいて: Inferential Case | *based on/upon ~; on the basis of ~*

この物語は伝説に基づいて書かれた: "This story was written based on a legend".

➤ **N ni tsurete** につれて: Translative Durative Case | *as ~*

年が経つにつれて街の様子が変わってきた: "As the years went by, the city changed".

➤ **N ni kagirazu** に限らず: [*for.*] Negative Lower Limitative Case | *not only/just ~*

学生に限らず先生も休みになるのを持っている: "Not only students, but teachers are looking forward the holidays too".

➤ **N/n/V/i ni chigai nai** に違いない: Assumptive Mood | *convinced that ~; surely ~*

❖ This structure expresses a strong conviction on the part of the speaker in the face of a fact, but based on deduction or intention rather than on objective evidence.

山田先生はきっと日本へ帰ったに違いありません: "I'm sure Yamada has come to Japan" / "Dr. Yamada must have returned to Japan".

1.3 Focal Particles Extensions

➤ **N to shite** として: Contrastive Correlative Case | *as ~; in the capacity of ~; in the role of ~*

マリアさんは英語の先生として日本へ行きました: "Maria went to Japan as an English teacher".

➤ **N to shtie wa** としては: Contrastive Concessive Case | *for ~; as for ~*

あの靴はイタリア製の靴としては安いよ: "Those shoes are too cheap for being Italian".

1.4 Delimitative Particles Extensions

➤ **N/na/V/i dake {D}** だけ: Lower Limitative Copula | *be just/only ~*

ちょっと見ているだけです: "I'm just looking".

➤ **N/na/U/i bakari {D}** だけ: Lower Limitative Copula | *be just/only ~*

❖ It usually has a somewhat neg. connotation.

この腐ったオレンジは捨てるばかりです: "These rotten oranges only can be thrown away".

➤ **TE bakari iru**: Lower Limitative Progressive Aspect | *be only ~ing*

あの子はテレビを見てばかりいて全然勉強しない: "That kid only watches TV and never studies" / "That kid always watching TV and never studies".

➤ **U shika nai** しかない: *there's no way but ~*

日本語を覚えるために勉強するしかありません: "The only way to learn Japanese is to study it". (Lit. "To learn Japanese there's no other way but study".)

2. MODAL PARTICLES EXTENSIONS

Derivations of modal particles [☞ VIII.3].

2.1 Interrogative Particles Extensions

These particles indicate a doubt, expressed in a familiar way by the speaker when calibrating the veracity of a fact.

➤ **N/n/V/i ka na** かしら: [*fam.*] Emphatic Dubitative Mood | *I wonder if ~*

明日晴れるかな: "I wonder if it'll clear up tomorrow". / "I hope it's sunny tomorrow".

➤ **N/n/V/i ka shira** かしら: [*fam.*][*fem.*] Emphatic Dubitative Mood | *I wonder if ~*

誰かしら: "I wonder who it is".

➤ **N/n/V/i ka mo shirenai** かもしれない: Deliberative Mood | *may ~; might ~; can't tell if ~*

彼は来ないかもしれない: "He may not come".

2.2 Final Particles Extensions

➤ **U yō ni iu** ように言う: Imperative Quotative Mood | *tell to ~*

✤ This extension of the combined final particle **yō ni** indicates an imperative or command in the indirect style.

友達にあそこに座るように言った: "I told my friend to sit over there".

2.3 Presumptive Particles Extensions

These forms can be used either to express one's own thoughts aloud or to express a question to the listener in an indirect and polite way.

➤ **N/n/V/i (no/n)* darō ka** だろうか: Dubitative Mood | *perhaps ~; I wonder if/ whether ~*

✤ *The nominalization marker [☞ X.1.3].

これは愛だろうか？ : "(I wonder if) this could be love?"

➤ **N/n/V/i (no/n)* deshō ka** でしょうか: [*pol.*] Dubitative Mood | *perhaps ~; I wonder if/whether ~*

✤ *The nominalization marker [☞ X.1.3].

❖ It expresses a personal doubt spoke aloud.

どのボタンを押せばいいんでしょうか: "Which button should I press?". (Lit. I wonder what button should I press?)

❖ It expresses an indirect and polite interrogation.

お茶はいかがでしゅか: "Would you like some tea?".

3. PHRASAL PARTICLES EXTENSIONS

Derivations of phrasal particles [☞ VIII.4].

3.1 Subordinators Extensions

Derivations of quotative subordinators [☞ VIII.4.2]

➤ **P to iu** という: Quotative Mood | *say(s) that ~*

原さんは熱があると言っています: "Hara says/is saying (that) he has a fever".

  ➤ **P tte iu** っていう: [*col.*] Quotative Mood | *say(s) that ~*

  山田さんはもうすぐ帰るって言ってる: "Yamada says/is saying (that) he'll be home soon".

    ➤ **P tte** って: [*col.*] Quotative Mood | *say(s) that ~*

    武君は来られないって: "Takeshi said (that) he can't come".

  ➤ **N to iu ⟨N⟩** という …: Attributive Quotative Subordinator | *so-called ~*

  ダンスというクラブ会ったことがある？: "Have you ever been to the club called *Dance*?".

➤ **P to omou** と思う: *think/believe that ~*

いいと思います: "I think (that) it's good".

  ➤ **Ō to omou** と思う: Intentional Mood | *think (that)/about/to ~; planning to ~* | ≈ U tsumori {D} [☞ XII.1.1]

  プールで泳ごうと思います: "I think I'm going to swim in the pool".

  ➤ **N/n/V/i darō to omou** だろうと思う: Intentional Mood | *think (that)/about/to ~; planning to ~* | ≈ U tsumori {D} [☞ XII.1.1]

たぶんコンサートに行くだろうと思います: "I think he'll probably go to the concert".

4. NOMINALIZATION MARKERS EXTENSIONS

Derivations of nominalization marks [☞ X.1.3].

4.1 Explanative Copulae

Explanatory copulae are used to express that the speaker is giving an explanation or making a statement in an emotive and emphatic way (roughly translated as "the thing is that ..."). They are constructed by means of the nominalization marker and dependent noun **no** placed before a copulative form.

Expressions made through the explanatory copulae are very common in Japanese and are constantly used in the colloquial language.

➤ **V/na/i no {D}** のだ/です: Explanative Copula | *the thing is ~; it's because ~*

❖ It expresses that the speaker intends to explain something to the listener based on certain circumstances that are more or less known to both the speaker and the listener.

夕べ子供に泣かれてあまり眠れなかったんです: "(The thing is that) I couldn't sleep much last night because the kids were crying".

❖ It is also used to give an explanation or statement in an emotional way.

テニスが大好きなのです: "I love tennis".

➤ **V/na/i n {D}** のだ/です: [*col.*] Explanative Copula | *the thing is ~; it's because ~*

最近忙しくてあまり寝ていないんです: "I've been so busy lately that I haven't slept much".

➤ **V/na/i n da** んだ: [*col.*][*fam.*][*mas.*] Explanative Copula | *the thing is ~; it's because ~*

頭が痛いんだ: "My head hurts".

➤ **V/na/i no** の: [*col.*][*fam.*][*fem.*] Explanative Copula | *the thing is ~; it's because ~*

田中さんはフランスへ行ったの: "Tanaka went to France, you know".

4.2 Derivaciones de la partícula Koto

➤ **U koto ni suru** ことにする: Decisive Mood | *decide to ~*

タバコを止めることにしました: "I've decided to quit smoking".

➤ **U koto ni naru** ことになる: Passive Decisive Mood | *it has been decided that ~*

学校が金曜日八時に閉まることになりました: "(It has been decided that) The school will close at eight o'clock on Fridays".

➤ **U koto ga dekiru** ことができる: Potential Mood | *can ~; be able to ~*

マリアさんは日本語を話すことができます: "Maria can speak Japanese".

➤ **U koto ga aru** ことがある: Occasional Aspect | *there are times when ~; sometimes ~*

朝ご飯を食べないで学校へ行くことがある: "Sometimes I go to school without eating breakfast".

➤ **TA koto ga aru** ことがある: Experiential Aspect | *have/has (the experience of) ~*

アメリカへ行ったことがありますか: "Have you ever been to the United States?".

XIV. CORRELATIVE CONSTRUCTIONS

Correlative constructions are grammatical structures that are used to contrast or compare two phrases.

The most common correlative constructions in Japanese can be grouped into the following categories:

1. **Binary & Open Choices**: Expressing contrast of several elements from which one can be chosen.

2. **Comparison**: Expressing comparison of various elements.

2. **The Superlative**: Expressing the prominence of one element over others.

1. BINARY & OPEN CHOICES

Binary and open options convey a contrast between several verbal or nominal elements that appear as possible choices to be made by the subject.

Binary options are expressed by alternative coordinators that indicate the option to choose only one option among several. Open options are expressed by enumerative coordinators and indicate the option to choose or not to choose several options at the same time.

1.1 Alternative Coordinators

The constructions that fulfill an alternative coordinator function express that there is an option to choose between two options. These phrases are translated in English by the expression "do something or not". In Japanese, these constructions are made by means of the interrogative subordinator **ka**.

➤ **N/n/V/i ka dō ka** かどうか: Alternative Coordinator | *if/whether ~ or not*

授業に出席したかどうか聞いた: "He asked him if I attended class (or not)".

➤ **V/i ka ⟨A/ku⟩ nai ka** か...なかったか: Alternative Coordinator | *if/whether ~ or not*

❖ V/i and ⟨A/ku⟩ are the same verbal.

授業に出席したかしなかったか聞いた: "He asked him if I attended class (or not)".

➤ **V/i ka** か: Alternative Coordinator | *if/whether ~ (or not)*

❖ Reduction of the form **ka dō ka**, formally equivalent to the interrogative subordinator **ka** [☞ VIII.4.2].

授業に出席したか聞いた: "He asked him if I attended class (or not)".

+ More alternative coordinators in Expressing Yourself in Japanese [☞ EY.III.4.2].

1.2 Enumerative Coordinators

Structures acting as enumerative coordinators provide an inexhaustive list of actions from which two or three are representatively chosen and performed in alternation without any temporal order or causal relationship.

➢ **TA ri ... ⟨TA⟩ ri suru** り...りする: Enumerative Coordinator | *(do) things like/as ~ and/or ...*

今朝掃除をしたり買い物に行ったりした: "This morning I did some cleaning and went shopping". (Lit. "This morning I did things like cleaning and going shopping".)

➢ **U to ka ... ⟨U⟩ to ka suru** とか...とかする: Enumerative Coordinator | (do) **things like/as ~ and/or ...**

本を読むとか映画に行くとかします: "I read a book or go to a movie".

+ More enumerative coordinators in Expressing Yourself in Japanese [☞ EY:III.1.3]

2. COMPARISON

Comparative structures contrast two elements by expressing that one has a higher degree than the other ("something is more than...")—upper comparison—or an equal one ("something is as ... as")—equal comparison.

In Japanese, there are no inferiority structures ("something is less than...").

2.1 Upper Comparison

Structures that indicate that a nominal or verbal element has a greater degree of a characteristic or is done to a greater degree.

➢ **V/na/i^A no hō ga ⟨V/na/i⟩^{B} yori (mo) ⟨P⟩^{C}** ほうが...より... | A *is more* C than B

地下鉄で行くのほうがバスで行くより早いです [subway–by go–more bus–by go–than fast is]: "Taking the subway is faster than taking the bus".

➢ **V/na/i^A no hō ga ⟨P⟩^{C} のほうが...** | A *is more* C

あのコートのほうが高い: "That coat is more expensive".

➢ **N^A no hō ga* ⟨N⟩^{B} yori (mo) ⟨P⟩^{C}** ほうが...より... | A *is more* C than B

391

飛行機のほうが電車より早いです: "The plane is faster than the train".

♣ *The particle **ga** can be replaced by the accusative particle **o** when the comparison is a direct complement.

魚のほうを肉よりよく食べます: "I eat more fish than meat".

➤ **N^A no hō ga ⟨P⟩^C のほうが...** | **A is more C**

あのコートのほうが高い: "That coat is more expensive".

➤ **N^A wa/ga ⟨N⟩^B yori ⟨P⟩^C {は/が}...より...** | **A is more C than B**

今日は昨日より暑いです [today TOP yesterday–than hot is]: "Today it's hotter than yesterday".

➤ **N^A wa/ga motto ⟨P⟩^C {は/が}もっと...** | **A is more C**

あのコートはもっと高い: "That coat is more expensive".

➤ **N^A wa/ga ⟨N⟩^B hodo ⟨P⟩^C* {は/が}...ほど...** | **A is not as C as B**

♣ *A verbal in the negative form.

今日は昨日ほど暑くない: "Today is not as hot as yesterday".

+ More related constructions in Expressing Yourself in Japanese [☞ EY:4]

2.2 Equitative Comparison

Structures that put one nominal element on the same level as another.

N^A wa/ga/mo ⟨N⟩^B (mo) onaji kurai ⟨P⟩^C {は/が/も}...も同じくらい... | **A is as C as B**

水泳もテニスも同じくらい好き: "I like swimming as much as tennis".

2.3 Comparative Questions

Comparative structures used when formulating questions.

➤ **N^A to ⟨N⟩^B to dochira (no hō) ga ⟨P⟩^C と...とどちらのほうが...** | **among A and B which one is more C?**

このスカートとあれとどちら{のほうが}高いですか: "What's more expensive, this skirt or that one?".

➤ **V/na/i^A no to ⟨V/na/i⟩^B no to dochira (no hō) ga ⟨P⟩^C のと...のとどちらのほうが...** | **among A and B which one is more C?**

家で食事をすうるのと外で食事をするのとどちら{のほうが}楽しいと思いますか: "What do you think is more enjoyable, eating at home or eating out?".

3. THE SUPERLATIVE

Structures that indicate that an element has the highest qualifying degree within a group of elements with which it is compared.

3.1 Superlative Declarations

Superlative structures made as statements.

(N^A wa) (N^B de) ichiban P^C ...一番... | (A) *is the most C* (*in* B)

エベレストは世界で一番高い山です: "The Everest is the tallest mountain in the world"

(N^A wa) (N^B de) mottomo P^C ...最も... | (A) *is the most C* (*in* B)

私は最も速い走者です: "I'm the fastest runner".

3.2 Superlative Questions

Superlative structures used in questions.

(N^A to) (N^B no naka de) N* ga ichiban/mottomo P^C ...が{一番/最も}... |
[*among B*] [*and A*] *which one is the most C*

♣ *An interrogative pronoun.

ペットの中で何が一番好きですか: "What is your favorite pet?" (Lit. "Among pets, which one do you like the most?)

3.3 Sino-Japanese Superlatives

There are some adjectival nouns formed with the prefix **sai-** that are already an intrinsic superlative. The most common are the following:

最高 (*highest; best*) • 最低 (*lowest*) • 最良 (*best*) • 最悪 (*worst*)

XV. FORMALITY

Formality in Japanese refers to the various verb forms and specific vocabulary used in the formal, polite, honorific, and humble registers.

So far, we have already seen the polite forms [☞ VI.1], but in this section, we will look at verb forms for the honorific and humble registers.

1. HONORIFIC & HUMBLE INFLECTIONS

In very formal contexts, both honorific and humble registers are used when speaking to a person with a higher social position.

The honorific register is used when talking about that higher second person or respected third parties, while the humble register is used when talking about oneself.

Here we will deal with grammatical verbal forms, but one should remember that there are also some specific proper verbs that are used only within these registers. C.f. Vocabulary [☞ VO:IV.3].

1.1 Honorific Verbs Inflections

Although there are some specific honorific verbs [☞ VO:IV.3], any verb can be made honorific in three ways:

➤ o **I** ni naru お...になる

先生は晩ご飯をお食べになる: "The professor will eat dinner".

➤ go **VN** ni naru ご...になる

➤ Ⓢ**A** rareru られる

❖ Ending, identical to the passive form, used to make an honorific verb.

先生は晩ご飯を食べられる: "The professor will eat dinner".

➤ Ⓦ**A** reru れる

❖ Ending, identical to the passive form, used to make an honorific verb.

先生は日本のことを話された: "The professor spoke about Japan".

1.2 Humble Verbs Inflections

As with honorific verbs, there are also specific humble verbs and three different ways to make any verb humble.

➤ o VN/I kudasai お...ください: [*hon.*] Directive Mood | *please ~*

❖ It expresses a request in an honorific and very formal register.

少々　お待ちください: "Please wait".

2. ARCHAIC FORMS

There are some formulas or idioms in Japanese that use archaic honorific grammatical forms no longer used in any other context.

The most common archaic form is as follows:

➤ o I お: [*obs.*] Imperative Mood | *do ~*

❖ Archaic form reserved for some fossilized expressions of politeness.

お休み: "Good night". (Lit. "(you) Rest".)

EXPRESSING
YOURSELF
IN JAPANESE

EXPRESSING YOURSELF IN JAPANESE

In this part of the book, different ways of saying things in Japanese are presented from the perspective of the English meaning of the grammatical forms to be used in Japanese.

All grammatical forms are grouped according to the following categories:

I. **Aspect**: Different temporal expressions that describe the time in which the action of the verbal is performed or occurs.

II. **Voice**: Verbal voices indicating whether the subject receives or performs the verbal action.

III. **Coordination**: Consecutive syntactic relations between two clauses.

IV. **Subordination**: Dependent syntactic relations between two clauses.

V. **Word Class Transformation**: Ways to transform one word class into another.

VI. **Mood**: Verbal modalities that express the attitude of the speaker with respect to the verbal action or state.

VII. **Case**: Cases of nouns marked with particles that establish a semantic or syntactic relationship between the noun and another part of the phrase.

I. ASPECT

Events (actions or states) expressed by a verb or adjectival verb have to be placed somewhere within a timeline. This point in time alluded by the different verbal forms or inflections is called **Aspect**.

There are several types of aspects depending on the time frame that is taken into account. The most important ones are the following:

1. **Imperfective Aspects** [present]: They refer to actions or states that occur at the time of speech.

2. **Perfective Aspects** [past]: They refer to actions or states that have already occurred at the time of speech.

3. **Continuous Aspects** [ongoing]: They refer to actions or states that are evolving or ongoing at the time of speech.

4. **Non-Continuous Aspects** [during]: They refer to actions or states that occur at a specific point in time.

5. **Inchoative Aspects** [starting]: They refer to actions that begin to take place.

6. **Cessative Aspects** [ending]: They refer to actions that have been or are being completed.

1. IMPERFECTIVE ASPECTS

The imperfective aspects are used when one speaks of events that have not yet concluded at the moment of the speech. Transposed to English grammar, these aspects would be equivalent to the present and future tenses.

The items listed in this section default to the indicative mood [☞ VI.1.1]. See the next section to delve deeper into grammatical moods [☞ II].

Important Imperfective Aspects

1.1 **Imperfective Aspect**: It refers to actions or states that happen in the present time at the moment of speech.

Ⓕ [*fam.*] **U/i ø**

Ⓕ Ⓥ [*pol.*] **I** masu ます

Ⓕ Ⓐ [*pol.*] **i** desu です

• **Negative Imperfective Aspect** [*not; don't; doesn't*]: It refers to actions or states that are not occurring in the present time at the moment of speech.

Ⓕ [*fam.*] **A/ku** nai ない

Ⓕ Ⓥ [*pol.*] **I** masen ません

Ⓣ [*pol.*] **A/ku** nai desu ないです

1.2 Imperfective Copula [*am*; *is*; *arə*]: It refers to entities or things that exist in the present time at the moment of speech.

Ⓣ [*fam.*] **N/n** da だ

Ⓣ [*pol.*] **N/n** desu です

• **Negative Imperfective Copula** [*am not*; *isn't*; *arən't*]: It refers to entities or things that do not exist in the present time at the moment of speech.

Ⓣ [*lit.*] **N/n** de wa nai ではない

Ⓣ [*col.*][*fam.*] **N/n** ja nai じゃない

Ⓣ [*for.*][*pol.*] **N/n** de wa arimasen ではありません

Ⓣ [*col.*][*pol.*] **N/n** ja arimasen じゃありません

1.1 Imperfective Aspect

❖ It expresses an unfinished event occurring in either the present or future time.

Ⓣ Ⓥ [*fam.*] **U** ø

Ⓣ Ⓐ [*fam.*] **i** ø

Ⓣ Ⓥ [*pol.*] **I** masu ます

Ⓣ Ⓐ [*pol.*] **i** desu です

Ⓢ [*hon.*] **A** rareru られる

Ⓦ [*hon.*] **A** reru れる

Ⓛ [*for.*][*hon.*] o **I** ni naru お...になる 〔...に成る〕

❖ V.s that have pol. or hon. f.s will use these f.s instead of the plain ones.

[*for.*][*hon.*] o **I** nasaru お...なさる 〔...為さる〕

❖ In declarative sentences, the pol. f. nasaimasu has to be u. The plain imperfective f. nasaru is only u. in dependent clauses.

[*for.*][*hon.*] go **VN** nasaru ...なさる 〔為さる〕

❖ In declarative sentences, the pol. f. nasaimasu has to be u. The plain

imperfective f. nasaru is only u. in dependent clauses.

[*hum.*] o **I** suru する

❖ M. u. in the pol. f. shimasu.

[*for.*][*hum.*] o **I** itasu お...いたす 〔...致す〕

❖ M. u. in the pol. f. itashimasu.

[*for.*][*hum.*] go **VN** itasu ご...いたす 〔致す〕

❖ M. u. in the pol. f. itashimasu.

Negative Imperfective

don't ~; not ~

❖ It negates an unfinished event or quality occurring in either the present or future time.

Ⓣ Ⓥ [*fam.*] **A** nai ない

Ⓣ Ⓐ [*fam.*] **ku** nai ない

Ⓣ Ⓥ [*pol.*] **I** masen ません

Ⓣ Ⓥ [*pol.*] **A** nai desu ないです

Ⓣ Ⓐ [*pol.*] **ku** nai desu ないです

Ⓐ [*pol.*] **ku** (wa) arimasen はありません

Ⓦ [*col.*][*fam.*][*mas.*] **A** ん

Ⓥ [*lit.*] **A** zu ず

Ⓥ [*obs.*] **A** nu ぬ

❖ M. u. nowadays in fossilized set phrases.

Ⓥ [*obs.*] **A** zaru ざる

❖ M. u. nowadays in fossilized set phrases.

1.2 Imperfective Copula

> *am ~; are ~; is ~*

❖ It expresses the ongoing existence of the marked noun.

Ⓕ [*fam.*] **N/n** da だ

Ⓕ [*pol.*] **N/n** desu です

[*lit.*][*for.*] **N/n** de aru である

[*for.*] **N/n** de {p*} aru である

 ❖ *Focal p.s such as *wa; mo; shika or sae*

[*for.*][*pol.*][*obs.*] **N/n** de arimasu であります

Ⓛ [*for.*][*pol.*][*hum.*] **N/n** de gozaimasu でございます

[*obs.*] **N/n** nari なり

❖ Only u. to qualify s.t.

❖ M. u. nowadays in fossilized set phrases.

[*obs.*] **N/n** ari あり〔有り〕

❖ M. u. nowadays in fossilized set phrases.

Negative Imperfective Copula

> *am/are/is not ~; aren't ~; isn't ~*

❖ It negates the ongoing existence of the marked noun.

Ⓕ [*lit.*] **N/n** de wa nai ではない

➤ Ⓕ [*col.*][*fam.*] **N/n** ja nai じゃない

Ⓕ [*for.*][*pol.*] **N/n** de wa arimasen ではありません

➤ Ⓕ [*col.*][*pol.*] **N/n** ja arimasen じゃありません

[*for.*][*pol.*] **N/n** de wa nai desu ではないです

➤ [*col.*][*pol.*] **N/n** ja nai desu じゃないです

[*for.*][*pol.*][*hum.*] **N/n** de (wa) gozaimasen ではございません

2. PERFECTIVE ASPECTS

Perfective Aspects are used to indicate that the event has already concluded at the time of speech. In English grammar, this would be equivalent to the simple past tense.

Important Perfective Aspects

2.1 **Perfective Aspect** [~ed; *did*]: It refers to actions or states that have occurred in the past.

Ⓕ Ⓥ [fam.] **TA** ø

Ⓕ Ⓐ [fam.] **s** katta かった

Ⓕ Ⓥ [pol.] **I** mashita ました

Ⓕ Ⓐ [pol.] **s** katta desu かったです

• **Negative Perfective Aspect** [*didn't*]: It refers to actions or states that have not occurred in the past.

Ⓣ [*fam.*] **A/ku** nakatta なかった

Ⓣ Ⓥ [*pol.*] **I** masen deshita ませんでした

Ⓣ Ⓐ [*pol.*] **ku** nakatta arimasen deshita なかったありませんでした

Ⓣ Ⓥ [*pol.*] **A/ku** nakatta desu なかったです

2.2 Perfective Copula [*was*; *were*]: It refers to entities or things that have existed or that have been so in the past.

Ⓣ [*fam.*] **N/n** datta だった

Ⓣ [*pol.*] **N/n** deshita でした

• **Negative Perfective Copula** [*wasn't*; *weren't*]: It refers to entities or things that have not existed or that have not been so in the past.

Ⓣ [*lit.*] **N/n** de wa nakatta ではなかった

Ⓣ [*col.*][*fam.*] **N/n** ja nakatta じゃなかった

Ⓣ [*for.*][*pol.*] **N/n** de wa arimasen deshita ではありませんでした

Ⓣ [*col.*][*pol.*] **N/n** ja arimasen deshita じゃありませんでした

2.6 Experiential Aspect [*have ~ed*; *has ~ed*]: It refers to actions that the speaker has the experience of having performed sometime in the past.

Ⓣ **TA** koto ga aru ことがある

- -

2.1 Perfective Aspect

~ed; did ~

❖ It expresses an event or quality occurring in the past that is understood as if it had already finished.

Ⓣ Ⓥ [*fam.*] **TA** ø

Ⓣ Ⓐ [*fam.*] **s** katta かった

Ⓣ Ⓥ [*pol.*] **I** mashita ました

Ⓣ Ⓐ [*pol.*] **s** katta desu かったです

Negative Perfective

didn't ~; hasn't/haven't ~

❖ It negates an event or quality occurring in the past.

Ⓣ Ⓥ [*fam.*] **A** nakatta なかった

Ⓣ Ⓐ [*fam.*] **ku** nakatta なかった

Ⓣ Ⓥ [*pol.*] **I** masen deshita ませんでした

Ⓣ Ⓐ [*pol.*] **ku** nakatta arimasen deshita なかったありませんでした

Ⓣ Ⓥ [*pol.*] **A** nakatta desu なかったです

Ⓣ Ⓐ [*pol.*] **ku** nakatta desu なかったです

2.2 Perfective Copula

was ~; were ~

❖ It expresses the past existence of the marked noun.

Ⓣ [*fam.*] **N/n** datta だった

Ⓣ [*pol.*] **N/n** deshita でした

[*lit.*] **N/n** de atta であった

401

[*for.*][*pol.*][*obs.*] **N/n** de arimashita であ
りました

[*for.*][*pol.*][*hum.*] **N/n** de gozaimashita
でございました

Negative Perfective Copula

wasn't ~; weren't ~

❖ It negates the past existence of the
marked noun.

Ⓕ [*lit.*] **N/n** de wa nakatta ではなかった

➤ Ⓕ [*col.*][*fam.*] **N/n** ja nakatta じゃな
かった

Ⓕ [*for.*][*pol.*] **N/n** de wa arimasen
deshita ではありませんでした

➤ Ⓕ [*col.*][*pol.*] **N/n** ja arimasen deshita
じゃありませんでした

[*for.*][*pol.*] **N/n** de wa nakatta desu ではな
かったです

➤ [*col.*][*pol.*] **N/n** ja nakatta desu じゃな
かったです

[*for.*][*pol.*][*hon.*] **N/n** de gozaimasen
deshita でございませんでした

2.3 Recent Perfective Aspect

have just ~(-ed); just ~(-ed)

❖ It indicates that something is freshly or
recently done.

⊕ **TA** tokoro {D} ところだ/です

➤ [*fam.*] **TA** tokoro ところ

➤ [*col.*][*fam.*] **TA** toko ({D}) とこだ/です

⊕ **TA** bakari {D} ばかりだ/です〔計り〕

❖ It indicates that the action has been
performed very recently.

➤ [*fam.*] **TA** bakari ばかり〔計り〕

2.4 Recent Perfective Copula

(is) just/newly/freshly ~(-ed)

❖ It indicates that something is freshly or
recently done.

I tate {D} たてだ/です〔立て〕

2.5 Preparatory Perfective Aspect

*~ in advance; ~ ahead; ~
beforehand*

❖ It expresses the something is done
beforehand for future convenience.

⊕ **TE** oku おく〔置く〕

➤ [*col.*][*fam.*] Toku とく

❖ For v.s whose gerundive f. ends in -**te**.

➤ [*col.*][*fam.*] Doku どく

❖ For v.s whose gerundive f. ends in -**de**.

2.6 Experiential Aspect

have ~; has ~

❖ It expresses that someone has the
experience of having done something at
least once.

Ⓕ **TA** koto ga aru ことがある

3. CONTINUOUS ASPECTS

Continuous aspects are used to talk about events that are not only taking place at the
moment of the speech but are also prolonged in time into the future, that is, they *continue*
to take place.

Important Continuous Aspects

3.1 Progressive Aspect [*bə ~ing*]: It refers to actions that are ongoing at the moment of speech.

    Ⓕ **TE iru** いる

- **Continuous Progressive Aspect** [*keep on*]: It refers to actions that are ongoing in the present and whose realization extends also into the future.

    ⊕ **TE iku** いく

- **Translative Progressive Aspect** [*been ~ing*]: It refers to actions that were started before the moment of speech but are still ongoing and changing at that moment of speech.

    ⊕ **TE kuru** いる

3.2 Continuative Aspect [*keep on*]: It refers to the continuation of an action.

    ⊕ **I tsudzukeru** 続ける

3.3 Stative Aspect [*have been ~əd; has been ~əd*]: It refers to ongoing states arisen by actions that were started in the past and whose result is palpable at the moment of speech.

    Ⓕ **TE aru** ある

    Ⓕ [*pol.*] **N/n deshita** でした

- **Continuous Stative Aspect** [*bə ~əd*]: It refers to ongoing states caused by a past action.

    Ⓕ **TE iru** いる

- **Progressive Stative Aspect** [*as it is*]: It refers to actions or states that remain unchanged at the time of speech.

    ⊕ **TA/na/no/i mama** (de/ni) ままで/に

- **Benefactive Stative Aspect** [*lət*]: It refers to states or actions whose continuation is allowed.

    ⊕ **TE oku** おく

- -

3.1 Progressive Aspect

bə ~ing

❖ It expresses that an action or state that began in the past is ongoing at the moment of speech.

Ⓕ **TE iru** いる

➤ [*col.*] **TE ru** る

[*for.*] **I tsutsu aru** つつある

    ❖ Not u. w. transitive v.s. that express everyday actions.

[*hum.*] **TE oru** おる

[*hon.*] **TE irassharu** いらっしゃる

Continuous Progressive

getting ~; getting to ~; go on ~; keep on ~; continue to ~

❖ It indicates that an action or state continues to change at the time of speech and that the change process is extended into the future.

⊕ **TE iku** いく〔行く〕

➤ [*col.*] **TE ku** く

Translative Progressive

been ~ing up to now; have ~ed up to now; come to ~

❖ It indicates that some action has continued in a process of some change up to the time of speech.

⊕ **TE kuru** くる〔来る〕

Egressive Progressive

have been ~ing; remain ~ing; leave ~ing

❖ It expresses that a state has been left ongoing since the past.

㊤ **I ppanashi {D}** っぱなし*だ/です*

  ❖ U. w. transitive v.s.

➤ [*col.*] **I ppa** っぱ

Lower Limitative Progressive

be only ~ing; be doing nothing but ~ing

㊤ **TE bakari iru** ばかりいる

na/i bakari {D} ばかり*だ/です*

Emphatic Progressive

is in fact ~ing

TE wa iru はいる

Simultaneous Progressive

~ing; while ~

❖ It indicates that an action takes place, in a progressive way, during the time that the action expressed by the marked verb occurs.

[*for.*] **I tsutsu** つつ

3.2 Continuative Aspect

keep on ~; continue to ~

❖ It expresses that an ongoing event or action extends indefinitely in time.

⊕ **I tsudzukeru** 続ける

I tsudzuke {D} 続け*だ/です*

㊤ **I ppanashi {D}** っぱなし*だ/です*

❖ U. w. intransitive v.s.

➤ [*col.*] **I ppa** っぱ

Protractive Continuative

~ continuously; ~ throughly; ~ on and on

❖ It expresses that something is done recursively for a long time until some satisfactory state is met.

㊤ **I komu** 込む

Exclusive Continuative

only ~; always ~; continue(s) to ~; ~ more and more

❖ It expresses that something is continuously done as the only option left.

㊤ **U ippō {D}** 一方*だ/です*

3.3 Stative Aspect

have/has been ~; be ~ed

❖ It indicates that an event has occurred and that the state resulting from that event remains in place.

㊦ **TE aru** ある ❖ U. w. transitive v.s.

Continuous Stative

be ~ed; have/has ~ed

❖ It expresses that someone or something is in a state initiated by a previous action.

Ⓣ **TE** iru いる

➤ [*col.*] **TE** ru る

Progressive Stative

. *~ as it is; remains ~; still ~; staying ~*

❖ It expresses that a state or action remains unchanged at the time of speech.

⊕ **TA/na/no/i** mama (de/ni) ままで/に

[*lit.*] **TA** nari (de) なりで

Preparatory Stative

leave ~ed

❖ It expresses that an action or state is deliberatively left to continue in the future.

⊕ **TE** oku おく〔置く〕

➤ [*col.*][*fam.*] Toku とく

   ❖ For v.s whose gerundive f. ends in -**te**.

➤ [*col.*][*fam.*] Doku どく

   ❖ For v.s whose gerundive f. ends in -**de**.

Benefactive Stative

let ~

❖ It expresses that someone is allowed to remain in a certain state.

⊕ **TE** oku おく〔置く〕

   ❖ U. w. causative v.s.

➤ [*col.*][*fam.*] TOKU とく

   ❖ For v.s whose gerundive f. ends in -**te**.

➤ [*col.*][*fam.*] DOKU どく

   ❖ For v.s whose gerundive f. ends in -**de**.

3.4 Frequentative Aspect

usually ~; ~ all the time

❖ It expresses that the subject of the sentence habitually or frequently does an action.

⊕ **TE** iru いる

➤ [*col.*] **TE** ru る

3.5 Iterative Aspect

to ~ again; to ~ over

❖ It expresses that an action is performed one more time so that the result is better than the previous one.

⊕ **I** naosu なおす〔直す〕

3.6 Reiterative Aspect

to ~ again; to ~ back

❖ It expresses that an action is repeated.

I kaesu 返す

I kaeru 替える

   ❖ It hans the sense that something is done again from scratch.

Continuous Reiterative

to ~ over and over again; to ~ relentlessly

❖ It expresses that an action is performed repeatedly and indefinitely.

I makuru まくる〔捲る〕

---

4. NON-CONTINUOUS ASPECTS

Non-continuous aspects are used to express that a particular action is performed during a limited period of time. Continuous aspects are technically a subgroup of imperfective aspects.

Important Non-Continuous Aspects

4.1 Punctual Aspect [*when*]: It refers to the specific moment when an action is performed.

ⓉV/na/no/i toki (ni) ときに

- **Approximative Punctual Aspect** [*around the time when*]: It refers to an approximate moment when an action is performed.

⊕ **V/i** koro ころ

4.2 Durative Aspect [*while*; *during (the time when)*]: It refers to a period of time during which an action is performed.

⊕ **U/na/no/i** aida (ni) 間に

- **Simultaneous Durative Aspect** [*while*; *(at the same time) as*]: It refers to an action that is performed at the time during which another action is also performed.

⊕ **I** nagara ながら

4.3 Occasional Aspect [*there are times when*]: It indicates that an action is performed occasionally.

⊕ **U/na/no/i** koto ga aru ことがある

4.1 Punctual Aspect

when ~; on the occasion of ~; at the time of/when ~

❖ It indicates that something happens at the specific moment when the action marked by the verb is performed.

Ⓣ **V/na/no/i** toki (ni) ときに〔時〕

Ⓔ [*for.*] **U/i** tokoro ところ

❖ U. to mark an action after which a non deliberate action or state occurs.

V/na/no/i tokoro {p*} ところで

❖ *Case p.s such as o, ni, e or de.

Ⓔ [*for.*] **V/no** sai (ni) 際に

[*for.*] **VN/U** ni atatte に当たって

➤ [*lit.*] **VN/U** ni atari に当たり

[*for.*] **VN/U** ni sai shite (wa) に際しては

[*for.*] **V/no** ori ni 折に

❖ M. u. when the occasion is desirable and special.

➤ [*lit.*] **I** nagara ni shite ながらにして

Approximative Punctual

around the time when ~

❖ It expresses that something happens approximately at the moment when the action marked by the verb is performed.

⊕ **V/no/i** koro ころ〔頃〕

Evidential Punctual

upon realizing that ~; once one notices that ~; as soon as one notices that ~

V/na/i to miru to/ya とみる{と/や}

V/i ka to omou to かと思うと

V/i ka to omoeba かと思えば

V/i ka to omotta ra かと思ったら

4.2 Durative Aspect

while ~; during (the time when) ~

❖ It expresses that the action of the predicate occurs during the time in which the action indicated by the marked verb is performed.

⊕ **U/na/no/i** aida (ni) 間に

ℒ **U/na/no/i** uchi ni うちに〔内〕

❖ Usually indicating a period of time that has to be made a good use of, or an action that happens spontaneously while the marked action develops.

➤ **I** no uchi ni のうちに

ℒ **TE** iru saichuu ni いる最中に

Simultaneous Durative

at the same time as ~; as ~; while ~

❖ It expresses that the action of the predicate is carried out simultaneously with the action indicated by the marked verb. Both actions are done by the same subject.

⊕ **I** nagara (ni) ながらに

[*for.*] **VN/U** to dōji ni と同時に

[*for.*] **VN** katagata かたがた

[*lit.*] **U/no** katawara かたはら〔傍ら〕

[*lit.*] **VN/U** to tomo ni と共に

VN/I gatera がてら

Intrative Durative

in the midst/middle of ~(ing); while ~

ℒ **VN** chuu 中

ℒ **U*/no** saichuu ni 最中に

❖ *The progressive f.s **TE** iru.

ℒ **U/no** tochuu de/ni 途中{で/に}

U/na/i naka o 中を

U/na/i naka de (wa) 中では は

Causative Durative

while ~; as ~; since ~

❖ It expresses that a second action is carried out at the same time as a first action, the first action being a cause to be taken as an opportunity.

ℒ **VN/I/n/no/V/s/i** tsuide ni ついでに〔次いでに〕

Punctual Durative

by the time ~

⊕ **U** made ni までに

Distributive Durative

every time (that) ~; whenever ~

ℒ **U** tabi ni たびに〔度に〕

U goto ni ごとに〔毎に〕

[*for.*] **VN/U** ni tsukete (mo) につけても〔に付けて〕

➤ [*for.*] **VN/U** ni tsuke につけ

Limitative Durative

as long as ~; as ~; as far as ~; while ~

❖ It expresses that the action or state of the predicate occurs as long as the marked action lasts.

U aida wa 間は

U uchi wa うちは〔内は〕

V kara ni wa からには

V ijō (wa) 以上は

Translative Durative

as ~

✤ It expresses that the action indicated by the marked verb occurs simultaneously with the action of the predicate which, in turn, progressively changes.

⊕ **VN/V ni tsurete** につれて

➣ [*for.*] **VN/V ni tsure** につれ

[*for.*] **VN/U ni tomonatte** に伴って

➣ **VN/U ni tomonai** に伴い

⊕ [*lit.*] **U ni shiitagatte** に従って

5. INCHOATIVE ASPECTS

Aspects that refer to the beginning of an action or actions performed before the beginning of an action.

Important Inchoative Aspects

5.1 **Antessive Aspect** [*before*]: It refers to the time before an action begins.

⊤ **U mae ni** 前に

5.2 **Prospective Aspect** [*about to*]: It indicates that an action is about to begin.

⊕ **U tokoro {D}** ところだ/です

6.3 **Inceptive Aspect** [*start to*]: It refers to the beginning of an action.

⊕ **I hajimeru** 始める

• **Non-Intentional Inceptive Aspect** [*start to*]: It refers to the unintentional beginning of an action.

⊕ **I dasu** だす

• **Resultative Inceptive Aspect** [*been ~ing*]: It refers to the beginning of an action as a result of a transformative process.

⊕ **TE kuru** くる

• **Deflective Inceptive Aspect** [*almost*]: It refers to an action that is almost done.

⊕ [*fam.*] **U tokoro datta** ところだった

⊕ [*pol.*] **U tokoro deshita** ところでした

⊕ **I kakeru** かける

➣ [*lit.*] **U ni shitagai** に従い

4.3 Occasional Aspect

there are times when ~; sometimes ~

✤ It expresses that an action is performed occasionally.

⊕ **U/na/no/i koto ga aru** ことがある

5.1 Antessive Aspect

before ~; prior to ~

✤ It indicates that the action of the predicate is performed before the action expressed by the marked verb.

⑤ **U** mae ni 前に

⑥ **A** nai uchi ni ないうちに〔ない内に〕

❖ It indicates that the marked action is uncontrollable and that the action of the second clause has to be done before that marked action starts.

[*for.*] **VN/U** ni atatte に当たって

➤ [*lit.*] **VN/U** ni atari に当たり

[*for.*] **VN/U** magiwa (ni) 間際に: *just before* ~

5.2 Prospective Aspect

> *(to be) about to* ~

❖ It refers to an action that is about to be done in the near future.

⊕ **U** tokoro {D} ところだ/です

➤ [*col.*][*fam.*] **TA** toko ({D}) とこだ/です

⑥ **Ō** to suru とする

[*lit.*] **A** n to suru んとする

I kakaru かかる〔掛かる〕

6.3 Inceptive Aspect

> *start to* ~; *begin to* ~

❖ It refers to an action that begins to be carried out at the moment of speech.

⊕ **I** hajimeru 始める

Non-Intentional Inceptive

> *start to* ~; *begin to* ~; *begin* ~*ing*

❖ It expresses that an action begins without the volition of someone being involved.

⊕ **I** dasu だす〔出す〕

Punctual Inceptive

> *as soon as* ~; *soon after* ~; *when* ~; *the moment* ~

❖ It expresses that an action begins to be performed just after the action defined by the marked verb has also started.

⑥ **TA** totan (ni) 途端に

VN/I shidai (ni) 次第に

V soba kara そばから〔傍から〕

TA ra sugu らすぐ

U nari なり

U ga hayai ka が早いか

U ka ⟨**A**⟩ nai ka no uchi ni かないかのうちに

[*for.*] **U** ya ina ya やいなや〔や否や〕

➤ **U** ya

Resultative Inceptive

> *been* ~*ing up to now*; *have* ~*ed up to now*; *come to* ~; *get* ~*ed*

❖ It expresses that an action begins as the result of a long transformative process.

⊕ **TE** kuru くる〔来る〕

Deflective Inceptive

> *almost* ~

❖ It expresses that an action has almost started to be carried out.

⊕ **U** tokoro {D*} ところ

❖ *In the perfective f.s datta or deshita.

⑥ **I** kakeru かける〔掛ける〕

I sō ni naru そうになる

6. CESSATIVE ASPECTS

Aspects that refer to the ending of an action or the beginning of an action once another action has already ended.

Important Cessative Aspects

6.1 **Terminative Aspect** [*finish*]: It refers to the completion of an action.

⊕ **I** owaru 終わる

6.2 **Postessive Aspect** [*after*]: It refers to the time after the completion of an action.

⊕ **TA** ato (de/ni) 後で/に

⊕ **TA** ra ら

6.4 **Limitative Aspect** [*until*]: It refers to an action that is set as a time limit.

⊤ **U** made まで

6.5 **Resultative Aspect** [*come to*]: It refers to an action understood as the result of another action.

⊕ **U/na/i** koto ni naru ことになる

⊕ **U** yō ni naru ようになる

⊕ **ku** naru なる

6.6 **Resultative Copula** [*become*]: It refers to the transformation into a state, thing, or entity.

⊤ **N/n/C** ni naru になる

6.1 Terminative Aspect

to finish ~

✤ It indicates that an action is finished.

⊕ **I** owaru 終わる

Active Terminative

to finish ~

✤ It indicates that someone finishes doing an action.

⊕ **I** ageru 上げる

✤ M. u. in the perfective f. ageta.

Passive Terminative

to finish ~; to end ~

✤ It indicates that an action has been completed by someone.

⊕ **I** agaru 上がる

✤ M. u. in the perfective f. agatta.

Complete Terminative

to have (finished) ~

❖ It denotes that an action has been fully completed.

⊕ **TE shimau** しまう

➤ [col.][mas.] CHimau ちまう

❖ For verbs whose gerundive f. ends in **-te**.

➤ [col.] CHau ちゃう

➤ [col.][mas.] Jimau じまう

❖ For verbs whose gerundive f. ends in **-de**.

➤ [col.] Jau じゃう

Deflective Terminative

start to ~ (and not finish); half ~; not yet ~

❖ It expresses that an action has started but has left undone.

Ⓔ **VN/I kakeru** かける〔掛ける〕

Ⓔ **VN/I kake {D}** かけだ/です〔掛け〕

VN/I gake {D} かけだ/です〔掛け〕

6.2 Postessive Aspect

after ~

❖ It indicates that an action is performed after another action has been already finished.

⊕ **TA ato (de/ni)** 後で/に

⊕ **TA ra** ら

❖ U. to point when an action not controlled by the subject occurs after the subject performs another action.

Ⓔ **TE kara** から

❖ It focuses in the sequential order.

[lit.] **TA nochi ni** の後に

TA sue (ni) 末に: *at the end of ~*

Prospective Postessive

after ~

❖ It introduces a preparatory action as a precedent for a relatively important event.

Ⓔ **TA ue de** 上で

➤ **VN no ue de** 上で

Resultative Postessive

after ~; finally ~; in the end ~; as a result of ~

❖ It expresses that some action is done as a result of a previous action or event that has been prolonged in time.

Ⓔ **TA ageku (ni)** あげくに

Ⓔ **TA/no kekka** 結果

Limitative Postessive

only after ~; not until ~; ~ for the first time

❖ It indicates that an action is performed, for the first time, only after another action has ended.

Ⓔ **TE hajimete** 始めて

6.3 Egressive Aspect

since ~

❖ It indicates that an action is performed from the moment the action expressed by the marked verb was carried out.

Ⓔ **TE kara** から

Ⓔ **TA kiri** きり

➤ [col.] **TA kkiri** っきり

[for.] **TE irai** 以来

Causal Egressive

since ~; now that ~

❖ It indicates that an action is performed from the moment in which the action expressed by the marked verb was carried out and also that this action is the cause of the former.

Ⓛ **TE** kara から

U ue wa 上は

TA tokoro de ところで

6.4 Limitative Aspect

until ~

♣ Aspect that indicates that the action of the predicate is performed until the marked action is carried out.

Ⓕ **U** made まで

6.5 Resultative Aspect

end up ~ ; come to ~; become able to ~

♣ It expresses that the marked verb is the result of the action indicated by the predicate.

⊕ **U/na/i** koto ni naru ことになる 〔事になる〕

⊕ **U** yō ni naru ようになる 〔様になる〕

⊕ **ku** naru なる

U hame ni naru 羽目になる

  ♣ U. when the result is unpleasant.

I tsuku つく 〔付く〕 : *become ~ed*

I dzuku づく 〔付く〕 : *become ~ed*

Negative Resultative

not ~ anymore

A/ku naku naru なくなる

➤ **N/n** de wa naku naru ではなくなる

  ➤ [*col.*] **N/n** ja naku naru じゃなくなる

6.6 Resultative Copula

become ~; turn into ~

♣ It expresses that the implicit or explicit subject of the sentence is transformed into the entity or state indicated by the marked noun or adjective.

Ⓕ **N/n/C** ni naru になる

[*lit.*] **N/n** to naru になる

II. VOICE

The grammatical voice describes the relationship that the action or the state marked by the verb has with the participants in it, that is, the subjects or objects of the sentence.

In Japanese, there are three main grammatical voices:

1. **Active Voice**: It refers to actions in which the doer is the subject of the sentence.
2. **Passive Voice**: It refers to actions in which the object of the verb is the subject of the sentence.
3. **Causative Voice**: It refers to actions that the subject of the sentence has been caused to do.

1. ACTIVE VOICE

The active voice indicates that the subject of the sentence is the agent (doer) of the action or state marked by the verb. Every verb is by default in the active voice unless it is expressly stated that it is in a passive or causative form [☞ II.2-3].

2. PASSIVE VOICE

The passive voice indicates that the subject of the sentence is the patient of the action or state marked by the verb, that is, that the subject is the one who undergoes or experiences said action or state, which is caused by an agent who is not the subject. In Japanese, the passive voice is marked by the inflection of the passive voice [☞ GE:VI.2.1].

2.1 Passive Voice Form

be ~ed; get ~ed

❖ It describes that the marked action is not performed by the subject of the sentence but occurs to him or her through the agency of another person or thing.

中 Ⓢ **A** rareru られる

中 Ⓦ **A** reru れる

3. CAUSATIVE VOICE

The causative voice indicates that the subject of the sentence causes someone or something to perform the action marked by the verb [☞ GE:VI.2.2] or that someone or something is the patient who is provoked to perform the action marked by the verb [☞ GE:VI.2.3].

3.1 Causative Voice Form

make s.o./s.t. ~; cause s.o./s.t. to ~

❖ It indicates that someone or something causes the subject to perform the marked action.

㊉ Ⓢ **A** saseru させる

㊉ Ⓦ **A** seru せる

㊉ **n** ni suru にする

㊉ **ku** suru する

Ⓢ **A** sasu さす

　❖ Regional or vulgar variant.

Ⓦ **A** su す

　❖ Regional or vulgar variant.

Permissive Causative Voice

let s.o./s.t. ~; allow s.o./s.t. to ~

❖ It indicates that someone or something causes the subject to perform the marked action.

㊉ Ⓢ **A** saseru させる

㊉ Ⓦ **A** seru せる

Passive Causative Voice

be made to ~

㊉ Ⓢ **A** saserareru させられる

㊉ Ⓦ **A** serareru せられる

III. COORDINATION

Coordination refers to the syntactic arrangement of sentences by which two clauses follow each other.

The main types of coordination are as follows:

1. **Conjunctive Coordination** [*and*]: It refers to a consecutive union of two clauses.

2. **Cumulative Coordination** [*also*]: It refers to the sum of two clauses, indicating simultaneity.

3. **Adversative Coordination** [*but*]: It refers to a contrast or contraposition between two clauses.

4. **Disjunctive Coordination** [*or*]: It refers to the availability of a choice between two clauses.

1. CONJUNCTIVE COORDINATION

Conjunctive coordination refers to the union of two clauses in a consecutive manner, expressed in English by the conjunction *and*.

Important Conjunctive Coordinators

1.1 **Conjunctive Coordinator** [*and*]: It joins two clauses.

Ⓣ Ⓥ **TE** ø

Ⓣ Ⓐ **ku te** て

⊕ **V/i shi** し

1.2 **Privative Coordinator** [*without*]: It refers to actions that are performed without performing another action.

Ⓣ [*fam.*] **A nai de** ないで

⊕ **A zu ni** ずに

1.3 **Enumerative Coordinator** [*and (things like)*]: It joins two actions understood as being within an inexhaustible list of actions.

Ⓣ **TA ri ⟨TA⟩ ri** (suru) り...りする

⊕ **U to ka ⟨U⟩ to ka** (suru) とか...とかする

1.1 **Conjunctive Coordinator**   ~ *and*

415

✤ It expresses that an action or state is performed or occurs and then another implicit or explicit action or state is subsequently introduced.

ⓕ Ⓥ TE ∅

❖ Referring to consecutive actions.

ⓕ Ⓐ ku te て

Ⓝ N/n de で

⊕ V/i shi し

❖ Putting the emphasis on the conjunction itself.

➤ N/n {D} shi し

Ⓥ I ∅

Ⓐ [*lit.*] ku

[*lit.*][*for.*] N/n de atte であって

Ⓝ [*lit.*] N/n de ari

[*for.*][*pol.*][*obs.*] N/n de arimashite でありまして

[*for.*] N/n ni shite にして

[*for.*][*pol.*] I mashite まして

Negative Conjunctive

not ~ and

✤ It expresses that an action or state is not performed or not occurring and then another action or state happens or not (depending on the polarity of that action).

A/ku nakute なくて

❖ U. to express causes or conditions.

A nai de ないで

N/n de (wa) nakute ではなくて

➤ [col.] N/n ja nakute じゃなくて

[lit.][for.] N/n de (wa) naku ではなく

[*lit.*] ku naku なく

Thematic Conjunctive

(only) ~ and

✤ It indicates that an action is performed and then another or the same action is also performed, being that first action the main topic of the discourse in the sense that it conveys a certain emotional emphasis, occasionally implicitly indicating a certain degree of repetition.

TE wa は

➤ [col.] cha ちゃ

❖ For verbs whose gerundive f. ends in -te

➤ [col.] ja じゃ

❖ For verbs whose gerundive f. ends in -de

N/n de wa では

Emphatic Conjunctive

now that ~; ~ and then; only after ~

✤ It refers to the fact that an action is carried out specifically in a way that is consecutive to the marked action.

TE koso こそ

Cumulative Conjunctive

both ~ and ...; neither ~ nor ...

VN/I mo ⟨VN/I⟩ mo suru も...もする

N/ku mo ⟨N/ku⟩ mo aru も...もある

N/n de mo ⟨N/n⟩ de mo aru でも...でもある

1.2 Privative Coordinator

without ~ing

✤ It expresses that the action of the predicate is carried out without the occurrence of the marked action.

ⓕ [*fam.*] A nai de ないで

[*lit.*][*for.*] N/n de wa naku なく

ⓙ [*for.*] A zu ni ずに

❖ The v. suru takes the f. sezu.

[*for.*] **A** zu shite ずして

❧ The v. **suru** takes the f. sezu.

[*for.*] **U** koto nashi de (wa) ことなしでは

[*for.*] **U** koto nashi ni (wa) ことなしには

[*for.*] **U** koto naku shite (wa) ことなくでは

VN ni yorazu によらず

Concessive Privative

even without ~ing; without even ~ing; even if not ~

A/ku nai de mo ないでも

A/ku nakute mo なくても

➚ **N/n** de wa nakute mo ではなくても

➚ [*col.*] **N/n** ja nakute mo じゃなくても

[*for.*] **A** zu to mo ずとも

➚ [*for.*] **N/n** nara zu to mo ならずとも

I mo shinai de もしないで

U koto (mo) naku こともなく: *without ~ing even once*

1.3 Enumerative Coordinator

(do) things like/as ~ and/or ...

❧ It introduces an inexhaustive list of actions or states.

Ⓣ **TA** ri ... ⟨**TA**⟩ ri (suru) り...りする

Ⓤ **U** to ka ... ⟨**U**⟩ to ka (suru) とか...とかする

V/n/i da no ... ⟨**V/n/i**⟩ da no to だの...だのと

U/n/i yara ... ⟨**U/n/i**⟩ yara

➚ **V/na/i** no yara ... ⟨**V/na/i**⟩ no yara

Alternative Enumerative

~ or (things like) ...

❧ It presents two choices as examples of an implicitly larger group of things.

Ⓣ **TA** ri ⟨**TA**⟩ ri (suru) り...りする

N/U nari ⟨**N/U**⟩ nari なり

Cumulative Enumerative

sometimes ~ and sometimes ~; may ~ or may ...; there are times when ~ and/or ...

❧ It expresses examples of two actions that may be performed alternately but are both equally feasible.

Ⓖ **VN/I** mo sureba ⟨**VN/I**⟩ mo suru もすれば...もする

U mo suru shi ⟨**U**⟩ mo suru もするし...もする

ku mo nareba ⟨**ku**⟩ mo naru もなれば...もなる

N mo areba ⟨**N**⟩ no mo aru もあれば...もある

➚ **n/i** no mo areba ⟨**n/i**⟩ no mo aru のもあれば...のもある

1.4 Lower Limitative Coordinator

just ~ing/to ~ (and)

❧ It indicates that only the marked action or state is performed or occurring.

Ⓖ **U/na/i** bakari de ばかりで

V/na/i dake de だけで

[*for.*] **VN/U** da ni だに

❧ Usually associated w. neg. impressions.

Negative Lower Limitative

not only ~ (but also/either)

❧ It indicates that not only the marked action or state is performed or occurring but also another one.

ⓔ **V/na/i** bakari de (wa) naku ばかりでは なく

➤ [*col.*] **V/na/i** bakari ja naku だけじゃ なく

V/na/i bakari ka ばかりか

U/n/na/i dokoro ka どころか

V/na/i dake de (wa) naku だけではなく

➤ [*col.*] **V/na/i** dake ja naku だけじゃな く

[*for.*] **V/na/i** nomi narazu のみならず

[*for.*] **V/na/i** nomi ka のみか

2. CUMULATIVE COORDINATION

Cumulative coordination refers to the union of two clauses by means of addition, expressed in English with the conjunctions *too* or *also*.

2.1 Cumulative Coordinator

(… and) also ~; (… and) either ~

❖ It presents a clause as a simultaneous addition to a previous clause.

VN/I mo suru もする

TA ri mo suru もする

N/n de mo aru でもある

ⓔ **N(p)** mo ⟨BA⟩ ⟨**N(p)**⟩ mo ⟨V⟩ も…も

❖ ⟨BA⟩ & ⟨V⟩ are the same v.

N mo ⟨U⟩ shi ⟨**N**⟩ mo ⟨V⟩ し…も

N mo ⟨s⟩ kereba ⟨**N**⟩ mo ⟨i⟩ も…ければ… も

N¹ mo ⟨**N/n**⟩ nara ⟨**N²**⟩ mo ⟨**N/n**⟩ {D} も…なら…だ/です

Emphatic Cumulative

~ as well; ~ in addition; ~ besides; ~ moreover; not only ~ but also

❖ It introduces a clause that is understood as an addition to the previous clause made in an emotional way.

V/na/no/i ue (ni) 上に

Contrastive Cumulative

~ on the other hand; ~ as well as; while ~, also

❖ It expresses that the marked action or state occurs while it is being compared with another action or state that also occurs.

ⓔ **V/na/no/i** ippō de 一方で

U/na/i hanmen 反面

3. ADVERSATIVE COORDINATION

Adverse coordination refers to the consecution of clauses through contrast, expressed in English by the conjunctions *but* or *however*.

Important Adversative Coordinators

3.1 **Adversative Coordinator** [*but*]: It contrasts two clauses.

ⓕ **V/i** ga が

Ⓕ [*for.*] **V/i** keredomo けれども

Ⓕ [*col.*] **V/i** kedo けど

3.2 Concessive Coordinator [*even though*]: It contrasts two clauses in an unexpected way.

⊕ **V/na/i** no ni のに

- -

3.1 Adversative Coordinator

~ but; ~ however

❖ It introduces an action or state upon which another state or action is presented, being the latter state or action contrasted with the former.

Ⓕ **V/i** ga が

❖ Emphasis goes to the marked v. or adj. v.

N/n da ga だが

Ⓕ [*for.*] **V/i** keredomo けれども

❖ Emphasis goes to the following clause.

➤ [*for.*] **N/n** da keredomo だけれども

➤ [*for.*] **V/i** keredo けれど

➤ [*for.*] **N/n** da keredo だけれど

➤ **V/i** kedomo けども

➤ **N/n** da kedomo だけども

➤ Ⓕ [*col.*] **V/i** kedo けど

➤ Ⓛ [*col.*] **N/n** da kedo だけど

3.2 Concessive Coordinator

even though ~; although ~; despite ~

❖ It expresses that an action is performed or a state occurs in such a way that another action or state subsequently occurs in an unexpected way.

⊕ **V/na/i** no ni のに

Ⓛ **V/na/no/i** kuse ni くせに〔癖に〕

❖ Only u. when the subject of the preceding and following clauses are the same.

❖ Not u. when the subject is the first person.

➤ **V/na/no/i** kuse shite くせして〔癖して〕

Ⓛ [*for.*] **VN/n/I/i** nagara (mo) ながらも

V/na/i mono no ものの

V/na/no/i tokoro o ところを

V/no kai mo naku 甲斐もなく

I koso sure こそすれ

N koso are こそあれ

N koso aru ga こそあるが

[*for.*] **V/i** ni (mo) kakawarazu にも関わらず

➤ [*for.*] **N/na/V/i** no ni (mo) kakawarazu にも関わらず

[*for.*] **N** wa atte mo はあっても

➤ [*lit.*] **N** wa are (do) はあれど

[*lit.*] **E** domo ども

Negative Concessive

don't even

VN/I mo shinai もしない

[*for.*] **VN** da n shinai だにしない

Contrastive Concessive

for ~; considering ~; despite ~

❖ It indicates that the action or state of the predicate is not proportional to what would be expected from the marked action or state.

ⓔ **V/na/no/i wari ni (wa)** わりには〔割には〕

4. DISJUNCTIVE COORDINATION

Disjunctive coordination refers to the consecution of clauses that represent an option or an alternative, expressed in English with the conjunction *or*.

Important Disjunctive Coordinator

4.1 Disjunctive Coordinator [*or*]: It presents two options among which one shall be obligatorily chosen.

ⓕ **N/n/V/i ka ⟨N/n/V/i⟩ ka** か...か

ⓗ **N/na/U/ku mata wa** または

4.2 Alternative Coordinator [*whether (or not)*]: It presents two options that are presented as an eligible but not necessarily obligatory choice.

ⓗ **N/n/V/i ka (dō ka)** かどうか

- -

4.1 Disjunctive Coordinator

(either) ~ or

❖ It presents an alternative to the marked action or state.

ⓕ **N/n/V/i ka ⟨N/n/V/i⟩ ka** か...か

ⓗ [*lit.*][*for.*] **N/na/U/ku mata wa** または〔又は〕

[*lit.*] **N/n/V/i (ka) nai shi (wa) ⟨N⟩** かない しは...〔乃至〕: *or (and what is in between)*

Negative Dependent Disjunctive

(regardless of) whether ~ or

❖ It indicates that the verb or state appearing in a clause is performed independently of another clause.

N/n/V/i ni shite mo ⟨N/n/v/i⟩ ni shite mo にしても...にしても

N/n/V/i ni shiro ⟨N/n/v/i⟩ ni shiro にし ても...にしても

[*lit.*] **N/n/V/i ni seyo ⟨N/n/v/i⟩ ni seyo** にしても...にしても

Ō to/ga ⟨Ō⟩ to/ga と/が...と/が

N/n/V/i ka ⟨N/n/V/i⟩ ka ni yorazu か... かによって

[*for.*] **N/n/V/i ka ⟨N/n/V/i⟩ ka ni kakawarazu** か...かに関わらず

[*for.*] **N/n/V/i ka ⟨N/n/V/i⟩ ka o towazu** か...かを問わず

4.2 Alternative Coordinator

whether ~ (or not)

❖ It points out to a clause that is presented as an optative choice.

ⓗ **N/n/V/i ka (dō ka)** かどうか

V/i ka ⟨A/ku⟩ nai ka か...ないか

N/n/V/i ka nai ka かないか

[*lit.*] **N/n/V/i ka ina ka** か否か

[*col.*][*fam.*] **U/n/i yara ⟨N/n/U/i⟩ yara** やら

Ō ka ⟨U/I⟩ mai ka かまいか

❖ 〖Ō〗 & 〈U〉 are the same v.

ku mo 〈**ku**〉 mo も...も

TA ra 〈**TA**〉 de ら...で

[*for.*] **N/n** de mo 〈**N/n**〉 de mo でも...でも

[*lit.*][*for.*] **N/n** de arō ga/to 〈**N/n**〉 de arō ga/to であろう{が/と}...であろう{が/と}

[*lit.*] **N/n** de are 〈**N/n**〉 de are であれ...であれ

[*lit.*] **s** karō to 〈**N/n**〉 karō to かろうと...かろうと

Dependent Alternative

depending on whether ~ (or not)

❖ It expresses that the verb or state of a clause is carried out optionally in dependence on another clause.

N/n/V/i ka dō ka ni yotte かどうかによって

➤ [lit.] **N/n/V/i** ka dō ka ni yori かどうかにより

Negative Dependent Alternative

(regardless of) whether ~ or not

❖ It expresses that the verb or state appearing in a clause is carried out independently whether the action or state of another clause is performed or not.

Ō ga/to 〈**U/I**〉 mai ga/to が/と...まい{が/と}

❖ 〖Ō〗 & 〈U/i〉 are the same v.

N/n/V/i ka (dō ka) ni yorazu かどうかによらず

[*lit.*] **N/n/V/i** ka ina ka ni yorazu か否かを問わず

[*for.*] **N/n/V/i** ka (dō ka) ni kakawarazu かどうかに関わらず

[*for.*] **N/n/V/i** ka (dō ka) o towazu かどうかを問わず

[*lit.*] **N/n/V/i** ka ina ka o towazu か否かを問わず

4.3 Exclusive Coordinator

except (for) ~; other than ~ ; (nothing) but ~; excluding ~

❖ It presents an action that remains the only possible option within an implicit alternative.

U/i igai **{p}** 以外

V ka dō ka wa betsu to shite かどうかは別として

4.3 Substitutive Coordinator

instead of ~ing; in place of ~ing; despite ~ing

❖ It presents an action or state as an alternative that should be changed to another.

Ⓔ **V/na/no/i** kawari ni 代わりに

V/na/i no ni hikikae のに引き換え

IV. SUBORDINATION

Subordination is an organizing principle within syntax [☞ GE:II.2.2]—the ordering of clauses and phrases—that describes the relationship that some parts of the sentence have with other parts in a position of dependence.

The types of subordination in Japanese are as follows:

1. **Attributive Subordination** [*that...*]: It refers to the relationship of dependence that a modifying verbal or verbal phrase has with respect to a modified noun.

2. **Interrogative Subordination** [*whether...*]: It refers to questions embedded within a sentence.

3. **Quotative Subordination** [*that...*]: It involves the reference made in the speech to what someone has thought, said or heard.

4. **Comparative Subordination** [*than...*]: It refers to the relationships of comparison of the degree or quantity of actions or states between two people or things.

5. **Limitative Subordination** [*as much as...*]: It refers to the dependence established between one predicate in relation to another predicate understood as a limitation to the first one.

1. ATTRIBUTIVE SUBORDINATION

Attributive subordination refers to the dependency of the nominal part of the sentence on the adjectival or verbal part. The attribute is, therefore, an adjective or verb that is positioned before a dependent noun, modifying it.

1.1 Imperfective Attributive

... that/which/who ~

❖ It indicates that an action is performed in the present or future time by the noun following the verb or adjective.

Ⓣ Ⓥ U ⟨N⟩ ø

Ⓣ Ⓐ i ⟨N⟩ ø

Ⓣ n na ⟨N⟩ な

N(p*)/n† no ⟨N⟩ の

　❖ *e, to, kara or made.

　❖ †Just some adj. n.s.

[*lit.*][*for.*] N/n de aru ⟨N⟩ である

[*lit.*][*obs.*] n naru ⟨N⟩ なる〔成る〕

Negative Imperfective Attributive

... that/which/who don't/doesn't ~

❖ It expresses that the noun following the inflection does not perform the action indicated by the preceding verb doesn't have the characteristics of the preceding adjectival verb.

Ⓣ Ⓥ A/ku nai ⟨N⟩ ない

Ⓣ Ⓐ ku nai ⟨N⟩ ない

Ⓣ N/n de (wa) nai ⟨N⟩ ではない

➤ [*col.*] N/n ja nai ⟨N⟩ じゃない

Ⓥ [*obs.*] A nu ⟨N⟩ ない

✤ M. u. nowadays in fossilized set phrases.

Ⓥ [*obs.*] **A** zaru ⟨N⟩ ざる

✤ M. u. nowadays in fossilized proverbs or sayings.

1.2 Perfective Attributive

> *... that/which/who ~ed/did ~*

✤ It indicates that an action was performed in the past by the noun following the verb or that the noun following the adj. v. had its characteristics in the past.

Ⓣ Ⓥ **TA** ⟨N⟩

Ⓣ Ⓐ **s** katta ⟨N⟩ かった

Ⓣ **N/n** datta ⟨N⟩ だった

[*for.*] **N/n** de atta ⟨N⟩ であった

Negative Perfective Attributive

> *... that/which/who didn't/hasn't/ haven't ~*

✤ It expresses that the noun following the inflection didn't perform the action indicated by the preceding verb or didn't have the characteristics indicated by the preceding adjectival verb.

Ⓣ Ⓥ **A** nakatta ⟨N⟩ なかった

Ⓣ Ⓐ **ku** nakatta ⟨N⟩ なかった

Ⓣ **N/n** de wa nakatta ⟨N⟩ ではなかった

➤ [*col.*] **N/n** ja nakatta ⟨N⟩ じゃなかった

2. INTERROGATIVE SUBORDINATION

Interrogative subordination refers to questions embedded within a sentence.

2.1 Interrogative Subordinator

> *(whether) if ~; whether ~*

✤ It indicates that the speaker is asking if the action or state marked takes place within the predicate.

Ⓣ **N/n/V/i** ka か

V/na/i no ka のか

✤ Only u. w. questions that have interrogative demonstratives.

[*fam.*] **V/na/i** no yara のやら

3. QUOTATIVE SUBORDINATION

Quotative subordination refers to the relationship of dependence that a sentence has with respect to a verb, indicating that the dependent part is a quotation (something someone has said), which is referred to by the verb (V), a verb that normally expresses a discursive action (i.e. 'saying', 'thinking', 'hearing', etc.).

3.1 Quotative Subordinator

> *that ~*

✤ It indicates that a clause has been expressed by another person or that has been or is being thought by the speaker.

Ⓣ **P** to

✤ *Usually followed by the v.s **iu** (*to say*); **omou** (*to think*); **kaku** (*to write*) or **kiku** (*to hear*).

⊕ [*col.*] **P** tte って

➤ [*col.*] **N/n** da tte だって

Interrogative Quotative

whether ~; if ~; what ~

♣ It introduces a renarrative question.

N*/n/V/i ka to かと

♣ *Indefinite pronouns.

♣ Usually followed by the v.s **iu** (*to say*); **omou** (*to think*); **kaku** (*to write*) or **kiku** (*to hear*).

Attributive Quotative

... what/that is called ~; ... that ~

♣ It expresses that the marked phrase identifies or explains the modified noun.

P to iu ⟨**N**⟩ という 〔と言う〕

[col.] **P tte iu** ⟨**N**⟩ っていう 〔って言う〕

[col.] **P tte** ⟨**N**⟩ って

[*lit.*] **P to no** ⟨**N**⟩ との

Emphatic Quotative

~ing; (in such a way) that ~; (thinking/saying) that ~

♣ It indicates that the marked phrase is a thought, feeling or quotation that is brought into the conversation and that affects, acting as an adverbial phrase, the following phrase.

P to と

[*col.*][*fam.*] **P tte** って

Thematic Quotative

the fact that ~; that ~; that is to say that ~

♣ It expresses that the marked phrase is the main topic upon which the following part of the sentence is developed or explained.

VN/n/V/i to wa とは

VN/n/V/i to iu mono wa というものは 〔と言う物は〕

VN/n/V/i to iu koto wa ということは 〔と言う事は〕

♣ Expressing s.t. factual or demonstrable.

[*col.*] **VN/n/V/i tte iu koto wa** っていうことは

[*col.*] **VN/n/V/i tte koto wa** ってことは

[*col.*][*fam.*] **VN/n/V/i tsuu koto wa** つうことは

㊤ [*col.*] **VN/n/V/i to iu no wa** というのは 〔と言うのは〕

3.2 Enunciative Subordinator

things like ~ (or)

♣ It enunciates an approximate quote of words or ideas.

V/i nado to などと

Emphatic Enunciative

things like ~

♣ It enunciates an approximate quote of words or ideas in an emphatic way.

㊤ **V/i nante** なんて

V/i nado to wa などとは

4. COMPARATIVE SUBORDINATION

Comparative subordination refers to the relationship of comparison of the degree or quantity of actions or states between two people or things.

+ *More details in Grammar Explanations* [☞ GE:XIV.2].

4.1 Comparative Subordinator

> *compared to ~; as opposed to ~*

✤ It indicates that a noun, verb or adjective is being compared to that of another noun, verb or adjective.

⊕ **N/na/V/i** yori (mo) よりも

Upper Comparative

> *B is/does more C than A; compared to A B is/does more C; B is/does more P as opposed to A.*

✤ It indicates that someone or something (*B*) has a higher degree of a quality or performs more an action (*C**) than another person or thing (*A*).

✤ **C is an adj. v. or a finite v.*

Ⓣ **N**A yori (mo) ⟨**N**⟩B no hō ga ⟨**P**⟩C より も...のほうが...〔より...の方が...〕

➢ **V/na/i**A yori (mo) ⟨**V/na/i**⟩B hō ga ⟨**P**⟩C ほうが...よりも...〔...の方が...より〕

NA yori ⟨**N**⟩B ga/wa ⟨**P**⟩C より...が/はもっと...

V/na/iA hō ga ⟨**V/na/i**⟩B yori (mo) ⟨**P**⟩ ほうが...よりも...〔...方が...より〕

➢ **N**A no hō ga ⟨**N**B⟩ yori (mo) ⟨**P**⟩C ほうが...よりも...〔...の方が...より〕

NA wa ⟨**N**⟩B yori (mo) ⟨**P**⟩C は...よりも...

➢ **V/na/i**A no wa ⟨**V/na/i**⟩B no yori (mo) ⟨**P**⟩C のは...のよりも...

N/na/V/i yori ⟨**P**⟩ より ...: *compared to N/na/V/i is more P*

V/na/i hō (ga) ⟨**P**⟩ ほうが...〔方が...〕: *V/na/i is more P*

➢ **N** no hō (ga) ⟨**P**⟩ のほうが...〔の方が...〕: *N is more P*

Equitative Comparative

> *A is/does P as much as B*

NA wa ⟨**N**⟩B to onaji kurai ⟨**P**⟩ は...と同じくらい

Superlative Comparative

> *A is/does the most P among B*

NA wa/ga ⟨**N**⟩B (no naka) de ichiban ⟨**P**⟩ は/が...の中で一番...

[*for.*] **N**A wa/ga ⟨**N**⟩B (no naka) de mottomo ⟨**P**⟩ は/が...の中で最も...

5. LIMITATIVE SUBORDINATION

Limitative subordination establishes a relationship of dependence between a phrase marked by a limiting particle and the rest of the sentence.

5.1 Upper Limitative Subordinator

> *as much as ~; to the extent of ~ing; to the extent that ~*

✤ It presents an action or state understood as a limit to be reached.

⊕ **U/na/i** hodo ほど〔程〕

Ⓛ **V/na/i** kurai くらい

Ⓛ **V/na/i** gurai くらい

U/na/i dake だけ

TE made まで

N/n/U/i ni mo hodo ga aru にもほどがある〔にも程がある〕

Comparative Upper Limitative

> *more than ~*

VN/V ijō ni 以上に

Translative Upper Limitative

the more ~ the more ...

Ⓔ BA ⟨U/na/i⟩ hodo ⟨U/na/i⟩ ...ほど...
〔...程...〕

♣ 〖BA〗 & ⟨U/i⟩ have to be the same v.
or adj. v.

➤ N nara ⟨na⟩ hodo なら...ほど〔なら...
程〕

V. WORD CLASS TRANSFORMATION

Transformation as a grammatical category refers to morphemes that fulfill a certain grammatical function that replaces the original grammatical function—class—of a word.

In Japanese, there are two main ways of transforming the grammatical function of a word into another:

1. **Nominalization**: It transforms a verb or adjective into a noun.

2. **Adverbialization**: It transforms an adjective into an adverb.

1. NOMINALIZATION

Nominalization refers to the transformation of verbs and adjectives into nouns.

1.1 Nominalization Marker

to ~; ~ing; a thing that ~; what ~; ~ one

❖ It transforms verbal or adjectival phrases into noun phrases.

Ⓣ **V/na/i no** の
　❖ M. u. for tangible or perceptible things.

Ⓜ **V/na/i koto** こと 〔事〕
　❖ M. u. for intangible or abstract things.

Ⓜ **V/na/i mono** もの 〔物/者〕
　❖ M. u. for things that convey some degree of emotion.

Ⓜ **n/s sa** さ: *~ness*
　❖ Expressing a degree or quality.

s mi み

❖ Non productive, meaning that only some adj. v.s allow this pattern.

❖ Expressing a tinge or trace of a quality or the quality itself.

I mono もの 〔物/者〕

❖ Non productive, meaning that only some v.s allow this pattern.

n ø

I ø

Thematic Nominalization

that ~; where ~; when ~; who ~; the reason why ~; the fact that ~

❖ It transforms any verbal phrase into a noun phrase while it brings the main focus of the discourse towards it.

Ⓜ **V/na/i no wa** のは

V/na/i koto wa ことは 〔事は〕
　❖ M. u. for abstract conceptualizations.

Causal Nominalization

~ because; it is ~ that

❖ It introduces a feeling that is the result of a cause expressed in the following clause.

Ⓔ **V/n/i koto ni** ことに 〔事に〕
　❖ Limited to v.s or adj. v.s related to emotions.

Quotative Nominalization

the thing called/named ~

✤ It presents the marked phrase as a quotation expressed as a nominal phrase.

⊕ **P** to iu koto ということ〔と言う事〕

[*for.*] **P** to no koto とのこと〔との事〕

P to iu mono というもの〔と言う物〕

Inferential Nominalization

the thing that ~

✤ It transforms the marked phrase into a nominal phrase that is understood as something to be inferred within a context.

⊕ **P** to iu koto ということ〔と言う事〕

[*for.*] **P** to no koto とのこと〔との事〕

P to iu mono というもの〔と言う物〕

2. ADVERBIALIZATION

It refers to the transformation of adjectives into adverbs.

2.1 Adverbialization Marker

~*ly*

✤ It transforms adjectival verbs and adjectival nouns into adverbs.

Ⓣ **s** ku く

n ni に

VI. MOOD

The mood is a grammatical category that identifies the modality of the verbs or adjectival verbs, that is, the attitude that the speaker takes with respect to the actions or states that he or she expresses, understanding the attitude, mainly, as his or her stance in relation to the degree of viability of the accomplishment of said action or state.

Three main categories can be distinguished within modalities:

1. **Realis Modality:** It indicates that actions or states are understood as experimentally real.

2. **Pseudo-Realis Modality:** It indicates that actions or states are understood as subjectively real, meaning that they are considered to be real but not experimentally so.

   Irrealis Modality: It indicates that actions or states are considered as possible, probable or necessary but they are not yet accomplished at the moment of speech.

Within the Irrealis Modality there are also five subgroups:

3. **Epistemic Moods** [*could*]: They refer to states and actions specifically considered as possible or probable.

4. **Volitional Moods** [*would*]: They refer to states and actions whose occurrence is desired.

5. **Deontic Moods** [*should*]: They refer to actions whose realization is considered obligatory or necessary.

6. **Purposive Moods** [*let's*]: They refer to actions whose performance the speaker suggests to the listener.

7. **Subjective Moods** [*!*]: They refer to states or actions in whose expression a certain emotion is inferred.

1. REALIS MODALITY

Moods that express events or actions that are understood to be experimentally real, meaning that they have actually happened or are happening.

Important Realis Moods

1.1 **Indicative Mood:** It refers to verbal or adjectival statements understood as factual. This is the default mood.

1.2 **Explanative Copula:** It refers to actions or states that are implied to be explanations.

ⓕ **V/na/i no {D}** のだ/です

1.2 **Causal Copula** [*it's because*]: It refers to actions or states that are understood as explicit causes for the preceding clause.

Ⓣ **V/i kara {D}** からだ/です

1.3 **Causal Mood** [*because*]: It refers to actions or states presented as causes for the following clause.

Ⓣ **V/i kara** から

Ⓣ [*for.*] **V/na/i no de** ので

1.4 **Quotative Mood** [*say that*]: It refers to things that somebody says.

⊕ **P to iu** という

- -

1.1 Indicative Mood

❖ The indicative mood expresses the declaration of a sentence that is understood to be true. The bulk of indicative is presented under the previous Aspects section [☞ I], since the indicative mood is the default mood when no other mood is mentioned.

1.2 Explanative Copula

the thing is ~; it's because ~; it is that ~; means that ~

❖ It presents a reliable explanation expressed by the marked verb or adjectival verb.

Ⓣ **V/na/i no {D}** のだ/です

➤ [*col.*] **V/na/i n {D}** んだ/です

➤ [*col.*][*fam.*][*mas.*] **V/na/i n da** んだ

➤ [*col.*][*fam.*][*fem.*] **V/na/i no** の

Ⓛ **V/na/i mono ({D})** ものだ/です

➤ [*col.*] **V/i mon** もんだ/です

N/n {D} mono ({D}) だ/ですもの

➤ [*col.*] **N/n {D} mon** だ/ですもん

V/na/i koto {D} ことだ/です

　❖ M. u. for abstract conceptualizations.

➤ **N/n no koto {D}** のことだ/です

Emphatic Explanative

its's because ~, you know

❖ It presents, in an emphatic way, the marked verb or adjective as an explanation for the predicate.

[*fam.*] **V/na/i no {D} mono ({D})** のだ/ですもの

➤ [*col.*][*fam.*] **V/na/i n {D} mono/mon** だ/ですもの/もん

Inferential Explanative

(so) that means that ~; that's why ~; so ~

❖ It presents an explanation for something that is deduced from a given context.

Ⓛ **V/na/i wake {D}** わけだ/です 〔訳〕

➤ **N to iu wake {D}** というわけだ/です 〔と言う訳〕

Ⓛ **V/i to iu koto {D}** ということだ/です 〔という事〕

V/i to iu mono {D} というものだ/です 〔と言う物〕

[*for.*] **V/i to no koto {D}** とのことだ/です 〔との事〕

Indirect Explanative

it's not that s.o. don't/doesn't ~

✤ It explains a clause in an indirect way using a double negative, denying the non-existence of the referred action or state.

Ⓔ **A/ku** nai koto mo/wa nai ないこと{も/は}ない

➢ **N/n** de wa nai koto mo/wa nai ではないこと{も/は}ない

➢ [*col.*] **N/n** ja nai koto mo/wa nai じゃないこと{も/は}ない

A/ku naku mo/wa nai なく{も/は}ない

➢ **N/n** ga naku mo/wa nai なく{も/は}ない

1.2 Causal Copula

it is because ~

✤ It states an explicit cause for the preceding clause.

Ⓣ **V/i** kara {D} からだ/です

Ⓔ **V/na/no/i** tame {D} ためだ/です〔為〕

1.3 Causal Mood

because ~; since ~; due to ~ing

✤ It introduces the cause of the predicate.

Ⓣ **V/i** kara ({D}) から

✤ Referring to a cause that leads the speaker to have an opinion or carry out a decision.

➢ ⊕ **N/n** {D} kara だ/ですから

Ⓣ **V/na/i** no de ので

✤ Referring to a cause of a state or action that occurred spontaneously.

➢ [*col.*] **V/na/i** n de んで

TE ø

Ⓔ **V/na/i** koto kara ことから

V/na/i koto de ことで

[*lit.*][*for.*] Ⓔ **V/na/no/i** tame (ni) ために〔為〕

V/na/i tokoro kara ところから

[*for.*] **V/na/no/i** sei de せいで: *as a result of ~*

[*lit.*] **V/na/no/i** yue (ni) ゆえに〔故〕

➢ [*lit.*] **N/n/V/i** ga yue (ni) がゆえに〔が故〕

[*lit.*] **N/n/V/i** to kite iru ときている

✤ Followed by other causal p.s such as kara or no de.

Thematic Causal

since ~; now that ~; once ~; because ~

✤ It points out the cause of the predicate while putting the focus on the predicate.

V kara ni wa からには

➢ [*col.*] **V** kara wa からは

V ijō (wa) 以上は

Benefactive Causal

thanks to ~

V/na/no/i okage de お陰で

Explanative Causal

it's because ~

✤ It emphatically introduces the cause of the predicate.

V/na/i no {D} kara のだ/ですから

➢ [*col.*] **V/na/i** n {D} kara んだ/ですから

V/na/i mono {D} kara ものだ/ですから

➢ [*col.*] **V/na/i** mon {D} kara もんだ/ですから

V/na/no/i koto {D} kara ことだ/ですから

[*for.*] **V/na/no/i** koto da shi ことだし

[*lit.*] **U/na/no** koto tote こととて

Expectative Causal

and as one would expect ~; so (naturally) ~

❖ It presents a cause that is expectedly deducted from what is inferred in the marked verb or adjective.

V/na/i dake ni だけに

[*for.*] **V/na/i** to atte とあって

Resultative Causal

and as one would expect ~; so (naturally) ~

❖ It expresses that the action or state marked is a reason for the result expressed in the following clause.

TA no/koto o kikkake ni {の/こと}をきっかけに〔...切っ掛けで〕

❖ Focusing on the time.

TA no/koto ga kikkake de {の/こと}がきっかけで〔...切っ掛けで〕

❖ Focusing on the cause.

[*for.*] **TA** no o ki ni のを機に

1.4 Quotative Mood

say(s) that ~

❖ It expresses that someone has said the marked phrase.

⊕ **P** to iu という

[*col.*] **P** tte iu っていう

[*col.*][fam.] **P** tte って

➤ [*col.*][fam.] **N/n** da tte だって

[*col.*][fam.] **P** tsuu つう

Imperative Quotative

tell to ~

❖ It expresses that someone tells another person to perform the action of the verb.

U yō ni iu ように言う〔様に言う〕

1.5 Enumerative Mood

do things like ~

❖ It presents an inexhaustive list of actions that are performed.

U to ka suru とかする

TA ri suru りする

1.6 Lower Limitative Copula

~ that's all; is just ~(ing); is/does nothing but ~

❖ It expresses, in an explanatory manner, that the action or state marked is the only one that is done or occurs.

⊕ **N/na/U/i** bakari {D} ばかり だ/です

❖ Usually w. a somewhat neg. connotation.

N/na/V/i dake {D} だけ だ/です

[*for.*] **N/V** nomi {D} のみ だ/です

N/C/U ni suginai に過ぎない

[*lit.*] **N** ni hoka naranai にほかならない〔に他ならない〕

➤ [*lit.*] **V/i** kara ni hoka naranai からにほかならない〔からに他ならない〕

[*lit.*] **N** ni hoka naranu にほかならぬ}〔に他ならぬ〕

➤ [*lit.*] **V/i** kara ni hoka naranu からにほかならぬ〔からに他ならぬ〕

1.7 Formal Mood

way of ~ing; how to ~

❖ It indicates the way something is done.

432

⊕ **I** kata 方

I hō 方

VN no shikata の仕方

I yō よう〔様〕

Correlative Formal

as (one) ~; the way ~

❖ It indicates that what is expressed in the predicate corresponds to the way in which the subject does the marked action.

㊤ **V** toori (ni) 通りに

➢ **VN** no toori (ni) 通りに

I doori 通り

TE no toori 通り

1.8 Benefactive Copula

be worth ~ing; ~ pays off

❖ It indicates that it is worth doing the marked action.

V/I/no kai ga aru 甲斐がある

1.9 Active Benefactive Mood

to ~ for the sake of s.o.

❖ It denotes that the subject of the sentence does something for the benefit of someone else, expressed from the viewpoint of the person who does the favor.

㊤ **TE** ageru 上げる/挙げる

❖ The receiver of the benefit (indirect complement) is in the second or third person.

➢ [*col.*] Tageru たげる

❖ For verbs whose gerundive f. ends in -**te**.

➢ [*hum.*] **TE** sashiageru 差し上げる

❖ The receiver is of a higher social status than the speaker.

➢ ⊕ [*fam.*] **TE** yaru やる

❖ The receiver is of inferior social status than the speaker.

⊕ **TE** kureru くれる

❖ The receiver of the benefit (indirect complement) is in the first person or is s.o. from his/her in-group, while the subject (the doer) is in the second or third person.

➢ ⊕ [*hon.*] **TE** kudasaru くださる〔下さる〕

❖ The doer is of superior social status than the speaker.

1.10 Passive Benefactive Mood

~ for s.o.; do s.o. a favor by ~

❖ It denotes that the subject of the sentence does something for the benefit of someone else, expressed from the viewpoint of the person who receives the favor.

⊕ **TE** morau もらう

❖ It has the nuance that the person receiving the favor feels good about it.

➢ ⊕ [*hum.*] **TE** itadaku いただく

❖ M. u. in the pol. f. itadakimasu.

1.11 Habitual Mood

get used to ~

㊤ **N/I** ni nareru になれる

I tsukeru つける〔付ける〕

2. PSEUDO-REALIS MODALITY

Moods that express entities, states or actions that are considered as possible or apparent.

Important Pseudo-Realis Moods

2.1 **Potential Mood** [*can*; *bͻ ablͻ to*]: It refers to actions whose realization is considered feasible.

⊕ Ⓢ **E** rareru られる

⊕ Ⓦ **E** ru る

⊕ **U** koto ga dekiru ことが出来る

2.2 **Semblative Mood** [*likͻ ~ing*; *as if*]: It refers to actions that are performed in a similar way to another action or state.

⊕ **V/na/no/i** yō ni ように

⊕ [col.][*fam.*] **N/n/V/i** mitai ni みたいに

2.3 **Semblative Copula** [*bͻ likͻ*; *sͻͻm*]: It indicates that the existence or occurrence of an entity, state or action is apparent.

⊕ **V/na/no/i** yō {D} よう*だ/です*

⊕ [col.][*fam.*] **N/n/V/i** mitai ({D}) みたい*だ/です*

- **Evidential Semblative Copula** [*look likͻ*]: It indicates that the speaker senses that the subject appears to perform an action or be in a certain state.

  ⊕ **TE/ku** mieru みえる

  ⊕ **I/n/s** sō ({D}) そう*だ/です*

- **Approximative Semblative Copula** [*(somewhat) likͻ*; *~ish*]: It indicates an approximate appearance.

  ⊕ **N/n/V/i** rashii らしい

2.4 **Inferential Mood** [*hͻ ard that*]: It refers to an action or state whose occurrence is inferred through what the speaker has heard from another person.

⊕ [*fam.*] **V/i** sō ({D}) そう*だ/です*

⊕ **N/n/V/i** to kiita と聞いた

2.5 **Provisional Mood** [*if*]: It refers to actions or states whose occurrence is considered as an hypothetical condition for the predicate.

⊤ Ⓢ **E** ba ば

⊤ Ⓦ **E** reba れば

⊤ Ⓐ **s** kereba ければ

⊕ **N/n/V/i** (no) nara のなら

2.6 **Conditional Mood** [*(only)* *if*]: It refers to actions or states whose occurrence is understood as an indispensable condition for the predicate.

⊕ **U/i** to と

⊕ **TA** ra ら

2.1 Potential Mood

can ~; be able to ~

❖ It expresses that the subject has the capacity to perform the marked action.

⊕ Ⓢ **E** rareru られる

❖ The potential f. of the irregular v. **kuru** (*to come*) is korareru, while the irregular v. **suru** (*to do*) has not a potential f. and uses instead the v. dekiru (*to be able to*).

➤ Ⓢ [*col.*] **E** reru れる

⊕ Ⓦ **E** ru る

⊕ **U** koto ga dekiru ことが出来る

➤ **VN** ga dekiru が出来る

I eru 得る

[*lit.*] **I** uru 得る

Negative Potential

can't ~; unable to ~

Ⓢ **E** rarenai られない

➤ Ⓢ [*col.*] **E** renai れない

Ⓦ **E** nai ない

U koto ga dekinai ことができない

[*for.*][*pol.*] **I** kaneru かねる 〔兼ねる〕

❖ Only u. w. human subjects.

I enai 得ない

TE kamawanai かまわない 〔構わない〕

U ni ⟨V⟩* に...

❖ *V. in the neg. potential f.

❖ 〖U〗 and ⟨V⟩ are the same v.

2.2 Semblative Mood

like (~ing); as (if) ~

❖ It points out that the action of the predicate is done in a similar way to the marked action, state or entity.

⊕ **V/na/no/i** yō ni ように 〔様に〕

➤ [*for.*] **V/i** ka no yō ni かのように 〔かの様に〕

⊕ [*col.*][*fam.*] **N/n/V/i** mitai ni みたいに

[*lit.*] **U** ga gotoku がごとく 〔が如く〕

➤ [*lit.*] **N** no gotoku のごとく 〔の如く〕

[*lit.*] **N/U** ka no gotoku かのごとく 〔かの如く〕

Formal Semblative

manner in which ~; behaving like ~; acting like ~; way in which ~

❖ It refers to the way in which the subject of the sentence seems to act.

I buri ぶり 〔振り〕

I bburi っぶり

I ppuri っぷり

N/n/s buru ぶる

❖ M. u. in the progressive f. butte iru.

N/n/s biru びる

Active Semblative

pretend to ~; act as if ~

❖ It indicates that the subject apparently and deliberately acts like the marked verb, adjective or noun.

⊕ **V/na/i** furi o suru ふりをする〔振りを
する〕

➤ **N** no furi o suru のふりをする〔の振り
をする〕

Inferential Semblative

as if ~

❖ It indicates that an action or event that
is inferred from a date or thought seems to
take place.

V to iu fuu ni というふうに〔と言う風
に〕

V to iu yō ni というように〔と言う様に〕

[*for.*] **V** to bakari ni とばかりに

[*lit.*] **V** to iwan bakari ni とばかりに

2.3 Semblative Copula

*be like ~; seem(s) (that) ~; appear(s)
(that) ~*

❖ It denotes that the realization,
occurrence or existence of the marked
action, state or entity is apparent.

⊕ **V/na/no/i** yō {D} ようだ/です〔様〕

⊕ [*col.*][*fam.*] **N/n/V/i** mitai ({D}) みた
いだ/です

[*lit.*] **U** ga gotoshi がごとし〔が如し〕

➤ [*lit.*] **N** no gotoshi のごとし〔の如し〕

[*lit.*] **U** ka no gotoshi かのごとし〔かの如

➤ **N** jimiru じみる〔染みる〕:

❖ M. u. in the progressive f. jiimite iru,
or in the perfective f. jimita when u. as
an attribute.

N/V mo dōzen {D} も同然だ/です: *be just
like ~*

- -

➤ **V/na/no/i** yō na ⟨N⟩ ような〔様な〕

➤ [*col.*][*fam.*] **N/V/i** mitai na ⟨N⟩ みたい
な

➤ [*lit.*] **U** ga gotoki ⟨N⟩ がごとき〔が如き〕

➤ [*lit.*] **N** no gotoki ⟨N⟩ のごとき〔の如
き〕

➤ [*lit.*] **N/U** ka no gotoki ⟨N⟩ かのごとき
〔が如き〕

N/V mo dōzen no ⟨N⟩ も同然の

Evidential Semblative

*look(s) like ~; seem to/that ~; have
the appearance of ~; akin to (being)
~*

❖ It indicates that the speaker sensorily
perceives that the subject of the sentence
seems to perform the marked action or be
similar to the characteristics indicated by
the marked adjective or noun.

⊕ **TE/ku** mieru みえる〔見える〕

➤ **N/n** ni mieru にみえる〔に見える〕

⊕ **U/na/no/i** yō ni mieru ようにみえる
〔様に見える〕

[*for.*] **V/i** ka no yō ni mieru かのようにみ
える〔かの様に見える〕

➤ [*for.*] **V/i** ka ni mieru かにみえる〔か
に見える〕

⊕ **I/n/s** sō ({D}) そうだ/です

❖ The neg. f. is **I/n/s** sō ni/mo nai or **A**
nasa sō ({D})

➤ **I/n/s** sō ni mieru そうにみえる〔そう
に見える〕

➤ **I/n/s** sō na ⟨N⟩ そうな...

⊕ **n/s** garu がる

❖ M. u. in the progressive f. gatte iru.

⊕ **N** meku めく

❖ M. u. in the progressive f. meite iru, or
in the perfective f. meita when u. as an
attribute.

I/n/s ge {D} げだ/です〔気〕

Inferential Semblative

it looks as if ~; it seems that ~

✤ It expresses that a state or action appears to be such according to one's inner feelings.

Ⓤ **U/i** to mieru とみえる〔と見える〕

[*for.*] **V/na/no/i** yō ni omowareru ように思われる〔様に思われる〕

[*for.*] **V/i** ka no yō {D} かのようだ/です〔かの様〕

➤ [*for.*] **V/i** ka no yō 〈**N**〉 かのような〔かの様な〕

Approximative Semblative

~ish; ~ful; ~like; somewhat ~; rather ~

✤ It indicates that the subject of the sentence has an approximate resemblance to the characteristic expressed by the adjective, verb or noun.

⊕ **N/n/V/i** rashii らしい

Ⓤ [*col.*][*fam.*] **N/n/s** ppoi っぽい

Ⓤ **VN/I** gimi {D} 気味だ/です

[*fam.*] **s** me め

Tendency Semblative

tends to ~; have a tendency to ~

✤ It expresses that the subject of the sentence seems to be inclined to do the marked action or have the qualities of the marked adjective.

⊕ **n/s** gari {D} がりだ/です

Ⓤ **VN/I** gachi {D} がちだ/です

V/na/no/i kēkō ga aru 傾向がある

V/no kirai ga aru 嫌いがある

✤ U. when the tendency is considered negative.

2.4 Inferential Mood

I heard (that) ~; people say (that) ~; apparently ~

✤ It expresses that the occurrence or existence of the marked action or state is deduced from what someone has told.

⊕ **V/i** sō ({D}) そうだ/です

➤ **N/n** {D} sō ({D}) だ/ですそうだ/です

⊕ **N/n/V/i** to kiita と聞いた: *I heard that ~*

Ⓤ [*col.*][*fam.*] **V/na/i** (n) da tte んだって

[*col.*][*pol.*] **V/na/i** (n) desu tte んですって

[*lit.*] **N/n/V/i** to iu という

[*col.*] **N/n/V/i** tte iu っていう

N/n/V/i to iu という

[*lit.*] **V/no/i** yoshi ({D}) 由

Evidential Inferential

have a feeling that ~; rather feel that/like ~; kind of ~; may ~

✤ It expresses that the occurrence or existence of the marked action or state is deduced from what the speaker has felt.

Ⓤ **V/na/i** yō na ki ga suru ような気がする〔様な気がする〕

Ⓤ **N/n** no yō na ki ga suru のような気がする〔の様な気がする〕

V/na/i ki ga suru 気がする

A nai de mo nai ないでもない

✤ M. u. w. v.s of perception such as **kanjiru** (*to feel*), **ki ga suru** (*to feel*), **omou** (*to think*), or **mieru** (*to look*).

2.5 Provisional Mood

if ~; provided that ~; supposing that ~

❖ It expresses that the marked action, state or entity is a hypothetical or actual provision with respect to the following clause.

Ⓣ Ⓢ **E reba** れば

  ❖ U. to express hypothetical provisions.

➢ Ⓢ [*col.*] **E rya** りゃ

Ⓣ Ⓦ **E ba** ば

➢ Ⓦ [*col.*] **S ya** や

Ⓣ Ⓐ **s kereba** ければ

➢ Ⓐ [*col.*] **s kerya** けりゃ

⊕ Ⓝ **N/n nara** なら

⊕ **V/i** (no) **nara** のなら

  ❖ U. to express provisions based on information of a context already known by both the speaker and the listener.

➢ Ⓦ [*col.*] **N/n/V/i ya** や

[*for.*] **N/n/V/i naraba** ならば

[*lit.*][*for.*] **N/n** (no) **de areba** のであれば

Negative Provisional

if not ~; supposing that not ~

A/ku nakereba なければ

➢ [*col.*] **A/ku nakerya** なけりゃ

➢ [*col.*][*fam.*] **A/ku nakya** なきゃ

➢ **A/ku nai nara** ないなら

➢ **N/n de nakereba** でなければ

Emphatic Provisional

provided that ~; as long as ~

❖ It denotes that the action or state expressed by the predicate is fulfilled as long as the action or state expressed by the marked verb is carried out.

Ⓣ **TE/I sae** ⟨**BA**⟩* さえ...

  ❖ *Usually the v.s **suru** (to do) or **iru** (to be).

ku sae areba さえあれば

N/n/V/i to areba とあれば

V kagiri 限り

[*lit.*] **Ō mono nara** ものなら

Concessive Provisional

even if ~; although ~; even though ~

❖ It indicates that the thing that the predicate states is not what is expected from what is inferred by the provision expressed by the marked verb, adjective or noun.

⊕ Ⓥ **TE mo** も

Ⓐ **ku te mo** ても

Ⓝ **N/n de mo** でも

[*lit.*][*for.*] **N/n de atte mo** であっても

[*lit.*][*for.*] **N/n de are** であれ

[*lit.*][*for.*] **N/n de arō ga/to** (mo) であろう{が/と}も

N/n de sae (mo) でさえも

Ⓥ [*col.*][*fam.*] **TA tte** たって

Ⓐ [*col.*][*fam.*] **ku tatte** たって

Ⓐ [*col.*][*fam.*] **ku ttatte** ったって

Ⓝ [*col.*][*fam.*] **N/n da tte** だって

n/i nari ni なりに

BA ⟨V/na/i⟩ **mono o** ものを

TA ra ⟨V/na/i⟩ **mono o** ら...ものを

TA tokoro de ところで

[*for.*] **N/n/V/i ni shita tokoro de** にしたところで

➢ [*col.*][*for.*] **N/n/V/i ni shita tte** にしたって

[*for.*] **V/i to shita tokoro de** にしたところで

➢ [*col.*][*for.*] **V/i to shita tte** にしたって

[*for.*] **I tsutsu mo** つつも

[*lit.*] **VN/V tote** とて

Quotative Provisional

when I/you hear ~; when I think of ~; if you say ~

Ⓔ **P to ieba** といえば〔と言えば〕

Resultative Provisional

when (it becomes) ~; once ~; if it is the case that ~

❖ It presents a hypothetical situation that is the result of a process.

N/na/V/i to (mo) nareba ともなれば

2.6 Conditional Mood

if ~

❖ It expresses that the occurrence of the predicate depends on the realization of the marked action without the input of the first person, a key difference with the Provisional Mood [☞ VI.2.5].

⊕ **U/i to** と

❖ U. to express results that are constant.

➣ **N/n {D} to** だ/ですと

⊕ **TA ra** ら

❖ U. to express one-time hypothetical or actual conditions.

➣ **N/n datta ra** だったら

➣ [*pol.*] **N/n deshita ra** でしたら

➣ moshi ⟨TA⟩ **ra** もし~ら

❖ Only u. w. hypothetical (not actual) conditions.

➣ [*lit.*][*obs.*] **TA raba** らば

Negative Conditional

if not ~; unless ~

❖ It expresses that the occurrence of the predicate depends on the non-realization of the marked action.

Ⓔ **A/ku nai to** ないと

N/n de nai to でないと

➣ [*col.*] **N ja nai to** じゃないと

A/ku nakatta ra んかあったら

N/n de nakatta ra でなかったら

Thematic Conditional

if ~; when ~; if it is the case that ~; if it's true that ~

❖ It presents an action or state as a topic of the discourse that is also a provision for the predicate.

Ⓥ **TE wa** は

❖ The predicate usually has a neg. nuance.

➣ [*col.*] **CHa** ちゃ

❖ For v.s whose gerundive f. ends in -**te**

➣ [*col.*] **Ja** じゃ

❖ For v.s whose gerundive f. ends in -**de**

Ⓐ **ku te wa** ては

➣ [*col.*] **ku CHa** ちゃ

N/n de wa では

➣ [*col.*] **ja** じゃ

⊕ **V/na/no/i baai {p}** 場合

[*for.*] **N/n/V/i to atte wa** とあっては

U/na/no/i yō de wa ようでは〔様では〕

❖ U. when the condition is understood as negative.

Negative Thematic Provisional

if not ~; supposing that not ~

A/ku nakute wa なくては

➣ [*col.*] **A/ku nakucha** なくちゃ

➣ **N de nakute wa** でなくては

A nai koto ni wa ないことには

Emphatic Conditional

if only ~

TE/I sae ⟨TA⟩* ra さえ...ら

❖ *Usually the v.s **suru** (*to do*) or **iru** (*to be*).

Enumerative Conditional

in the case that ~ (one does s.t. like)

❖ It indicates that a hypothetical situation or provision is presented as an action that is illustrative of something that one normally wants to avoid.

TA ri shita ra りしたら

Concessive Conditional

even if ~; no matter what/who/how ~; even supposing (that) ~

Ⓛ VN/V ni shite mo にしても

V/i to shite mo としても

[*for.*] N/n/V/i ni shiro にしろ

[*lit.*] N/n/V/i ni seyo にせよ

[*lit.*] Ō/ku to mo とも

[*lit.*] s karō to mo かろう

Ō to と

N/n darō to (mo) だろうとも

➤ [*lit.*][*for.*] N/n de arō to (mo) であろうとも

Ō ga が

N/n darō ga だろうが

➤ [*lit.*][*for.*] N/n de arō ga であろうが

Negative Concessive Conditional

even if not ~

U mai to (mo) まいとも

U mai ga まいが

Quotative Conditional

when I/you hear ~; when I think of ~; if you say ~

P to iu to というと 〔と言うと〕

P to itta ra といったら 〔と言ったら〕

➤ [*col.*] P tta ra ったら

Resultative Conditional

when (it becomes) ~; once ~; if it is the case that ~

❖ It presents an uncontrollable hypothetical condition as the main theme of the speech.

N/na/V/i to (mo) naru to ともなると

3. IRREALIS MODALITY: EPISTEMIC MOODS

Moods that express the probability of the occurrence of an action or event.

Important Epistemic Moods

3.1 **Presumptive Mood** [*will (probably)*]: It refers to actions or states whose future occurrence is considered probable.

Ⓕ [*fam.*] N/n/V/i darō だろう

Ⓕ [*for.*] N/n/V/i deshō でしょう

Ⓣ [*pol.*] **I** mashō ましょう

3.4 Deliberative Mood [*may*; *might*]: It refers to actions or states whose occurrence is considered unlikely.

⊕ **N/n/V/i** ka mo shirenai かもしれない

3.5 Interrogative Mood [*?*]: It refers to actions or states whose occurrence is questioned to the listener.

Ⓣ [*for.*] **N/n/V/i** ka か

Ⓣ [*fam.*] **P ?** ø

3.6 Inquisitive Mood [*right?*]: It refers to statements that the speaker expresses by seeking reassurance from the listener.

Ⓣ **N/n/V/i** ne ね

3.1 Presumptive Mood

will (probably) ~

❖ It expresses the expected possibility that the marked action or state will be realized.

Ⓣ [*fam.*] **N/n/V/i** darō だろう

Ⓣ [*for.*] **N/n/V/i** deshō でしょう

[*for.*][*pol.*][*obs.*] **N/n/V/i** de arimashō でありましょう

[*for.*][*pol.*][*hum.*] **N/n/V/i** de gozaimashō でございましょう

[*lit.*] **N/n/V/i** de arō であろう

Ⓣ [*pol.*] **I** mashō ましょう

Ⓥ **Ō** ø

❖ M. u. only w. the cop. or stative v.s., otherwise considered as lit.

Ⓐ [*lit.*][*for.*] **s** karō かろう

Negative Presumptive

don't think that ~; *(probably) won't* ~

❖ It expresses the high probability that the marked action is not going to be realized.

[*fam.*] **A/ku** nai darō ないだろう

➤ [*lit.*] **N/n** de wa nai darō ではないだろう

➤ [*col.*][*fam.*] **U** ja nai darō じゃないだろう

[*pol.*] **A/ku** nai deshō ないでしょう

➤ [*pol.*] **N/n** de wa nai deshō ではないでしょう

➤ [*col.*][*pol.*] **U** ja nai deshō じゃないでしょう

[*for.*] **U** mai まい

➤ [*for.*] **ku** wa aru mai くはあるまい

➤ [*for.*] **N/n** de wa aru mai ではあるまい

➤ [*col.*][*for.*] **N/n** ja aru mai じゃあるまい

[*lit.*][*for.*] **ku** (wa) nakarō はなかろう

➤ [*lit.*][*obs.*] **N/n** de wa nakarō ではなかろう

3.2 Assumptive Mood

convinced that ~; *feel sure that* ~; *there's no doubt that* ~; *must (be)* ~; *surely* ~

❖ It expresses that the realization of the marked action or state is assumed to be very probable.

㊤ **N/n/V/i** ni chigai nai に違いない

N/n/V/i ni kimatte iru に決まっている

TA/na/i tsumori {D} つもりだ/です

N/n/V/i ni sōi nai に相違ない

N/n de nakute nan darō でなくてなんだ ろう

A nai de wa okanai ないではすまない

➤ [*lit.*] **A** zu ni wa okanai ずにはおかな い

Evidential Assumptive

it's only natural (that) ~; no wonder ~; it's normal that ~

❖ It expresses the certainty the speaker has about the realization of the marked state or action based on an observation.

TE (mo) tōzen {D} も当然だ/です

➤ **U** no mo tōzen {D} のも当然だ/です

VN/U no mo (wa) motto mo {D} のはも もっともだ/です

3.3 Tentative Mood

can ~; may ~; might ~; possible to ~; it's not impossible that ~

❖ It expresses that there is a possibility that the marked action will occur.

U/no kanōsē ga aru 可能性がある: *there's the possibility of ~*

A nai to mo kagiranai ないとも限らない: *it's not (entirely) possible that ~*

A nai mono de mo nai ないとも限らない: *it's not (entirely) possible that ~*

I kanenai かねない〔兼ねない〕

❖ Only u. for the third person.

❖ It is implied that the possibility is not wanted.

I eru 得る

[*lit.*] **I** uru 得る

Negative Tentative

cannot ~; can't ~; not possible to ~; there's no way of ~ing

㊤ **U** yō ga nai ようがない〔様がない〕

U* mono de wa nai ものではない

❖ *When u. w. the realis f.《U》it shall be done w. the potential m.

➤ [*col.*] **U** mono ja nai ものじゃない

➤ [*col.*] **U** mon ja nai もんじゃない

㊤ **U** koto wa nai ことはない

U kanōsē ga nai 可能性がない

VN/n/U/i dokoro de wa nai どころでは ない

➤ [*col.*] **VN/n/U/i** dokoro ja nai もの じゃない

I enai 得ない

[*lit.*][*for.*] **U** beku mo nai べくもない

3.4 Deliberative Mood

may ~; might ~; can't tell if ~; I wonder if it's not ~

❖ It indicates that the speaker is not completely sure of the accomplishment of the marked action or state.

⊕ **N/n/V/i** ka mo shirenai かもしれない

➤ [*col.*][*fam.*] **N/n/V/i** ka mo かも

V/na/i no de wa nai darō ka のではないだ ろうか

➤ **N/n** de wa nai darō ka ではないだろう か

[*pol.*] **V/na/i** no de wa arimasen ka のでは ありませんか

➤ [*pol.*] **N/n** de wa arimasen ka ではあり
ません か

[*for.*] **V/na/i** no de wa aru mai ka のでは
あるまいか

➤ [*for.*] **N/n** de wa aru mai ka ではあるま
いか

3.5 Interrogative Mood

> **~?**

❖ It denotes a question.

Ⓕ **N/n/V/i** ka か

Ⓕ [*fam.*] **P** ? ø

V/na/i no ka のか

  ❖ Only u. w. questions that have
interrogative pronouns.

[*fam.*] **V/na/i** no の

⊕ [*fam.*][*mas.*] **N/n/V/i** kai かい

  ❖ Only u. for yes-no questions.

[*fam.*][*mas.*] **V/na/i** no kai のかい

  ❖ Only u. for yes-no questions.

[*fam.*][*mas.*] **N/n** dai だい

  ❖ Only u. w. questions that have
interrogative pronouns.

[*fam.*][*mas.*] **V/na/i** n dai んだい

  ❖ Only u. w. questions that have
interrogative pronouns.

Ⓔ [*col.*][*fam.*] **TA** kke っけ

Ⓔ [*col.*][*fam.*] **V/na/i** n da kke んだっけ

[*col.*][*fam.*] **N/n** da kke だっけ

3.6 Inquisitive Mood

> **~, don't you?; ~, doesn't it?;**
> **~right?; ~ isn't it?; ~is it?**

❖ It signals the speaker's search for
reassurance towards the listener.

Ⓕ **N/n/V/i** ne ね

N/n/V/i nee ねえ

⊕ [*lit.*] **N/n** de wa nai ka ではないか

➤ [*col.*][*fam.*] **N/n/V/i** ja nai (ka) じゃな
いか

  ➤ [*col.*][*fam.*] **N/n/V/i** jan じゃん

⊕ [*for.*] **N/n** de wa arimasen ka ではあ
りませんか

➤ [*col.*][*for.*] **N/n** ja arimasen ka じゃあ
りませんか

⊕ [*lit.*] **V/i** no de wa nai ka のではない
か

➤ [*col.*][*fam.*] **V/i** no ja nai ka のじゃな
いか

➤ [*col.*][*fam.*] **V/i** n ja nai ka んじゃない
か

⊕ [*for.*] **V/i** no de wa arimasen ka ので
はありませんか

➤ [*col.*][*for.*] **V/i** no ja arimasen ka の
じゃありませんか

Assertive Inquisitive

> **~ right?**

❖ It shows that the speaker insists on his
statement but at the same time seeks
confirmation from the listener.

[*col.*] **N/n/V/i** yo ne よね

3.7 Dubitative Mood

> **perhaps ~; I wonder if/whether ~;**
> **don't know if ~**

❖ It indicates that the speaker has certain
doubt in regards to the execution of the
marked action or state.

Ⓔ [*fam.*] **V/n/i** no darō ka のだろうか

➤ [*col.*][*fam.*] **V/n/i** n darō ka んだろう
か

Ⓔ [*for.*] **V/n/i** no deshō ka のでしょうか

➤ [*col.*][*for.*] **V/n/i** n deshō ka んでしょ
うか

[*fam.*] **N/n/V/i** darō ka だろうか

[*for.*] **N/n/V/i** deshō ka でしょうか

[*fam.*] **V/na/i** (no) yara のやら

[*fam.*] **V/i** koto yara ことやら

[*fam.*] **V/na/i** mono yara ものやら

TA* mono ka ものか

❖ *W. clauses that start w. interrogative pronouns.

➤ [*pol.*][*fam.*] **TA** mon desu ka もんです か

➤ [*col.*][*mas.*] **TA** mon ka もんか

Emphatic Dubitative

I wonder if ~

❖ It expresses a doubt in an emotional way.

⊕ [*fam.*] **N/n/V/Ō/i** ka na かな

[*fam.*] **N/n/V/Ō/i** ka naa かなあ

⊕ [*fam.*][*fem.*] **N/n/V/i** ka shira かしら

4. IRREALIS MODALITY: VOLITIONAL MOODS

Moods that express the desire or willingness for an action or event to take place.

Important Volitional Moods

4.1 **Volitive Mood** [*want to*]: It expresses that someone wants to perform an action.

Ⓕ **I** tai たい

• **Semblative Volitive Mood** [*wants to*]: It indicates that someone other than the speaker seems to want to perform an action.

⊕ **I** tagaru たがる

• **Patient Volitive Mood** [*want s.o. to*]: It indicates that someone wants someone else to perform an action.

⊕ **TE** hoshii 欲しい

4.2 **Desiderative Mood** [*would be good if*]: It refers to actions that are considered as desirable.

⊕ **BA** ii いい

⊕ **TA** ra ii らいい

4.3 **Expectative Mood** [*hope*]: It expresses that an action or state is expected to be carried out.

⊕ **U/na/no/i** hazu {D} はずだ/です

- -

4.1 Volitive Mood

want to ~

❖ It expresses the explicit desire to perform the marked action.

Ⓕ **I** tai たい

❖ Only u. in the first person singular ('I') in declarative sentences or in the second person ('you') in interrogative sentences.

Semblative Volitive

(seems to) want to ~; wants to ~

❖ It expresses that the subject of the sentence seems to have the will to perform the marked action.

⊕ **I** tagaru たがる

❖ Only u. w. the second person (you) or the third person (he; she; it; they).

❖ Usually appearing in the progressive f. tagatte iru.

Patient Volitive

want s.o. to ~

❖ It expresses the desire for someone to do something.

⊕ **TE** hoshii 欲しい

❖ U. towards people of equal or lower social status.

[*pol.*] **TE** moraitai もらいたい〔貰いたい〕

[*hum.*] **TE** itadakitai いただきたい〔頂きたい〕

❖ U. towards people of superior social status.

Evidential Volitive

feel like ~

U ki ga aru 気がある

U ki ni naru 気になる

4.2 Desiderative Mood

hope (to) ~; wish ~; would like to ~; would be nice if ~

❖ It expresses the hope that the marked action will be carried out.

⊕ **BA** ii いい

⊕ **TA** ra ii らいい

Ⓔ **U** to ii といい

A* nai mono (darō) ka ないものだろうか

❖ *The neg. potential f.s (Ⓢ E-ranai; Ⓦ E-rarenai).

4.3 Expectative Copula

expect to ~; no wonder ~

❖ It indicates that the marked action is expected to be performed.

⊕ **U/na/no/i** hazu {D} はずだ/です

➢ **U/na/no/i** hazu no ⟨N⟩ はずの...

Negative Expectative

don't expect to/that ~

⊕ **U/na/no/i** hazu ga nai はずがない

Prospective Expectative

it is expected that ~

N/n/V/i to mirareru とみられる

Evidential Expectative

~ as is expected; ~ no wonder

❖ It indicates that the marked action is assumed as expected and hence its realization is not surprising.

N/na/V/i dake no koto wa aru だけのことはある

➢ **N/na/V/i** dake aru だけある

- -

N/na/V/i dake no koto wa atte atte だけあって

N/na/V/i dake atte だけあって

[*lit.*][*for.*] **U** beku shite べくして: ~ *exactly as expected*

Emphatic Negative Expectative

there is no way that ~

Ⓛ **U/na/no/i** wake ga nai わけがない
〔訳がない〕

5. IRREALIS MODALITY: DEONTIC MOODS

Moods that express an assumed necessity for the events or actions to occur.

Important Deontic Moods

5.1 **Obligative Mood** [*have to*; *must*]: It refers to actions or states that must take place.

　Ⓣ **A/ku** nakute wa naranai/ikenai なくては{ならない/いけない}

　⊕ [*col.*][*fam.*] **A/ku** nakucha (naranai/ikenai) なくちゃならない/いけない

　⊕ **A/ku** nakereba naranai/ikenai なければ{ならない/いけない}

　Ⓣ **A/ku** nai to ikenai ないといけない

　⊕ [*fam.*] **A/ku** nai to dame ({D}) ないとだめだ/です

　⊕ [*col.*][*fam.*] **A/ku** nakucha dame ({D}) なくちゃだめだ/です

• **Negative Obligative Mood** [*don't have to*]: It indicates the non-obligation to perform an action.

　Ⓣ **A** nakute (mo) ii なくてもいい

5.3 **Necessitative Mood** [*need to*]: It refers to actions that are considered to be necessary.

　⊕ **VN/U** hitsuyō ga aru 必要がある

5.4 **Directive Mood** [*please*]: It refers to actions that the speaker asks the listener to do.

　Ⓣ [*pol.*] **TE** kudasai ください〔下さい〕

　Ⓣ [*fam.*] **TE** ø

　⊕ [*pol.*] **I** nasai なさい

　⊕ [*col.*][*fam.*] **I** na な

• **Negative Directive Mood** [*please don't*]: It refers to actions that the speaker asks the listener not to do.

　Ⓣ [*pol.*] **A** nai de kudasai ないでください

　Ⓣ [*fam.*] **A** nai de ないで

5.5 **Imperative Mood** [*do*]: It refers to actions that the speaker commands the listener to do.

　⊕ Ⓢ **E** ro ろ

　⊕ Ⓢ [*lit.*] **E** yo よ

⊕ Ⓦ E ø

5.6 Prohibitive Mood [*don't*]: It refers to actions that the speaker commands the listener not to do.

Ⓔ **TE wa** naranai/ikenai は{ならない/いけない}

⊕ [*col.*] cha/ja naranai/ikenai {ちゃ/じゃ}{ならない/いけない}

Ⓕ [*fam.*] **TE wa dame** ({D}) はだめだ/です

⊕ [*col.*][*fam.*] cha/ja dame ({D}) ちゃだめだ/です

5.7 Permissive Mood [*can*]: It refers to actions that the listener has permission to perform.

Ⓕ **TE mo ii** もいい

5.1 Obligative Mood

should ~; have to ~; must ~

❖ It expresses an obligation in a neutral or indirect manner.

Ⓕ **A/ku nakute wa** naranai なくてはならない

  ❖ Usually it expresses a logical or common-sense obligation.

➤ ⊕ [*col.*] **A/ku** nakucha naranai なくちゃならない

N/n de nakute wa naranai でなくてはならない

Ⓕ **A/ku nakute wa** ikenai なくてはいけない

  ❖ Usually it expresses a rather personal obligation.

➤ ⊕ [*col.*] **A/ku** nakucha ikenai なくちゃいけない

N de nakute wa ikenai 出なくてはいけない

⊕ **A/ku** nakereba naranai なければならない

➤ [*col.*] **A/ku** nakerya naranai なけりゃならない

➤ [*col.*] **A/ku** nakya naranai なきゃならない

N/n de nakereba naranai でなければならない

⊕ **A/ku** nakereba ikenai なければいけない

➤ [*col.*] **A/ku** nakerya ikenai なけりゃいけない

➤ [*col.*] **A/ku** nakya ikenai なきゃいけない

N/n de nakereba ikenai でなければならない

⊕ [*col.*] **A/ku** nakucha なくちゃ

[*col.*] **A/ku** nakya なきゃ

[*lit.*] **A/ku** neba naranai ねばならない

  ❖ The v. **suru** takes the f. seneba naranai.

[*lit.*] **A/ku** neba naranau ねばならなう

  ❖ The v. **suru** takes the f. seneba naranai.

Ⓕ **A/ku** nai to ikenai ないといけない

⊕ [*fam.*] **A/ku** nai to dame ({D}) ないとだめだ/です

⊕ [*col.*][*fam.*] **A/ku** nakucha dame ({D}) なくちゃだめだ/です

Ⓔ [*lit.*] **U koto** こと

➤ **VN no koto** のこと

A nai de wa sumanai ないではすまない

447

➤ [*lit.*] **A** zu ni wa sumanai ずにはすまない

TE shikaru beki {D} しかるべきだ/です〔然る可き〕

Negative Obligative

> *don't have to ~*

✤ It expresses the non-obligation to perform the marked action.

Ⓕ **A** nakute mo ii なくてもいい

[*lit.*] **A** nai koto ないこと

5.2 Jussive Mood

> *(one) should ~; let's ~*

✤ It expresses the obligation to perform an action in an impersonal manner.

Ⓤ **U** beki ({D}) べきだ/です

> ✤ suru beki can be contracted to su beki.

Ⓤ **U** mono {D} ものだ/です

> ✤ U. for generic statements.

Negative Jussive

> *(one) shouldn't ~; let's not ~*

✤ It expresses the non-obligatory nature of performing an action in an impersonal manner.

Ⓤ **U** beki de (wa) nai べきではない

➤ [*col.*] **U** beki ja nai べきじゃない

[*lit.*] **U** bekarazu べからず

> ✤ suru bekarazu can be contracted to su bekarazu.

U mono de wa nai ものではない

➤ [*col.*] **U** mono ja nai ものじゃない

➤ [*col.*] **U** mon ja nai もんじゃない

5.3 Necessitative Mood

> *need to ~; it's necessary to ~*

✤ It expresses the explicit need to carry out the marked action.

⊕ **VN/U** hitsuyō ga aru 必要がある

⊕ **VN** ga hitsuyō {D} が必要だ/です

Negative Necessitative

> *don't need to ~; there's no need to ~; not necessary to ~*

✤ It expresses that the marked action does not need to be carried out.

Ⓤ **U** koto wa nai ことはない

➤ [*col.*] **U** koto nai ことない

➤ **U** hodo no koto wa/mo nai ほどのことはない

VN/U hitsuyō wa nai 必要はない

U made mo nai までもない

U ni (wa) oyobanai には及ばない

U hodo no koto mo nai ほどのこともない

Emphatic Negative Necessitative

> *there's no point to ~; it's no use to ~*

Ⓤ **TE** mo hajimaranai も始まらない

TE mo dō ni mo naranai もどうにもならない

5.4 Directive Mood

> *(please) ~; will you ~*

✤ It expresses the request made to the listener to perform the marked action.

Ⓕ [*pol.*] **TE** kudasai ください〔下さい〕

➤ Ⓕ [*fam.*] **TE** ∅

➤ [*hon.*] o **I** kudasai お...ください〔下さい〕

➤ [*hon.*] go **VN** kudasai ご…ください 〔…下さい〕

[*fam.*][*mas.*] **TE** kure くれ

⊕ [*pol.*] **I** nasai なさい

❖ U. by people of a superior social status toward people of equal or inferior social status.

➤ [*hon.*] o **I** nasai お…なさい

➤ [*hon.*] go **VN** nasai ご…なさい

➤ ⊕ [*col.*][*fam.*] **I** na な

[*hon.*] go **VN** negai ご…願う

❖ M. u. w. the pol. f. negaimasu.

[*hon.*] o **I** negau ご…願う

❖ M. u. w. the pol. f. negaimasu.

㊤ [*fam.*][*fam.*] **TE** chōdai ちょうだい 〔頂戴〕

Negative Directive

please don't ~

❖ It expresses the request made to the listener to not perform the marked action.

㊦ [*pol.*] **A** nai de kudasai ないでくださ い

➤ ㊦ [*fam.*] **A** nai de ないで

5.5 Imperative Mood

~; do ~; you must ~

❖ It expresses an explicit command made to the listener.

⊕ Ⓢ **E** ro ろ

⊕ Ⓢ [*lit.*] **E** yo よ

⊕ Ⓦ **E** ø

Ⓐ [*obs.*] **s** kare かれ

N/n ni shite にして

[*lit.*][*for.*] **N/n** de are であれ

[*mas.*] **I** tamae たまえ

[*pol.*] **I** mase ませ

❖ Only. u. w. hon. v.s.

[*obs.*] o **I** お

5.6 Prohibitive Mood

don't ~; you can't ~; must not ~

❖ It expresses a prohibition to perform the marked verb made towards the listener.

㊤ **TE** wa naranai はならない

➤ ⊕ [*col.*] cha naranai ちゃならない

❖ For v.s whose gerundive f. ends in **-te**

➤ ⊕ [*col.*] ja naranai じゃならない

❖ For v.s whose gerundive f. ends in **-de**

㊤ **TE** wa ikenai はいけない

➤ ⊕ [*col.*] cha ikenai ちゃいけない

❖ For v.s whose gerundive f. ends in **-te**

➤ ⊕ [*col.*] ja ikenai じゃいけない

❖ For v.s whose gerundive f. ends in **-de**

㊤ [*fam.*] **TE** wa dame ({D}) はだめだ/です

➤ ⊕ [*col.*][*fam.*] cha dame ({D}) ちゃだ めだ/です

❖ For v.s whose gerundive f. ends in **-te**

➤ ⊕ [*col.*][*fam.*] ja dame ({D}) じゃだめ だ/です

❖ For v.s whose gerundive f. ends in **-de**

㊤ [*mas.*] **U** na な

U majiki ⟨N⟩ まじき

5.7 Permissive Mood

you can ~; it's okay if ~; allowed to ~; it doesn't matter if ~

❖ It expresses permission to perform the marked action.

㊦ Ⓥ **TE** mo ii もいい

➤ [*fam.*] **TE** ii いい

➤ [*for.*] **TE** mo yoroshii もよろしい

➤ [*lit.*] **A** zu to mo yoi ずとも良い

Ⓐ **ku** te mo ii てもいい

Ⓝ **N/n** de mo ii でもいい

Ⓔ **TE** mo kamawanai も構わない

[*for.*] **TE** mo sashitsukenai も差付けない

5.8 Negative Optative Mood

> *cannot keep from ~; cannot help but ~ ;*

❖ It expresses that the subject cannot stop to avoid doing the marked action.

Ⓔ **U** wake ni wa ikanai 訳にはいかない

> ❖ It implies that there is no other choice.

A nai de wa irarenai ないではいられない

➤ [*lit.*] **A** zu ni wa irarenai ずにはいられない

N/n de wa irarenai ではいられない

[*lit.*] **A** zu ni wa orarenai ずにはおられない

[*lit.*] **A** zu ni wa orenai ずには折れない

6. IRREALIS MODALITY: PURPOSIVE MOODS

Moods that express the proposal, suggestion or intention to perform an action.

Important Purposive Moods

6.1 **Hortative Mood** [*let's*]: It indicates that the speaker urges the listener to perform an action together.

Ⓣ [*fam.*] **Ō** ø

Ⓣ [*pol.*] **I** mashō ましょう

6.2 **Propositive Mood** [*how about*; *shall we*]: It indicates that the speaker proposes the listener to perform an action.

Ⓣ [*fam.*] **Ō** ka か

Ⓣ [*pol.*] **I** mashō ka ましょうか

Ⓣ [*pol.*] **I** masen ka ませんか

⊕ [*lit.*] **Ō** de wa nai ka ではないか

⊕ [*col.*][*fam.*] **Ō** ja nai ka じゃないか

⊕ [*fam.*] **TA** ra dō らどう

6.3 **Suggestive Mood** [*you'd better*]: It indicates that the speaker indirectly suggests the listener to perform an action.

Ⓣ **V** hō ga ii ほうがいい

6.4 **Intentional Mood** [*intend to*; *will*]: It indicates that the speaker intends to perform an action.

Ⓣ **U/no** tsumori {D} つもりだ/です

⊕ **U yotē** {D}

⊕ **Ō to omou** と思う

6.5 **Determinative Mood** [*make sure that*]: It indicates the strong determination to perform an action.

⊕ **U yō ni suru** ようにする

6.6 **Probationary Mood** [*try to*]: It points out the attempt to perform an action.

⊕ **TE miru** みる

6.7 **Decisive Mood** [*decide to*]: It points out the decision to perform an action.

⊕ **U koto ni naru** ことになる

6.8 **Final Mood** [*(in order) to*; *so that*]: It refers to the performance of an action understood as the objective for which another action is performed.

下 **VN/I ni** に

⊕ **V tame (ni)** ために

⊕ **U yō ni** ように

⊕ **U no ni** のに

6.1 **Hortative Mood**

let's ~

❖ It expresses that the listener is invited to do the marked action together with the speaker.

下 [*fam.*] **Ō ø**

下 [*pol.*] **I mashō** ましょう

Emphatic Hortative

let's ~ okay?

Ō yo よ

6.2 **Propositive Mood**

how/what about ~?; shall we ~?; why don't you ~

❖ It presents the proposal to carry out the marked action.

下 [*fam.*] **Ō ka** か

下 [*pol.*] **I mashō ka** ましょうか

❖ U. to propose an action performed by the speaker.

下 [*pol.*] **I masen ka** ませんか

❖ U. to propose an action performed by the listener.

⊕ [*lit.*] **Ō de wa nai ka** ではないか

➤ ⊕ [*col.*][*fam.*] **Ō ja nai ka** じゃないか

⊕ [*fam.*] **TA ra dō** らどう

➤ [*fam.*] **N wa dō** はどう

[*pol.*] **TA ra dō desu ka** らどうですか

➤ [*pol.*] **N wa dō desu ka** はどうですか

[*fam.*] **A nai mono (darō) ka** ないものだろうか: *can't I/we?*

6.3 Suggestive Mood

> *would be good if ~; you'd better ~; you should ~*

❖ It presents the strong suggestion to perform the marked action.

⊤ **V hō ga ii** ほうがいい

➤ **U koto {D}** ことだ/です

➤ **VN no koto {D}** のことだ/です

Negative Suggestive

> *you'd better not ~*

A nai hō ga ii ないほうがいいい

6.4 Intentional Mood

> *intend/plan to ~; will ~; going to ~*

❖ It expresses the clear intention to carry out the marked action in the future or the clear conviction that a state is such.

⊤ **V/no tsumori {D}** つもりだ/です

⊕ **U yotē {D}** 予定だ/です

➤ **VN no yotē {D}** の予定だ/です

⊕ **Ō to omou** と思う: *think about ~ing; plan to ~*

N/n/V/i darō to omu だろうとむ

TE miseru みせる

6.5 Determinative Mood

> *make sure that ~*

❖ It expresses a strong determination to perform the marked action.

⊕ **U yō ni suru** ようにする〔様にする〕

6.6 Probationary Mood

> *try to ~*

❖ It points out the intent to perform the marked action.

⊕ **TE miru** みる

⊥ **Ō to suru** とする

[*lit.*] **A n to suru** んとする

6.7 Decisive Mood

> *decide to ~*

❖ It expresses that someone decides to perform the marked action.

⊕ **U koto ni suru** ことにする

U koto ni kimeru ことに決める

Passive Decisive

> *has been decided that ~*

⊕ **U koto ni naru** ことになる

6.8 Final Mood

> *to ~; in order to ~; so that ~*

❖ It expresses that the marked action is the objective for which the action of the predicate is performed.

⊤ **VN/I ni** に

  ❖ Only u. before motion v.s such as **iku** (*to go*) or **kuru** (*to come*).

⊕ **U tame ni** ために〔為に〕

  ❖ Referring to action or states that are controlled by the subject.

➤ **U tame no ⟨N⟩** ための...〔為の...〕

⊕ **U* yō ni** ように〔様に〕: *so that ~*

  ❖ *U. w. the potential or neg. f.s of the v. when the subject is the first person.

  ❖ Referring to action or states that are not controlled by the subject.

⊕ **U no ni** のに: *for the purpose of ~*

  ❖ It implies a process in order to approach the goal.

Ⓔ **U** (no) ni wa のには

❖ It implies a process in order to approach the goal that is morally or practically judged

[*lit.*][*for.*] **U** beku べく

❖ suru beku can be contracted to su beku.

[*for.*] **VN** katagata かたがた

[*lit.*] **A** n ga tame ni んがために〔んが為に〕

Negative Final

(in order) *not to* ~

Ⓔ **TE** wa ikenai kara はいけないから

U/na/i koto no nai yō (ni) ことのないよ うに〔事のな様〕

6.9 Preferential Mood

would rather ~; would better ~

❖ It expresses a preference to perform the marked action over another one.

V hō ga mashi {D} ほうがまし だ/です: *would rather ~*

V hō ga ii ほうがいい: *would be better to ~*

Comparative Preferential

rather than ~

❖ It expresses a preference to perform the action of the predicate rather than the marked action.

U kurai nara くらいなら

U gurai nara ぐらいなら

U yori より

Negative Preferential

there's no choice but ~

❖ It expresses that there is no alternative to the option expressed through the marked noun or verb.

U (yori) hoka (ni) (wa) ⟨**A**⟩ nai より他に/は ない

6.10 Instrumental Mood

by ~ing

❖ It indicates that the marked verb is a method to reach an objective.

V koto de ことで

V koto ni yotte ことによって

V koto ni yori ことにより

7. IRREALIS MODALITY: SUBJECTIVE MOODS

Moods that denote certain emotions inferred in the statements.

Important Subjective Moods

7.1 Assertive Mood [*you know*]: It expresses that the speaker makes a statement in an assertive or insistent manner.

Ⓣ **N/n/V/i** yo よ

7.2 Admirative Mood [*!*]: It expresses that the speaker feels a surprise in his or her statement.

Ⓣ [*fam.*] **N/n/V/i** na な

7.1 Assertive Mood

~ you know; I tell you ~; sure ~; ~!

❖ It indicates that the speaker insists on his or her statement.

Ⓣ **N/n/V/i** yo よ

[*col.*][*fam.*] **V/na/i** no yo のよ

[*col.*][*fam.*][*mas.*] **N/n/V/i** sa さ

[*col.*][*fam.*][*mas.*] **V/i** zo ぞ

[*col.*][*fam.*][*mas.*] **V/i** ze ぜ

[*col.*][*fam.*][*fam.*] **V/i** wa わ

Ⓤ tomo とも

Quotative Assertive

I'm telling you (that) ~; I told you that ~

❖ It expresses in a strong and reiterative way something that the speaker wants to make clear and that has been mentioned before.

[*col.*][*fam.*] **P** tte って

[*col.*][*fam.*] **P** tteba ってば

7.2 Admirative Mood

~!

❖ It expresses a certain surprise on the part of the speaker.

Ⓣ [*fam.*] **N/n/V/i** na な

[*fam.*] **N/n/V/i** naa なあ

[*fam.*][*fam.*] **V/i** wa nee わねえ

[*fam.*][*fam.*] **N/n** nee ねえ

Ⓛ [*lit.*] **V/na/i** koto ka ことか

7.3 Emphatic Mood

do ~; even ~; indeed ~

❖ It indicates that the marked action is reaffirmed, putting an emphasis on it.

I wa suru はする

ku wa aru はある

n de wa aru ではある

V/na/i koto wa ⟨V/{D}/i⟩* ことは...

 ❖ *The same v., adj. v. or adj. n. as ⟦V/na/i⟧ .

Negative Emphatic

definitely not ~; absolutely not ~; there's no way (that) ~; as if ~

❖ It expresses a negation in an emphatic way.

U mono ka ものか

➤ [*pol.*][*fam.*] **U** mon desu ka もんですか

➤ [*col.*][*mas.*] **U** mon ka もんか

I ya/wa shinai {や/は}しない

7.4 Superlative Mood

(is) very/extremely/so ~

❖ It denotes that the qualities expressed by the marked verb or adjective are present to a higher degree than usual.

U/n/i to itta ra nai と言ったらない

➤ [*col.*] **U/n/i** tta ra nai ったらない

n/s sa to itta ra nai さと言ったらない

U/na/i koto to itta ra nai ことと言ったらない

➤ [*col.*] **U/na/i** koto tta ra nai ことった
らない

[for.] **V/na/i** nado to iu mono de wa nai
などというものではない

[*col.*] **V/na/i** nante mon ja nai なんても
んじゃない

[*col.*] **V/na/i** no nan no tte のなんのって

i kagiri {D} 限り だ/です

[*for.*] **N** no itari {D} の至り だ/です

[*for.*] **N** no kiwami {D}/ni に極み だ/です/に

[*for.*] **n** kono ue nai この上ない

[*for.*] **na/i** koto kono ue nai ことこの上
ない

7.5 Derogatory Mood

have the nerve to ~

❖ It indicates a sensation of disdain
expressed towards the marked action.

[*col.*] **TE/I** yagaru やがる

VII. CASE

The term 'case' refers to how nominals establish syntactic or semantic relationships with verbals or other nouns.

Cases can be separated into six main categories that refer to the type of those relationships. The six categories, or 'alignments', are the following:

1. **Syntactic Alignment**: It refers to the relations of grammatical functionality that the verb of the clause (predicate) has with respect to a nominal word.

2. **Complementary Alignment**: It refers to the semantic relations of dependence that a noun has with respect to another explicit or implicit noun.

3. **Focal Alignment**: It refers to the relationship between the main topic or 'focus' of the sentence with respect to the rest of it.

4. **Delimitative Alignment**: It refers to quantitative relationships.

5. **Conjunctive Alignment**: It refers to the conjunction of two or more nouns.

6. **Adjunctive Conjuncts**: It refers to the semantic extra information that a noun gives in relation to the verb.

1. SYNTACTIC ALIGNMENT

Cases that place the noun in a distinctive syntactic relationship with regard to the verb in the predicate, referring to the subject or arguments other than the complements, i.e. objects or agents in passive or causative constructions.

Important Syntactic Cases

1.1 **Nominative Case**: It refers to the subject of the sentence.

ⓕ N ga が

1.2 **Accusative Case**: It refers to the direct object of the sentence.

ⓕ N o を

1.3 **Dative Case** [*to; for*]: It refers to the indirect object of the sentence.

ⓕ N ni に

1.4 **Agentive Case** [*by*]: It refers to the agent of a passive or causative verb.

ⓕ N ni に

- -

1.1 Nominative Case

a(n) ~; the ~

❖ Case that points to the subject of the sentence, that is, 'what' or 'who' does the action defined by the verb of the sentence.

Ⓣ **N ga** が

Attributive Nominative

> *that ~*

❖ It marks the subject of a relative clause.

N ga が

N no の

1.2 Accusative Case

> *a(n) ~; the ~*

❖ Case that points out the direct object of the sentence, that is, the object on which the action of the verb is focused.

Ⓣ **N o** を

Thematic Accusative

> *focusing on ~; on ~; over ~*

❖ It points to the direct object of the verb, making it the focal point on which the verb is centered. It can sometimes overlap with the correlative case [☞ VII.1.5]

Ⓔ [*for.*] **N o chuushin ni** を中心に

➤ [*for.*] **N o chuushin ni/to shite** を中心にして

[*for.*] **N o megutte** をめぐって〔を巡って〕

➤ [*lit.*] **N o meguri** をめぐり〔を巡り〕

- -

➤ **N o meguru** 〈**N**〉

➤ **o chuushin to shita** 〈**N**〉

➤ **o chuushin to suru** 〈**N**〉

1.3 Dative Case

> *to ~; for ~*

❖ Case that highlights the indirect object of the sentence, that is, 'to what or who' or 'for what or who' the action of the verb is performed.

Ⓣ **N ni** に

Thematic Dative

> *to ~; for ~*

❖ It identifies the indirect object of the sentence while making it the main focus of the discourse.

Ⓔ **N ni wa** には

Ⓔ **N ni totte** にとって

N ate ni あてに〔宛てに〕: *addressed to ~*

Purposive Dative

> *oriented to ~; aimed at; intended for ~; for ~*

❖ It identifies the marked noun as the indirect object of the sentence for which or for the benefit of which the verb in the sentence acts.

Ⓔ **N muke ni** 向けに

Correlative Dative

> *suitable for ~; designed for ~; for ~*

❖ It identifies the marked noun as the indirect object of the sentence for which something is designed for.

Ⓔ **N muki ni** 向きに

Contrastive Dative

> *compared to ~; in contrast to ~; in comparison to/with ~; whereas ~; while ~*

❖ It identifies the marked noun as an object to which something is compared.

Ⓔ **N ni/to kurabete** に比べて: *compared to ~*

➤ N ni kurabe に比べ

➤ N ni kurabereba に比べれば

➤ N ni/to kuraberu to に比べると

N ni hikikae に引き換え: *in contrast to ~*

Ⓛ **N** ni tai shite に対して: *as opposed to ~; in contrast to ~*

➤ [*lit.*] **N** ni tai shi に対し

- -

➤ N ni tai suru ⟨**N**⟩

➤ N ni tai shite no ⟨**N**⟩

Oppositive Dative

against ~; opposing ~

❖ It expresses that the marked noun is something against which the subject of the sentence is positioned.

Ⓛ **N** ni han shite に反して: *against ~; contrary to ~; in contrast to ~*

➤ [*lit.*] **N** ni han shi に反し

➤ [*lit.*] **N** ni tai shi に対し

Substitutive Essive

in place of ~; in exchange for ~; in spite of ~; on behalf of ~; instead of ~

Ⓛ **N** ni kawatte に代わって

➤ Ⓛ [*lit.*] **N** ni kawari に代わり

N ni hikikae に引き換え

Lower Limitative Dative

only for ~

N ni kagitte に限って

➤ [*lit.*] **N** ni kagiri に限り

1.4 Agentive Case

by ~

❖ Case that identifies the agent of a passive or causative phrase, showing 'what or who' is the performer of a passive or causative verb.

Ⓕ **N** ni に

Ⓛ **N** ni yotte によって〔に　因って〕

❖ When the subject of the sentence is a creation, invention or discovery made by the agent complement.

➤ [*lit.*] **N** ni yori により

- -

➤ N ni yoru による

➤ N ni yoru ⟨**N**⟩ による

2. COMPLEMENTARY ALIGNMENT

Cases that mark nominals as nominal complements to other explicit nominals in a semantically dependent relation.

Important Complementary Cases

2.1 **Genitive Case** [*of*; *'s*]: It indicates that a noun has a dependent relationship to another noun.

Ⓕ **N** no の

2.2 **Comitative Case** [*(together) with*]: It establishes a relationship of joint participation in the action of the verb among two or more nouns.

Ⓣ **N to** と: *with* ~

2.3 Privative Case [*without*]: It indicates a lack of participation in the action of the verb.

⊕ **N nashi** なし

4.1 Genitive Case

of ~; ~'*s*

❖ Case that establishes a dependent relationship between the marked noun and the noun that follows the particle, making the latter dependent on the former.

Ⓣ **N no** の

[*lit.*][*obs.*] N ga が

2.2 Comitative Case

(together) with ~; *along with* ~

❖ Case that identifies a noun as an element or individual that is physically or metaphorically accompanied by the subject of the sentence.

Ⓣ **N to** と: *with* ~

N to issho ni と一緒に: *together with* ~

Ⓤ [*for.*] **N to tomo ni** とともに〔と共に〕: *together with* ~

[*for.*] **N ni tomonatte** に伴って: *along with* ~; *accompanied by* ~

❖ M. u. w. abstract n.s.

➤ [*for.*] **N ni tomonai** に伴い

[*for.*] **N o/mo kanete** を兼ねて: *combined with* ~

[*lit.*] **N to aimatte** と相まって: *coupled with* ~

2.3 Privative Case

without ~; *no* ~

❖ Case that indicates the absence of the marked element.

⊕ **N nashi** なし〔無し〕

➤ [*for.*] **N nashi de/ni (wa)** なしでは

N (koto) naku ことなく

❖ It expresses the lack of s.t. in an adverbial manner, that is, always in connection to a verb.

N nuki de/ni (wa) 抜きでは

➤ [*for.*] **N nuki de/ni shite (wa)** 抜にしては

N naku shite (wa) なくしては

N ni yorazu によらず〔に寄らず〕: *without (depending on)* ~

3. FOCAL ALIGNMENT

Cases that point out the main or secondary topics of a sentence.

Important Focal Cases

3.1 **Thematic Case**: It shows the main theme or focus of the discourse.

Ⓣ **N wa** は

459

3.3 **Cumulative Case** [*too*]: It shows the theme or focus of the speech understood as an implicit addition to another theme.

Ⓣ **N mo** も

3.4 **Concessive Case** [*even*]: It expresses a concession, that is, something that is not expected.

⊕ **N(p) mo** も

⊕ **N made** まで

3.5 **Correlative Case** [*about*]: It denotes a relationship with respect to a specific topic.

⊕ **N ni tsuite (wa)** について は

3.6 **Enunciative Case** [*such as*]: It presents a noun as a representative example within a category of things that usually acts as the topic of the sentence.

⊕ **N nado {p}** など

3.1 Thematic Case

as for ~; the ~; talking about ~; speaking of ~

❖ Case that introduces the main theme of the sentence, that is, 'what' or 'who' is the sentence about, which can be the subject but not necessarily.

Ⓣ **N wa** は

Contrastive Thematic

that ~

❖ It turns the marked noun into the focus of the discourse insofar as it is contrasted with another element mentioned before.

Ⓣ **N wa** は

Emphatic Thematic

when it comes to ~; speaking of ~; as for ~

❖ It introduces a new topic to the discourse with the intention of drawing all the attention to it.

Ⓣ **N to ieba** といえば 〔と言えば〕

N to iu to というと 〔と言うと〕

N to itta ra といったら 〔と言ったら〕

N to kita ra と来たら

➤ [*col.*][*fam.*] **N tta ra** ったら

N ni/to naru to {に/と}なると

N to iu ⟨N⟩ wa という...は

  ❖ Usually having neg. implications.

[*for.*] **N ni itatte (wa)** に至っては

[*lit.*] **N taru ya** たるや

[*lit.*] **N taru mono** たるもの

Quotative Thematic

speaking of ~; something called/named ~

❖ It introduces a new topic to the discourse that is about to be defined or explained.

N to wa とは ❖ M. u. for definitions.

[*col.*] **N tte** って

[*col.*] **N** tte ieba っていえば〔って言えば〕

➤ [*col.*] **N** tteba ってば

N to iu mono wa というものは〔と言う物は〕

[*col.*] **N** to iu no wa というのは〔と言うのは〕

3.2 Emphatic Case

(the) very ~; precisely ~; ~ in particular

❖ It points out the topic of the discourse and places a strong emphasis on it.

Ⓔ **N(p*)** koso こそ

❖ *ni, e, de, to, kara and *made*.

3.3 Cumulative Case

also ~; ~ too; either ~

❖ It makes the marked noun the main focus of the discourse while indicating that the noun is an addition to another explicit or implicit central element inferred in the discourse.

Ⓣ **N(p*)** mo も

❖ *ni, e, de, to, kara and *made*.

[*col.*][*fam.*] **N(p*)** datte だって

❖ *ni, e, de, to, kara and *made*.

[*for.*] **N** ni kuwaete にくわえて〔に加えて〕: *in addition to ~*

[*lit.*] **N** ni kuwae: に加え

3.4 Concessive Case

even ~

❖ Case that marks a noun in order to define it as a subjectively unexpected element or circumstance within the discourse.

Ⓜ **N(p*)** mo も

❖ *ni, e, de, to, kara or *made*.

Ⓜ **N** made まで

Ⓤ **N(p*)** sae さえ

❖ *ni, e, de, to, kara or *made*.

[*col.*][*fam.*] **N(p*)** datte だって

❖ *ni, e, de, to, kara or *made*.

[*for.*] **N(p*)** sura すら

❖ *ni, e, de, to, kara or *made*.

[*for.*] **N** ni shita tokoro de にしたところで

[*for.*] **N** ni shita tte にしたって

[*lit.*] **N** tote とて

C tari to mo たりとも: *(not) even ~*

❖ Only u. before neg. v.s.

Contrastive Concessive

(as) for ~; considering that is ~

❖ It indicates that the qualities of the marked noun do not correspond comparatively to what would be expected of it.

Ⓔ **N** ni shite wa にしては

[*col.*] **N** no wari ni (wa) のわりには〔の割には〕

N to shite wa にしては

N no temae の手前

3.5 Correlative Case

about ~; concerning ~; regarding ~; in regards to ~; in relation to ~; on ~

❖ It marks a noun by semantically indicating that it is the topic which the discourse is concerned 'about'.

Ⓜ **N** ni tsuite (wa) については〔に就いて/に付いて〕: *about ~*

N no koto {p} のこと〔の事〕: *(things) about ~*

Ⓛ **N** ni kakete (wa) にかけては〔に掛けて〕: *concerning ~; regarding ~*

❖ Usually occurring w. pos. elements.

Ⓛ [*for.*] **N** ni kan shite (wa) に関しては: *in relation to ~*

➤ [*lit.*] **N** ni kan shi に関し

Ⓛ **N** ni tai shite に対して: *with respect to ~*

N ni kakawatte に関わって: *related to ~; in connection with ~*

➤ [*lit.*] **N** ni kakawari に関わり

N ni tera shite に照らして: *in light of ~*

- -

➤ **N** ni tsuite no ⟨**N**⟩

➤ **N** ni kan suru ⟨**N**⟩

➤ **N** ni kakawaru ⟨**N**⟩

➤ **N** ni matsuwaru ⟨**N**⟩

Dependent Correlative

depending on ~

❖ It establishes that the marked noun is the object on which the predicate depends.

Ⓛ **N** ni yotte によって〔に依って〕

➤ [*lit.*] **N** ni yori により

N (no) ikan de (wa) のいかんでは〔如何で〕

➤ **N** (no) ikan ni yotte (wa) のいかんによっては〔如何によって〕

N shidai de 次第で

Negative Dependent Correlative

regardless of ~; despite ~

❖ It establishes that the predicate of the sentence unfolds independently of the marked noun.

N ni yorazu によらず〔に寄らず〕

N mo/o kaerimizu を顧みず

[*for.*] **N** ni (mo) kakawarazu にも関わらず

[*for.*] **N** o towazu を問わず

[*for.*] **N** o yoso ni をよそに: *indifferent to ~*

[*for.*] **N** ni kankē naku に関係なく

[*for.*] **N** (no) ikan ni yorazu のいかんによらず〔にいかんに依らず〕

[*for.*] **N** (no) ikan ni kakawarazu のいかんに関わらず

[*for.*] **N** (no) ikan o towazu のいかんを問わず

Perlative Correlative

in accordance with ~; according to ~; following ~; as ~

❖ It indicates that the marked noun refers to something whose parameters are followed.

N ni sotte に沿って: *following ~; in accordance with ~*

N ni soi に沿

N ni ōjite に応じて: *complying with ~; according to ~*

N ni shitagatte に従って: *following ~*

N ni shitagai に従い

N ni nottotte に則って: *following ~; in accordance with ~*

N (no) toori (ni) の通りに: *(in the same way) as ~*

N doori (ni) 通りに

N no ten {p*} の点: *in terms of ~*
　❖ **de, ga* or *o*.

[*for.*] **N** ni tomonatte に伴って: *associated with ~*

[*for.*] **N** ni tomonai に伴い

[*lit.*] **N** ni soku shite に即して: *in line with ~*

Contrastive Correlative

in the role of ~; in the capacity of ~; as ~

❖ It indicates that the marked noun is a role that someone plays.

Ⓔ **N to shite** として

Equivalent Correlative

on par with ~; equivalent to ~; equal to ~; at the same level as ~

❖ It indicates that the marked noun is something with respect to which the subject is equated.

N nami ni 並みに

- -

➤ **N nami** {D}

➤ **N nami no** ⟨N⟩

Quotative Correlative

according to ~; based on ~ (what s.o. has said)

❖ It indicates that the marked noun is a person or entity that has said something on which the discourse of the predicate of the sentence is based.

Ⓔ **N ni yotte** によって〔に因って〕

Ⓔ **N ni yoru to** によると

Ⓔ **N ni yoreba** によれば

N no ue de wa の上では: *as far as ~ is concerned* ❖ U. for abstract n.s.

3.6 Enunciative Case

such as ~; for example ~; ~ or the like; ~ or something/anything

❖ Case used to enunciate a noun as a representative example of something.

⊕ **N nado** {p} など〔等〕

Ⓔ **N ka nani ka** か何か

➤ [*col.*] **N ka nanka** かなんか

[*for.*] **N tō** 等: *~ etc*

[*col.*][*fam.*] **N datte** だって

N da no だの

❖ M. u. when the speaker is complaining about s.t.

N de mo でも

Emphatic Enunciative

(even) things like ~; even ~

❖ Used to give the marked noun a hint of emotion, be it astonishment, envy, disgust or admiration.

Ⓔ **N nante** なんて

Ⓔ [*col.*] **N nanka** {p} なんか

N nado to wa などとは

4. CONJUNCTIVE ALIGNMENT

Cases that identify conjunct relationships, that is, syntactic and semantic relationships that conjoin two or more nouns that convey the same function within the sentence.

Important Conjunctive Cases

4.1 Conjunctive Case [*and*]: It indicates a succession of two or more nouns.

Ⓕ **N to** と

4.2 Enumerative Case [*and (things like)*]: It indicates that a noun succeeds other nouns within an incomplete list.

㊦ **N ya** や

㊥ **N to ka** とか

4.3 Alternative Case [*or*]: It presents an alternative.

㊥ **N mata wa** または

- **Alternative Enumerative Case** [*or (things like)*]: It points out a noun that is considered an alternative within an implicit or explicit list of nouns.

㊦ **N ka** か

4.1 Conjunctive Case

> *~ and*

❖ Case indicating that a noun precedes in succession one or more other nouns.

㊦ **N to** と

[*lit.*][*for.*] **N oyobi** および 〔及び〕

Cumulative Conjunctive

> *both ~ and ...; neither ~ nor ...*

N(p) mo ⟨N(p)⟩ mo も... も

4.2 Enumerative Case

> *(such as) ~ and; and things like ~*

❖ It indicates that a noun precedes in succession one or more other nouns that appear within an incomplete list, this list being understood as a given example.

㊦ **N ya** や

㊥ **N to ka** とか

[*fam.*] **N yara {p}** やら

4.3 Alternative Case

> *~ or*

❖ Case indicating that a noun is an alternative.

㊥ **N mata wa** または 〔又は〕

Alternative Enumerative

> *~ or; or things like ~*

❖ It indicates that a noun is understood as an alternative within an explicit or implicit set of things.

㊦ **N ka** か

5. ADJUNCTIVE ALIGNMENT

Cases that identify the marked noun as a verbal complement that is not essential for the meaning of the predicate, something which is referred as an 'adjunct'.

Important Adjunctive Cases

5.1 Essive Case [*in*; *on*; *at*]: It indicates a location in time or space.

> ⓣ **N de** で
>
> ⓣ **N ni** に

5.2 Lative Case [*to*; *towards*]: It indicates a direction in time or space.

> ⓣ **N e** へ
>
> ⓣ **N ni** に

5.4 Elative Case [*out of*]: It indicates an exit point in space.

> ⓣ **N kara** から

5.5 Ablative Case [*from*; *since*]: It indicates a starting point in space or time.

> ⓣ **N kara** から

5.7 Instrumental Case [*by (means of)*; *with*]: It points out the instrument or method by which an action is performed.

> ⓣ **N de** で

5.8 Benefactive Case [*for (the sake of)*]: It refers to the person who receives a favor.

> ⊕ **N no tame (ni)** のために

5.9 Causal Case [*because of*; *due to*]: It indicates the cause of the action expressed by the verb.

> ⓣ **N de** で
>
> ⊕ **N no tame (ni)** のために

5.12 Semblative Case [*like*]: It indicates a relationship of similarity.

> ⊕ **N no yō ni** のように
>
> ⊕ [*col.*][*fam.*] **N mitai ni** みたいに

5.1 Essive Case

> *in ~; on ~; at ~*

❖ Case indicating that the marked noun is located 'at' a specific point in time or space where the action of the verb is performed.

ⓣ **N/C de** で

❖ When u. w. time expressions, it indicates the amount of time required to perform the action of the v.

ⓣ **N/C ni** に

❖ When u. w. spatial expressions, it also can indicate the place where a state occurs.

[*lit.*] **N/C nite** にて

Thematic Essive

in ~; on ~; at ~

❖ It indicates the place or point in time or space in which an action is performed as it is identified as the main focus of the discourse.

㊤ **N** ni wa には

N de wa では

㊤ [*for.*] **N** ni oite において〔に於いて〕

  ❖ Only u. w. spaces.

[*lit.*] **N** ni shite にして

N ni atte (mo/wa) にあっても/は

  ❖ M. u. w. abstract n.s.

N ni atatte にあたって〔に当たって〕

➢ [*lit.*] **N** ni atari にあたり〔に当たり〕

Lower Limitative Essive

only in ~; only when ~

N dake ni だけに

N ni kagitte に限って

➢ [*lit.*] **N** ni kagiri に限り

Perlative Essive

over ~; through ~; throughout ~; extending for ~; along ~; during ~; for ~

❖ It indicates a space or time that extends along an implicit boundary in which the action defined by the verb is performed.

㊤ **N/C** chuu 中

㊤ **N/C** juu 中

[*for.*] **N/C** ni watatte にわたって〔に渡って〕

➢ [*lit.*] **N** ni watari にわたり〔に渡り〕

㊤ **N** ni kakete (wa) にかけては〔に掛けて〕❖ Only u. for time.

㊤ **N** o too shite を通して ❖ Only u. for time.

㊤ **C** rai 来 ❖ Only u. for time.

N ni sotte に沿って: *along ~* ❖ Only u. for spaces.

N no uchi wa のうちは〔の内は〕❖ Only u. for time.

[*lit.*] **N** o hete お経て: *along ~* ❖ Only u. w. time.

[*lit.*] **C** ni shite お経て: *along ~* ❖ Only u. w. time.

[*lit.*] **N** zoi ni 沿い

Inchoative Essive

starting with/from ~

㊤ **N** o hajime (to shite) を始めとして

[*for.*] **N** o kawakiri ni/to (shite) を皮切り{に/と}して

Inessive

inside ~; within ~

㊥ **N** no naka de/ni の中で/に

N no uchi (ni) の内に

  ❖ M. u. fig. for units within groups.

㊥ **C** inai (de/ni) 以内で/に: *within ~*

  ❖ Only u. for quantities.

[*lit.*] **N** nai (de/ni) 内で/に

Intrative Essive

① *amidst ~; in the middle/midst of ~; among ~* ② *between ~*

❖ It highlights a space in the middle of which an action occurs.

㊥ **N** no naka de/o の中で/を: *amidst ~*)

N no chuushin ni の中心に: *in the center of ~*

N no aida ni の間に: *between ~*

Subessive

below ~; under ~; beneath ~

N no shita ni の下に

N no moto de/ni の下で/に

Superessive

on top of ~; on ~; in ~

N no ue de/ni の上に

[*for.*] **N** jō 上

❖ Frequently u. w. n.s that are related to a field or domain of knowledge.

Adessive

next to ~; beside ~; by ~

N no yoko ni の横に: *beside ~*

N no tonari ni の隣に: *next to ~*

Apudessive

near ~; around ~

N no chikaku ni の近くに (*near ~*)

N no mawari ni の周りに•の回りに (*around ~*)

Antessive

① *in front of ~* ② *before ~*

Ⓕ **N** no mae ni の前に

C mae ni 前に ❖ Only u. for time.

[*for.*] **N** izen (ni) 以前に ❖ Only u. for time.

[*for.*] **N** ni saki dachi に先立ち: *prior to ~* ❖ Only u. for time.

[*for.*] **N** ni saki datsu に先立つ

[*for.*] **N** ni saki datte に先立って

Postessive

① *behind ~* ② *after ~*

Ⓗ **N** no ato de/ni の後で/に

C ato de/ni の後で/に ❖ Only u. for time.

N no ushiro ni の後ろに ❖ Only u. for spaces.

[*lit.*] **N** no nochi ni の後に ❖ Only u. for time.

N ikō (ni) 以降に

❖ Only u. after time-related nominal adv.s or classifiers.

[*for.*] **N** igo (ni) 以後に ❖ Only u. for time.

N no sue (ni) の末に: *at the end of ~* ❖ Only u. for time.

Ⓙ **C** buri (ni) ぶり〔振り〕: *for the first time after ~* ❖ Only u. for time.

C ppuri っぷり

C kagiri de 限りで: *as of the end of ~* ❖ Only u. for time.

[*for.*] **C** o kagiri ni を限りに: *as of the end of ~; starting from ~* ❖ Only u. for time.

5.2 Lative Case

to ~; towards ~

❖ Case indicating that the marked noun is a direction towards which a movement takes place.

Ⓕ **N** e へ ❖ Focuses on direction.

Ⓕ **N** ni に ❖ Focuses on location.

N ni mukete に向けて: *heading to ~; aiming at ~*

N ni mukatte に向かって: *addressing ~; facing ~; heading to ~*

5.3 Illative Case

into ~

N no naka ni の中に

5.4 Elative Case

out of ~

Ⓕ **N** kara から

N o を

5.5 Ablative Case

from ~; since ~

✣ Case indicating that the marked noun is separated 'from' a specific point in space or time.

Ⓕ **N** kara から

[*for.*] **N** yori より

[*for.*] **N/C** irai 以来 ✣ Only u. w. time.

Ⓛ **C** rai 来 ✣ Only u. w. time.

5.6 Prolative Case

through ~; throughout ~; via ~; by (means of) ~

✣ Case that identifies a noun as a means 'through' which one passes physically or metaphorically. In the metaphorical sense, the semantic sense of this case may overlap with that of the instrumental case (*by means of ~*) [☞ VII.4.2].

N o を

N o tootte を通って

Ⓛ [*for.*] **N** o too shite を通して

Ⓛ [*lit.*] **N** o tsuujite を通じて

Ⓛ [*for.*] **N** kēyu 経由: *via ~*

[*lit.*] **N** o kai shite を介して

[*lit.*] **N** o hete を経て

- -

➢ **N** o tsuujite no ⟨**N**⟩

➢ **N** o tsuujita ⟨**N**⟩

➢ **N** o kai shite no ⟨**N**⟩

5.7 Instrumental Case

by (means of) ~; with ~

✣ Case that identifies a noun as a tool or element used in order to perform the action marked by the verb, answering to the questions 'with what?' or 'by what means?'.

Ⓕ **N** de で

[*for.*] **N** o motte をもって〔を以て〕

Ⓛ [*for.*] **N** ni yotte によって〔に因って〕

[*lit.*] **N** ni yori により

[*lit.*] **N** nite にて

N o tsukatte を使って (*using ~*)

[*lit.*] **N** o mochiite を用いいて (*using ~*)

- -

➢ **N** de no ⟨**N**⟩

➢ **N** ni yoru ⟨**N**⟩

➢ [*for.*] **N** nite no ⟨**N**⟩

➢ [*for.*] **N** o motte no ⟨**N**⟩

Lower Limitative Instrumental

only with ~; using only ~

N dake de だけで

5.8 Benefactive Case

for (the sake of) ~

✣ Case that indicates the person or thing for the benefit of which an action is performed.

⊕ **N** no tame (ni) のために〔の為〕

5.9 Causal Case

because of ~; due to ~

✣ Case that highlights the reason why an event occurs or an action is performed.

Ⓕ **N** de で

⊕ [*lit.*][*for.*] **N** no tame (ni) のために〔の 為〕

[*for.*] **N** ni tsuki につき〔に就き〕

[*lit.*] **N** (ga/no) yue (ni) が/のゆえに

Correlative Causal

because of ~; in relation to ~

[*for.*] **N** no kankē de の関係で: *in relation to ~*

Benefactive Causal

thanks to ~

❖ It identifies a noun as the object of gratitude for which a positive consequence is assumed.

N no okage de のお陰で

- -

➤ **N** no okage {D} のお陰

Resultative Causal

thanks to ~; as a result of ~; taking advantage of ~

❖ It identifies a noun as the fortuitous or unplanned cause of a positive consequence.

N o kēki ni を契機に

N o kēki to shite を契機として

N o kikkake ni を切っ掛けに

N o kikkake to shite を切っ掛けとして

N ga kikkake de が切っ掛けで

Expectative Causal

as expected from/of ~; precisely because ~

❖ It marks a noun as the expected cause of the consequence defined by the verb of the sentence.

N dake ni だけに

[*for.*] **N** to atte とあって

5.10 Final Case

for (the purpose/sake of) ~

❖ Case that marks the objective for which an action is performed.

N no tame ni のために〔の為に〕

N ni mukete に向けて

[*lit.*] **N** o meza shite を目指して

[*lit.*] **N** o mokuhyō ni を目標に

- -

➤ **N** ni muketa 〈**N**〉

➤ **N** ni mukete no 〈**N**〉

5.11 Inferential Case

based on ~; on the basis of ~

❖ It identifies a noun as the element on which what is explained in the rest of the sentence is based.

N o moto ni (shite) をもとにして〔元に〕

N ni moto dzuite に基づいて

[*lit.*] **N** ni moto dzuki に基づき

[*for.*] **N** o kihon ni (shite) を基本にして

[*lit.*] **N** o fumaete を踏まえて

[*lit.*] **N** o fumae を踏まえ

[*lit.*] **N** ariki ありき

- -

➤ **N** o fumaeta 〈**N**〉

➤ **N** ni moto dzuku

➤ **N** ni moto dzuku 〈**N**〉

➤ **N** ni moto dzuita 〈**N**〉

➤ **N** o kihon ni suru

Ablative Inferential

in terms of ~; judging from ~; judging by ~; from the standpoint of ~; from the point of view of ~

❖ It indicates that the marked noun is a speculative but well-founded (inferential) source of reasonable judgment.

N kara iu to から言うと

N kara itte から言って

N kara ieba から言えば

N kara suru to からすると

N kara shite からして

N kara sureba からすれば

N kara mite から見て

N kara miru to から見ると

N kara miireba から見れば

Subjective Inferential

in the position of ~; in ~'s position; from ~'s perspective

❖ It indicates that the subject of the sentence is placed under the point of view of the entity or person defined by the marked noun.

N ni shita ra にしたら

N ni sureba にすれば

N ni suru to にすると

5.12 Semblative Case

like ~; as ~; similar to ~; resembling ~

❖ Case that indicates that the marked noun is understood as something in whose similarity the action referred by the verb is carried out.

⊕ N no yō ni のように〔の様に〕

⊕ [*col.*][*fam.*] N mitai ni みたいに

[*lit.*] N no gotoku の如く

- -

➢ N no yō na ⟨N⟩

➢[*col.*][*fam.*] N mitai na ⟨N⟩

[*lit.*] N no gotoki ⟨N⟩ の如き

Formal Semblative

~'s way; ~'s manner; ~'s style

❖ It indicates that something is done in the manner or form of the marked noun.

N buri ぶり〔振り〕

N fuu ni 風に

N nari ni なりに

- -

➢ N fuu no ⟨N⟩

➢ N nari no ⟨N⟩

Negative Semblative

unlike ~

N to wa chigatte と違って

Approximative Semblative

(somewhat) like ~; ~ish

❖ It indicates that the noun is the basis of an approximate appearance.

⊕ N rashii らしい

Ⓛ [*col.*][*fam.*] N ppoi っぽい

---

6. DELIMITATIVE ALIGNMENT

Cases that semantically place the noun within a specific quantitative or physical limitation.

Important Delimitative Cases

6.1 **Limitative Case** [*until*]: It sets a quantitative limit.

⑦ **N/C made** まで

6.2 **Upper Limitative Case** [*as much as; up to*]: It Indicates a quantitative limit not yet reached.

⊕ **N hodo** ほど

6.3 **Lower Limitative Case** [*only; just*]: It indicates a quantitative limit that has already been reached and cannot be exceeded, usually referring to a comparatively small amount.

⑦ **N(p)/C dake {p}** だけ

⊕ **N bakari** ばかり

6.4 **Approximative Case** [*approximately; about*]: It indicates an approximate amount.

⊕ **N/C kurai/gurai** くらい/ぐらい

⊕ **N goro/koro (ni)** 頃に

⊕ [*for.*] **yaku N** 約

6.1 Limitative Case

until ~; up to ~; as far as ~; to ~

❖ It indicates that the marked noun is a temporal, spatial or abstract limit to be reached by the action or state defined by the predicate.

⑦ **N/C made** まで

[*lit.*] **N ni itaru made** に至るまで

Punctual Limitative

by (the time when) ~

⊕ **N/C made ni** までに

6.2 Upper Limitative Case

as much as ~; up to ~; to the extent of/that ~

❖ It indicates that the marked noun has an "upward" quantitative limit, that is, a limit not yet reached.

⊕ **N hodo** ほど 〔程〕

❖ Only u. w. neg. verbal f.s.

C mo も

C kara aru/suru/no 〈N〉 から{ある/する/の}

N made shite までして

Concessive Upper Limitative

at least ~; even as much as ~

N nari to mo なりとも

Comparative Upper Limitative

more than ~; over ~; above ~

⊕ **C ijō** 以上

C amari あまり〔余り〕

6.3 Lower Limitative Case

> *only ~; just ~; ~ alone; as few as ~*

❖ It indicates that the marked noun has a "downward" quantitative limit, that is, a limit that has already been reached and cannot be exceeded, usually considered a small amount.

Ⓕ **N(p*)/C** dake {p*†} だけ

❖*ni, e, to, de, kara* or *made*; †*ga* or *o* are optional.

[*for.*] **N(p*)** nomi {p*†} のみ

❖*ni, e, to, de* or *kara*; †*ga* or *o* are optional.

Ⓜ **N(p*)** bakari ばかり〔計り〕

❖*ni, e, to, de, kara* or *made*

❖ Usually has neg. connotations.

➤ [*col.*] **N** bakkari ばっかり

➤ [*col.*] **N** bakka ばっか

➤ [*col.*] **N** bakashi ばかし

Ⓛ **N/C** kiri きり〔切り〕

➤ [*col.*] **N/C** kkiri っきり

Exclusive Lower Limitative

> *nothing but ~; nobody but ~; as few as ~; only ~*

❖ It indicates that the marked noun has a limit already reached that cannot be exceeded and is associated only with negative predicates, thus indicating exclusivity.

Ⓛ **N(p*)/C** shika しか

❖ U. before neg. predicates.

❖ *ni, e, de, to, kara* or *made*.

Negative Lower Limitative

> *not only/just ~ (but also/as well as/either) ...*

Ⓛ **N** bakari de (wa) naku ばかりではなく

➤ [*col.*] **N** bakari ja naku だけじゃなく

N bakari ka ばかりか

N dake de (wa) naku だけではなく

➤ [*col.*] **N** dake ja naku だけじゃなく

N dokoro ka どころか

[*for.*] **N** nomi ka のみか

[*for.*] **N** nomi narazu にのみならず

[*for.*] **N** mo saru koto nagara もさることながら〔もさる事ながら〕

[*for.*] **N** ni kagirazu に限らず: *not limited to ~*

[*lit.*] **N** ni todomarazu に留まらず: *doesn't stop with ~*

Negative Exclusive Lower Limitative

> *let alone ~; not to mention ~*

Ⓛ **N** wa mochiron はもちろん〔は勿論〕

[*for.*] **N** wa iu made mo naku は言うまでもなく

[*for.*] **N** wa oroka は愚か

[*for.*] **N** wa moto yori はもとより〔は元より〕 ❖ U. before neg. v.s.

[*lit.*] **N** wa iu ni oyobazu は言うに及ばず

Comparative Lower Limitative

> *less than ~; under ~; below ~*

Ⓜ **N/C** ika 以下

C miman 未満

❖ Less than X without X included.

6.4 Approximative Case

> *approximately ~; about ~; about ~*

❖ It indicates that a specific amount or time given by the marked noun is not exact but approximate.

⊕ **N*/C kurai** くらい

❖ *Only demonstrative pronouns.

❖ Only u. w. quantities.

⊕ **N*/C gurai** くらい

❖ *Only demonstrative pronouns.

❖ Only u. w. quantities.

⊕ **N/C goro** (ni) 頃に

❖ Only u. w. time.

⊕ **N/C koro** (ni) 頃に

❖ Only u. w. time.

⊕ [*for.*]**C hodo** ほど 〔程〕

⊕ [*for.*] **yaku N*+C** 約

❖ *Number.

⊕ [*for.*] **oyoso N*+C** およそ 〔凡そ〕

❖ *Number.

C tēdo 程度

C zengo 前後

C bakari ばかり 〔計り〕

Limitative Approximative

close to ~; nearly ~; a little less than ~; almost ~

C chikaku 近く

C tarazu 足らず

6.5 Distributive Case

for (each) ~; per ~; a ~

❖ It indicates that the marked noun or classifier is a fixed amount or time to which a given amount corresponds.

C atari あたり 〔当たり〕

C ate あて 〔充て〕

C ni tsuki につき 〔に就き〕

C ni tsuite (wa) については 〔に付いて〕

Equative Distributive

each ~; ~ at a time; per ~; ~ apiece

❖ It expresses that the marked quantity refers to an equal amount for each person or thing to which it corresponds.

⊕ **C zutsu** ずつ

Temporal Distributive

every (instance of) ~; each ~; at intervals of ~

❖ It expresses that something is repeated at a certain interval.

C goto (ni) ごとに 〔毎〕

❖ It focuses on the moment that s.t. happens.

C oki ni おきに 〔置きに〕

❖ It focuses on the interval.

6.6 Exclusive Case

excluding ~; except for ~; other than ~; apart from ~

❖ It marks a noun that is excluded from the rest of the discourse, placing it outside the semantic context of the predicate.

⊕ **N no/yori hoka** (ni) **wa** {の/より}他には: *other than ~*

⊕ **N wa betsu to shite** は別として: *apart from ~*

N o nozoite (wa) を除いては: *excluding ~; except for ~*

N o nozokeba を除けば

N o oite をおいて 〔を措いて〕: *excluding ~; setting aside ~*

N igai {p} 以外: *with the exception of ~*

[*lit.*] **N wa sate oki** はさておき 〔はさて置き〕: *setting apart ~*

GRAMMAR DICTIONARY

In this part of the book, the plethora of grammatical endings and particles, simple and compound, used in the Japanese language are comprehensively represented in alphabetical order.

A

AGARU 上がる: [*v.*] to go up

㊤ 【I】 Passive Terminative a.

to finish ~; to end ~

❖ Aux. v. indicating that an action has been finished by s.o.

❖ M. u. in the perfective f. **agatta**.

AGEKU あげく〔挙句〕: [*adv.*] in the end; finally; eventually

➤ ㊤ ageku (ni): 【TA】 Resultative Postessive a.

after ~; finally ~; in the end ~

❖ Adverbial p. that expresses that s.t. is done as a result of a previous action or event that has been prolonged in time.

AGERU 上げる/挙げる: [*v.*] to give

㊤ 【TE】 Active Benefactive m.

to do ~ for (the sake of s.o. else)

❖ Subsidiary v. expressing that the subject does s.t. for the benefit of s.o. of equal status who is not part of his or her in-group.

❖ The subject of the modified v. is expressed in the active voice, marked w. the p. **ga**, and the patient is not a member of the agent's in group but is of equal status, and it is marked w. the p. **ni**.

❖ The v. *ageru* is stated from the viewpoint of the person doing the favor.

㊤ 【I】 Active Terminative a.

to finish ~

❖ Aux. v. indicating that s.o. has finished an action.

❖ M. u. in the perfective f. **ageta**.

AIDA 間: [*adv.*] between

➤ ㊥ aida (ni): 【U*/na/i】 Durative a.

while ~; during ~; for ~

❖ Adverbial p. that expresses that two events occur in the same span of time.

❖ *It usually gets attached to the f. **TE iru**.

➤ aida wa: ❶ 【U/na/i】 Durative a. ❷ 【U】 Limitative Durative a.

① *while ~; during ~*

② *as long as ~; as far as ~; while ~*

❖ ❷ Construction that expresses that the action or state of the predicate occurs as long as the marked action lasts.

AMARI あまり〔余り〕: [*adv.*] (not) very (much)

(I) *amaru* 余る (*to remain*)

【C】 Comparative Upper Limitative c.

more than ~; over ~; above ~

ARI あり〔有り〕: [*v. n.*]

O.J. indicative f. of the v. *aru* (*to be*)

【N】 [*obs.*] ≈ **da**

ARIKI ありき〔有き〕: [*aux n.*]

O.J. adjectival f. of the v. *aru* (*to be*)

【N】 [*lit.*] Inferential c.

based on ~; originating from ~

ARIMASEN ありません〔有りません〕: [*i.*]

Neg. f. of the pol. v. *arimasu* (*to have; to exist*)

【ku】 [*pol.*] ≈ **nai**

ARU ある〔在る/有る 〕: [*v.*] to be; to exist; to have

㊦ 【TE】 Stative a.

have/has been ~; be ~ed; be ~ing

❖ Subsidiary v. that marks that an event has occurred and that the state resulting from that event remains.

❖ M. u. w. transitive v.s.

❖ The neg. f. of this v. is irregular: nai.

ATARI あたり〔当たり〕: [n.] hit

(I) *ataru (to hit)*

【C】 Distributive c.

per ~; a ~; for (each) ~

ATE あて〔充て〕: [n.] aim

(I) *ateru (to apply)*

【N】 Thematic Dative c.

addressed to ~; to ~

【C】 Distributive c.

per ~; a ~; for (each) ~

ATO 後: [*adv.*] later; after; behind

➤ ⊕ ato (de/ni)*: 【TA/C】 Postessive a./ c.

after ~

❖ Adverbial p. indicating that one event takes place after another.

❖ *Usually **de** after a v. and **ni** after a classifier.

AU 会う: [*v.*] to come together

Ⓛ 【I】 *to ~ together; to ~ each other*

B

BA ば: [*i.*]

← n. *hakari* 計り (*measurement*)

Ⓣ Ⓦ 【E】 Provisional m. | Ⓢ ☞ **reba**

if ~; provided that ~

❖ Inflection that indicates that the preceding clause is a hypothetical provision for the following clause.

BAAI 場合: [*n.*] case

➤ ⊕ baai {p}: 【V/na/i】 Thematic Conditional m.

in the case/event of ~; if ~

❖ Nominal p. that introduces the moment or circumstance in which a specific event occurs.

❖ M. u. in suppositional circumstances, events that may or may not take place.

BAKARI ばかり〔許り〕: [*p.*]

← n. *hakari* 計り (*measurement*)

⊕ 【N(p*)】 Lower Limitative c.

only ~; just ~; nothing but ~

❖ Delimitative p. indicating that the marked element is the only thing that exists or takes place.

❖ *ni, e, to, de, kara or made.

❖ It has neg. or critizising connotations.

【C】 Approximative c.

about ~; approximately ~; roughly ~; ~ or so

【TA】 [*fam.*] ≈ 〚TA〛 **bakari** {D}

➤ ⊕ bakari {D}: ❶ 【N/na/U/i】 Lower Limitative cop. || ❷ 【TA】 Recent Perfective a.

① *(is) just ~ing; is nothing but ~ing*

477

② *have just ~(ed); just ~(ed)*

❖ ❶ It usually has a somewhat neg. connotation.

➤ ㊤ bakari de: 【V/na/i】 Lower Limitative coordinator

just ~ and

❖ Construction u. to indicate that only the marked action or state occurs.

➤ ㊤ bakari de (wa) naku: ❶ 【N】 Negative Lower Limitative c. ❷ 【V/na/i】 Negative Lower Limitative coordinator

not only ~ (but also)

➤ ㊤ bakari iru: 【TE】 Lower Limitative Progressive a.

be only ~ing; do nothing but ~

➤ bakari ja naku: 【N】 [*col.*] ≈ **bakari de** (wa) **naku**

➤ bakari ka: 【N】 ≈ 〖N〗 **bakari de** (wa) **naku**

➤ bakari ni: 【V/na/i】 Lower Limitative Causal m.

simply/only/just because (of) ~

❖ A single factor causes a neg. situation.

BAKASHI ばかし: [*col.*] ≈ **bakari**

BAKKA ばっか: [*col.*] ≈ **bakari**

BAKKARI ばっかり: [*col.*] ≈ **bakari**

BBURI っぶり: 【I】 = 〖I〗 **buri**

BEKARAZU べからず〔可からず〕: [*p.*]

Neg. f. of the O.J. v. *beku (must)*

【U】 [*lit.*] ≈ **beki de** (wa) **nai**

❖ suru bekarazu can be contracted to su bekarazu.

BEKI べき〔可き〕: [*dep. adj. v.*]

(I) dep. v. beku (must)

➤ ㊤ beki ({D}): 【U】 Jussive m.

(one) should ~; ought to ~

❖ Verbal p. indicating the belief that a state or action should take place.

❖ When referring to people, it is impolite for the speaker to use this expression if the hearer is older or of higher status.

❖ suru beki can be contracted to su beki.

➤ ㊤ beki de (wa) nai: 【U】 Negative Jussive m.

(one) shouldn't ~; mustn't ~

❖ Structure indicating the strong belief that a state or action should not occur.

➤ beki ka: 【U】 Jussive Deliberative m.

wonder if should ~; should ~

➤ beki ja nai: 【U】 [*col.*] ≈ **beki de** (wa) **nai**

BEKU べく〔可く〕: [*dep. v.*] must

【U】 [*lit.*][*for.*] Final m.

in order to ~; to ~

❖ Verbal p. indicating a necessary purpose of an event or action.

❖ suru beku can be contracted to su beku.

➤ beku mo nai: 【U】 [*lit.*][*for.*] Negative Tentative cop.

it is impossible to ~; can't ~; no way ~

➤ beku shite: 【U】 [*lit.*][*for.*] Evidential Expectative m.

~ as expected

❖ 【U】 & ⟨U⟩ are the same verb

❖ U. only w. intransitive v.s

BIRU びる: 【N/n/s】 = **buru**

(for the first time) after ~

BURI ぶり〔振り〕: [*dep. n.*]

(I) dep. v. *buru (to act like)*

【N】 Formal Semblative c. 【I】 Formal Semblative m.

style/manner/method/way of ~

➤ ㊤ buri (ni): 【C】 Postessive c.

BURU ぶる〔振る〕: [*dep. v.*] to act like

← *furu* 振る *(to shake; to swing)*

【N/n/s】 Formal Semblative cop.

behaving like ~; *acting like* ~

❖ M. u. in the progressive f. butte iru.

C

CHA ちゃ: ❶ [*col.*] ≈ 〖TE〗 **wa** ‖
❷ 【ku】 [*col.*] ≈ 〖ku〗 **te wa**

❖ For v.s whose gerundive f. ends in -te

➤ ㊉ cha dame ({D}): [*col.*] ≈ 〖TE〗 **wa dame ({D})**

➤ ㊉ cha ikenai: [*col.*] ≈ 〖TE〗 **wa ikenai**
❖ For v.s whose gerundive f. ends in -te

➤ ㊉ cha naranai: [*col.*] ≈ 〖TE〗 **wa naranai**
❖ For v.s whose gerundive f. ends in -te

CHAU ちゃう: [*col.*] ≈ 〖TE〗 **shimau**
❖ For v.s whose gerundive f. ends in -te.

CHIKAKU 近く: [*adv. n.*] nearly

【C】 Limitative Approximative c.

nearly ~; *close to* ~; *almost* ~

CHIMAU ちまう: [*col.*][*mas.*] ≈ 〖TE〗 **shimau**

❖ For verbs whose gerundive f. ends in -te

CHUU 中: [*n.*] medium

㊤ ❶ 【N/C】 Perlative Essive c. ‖ ❷ 【VN】 Intrative Durative a.

① *throughout* ~; *(extending) for* ~; *during* ~

② *while* ~; *in the middle of* ~

D

DA だ: [*cop.*]

← lit. cop. *de aru (to be)*

㊦ 【N/n】 [*fam.*] Imperfective cop.

am/are/is ~

❖ Copulative f. indicating that the marked n. or adj. n. *is* in respect to the implicit or explicit subject.

❖ This version of the copula is u. in a fam. register when spoken, but in the written language it is understood as a plain f. (not necessarily implying familiarity).

➤ da ga: 【N/n】 Adversative cop.

am/are/is ~ *but*

➤ ㊉ da kara: 【N/n】 [*fam.*] Causal cop.

because (s.o./s.t.) is ~; since (s.t./s.o). is ~.
is ~ so

➤ ㊤ da kedo: 【N/n】 Adversative cop.

am/are/is ~ but; am/are/is ~ however

➤ da kke: 【N/n】 [*col.*][*fam.*]
Interrogative cop.

is it ~?

✤ M. u. when the speaker tries to remember s.t.

➤ da mono ({D}): 【N/n】 [*fam.*] ≈ 〚V/i〛 mono ({D})

➤ da mon: 【N/n】 [*col.*] ≈ da mono ({D})

➤ da ni: 【VN/U】 [*for.*] Lower Limitative coordinator

just to ~; just ~ing

✤ Usually associated w. neg. impressions.

　➤ da ni shinai: 【VN】 [*for.*] Negative Concessive coordinator

　　not even ~; don't/doesn't even ~

➤ da no: 【N】 Enunciative c.

~ and ...; ~ or ...; ~ and things like that;
~ and the like; ~ and so forth

✤ Compound copulative p. u. to enunciate elements of a list in an inexhaustive manner.

✤ M. u. when the speaker is complaining about s.t.

➤ da no ⟨V/n/i⟩ da no to: 【V/n/i】 Enumerative coordinator

(do) things like/as ~ and ...

➤ da tte: 【N/n】 [*col.*] ❶ Quotative subordinator ≈ ① tte | [*col.*][*fam.*] ❷ Quotative m. ≈ ① tte iu ❸ Concessive Provisional cop. ≈ 〚TA〛 tte || ❹ 【N】 ≈ datte || ❺ 【V/na/i】 [*col.*][*fam.*] Inferential m. ≈ n da tte

① *that ~*

② *say(s) that ~; said that ~*

③ *even if (it is) ~*

⑤ *heard that ~*

___

DAI だい: [*p.*]

fam. cop. *da (to be)* + O.J. emphatic assertive p. *i*

【N/n】 [*col.*][*fam.*][*mas.*] Interrogative cop.

is/are ~?

✤ Emphatic p. used to ask questions informally.

✤ Only u. w. questions that have interrogative pronouns.

___

DAKE だけ 〔丈〕: [*p.*]

← n. *take* 丈 (*length*)

① 【N(p*)/C】 Lower Limitative c.

only ~; just ~; ~ alone; nothing but ~

✤ Delimitative p. expressing a limit imposed upon s.t. while putting an emphasis on the limitation.

✤ *ni, e, to, de, kara or made.

【U/na/i】 Upper Limitative subordinator

as much as ~

✤ It establishes an extent up to which an action is performed.

✤ Usually followed by the same v.

➤ dake {D}: 【N/na/V/i】 Lower Limitative cop.

~ that's all; is just ~; is only ~

➤ ① dake {p*}: 【N】 ≈ 〚N〛 dake

✤ *ni, e, to, de or kara; ga or o are optional.

➤ dake aru: 【N/na/V/i】 ≈ dake no koto wa aru

➤ dake atte: 【N/na/V/i】 ≈ dake aru

➤ dake de: ❶ ⊕ 【N】 Lower Limitative Instrumental c. || ❷ 【V】 Lower Limitative Instrumental m. || ❸ 【V/na/i】 Lower Limitative coordinator ≈ bakari de

① *with only ~; using only ~*

② *just by ~ing*

③ *just ~ing*

❖ ❷ It expresses the idea that doing s.t. is enough in order to achieve s.t.

➤ dake de (wa) naku: ❶ 〖N/na/V/i〗 ≈ **bakari de** (wa) **naku**

➤ dake ja naku: 〖N/na/V/i〗 [*col.*] ≈ **dake de** (wa) **naku**

➤ dake ni: ❶ 〖N〗 Expectative Causal c. | ❷ Lower Limitative Essive c. ‖ ❸ 〖V/na/i〗 Expectative Causal m.

① *as expected from/of ~; precisely because ~*

② *only in ~*

③ *and as one would expect ~; so (naturally) ~*

❖ ❶ ❸ Compound p. u. to express that s.t. is the expected cause of a latent result.

➤ dake no koto {D}: 〖U〗 Lower Limitative Necessitative m.

just need to ~

➤ dake no koto wa aru: ❶ 〖N〗 Evidential Expectative cop. ❷ 〖V/na/i〗 Evidential Expectative m.

① *as it is expected of ~*

② *no wonder ~; it's not surprising that ~*

❖ Structure u. to express that an action or state was the expected one.

❖ Only u. when the expected action or state is somehow positive.

➤ dake no koto wa atte: 〖N/na/V/i〗 ≈ **dake no koto wa aru**

➤ dake wa ⟨TA/TE⟩: 〖U〗 Upper Limitative Potential m.

to ~ all that one can; as much as one can ~

❖ 〖U〗 & ⟨TA/TE⟩ are the same verb.

DARŌ だろう: [*cop.*]

← de arō: Presumptive f. of the lit. cop. *de aru*.

Ⓣ 〖N/n〗 [*fam.*] Presumptive cop.

probably is/are ~; surely ~

❖ Presumptive f. of the cop. that casually expresses the speaker's conjecture on the 'being' or existence of s.t.

Ⓣ 〖V/i〗 [*fam.*] Presumptive m.

probably ~; surely ~, I think/guess/assume (that) ~; will likely ~

❖ Presumptive f. of the cop. that casually expresses a speaker's conjecture which is not based on any particular evidence.

➤ darō ga: 〖N/n〗 Concessive Conditional cop.

no matter whether (s.t.) is ~ or ...; even if it is ~ or ...

➤ darō ka: ❶ 〖N/n〗 Dubitative cop. ❷ 〖V/i〗 Dubitative m.

① *I wonder if it is ~*

② *I wonder if ~*

❖ M. u. when the first person asks questions to him or herself.

➤ darō ni: 〖V/i〗 Presumptive Concessive coordinator

even though (it) would ~

❖ M. u. to imbue a statement w. some degree of regret.

➤ darō to (mo): 〖N〗 Concessive Conditional cop.

no matter what/how/who/if ~ is; even if s.t. (is assumed that it). is ~

➤ darō to omu: 〖N/n/V/i〗 ≈ 〖Ō〗 **to omu**

DASU だす 〔出す〕: [*v.*] to take out; to emit

⊕ 〖I〗 Non Intentional Inceptive a.

to start to ~; to begin ~ing; ~ out

❖ Aux. v. indicating that some latent action 'starts' without any personal volition involved.

DATTA だった: [*cop.*]

Perfective f. of the plain cop. *da*.

Ⓣ 【N/n】 [*fam.*] Perfective cop.

was/were ~

➢ Ⓣ datta ⟨N⟩: 【N/n】 Perfective a. Attributive cop.

that/which/who was/were ~

➢ datta ra: 【N/n】 Provisional cop.

if s.t/s.o. was/were ~

DATTE だって: [*p.*]

cop. *da* (*to be*) + col. quotative p. *tte* (*say that*)

【N(p*)】 [*col.*][*fam.*] ❶ Concessive c. ≈ ① de mo ❷ Cumulative c. ≈ ① mo ‖ ❸ 【N】 [*col.*][*fam.*] Enunciative c. ≈ ① nado {p} | ❹ ≈ da tte

① *even* ~

① † ~*ever; any* ~

② *also* ~; ~ *too*

③ *whether* ~ *or* (*not*)

❖ *ni, e, de, to, kara or made.

❖ †When u. w. indefinite pronouns [☞ VO:I.2].

DE₁ で: [*cop.*]

← de atte: Gerundive f. of the lit. cop. *de aru*

【N/n】 Conjunctive cop.

am/are/is ~ *and*

- -

DE₂ で: [*p.*]

Ⓣ ❶ 【N/C】 Essive c. | 【N】 ❷ Instrumental c. | ❸ Causal c.

① *in* ~; *at* ~; *on* ~

② *by* (*means of*) ~; *with* ~

③ *because of* ~; *due to* ~; *by* ~

❖ ❶ It expresses a location in which some activity is performed. This p. cannot be u. to indicate location of existence.

❖ ❶ It indicates the time required to perform the action of the v.

❖ ❷ It marks the instrument or means through the use of which an action is performed.

❖ ❸ It shows that the marked n. is a weak cause or reason for the following part of the sentence.

- -

➢ de are: 【N/n】 ❶ [*lit.*] Concessive Provisional cop. ≈ ② de mo ‖ ❷ [*lit.*] [*for.*] Imperative cop. ≈ 〖E〗 ro

① *even if it is* ~

② *be* ~

➢ de are ⟨N/n⟩ de are: 【N/n】 [*lit.*] Alternative coordinator ≈ de mo ⟨N/n⟩ de mo

➢ de areba: 【N/n】 [*lit.*][*for.*] Provisional m. ≈ nara

➢ de ari: [*lit.*] ≈ de₁

➢ de arimasu: [*for.*][*pol.*][*obs.*] ≈ da

➢ de arimashita: 【N/n】 [*for.*][*pol.*] [*obs.*] ≈ datta

➢ de arimashite: 【N/n】 [*for.*][*pol.*] [*obs.*] ≈ de₁

➢ de arimashō: 【N/N/na/V/i】 [*for.*] [*pol.*][*obs.*] ≈ darō

➢ de arō: 【N/N/na/V/i】 [*lit.*][*for.*] ≈ darō

➢ de arō ga: 【N/n】 [*lit.*][*for.*] ≈ darō ga

➢ de arō ga ⟨N/n⟩ de arō ga: 【N/n】 [*for.*] ≈ de mo ⟨N/n⟩ de mo

➢ de arō to (mo): 【N/n】 [*lit.*][*for.*] ≈ darō to (mo)

➤ de arō to ⟨N/n⟩ de arō to: 【N/n】 [*for.*] ≈ **de mo** ⟨N/n⟩ **de mo**

➤ de {p*} aru: 【N/n】 [*for.*] ≈ **da**

❖ **de* can be followed by focal p.s such as wa; mo; shika; sae or koso.

➤ de aru: [*lit.*][*for.*] ≈ **da**

➤ de aru ⟨N⟩: 【N/n】 [*lit.*][*for.*] Imperfective a. Attributive cop.

… that/which/who is/are ~

➤ de atta: 【N/n】 [*lit.*][*for.*] ≈ **datta**

➤ de atta ⟨N⟩: 【N/n】 [*lit.*][*for.*] ≈ **datta** ⟨N⟩

➤ de atte: 【N/n】 [*lit.*][*for.*] ≈ **de₁**

➤ de atte mo: [*lit.*][*for.*] 【N/n】 ≈ ② **de mo**

➤ de gozaimasen: 【N/n】 = **de wa gozaimasen**

➤ de gozaimashita: 【N/n】 [*for.*] [*pol.*] [*hum.*] ≈ **datta**

➤ de gozaimashō: 【N/n/V/i】 [*for.*] [*pol.*][*hum.*] ≈ **darō**

➤ Ⓔ de gozaimasu: 【N/n】 [*for.*] [*pol.*] [*hum.*] ≈ **da**

❖ M. u. in very formal situations such as vendor-customer relationships.

➤ de mo: ❶ 【N/n】 Concessive Provisional cop. ‖ ❷ 【N】 Enunciative c. | ❸ Cumulative Essive c. ‖ ❹ 【TE】 Concessive Provisional m. = 〖TE〗 **mo**

① *even ~*

① † *~ever; any ~*

② *even (if it is) ~*

③ *something like ~; ~ or something*

④ *also in ~*

⑤ *even if/though ~; although ~*

⑤ ‡ *no matter what/how/when/who ~*

❖ *ni, e, de, to, kara or made.

❖ †When u. w. indefinite pronouns [☞ VO:I.2].

❖ ‡When u. after phrases starting w. interrogative pronouns. [☞ VO:I.2].

➤ de mo aru: 【N/n】 ≈ **mo aru**

➤ de mo ⟨N/n⟩ de mo: 【N/n】 Alternative coordinator

whether it is ~ or …

➤ de mo ⟨N/n⟩ de mo aru: 【N/n】 ≈ **mo** ⟨N/ku⟩ **mo aru**

➤ de mo ii: 【N/n】 Permissive cop.

it's okay if it is ~

➤ de nai ⟨N⟩: Negative Imperfective a. Attributive cop. = **de wa nai** ⟨N⟩

➤ de nai to: 【N/n】 Negative Conditional cop.

if is/are not ~

➤ de nakatta ra: 【N/n】 Negative Postessive Provisional cop.

if it isn't ~

➤ de nakereba: 【N/n】 Negative Provisional cop.

if is/are not ~; unless is/are ~

➤ de nakereba ikenai: 【N/n】 = **de nakereba naranai**

➤ de nakereba naranai: 【N/n】 Obligative cop.

have/has to be ~

➤ de naku: 【N/n】 = **de wa naku**

➤ de nakute: 【N/n】 = **de wa nakute**

➤ de nakute nan darō: 【N/n】 Assumptive cop.

must be ~; is definitely ~

➤ de nakute wa: 【N/n】 Negative Thematic Provisional cop.

if (is/are) not ~

➤ de nakute wa ikenai: 【N/n】 = **de nakute wa naranai**

➤ de nakute wa naranai: 【N/n】
Obligative cop.

have/has to be ~

➤ de sae (mo): 【N/n】 = ② de mo

➤ de tamaranai: 【n】 ≈ te tamaranai

➤ de wa: ❶ 【N】 Thematic Essive c. ‖ 【N/
n】 ❷ Thematic Conjunctive cop. ❸
Thematic Conditional cop.

① *in ~; at ~*

② *is ~ and*

③ *if it is ~*

✢ ❶ Compound thematic essive p. that
makes a place where an action occurs the
main topic of a statement.

➤ ⓕ de wa arimasen: 【N/n】 [*for.*]
[*pol.*] ≈ de wa nai

   ➤ ⓕ de wa arimasen deshita: 【N/
   n】 [*for.*][*pol.*] ≈ de wa nakatta

   ➤ ⊕ de wa arimasen ka: 【N/n】
   [*pol.*] ≈ ① de wa nai ka

➤ de wa aru: 【n】 ≈ 〚ku〛 wa aru

   ➤ de wa aru mai: 【N/n】 [*for.*] ≈
   de wa nai darō

     ➤ de wa aru mai ka: 【N/n】
     [*for.*] ≈ ① de wa nai ka

➤ de wa gozaimasen: 【N/n】 [*for.*]
[*pol.*][*hum.*] ≈ de wa nai

   ➤ de gozaimasen deshita: 【N/n】
   [*for.*][*pol.*][*hon.*] ≈ de wa nakatta

➤ de wa irarenai: 【N/n】 ≈ nai de wa
irarenai

➤ ⓕ de wa nai: 【N/n】 [*lit.*] Negative
Imperfective cop.

am/is/are not ~; isn't ~; aren't ~

   ➤ ⓕ de wa nai 〈N〉: 【N/n】 [*lit.*]
   Negative Attributive cop.

   that is/are not ~; which is/are not ~

   ➤ de wa nai darō: 【N/n】 [*lit.*]
   Negative Presumptive cop.

*probably am/is/are not ~; probably
isn't ~; probably aren't ~*

   ➤ de wa nai darō ka: 【N/n】
   [*lit.*] Deliberative cop.

may be ~

➤ de wa nai deshō: 【N/n】 [*for.*] ≈
de wa nai darō

➤ de wa nai desu: 【N/n】 [*for.*]
[*pol.*] ≈ de wa nai

➤ ⊕ de wa nai ka: ❶ 【N/n】 [*lit.*]
Inquisitive ‖ ❷ 【Ō】 [*lit.*]
Propositive m.

   ① *isn't it ~?; ~ right?; I wonder if
   it's not ~*

   ② *why don't we ~?; let's …*

➤ de wa nai koto mo/wa nai: 【N/
n】 ≈ nai koto mo nai

➤ de wa nai made mo: 【N/n】 ≈
nai made mo

➤ de wa nakarō: 【N/n】 [*lit.*][*obs.*] ≈
de wa nai darō

➤ ⓕ de wa nakatta: 【N/n】 [*lit.*]
Negative Perfective cop.

was/were not ~; wasn't/weren't ~

   ➤ ⓕ de wa nakatta 〈N〉: 【N/n】
   [*lit.*] Negative Perfective a.
   Attributive cop.

   … that/which/who wasn't/weren't ~

   ➤ de wa nakatta desu: 【N/n】
   [*for.*][*pol.*] ≈ de wa nakatta

➤ de wa naku: 【N/n】 [*lit.*][*for.*] ≈ de
wa nakute

   ➤ de wa naku naru: 【N/n】 ≈ naku
   naru

➤ de wa nakute: 【N/n】 Negative
Conjunctive cop.

am/is/are not ~ and

➢ de wa nakute mo: 【N/n】 ≈ **nakute mo**

Ⓣ DESHITA でした: [*pol.*] ≈ **datta**

➢ deshita ra: 【N/n】 [*pol.*] ≈ **datta ra**

Ⓣ DESHŌ でしょう: [*for.*] ≈ **darō**

➢ deshō ka: [*for.*] ≈ **darō ka**

➢ deshō ni: [*for.*] ≈ **darō ni**

DESU です: [*cop.*]

Ⓣ 【N/n】 [*pol.*] ≈ **da**

Ⓣ 【i】 [*pol.*] ≈ 〖I〗 **masu**

➢ desu kara: 【N/n】 [*pol.*] ≈ **da kara**

➢ desu mono: 【N/n】 [*pol.*] ≈ **da mono** ({D})

➢ desu tte: 【V/na/i】 [*pol.*] ≈ ⑤ **da tte**

DOKORO どころ: [*n.*]

← n. *tokoro (place)*

➢ dokoro de wa nai: 【VN/n/U/i】 Negative Tentative cop.

cannot ~; impossible to ~; far from ~; anything but ~; no way ~; not the time/ occasion for ~

❖ Delimitative p. indicating that an action or state is impossible due to an adverse situation.

➢ dokoro ja nai: 【VN/n/U/i】 [*col.*] ≈ **dokoro de wa nai**

➢ dokoro ka: 【N】 ≈ **bakari ka** 【U/n/na/i】 Negative Lower Limitative coordinator

not just ~ (but also/either); let alone ~; far from ~

❖ Delimitative p. indicating that s.o. or s.t. is very far from an expected state.

DOKU どく: [*col.*][*fam.*] ≈ 〖TE〗 **oku**

❖ For v.s whose gerundive f. ends in -**de**.

DOMO ども: [*p.*]

Obs. concessive p. *do* + thematic concessive p. *mo*

【E】 [*lit.*] Concessive coordinator

even though ~; although ~

DOORI 通り: 【N/I】 = **toori**

DZUKU づく 〔付く〕: 【I】 = **tsuku**

DZURAI づらい 〔辛い〕: [*dep adj. v.*]

⊕ 【I】 *difficult to ~; hard to ~*

E

E へ: [*p.*]

← O.J. n. *he (vicinity)*

Ⓣ 【N】 Lative c.

towards ~; to ~

❖ Case p. indicating the direction toward which a movement is going.

❖ Written へ (*he*) but pronounced e (え).

ENAI 得ない: [*neg. adj. v.*] to not get

Neg. f. of *eru (to get)*

【I】 ❶ Negative Tentative m. ❷ Negative Potential m.

① *cannot ~; it is not possible to ~*

② *cannot* ~

❖ U. to talk about s.t. that is not supposed to happen (**❶**) or cannot be done (**❷**).

ERU える 〔得る〕 : [*v.*] to get; to obtain

【I】 ❶ Tentative m. **❷** Potential m.

① *can* ~; *it is possible (that)* ~

② *can* ~

❖ U. to talk about s.t. that one considers that can happen (**❶**) or can do (**❷**).

F

FUU 風: [*n.*] wind

➤ fuu ni: **【N】** Formal Semblative c.

in ~ *manner;* ~ *style; like* ~

➤ fuu no ⟨**N**⟩: **【N】** Attributive ☞ **fuu ni**

FURI 振り [*p.*]

(I) *furu (to swing)*

➤ ⓔ furi o suru: **【V/na/i】** Active Semblative m.

to pretend (to/that) ~; *to act as if* ~

❖ Expression that indicates that the subject of the sentence acts apparently and deliberately in the indicated manner.

G

GA₁ が: [*p.*]

❶ ⓕ **【N】** Nominative c. | **❷** [*lit.*][*obs.*] Genitive c. ≈ **no₁**

❖ **❶** Case p. that marks the subject of a sentence when that subject is introduced for the first time in the discourse.

❖ **❶** There are some commonly u. adj. v.s such as *to like* or *to want* (*suki; hoshii…*) whose semantic counterparts in English are v.s. What in English would be the object of such v.s, in Japanese are actually passive subjects and therefore take the particle **ga**.

❖ **❷** Only found in fossilized expressions, topography, historical records or historical literature.

❖ **❶** This p. is frequently pronounced *nga* (w. a nasal *n*).

- -

GA₂ が: [*p.*]

ⓕ **【V/i】** Adversative coordinator

~ *but;* ~ *however;* ~ *still*

❖ Subordinate p. u. to join two clauses expressing contrastive information.

【Ō】 = 〖Ō〗 **to₃**

- -

➤ ga ⟨**N**⟩ᴮ de ichiban ⟨**P**⟩: **【Nᴬ】** ≈ **wa** ⟨**N**⟩ **de ichiban** ⟨**P**⟩

➤ ga dekiru: **【VN】** ≈ **koto ga dekiru**

➤ ga ⟨**N**⟩ᴮ de motto mo ⟨**P**⟩: **【Nᴬ】** [*for.*] ≈ **ga** ⟨**N**⟩ **de ichiban** ⟨**P**⟩

➤ ga ⟨**Ō**⟩ ga: **【Ō】** = **to** ⟨**Ō**⟩ **to**

➤ ga gotoki ⟨**N**⟩: **【N】** ≈ **ga gotoku**

➤ ga gotoku: **【U】** [*lit.*] Semblative m.

like ~; *looking like* ~

➤ ga gotoshi: **【U】** [*lit.*] Semblative cop.

be like ~; *look like* ~

➤ ga hayai ka: **【U】** Punctual Inceptive a.

as soon as ~; *the moment* ~

➤ ⊕ ga hitsuyō {D}: 【VN】 ≈ **hitsuyō ga aru**

➤ ga naku mo/wa nai: 【N】 ≈ **naku mo nai**

➤ ga kikkake de: 【N】 ≈ **o kikkake ni**

✿ The p. *ni* here focuses on the cause.

➤ ga ⟨U/I⟩ mai ga: 〖Ō〗 Negative Dependent Alternative coordinator

regardless of whether ~ *or not*

✿ 〖Ō〗 & ⟨U/I⟩ are the same v.

➤ ga ⟨N⟩ᴮ no naka de ichiban ⟨P⟩: 【Nᴬ】 ≈ **ga ⟨N⟩ de ichiban ⟨P⟩**

➤ ga ⟨N⟩ᴮ no naka de motto mo ⟨P⟩: 【Nᴬ】 [*for.*] ≈ **ga ⟨N⟩ no naka de ichiban ⟨P⟩**

➤ ga sugiru: 【N】 = 〖VN〗 **sugiru**

➤ ga yue (ni): 【N/n/V/i】 ≈ **yue** (ni)

GACHI がち〔勝ち〕: [*dep. n.*]

← *kachi:* (I) *katsu (to win)*

➤ ① gachi {D}: 【VN/I】 Tendency Semblative cop.

tends to ~; *be prone to* ~; *be liable to* ~; *be apt to* ~; *easy to* ~

✿ Expresses that the tendency is somehow undesirable.

GAKE がけ〔掛け〕: 【VN/I】 = **kake**

GARI がり: [*dep. n.*]

(I) dep. v. *garu (to show signs of)*

⊕ 【n/s】 Tendency Semblative cop.

tend(s) to be ~

GARU がる: [*dep. v.*]

① 【n/s】 Evidential Semblative cop.

shows signs of ~; *seems to feel/be* ~; *to seem* ~; *to behave as if* ~

✿ Not frequently u. when talking about oneself.

✿ A common rendition of this verb is in the progressive f. gatte iru.

GATAI がたい〔難い〕: [*dep adj. v.*]

← Obs. adj. *katai (to be difficult)*

① 【I】 [*for.*] *(very) difficult to* ~; *(very) hard to* ~; *can hardly* ~; *cannot* ~; *unable to* ~; *impossible to* ~

GATERA がてら: [*p.*]

【VN/I】 Simultaneous Durative a.

while ~; *as* ~; ~ *at the same time; coincidentally* ~

GE げ〔気〕: [*dep. n.*]

← Ⓒ n. *ke* 気 *(feeling)*

➤ ge {D} 【I/n/s】 Semblative cop.

looks like ~; *seems (like)* ~; *appears to* ~

✿ Not u. when talking about oneself.

✿ M. u. to describe things like human emotions or states of being.

GIMI ぎみ〔気味〕: [*dep. n.*]

← Ⓒ n. *kimi* 気味 *(sensation)*

➤ ① gimi {D}: 【VN/I】 Approximative Semblative cop.

looking/feeling (somewhat) like ~; *feeling like* ~; *looks* ~; *have a touch of* ~

✿ Expresses an observable sensation or feeling.

GORO 頃: [*dep. n.*]

← n. *koro (such a time)*

➤ ⊕ goro (ni): 【N/C】 Approximative c.

about ~; around ~

❖ Only u. w. expressions of time.

GOTO ごと〔毎〕: [*dep. n.*] every

➤ goto ni: ❶ 【C】 Temporal Distributive c. ‖ ❷ 【U】 Distributive Durative a.

① *each ~; every (instance of) ~; at intervals of ~*

② *every time ~*

❖ Expressing temporal intervals.

⊕ GURAI ぐらい: 【N/C】 = kurai

H

HAJIMERU はじめる〔始める〕: [*v.*] to start

⊕ 【I】 Inceptive a.

to begin (to) ~; to start (to) ~

❖ Aux. v. indicating that s.o. or s.t. starts an action.

HAJIMETE 始めて: [*adv.*]

Gerundive f. of the v. *hajimeru* (to start)

⊥ 【TE】 Limitative Postessive a.

not until ~; only after ~; ~ for the first time

HAME 羽目: [*n.*] difficult situation

➤ hame ni naru: 【U】 Resultative a.

to end up with ~

❖ This construction is u. when the result is unpleasant.

HANMEN 反面: [*n.*] reverse

➤ hamen: 【U/na/i】 [*for.*] Contrastive Cumulative coordinator

~ on the other hand; ~ as well as; while ~, also

HAZU はず〔筈〕: [*dep. n.*]

➤ ⊕ hazu {D}: 【V/na/i】 Expectative cop.

I expect that ~; it is expected that ~; is expected to ~; should ~; must ~ought to ~; no wonder ~; it is natural that ~; certainly ~

❖ Dep. n. expressing the speaker's certain expectation insofar as he or she expects s.t. to happen.

➤ ⊕ hazu ga/wa nai: 【U/na/i】 Negative Expectative m.

it isn't expected (to be possible) that ~; I don't expect that ~; it is impossible that ~; cannot ~

➤ hazu no ⟨N⟩: 【V/na/i】 Attributive ☞ hazu {D}

HITSUYŌ 必要: [*n.*] necessity; need

➤ ⊕ hitsuyō ga aru: 【VN/U】 Necessitative m.

need/needs to ~; have/has to ~; it is necessary to ~

➤ hitsuyō ga/wa nai: 【VN/U】 Negative Necessitative m.

there's no need to ~

HŌDAI 放題: [*dep. n.*]

ⓒ *hō* 放 (releasing) + *dai* 題 (topic)

⊕ 【VN/I】 Upper Limitative Potential m.

as much as one would like to ~; all you can ~

HODO ほど〔程〕: [*n.*] extent; degree; limit

⊕ 【N】 Upper Limitative c.

① *as much (so) as ~*

❖ Delimitative p. indicating an extent or degree to which s.o. or s.t. does s.t.

❖ Only u. w. neg. verbal f.s.

⊕ 【C】 [*for.*] Approximative c.

about ~; around ~

⊕ 【U/na/i】 Upper Limitative subordinator

to the extent that ~; as much as ~

➤ ㊤ ⟨U/na/i⟩ hodo ⟨U/na/i⟩: 【BA】 Translative Upper Limitative subordinator

the more ~ the more ...

❖ 〖BA〗 & ⟨U/i⟩ have to be the same v. or adj.

➤ hodo no koto wa/mo nai: 【U】 = ① **koto wa nai**

HŌ ほう〔方〕: [*n.*] direction

【V/na/i】 ≈ hō ga ⟨P⟩

【I】 ≈ kata

➤ hō ga ⟨P⟩: 【V/na/i】 Upper Comparative subordinator

V/na/i is more P

➤ hō ga ii: ❶ ㊦ 【V】 Suggestive m. | ❷ Preferential m.

① *would better ~; should ~*

② *would be better (to) ~; would rather ~*

❖ Construction u. to strongly suggest that s.o. should do s.t. (❶) or to say that some action would be better (❷).

➤ hō ga mashi {D}: 【V】 Preferential m.

would rather ~; better ~; would prefer to ~

➤ hō ga ⟨V/na/i⟩ yori (mo) ⟨P⟩: 【V/na/i】 ≈ yori ⟨V/na/i⟩ hō ga ⟨P⟩

HOKA 他: [*n.*] other

➤ hoka (ni) (wa) ⟨A⟩ nai: 【U】 Negative Preferential m.

there's no choice but ~; there's no other option but ~

❖ U. before neg. v.s.

HOSHII 欲しい: [*adj. v.*] to be wanted

⊕ 【TE】 Patient Volitive m.

want (s.o.) to ~

❖ U. to express that one wants another person (patient) to do s.t.

❖ When the patient appears in the sentence, it is marked by the p. **ni**.

❖ The patient of the adj. v. is of equal or lower status than the speaker.

HYŌSHI 拍子: [*n.*] instance

➤ hyōshi ni: 【TA】 Emphatic Punctual a.

the moment ~; the instance ~

I

IGAI 以外: [*aux. n*] exception

➤ igai {p}: 【N】 Exclusive c. 【U/i】 Exclusive coordinator.

except (for) ~; other than ~; (nothing) but ~; (nothing) besides ~; outside ~

IGO 以後: [*adv. n.*] thereafter

➤ igo (ni): 【N】 [*for.*] Postessive c.

after ~; since ~

II いい: [*adj. v.*] good

← *yoi (good)*

⊕ 【BA】 Desiderative m.

it would be good if ~; (you) could ~

【TE】 [*fam.*] ≈ **mo ii**

IJŌ 以上: [*adv. n.*] beyond

⊕ 【C】 Comparative Upper Limitative c.

more than ~; over ~; above ~

➤ ijō ni: 【VN/V】 Comparative Upper Limitative subordinator

more than ~ed

➤ ijō (wa): 【V】 ❶ Thematic Causal m. | ❷ Limitative Durative a.

① *since ~; now that ~; once ~; seeing that ~*

② *as long as ~*

❖ ❶ Aspect p. used to express that the speaker considers that there is a strong logical or natural connection between the preceding action and the subsequent action.

IKA 以下: [*adv. n.*] below

⊕ 【N/C】 Comparative Lower Limitative c.

below ~; less than ~

IKAN いかん 〔如何〕: [*adv.*] howsoever

← *ikan ni*: adj. *ika (what kind of)* + adverbializing suf. *ni*

➤ ikan de (wa): 【N】 Dependent Correlative c.

depending on ~

➤ ikan ni yotte (wa): 【N】 = **ikan de (wa)**

➤ ikan ni kakawarazu: 【N】 = **no ikan ni kakawarazu**

➤ ikan ni yorazu: 【N】 = **no ikan ni yorazu**

➤ ikan o towazu: 【N】 = **no ikan o towazu**

IKŌ 以降: [*adv. n.*] hereafter

【N/C】 Postessive c.

after ~; since ~

❖ Only u. w. adv. n.s or classifiers related to time.

IKU 行く: [*v.*] to go

⊕ 【TE】 ❶ Continuous Progressive a. ❷ Connective Egressive Motion marker

① *go/goes on ~ing; continue(s) to ~*

② *go as ~; ~ and go*

❖ ❶ Subsidiary v. indicating that the action or state continues to change at the time that the speaker describes it and that that change process is extended into the future.

INAI 以内: [*n.*] inside

➤ ⊕ inai (de/ni): 【C】 Inessive c.

within ~

❖ Only u. for quantities.

IPPŌ 一方: [*adv. n.*] one direction

➤ ⊕ ippō {D}: 【U】 Exclusive Continuative a.

only ~; always ~; continue(s) to ~; keep(s) ~ing ; ~ more and more

❖ Construction indicating that s.t. happens or is done continuously as an unavoidable result.

➤ Ⓔ **ippō de:** 【V/na/i】 Contrastive Cumulative coordinator

~ *on the other hand; ~ as well as; while ~, also*

❖ Construction indicating that an action or state happens while it is being compared w. another action or state that also happens.

IRAI 以来: [*adv. n.*] since

【N/C】 [*for.*] Ablative c. 【TE】 [*for.*] Egressive a.

(ever) since ~; henceforth ~

❖ Only u. w. expressions of time.

IRASSHARU いらっしゃる: [*v.*] ① to be ② to go ③ to come

Potential f. of the v. *kiru (to cut)*

【TE】 [*hon.*] ≈ ① 〖TE〗 **iru**

IRU いる〔居る〕: [*v.*] to be; to exist

【TE】 ❶ Ⓣ Progressive a. | ❷ Continuous Stative a. | ❸ Ⓔ Frequentative a. | ❹ Connective Stative Motion marker

① *be ~ing*

② *have/has ~ed; be ~ed*

③ *~ all the time; usually ~*

④ *~ and is/are/remains here/there*

❖ ❶ Subsidiary v. used to express that an action or state that began in the past is ongoing at the time of speech.

❖ ❷ It specifies that s.o. or s.t. is in a state initiated by a previous action.

❖ ❸ This v. is also u. to express that s.t. is habitually done.

ITADAKITAI いただきたい〔頂きたい〕: [*adj. v.*]

Volitional f. of the hum. v. *itadaku (to receive)*

【TE】 [*hum.*] ≈ 【TE】 **hoshii**

❖ M. u. in the pol. f. itadakitai desu.

ITADAKU いただく〔頂く〕: [*v.*] [*hum.*] to receive

⊕ 【TE】 [*hum.*] ≈ 〖TE〗 **morau**

❖ M. u. in the pol. f. itadakimasu.

ITASU いたす〔致す〕: [*v.*] to do

O.J. passive f. of the v. *naru (to do)*

【VN*/I†】 [*for.*][*hum.*] Imperfective a. Indicative m.

❖ U. to respectfully say, in a humble way, that oneself is doing s.t.

❖*The nominal part of Sino-Japanese v.s attached to the hon. pre. **go**.

❖ †After the hon. pre. **o**.

❖ M. u. in the pol. f. itashimasu.

IZEN 以前: [*adv. n.*] before

➤ **igo** (ni): 【N】 [*for.*] Antessive c.

before ~

J

JA₁ じゃ: 【N/n】 [*col.*] ≈ **de wa**

- -

JA₂ じゃ: [*col.*] ≈ 〖TE〗 **wa**

❖ For v.s whose gerundive f. ends in -**de**.

- -

➤ Ⓣ **ja arimasen:** 【N/n】 [*col.*] ≈ **de wa arimasen**

➤ Ⓣ **ja arimasen deshita:** 【N/n】 [*col.*] ≈ **de wa arimasen deshita**

➤ ja arimasen ka: 【N/n】 [*col.*] ≈ de wa arimasen ka

➤ ja aru mai: 【N/n】 [*col.*] ≈ de wa aru mai

➤ ⊕ ja dame ({D}): [*col.*] ≈ 〖TE〗 wa dame

➤ ⊕ ja ikenai: [*col.*] ≈ 〖TE〗 wa ikenai

➤ ja nai: [*col.*] 【N/n】 ❶ ⓣ Negative Imperfective cop. ≈ de wa nai | ❷ Inquisitive m. = ja nai ka

① *am/are/is not ~*

② *~ right?; ~ isn't it?*

  ➤ ja nai ⟨N⟩: 【N/n】 [*col.*] ≈ de wa nai ⟨N⟩

  ➤ ja nai darō: 【N/n】 [*col.*] ≈ de wa nai darō

  ➤ ja nai deshō: 【N/n】 [*col.*][*for.*] ≈ de wa nai darō

  ➤ ja nai desu: 【N/n】 [*col.*] ≈ de wa nai desu

  ➤ ja nai ka: [*col.*] 【N/n/V/i】 ≈ de wa nai ka

  ➤ ja nai koto mo/wa nai: 【Ō/N/n】 [*col.*] ≈ de wa nai koto mo/wa nai

  ➤ ja nai made mo: 【N/n】 [*col.*] ≈ de wa nai made mo

➤ ⓣ ja nakatta: 【N/n】 [*col.*] ≈ de wa nakatta

  ➤ ja nakatta ⟨N⟩: 【N/n】 [*col.*] ≈ de wa nakatta ⟨N⟩

  ➤ ja nakatta desu: 【N/n】 [*col.*] ≈ de wa nakatta desu

➤ ja naku naru: 【N/n】 [*col.*] ≈ de wa naku naru

➤ ja nakute: 【N/n】 [*col.*] ≈ de wa nakute

  ➤ ja nakute mo: 【N/n】 [*col.*] ≈ de wa nakute mo

➤ ⊕ ja naranai: [*col.*] ≈ 〖TE〗 wa naranai

JAN じゃん: [*col.*][*fam.*] Inquisitive m. ≈ ja nai ka

~ right?; ~ isn't it?

JAU じゃう: [*col.*] ≈ 〖TE〗 shimau

❖ For v.s whose gerundive f. ends in -**de.**

JIMAU じまう: [*col.*][*mas.*] ≈ 〖TE〗 shimau

❖ For v.s whose gerundive f. ends in -**de.**

JIMIRU じみる 〔染みる〕: [*dep. v.*] to appear like

【N】 [*lit.*] Semblative cop.

look(s) like ~; behave(s) like ~

❖ Usually in the perfective f. jimita when u. before n.s or the progressive f. jimite iru if u. at the end of the sentence.

JŌ 上: [*adv. n.*] hereafter

ⓛ 【N】 [*for.*] Superessive c.

on top of ~; on ~; in ~; within (the context of) ~; in terms of ~

❖ Frequently u. w. n.s that are not referring to a physical location but to a field or domain of knowledge.

JUU 中: 【N/C】 = ① chuu

K

KA₁ か: [*p.*]

ⓣ ❶ 【N】 Alternative Enumerative c. ‖

❷ 【N/n/V/i】 Disjunctive coordinator |
❸ ⊕ Alternative coordinator ≈ **ka dō ka**

① ~ *or*

② *(either)* ~ *or*

③ *whether* ~ *(or not)*

✣ ❶ It indicates that the marked noun is presented as an alternative within an explicit or implicit set of things.

✣ ❷ Coordinate p. u. to mark an alternative choice between two or more things or actions.

- -

KA₂ か: [*p.*]

【N/n/V/i】 ❶ ⓉInterrogative m. | ❷ Ⓣ Interrogative subordinator

① ~ *?*

② *whether* ~*; ... if* ~*; ... what* ~

✣ ❶/❷ Phrasal p. indicating that the preceding clause is interrogative.

✣ ❶ This p. cannot follow the informal version of the cop. (*da*).

【Ō】 Propositive m.

shall we ~*; let's* ~

- -

➤ ⊕ ka dō ka: 【N/n/V/i】 Alternative coordinator

whether ~ *or not*

➤ ka dō ka ni kakawarazu: 【N/n/V/i】 [*for.*] ≈ **ka dō ka ni yorazu**

➤ ka dō ka ni yorazu: 【N/n/V/i】 Negative Dependent Alternative coordinator

(regardless of) whether ~ *(or not)*

➤ ka dō ka ni yotte: 【N/n/V/i】 Dependent Disjunctive coordinator

depending on whether ~

➤ ka dō ka o towazu: 【N/n/V/i】 [*for.*] ≈ **ka dō ka ni yorazu**

➤ ka dō ka wa betsu to shite: 【V】 Exclusive coordinator

other than ~*ing*

➤ ka ina ka: 【N/n/V/i】 [*lit.*] ≈ **ka dō ka**

➤ ka ina ka ni yorazu: 【N/n/V/i】 [*lit.*] ≈ **ka dō ka ni yorazu**

➤ ka ina ka o towazu: 【N/n/V/i】 [*lit.*] ≈ **ka dō ka o towazu**

➤ Ⓣ ka ⟨N/n/V/i⟩ ka: 【N/n/V/i】 Disjunctive coordinator

whether ~ *or ...*

➤ ka ⟨N/n/V/i⟩ ni kakawarazu: 【N/n/V/i】 [*for.*] ≈ **ka dō ka ni yorazu**

➤ ka ⟨N/n/V/i⟩ ka ni yorazu: 【N/n/V/i】 Negative Dependent Disjunctive coordinator

regardless of whether ~ *or ...*

➤ ka ⟨N/n/V/i⟩ ka o megutte: 【N/n/V/i】 Correlative Dependent Alternative coordinator

concerning whether ~ *or not*

➤ ka ⟨N/n/V/i⟩ ka o towazu: 【N/n/V/i】 [*for.*] ≈ **ka ⟨N/n/V/i⟩ ka ni yorazu**

➤ ka ⟨A/ku⟩ nai ka: 【V/i】 = **ka dō ka**

➤ ka nai ka: 【N/n/V/i】 = **ka dō ka**

➤ ka nai shi (wa) ⟨N/n/V/i⟩: 【N/n/V/i】 = ① **nai shi ⟨N/n/V/i⟩**

➤ ka ⟨A⟩ nai ka no uchi ni: 【U】 Punctual Inceptive a.

just as ~*; right after* ~*; as soon as* ~

➤ ka ni kakawarazu: 【N/n/V/i】 = **ka dō ka ni kakawarazu**

➤ ka ni yorazu: 【N/n/V/i】 = **ka dō ka ni yorazu**

➤ ka ⟨U/I⟩ mai ka: 【Ō】 Alternative coordinator

whether ~ *or not*

❖ 〖Ō〗 & ⟨U⟩ have to be the same v.

➤ ka mo: 【N/n/V/i】 [col.][fam.] ≈ ka mo shirenai

➤ ⊕ ka mo shirenai: 【N/n】 Deliberative cop. 【V/i】 Deliberative m.

can't tell if ~; might ~; perhaps ~

❖ Construction indicating a doubt concerning an action or event which probability is rather low.

➤ ⊕ ka na: 【N/n/V/Ō/i】 [fam.] Emphatic Dubitative m.

I wonder if ~; I guess ~

❖ Usually u. when the speaker asks questions to him or herself.

➤ ka naa: 【N/n/V/Ō/i】 = ka na

➤ ⊕ fn: 【N】 Enunciative c.

~ or something

➤ ka ni mieru: 【V/i】 ≈ ka no yō ni mieru

➤ ka no gotoki ⟨N⟩: 【N/U】 ≈ ga gotoki ⟨N⟩

➤ ka no gotoku: 【N/U】 ≈ ga gotoku

➤ ka no gotoshi: 【U】 = ga gotoshi

➤ ka no yō {D}: 【V/i】 [for.] Semblative cop.

be like ~

➤ ka no yō na ⟨N⟩: 【V/i】 Attributive ☞ ka no yō ni

➤ ka no yō ni: 【V/i】 [for.] Semblative m.

as if ~; just like ~

  ➤ ka no yō ni mieru: 【V/i】 [for.] Evidential Semblative cop.

  look as if ~

➤ ⊕ ka shira: 【N/n/V/i】 [fam.][fem.] Emphatic Dubitative m.

I wonder if ~

➤ ⊤ ka to: 【N*/n/V/i】 Interrogative Quotative subordinator

… whether ~; … if ~; … what ~

❖ It indicates a question about what s.o. has said.

❖ Usually followed by the v.s **iu** (*to say*); **omou** (*to think*); **kaku** (*to write*) or **kiku** (*to hear*).

❖ *Indefinite pronouns [☞ VO:I.2].

  ➤ ka to iu to: 【N*/n/V/i】 Interrogative Quotative Conditional m.

  if you ask if ~ (the reason is)

  ❖ Quotative conditional expression m. u. to give explanations.

  ❖ *Indefinite pronouns [☞ VO:I.2].

➤ ka to omoeba: 【V】 = ka to omou to

➤ ka to omotta ra: 【V】 = ka to omou to

➤ ka to omou to: 【V】 Evidential Punctual a.

just when you think that ~; as soon as (one notices that) ~; soon after ~

❖ Quotative conditional expression u. to indicate that an action or state follows another action or state that one has just noticed.

➤ ka o towazu: 【N/n/V/i】 = ka dō ka o towazu

KAERU 替える: [v.] to replace

【I】 Reiterative a.

to ~ again; to ~ over

❖ It indicates that an action is done again from scratch.

KAESU 返す: [v.] to return

【I】 Reiterative a.

to ~ again; to ~ over

❖ It indicates that an action is repeated.

KAGIRI 限り : [n.] limit; extent

(I) *kagiru (to be limited)*

【V】 Emphatic Provisional m.

as long as ~; as far as ~; while ~; to the extent ~; until ~; unless ~

❖ P. expressing the existence of an event or action conditioned to the duration of the action or event marked by it.

➤ kagiri {D}: ❶ 【i】 Superlative cop. ❷ 【C】 Postessive c. ≈ **kagiri de**

① *extremely ~; as much as ~ as can be*

② *after ~; starting from ~*

❖ ❶ P. indicating that the degree of emotion expressed by an adj. is extreme or deeply felt.

➤kagiri de: 【C*】 Postessive c.

after ~; as of the end of ~; starting from ~

❖ *Classifiers related to time.

KAI₁ かい: [p.]

⊕ 【N/n/V/i】 [*fam.*][*mas.*] Interrogative m.

~?

❖ Only u. w. yes-no (closed) questions.

❖ M. u. by men towards children or girlfriends.

- -

KAI₂ かい 〔甲斐〕 : [n.] value; worth

- -

➤ kai ga aru: 【V/I】 Benefactive cop.

(it's) worth ~; ~ pays off

➤ kai mo naku: 【V】 Concessive coordinator

even though ~

KAKARU かかる 〔掛かる〕 : [v.] to be hung

【I】 Prospective a.

to be on the verge of ~; to be about to ~

❖ Aux. v. indicating that an action is about to be started.

KAKE かけ 〔掛け〕 : [n.] proportion

(I) *kakeru (to hang)*

➤ ㊤ kake {D}: 【VN/I】 ≈ **kakeru**

➤ ㊤ kake no 〈N〉: Attributive ☞ **kakeru**

KAKERU かける 〔掛ける〕 : [v.] to hang

㊤ 【VN/I】 ❶ Deflective Terminative a. ❷ Deflective Inceptive a.

① *stopped to ~; half ~; started to ~ (but not finished); be in the midst of ~*

② *almost ~; be on the verge of ~ing*

❖ ❶ Aux. v. expressing that an action or state has started but has been left without completion.

❖ ❷ It indicates that an action is about to start.

KANAWANAI かなわない 〔敵わない〕 : [*neg. adj. v.*] to be no match for

【TE】 Negative Potential m.

to be unable to ~; can't stand ~

KANENAI かねない:[*adj. v.*] to be possible

Neg. f. of the aux. v. *kaneru (to be unable to)*

【I】 [*for.*] Tentative m.

be possible to ~; might ~

KANERU かねる 〔兼ねる〕 : [v.] to be unable to

【I】 [*for.*][*pol.*] Negative Potential m.

cannot ~; be difficult to ~; be in no position to ~

❖ This v. is only u. when the subject is a human being.

KANŌSĒ 可能性: [n.] possibility

➤ kanōsē ga aru: 【U】 Tentative m.

there's a possibility that ~; might ~

KARA から: [p.]

O.J. n. *kara (inherent quality)*

Ⓕ 【N】 ❶ Ablative c. ❷ Elative c.

① *from ~; since ~*

② *out of ~*

✢ Case p. indicating a temporal or spatial starting point.

Ⓕ 【V/i】 Causal m.

because ~; since ~; ~ so

✢ It expresses a reason or a cause that leads the speaker to have an opinion or carry out a decision.

Ⓛ 【TE】 ❶ Postessive a. ❷ Egressive a. ❸ Causal Egressive a.

① *after ~*

②③ *since ~*

✢ Gerundive p. indicating an action after which s.t. is done or takes place.

➤ kara {D}: 【V/i】 Causal cop.

it is because ~

➤ kara aru ⟨N⟩: 【C】 Attributive Upper Limitative m.

at least ~; about ~ or more; as much as ~; as many as ~

➤ Ⓛ kara de nai to: 【TE】 Tentative Conditional m.

unless ~; until ~; cannot do without first ~

✢ Construction that expresses that until or unless s.t. is done the subsequent action or event cannot occur.

➤ Ⓛ kara de nakereba: 【TE】 Tentative Provisional m. ≈ **kara de nai to**

➤ kara ieba: 【N】 = **kara iu to**

➤ kara itte: 【N】 = **kara iu to**

➤ kara iu to: 【N】 Ablative Inferential c.

in terms of ~; judging from ~; from the standpoint of ~

➤ kara koso: 【U】 Emphatic Causal m.

(it is) precisely because ~; only because ~; to the extent that ~

➤ kara mireba: 【N】 = **kara miru to**

➤ kara miru to: 【N】 Ablative Inferential c.

judging from ~; judging by ~

➤ kara mite: 【N】 = **kara miru to**

➤ kara ni hoka naranai: 【V/i】 ≈ **ni hoka naranai**

➤ kara ni wa: 【V】 ❶ Thematic Causal m. | ❷ Limitative Durative a.

① *since ~; because ~; now that ~*

② *as long as ~*

➤ kara no ⟨N⟩: 【C】 = **kara aru ⟨N⟩**

➤ kara shite: 【N】 = **kara suru to**

➤ kara sureba: 【N】 = **kara suru to**

➤ kara suru ⟨N⟩: 【C】 = **kara aru ⟨N⟩**

➤ kara suru to: 【N】 Ablative Inferential c.

judging from ~; from ~; from the point of view of ~; from ~'s point of view; from the standpoint of ~

✢ Construction that states the source of a reasoning in a speculative but well-founded (inferential) way.

➤ kara to itte: 【V/i】 Concessive Causal m.

just because ~; even if ~; even though ~

✢ Construction that introduces a reasoning that explains an action or fact that the speaker does not approve of.

✤ U. w. neg. verbal f.s.

➤ kara to iu mono: 【TE】 Emphatic Egressive a.

(ever) since ~

➤ kara tte: 【V/i】 [*col.*] ≈ **kara to itte**

➤ kara wa: 【V】 [*col.*] ≈ **kara ni wa**

KARE かれ: [*i.*]

【s】 [*obs.*] ≈ 〖E〗 **ro**

KARŌ かろう: [*i.*]

【s】 [*lit.*][*for.*] ≈ 〖i〗 **darō**

➤ karō to ⟨s⟩ karō to: 【s】 [*lit.*] ≈ **de mo** ⟨N/n⟩ **de mo**

➤ karō to mo: 【s】 ≈ **to mo**

KATA 方: [*n.*] way

⊕ 【I】 Formal m.

way of ~; method of ~; how to ~

KATAGATA かたがた〔方々〕: [*adv.*] various

kata (way) ×2

【VN】 [*for.*] ❶ Final m. ❷ Simultaneous Durative a.

① *for ~*

② *while ~; at the same time ~*

✤ Nominal p. indicating that an action w. a purpose in mind is performed while another action is being performed too.

KATAWARA かたわら〔傍ら〕: [*n.*] side

kata (way) + wara (straw)

[*lit.*] 【U】 Simultaneous Durative a.

while ~; at the same time ~; in addition ~; besides ~ also

✤ This nominal p. is u. to express that two actions are being done at the same time but not at the same instant.

KATTA かった: [*i.*]

Ⓣ 【s】 [*fam.*] Perfective a. Indicative m.

was ~; were ~

➤ Ⓣ katta desu: 【s】 [*pol.*] ≈ **katta**

KAWARI 代わり: [*n.*] change

(I) *kawaru (to change)*

➤ Ⓙ kawari ni: 【V/na/i】 Substitutive coordinator

instead of ~; in place of ~; but ~; to make up for ~

Ⓣ KEDO けど: 【V/i】 [*col.*] ≈ **keredomo**

KEDOMO: 【V/i】 ≈ **keredomo**

KEKKA 結果: [*n.*] result

Ⓙ 【TA】 Resultative Postessive a.

as a result of ~; after ~

KĒKŌ 傾向: [*n.*] tendency; trend

➤ kēkō ga aru: 【V/na/i】 Tendency Semblative cop.

have a tendency to ~; tend to ~; be slightly ~; be inclined to ~

KEREBA ければ: 【s】 ≈ **ba**

KEREDO: 【V/i】 = **keredomo**

KEREDOMO けれど: [*p.*]

Ⓣ 【V/i】 [*for.*] Adversative coordinator

~ but

KERYA けりゃ: 【s】 [*col.*] ≈ **kereba**

KĒYU 経由: [*dep. n.*]

C *kē* 経 *(lapsing)* + *yu* 由 *(cause)*

㊤ 【N】 [*for.*] Prolative c.

via ~; through ~; by way of ~

KI 気: [*n.*] mood

➤ ki ga aru: 【U】 Evidential Volitive m.

feel like ~

➤ ki ga suru: 【V/na/i】 Evidential Inferential m.

have a feeling that ~

➤ ki ni naru: 【U】 Evidential Volitive m.

feel like ~

KIRAI 嫌い: [*adj. v.*] disliked

➤ kirai ga aru: 【V】 Tendency Semblative cop.

have a tendency to ~; tend to ~; be slightly ~

❖ This structure expresses that s.o. has an undesirable tendency to do s.t.

KIRENAI 切れない: [*adj. v.*]

Neg. f. of the v. *kireru (to be cut)*

㊤ 【I】 *cannot (finish) ~; unable to (finish) ~*

❖ Aux. v. that expresses the impossibility of completing an action.

KIRERU 切る: [*v.*] to be able to cut

Potential f. of the v. *kiru (to cut)*

【I】 *to be able to ~ completely; to be able to finish ~*

KIRI きり 〔切り〕 : [*n.*] end; finish

(I) *kiru (to cut)*

㊤ 【TA】 Egressive a.

since ~

❖ Nominal p. that expresses that since s.t. has happened the resulting state remains unchanged.

㊤ 【N/C】 Lower Limitative c.

only ~; just ~

❖ Nominal p. that expresses a limitation in quantity.

KIRU 切る: [*v.*] to cut

㊤ 【I】 *to ~ completely; to finish ~; to ~ through*

❖ Aux. v. expressing that an action is completed to the end.

KIWAMARI きわまり 〔極まり〕 : [*n.*] extremity

(I) *kiwamaru (to reach an extreme)*

➤ kiwamari nai 〈N〉: 【n】 = **kiwamaru** 〈N〉

KIWAMARU きわまる 〔極まる〕 : [*v.*] to reach an extreme

➤ kiwamaru 〈N〉: 【n】 Superlative m.

extremely ~

KKE っけ: [*p.*]

㊤ 【TA】 [*col.*][*fam.*] Inquisitive Dubitative m.

did ~?; have ~?; ~ again?

❖ M. u. when the speaker tries to remember s.t.

KKIRI っきり: 【N】 [*col.*] ≈ kiri

KKONAI っこない: [*dep adj. v.*]

【I】 [*fam.*] Emphatic Negative Potential m.

no chance of ~; no way that ~; will never ~; is definitely not possible to ~

❖ Aux. adj. v. that expresses the certainty that s.t. cannot happen or be done.

KOMU 込む: [v.] to get packed

㊤ 【I】 ❶ Protractive Continuative a.

① ~ continuously; ~ thoroughly; ~ on and on

❷ ~ into; ~ thoroughly

❖ ❶ Aux v. expressing that an action is carried out for a long time until a satisfactory result is met.

❖ ❷ Aux. v. expressing that s.t. moves, either fig. or lit., into s.t. else.

KONO この: [pronoun] this

➤ kono ue nai: 【n】 [for.] Superlative m.

extremely ~; utterly ~; very ~

KORO ころ 〔頃〕: [n.] such a time

㊥ 【N/C】 Temporal Approximative c. = goro (ni)

㊥ 【V/i】 Approximative Punctual a.

(around the time) when ~

KOSO こそ: [p.]

Proximal pre. ko + O.J. emphatic p. so

㊤ 【N(p*)】 Emphatic c.

precisely ~; the very ~; it is ~; definitely ~; ~ for sure

❖ Focal p. u. to emphasize a word or nominal phrase.

❖ *This p. replaces the p.s ga, wa and o, while it can optionally be added to the p.s ni, de, to, kara or made.

㊤ 【TE】 Emphatic Conjunctive coordinator

now that ~; ~ and then; only after ~

【BA】 [for.] Emphatic Causal m.

it is precisely because ~; it is only because ~

➤ koso are: 【N】 Concessive cop.

although there is ~; even though there is ~

➤ koso aru ga: 【N】 = koso are

➤ koso sure: 【I】 ≈ koso are

KOTO こと 〔事〕: [n.] (intangible) thing

㊥ 【V/na/i】 Nominalization marker

to ~; ~ing; (a thing) that ~; what ~;

❖ Nominalizer u. to denote things that are intangible (that cannot be seen or touched).

❖ This nominalizer is m. u. when referring to s.t. that the speaker does not feel very close to. This usually implies that the action which is referred is not performed by the speaker himself.

㊤ 【U】 [lit.] Obligative m.

should ~

❖ M. u. when giving advice or suggestions to another person.

➤ koto {D}: ❶ 【V/na/i】 Explanative cop. ❷ 【U】 Suggestive m.

① means that ~

② you should ~

➤ koto {D} kara: 【V/na/i】 Explanative Causal m.

because (of) ~; since ~

❖ Construction that serves to give a reason that is based on s.t. habitual for or characteristic of what is referenced by the marked n.

❖ M. referring to an action or state that is presumably going to occur in the future.

➤ koto da shi: 【V/na/i】 [for.] ≈ koto {D} kara

➤ koto de: ❶ 【U】 Instrumental m. ‖ ❷ 【V/na/i】 Causal m.

① by ~ing

② because ~

➤ koto ga aru: ❶ ⊕ 【U/na/i】 Occasional a. ‖ ❷ ⊤ 【TA】 Experiential a.

① *there are times when ~; sometimes ~*

② *have/has ~; have/has (the experience of) ~; there was a time when ~*

✦ ❷ It expresses that s.t. has been done sometime in the past.

➤ ⊕ koto ga dekiru: 【U】 Potential m.

can ~; be able to ~

➤ koto to itta ra nai: 【U/na/i】 ≈ to itta ra nai

➤ ① koto ka: 【V/na/i】 [*lit.*] Admirative m.

how ~!; what a(n) ~!

➤ ① koto kara: 【V/na/i】 Causal m.

because ~; due to ~; from the fact that ~

➤ koto kono ue nai: 【na/i】 ≈ kono ue nai

➤ koto mo naku: 【U】 = 【U】 koto naku

➤ koto nai: 【U】 [*col.*] ≈ ① koto wa nai

➤ koto naku: ❶ 【U】 Concessive Privative m. ‖ ❷ 【N】 Privative c. ≈ nashi

① *without ~ even once*

② *without ~*

✦ ❶ Construction that expresses that an action has not been performed for a long time.

➤ koto naku shite (wa): 【U】 = koto nashi de/ni (wa)

➤ koto nashi de/ni (wa): 【U】 [*for.*] Privative coordinator

without ~

➤ ① koto ni: 【V/na/i】 Causal nominalization

it is ~ that; ~ because

✦ This construction is limited to verbs and adjectives related to emotion.

➤ koto ni kimeru: 【U】 = koto ni suru

➤ ⊕ koto ni naru: ❶ 【V/na/i】 Resultative a. ❷ 【U】 Passive Decisive m.

① *end up (with) ~; turns out that ~; come to mean that ~*

② *it has been decided that ~; it has been the case that ~*

✦ ❶ Construction that expresses a result of a past action or event.

✦ ❷ This form indicates that some decision has been made.

➤ ⊕ koto ni suru: 【U】 Decisive m.

decide to ~

✦ Most commonly referring to the speaker's decision.

➤ koto ni yori: 【V】 = koto ni yotte

➤ koto ni yoru ⟨N⟩: 【V】 Attributive ☞ koto ni yotte

➤ koto ni yotte: 【V】 Instrumental m.

by ~ing

➤ koto no nai yō (ni): 【U/na/i】 Negative Final m.

so as not to ~; to not ~

➤ koto tote: 【U/na】 [*lit.*] Explanative Causal m.

because ~ ; since ~

➤ koto tta ra nai: 【U/na/i】 [*col.*] ≈ koto itta ra nai

➤ koto wa: 【V/na/i】 Thematic Nominalization marker

the fact that ~; that ~

✦ The n. *koto* implies that this structure is u. to talk about concrete or demonstrable conceptualizations.

➤ koto wa ⟨V/na/i⟩: 【V/na/i】 Emphatic m.

indeed ~; do ~

❖ Construction u. to reaffirm the certainty of one statement.

❖ 【V/na/i】 & 〈V/na/i〉 have to be the same word.

➢ ⒠ koto wa 〈V/na/i〉 ga: 【V/na/i】 Emphatic Adversative coordinator

although ~; but ~

❖ 【V/na/i】 & 〈V/na/i〉 have to be the same word.

➢ ⒠ koto wa nai: 【U】 ❶ Negative Necessitative m. ❷ Negative Tentative cop.

① *(there is) no need to ~; not necessary (to) ~*

② *there is no chance to ~*

❖ The verb to which this construction is added must be affirmative.

➢ koto yara: 【V/i】 ≈ **no yara**

❖ It expresses a strong concern or anxiety.

KU₁ く: [*i.*]

【s】 ❶ Adverbialization marker | ❷ [*lit.*] Conjunctive coordinator ≈ 【ku】 **te**

① *~ly*

② *~ and*

❖ ❶ It turns adj.s into adverbs.

- -
- - - -

KU₂ く

【TE】 [*col.*] ≈ ① 【TE】 **iku**

KUDASAI ください〔下さい〕[*i.*]

Imperative f. of the hon. v. *kudasaru (to give)*

Ⓣ 【TE】 [*pol.*] Directive m.

please ~

❖ Subsidiary adj. indicating a request asked to the listener.

⊕ 【VN*/I†】 [*hon.*] ≈ 【TE】 **kudasai**

❖ *Is the nominal p. of a Sino-Japanese n. v. and goes after the hon. pre. **go**.

❖ †Goes after the hon. pre. **o**.

KUDASARU 下さる: [*v.*] [*hon.*] to be given

⊕ 【TE】 [*hon.*] ≈ 【TE】 **kureru**

KURAI くらい: [*p.*]

O.J. n. *kurai (position)* ← O.J. *kura (seat)* + O.J. *i (being)*: posit

⊕ 【N*/C】 Approximative c.

about ~; approximately ~

❖ *Only demonstrative or interrogative pronouns.

⒠ 【U/na/i】 = 【U/na/i】 **hodo**

➢ kurai nara: 【U】 Comparative Preferential m.

rather than ~ do

➢ kurai na/no mono {D}: 【N】 Emphatic Lower Limitative cop.

only ~

KURE くれ: [*fam.*][*mas.*] ≈ **kudasai**

KURERU くれる〔呉れる〕: [*v.*] to be given

⊕ 【TE】 Active Benefactive m.

to be done the favor of ~; ~ for s.o.; do s.o. a favor by ~

❖ Subsidiary v. indicating that s.o. (the subject) does s.t. for the sake of s.o. else (the object).

❖ The person receiving the benefit of the action, when appearing in the sentence, is the object of a transitive v., hence it is marked w. the p. **ni**.

❖ The v. *kureru* is stated from the viewpoint of the person who receives the favor, so usually the receiver is the first person or s.o. close to him or her.

KURU くる〔来る〕: [*v.*] to come

⊕【TE】❶ Translative Progressive a. ❷ Resultative Inceptive a. ❸ Connective Regressive Motion marker

① *come (about) to ~; grown to ~; begin/ start to ~*

② *been ~ing up to now; have ~ed up to now; come to ~; get ~ed*

③ *to ~ and come back*

❖ ❶ Subsidiary v. describing the continuation and change of some action up to the present time.

❖ ❷ Describing the beginning of some continuative process.

❖ M. referring to the speaker or s.o. close to the speaker.

KUSE 癖: [*n.*] habit

➤ ⊕ kuse ni: 【V/na/i】 Concessive coordinator

although ~; even though ~; despite the fact that ~; and yet ~; but ~

❖ Nominal p. expressing the speaker's dissatisfaction or disagreement w. an action or state.

❖ P. not u. when the subject is the first person.

➤ kuse shite: 【V/na/i】 = kuse ni

M

MADE₁ まで : [*p.*]

⊕【N】Concessive c.

even ~

❖ Subjective p. marking an unexpected object or situation.

- -

MADE₂ まで : [*p.*]

⊤ ❶【N/C】Limitative c. 【U】Limitative a.

until ~; to ~; as far as ~; up to ~; through ~

❖ Delimitative p. indicating a spatial, temporal or quantitative limit.

【TE】Upper Limitative subordinator

as far as to ~; to the point of ~; to the extent of ~

- -

➤ made {D}: 【V】❶ Emphatic Determinative m. ❷ Emphatic Explanative cop.

① *I'll just ~*

② *just ~; only ~; merely ~*

❖ ❶ Construction that indicates that the speaker makes a decision to do s.t. when faced w. a negative situation.

❖ ❷ It expresses an explanation that does not require a specific logical reason.

➤ made mo nai: 【U】Negative Necessitative m.

(it is) not necessary to ~; (there's) no need to ~

➤ made no koto {D}: 【V】= made {D}

➤ ⊕ made ni: 【N/C】Punctual Limitative c. 【U】Punctual Durative a.

by (the time when) ~

❖ Compound p. indicating a time limit for an action.

➤ made shite: 【N】Upper Limitative c.

to the extent of ~

MAE 前: [*adv.*] ① before ② in front of

➤ ⊤ mae ni: 【U/C/no】Antessive a./c.

before ~

❖ ❶ M. u. when the speaker knows when s.t. is going to take place.

MAGIWA 間際: [*dep. n.*]

ma (just) + *giwa* ← *kiwa (verge)*

➢ magiwa (ni): 【VN/U】 [*for.*] Antessive a.

just before ~

MAI まい: [*i.*]

【U*】 [*for.*] Negative Presumptive m.

will not ~; *probably won't* ~

❖ Verbal ending that expresses a confident guess that s.t. is not going to happen.

❖ *Strong v.s originally add the ending -**mai** to their root 〖S〗, but currently, by analogy w. weak v.s, they also add the ending to the indicative f. 〖U〗.

❖ The irregular v. **kuru** (*to come*) can take the f. komai or kurumai and the irregular v. **suru** (*to do*) can take the f.s shimai, sumai or surumai.

➢ mai ga: 【U】 = **mai to**

➢ mai ka: 【U】 Negative Dubitative m.

won't I ~

➢ mai to: 【U】 Negative Concessive Conditional m.

even if not ~

  ➢ mai to mo: 【U】 = **mai to**

  ➢ mai to suru: 【U】 [*lit.*] Negative Probationary m.

try not to ~

MAJIKI まじき: [*dep. adj. v.*]

adj. *maji (serious)* + O.J. adjectival attributive ending *ki*

➢ majiki ⟨N⟩: 【U】 Prohibitive m.

should not ~; *must not* ~

❖ Expression u. to express that s.t. is not acceptable and should not be done.

MAKURU まくる 〔捲る〕: [*v.*] to turn up

【I】 Continuous Reiterative a.

to ~ *over and over again; to* ~ *relentlessly*

MAMA まま: [*dep. n.*] condition

⊕ 【TA/na/i】 Progressive Stative a.

as it is ~; *remains* ~; *still* ~

❖ Nominal p. expressing that a condition or action remains unchanged at the time of speech.

➢ mama de/ni: 【TA/na/i】 ≈ **mama**

MASE ませ: [*i.*]

【I】 [*pol.*] Imperative m.

❖ Only u. w. hon. v.s.

MASEN ません: [*i.*]

⒡ 【I】 [*pol.*] **nai**

➢ ⒡ masen deshita: 【I】 [*pol.*] ≈ 〖A〗 **nakatta**

➢ ⒡ masen ka: 【I】 [*pol.*] Propositive m.

wouldn't you ~?; *would you* ~?; *shall we* ~?

❖ U. to propose an action performed by the listener.

MASHITA ました: [*i.*]

⒡ 【I】 [*pol.*] Perfective a. Indicative m.

❖ Inflection u. to make perfective sentences polite.

MASHITE まして: [*i.*]

【I】 [*for.*][*pol.*] Conjunctive coordinator

~ *and*

❖ Inflection u. to make conjunctive sentences polite.

❖ R. u. when inferring respect to the person who does the action.

MASHŌ ましょう: [*i.*]

Ⓣ 【I】 [*pol.*] ❶ Presumptive m. ❷ Hortative m.

① *will ~*

② *let's ~; shall we ~*

❖ Pol. verbal ending u. to express that a certain action is to be performed by the speaker (❶) or to politely suggest to the listener to perform an activity together (❷).

➤ Ⓣ mashō ka: 【I】 [*pol.*] Propositive m.

shall (I/we) ~?

❖ U. to propose an action performed by the speaker.

MASU ます: [*dep. v.*]

Ⓣ 【I】 [*pol.*] Imperfective a. Indicative m.

❖ Aux. v. u. to make imperfective sentences polite.

MATA また 〔又〕: [*adv.*] again

➤ Ⓗ mata wa: ❶ 【N】 Alternative c. ≈ ① **ka₁** ‖ ❷ 【N/n/V/i】 [*lit.*][*for.*] Disjunctive coordinator ≈ ② **ka₁**

① *~ or*

② *(either) ~ or*

MAWARU 回る: [*v.*] to turn

【TE】 *to go around ~*

ME め 〔目〕: [*dep. n.*]

Ⓒ *mi* 未 (*not yet*) + *man* 満 (*fulfilling*)

【s】 [*fam.*] Approximative Semblative m.

~ish; somewhat ~; rather ~

MEKU めく 〔貰う〕: [*v.*] to receive

Ⓤ 【N】 Evidential Semblative cop.

to show signs of ~; to have the air of ~; to look like ~

❖ U. to express that s.t. gives the impression or feeling of being like what is defined by the marked n.

❖ Usually in the perfective f. meita when u. before n.s or the progressive f. meite iru if u. at the end of the sentence.

MI み: [*suf.*]

【s】 Nominalization marker

~ness

❖ It transforms some limited—usually related to emotions—adj. v.s into n.s.

MIERU みえる 〔見える〕: [*v.*] to be seen; to show

Ⓗ 【TE/ku】 Evidential Semblative cop.

look like ~; seem to ~

MIMAN 未満: [*suf.*]

Ⓒ *mi* 未 (*not yet*) + *man* 満 (*fulfilling*)

【C】 Comparative Lower Limitative c.

less than ~; under ~

MIRU みる 〔見る〕: [*v.*] to see; to look

Ⓗ 【TE】 Probationary m.

try to ~; try ~ing

❖ Subsidiary v. indicating that an action is performed in a tentative way to check what happens.

MISERU みせる 〔見せる〕: [*v.*] to show

【TE】 Intentional m.

will definitely ~; can manage to ~; (be) determined to ~

❖ Subsidiary v. indicating that the speaker has a strong determination to do s.t.

❖ Always u. w. the first person.

MITAI みたい: [*dep. adj. v.*] resembling

← mita* Ⓒ yō 様 (way) | *Perfective f. of the v. *miru* (to see)

➤ mitai ({D}): [*col.*][*fam.*] 【V/na/i】 Semblative cop.

be like ~; be as ~

➤ mitai na ⟨N⟩: Attributive ☞ **mitai ni**

➤ ⊕ mitai ni: [*col.*][*fam.*] 【N】 Semblative c. 【V/i】 Evidential Semblative m.

like ~; as ~; similar to ~

MO も: [*p.*]

【N(p*)】 ❶ Ⓣ Cumulative c. | ❷ ⊕ Concessive c.

① ~ *too; also ~; ~ either*

② *even ~*

② † *not even ~; not a single ~*

② ‡ *no ~; any ~*

❖ ❶ Focal p. that puts focus on the marked n. while indicating that this element is added, in an inclusive manner, to another implicit or explicit element.

❖ ❷ Adds focus to the marked entity or quantity while emphasizing it in order to highlight its quality or volume.

❖ *ni, e, de, to, kara or made.

❖ †When u. w. neg. clauses.

❖ ‡When u. w. indefinite pronouns [☞ VO:I.2].

【C】 Upper Limitative c.

as many/much/long as ~; any ~

⊕ 【TE】 Concessive Provisional m.

even if/though ~; although ~; whether ~ or (not)

* *no matter how/what/who/when ~*

❖ P. u. to indicate that what is established in a subordinate clause is carried out despite not being in accordance w. what is expected from the preceding clause.

❖ *When u. after phrases starting w. interrogative pronouns [☞ VO:I.2].

- -

➤ mo areba ⟨N⟩ mo aru: 【N】 ≈ mo sureba ⟨VN/I⟩ mo suru

➤ mo aru: 【ku】 Cumulative coordinator

(and) is also ~; (and) is neither ~

❖ M. u. after conjunctive coordinators.

➤ mo dō ni mo naranai: 【TE】 Emphatic Negative Necessitative m.

it's no use ~; it's no good ~

➤ mo dōzen {D}: 【N/V】 Semblative cop.

it is just like ~; it is the same as ~

➤ mo dōzen no ⟨N⟩: Attributive ☞ **mo dōzen {D}**

➤ Ⓔ mo hajimaranai: 【TE】 Emphatic Negative Necessitative m.

it's no use to ~; there's no point to ~

➤ Ⓣ mo ii: 【TE】 Permissive m.

may ~; it is alright if ~; can ~

❖ Construction expressing permission or concession.

➤ Ⓣ mo ii desu: 【TE】 [*pol.*] ≈ mo ii

➤ mo kaerimizu: 【N】 = o kaerimizu

➤ mo ⟨s⟩ kereba ⟨N⟩ mo ⟨i⟩: 【ku】 ≈ mo ⟨BA⟩ ⟨N/p⟩ mo ⟨V⟩

➤ Ⓔ mo kamawanai: 【TE】 Permissive m.

it doesn't matter if ~; wouldn't mind (if) ~; may ~; can ~; it's okay if ~

➤ mo kanete: 【N】 = o kanete

➤ Ⓔ mo ⟨BA⟩ ⟨N(p)⟩ mo ⟨V⟩: 【N(p)】 Cumulative coordinator

~ and also ...; either ~ or/nor ...

❖ ⟨BA⟩ & ⟨V⟩ are the same v.

➤ Ⓔ mo ⟨N(p)⟩ mo: 【N(p)】 Cumulative Conjunctive c.

both ~ and ...; neither ~ nor ...

➤ mo ⟨ku⟩ mo: 【ku】 Alternative Coordinator

whether ~ (or not)

➤ mo ⟨N/ku⟩ mo aru: 【N/ku】 Cumulative Conjunctive coordinator

is/am/are both ~ and ...; is/am/are) neither ~ nor ...

➤ mo ⟨VN/I⟩ mo suru: 【VN/I】 Cumulative Conjunctive coordinator

both ~ and ...; neither ~ nor ...

➤ mo ⟨N/n⟩ nara ⟨N²⟩ mo ⟨N/n⟩ {D}: 【N¹】 ≈ mo ⟨BA⟩ ⟨N(p)⟩ mo ⟨V⟩

❖ Both ⟨N/n⟩ are the same adj. n

➤ mo nareba ⟨ku⟩ mo naru: 【ku】 ≈ mo sureba ⟨VN/I⟩ mo suru

➤ mo saru koto nagara: 【N】 [*for.*] Negative Lower Limitative c.

~ is one thing, but; it is true that ~, but; it is the case that ~, but; not only ~ but also

❖ Construction u. to acknowledge some important fact to introduce yet another more important fact.

➤ mo sashitsukenai: 【TE】 [*for.*] Permissive m.

can ~; it's okay if ~

➤ mo ⟨U⟩ shi ⟨N/(p)⟩ mo ⟨V⟩: 【N(p)】 = mo ⟨BA⟩ ⟨N(p)⟩ mo ⟨V⟩

❖ ⟨U⟩ & ⟨V⟩ are the same v.

➤ mo shinai: 【VN/I】 Negative Concessive coordinator

don't even ~

　➤ mo shinai de: 【I】 Concessive Privative coordinator

　　without even ~

➤ ⊕ mo sureba ⟨VN/I⟩ mo suru: 【VN/I】 Cumulative Enumerative coordinator

sometimes ~ and sometimes ~; may ~ or may ...; there are times when ~ and/or ...

❖ Structure that expresses examples of two actions or events that are simultaneously feasible.

➤ mo suru: 【VN/I】 Cumulative coordinator

(and) also ~; (and) neither ~

❖ M. u. after conjunctive coordinators.

　➤ mo suru shi ⟨U⟩ mo suru: 【U】 = mo sureba ⟨VN/I⟩ mo suru

➤ mo tōzen {D}: 【TE】 Evidential Assumptive m.

it's only natural (that) ~; no wonder ~; might as well ~

➤ mo yoroshii: [*for.*] ≈ mo ii desu

MON もん: [*col.*] ≈ mono

➤ mon: [*col.*] ≈ mono {D}

➤ mon {D} kara: 【V/na/i】 [*col.*] ≈ mono {D} kara

➤ mon desu ka: [*pol.*][*fm.*] ≈ mono ka

➤ mon ja nai: 【U】 [*col.*] ≈ mono de wa nai

➤ mon ka: [*col.*] ≈ mono ka

MONO もの 〔物/者〕: [*n.*] (tangible) thing

【I】 Nominalization marker

❖ Only a limited number of v.s allow this way of nominalization.

【V/na/i】 ❶ ⊕ Nominalization marker | ❷ Explanative cop. = ② mono {D}

① *to ~; ~ing*

② *the thing is ~; it's because ~*

❖ ❶ Referring to things that may arise some degree of emotion. M. u. w. adj.s.

➤ ⊕ mono {D}: ❶ 【U】 Jussive m. ‖ ❷ 【V/na/i】 Explanative cop.

① *(s.o.) should ~*

② *the thing is ~; it's because ~*

❖ ❶ Verbal nominalization marker u. to indicate that s.t. should be done without personal involvement.

❖ ❷ Structure u. to introduce an explanative clause upon a subject matter.

❖ ❶ M. u. for generic statements.

❖ ❷ The word *mono* actually refers to a tangible object, so this construction confers the explained event or action a remarkable degree of emotion, similar to that which could be evoked by a tangible thing.

➢ mono {D} kara: 【V/na/i】 Explanative Causal m.

so ~; therefore ~; because ~

❖ *After both n.s and the nominal part of adj. n.s.

➢ mono de: 【V/na/i】 Explanative causal coordinator

it's because ~ (and)

➢ mono de wa nai: ❶ 【U】 Negative Jussive m. ≈ **beki de** (wa) **nai** ‖ ❷ 【U*】 Negative Tentative cop.

① *(one) shouldn't ~*

② *naturally cannot ~*

❖ Construction formed to indicate that s.t. should not (❶) or presumably cannot or could not be done (❷).

❖ *U. w. the potential f. of the v.s.

➢ mono ja nai: 【U】 [*col.*] ≈ **mono de wa nai**

➢ mono ka: ❶ 【N/na/U/i】 Negative Emphatic m. ‖ ❷ 【TA*】 Dubitative m.

① *definitely not ~; absolutely not ~; there's no way (that) ~*

② *I wonder if ~*

❖ ❶ Grammatically interrogative construction that indicates, in an ironic way, a strong negation.

➢ mono nara: ❶ 【U*】 Tentative Provisional m. ‖ ❷ 【Ō】 [*lit.*] Emphatic Provisional m.

❶ *If I can/could ~ then*

❷ *if ~ at all*

❖ *Usually in the potential f. (Ⓢ **E-ru**; Ⓦ **E-rareru**)

➢ mono no: 【V/na/i】 Concessive coordinator

although ~; though ~; even though ~; but ~

❖ This construction usually expresses, in an adverse way, an unexpected action or event.

➢ ⟨V/na/i*⟩ mono o: 【BA】 Provisional Concessive Adversative m.

if ~ would … but; if ~ I wish …

❖ *M. the adj. ii (*good*) or in its perfective f. yokatta (*was good*), making the sentence mean s.t. like: "if ~ would be/have been good but …"

➢ mono yara: 【V/na/i】 = **no yara**

MORAITAI もらいたい〔貰いたい〕: [*adj. v.*]

Volitional f. of the v. *morau (to receive)*

【TE】 [*pol.*] ≈ **hoshii**

MORAU もらう〔貰う〕: [*v.*] to receive

⊕ 【TE】 Passive Benefactive m.

s.o. ~ for me/for one's sake

❖ Subsidiary v. that expresses that oneself or s.o. close to one receives a favor or gets s.t. done on his or her behalf by s.o. else of equal or lower status.

❖ The patient subject of the sentence (the person receiving the favor) takes the p. **ga** and the agent, if appearing in the sentence, takes the p. **ni**.

❖ This v. has the nuance that the person receiving the favor feels good about receiving that favor.

MUKE 向け: [*dep. n.*]

(I) *mukeru (to turn towards)*

➤ muke {D}: 【N】 Purposive Dative cop.

it is for ~; it is intended for ~

➤ Ⓔ muke ni: 【N】 Purposive Dative c.

oriented towards ~; aimed at ~; intended for ~

MUKI 向き: [*n.*] orientation

(I) *muku (to face)*

➤ muki {D}: 【N】 Correlative Dative cop.

it is suited to ~; it is designed for ~

➤ Ⓔ muki ni: 【N】 Correlative Dative c.

suited to ~; suitable for ~; designed for ~

N

N_1 ん: [*col.*] ≈ no_2

- -

N_2 ん: 【A】 [*col.*][*mas.*] ≈ nai

← O.J. neg. i. *(not be)*

❖ This version of the neg. f. of the v. **suru** (*to do*) is sen.

- -

N_3 ん: [*i.*]

← O.J. neg. i. *(not be)*

❖ This version of the neg. f. of the v. **suru** (*to do*) is sen.

- -

➤ n bakari {D}: 【A】 [*for.*] Prospective a. Prospective Evidential cop.

it is/was as if s.t./s.o. was/were about to ~

➤ n bakari ni: 【A】 [*for.*] Prospective a. Evidential Semblative m.

as if s.t./s.o. was/were about to ~; almost ~

❖ Structure u. to indicate that it looks like s.o. is about to do s.t. or that s.t. is about to happen.

➤ n {D}: 【V/na/i】 [*col.*] ≈ no {D}

  ➤ n {D} kara: 【V/na/i】 [*col.*] ≈ no {D} kara

  ➤ n {D} mon: 【V/na/i】 [*col.*] ≈ no {D} mono ({D})

➤ n {D} mono: 【V/na/i】 [*col.*] ≈ no {D} mono ({D})

➤ n dai: 【V/na/i】 [*fam.*][*mas.*] Interrogative m.

~?

❖ Only u. w. questions that have interrogative pronouns.

➤ n da: 【V/na/i】 [*fam.*][*mas.*] ≈ n {D}

  ➤ Ⓔ n da kke: 【V/na/i】 [*col.*] [*fam.*] Interrogative m.

  ~?

  ➤ Ⓔ n da tte: 【V/na/i】 [*col.*] [*fam.*] Inferential m.

  I hear that ~; heard that ~

➤ n de: 【V/na/i】 [*col.*] ≈ no de

➤ n darō ka: 【V/na/i】 [*col.*] ≈ no darō ka

➤ n deshō ka: 【V/na/i】 [*col.*] ≈ no deshō ka

➤ n desu: 【V/na/i】 [*pol.*] ≈ n {D}

  ➤ n desu tte: 【V/na/i】 [*pol.*] ≈ n da tte

➤ n ga tame (ni): 【A】 ≈ ② 〖V〗 tame (ni)

➤ n ja nai ka: 【V/na/i】 [col.] ≈ no de wa nai ka

➤ n to suru: 【A】 [lit.] ≈ 〖Ō〗 to suru

NA₁ な: [cop.]

← O.J. naru* (to be) → C.J. naru (to become) | *← ni aru: essive p. ni + v. aru (to be)

➤ Ⓣ na 〈N〉: 【n】 Indicative Imperfective a. Attributive cop.

… that/which/who is/are ~

❖ Copulative p. that makes an adj. n. an attribute (modifying another n.).

- -

NA₂ な: [p.]

← emphatic p. ne

Ⓣ 【N/n/V/i】 [fam.] Admirative m.

how ~!; what ~!; ~!

❖ An emphatic particle u. to imbue the sentence w. strong feelings, indicating admiration or hope.

- -

NA₃ な: [i.]

← adj. nai (not to be)

Ⓛ 【U】 [mas.] Prohibitive m.

don't ~; do not ~

❖ Ending u. to state a strong prohibition. Only u. in very informal and emotional contexts, m. by men.

- -

NA₄ な: [i.]

← nasai: Imperative f. of the hon. nasaru (to do)

⊕ 【I】 [col.][fam.] ≈ nasai

NAA なあ: [p.]

Ⓣ 【P】 = na₂

NADO など 〔等〕: [p.]

← nando ← nanito: pron. nani (what) + quotative p. to

➤ ⊕ nado {p}: 【N】 Enunciative c.

such as ~; things like ~; ~ or the like; for example ~; ~ etc.

❖ P. indicating some sort of exemplification.

➤ nado to: 【N】 Quotative Enunciative c. 【V/i】 Enunciative subordinator

(things) like ~; ~ or something

❖ Compound p. that enunciates an approximate quote of words or ideas.

  ➤ nado to iu mono de wa nai: 【V/na/i】 [for.] ≈ no nan no tte

  ➤ nado to wa: 【N】 Emphatic Enunciative c. 【V/i】 Emphatic Enunciative m.

  things like ~; that ~

NAGARA ながら 〔乍ら〕: [p.]

Probably from attributive cop. na (to be) + gara: (I) aux. v. garu (to show sings of)

❶ ⊕ 【I】 Simultaneous Durative a. ‖
❷ 【VN/n/I/i】 Concessive Adversative m. = nagara mo

① while ~; at the same time as ~; as ~

② although ~; even though ~; despite ~; nevertheless; while ~

❖ Subordinate p. indicating that an action takes place simultaneously w. another action.

❖ The subject of the two actions that take place simultaneously has to be the same.

➤ Ⓛ nagara mo: 【VN/n/I/i】 [for.] Concessive Adversative m.

although ~; even though ~; despite ~; nevertheless; while ~

➤ nagara ni shite: 【I】 ≈ ① ni shite

➤ nagara ni: 【I】 = ① nagara

NAI ない〔無い〕: [i.]

← O.J. *nashi (not to be)*

Ⓕ 【A/ku】 [*fam.*] Negative Imperfective a. Indicative m.

not ~; don't ~

❖ Inflection that negates the action or description given by a v. or an adj.

➢ Ⓕ nai ⟨N⟩: 【A/ku】 Negative Imperfective a. Attributive subordinator

〖A〗 *that/which/who don't/doesn't ~*

〖ku〗 *that/which/who is/are not ~*

➢ nai darō: 【A/ku】 [*fam.*] Negative Presumptive m.

(probably) won't ~

➢ Ⓕ nai de: 【A/ku】 ❶ [*fam.*] Negative Directive m. | ❷ [*fam.*] Privative coordinator | ❸ Negative Conjunctive coordinator

① *don't ~*

② *without ~*

③ *not ~ and*

❖ If this structure is not followed by any clause it is understood that the sentence is a neg. request (❶); telling s.o. not to do s.t.

❖ If this structure is followed by a clause the meaning of this structure is m. understood as 'without' (❷), but sometimes it can take the meaning of a negative declarative mood (❸).

➢ nai de hoshii: 【A】 Negative Patient Volitive m.

don't want (s.o.) to ~

➢ Ⓕ nai de kudasai: 【A】 [*pol.*] Negative Directive m.

please don't ~

➢ nai de mo: 【A/ku】 Concessive Privative coordinator

without even ~

➢ nai de mo nai: 【A】 Evidential Inferential m.

seem to ~; somewhat ~; rather feel that/like ~; kind of ~; may ~

❖ Double neg. construction u. to express, in a hesitant way, that s.t. seems to be the case.

❖ M. u. w. v.s of perception such as **kanjiru** (*to feel*), **ki ga suru** (*to feel*), **omou** (*to think*), or **mieru** (*to look*).

➢ nai de moraitai: 【A】 [*pol.*] ≈ **nai de hoshii**

➢ nai de wa irarenai: 【A】 Negative Optative m.

can't help but ~; cannot keep from n

➢ nai de wa okanai: 【A】 Assumptive m.

will definitely ~; cannot not ~; undoubtedly ~; ~ without fail; ~ without a doubt

❖ Double neg. construction u. to express that s.t. inevitably will happen.

➢ nai de wa sumanai: 【A】 Obligative m.

must ~; have to ~

➢ nai (de/ni): 【N】 [*lit.*] Inessive c.

inside ~; within ~

➢ nai deshō: 【A/ku】 [*for.*] ≈ **nai darō**

➢ Ⓕ nai desu: 【A/ku】 [*pol.*] ≈ **nai**

➢ nai hō ga ii: 【A】 Negative Suggestive m.

you would better/rather not ~

➢ nai kara koso: 【A】 Negative Emphatic Causal m.

precisely because (not) ~

➢ nai koto: 【A】 [*lit.*] Negative Obligative m.

should not ~; do not ~; may not ~

➤ Ⓔ nai koto mo nai: 【A/ku】 Indirect Explanatory cop.

it is not impossible to ~; it isn't the case that s.o. don't/doesn't ~; it is not that s.o. don't/doesn't ~; can ~; may

❖ Double negative construction u. to recognize the actuality of s.t. in a humble way.

➤ nai koto ni wa: 【A】 Negative Provisional m.

if not ~ (then); unless ~

❖ Structure that indicates that an event will not take place if a given condition is not met.

➤ Ⓔ nai koto wa nai: 【A/ku】 = nai koto mo nai

➤ nai made mo: 【A/ku】 Negative Concessive Provisional m.

may not ~ but; even though ~ not; although ~ not

❖ Construction u. to give a choice after declaring the impossibility of an action or state.

➤ nai mono darō ka: 【A】 = nai mono ka

➤ nai mono de mo nai: 【A】 Tentative m.

it is not impossible (that) ~

➤ nai* mono ka: 【A】 Desiderative m.

I wish ~; would be good if ~

❖ This construction also indicates, in a subjective manner, a doubt towards a possible action.

❖ *The neg. potential f.s (Ⓢ E-ranai; Ⓦ E-rarenai).

➤ nai nara: 【A/ku】 Negative Provisional m.

if don't/doesn't ~

➤ nai shi (wa) ⟨N/n/V/i⟩: [lit.] ❶ [N/n/V/i] Disjunctive coordinator. ❷ [C] Range marker

① ~ or

② *from ~ to …; between ~ and*

❖ ❶ Compound p. u. to present two different choices.

❖ ❷ Compound p. u. to introduce possible quantitative choices between a numerical range.

➤ Ⓔ nai to: 【A/ku】 Negative Provisional m.

if not ~; unless ~

➤ ⊕ nai to dame ({D}): [fam.] ≈ nai to ikenai

➤ Ⓣ nai to ikenai: 【A/ku】 = nakute wa ikenai

➤ nai to mo kagiranai: 【A】 Tentative m.

might ~; may ~; it's not impossible that ~

➤ nai uuchi ni: 【A】 Antessive a.

before ~

❖ It indicates that the marked action is uncontrollable and the following action has to be done before the marked action starts.

NAKA 中: [n.] middle

➤ naka de (wa): 【U/na/i】 ≈ naka o

➤ naka o: 【U/na/i】 Intrative Durative a.

in the midst of ~; while ~; when ~; through ~

❖ Combined p. that indicates the time in the midsts of which s.t. is done or happens.

NAKARŌ なかろう: [i.]

Presumptive f. of the adj. *nai (not to be)*

【A】 [lit.][obs.] ≈ 〖A〗 nai darō

【ku】 [lit.][for.] ≈ 〖ku〗 nai darō

➤ wa nakarō: 【ku】 = nakarō

NAKATTA なかった: [i.]

Perfective f. of the adj. *nai (not to be)*

Ⓣ 【A/ku】 [*fam.*] Negative Perfective a.

〖A〗 *did not ~; didn't ~; hasn't/haven't ~*

〖ku〗 *was/were not ~*

➤ Ⓣ nakatta 〈N〉: 【A/ku】 Negative Perfective a. Attributive subordinator

〖A〗 *... that/which/who wasn't/weren't ~*

〖ku〗 *... that/which/who wasn't/weren't ~*

➤ Ⓣ nakatta arimasen deshita: 【ku】 = nakatta desu

➤ Ⓣ nakatta desu: [*pol.*] 【A/ku】 ≈ nakatta

➤ Ⓣ nakatta ra: 【A/ku】 Negative Postessive Provisional m.

if not ~ (then); when not ~; after not having ~

NAKEREBA なければ: [*i.*]

Provisional f. of the adj. *nai (not to be)*

❶ 【A/ku】 Negative Provisional m.

if not ~

✤ Inflection that presents the provision that s.t. does not happen.

❷ 【A/ku】 = nakereba naranai

➤ ⊕ nakereba ikenai: 【A/ku】 ≈ nakereba naranai

✤ M. expressing a personal obligation.

➤ ⊕ nakereba naranai: 【A/ku】 Obligative m.

have to ~; must ~; need (to) ~; got to ~

✤ M. expressing a general or common-sense obligation.

NAKERYA なけりゃ: 【A/ku】 [*col.*] ≈ nakereba

➤ nakerya naranai: 【A/ku】 [*col.*] ≈ nakereba naranai

NAKU なく: [*i.*]

Infinitive f. of adj. v. *nai (not to be)*

【ku】 [*lit.*] ≈ nakute

➤ naku mo nai: 【A/ku】 = nai koto mo nai

➤ naku naru: 【A/ku】 Negative Resultative a.

not ~ anymore

➤ naku shite (wa): 【N】 Privative c.

without ~

➤ naku wa nai: 【A/ku】 = naku mo nai

NAKUCHA なくちゃ: [*i.*]

⊕ 【A/ku】 ❶ Obligative m. = nakucha naranai | ❷ [*col.*] Negative Thematic Provisional m. ≈ nakute wa

① *have to ~; must ~; need (to) ~; got to ~*

② *if not ~ (then); unless ~*

✤ ❶ When ending a sentence.

✤ ❷ Before another clause.

➤ ⊕ nakucha dame: 【A/ku】 = nai to dame ({D})

➤ ⊕ nakucha ikenai: 【A/ku】 [*col.*] [*fam.*] ≈ nakute wa ikenai

➤ ⊕ nakucha naranai: 【A/ku】 [*col.*] [*fam.*] ≈ nakute wa naranai

NAKUTCHA なくっちゃ: 【A/ku】 = nakucha

NAKUTE なくて: [*i.*]

Gerundive f. of the adj. *nai (not to be)*

【A/ku】 Negative Conjunctive coordinator

not ~ and; is not ~ and; not ~ but

❖ Inflection that negates an action or state as a cause or condition that introduces a subsequent action or state.

➢ nakute ii: 【A】 = nakute mo ii

➢ nakute mo: 【A/ku】 Concessive Privative coordinator

without even ~; even if not ~

➢ ⑤ nakute mo ii: 【A】 Negative Obligative m.

don't have to ~; no need to ~; it's alright if ~

➢ nakute wa: 【A/ku】 Negative Thematic Provisional m.

if not ~ (then); unless ~

➢ ⑤ nakute wa ikenai: 【A/ku】 = nakereba ikenai

➢ ⑤ nakute wa naranai: 【A/ku】 = nakereba naranai

NAKYA なきゃ: [col.][fam.] ❶ Obligative m. = nakya naranai | ❷ Negative Provisional m ≈ nakereba

① *have to ~; must ~; need (to) ~; got to ~*

② *if not ~ (then); unless ~*

❖ ❶ When ending a sentence.

❖ ❷ Before another clause.

➢ nakya naranai: 【A/ku】 [col.] ≈ nakereba naranai

NAMI 並み: [n.] average

➢ nami {D}: 【N】 Equitative Correlative cop.

to be on par with ~; to be equivalent to ~

➢ nami ni: 【N】 Equitative Correlative c.

on par with ~; equivalent to ~; equal to ~; at the same level as ~

NANKA なんか: [p.]

nan + interrogative p. ka | *← nani (what)

Ⓔ 【N】 [col.] Emphatic Enunciative c.

~ or the like; ~ or anything

NANTE なんて: [p.]

← *nado* tote† | *Semblative enunciative p. nado (things like) | †Concessive p. tote (even)*

Ⓔ ❶ 【N】 Emphatic Enunciative c. ‖ ❷ 【V/i】 Emphatic Enunciative subordinator

even (that) ~; thinks like ~

❖ U. to give the marked part of speech a hint of emotion, be it astonishment, envy, disgust or admiration.

➢ nante mon ja nai: 【V/na/i】 = no nan no tte

NAOSU なおす〔直す〕: [v.] to fix

Ⓔ 【I】 Iterative a.

to ~ again; to ~ over

❖ It expresses that an action is redone in order to improve its result.

NARA なら: [cop.]

Irrealis f. of O.J. v. *naru (to be)*

⊕ 【N/n】 Provisional cop.

if be ~

⊕ 【V/i】 Provisional m.

if (it's true that) ~; if (it's the case that) ~; if ~

❖ Copulative structure u. to indicate that the marked phrase is an assumption ('provision') of the speaker regarding the truth or actualization of a deed or situation in the present or future.

❖ This f. is u., then, when there is already a given context known by both the speaker and the listener listener concerning the provision.

➣ nara de wa {D}: 【N】 ❶ Exclusive Provisional cop.❷ Exclusive Correlative cop.

① *only if ~; impossible unless it is ~*

② *is uniquely applying to ~; is distinctive of ~; is characteristic of ~*

➣ nara mada shi mo: 【N】 Preferential cop.

rather be ~; better be ~

➣ nara zu to mo: 【N】 ≈ zu to mo

NARABA ならば: [*cop.*]

Provisional f. of the O.J. v. *nari (to be)*

【N/n/V/i】 [*for.*] ≈ nara

NARANAI ならない [*subsidiary adj*]

Neg. f. of the v. *naru (to become)*

【TE】 *cannot help ~ing; irresistibly ~; dying to ~*

❖ Subsidiary adj. that expresses the irrepressible psychological or physical desire to do s.t.

NARERU 慣れる: [*v.*] to get used to

⊕ 【I】 *to get used to ~*

NARI なり: [*p.*]

From O.J. v. *nari* ← *ni ari*: dative p. *ni (to)* + O.J. v. *ari (to be)* → C.J. → *aru*

【N】 ❶ ≈ nari 〈N/U〉 nari ‖ ❷ 【N/n】 [*obs.*] Imperfective cop. ≈ da

❖ ② Only u. to qualify s.t.

【TA】 [*lit.*] Progressive Stative a.

while staying ~; keep ~ing

❖ It indicates that a state remains unchanged.

【U】 ❶ Punctual Inceptive a. ‖ ❷ ≈ nari 〈N/U〉 nari

the moment ~; as soon as ~; soon after ~; when ~

❖ P. which expresses that an action begins to be performed just after a previous action 〈U〉.

➣ nari 〈N/U〉 nari: 【N/U】 Alternative Enumerative coordinator

~ or ...; either ~ or ...

❖ U. to present two choices as examples of an implicitly larger group of things.

➣ nari de: 【TA】 = 〘TA〙 nari

➣ nari ni: ❶ 【N】 Formal Semblative c. ‖ ❷ 【n/i】 Concessive Provisional m.

① *in ~ style/way*

② *though ~; even if ~*

➣ nari to mo: 【N】 Concessive Upper Limitative c.

at lest ~; even a little ~

NARU なる 〔成る〕: [*v.*] to become

← *ni aru*: Essive p. *ni* + v. *aru (to be)*

⊕ 【ku】 ≈ yō ni naru

➣ naru 〈N〉: 【n】 [*lit.*][*obs.*] ≈ na₁

NASAI なさい: [*i.*]

Imperative f. of the hon. v. *nasaru (to do)*

⊕ 【I】 [*pol.*] Directive m.

please do ~

❖ Inflection u. to give orders, in a pol. way, to people of an equal or inferior social position.

NASARU なさる 〔為さる〕: [*v.*] to do

O.J. passive f. of the v. *naru (to do)*

【VN*/I†】 [*for.*][*hon.*] Imperfective a. Indicative m.

❖ U. to formally show respect or reverence towards the person—of a higher social position than the speaker—indicated by the subject of the sentence.

✤*The nominal part of Sino-Japanese v.s attached to the hon. pre. **go**.

✤ †After the hon. pre. **o**.

✤ In declarative sentences, the pol. f. nasaimasu has to be u. The plain imperfective f. nasaru is only u. in dependent clauses.

✤ V.s that have pol. or hon. f.s will u. these f.s instead of the plain ones.

NASHI なし 〔無し〕: [*dep. adj. v.*] not be

Fossilized O.J. attributive f. of the C.J. adj. *nai (not be)*

⊕ 【N】 Privative c.

without ~; no ~; ~less

✤ Understood as a n. phrase.

➢ **nashi de/ni** (wa): 【N】 [*lit.*] ≈ **nashi**

NE ね: [*p.*]

Ⓣ 【N/n/V/i】 Inquisitive m.

~ isn't it?; ~ is it?; ~ right?; ~ you know

✤ Emphatic p. that subtly indicates that the speaker is asking for confirmation or agreement from the listener.

✤ This p., especially when pronounced w. a long vowel (*nee*), can add an admirative overtone to the sentence.

NEBA ねば: [*i.*]

➢ **neba naranai**: 【A】 [*lit.*] ≈ **nakereba naranai**

✤ The v. **suru** takes the f. seneba naranai

NEE ねえ: 【P】 ❶ Inquisitive m. = **ne** | ❷ [*fam.*] Admirative m. ≈ **na₂**

① *~ isn't it?; ~ is it?; ~ right?; ~ you know*

② *how ~!; what ~!; ~!*

NEGAU 願う: [*v.*] to hope

【VN*/I†】 [*hon.*] Directive m.

please ~

✤ U. to respectfully give directions or soft commands.

✤*The nominal part of Sino-Japanese v.s attached to the hon. pre. **go**.

✤ †Goes after the hon. pre. **o**

✤ In declarative sentences the pol. f. negaimasu has to be u. The plain imperfective f. negau is only u. in dependent clauses.

✤ V.s that have pol. or hon. f.s will u. these f.s instead of the plain ones.

NI₁ に: [*p.*]

Ⓣ 【N】 ❶ Dative c. ❷ Lative c. ❸ Agentive c.

① *to ~; for ~*

② *to ~; toward ~*

③ *by ~; from ~*

✤ ❶ It marks the indirect object, i.e. the person for whom an action is performed.

✤ ❶ U. w. transitive v.s.

✤ ❷ It indicates a place towards which s.t. or s.o. moves.

✤ ❸ It marks the agent of an action in a passive or causative construction, that is, it indicates the person who performs the action in a passive or causative sentence.

Ⓣ 【VN/I】 Final m.

to ~; in order to ~

✤ It indicates the intention w. which s.o. moves from one place to another.

✤ Only u. before v.s of motion such as **iku** (*to go*) or **kuru** (*to come*).

- -

NI₂ に: [*p.*]

Ⓣ 【N/C】 Essive c.

in ~; at ~; on ~

✤ Case p. that marks a specific point in space or time. In the case of being a space, it refers to either a location where s.o. or s.t. exists or the surface of s.t. upon which an action takes place. In the case of being a point in time, it usually refers to temporary periods that can be defined by digits.

	ni_1			ni_2
State:	Progression		Regression	Station
Case:	① Dative	② Lative	③ Agentive	Essive
Explanation:	to s.o.	to some place	by/from s.o.	at some place or time
Meaning:	to		by; from	in; at; on
	for	toward		

NI₃ に: [*suf.*]

Probably from *nari*: gerundive f. of the O.J. v. *naru (to be)*

【n】 Adverbialization marker

~*ly*

❖ Turns an adj. n into an adv.

➤ ni ⟨V⟩*: **【U】** Negative Potential m.

cannot (manage to) ~; (just) can't ~

❖ U. to express that s.o. cannot do s.t. due to external causes.

❖ *V. in the neg. potential f.

❖ 【U】 & ⟨V⟩ are the same v.

➤ ni atari: [*lit.*] ≈ **ni attate**

➤ ni atatte: [*for.*] **【N】** ❶ Thematic Essive c. ‖ **【VN/U】** ❷ Punctual a. ❸ Antessive a.

① *at ~; in ~*

② *on the occasion of ~; when ~*

③ *before ~; prior to ~*

➤ ni atte (mo/wa): **【N】** Thematic Essive c.

in ~; at ~

❖ M. u. w. abstract nouns.

➤ Ⓔ ni chigai nai: **【N/n】** Assumptive cop. **【V/i】** Assumptive m.

I'm sure ~; I'm certain ~; (there is) no doubt that ~; must ~

❖ Construction that expresses that the speaker is completely convinced of his or her guess.

➤ ni han shi: **【N】** = **ni han shite**

➤ Ⓔ ni han shite: **【N】** Oppositive Dative c.

against ~; contrary to ~; in contrast to ~

❖ U. for presenting two propositions in opposition.

➤ ni han suru ⟨N⟩: **【N】** Attributive ☞ **ni han shite**

➤ ni hikikae: **【N】** ① Contrastive Dative c. ② Substitutive Essive c.

① *in contrast to ~; while ~; whereas ~*

② *in exchange for ~*

❖ Nominal combined p. u. to present a sharp contrast between two people or things.

➤ ni hoka naranai: **【N】** [*lit.*] Lower Limitative cop.

is/are nothing but ~; is/are simply ~

➤ ni hoka naranu: 【N】 = ni hoka naranai

➤ ni itaru made: 【N】 [*lit.*] Upper Limitative c.

until ~; as far as ~

➤ ni itatte (wa): 【N】 [*for.*] Emphatic Thematic c.

as for ~; when it comes to ~

➤ ni kagirazu: 【N】 [*for.*] Negative Lower Limitative c.

not just ~; not only ~ (but also); not limited to ~ (but also)

➤ ni kagiri: 【N】 [*lit.*] ≈ ni kagitte

➤ ni kagitte: 【N】 ❶ Lower Limitative Essive c. ❷ Lower Limitative Dative c.

① *only in ~; only when ~*

② *only for ~*

➤ ni kakatte iru: 【N】 Dependent Correlative cop.

depending on ~

➤ ni kakawarazu: 【N】 = ni mo kakawarazu

➤ ni kakawari: 【N】 [*lit.*] ≈ ni kakawatte

➤ ni kakawaru 〈N〉: 【N】 Attributive ☞ ni kakawatte

➤ ni kakawatte: 【N】 Correlative c.

related to ~; having to do with ~

➤ ⓔ ni kakete (wa): 【N】 ❶ Correlative c. ❷ Perlative Essive c.

① *concerning ~; regarding ~as for ~; when it comes to ~; about ~*

② *over ~; through ~*

❖ ❶ This compound p. implies that the marked theme involves some sort of praise or recognition in regards to ability or competence.

➤ ni kankē naku: 【N】 [*for.*] = o towazu

➤ ni kan shi: 【N】 [*lit.*] ≈ ni kan shite

➤ ⓔ ni kan shite (wa): 【N】 [*for.*] Correlative c.

related to ~; concerning ~; with regard to ~; about ~; on ~

➤ ⓔ ni kan suru 〈N〉: 【N】 Attributive ☞ ni kan shite

➤ ⓔ ni kawari: 【N】 [*lit.*] ≈ ni kawatte

➤ ⓔ ni kawatte: 【N】 Substitutive Essive c.

in place of ~; on behalf of ~; instead of ~

❖ M. u. w. people.

➤ ni kimatte iru: 【N/n】 Assumptive cop. 【V/i】 Assumptive m.

surely ~; certainly ~; of course ~; must (be the case that) ~

➤ ni kurabe: 【N】 = ni kurabete

➤ ni kurabereba: 【N】 = ni kurabete

➤ ni kuraberu to: 【N】 = ni kurabete

➤ ⓔ ni kurabete: 【N】 Contrastive Dative c.

compared with/to ~; in comparison to ~

➤ ni kuwae: 【N】 [*lit.*] ≈ ni kuwaete

➤ ni kuwaete: 【N】 [*for.*] Cumulative c.

in addition (to) ~

➤ ni matsuwaru 〈N〉: 【N】 = ni kan suru 〈N〉

➤ ⊕ ni mieru: 【N/n】 ≈ 〖TE/ku〗 mieru

➤ ni mo: 【N】 ❶ Essive Cumulative c. ❷ Lative Cumulative c. ❸ Dative Cumulative c. ‖ ❹ 【Ō】 Concessive Presumptive m.

① *also in ~*

②③ *also to ~*

④ *even if s.o. tries to/wants to ~; although s.o. tries to/wants to ~*

✧ ❹ U. w. the first person or when speaking about s.o. towards whom the speaker feels empathically close.

✧ ❹ M. u. before neg. v.s.

➤ ni mo hodo ga aru: 【N/n/U/i】 Upper Limitative cop.

there is a limit to ~; ~ too far

➤ ni mo kakawarazu: [for.] ❶ 【N】 Negative Dependent Correlative c. ‖ ❷ 【V/i】 Concessive coordinator

① *regardless of ~; in spite of ~*

② *even though ~; although ~; despite (the fact that) ~; ~ nevertheless; in spite of ~*

✧ Construction u. to indicate that an action or state is unrelated to another action or state.

➤ ni mo mashite: 【N】 Concessive Comparative c.

(even) more than ~; above ~

➤ ni mo nareba: 【N/U】 Emphatic Provisional m.

when ~; if ~; as ~

✧ Phrase u. to express that the speaker would feel a special emotion if the marked element took place.

➤ ni mo naru to: 【N/U】 Emphatic Conditional m.

when ~; if ~; as ~

✧ Structure u. to express that the speaker would feel a special emotion if the uncontrollable or unexpected marked element took place.

➤ ni moto dzuita ⟨N⟩: 【N】 Attributive ☞ ni moto dzuite

➤ ni moto dzuite: 【N】 Inferential c.

based on/upon ~; on the basis of ~

➤ ni moto dzuki: 【N】 [lit.] ≈ ni moto dzuite

➤ ni moto dzuku: 【N】 ≈ ni moto dzuite

➤ ni moto dzuku ⟨N⟩: 【N】 Attributive ☞ moto dzuite

➤ ni mukatte: 【N】 Lative c.

toward ~; to ~; aiming at; facing ~; heading to ~; addressing ~

➤ ni muketa ⟨N⟩: 【N】 Attributive ☞ ni mukete

➤ ni mukete: 【N】 ❶ Lative c. ❷ Final c.

① *toward ~; to ~; aiming at*

② *for (the purpose of) ~*

✧ ❷ M. u. for events.

➤ ni mukete no ⟨N⟩: Attributive ☞ ni mukete

➤ ㊤ ni nareru: 【N/I】 Habitual m.

to get used to ~

➤ ni naru: ❶ ㊦ 【N/n/C】 Resultative cop. ‖ ❷ ㊤ 【I*/n*】 [for.][hon.] Imperfective a. Indicative m.

① *to become ~*

✧ ❷ This structure is u. to make the sentence honorific, that is, to show a certain degree of respect towards the person indicated by the subject.

✧ *After the hon. p. o.

✧ ❷ V.s that have pol. or hon. f.s will u. these f.s instead of the plain ones.

➤ ni naru to: 【N】 ❶ Resultative Conditional m. ❷ Emphatic Thematic c.

① *when it becomes ~; when it is ~; if s.o./s.t. becomes ~*

② *when it comes to ~*

✧ ❶ Construction u. to indicate the time when an uncontrollable state or habitual action occurs.

➤ ni nottotte: 【N】 Perlative Correlative c.

following ~; by ~; in accordance with ~; according to ~

➤ ㊤ ni oite: 【N】 [for.] Thematic Essive c.

at ~; on ~; in ~

❖ It indicates, while putting the focus on the marked n., an abstract or concrete place in space or point in time.

➢ ni ōjita ⟨N⟩: 【N】 Attributive ☞ ni ōjite

➢ ni ōjite: 【N】 Perlative Correlative c.

according to ~; in accordance with ~; appropriate for ~

❖ It indicates that s.t. is suitable to another thing.

➢ ⊕ ni okeru ⟨N⟩: 【N】 Attributive ☞ ni oite

➢ ni oyobanai: 【N/U】 = ni wa oyobanai

➢ ni sai shite (wa): 【VN/U】 [*for.*] Punctual a.

on the occasion of ~; at the time of ~

➢ ni saki dachi: 【N】 Antessive c.

before ~; prior to ~

➢ ni saki datsu: 【N】 = ni saki dachi

➢ ni saki datte: 【N】 = ni saki dachi

➢ ni seyo: 【N/n/V/i】 [*lit.*] ≈ ni shiro

  ➢ ni seyo ⟨N/n/V/i⟩ ni seyo: 【N/n/V/i】 [*lit.*] ≈ ni shite mo ⟨N/n/V/i⟩ ni shite mo

➢ ni shiro: 【N/n/V/i】 Decisive Provisional m.

even if (s.o. decides to) ~; even though ~

  ➢ ni shiro ⟨N/n/V/i⟩ ni shiro: 【N/n/V/i】 [*for.*] ≈ ni shite mo ⟨N/n/V/i⟩ ni shite mo

➢ ni shitagai: 【N】 =ni shitagatte

➢ ni shitagatte: ❶ ⊕ 【N】 Perlative Correlative c. ‖ ❷ 【U】 [*lit.*] Translative Durative a. ≈ ni tsurete

① *following ~; in accordance with ~*

② *as ~*

➢ ni shita ra: 【N】 Subjective Inferential c.

in the position of ~; in ~'s position; from ~ perspective

➢ ni shita tokoro de: [*for.*] ❶ 【N】 Concessive c. ❷ 【V/i】 Concessive Provisional m. = to shita tokoro de

① *even (for) ~*

② *even if ~*

➢ ni shita tte: [*col.*] ≈ ni shita tokoro de

➢ ni shite: ❶ 【C】 [*lit.*] Perlative essive c. ‖ ❷ 【N】 [*lit.*] Thematic Essive c. ‖ 【N/n】 [*for.*] ❸ Conjunctive cop. ❹ Imperative cop.

① *while ~; over ~; during ~; as ~*

② *in ~; at ~*

③ *being ~; am/is/are ~ and*

④ *be ~*

❖ ❶ It indicates the time during which an action takes place.

  ➢ ⊕ ni shite mo: 【VN/N/V】 Concessive Conditional m.

  even if (s.o. decides to) ~; although (it's true that) ~; even if it's true that ~

  **no matter what/who/when*

  ❖ *W. phrases that start w. interrogative pronouns [☞ VO:I.2].

    ➢ ni shite mo ⟨N/n/V/i⟩ ni shite mo: 【N/n/V/i】 Negative Dependent Disjunctive coordinator

    regardless of whether ~ or

  ➢ ⊕ ni shite wa: ❶ 【N】 Contrastive Concessive c. ‖ ❷ 【V*】 Contrastive Concessive m.

  ① *for ~; considering that (is) ~*

  ② *for having ~; considering that you ~*

  ❖ Structure indicating that s.t. is subject to an implicitly agreed-upon standard and that the subsequent phrase expresses a deviation from it.

  ❖ *The perfective f. 〖TA〗 or the progressive f. TE iru.

➤ ni soi: 【N】 = ni sotte

➤ ni sōi nai: 【N/n】 Assumptive cop. 【V/i】 Assumptive m.

without a doubt ~; certainly ~; surely ~

➤ ni soku shite: 【N】 [*lit.*] Perlative Correlative c.

following ~; in accordance with ~; in line with ~

➤ ni sotta ⟨N⟩: 【N】 Attributive ☞ ni sotte

➤ ni sotte: 【N】 ① Perlative c. ② Perlative Correlative c.

① *along with ~; through ~*

② *along with ~; in accordance with ~; following ~*

➤ ni sou ⟨N⟩: 【N】 Attributive ☞ ni sotte

➤ ni sureba: 【N】 = ni shita ra

➤ ni suru: ❶ ⊤ 【N(p)】 Decisive c. ‖ ❷ ⊕ 【n】 Causative voice f.

① *decide on ~*

② *to make ~*

❖ ❷ It indicates that s.o. makes s.t. or s.o. as it is described by the marked adj. n.

➤ ni suru to: 【N】 = ni shita ra

➤ ni suginai: 【N/C/U】 Lower Limitative cop.

nothing but ~; nothing/not more than ~; mere ~; merely ~; only ~; just ~

❖ Compound p. that expresses a limit imposed upon s.t.

➤ ni tai shi: 【N】 [*lit.*] ≈ ni tai shite

➤ ⊕ ni tai shite: 【N】 ❶ Correlative c. ❷ Contrastive Dative c

① *in regard to ~; toward ~; to ~; reg ~; with respect to ~*

② *in contrast to ~; as opposed to ~*

❖ Construction u. to draw attention to s.t. (❶) or to show a comparison or contrast w. s.t. (❷).

➤ ni tai shite no ⟨N⟩: 【N】 Attributive ☞ ni tai shite

➤ ni tai suru ⟨N⟩: 【N】 Attributive ☞ ni tai shite

➤ ni tera shite: 【N】 Correlative c.

① *in light of ~; about ~; in relation to ~; in view of ~*

➤ ni todomarazu: 【N/U】 [*lit.*] Negative Lower Limitative c.

not limited to ~; doesn't stop/end with ~

➤ ni tomonai: 【N】 = ni tomonatte

➤ ni tomonatte: [*for.*] ❶ 【N】 Comitative c. | ❷ Perlative Correlative c. ‖ ❸ 【VN/U】 Translative Durative a.

① *along with ~*

② *as ~; along with ~; following ~; accordingly ~*

③ *as ~*

❖ M. u. w. abstract n.s.

➤ ni tomonau ⟨N⟩: Attributive ☞ ni tomonatte

➤ ⊕ ni totte: 【N】 Thematic Dative c.

to ~; for ~

❖ Compound p. that puts focus on the point of view of s.o. or s.t.

➤ ni tsuite (wa): ❶ ⊕ 【N】 Correlative c. ‖ ❷ 【C】 Distributive c.

① *about ~; regarding ~; concerning ~*

② *per ~; for ~; to ~; a ~; on ~*

➤ ni tsuke: 【N/U】 [*for.*] Distributive Durative a.

whenever ~; every time ~; as ~

➤ ni tsukete (mo): 【N/U】 = ni tsuke

➤ ni tsuki: ❶ 【C】 Distributive c. ≈ *atari* ❷ 【N】 [*for.*] Causal c.

① *per ~; for ~; to ~; a ~; on ~*

② *due to ~; because of ~*

➤ ni tsure: 【VN/V】 [for.] ≈ ni tsurete

➤ ⓔ ni tsurete: 【VN/V】 Translative
Durative a.

as ~

❖ Construction that expresses that an
event occurs gradually according to a
parallel, continuous process of change
that is beyond human control.

➤ ⓔ ni wa: ❶ 【U】 Final m. ‖ ❷ 【N】
Thematic Essive c. | ❸ = ni totte

① *to ~; in order to ~; for (the purpose of)*
~

② *in ~; on ~; at ~*

❖ ❶ It expresses a purpose for the
realization of an action that is developed
through a process that is judged morally
or practically.

➤ ni wa oyobanai: 【N/U】 Negative
Necessitative m.

there is no need to ~

➤ ni watari: 【N】 [lit.] ≈ ni watatte

➤ ni wataru ⟨N⟩: 【N】 Attributive ☞ ni
watatte

➤ ni watatte: 【N】 [for.] Perlative Essive
c.

for ~; extending ~; over ~

❖ Compound p. that expresses that s.t.
takes place in a delimited span of time or
space.

➤ ni yorazu: 【N】 ❶ Negative Dependent
Correlative c. ❷ Privative c. ‖ ❸ 【VN】
Privative coordinator

① *regardless of ~; independently of ~;
despite ~*

② *without ~*

③ *without ~ing*

❖ Compound p. that indicates that s.t.
has no dependence on s.t. else or that it is
(occurs) unrelated to that other thing.

➤ ⓔ ni yoreba: 【N】 = ni yoru to

➤ ni yori: 【N】 [lit.] ≈ ① ② ni yotte

➤ ⓔ ni yoru ⟨N⟩: 【N】 Attributive ☞ ni
yotte

➤ ⓔ ni yoru to: 【N】 = ③ ni yotte

➤ ⓔ ni yotte: 【N】 ❶ [for.] Instrumental
c. | ❷ Dependent Correlative c. | ❸
Quotative Correlative c. | ❹ Agentive c.

① *by means of ~; with ~; by ~*

② *depending on ~*

③ *according to ~*

③ *by ~*

❖ Multi-functional compound p. that can
be u. to indicate means (❶), dependency
(❷), correlation to what s.o. has said (❸)
or the agent of a passive sentence (❹).

NIKUI にくい 〔難い〕 : [adj. v.] to be
difficult

⊕ 【I】 *difficult to ~; hard to ~; not prone
to ~*

❖ Aux. adj. v. u. to express that s.t. is
difficult to do.

NITE にて: [i.]

【N】 [lit.] ❶ Essive c. ❷ Instrumental c.

① *in ~; on ~; at ~*

② *with ~; by ~*

NO₁ の: [p.]

ⓕ 【N】 ❶ Genitive c. | ❷ Relative
Nominative c. ≈ ga

① *of ~; ~'s*

❖ ❶ Case p. which combines two n.s or
nominal phrases (A *no* B) insofar as the
second n. or phrase (B) modifies the first
one (A) establishing, m., a subordinate or
possessive relationship. The most
common translation would be A *no* B → B
of A or A's B.

❖ ❷ It can optionally substitute the
nominative p. **ga** to mark the subject of a

subordinate (relative) clause within a compound sentence.

- -

NO₂ の: [*dep. n.*]

← Attributive cop. p. *no*

Ⓕ 【V/na/i】 ❶ Nominalization marker | ❷ [*col.*][*fam.*][*f°m.*] Explanative cop. ≈ **no** {D} | ❸ [*fam.*] Interrogative m.

① *that ~; to ~; ~ing; ~ one*

② *the fact/reason/explanation is that ~; it is that ~*

③ *~?*

❖ ❶ P. u. to transform a phrase into a n. that expresses s.t. tangible or perceptible.

- -

NO₃ の: [*cop.*]

Cognate w. the attributive cop. *na*

Ⓕ 【N(p)/n】 Imperfective a. Attributive cop. ☞ **no** ⟨N⟩

- -

➤ no ⟨N⟩: 【N(p*)/n†】 Imperfective a. Attributive cop.

... that/which/who is/are ~

❖ Copulative p. that makes some adj. n.s function as an attribute.

❖ *e, to, kara or made.

❖ †Just some adj. n.s (*no* adj. n.s [☞ GE:I.7.2]).

➤ no ⟨V/i⟩*: 【N】 Attributive Nominative c.

that ~

❖ It transforms the modified n. in the topic of a relative clause, meaning that this p. cannot be u. as a nominative c. marker in an independent sentence. The structure u. of this p. acting as a nominative marker is the following: A *no* ⟨V/i⟩ B; translated as: *the B that* ⟨V/i⟩ *A.*

❖ *Always acting as an attribute before a n.

➤ Ⓕ no {D}: 【V/na/i】 Explanative cop.

the fact/reason/explanation is that ~; it is that ~

❖ Copulative construction that indicates that the speaker explains s.t. or asks for an explanation about s.t. in an emotional way, meaning that the speaker wants to involve the listener in the affairs being discussed.

➤ no {D} kara: 【V/na/i】 Explanative Causal m.

because ~

➤ no {D} mono ({D}): 【V/na/i】 [*fam.*] Emphatic Explanative cop.

it's because ~, you know

❖ This construction is u. to give an explanation about s.t. inferring an emotional involvement to it.

➤ no {D} mon: 【V/na/i】 ≈ **no** {D} **mono** ({D})

➤ no aida (ni): ❶ 【N】 Intrative Essive c. ❷ 【VN】 Durative a. ≈ **aida** (ni)

① *between ~; among ~*

② *while ~; during ~; for ~*

➤ no amari: 【N/n/V】 Superlative Causal m.

so much ~that/so ~

➤ ⊕ no ato de/ni: 【N】 Postessive c.

after ~; behind ~

➤ no baai {p}: 【N】 ≈ **baai** {p}

➤ no chikaku ni: 【N】 Apudesssive c.

near ~

➤ no chuushin ni: 【N】 Intrative Essive c.

in the middle/center of ~

➤ Ⓛ no darō ka: 【V/na/i】 ≈ **darō ka**

➤ Ⓕ no de: 【V/na/i】 Causal m.

so ~; since ~; because (of) ~; given that ~

❖ Compound p. u. to express a reason or cause that is considered as natural or logical.

➤ no de areba: 【N/n】 = de areba

➤ no de wa arimasen ka: 【V/na/i】 ≈ de wa arimasen ka

➤ no de wa aru mai ka: 【V/na/i】 ≈ 〖N/n〗 de wa aru mai ka

➤ no de wa nai darō ka: 【V/na/i】 Deliberative m.

may ~; might ~; can't tell if ~

➤ no de wa nai ka: 【V/na/i】 ≈ 〖N/n〗 de wa nai ka

➤ ⊕ no deshō ka: 【V/na/i】 [*for.*] ≈ no darō ka

➤ no furi o suru: 【N】 ≈ no furi o suru

➤ no gotoki ⟨N⟩: 【N】 Attributive ☞ no gotoku

➤ no gotoku: 【N】 ≈ ga gotoku

➤ no gotoshi: 【N】 Semblative Declarative cop.

be like ~; be as ~

➤ no hazu {D}: 【N】 ≈ hazu {D}

➤ no hō (ga): 【N】 ≈ V/na/i hō ga

➤ no hō ga ⟨N⟩ yori (mo): 【N】 ≈ hō ga ⟨V/na/i⟩ yori

➤ ⊕ no hoka (ni) (wa): 【N】 Exclusive c.

except for ~; other than ~; apart from ~

➤ no ikan de (wa): 【N】 = ikan de (wa)

➤ no ikan ni kakawarazu: 【N】 = no ikan ni yorazu

➤ no ikan ni yorazu: 【N】 [*for.*] Negative Dependent Correlative c.

regardless of ~

➤ no ikan ni yotte (wa): 【N】 = ikan ni yotte (wa)

➤ no ikan o towazu: 【N】 = no ikan ni yorazu

➤ no ippō de: 【VN】 ≈ ippō de

➤ no itari {D}: 【N】 [*for.*] Superlative cop.

is the utmost ~

➤ no ja arimasen ka: 【V/na/i】 [*col.*] ≈ no de wa arimasen ka

➤ no ja nai ka: 【V/na/i】 [*col.*] ≈ no de wa nai ka

➤ no ka: 【V/na/i】 ❶ [*fam.*] Interrogative m. ‖ ❷ Interrogative subordinator m.

① ~?

② *whether ~; if ~*

❖ Shows a certain degree of surprise about s.t. that is different from what one thought.

❖ Only u. w. questions that have interrogative pronouns.

➤ no ka dō ka: 【na】 ≈ no ka dō ka

➤ no kai: 【V/na/i】 = kai₁

➤ no kai mo naku: 【N】 ≈ kai mo naku

➤ no kai ga aru: 【N】 ≈ kai ga aru

➤ no kai mo naku: 【N】 ≈ kai mo naku

➤ no kankē de: 【N】 Correlative Causal c.

because of ~; in relation to ~

➤ no kanōsē ga aru: 【N】 ≈ kanōsē ga aru

➤ no katawara: 【N】 ≈ katawara

➤ no kawari ni: 【N】 ≈ kawari ni

➤ no kekka: 【N】 ≈ kekka

➤ no kēkō ga aru: 【N】 ≈ kēko ga aru

➤ no kirai ga aru: 【N】 ≈ kira ga aru

➤ no kiwami {D}/ni: 【N】 [*for.*] Superlative cop.

(is) the utmost ~

➤ no koro: 【N】 ≈ 〚V/i〛 koro

➤ no koto: 【VN】 ≈ 〚U〛 koto

  ➤ no koto {p}: 【N】 Correlative c.

  about ~; related to ~; in terms of ~

  ➤ no koto {D}: 【VN】 ≈ koto {D}

    ➤ no koto {D} kara: 【N】 ≈ koto {D} kara

  ➤ no koto ga aru: 【N】 ≈ ① koto ga aru

  ➤ no koto tote: 【N】 ≈ koto tote

➤ no kuse ni: 【N】 ≈ kuse ni

➤ no mae ni: 【N】 ❶ Antessive c. ❷ ≈ mae ni

in front of ~; before ~

➤ ⊕ no mama (de/ni): 【N】 ≈ mama

➤ no mawari ni: 【N】 Apudesssive c.

around ~

➤ no mo: 【V/na/i】 ≈ mo

  ➤ no mo areba ⟨n/i⟩ no mo aru: 〚n/i〛 ≈ mo sureba ⟨VN/I⟩ mo suru

  ➤ no mo tōzen {D}: 【U】 ≈ mo tōzen {D}

  ➤ no mo motto mo {D}: 【VN/U】 Evidential Assumptive cop.

  no wonder ~; is only natural ~

  ➤ no mo wa motto mo {D}: 【VN/U】 = no mo motto mo {D}

➤ no moto de/ni: 【N】 = no shita ni

➤ no ⟨A⟩ nai no tte: 【V/na/i】 ≈ no nan no tte

✤ When u. w. neg. verbal f.s.

➤ ⊕ no naka de: 【N】 ❶ Intrative Essive c. ❷ Inessive c.

① *among ~; in ~* ② *inside ~*

✤ ❶ Roughly expresses that s.t. is in the middle of another thing.

➤ no naka ni: 【N】 Illative c.

into ~

➤ no naka o: 【N】 = no naka de

➤ no nan no tte: 【V/na/i】 [*col.*] Superlative m.

so (much) ~; extremely ~

✤ It indicates that s.t. is in an extreme state or has been done in excess.

➤ no nara: 【N/n/V/i】 = nara

➤ ⊕ no ni: ❶ 【V/na/i】 Concessive coordinator ❷ 【U】 Final m.

① *although ~; even though ~; despite ~ in spite of; ~ but*

② *in order to ~; for the purpose of ~*

✤ ❷ It expresses a purpose for which a process has been developed through a medium, instrument or time interval.

  ➤ no ni hikikae: 【V/na/i】 ≈ ni hikikae

  ➤ no ni mo kakawarazu: 【N/na/V/i】 ≈ ni mo kakawarazu

  ➤ no ni wa: 【U】 = 〚U〛 ni wa

➤ no nochi ni: 【N】 [*lit.*] ≈ no ato de/ni

➤ no o ki ni: 【TA】 [*for.*] ≈ no o kikkake ni

➤ no okage de: 【N】 ≈ okage de

➤ no ori ni: 【N】 ≈ ori ni

➤ no sai (ni): 【VN】 ≈ sai (ni)

➤ no saichuu ni: 【N/VN/I】 ≈ saichuu ni

➤ no sei de: 【N】 ≈ sei de

➤ no sei ka: 【N】 ≈ sei ka

➤ no shikata: 【VN】 ≈ 〚I〛 kata

➤ no shita ni: 【N】 Subessive c.

under ~; bellow ~; beneath ~

✤ U. both in a lit. and fig. way.

➤ no sue (ni): 【N】 Postessive c.

at the end of ~; after ~

➤ no tabi ni: 【N】 ≈ **tabi ni**

➤ no tame: 【N】 = **no tame ni**

> ➤ no tame {D}: 【N】 ❶ Benefactive cop. ❷ Causal cop.

> ① *it's for the benefit/sake of ~*

> ② *it's because of (the) ~*

> ➤ ⊕ no tame ni: 【N】 ❶ Final c. ≈ 〖U〗 **tame (ni)** | ❷ [*lit.*][*for.*] Causal c.

> ① *for the benefit/sake of ~*

> ② *because of (the) ~*

> ➤ no tame no ⟨N⟩: 【N】 Attributive ☞ **no tame ni**

➤ no temae: 【N】 Concessive Correlative c.

considering ~; in regard to ~; for ~

➤ no ten {p*}: 【N/n】 Perlative Correlative c.

in terms of ~; as far as ~ is concerned; ~ in that respect; in regard to ~

❖ *de, ga or o.

➤ Ⓔ no tochuu de/ni: 【N】 ≈ **tochuu de/ni**

➤ no toki (ni): 【N】 ≈ **toki** (ni)

➤ no tokoro {p}: 【N】 ≈ **tokoro {p}**

➤ no tokoro o: 【N】 ≈ **tokoro o**

➤ no tonari ni: 【N】 Adesssive c.

next to ~; beside ~; by ~

➤ no toori (ni): 【N/V】 ≈ **toori** (ni)

➤ no tsuide ni: 【N】 ≈ **tsuide ni**

➤ no tsumori {D}: 【N】 ≈ 〖U〗 **tsumori {D}**

➤ no uchi ni: ❶ 【N】 = ② **no naka de/ni** ❷ 〖I〗 ≈ **uchi ni**

➤ no uchi wa: 【N】 Perlative Essive c.

throughout ~; while ~; during ~

➤ no ue de (wa): ❶ 【N】 Quotative Correlative c. ❷ 【VN】 Prospective Postesive a. ≈ **ue de**

① *as far as ~ (is concerned); as ~ goes; in terms of ~; according to ~*

② *after ~*

❖ U. for abstract n.s.

➤ no ue ni: 【N】 ❶ Superessive c. | ❷ Emphatic Cumulative coordinator

① *on top of ~; on ~*

② *~ as well; ~ in addition; ~ besides*

➤ no ushiro ni: 【N】 Postessive c.

behind ~

➤ ⊕ no wa: 【V/na/i】 Thematic Nominalization marker

that ~

❖ Transforms a verbal clause into a nominal phrase while bringing the focus to it.

> ➤ no wa ⟨V/na/i⟩ᴮ no yori (mo) ⟨P⟩: 【V/na/iᴬ】 ≈ **wa ⟨N⟩ yori** (mo) ⟨P⟩

> ➤ no wari ni (wa): 【N】 ≈ **wari ni (wa)**

➤ no yara: 【V/na/i】 [*fam.*] ❶ Dubitative m. ❷ Interrogative subordinator

① *i wonder if ~*

② *whether ~*

❖ ❷ Only u. in subordinate clauses, marking embedded questions when there are interrogative pronouns.

❖ ❶ It expresses a strong concern or anxiety.

> ➤ no yara ⟨V/na/i⟩ no yara: 【V/na/i】 ≈ **yara ⟨U/n/i⟩ yara**

➤ no yō {D}: 【N】 ≈ **yō {D}**

➤ no yō de wa: 【N】 ≈ **yō de wa**

➤ ⊕ no yō na ki ga suru: 【N/n】 Evidential Inferential cop.

feel like s.t. it is ~; have a feeling that s.t. is ~

➤ ⊕ no yō ni: 【N】 ≈ yō ni

   ➤ no yō ni omowareru: 【N】 ≈ yō ni omowareru

   ➤ ⊕ no yō ni mieru: 【N】 ≈ yō ni mieru

➤ no wake ga nai: 【N】 ≈ wake ga nai

➤ no yo: 【V/na/i】 [*col.*][*fem.*] ≈ yo₁

➤ no yoko ni: 【N】 Adesssive c.

next to ~; beside ~; by ~

➤ ⊤ no yori ⟨N⟩ hō ga ⟨n/i⟩: 【V】 Comparative Upper Limitative subordinator

… more than ~

➤ no yoshi: 【N】 ≈ yoshi

➤ ⊕ no yotē {D}: 【VN】 ≈ yotē {D}

➤ no yue (ni): 【N】 ≈ yue (ni)

NOCHI 後: [*adv.*] after

➤ nochi ni: 【TA】 [*lit.*] Postessive a.

after ~

NOGASU 逃す: [*v.*] to miss

  【I】 *to fail to ~*

NOKORU 残る: [*v.*] to be left behind

  【I】 *to ~ leaving s.t. behind*

  ❖ U. w. intransitive v.s.

NOKOSU 残す: [*v.*] to leave behind

  【I】 *to ~ leaving s.t. behind*

  ❖ U. w. intransitive v.s.

NOMI のみ: [*p.*]

➤ nomi {D}: 【N/V】 [*for.*] ≈ nomi {p}

➤ nomi {p*}: 【N(p†)】 [*for.*] ≈ ① 〖N(p)〗 dake

  ❖ *ni, e, to, de or kara; ga or o are oprtional.

  ❖ †ni, e, to, de or kara

➤ nomi ka: 【N】 [*for.*] ≈ bakari ka

➤ nomi narazu: 【N/na/V/i】 [*for.*] ≈ bakari de (wa) naku

NU ぬ: [*i.*]

  O.J. neg. cop.

  【A】 [*lit.*][*obs.*] ≈ nai

  ❖ M. u. nowadays in fossilized set phrases.

  ❖ The v. **suru** (*to do*) becomes senu; and the v. **aru** (*to be; to exist*) becomes aranu.

➤ nu ⟨N⟩: Attributive ☞ nu

NUKERU 抜ける: [*v.*] to come out

  【I】 *to ~ completely; to ~ through*

  ❖ V. indicating that s.t. is done from beginning to end.

  ❖ U. w. intransitive v.s.

NUKI 抜き: [*n.*] leftover

  (I) *nuku (to leave out)*

➤ nuki de/ni (wa): 【N】 = nashi

➤ nuki de/ni shite (wa): 【N】 [*for.*] = nuki de/ni (wa)

NUKU 抜く: [*v.*] to take out

  【I】 *to ~ completely; to ~ through*

  ❖ V. indicating that s.t. is done from beginning to end.

  ❖ U. w. transitive v.s.

  ❖ M. u. w. things that require a great effort.

O を: [*p.*]

Ⓣ ❶ 【N】 ❶ Accusative c. ❷ Prolative c. ❸ Elative c. | ❹ [*lit.*] Emphatic Causal c.

② *in ~; on ~; across ~; through ~; along ~; over ~*

③ *from ~*

④ *about ~; that ~*

❖ ❶ Case p. u. to mark the direct object of the sentence, that is, the object or person towards which a transitive v. performs the action.

❖ ❷ It indicates a space across which s.o. or s.t. moves.

❖ ❸ It indicates a location from which some movement starts.

❖ ❷ ❸ U. only. w. motion v.s.

❖ ❹ It indicates the cause of some human emotion.

➤ Ⓔ o chōdai: 【N】 [*fam.*][*f°m.*] ≈ o kudasai

➤ Ⓔ o chuushin ni: 【N】 Thematic Accusative c.

focusing on ~; centered on ~

❖ This structure is u. to indicate that s.o. or s.t. is the center of the attention of the sentence; i.e. the 'topic'.

➤ o chuushin ni/to shita ⟨N⟩: 【N】 Attributive ☞ o chuushin ni/to shite

➤ o chuushin ni/to shite: 【N】 = o chuushin ni

➤ o chuushin ni/to suru ⟨N⟩: 【N】 Attributive ☞ o chuushin ni/to shite

➤ o fumae: 【N】 = o fumaete

➤ o fumaeta ⟨N⟩: 【N】 ≈ o fumaete

➤ o fumaete: 【N】 [*lit.*] Inferential c.

based on ~

➤ Ⓔ o hajime (to shite): 【N】 Inchoative Essive c.

starting with ~

➤ o hajime to suru ⟨N⟩: 【N】 Attributive ☞ o hajime (to shite)

➤ o hete: 【N】 [*lit.*] ❶ Prolative c. ❷ Perlative Essive c.

① *through ~; via ~*

② *throughout ~; extending for ~*

➤ o kaerimizu: 【N】 Negative Dependent Correlative c.

regardless of ~; despite ~

➤ o kagiri ni: 【C】 [*for.*] ≈ kagiri de

➤ o kai shite: 【N】 [*lit.*] ≈ o tootte

➤ o kai shite no ⟨N⟩: 【N】 Attributive ☞ o kai shite

➤ o kanete: 【N】 Cumulative c.

combined with ~

➤ o kawakiri ni (shite): 【N】 Inchoative Essive c.

starting with/from ~

➤ o kawakiri to shite: 【N】 = o kawakiri ni (shite)

➤ o kēki ni: 【N】 Resultative Causal c.

thanks to ~; as a result of ~; taking advantage of ~

❖ U. when talking about s.t. that is the consequence of s.t. done w. good intentions.

➤ o kēki to shite: 【N】 = o kēki ni

➤ o kikkake ni: 【N】 Resultative Causal c.

as a result of ~

❖ Construction u. to express that s.t. is the motivation or cause as a result upon which an action or state is developed.

❖ The p. *ni* here focuses on time.

➤ o kikkake to shite: 【N】 = o kikkake ni

➤ o kihon ni (shite): 【N】 [*for.*] Inferential c.

based on ~; on the basis of ~

➤ o kihon ni suru: 【N】 ≈ o kihon ni (shite)

➤ o meguri: 【N】 [*lit.*] ≈ o megutte

➤ o meguru ⟨N⟩: 【N】 Attributive ☞ o megutte

➤ o megutte: 【N】 [*for.*] Thematic Accusative c.

focusing on ~; over ~

✦ M. u. when talking about a topic or subject that is considered as a source of conflict.

➤ o meza shite: 【N】 Final c.

with the objective of ~

➤ o mochiite: 【N】 [*lit.*] ≈ o tsukatte

➤ o mokuhyō ni: 【N】 = o meza shite

➤ o mono to mo sezu (ni): 【N】 [*lit.*] Substitutive Accusative c.

in spite of ~; in defiance of ~

➤ o moto ni (shite): 【N】 Inferential c.

based on ~

➤ o motte: 【N】 [*for.*] Instrumental c.

by means of ~; with ~

➤ o nozoite (wa): 【N】 Exclusive c.

excluding ~; except for ~

➤ o nozokeba: 【N】 = o nozoite (wa)

➤ o oite: 【N】 Exclusive c.

excluding ~; other than ~

➤ Ⓔ o too shite: 【N】 ❶ [*for.*] Prolative c. ≈ o tootte | ❷ Perlative Essive c.

① *through ~*

② *through ~; throughout ~*

✦ It marks the medium through which s.t. is done (❶) or the period of time throughout which s.t. happens (❷).

➤ o tootte: 【N】 Prolative c.

through ~

➤ o towazu: 【N】 [*for.*] Negative Dependent Correlative c.

regardless of ~; irrespective of ~; no matter ~

➤ o tsukatte: 【N】 Instrumental c.

with ~; using ~

➤ Ⓔ o tsuujite: 【N】 [*lit.*] ≈ o tootte

➤ o yoso ni: 【N】 [*for.*] Negative Dependent Correlative c.

indifferent to ~; despite ~; without regards to ~

OKAGE おかげ 〔お陰〕: [*n.*] grace; benevolence

hon. pre. o + kage (shade)

➤ Ⓔ okage de: 【V/na/i】 Benefactive Causal m.

thanks to ~; owing to ~

✦ U. to express gratitude towards s.o. or s.t.

OKI おき 〔置き〕: [*dep. n.*]

(I) *oku (to put)*

➤ oki ni: 【C】 Temporal Distributive c.

each ~; every (instance of) ~; at intervals of ~; every other~; skipping (every so many)

✦ It expresses that s.t. is repeated at a certain interval.

✦ This dep. n. focuses on the interval itself (the gap).

OKU おく 〔置く〕: [*v.*] to put

⊕ 【TE】 ❶ Preparatory Perfective a. ❷ Preparatory Stative a. ❸ Benefactive Stative a.

① *~ in advance; ~ beforehand; ~ ahead*

② *leave ~ed*

③ *let ~*

✤ ❶ Subsidiary v. that expresses the idea of doing s.t. beforehand and leaving the resultant state of the action for future convenience.

✤ ❷ It expresses that an action or state is deliberatively left to continue in the future.

✤ ❸ If u. w. causative v.s., it expresses the idea that s.o. is allowed to remain in a certain state.

___

ORI 折: [*n.*] opportunity; occasion

(I) oru (*to break*)

➢ ori ni: 【V】 [*for.*] Punctual a.

on (the occasion of) ~; when ~

✤ M. u. w. the occasion is desirable and special.

___

ORU おる 〔居る〕: [*v.*] to be

【TE】 [*hum.*] ≈ ① 〖TE〗 **iru**

___

OYOBI および 〔及び〕: [*p.*]

(I) oyobu (*to reach*)

【N】 [*lit.*][*for.*] ≈ ② **to₁**

___

OWARU 終わる: [*v.*] to finish

⊕ 【I】 Terminative a.

to finish/end ~

✤ U. w. intransitive v.s.

P

PPA っぱ: 【I】 [*col.*] ≈ ① **ppanashi**

___

PPANASHI っぱなし 〔っ放し〕: [*dep. n.*]

← hanashi: (I) hanasu (*to leave*)

➢ ⊕ ppanashi {D}: 【I】 ❶ Egressive Progressive a. ❷ Continuative a.

① *have been ~ing; leave ~*

② *keep ~ing*

✤ ❶ U. w. transitive v.s, it expresses that s.o. or s.t. has left s.t. in an unfinished state.

✤ ❷ U. w. intransitive v.s, it expresses the idea that s.t. or s.o. is continuing to do s.t.

✤ When this dep. n. is u. w. transitive v.s (❶) it usually has the connotation that s.t. is left in an improper state.

___

PPOI っぽい: [*dep. adj. v.*]

← poi ← O.J. ohoi (*many*) → C.J. ooi

⊕ 【N/n/s】 [*col.*][*fam.*] Approximative Semblative cop.

~ish; ~like

⊕ 【I】 [*col.*][*fam.*] Tendency Semblative cop.

easy to ~

___

PPURI っぷり: 【I/C】 = 〖I/C〗 **buri**

R

RA ら: [*i.*]

← i. *raba*

⊕ 【TA】 ❶ Provisional m. ❷ Postessive a.

① *if ~; when ~*

② *after ~*

❖ Inflection that expresses that a state or action takes or would take place in case another concrete action or state hypothetically (①) or actually (②) occurs before.

➤ ra ⟨TA⟩ de: 【TA】 Alternative coordinator

whether ~ or not

➤ ⊕ ra dō: 【TA】 [*fam.*] Propositive m.

why don't you ~?; what about ~?

➤ ra dō desu ka: 【TA】 [*pol.*] ≈ **ra dō**

➤ nara ⟨na⟩ hodo: 【N】 ≈ ⟨U/na/i⟩ hodo ⟨U/na/i⟩

➤ ra ii: 【TA】 ⊕ Desiderative m.

It would be nice if ~; I hope ~

➤ ra ⟨U/i⟩ mono o: 【TA】 ≈ **mono o**

➤ ra sugu: 【TA】 Punctual Inceptive a.

as soon as ~; following ~

RABA らば: [*i.*]

【TA】 [*for.*] ≈ **ra**

RAI 来: [*suf.*] coming

Ⓔ 【C】 ① Ablative c. ② Perlative Essive c.

① *since ~*

② *(extending) for ~*

❖ It describes that s.t. has continued up until the moment of speech.

RARERU られる: [*i.*]

Ⓢ 【A】 ❶ ⊕ Passive voice f. | ❷ [*hon.*] Imperfective a. Indicative m.

① *be ~ed; get ~ed*

❖ ❶ It transforms a v. into the passive voice, that is, it makes it describe an action that is not controlled by the subject but happens to him or her through another agent. This agent, if it appears stated in the sentence, is marked by the agentive p. **ni**; while the subject who receives the action is marked by the focal p. **wa**.

❖ ❷ The passive f. can be u. as a mild way of expressing respect (acting as an hon. f.) towards the subject of the sentence since it is seen as an indirect way of making statements.

❖ The verbal f.s resulting from this inflection are always strong v.s (Ⓢ).

❖ The passive f. of the irregular v. **suru** (*to do*) is sareru, while the passive f. of the irregular v. **kuru** (*to come*) is korareru.

⊕ Ⓢ 【E】 Potential m.

be able to ~; can ~

❖ It indicates that an action can be performed.

❖ In sentences w. the potential f. the object of the action can be marked by the accusative p. **o** or the nominative p. **ga** in case that the potential action is understood as s.t. independent of the individual will.

❖ The verbal f.s resulting from this inflection are always strong v.s (Ⓢ).

❖ The potential f. of the irregular v. **kuru** (*to come*) is korareru, while the irregular v. **suru** (*to do*) has not a potential f. and uses instead the v. dekiru (*to be able to*).

RASHII らしい: [*dep. adj. v.*]

⊕ 【N/n/V/i】 Approximative Semblative cop.

like ~; equivalent to ~; perceived as ~

❖ Dep. adj. v. indicating that the subject of the sentence has a similar appearance or acts similarly to the marked state, action or noun.

REBA れば: [*i.*]

Ⓢ 【E】 ≈ Ⓦ 〖E〗 **ba**

RERU れる: [*i.*]

Ⓦ 【A】 ≈ 〖A〗 **rareru**

Ⓢ 【E】 [*col.*] ≈ 〖E〗 **rareru**

RI り: [*i.*]

← O.J. predicative f. *ari* (*to be*) → C.J. *aru*

【TA】 ☞ ri 〈TA〉 ri (suru)

➣ Ⓕ ri 〈TA〉 ri (suru): 【TA】 ❶ Enumerative coordinator ❷ Alternative Enumerative coordinator

① *do things like/such as ~ and ...; sometimes ~ and sometimes ...*

② *do things like/such as ~ or ...*

❖ Structure that introduces a list of actions or states in an inexhaustive manner, that is, without an explicit limit.

➣ ri suru: 【TA】 Enumerative m.

do things like/as ~

➣ ri suru: 【TA】 Cumulative Coordinator

and also ~

➣ ri shita ra: 【TA】 Enumerative Provisional m.

if ~ (at all); in the case that ~ (one does s.t. like)

❖ Structure u. to introduce an undesirable hypothetical situation.

RO ろ: [*i.*]

⊕ Ⓢ 【E】 Imperative m.

~; do ~; you must ~

❖ Inflection u. to give commands.

RŌ ろう: [*i.*]

【TA】 [*lit.*][*obs.*] Perfective Presumptive m.

probably will have ~

RU る: [*i.*]

⊕ Ⓦ 【E】 ≈ 〖E〗 **rareru**

【TE】 [*col.*] ≈ ① 〖TE〗 **iru**

RYA りゃ: Ⓢ 【E】 [*col.*] ≈ Ⓢ 〖E〗 **reba**

S

SA₁ さ: [*suf.*]

⊕ 【n/s】 Nominalization marker

~ness; ~ly

❖ It converts numerous adj. v.s and some adj. n.s into n.s, describing the degree of the characteristics represented by those adjectives.

➣ sa to itta ra nai: 【n/s】 ≈ **to itta ra nai**

- -

SA₂ さ: [*p.*]

【N/n/V/i】 [*col.*][*fam.*][*mas.*] Assertive m.

~, you know; sure ~; I tell you that ~

❖ Emphatic p. u. in informal contexts by males to express an assertion.

- -

➤ sa no amari: 【s】 ≈ no amari

SAE さえ: [*p.*]

(I) O.J. v. *saeru (to add)* → C.J. *soeru*

Ⓔ 【N(p*)】 = ① 〖N(p)〗 mo

❖ *ni, e, de, to, kara or made.

➤ sae ⟨BA⟩*: 【TE/I】 Emphatic Provisional m.

as long as ~; provided that ~

❖ *Usually the v.s suru (to do) or iru (to be).

➤ sae ⟨TA⟩* ra: Emphatic Conditional m.

as long as ~; provided that ~

❖ *Usually the v.s suru (to do) or iru (to be).

➤ sae areba: 【ku】 ≈ sae ⟨BA⟩

SAI 際: [*n.*] circumstances; juncture

➤ Ⓔ sai (ni): 【V】 [*for.*] Punctual a.

when ~; on the occasion of ~; at the time of ~

❖ It points to a specific occasion when s.o. does s.t.

SAICHUU 最中: [*n.*] middle (of)

➤ Ⓔ saichuu ni: 【U*】 Durative a.

while ~; during ~; in the middle of ~

❖ *The progressive f.s TE iru.

SASERARERU させる: [*i.*]

⊕ Ⓢ 【A】 Passive Causative voice f.

to be made to ~

❖ It expresses, in a passive way, that s.o. is made to do s.t.

SASERU させる: [*i.*]

⊕ Ⓢ 【A】 ❶ Causative voice f. ❷ Permissive m. Causative voice f.

① *make s.o. ~; cause (to) ~*

② *let s.o. ~*

❖ ❶ Inflection indicating that s.t. or s.o. makes another person or thing do the action or become in the state marked by the v.

❖ ❷ It indicates that s.o. is allowed to do s.t.

❖ The agent subject of the causative sentence, that is, the person who makes the action happen, is marked by the focal p. wa when it is the focus of the sentence or the nominative p. ga when it is not. W. intransitive v.s, the patient subject, i.e., the person or object to whom the action is made to be performed, can be marked by the accusative p. o or the dative p. ni; *ni* is u. when the action is voluntary and *o* when it is not. If the v. is transitive the patient is always marked w. the dative p. ni.

❖ The resulting v.s of this causative f. are always strong v.s (Ⓢ).

SASHIAGERU 差し上げる: [*v.*] [*hum.*] to give

*sashi** + pol. v. *ageru (to give)* |*(I) *sasu (to shine)*

【TE】 [*hum.*] ≈ 〖TE〗 ageru

SASU さす: [*i.*]

Ⓢ 【A】 = saseru

❖ Considered dialectal or somewhat vulgar.

SEI せい 〔所為〕: [*dep. n.*] outcome

➤ sei de: 【V/na/i】 Causal m.

because ~; due to ~; as a result of ~

❖ Dep. n. u. to indicate that s.t. undesirable occurs for the defined by the marked v.

➤ sei ka: 【TA】 Dubitative Causal m.

perhaps because ~

SERARERU せられる: [*i.*]

⊕ Ⓦ 【A】 ≈ **saserareru**

SERU せる: [*i.*]

⊕ Ⓦ 【A】 ≈ **saseru**

SHI し: [*i.*]

(I) *suru (to do)*

⊕ 【V/i】 Conjunctive coordinator

~ and; ~ so

SHIDAI 次第: [*n.*] order

【VN/I】 Punctual Inceptive a.

as soon as ~

❖ U. to express that an action is done expressly after another action.

❖ The infinitive f.s of the hon. v.s **irassharu**, **ossharu** y **nasaru** appear irregularly in this structure as irasshari-, osshari and nasari- respectively.

➤ shidai {D}: 【N】 Dependent Correlative cop.

depends on ~

❖ The marked n. denotes s.t. that has happened before.

➤ shidai de: 【N】 Dependent Correlative c.

depending on ~

SHIKA しか: [*p.*]

① 【N(p*)/C】 Exclusive Lower Limitative c.

nothing but ~; nobody but ~; only ~

❖ U. before neg. v.s.

❖ *ni, e, de, to, kara or made.

【U】 ☞ **shika nai**

➤ shika nai: 【U】 *there's no way but ~*

SHIKARUBEKI しかるべき〔然る可き〕: [*dep. adj. v.*] suitable

O.J. v. *shikaru** (*to be certain*) + dep. adj. v. *beki*†|*Derivative of p. *shika* (*only*) |†(I) dep. v. *beku* (*must*)

➤ shikaru beki {D}: 【TE】 [*for.*] Obligative m.

should ~

SHIMAU しまう〔仕舞う〕: [*v.*] to finish; to end

⊕ 【TE】 Complete Terminative a.

to finish ~ (up); to have ~

❖ Subsidiary v. u. to indicate the completion of an action.

❖ Sometimes this subsidiary v. is u., metaphorically, to indicate that an action or event has occurred involuntarily w. consequences perceived as negative.

SŌ そう〔相〕: [*aux. n*] appearance

➤ ⊕ sō ({D}): ❶ 【V/i】 [*fam.*] Inferential m. ‖ ❷ 【I/n/s】 Evidential Semblative cop.

① *I heard that ~; people say that ~*

② *It seems that ~; it looks like ~*

❖ ❶ Formula u. to express that what is stated by the marked v. or adj. is s.t. the speaker has heard before.

❖ ❷ It expresses a guess by the speaker based on what he or she feels or perceives in relation to a present or future event.

❖ The adj.s **ii** (*good*) and **nai** (*not be*) take the roots yo- and nasa- when u. w. this structure.

❖ The neg. f. is **I/n/s** sō ni/mo nai.

➤ ① sō mo nai: 【I/n/s】 Negative Evidential cop.

it doesn't seem that ~; it doesn't look like ~; is unlikely to ~

➤ ⊕ sō na ⟨N⟩: Attributive ☞ **sō ni**

➤ ⊕ sō ni: 【I/n/s】 Evidential m.

looks like ~; seems like ~

  ➤ sō ni mieru: 【I/n/s】 = 〖I/n/s〗 **sō** ({D})

  lool(s) like ~

  ➤ sō ni mo nai: 【I/n/s】 = **sō mo nai**

  ➤ sō ni nai: 【I/n/s】 = **sō mo nai**

  ➤ sō ni naru: 【I】 Deflective Inceptive a.

  almost ~

SOBA 側: [*n.*] near

➤ soba kara: 【V】 Punctual Inceptive a.

as soon as ~

SOKONAU 損なう: [*v.*] to forget

  【I】 *to fail to ~*

SU す: [*i.*]

Ⓦ 【A】 ≈ sasu

SUE 末: [*n.*] end; tip

➤ sue (ni): 【TA】 Postessive a.

after ~; at the end of ~; as a conclusion of ~

SUGI すぎ〔過ぎ〕: [*col.*] ≈ **sugiru**

SUGIRU すぎる〔過ぎる〕: [*v.*] to pass

  Ⓣ 【VN/I/n/s】 *too ~; ~ too much*

SUMIMASEN すみません: [*interjection*] sorry

  ⊕ 【TE】 *I'm sorry for ~*

SUMU 済む: [*v.*] to pass

  Ⓛ 【TE】 ~ *without any problem; no problem to ~*

❖ Subsidiary v. which states that an action has been taken or completed without any negative consequences.

SURA すら: [*p.*]

【N(p*)】 [*for.*] ≈ ② 〖N(p)〗 **mo**

❖ *ni, e, de, to, kara or made.

SURU する [*v.*] to do

【I*】 [*hum.*] Imperfective a. Indicative m.

❖ Describes the action of the speaker or s.o. of the speaker's in-group in a humble manner in order to show respect towards the listener.

❖ *After the hon. p. **o**.

❖ Usually in the pol. v. shimasu.

❖ There are some v.s who have specific humble versions which should be u. w. this f.

⊕ 【ku】 ≈ 〖n〗 **ni suru**

T

TABI たび〔度〕: [*n.*] (number of) times

➤ Ⓛ tabi ni: 【U】 Distributive Durative m.

each time (that) ~; every time that ~; whenever ~

TAGARU たがる: [*dep. v.*]

Stem of the dep adj. v. *tai (to want)* + dep. v. *garu (to seem)*

⊕ 【I】 Semblative Volitive m.

(it seems that) s.o. wants to ~

❖ Compound aux. v. u. to express that it seems that s.o. wants to do s.t. Only u. w. the second person (you) or the third person (he; she; it; they).

❖ Usually appearing in the progressive f. tagatte iru.

TAGERU たげる: [col.] ≈ 〖TE〗 **ageru**

❖ For v.s whose gerundive f. ends in **-te**.

TAI たい: [dep adj. v.]

㋓ 【I】 Volitive m.

want to ~

❖ It expresses s.o.'s desire or willingness to do a certain action.

❖ Only u. in the first person singular ('I') in declarative sentences or in the second person ('you') in interrogative sentences.

➤ tai desu: 【I】 [pol.] ≈ **tai**

TAKUTE たくて: [dep adj. v.]

Gerundive f. of the dep adj. v. *tai (to want)*

➤ takute mo: 【I】 Concessive Negative Potential

cannot even ~

❖ U. before neg. v.s.

TAMAE たまえ 〔給え〕: [dep. n.]

Imperative f. of the obs. v. *tamau (to do)*

【I】 [mas.] Imperative m.

do ~

TAME ため 〔為〕: [dep. n.] benefit

【V/na/i】 = 〖V/na/i〗 **tame ni**

➤ tame {D}: 【V/na/i】 ❶ Final cop. ❷ Causal cop.

① *it is for (the purpose of) ~ing*

② *it is because ~*

➤ tame ni: ❶ ⊕ 〖U〗 Final m. ‖ ❷ ㊤ 【V/na/i】 [lit.] [for.] Causal m.

① *(in order) to ~; for (the purpose of) ~*

② *because of ~; owing to ~*

❖ N. p. u. to express that s.t. is done in order to achieve s.t. (❶) or due to s.t. (❷).

❖ ❶ The marked v. has to be controllable or doable by the subject of the sentence.

➤ tame no ⟨N⟩: ⊕ 〖U〗 Attributive ☞ 〖U〗 **tame ni**

TARAZU 未満: [suf.]

Neg. f. of the v. *taru (to be sufficient)*

【C】 Limitative Approximative c.

(a little) less than ~; (just) under ~; close to ~; almost ~

TARI たり 〔足り〕: [dep. n.]

(I) *taru (to be enough)*

➤ tari to mo: 【C】 Concessive c.

(not) even ~

❖ Only u. before neg. v.s.

TARU たる: [p.]

Attributive f. of O.J. v. *tari (to be)*: ← comitative p. *to* + O.J. v. *ari (to be)*

➤ taru mono: 【N】 = **taru ya**

➤ taru ya: 【N】 [lit.] Emphatic Thematic c.

when it comes to ~; speaking of ~

❖ Compound p. that introduces a topic that contains surprising or unexpected information.

TATE たて 〔立て〕: [dep. n.]

(I) *tateru (to put up)*

➤ tate {D}: 【I】 Recent Perfective cop.

is just ~ed; is newly/freshly ~ed

✿ Dep. n. u. to indicate that s.t. has just been done. The resulting f. is grammatically a nominal construction.

TATTE たって: [p.]

【ku】 ≈ 〖TA〗 tte

【N/n/V/i】 [col.] ❶ ≈ to itte mo | ❷ ≈ to shite mo

〖Ō〗 = 〖Ō〗 ni mo

TE て: [i.]

【I/ku】 Conjunctive coordinator

~ and

➤ te mo: 【ku】 ≈ 〖TE〗 mo

  ➤ te mo ii: 【ku】 ≈ 〖TE〗 mo ii

➤ te tamaranai: 【ku】 Emphatic Negative Tentative m.

unbearably ~; extremely ~; awfully ~; can't help but ~

✿ It indicates that a quality is so extreme that it cannot be endured.

✿ *U. only w. adj. v.s.

➤ te wa: 【ku】 ≈ 〖TE〗 wa

TĒDO 程度: [n.] degree

【C】 ≈ 〖C〗 hodo

TEMAE 手前: [n.] before; in front of

【V/i】 considering ~; since ~

TO₁ と: [p.]

Ⓕ 【N】 ❶ Comitative c. ❷ Conjunctive c.

① with ~; as ~

② ~ and

✿ ❶ Complementary p. indicating a reciprocal, bidirectional relationship between the marked subject and the predicate that follows.

✿ ❷ Conjunctive p. u. to list things in an exhaustive manner, meaning that what is listed is all that it is.

TO₂ と: [p.]

【P】 ❶ Ⓣ Quotative subordinator | ❷ Emphatic Quotative subordinator

① that ~

① * with a ~ sound

② ~ing; (in such a way) that ~; (thinking/ saying) that ~

✿ ❶ Subordinate p. u. to express what has been said in a quotation, what has been thought, or the way s.t. has sounded.

✿ ❶ Usually followed by the v.s iu (to say); omou (to think); kaku (to write) or kiku (to hear). Sometimes these v.s do not appear explicitly but are implicitly understood.

✿ ❷ It transforms a clause into an adverbial phrase, inferring some degree of emotion derived from its grammatically original quotative nature, which lit. as 'thinking/saying that'.

✿ *When u. w. ideophone adv.s [☞ GE:I.6.1]

✿ ❷ This f. is actually an ellipsis of the constructions to itte (saying) or to omotte (thinking).

TO₃ と: [p.]

【U/i】 ⊕ Conditional m.

if ~

✿ U. to introduce a condition that brings up a state or event that is considered as a natural consequence derived without input from the subject.

✿ The neg. f. takes the f. de nai to instead of de wa nai to.

〖Ō〗 Concessive Conditional m.

even if ~; no matter what/who/how ~

to_1	*Union of Nouns by*	*Case:*	Comitative	**with**
			Conjunctive	**and**
to_2	*Union of Clauses by*	*Subordination:*	Quotative	**that**
to_3		*Modality:*	Conditional	**if**

➤ to aimatte: 【N】 [*lit.*] Comitative c.

together with ~; along with ~

➤ to areba: 【N/n/V/i】 ≈ sae 〈BA〉

➤ to atte: [*for.*] 【N】 Expectative Causal c. 【V/n/i】 Expectative Causal m.

because ~; since ~; due to the fact that ~

❖ Structure u. to introduce a reason or cause that the speaker considers natural or to be expected.

  ➤ to atte wa: 【N/n/V/i】 [*for.*] Thematic Provisional m. ≈ 〖TE〗 *wa*

  if it's true that ~; if it's the case that ~; being the case that ~

  ❖ Structure u. to expose a condition understood as factual.

➤ to bakari ni: 【P】 [*for.*] ❶ Quotative Semblative m. ❷ Inferential Semblative m.

① *as if to say ~; as if s.o. were saying ~*

② *as if s.o. was convinced that ~; as if s.o. believes that ~*

➤ to de mo iu beki 〈N〉: 【N】 [*for.*] Tentative Attributive Quotative subordinator

which could be called ~; which could be described as ~; which should be called ~

➤ to dōji ni: 【VN/U】 [*for.*] Simultaneous Durative a.

at the same time as ~; at the time when ~; while ~; as well as ~; ~ simultaneously

❖ Structure that introduces an action or state that is performed or takes place at the same time as another action or state.

➤ ⊕ to ieba: ❶ 【P】 Quotative Provisional m. ‖ ❷ 【N】 Emphatic Thematic c.

① *if s.o. say(s) ~*

② *speaking of ~*

➤ to ie domo: 【N/V】 [*lit.*] ≈ to itte mo

➤ ⊕ to ii: 【U】 Desiderative m.

it would be nice if ~; I hope ~

➤ to issho ni: 【N】 Comitative c.

with ~; along with ~

❖ Structure u. to express that two people or things do s.t. together.

➤ to itta 〈N〉: 【N/n/V/i】 Enunciative Attributive subordinator

like ~; such as ~; ~ among others

  ➤ to itta ra: ❶ 【P】 Quotative Conditional m. = ① to iu to ‖ ❷ 【N】 Quotative Thematic c. = ③ to iu to

  ① *If I say that ~*

  ② *speaking of ~; when it comes to ~*

➤ to itta ra nai: 【U/n/i】 Superlative m.

so ~; extremely ~; awfully ~

➤ ⊕ to itte mo: ❶ 【N】 Emphatic Concessive c. ‖ ❷ 【V/i】 Quotative Concessive coordinator

① *even ~*

② *even if s.o. says ~; although s.o. says ~; admitting that ~; ~ nonetheless*

➤ to iu: 【P】 ❶ ⊕ Quotative m. ‖ ❷ 【N/ n/V/i】 [*lit.*] Inferential m. ‖ ❸ ☞ to iu ⟨N⟩

① *say(s) that; say that ~*

② *heard that ~; they say that ~*

❖ Quotative structure used to state that s.o. says or thinks s.t.

➤ to iu ⟨N⟩: Attributive Quotative subordinator

* *... what/that is called ~; ... called ~; ... named ~*

† *all ~; every ~*

‡ *saying that ~; the fact that ~*

❖ Subordinator indicating by means of a quotation that s.t. is called in some way or that a noun is identified w. a fact said by s.o. or inferred in some way.

❖ *When 〖P〗 is a n.

❖ †When 〖P〗 & ⟨N⟩ are the same n.

❖ ‡When 〖P〗 is a v.

➤ to iu fuu ni: 【V】 Inferential Semblative m.

in such a way that ~; as if ~; as if to say ~

❖ It expresses the manner in which s.o. does s.t. while inferring it from some context.

➤ to iu ka: 【P】 ❶ Quotative Interrogative m. ❷ Quotative Disjunctive coordinator

① *say(s) that ~ ?*

② *or (I'd rather call it) ~; or rather ~; I'd (rather) say ~*

➤ to iu ka ⟨N/V/i⟩ to iu ka: 【N/V/ i】 Dubitative Quotative Adversative m.

not sure whether ~ or ...

➤ ⊕ to iu koto: 【P】 ❶ Inferential Nominalization marker ❷ Quotative Nominalization marker

① *the thing that ~*

② *the thing called/named ~*

❖ U. to convert clauses into nominal phrases that are understood to be s.t. inferred, thought or said by s.o.

➤ ⊕ to iu koto {D}: 【P】 ❶ Inferential Explanative cop. ❷ Quotative Explanative cop.

① *I heard that ~; (so) it means that ~*

② *so it means that ~; is something called ~*

➤ to iu koto mo naku: 【U】 = to mo naku

➤ to iu koto ni naru: 【P】 ≈ ① koto ni naru

➤ to iu koto wa: 【VN/n/V/i】 Thematic Quotative subordinator

the fact that ~; that ~; that is to say that ~

❖ The word *koto* here alludes to facts that are factual or demonstrable.

➤ to iu mono: 【P】 ❶ Quotative Nominalization marker ❷ Inferential Nominalization marker ≈ to iu koto ‖ ❷ 【C】 Perlative Essive c.

① *the thing called/named ~*

② *the thing that ~*

③ *(extending) for ~; during ~*

➤ to iu mono {D}: 【P】 ❶ Inferential Explanative cop. ❷ Quotative Explanative cop.

① *is something like ~; the thing is*

② *so it means that ~; is something called ~*

➤ to iu mono wa: ❶ 【N】 Quotative Thematic c. ‖ ❷ 【VN/n/V/i】 Thematic Quotative subordinator

① *something called /named ~; speaking of ~*

② *something like ~; the fact that ~*

❖ Structure u. to introduce a phrase that is interpreted as the focus of the entire sentence.

❖ *When u. after a n.

➤ to iu no ni: 【V/i】 Quotative Concessive coordinator

but ~; although ~; despite the fact that ~

➤ ⊕ to iu no wa: 【N/n/V/i】 [*col.*] ≈ to iu mono wa

➤ ⊕ to iu no wa 〈N/na/U/i〉 (no*) koto {D}: 【P】 Explanative cop.

~ means; the meaning of ~ is; what ~ means is

❖ *After 〈N〉.

➤ to iu no wa 〈U/i〉 to iu koto {D}: 【P】 = to iu no wa 〈N/na/U/i〉 koto {D}

➤ ⊕ to iu to: 【P】 ❶ Quotative Conditional m. ❷ Quotative Interrogative m. ‖ ❸ 【N】 Emphatic Thematic c.

① *when you mention ~; if s.o. say(s) ~; when it comes to ~; speaking of ~; when you say ~*

② *what do you mean by ~?*

③ *when it comes to ~; speaking of ~*

❖ ❶ Structure m. u. to express that s.t. that has been mentioned brings s.t. to the speaker's memory or that he or she wants to emphasize s.t. not expected about the mentioned thing.

➤ to iu tokoro {D}: 【N】 Approximative cop.

about ~; approximately ~

➤ to iu yō na 〈N〉: 【N/n/V/i】 ≈ to itta 〈N〉

➤ to iu yō ni: 【V】 Inferential Semblative m.

as if to say that ~; in such a way that ~

➤ ⊕ to iu yori (wa): 【N/n/V/i】 Emphatic Comparative m.

rather than ~

➤ to iu 〈N〉 wa: 【N】 Emphatic Thematic c.

❖ Structure that brings the focus to a n. while giving special emphasis to it.

❖ 〖N〗 & 〈N〉 are the same n.

❖ It usually infers negative implications.

➤ to iu wake {D}: 【N】 ≈ wake {D}

➤ to iwan bakari ni: 【P】 [*lit.*] ≈ to bakari ni

➤ to iwazu 〈N〉 to iwazu: 【N】 Enunciative Cumulative coordinator

~, ... and many other; including ~ and ...; ~, whether ~ or ...; both ~ and ...; ~ and .. among others

➤ ⊕ to ka: ❶ 【N】 Enumerative c. ‖ ❷ 【U】 ☞ to ka 〈U〉 to ka (suru)

~ and; such as ~ and

❖ Compound p. u. to introduce an inexhaustive list of things.

➤ to ka de: 【V】 Enumerative Causal m.

for some reason like ~; saying s.t. like ~; because ~ or s.t. like that

❖ Compound p. u. to introduce a somehow uncertain reason or cause.

➤ to ka iu: 【P】 Enumerative Quotative m.

say(s) that ~ or something

➤ to ka suru: 【U】 Enumerative m.

do things like ~

➤ ⊕ to ka 〈U〉 to ka (suru): 【U】 Enumerative coordinator

(do) things such as ~ and ...

➤ ⊕ to kiita: 【P】 Inferential m.

I heard that ~

➤ to kita ra: 【N】 Emphatic Thematic c.

when it comes to ~; speaking of ~

❖ Compound p. that introduces a topic that contains surprising or unexpected information.

➤ to kite iru: [*lit.*] ❶ 【N/n】 Causal cop. ‖ ❷ 【V/i】 Causal m.

① *because it is ~*

② *because ~; since ~*

❖ Followed by other causal p.s such as kara or no de.

➤ to kuraberu to: 【N】 = ni kuraberu to

➤ to kurabete: 【N】 = ni kuraberu to

➤ to 〈U/I〉 mai to: 【Ō】 = ga 〈U/I〉 mai ga

➤ Ⓔ to mieru: 【U/i】 Inferential Semblative cop.

it seems that ~; it looks as if ~

➤ to mirareru: ❶ 【N/n/V/i】 Expectative Semblative cop. ‖ ❷ 【V/i】 Prospective a. Expectative m.

① *appears that it will be ~*

② *it is expected to ~; it seems that will ~*

➤ to miru to: 【V/na/i】 Evidential Punctual a.

upon realizing that ~; as soon as one notices that ~

➤ to miru ya: 【V/na/i】 = to miru to

➤ to mo: 【Ō/ku】 [*lit.*] ≈ 〖Ō〗 to

➤ to mo naku: 【U】 [*for.*] Negative Intentional m.

without intending to ~; unconsciously ~

➤ to mo nareba: 【N/n/V/i】 = to nareba

➤ to mo naru to: 【N/n/V/i】 = ② to naru to

➤ to mo nashi ni: 【U】 = to mo naku

➤ to nareba: 【N/n/V/i】 Resultative Provisional m.

being the case that ~; when (it becomes) ~; once ~; when ~

➤ to naru: 【N/n】 [*lit.*] ≈ ni naru

➤ to naru to: ❶ 【N】 Emphatic Thematic c. ‖ ❷ 【N/n/V/i】 Resultative Conditional m.

① *when it comes to ~*

② *when (it becomes) ~; once ~; if it is the case that ~*

➤ to no 〈N〉: 【P】 [*for.*] ≈ to iu 〈N〉

➤ to no koto: 【P】 [*for.*] ≈ to iu koto

➤ to no koto {D}: 【P】 [*for.*] ≈ to iu koto {D}

➤ ⊕ to omou: 【Ō】 Intentional m.

think (that)/about/to ~; planning to ~

➤ to omowareru: 【V/Ō/i】 ≈ yō ni omowareru

➤ to sae: 【P】 Concessive Quotative m.

even said that ~

➤ Ⓔ to shita ra: 【V/i】 ≈ to sureba

➤ to shita tokoro de: 【V/i】 Concessive Provisional m.

even if ~

➤ to shita tte: 【V/i】 [*col.*] ≈ to shita tokoro de

➤ Ⓔ to shite: 【N】 Contrastive Correlative c.

as ~; in the capacity of ~; in the role of ~

➤ to shite mo: ❶ 【V/i】 Concessive Conditional m. ❷ 【N/Ō】 Concessive Probationary m.

① *even if ~; assuming ~*

② *even if s.o. tries to ~*

➤ to shite wa: 【N】 Contrastive Concessive c.

for ~; as for ~

❖ Indicates a standard for comparisons, indicating that what is discussed is not excepted for the marked n.

➤ ⓔ **to sureba**: 【V/i】 Assumptive Provisional m.

supposing that ~; assuming that ~

➤ **to suru**: ❶ ⓔ 【Ō】 ❶ Probationary m. ❷ Prospective a. ‖ 【N/n/V/i】 ❸ Hortative Assumptive m. ‖ 【N】 ❹ Decisive m. = ① *ni suru* | ❺ Contrastive Correlative c. ≈ **to shite**

① *try to ~*

② *be about to ~*

③ *let's assume/suppose that ~*

④ *decide on ~*

⑤ *in the capacity of ~; as ~*

➤ ⓔ **to suru to**: 【V/i】 Assumptive Conditional m.

supposing that ~; assuming that ~

➤ **to ⟨Ō⟩ to**: 【Ō】 Negative Dependent Disjunctive coordinator

regardless of whether ~ or …

➤ **to tomo ni**: ❶ ⓔ 【N】 [*for.*] ≈ **to issho ni** ‖ ❷ 【VN/U】 [*lit.*] Simultaneous Durative a.

② *at the same time ~; when ~; as ~; as well as ~*

❖ Structure u. to express that two people or things do s.t. together or share the same characteristic (❶) or that two actions or states occur at the same time (❷).

➤ **to wa**: 【N】 ❶ Quotative Thematic c. ≈ ① **to iu mono wa** | ❷ Thematic Comitative c. ‖ 【VN/n/V/i】 ❸ Thematic Quotative subordinator ≈ ② **to iu mono wa** | ❹ Quotative Admirative m.

① *speaking of ~; something called/named ~*

② *(also) with ~*

③ *that ~; the fact that ~*

④ *how come ~!*

❖ ❶ M. u. to refer to a word that is being defined.

❖ ❹ Inferring surprise towards s.t. that the speaker has experienced, seen or heard.

➤ **to wa chigatte**: 【N】 Negative Semblative c.

unlike ~

➤ **to wa ie**: [*lit.*] ≈ **to wa itte mo**

➤ **to wa itte mo**: 【N/V/i】 = **to itte mo**

➤ ⓔ **to wa kagiranai**: 【U/i】 Negative Evidential m.

not always ~; not necessarily ~

➤ **to wa** ⟨N/na/U/i⟩ (no) **koto** {D}: 【P】 = **to iu no wa** ⟨N/na/U/i⟩ (no) **koto** {D}

TŌ 等: [*n.*] rank

【N】 [*for.*] Enunciative c.

~ et cetera; ~ etc; ~ and the like

TOCHUU 途中: [*n.*] midway

➤ ⓔ **tochuu de/ni**: 【U】 Intrative Durative m.

in the middle of ~; while ~

TOKI とき〔時〕: [*n.*] time

➤ ⓣ **toki (ni)**: 【V/na/i】 Punctual a.

at the time when ~; when ~

TOKO とこ: [*col.*][*fam.*] ≈ **tokoro**

TOKORO ところ〔所〕: [*n.*] place

【U/i】 ⓔ [*for.*] Punctual a.

when ~

❖ U. to indicate a moment when s.t. not deliberate happens as a result of an action.

【TA】 [*fam.*] ≈ 〖TA〗 **tokoro** {D}

➤ ⊕ tokoro {D}: 〖U〗 ❶ Prospective a. ❷ *Deflective Inceptive a. ❸ †Durative Progressive a. ‖ ❹ 〖TA〗 Recent Perfective a.

① *be (just) about to~*

② *almost ~*

③ *be in the midst of ~ing; be on the course of ~ing*

④ *have just ~; just ~(-ed)*

✤ ❷ *When {D} is in the perfective f.s datta or deshita.

✤ ❸ †When 〖U〗 is in the progressive f.s TE iru and TE ita.

➤ tokoro {p*}: 〖V/na/i〗 Punctual a.

when ~; on the occasion of ~

✤ *Case p.s such as o, ni, e or de.

✤ *The p. de focuses on the point of time; the p. ni implies a fig. destination, the p. e implies a fig. direction; and the p. o is u. when the marked action or state is a direct object for the predicate.

➤ tokoro de: 〖TA〗 ❶ Concessive Provisional m. ❷ Causal m. Egressive a. | ❸ 〖V/na/i〗 Punctual a.≈ tokoro {p}

① *even if ~*

② *since ~*

③ *when ~*

✤ ❶ The following clause has to be neg. either explicitly or implicitly.

➤ tokoro kara: 〖V/na/i〗 Causal m.

from the fact that ~; caused by the fact that ~; because ~

➤ tokoro o: 〖V/na/i〗 ❶ Concessive coordinator ❷ Punctual a. ≈ tokoro {p}

① *despite ~; although ~*

② *when ~*

TOKU とく: [col.][fam.] ≈ 〖TE〗 oku

✤ For v.s whose gerundive f. ends in -te.

TOMO とも 〔共〕: [p.] all; both

Comitative p. *to (with)* + cumulative p. *mo (and)*

〖C〗 Inclusive Cumulative c.

all of the ~; both ~; ~ included

〖U〗 Assertive m.

I assure that ~; of course ~

〖N〗 ≈ to mo

TOORI 通り: [n.] way

(I) *tooru (to go through)*

➤ ⊕ toori (ni): ❶ 〖N〗 Perlative Correlative c. | ❷ 〖V〗 Correlative Formal m.

① *in ~'s way; in the same way as ~; as ~; in accordance with ~;*

② *as (one) ~; the way ~*

TOOSU 通す: [v.] to let s.t. through

⊕ 〖I〗 Perlative Upper Limitative m.

to ~ until the end; to continually ~; to ~ through

TOTAN 途端: [adv. n.] just (at the moment)

Ⓒ *to 途 (way)* + *tan 端 (edge)*

➤ ⊕ totan (ni): 〖TA〗 Punctual Inceptive a.

the moment ~; just as ~; as soon as ~

TOTE とて: [p.]

← to itte: Quotative p. *to* + *itte** | *Gerundive f. of the v. iu (to say)*

〖N〗 [lit.] Concessive c.

even ~

〖VN/V〗 [lit.] Concessive Provisional m.

even if ~; even though ~

TŌZEN 当然: [*adj. n.*] natural

➤ tōzen {D}: 【TE】 ≈ mo tōzen {D}

TSU つ: [*p.*]

➤ tsu ⟨I⟩ tsu: 【I】 Contrastive Enumerative coordinator

❖ It expresses a contrast between two parallel actions.

TSUDZUKE 続け: [*dep. n.*]

(I) *tsudzukeru (to continue)*

➤ tsudzuke {D}: 【I】 = 〖I〗 **tsudzukeru**

TSUDZUKERU 続ける: [*v.*] to continue

⊕ 【I】 Continuative a.

to keep on ~; to continue ~

TSUIDE ついで 〔序で〕: [*n.*] opportunity

➤ ⊕ tsuide ni: 【VN/I/n/s/V/i】 Causative Durative a.

when ~; while ~; since ~

❖ Compound p. u. to express that s.o. has the opportunity to do an action at the same time as another action in order to reduce effort.

TSUKERU 付ける: [*v.*] to attach

【I】 Habitual m.

① *to become accustomed to ~; to get used to ~* ② *to usually ~* ③ *to ~ vigorously*

TSUKU 付く: [*v.*] to be attached

【I】 Translative m.

to become ~ed

TSUMORI つもり 〔積もり〕: [*n.*] intention

(I) *tsumoru (to estimate)*

➤ ⊤ tsumori {D}: ❶ 【U】 Intentional m. ❷ 【TA/na/i】 Assumptive m.

① *intend to ~; going to ~; plan to ~*

② *be convinced that ~; believe (that) ~; feel sure that ~*

❖ N. u. to express an intention about future actions (❶) or a conviction about present states or past actions (❷).

❖ ❶ The subject, in declarative sentences, is the first person ('I') for s.o. w. whom the speaker sympathizes. In interrogative sentences, however, the subject is the second person ('you') or s.o. w. whom the listener sympathizes.

TSUTSU つつ: [*p.*]

【I】 [*for.*] Simultaneous Progressive a.

(be) ~ing; while ~

❖ P. u. to express an action in progress during the time another action is done or state is occurring.

➤ [*for.*] tsutsu aru: 【I】 ≈ ① 〖TE〗 iru

❖ Not u. w. everyday actions

➤ tsutsu mo: 【I】 [*for.*] Concessive Provisional m.

② *although ~; even if ~; in spite of ~*

TSUU つう: [*col.*][*fam.*] ≈ **to iu**

➤ tsuu ka: 【P】 [*col.*][*fam.*] ≈ **to iu ka**

➤ tsuu koto wa: 【P】 [*col.*][*fam.*] ≈ **to iu koto wa**

TTA ったらない: [*i.*]

← *to itta*: Quotative p. *to* + *itta** | *Perfective f. of the v. *iu (to say)*

➤ tta ra: ❶ 【N】 [*col.*][*fam.*] Emphatic Thematic c. ≈ **to kita ra** ‖ ❷ 【P】 [*col.*] Quotative Conditional m. ≈ **to itta ra**

① *when it comes to ~; speaking of ~; as for ~*

② *when I/you hear ~; when I think of ~; if you say ~*

➤ **tta ra nai**: 【U/n/i】 [*col.*] ≈ **to ittaranai**

TTATTE って: [*i.*]

【ku】 ≈ 〖TA〗 **tte**

TTE って: [*p.*]

← *tote*: Quotative p. *to* + Conjuctive p. *te*

【P】 [*col.*] ⊕ ❶ Quotative subordinator ≈ to₂ | [*col.*][*fam.*] ❷ Quotative m. ≈ **tte iu** ❸ Quotative Assertive m. ❹ Emphatic Quotative subordinator ≈ ② **to₂** | ❺ ☞ **tte ⟨N⟩ tte**

① *that ~*

② *say(s) that ~*

③ *I'm telling you (that) ~; I told you that ~*

④ *~ing; (in such a way) that ~; (thinking/ saying) that ~*

【N】 [*col.*] Quotative Thematic c.

speaking of ~; when it comes to ~

【TA*】 ❶ [*col.*][*fam.*] Concessive Provisional m. ≈ 〖TE〗 **mo** ‖ ❷ ≈ 〖P〗 **tte**

① *even if ~*

❖ **Only the perfective f. of v.s but not not adj. v.s. Adj.s take the form ≈ **ku tatte**.

➤ **tte ⟨N⟩**: 【P】 ≈ **tte iu ⟨N⟩**

➤ **tte ieba**: 【P】 [*col.*] ≈ **to ieba**

➤ **tte iu**: ❶ 【P】 [*col.*] Quotative m. ‖ ❷ 【N/n/V/i】 [*col.*] Inferential m. ≈ **to iu** | ❷ ☞ **tte iu ⟨N⟩**

① *say(s) that ~; said that ~*

② *heard that ~; they say that ~*

➤ **tte iu ⟨N⟩**: 【P】 [*col.*] ≈ **to iu ⟨N⟩**

➤ **tte iu ka**: 【P】 [*col.*] ≈ **to iu ka**

➤ **tte iu koto wa**: 【P】 [*col.*] ≈ **to iu koto wa**

➤ **tte ka**: 【P】 [*col.*] ≈ **tte iu ka**

➤ **tte koto wa**: 【P】 ≈ **tte iu koto wa**

TTEBA ってば: [*p.*]

← *tte ieba* ← *to ieba*: Quotative p. *to* + *ieba** | **Provisional f. of the v. iu (to say)*

【P】 ❶ = **tte ieba** | ❷ [*col.*][*fam.*] Quotative Assertive ≈ ③ **tte**

② *I said ~; I told you ~*

U

UCHI うち 〔内〕: [*n.*] inside

➤ ㊤ **uchi ni**: ❶ 【U*/na/i】 Durative a. ‖ ❷ Antessive a. ☞ **nai uchi ni**

① *while ~*

❖ ❶ It refers to the time during which an action or state takes place.

❖ ❶ Usually indicating a period of time that has to be made a good use of, or an action that happens spontaneously while the marked action develops.

❖ *Frequently u. w. the progressive f. **TE iru**.

➤ **uchi wa**: 【U】 = **aida wa**

UE 上: [*n.*] above

➤ ㊤ **ue de**: 【TA】 Prospective Postessive a.

after ~

❖ It introduces a preparatory action as a precedent for a relatively important event.

➤ ㊤ **ue (ni)**: 【V/na/i】 Emphatic Cumulative coordinator

~ as well; ~ in addition; ~ besides; ~ moreover; not only ~ but also

❖ U. to introduce an emotional statement.

➣ ue wa: 〖V〗 Causal Egressive a.

now that ~; since ~

URU うる 〔得る〕 : [v.] [lit.] to get

〖I〗 = 〖I〗 eru

W

WA₁ は: [p.]

① 【N(p*)】 ❶ Thematic c. ❷ Contrastive Thematic c.

as for ~; the ~; talking/speaking about ~

❖ ❶ Focal p. u. to introduces a new topic to the conversation or text, putting the focus on the marked n.

❖ ❶ U. w. generic n.s, n.s that refer to s.t. that there is only one of a kind, proper n.s or common n.s referring to s.t. that has already been introduced to the conversation or is understood contextually.

❖ ❷ It introduces a contrast in the discourse, indicating that the marked n. is highlighted as opposed to another explicit or implicit n.

❖ It replaces the nominative p. **ga** when the n. is the subject of the sentence and a topic already known by the interlocutors, or the accusative p. **o** if the known topic is a direct object.

❖ *It can be added to some other p.s when the modified noun is a known topic.

❖ Written w. the hiragana character は (originally pronounced *ha*) but always pronounced as **wa** (わ).

- -
- - - -

WA₂ は: [p.]

【TE】 ❶ Thematic Conditional m. ❷ Thematic Conjunctive coordinator

① *if ~; when ~; whenever ~; because ~*
② *(only) ~ and*

❖ ❶ Subordinate p. u. to introduce an action or state as a condition for some other action or state to happen.

❖ Written w. the hiragana character は (originally pronounced *ha*) but always pronounced as **wa** (わ).

❖ The predicate usually has a neg. nuance.

- -
- - - -

WA₃ わ: [p.]

【V/i】 [*fam.*] ≈ **zo**

- - - -

➣ wa are (do): 〖N〗 [*lit.*] ≈ **wa atte mo**

➣ wa arimasen: 〖ku〗 = 〖ku〗 **arimasen**

➣ wa aru: 〖ku〗 Emphatic m.

is indeed ~

➣ wa aru mai: 〖ku〗 ≈ **mai**

➣ wa atte mo: 〖N〗 [*for.*] Concessive cop.

even though/although there is/are ~

➣ ⬆ wa betsu to shite: 〖N〗 Exclusive c.

other than ~; apart from ~; aside from ~; except for ~

❖ Structure u. to introduce an exception within the sentence.

➣ ⬆ wa dame ({D}): 【TE】 [*fam.*] Prohibitive m.

must not ~; may not ~; cannot ~

➣ wa 〈N〉ᴮ de ichiban 〈P〉: 〖NA〗 Superlative Comparative subordinator

545

A is/does then most P among B

➤ wa ⟨N⟩ᴮ de motto mo ⟨P⟩: 【Nᴬ】 [for.] ≈ wa ⟨N⟩ de ichiban ⟨P⟩

➤ ① wa dō: 【N】 ≈ 〖TA〗 ra dō

➤ wa dō desu ka: [pol.] ≈ wa dō

➤ ① wa ikenai: 【TE】 Prohibitive m.

must/may not ~; shouldn't ~ cannot ~

❖ Combined verbal p. u. to strongly indicate that s.t. shouldn't be done.

➤ ① wa ikenai kara: 【TE】 Negative Final m.

in order to not ~; to prevent ~

➤ wa irarenai: 【TE】 Negative Progressive a. Potential m.

cannot be ~ing; shouldn't be ~ing; cannot/ shouldn't keep ~ing; unable to ~

❖ Combined verbal p. u. to express that s.o. cannot continue to be in a certain state or do a certain action.

➤ wa iru: 【TE】 Emphatic Progressive a.

s.o. is (in fact) ~

➤ wa iu made mo naku: 【N】 [for.] ≈ wa mochiron

➤ wa iu ni oyobazu: 【N】 [lit.] ≈ wa mochiron

➤ wa mada shi mo: 【N】 = nara mada shi mo

➤ ① wa mochiron: 【N】 Negative Exclusive Lower Limitative c.

let alone ~; not to mention ~; to say nothing of ~

❖ U. before neg. v.s.

➤ wa moto yori: 【N】 Negative Exclusive Lower Limitative c.

let alone ~; not to mention ~

➤ ① wa naranai: 【TE】 Prohibitive m.

cannot ~; must not ~; should not ~

➤ wa nee: 【V/i】 [fam.] ≈ na₂

➤ wa ⟨N⟩ᴮ no naka de ichiban ⟨P⟩: 【Nᴬ】 ≈ wa ⟨N⟩ de ichiban ⟨P⟩

➤ wa ⟨N⟩ᴮ no naka de motto mo ⟨P⟩: 【Nᴬ】 [for.] ≈ wa ⟨N⟩ no naka de ichiban ⟨P⟩

➤ wa oroka: 【N】 [for.] ≈ wa mochiron

➤ wa sate oki: 【N】 Exclusive c.

putting/setting aside ~

➤ wa shinai: 【I】 = ya shinai

➤ wa suru: 【I】 Emphatic m.

s.o. do/does ~

➤ wa ⟨U⟩ wa (de): 【U】 [col.] Emphatic Enumerative coordinator

~ and ...; because ~ and ...; for example ~ and ..

❖ Structure u. to present, in an emphatic way, an inexhaustive series of actions that, usually, entail a reason or example.

➤ wa ⟨N⟩ᴮ yori (mo) ⟨P⟩: 【Nᴬ】 ≈ yori ⟨N⟩ wa ⟨P⟩

WAKE わけ〔訳〕: [n.] reasoning

(I) *wakeru (to understand)*

➤ ① wake {D}: 【V/na/i】 Inferential Explanative cop.

(so) that means that ~; that's why ~; so ~

❖ It expresses an explanation made from a logical reasoning or based on s.t. that has been heard or read.

➤ ① wake ga nai: 【U/na/i】 Emphatic Negative Expectative m.

there is no reason to believe that ~ is possible; there is no reason why ~; it is impossible to ~; cannot ~

❖ It negates the existence of a reason to believe that some event, action or state takes place.

➤ ① wake ni wa ikanai: 【U】 Negative Optative m.

cannot help but ~ing; have no other choice but ~

❖ It negates the existence of a reason to believe that some event, action or state takes place.

WARI わり: [*n.*] rate

(I) *waru (to divide)*

➢ ⊕ wari ni (wa): 【V/na/i】 Contrastive Concessive m.

despite ~; although ~; considering ~

❖ Structure u. to express that s.t. is not in proportion to what one would expect.

WASURERU 忘れる: [*v.*] to forget

【I】 *to forget ~ing; to forget to ~*

Y

YA や: [*p.*]

⑦ 【N】 Enumerative c.

~ and

❖ Conjunctive p. u. to list two or more things within an inexhaustive list of things.

【U】 ≈ **ya ina ya**

➢ ya ina ya: 【U】 [*for.*] Punctual Inceptive a.

as soon as ~; the moment ~; immediately after ~

➢ ya shinai: 【I】 Negative Emphatic m.

no way ~

YAGARU やがる: [*dep. v.*]

← *agaru (to rise)*

【TE/I】 [*col.*] Derogatory m.

have the nerve to ~

❖ Subsidiary v. u. to make the sentence derogatory and disrespectful towards the listener.

YAMANAI やまない: [*dep. adj. v.*]

Neg. f. of the v. *yamu (to stop)*

【TE】 *never stop ~; always ~*

YARA やら: [*p.*]

Inexhaustive Enumerative p. *ya (and)* + plural suf. *ra*

【N】 [*fam.*] Enumerative c.

(such as) ~ and; ~ and the like

❖ Conjunctive p. u. to express an inexhaustive list of several actions or states.

【V/na/i】 = **no yara**

➢ yara {p}: ☞ **yara**

➢ yara ⟨U/n/i⟩ yara: 【U/n/i】 [*fam.*] ❶ Enumerative coordinator ❷ Alternative coordinator

① *~ and (things like) ~*

② *whether ~ or (not)*

YARU やる: [*v.*] to give

⊕ 【TE】 [*fam.*] ≈ 〖TE〗 **ageru**

YASUI やすい 〔易い〕: [*adj. v.*] easy

⊕ 【I】 *easy to ~*

YO₁ よ: [*p.*]

⑦ 【N/n/V/i】 Assertive m.

~ you know; ~ right?

❖ Emphatic p. u. to convey an affirmation or to draw attention to s.t.

【Ō】 Emphatic Hortative m.

let's ~, ok?

- -

YO よ: [*i.*] ⊕ Ⓢ 【E】 [*lit.*] = 〚E〛 ro

- -

➤ yo ne: 【N/n/V/i】 [*col.*] Assertive Inquisitive m.

~ isn't that right?; isn't it ~?

────────────────────────────

YŌ よう 〔様〕: [*dep. n.*] form

【I】 Formal m.

way of~; method of ~

➤ ⊕ yō {D}: 【V/na/i】 Semblative cop.

look like ~; look as if ~; it appears that ~; seems that ~

➤ yō de wa: 【U/na/i】 Thematic Conditional m.

if ~; if it is true that ~; if it is the case that ~

❖ Structure u. to present an undesirable state or action provided as a condition that is assumed to be true.

➤ ⊕ yō ga nai: 【I】 Negative Tentative cop.

there's no way to ~; it's impossible to ~

➤ ⊕ yō na 〈N〉: 【V/na/i】 Attributive ☞ yō {D}

➤ ⊕ yō na ki ga suru: 【V/na/i】 Evidential Inferential m.

have a feeling that ~

➤ ⊕ yō ni: ❶ 【V/na/i】 Semblative m. ‖ ❷ 【U*】 Final m.

① *as if ~; like ~*

② *so that ~; in order to ~*

❖ ❶ It expresses that the marked action or state is s.t. similar to what is expressed in the following clause.

❖ ❷ It expresses that the marked v. is an action or state not controlled by the subject, understood as an objective or purpose.

❖ *If the subject is the first person the v. has to be in the potential or neg. f.

➤ yō ni iu: 【U】 Imperative Quotative m.

tell to ~

❖ It expresses that s.o. is telling another person to do s.t.

➤ yō ni omowareru: 【V/na/i】 [*for.*] Inferential Semblative m.

seems (that) ~; appears (that) ~

❖ Usually concerning some sort of spontaneous feeling or u. as an indirect way of expressing s.t. that the speaker is hesitant to convey.

➤ ⊕ yō ni mieru: 【U/na/i】 Evidential Semblative cop.

to look like ~; to seem ~; to appear ~

➤ ⊕ yō ni naru: 【U】 Resultative a.

come to ~; have finally become ~; reach the point where ~; get ~ed

❖ It indicates that the action stated by the marked v. has become such at the moment of speech after having gone through a gradual transformative process.

➤ ⊕ yō ni suru: 【U】 Determinative m.

to ~ in such a way that ~; make sure that ~

❖ It indicates that there is a strong intention and determination to do the marked action.

────────────────────────────

YOI よい 〔良い〕: [*adj. v.*] good

【I】 *easy to ~*

【TE】 = 〚TE〛 ii

────────────────────────────

YORI より: [*p.*]

(I) *yoru (to be based on)*

【N/na/V/i】 ❶ ⊕ Comparative subordinator | ❷ ≈ yori 〈P〉 | ❸ ☞ 〚N〛 yori

① *compared to ~; as opposed to ~*

① 【U】 *rather than* ~

❖ ❶ P. u. to compare s.t. or s.o. to another person or thing.

❖ Only u. w. verbals in positive f.s.

【N】 [*for.*] Ablative c.

from ~; *past* ~

❖ It indicates that s.t. or some point in time or space is the origin from which the action of the verb develops.

➤ yori ⟨P⟩: 【N/na/V/i】 ≈ yori ⟨N⟩ no hō ga ⟨P⟩

➤ yori ⟨N^B⟩ ga ⟨P⟩: 【N/na/V/i】 ≈ yori ⟨N⟩ no hō ga ⟨P⟩

➤ yori ⟨V/na/i^B⟩ hō ga ⟨P⟩: 【V/na/i^A】 ≈ yori ⟨N⟩ no hō ga ⟨P⟩

➤ Ⓣ yori ⟨N^B⟩ no hō ga ⟨P⟩: 【N^A】 Upper Comparative subordinator

compared to A, B am/are/is/does more P; B is/does more P than A

❖ ⟨P⟩ is an adj. or a finite v.

➤ yori hoka (ni) wa: 【N】 ≈ no hoka (ni) wa

➤ yori hoka (ni) (wa) ⟨A⟩ nai: 【U】 Negative Preferential m.

there is no other option but ~; *there's no choice but* ~

❖ U. before neg. v.s.

➤ ① yori mo: 【N/na/V/i】 ≈ ① yori

➤ yori mo ⟨V/na/i⟩^{B} hō ga ⟨P⟩: 【V/na/i^A】 ≈ yori ⟨N⟩ no hō ga ⟨P⟩

➤ yori mo ⟨N^B⟩ no hō ga ⟨P⟩: 【N^A】 ≈ yori ⟨N⟩ no hō ga ⟨P⟩

➤ yori ⟨N^B⟩ wa ⟨P⟩: 【N/na/V/i】 ≈ yori ⟨N⟩ no hō ga ⟨P⟩

YOSHI 由: [*n.*] reason

➤ ⊕ yoshi ({D}) 【V/i】 [*lit.*] Inferential m.

I heard that ~; *it is said that* ~

YOTĒ 予定: [*n.*] plan

➤ ⊕ yotē {D}: 【U】 Intentional m.

I'm planning to ~; *I intend to* ~

YUE ゆえ 〔故〕: [*n.*] cause

➤ yue (ni): [*lit.*] 【N】 Causal c. 【V/na/i】 Causal m.

① *because of* ~; *due to* ~

② *because* ~

Z

ZARU ざる: [*i.*]

【A】 [*obs.*] ≈ nai

❖ M. u. nowadays in fossilized proverbs or sayings.

❖ The v. **suru** takes the f. sezaru.

ZE ぜ: 【V/i】 = zo

ZENGO 前後: [*n.*] front and rear

【C】 Approximative c.

about ~; *around* ~; *approximately* ~

ZO ぞ: [*p.*]

【V/i】 [*col.*][*fam.*][*mas.*] Assertive m.

I tell you that ~; ~ *you know*

❖ Emphatic p. u. to convey a strong affirmation or a strong desire to draw attention to s.t.

❖ Only u. by males towards equals or inferiors.

ZOI 沿い: [*dep. n.*]

← soi: (I) *sou (to run along)*

[N] [*lit.*] Perlative Essive c.

along ~; through ~

ZU ず: [*i.*]

[A] ☞ **zu ni**

➤ Ⓔ zu ni: **[A]** [for.] Privative coordinator

without ~

❖ The v. **suru** takes the f. sezu.

　➤ Ⓔ zu ni wa irarenai: **[A]** [*lit.*] ≈ **nai de wa irarenai**

　➤ zu ni wa okanai: **[A]** [*lit.*] ≈ **nai de wa okanai**

　➤ zu ni wa orarenai: **[A]** = **zu ni wa irarenai**

　➤ zu ni wa orenai: **[A]** = **zu ni wa irarenai**

　➤ zu ni wa sumanai: **[A]** = **nai de wa sumanai**

➤ zu shite: **[A]** = **zu ni**

➤ zu to mo: **[A]** [for.] ≈ **nakute mo**

　➤ zu to mo yoi: **[A]** [*lit.*] = 〖TE〗 **mo ii**

ZUTSU ずつ: [*p.*]

Ⓔ **[C]** Equative Distributive c.

each ~; ~ at a time; ~ apiece

❖ It expresses that the marked quantity corresponds to an equal amount for each person or thing to which it corresponds.

CPSIA information can be obtained
at www.ICGtesting.com
Printed in the USA
BVHW010122110821
613873BV00028B/77